Barley:
Chemistry and Technology

Edited by

Alexander W. MacGregor
Canadian Grain Commission
Grain Research Laboratory
Winnipeg, Manitoba, Canada R3C 3G8

Rattan S. Bhatty
Department of Crop Science
University of Saskatchewan
Saskatoon, Saskatchewan, Canada S7N 0W0

Published by the
American Association of Cereal Chemists, Inc.
St. Paul, Minnesota, USA

Front cover: heads of malting barley; courtesy of the Canadian International Grains Institute, Winnipeg, MB, Canada. Back cover: six-rowed malting barley; courtesy of Donald C. Rassmussen, Department of Agronomy and Plant Genetics, University of Minnesota, St. Paul, MN.

Library of Congress Catalog Card Number: 93-72889
International Standard Book Number: 0-913250-80-5

Printed in the United States of America on acid-free paper

American Association of Cereal Chemists, Inc.
3340 Pilot Knob Road
St. Paul, MN 55121-2097, USA

10000659441

CONTRIBUTORS

C. W. Bamforth, BRF International, Nutfield, Surrey, RH1 4HY England

A. H. P. Barclay, Bass Maltings Ltd., Alloa, FK10 1NU Scotland

R. S. Bhatty, Crop Development Centre, Department of Crop Science and Plant Ecology, University of Saskatchewan, Saskatoon, Saskatchewan, Canada S7N 0W0

M. P. Cochrane, Crop Science and Technology Department, The Scottish Agricultural College, Edinburgh EH9 3JG, Scotland

C. M. Duffus, Crop Science and Technology Department, The Scottish Agricultural College, Edinburgh EH9 3JG, Scotland

D. E. Falk, Crop Science Department, University of Guelph, Guelph, Ontario, Canada N1G 2W1

G. B. Fincher, Department of Plant Science, University of Adelaide, Waite Campus, Glen Osmond, South Australia, Australia 5064

K. J. Kasha, Crop Science Department, University of Guelph, Guelph, Ontario, Canada N1G 2W1

A. W. MacGregor, Grain Research Laboratory, Canadian Grain Commission, Winnipeg, Manitoba, Canada R3C 3G8

W. R. Morrison, Department of Bioscience and Biotechnology, University of Strathclyde, Glasgow, Scotland

L. Munck, Carlsberg Research Laboratory, DK-2500 Valby, Copenhagen, Denmark (*present affiliation*, Department of Dairy and Food Science, Royal Veterinary and Agricultural University, Frederiksberg C, Denmark)

R. A. Nilan, Department of Crop and Soil Sciences and Department of Genetics and Cell Biology, Washington State University, Pullman, Washington 99164-6420, USA

P. Bjørn Petersen, Carlsberg Research Laboratory, DK-2500 Valby, Copenhagen, Denmark

P. R. Shewry, Department of Agricultural Sciences, University of Bristol, Agricultural and Food Research Council, Institute of Arable Crops Research, Long Ashton Research Station, Bristol, BS18 9AF, United Kingdom

B. A. Stone, Commonwealth Special Research Centre for Protein and Enzyme Technology and Department of Biochemistry, La Trobe University, Bundoora, Victoria, Australia 3083

S. E. Ullrich, Department of Crop and Soil Sciences, Washington State University, Pullman, Washington 99164-6420, USA

A. Ziauddin, Crop Science Department, University of Guelph, Guelph, Ontario, Canada N1G 2W1

PREFACE

With the publication of the present volume, the American Association of Cereal Chemists has completed monographs on six of the eight major cereals in the family Gramineae, some in second (rice) and third (wheat) editions. Barley, although the fourth major cereal in the world (after wheat, rice, and corn), has been late making it to the list of AACC published titles. Part of the reason for this delay was the perception of barley as, first, a major raw material for the production of alcoholic beverages (hence of interest largely to the malting and brewing industries) and, second, a livestock feed. Animal feeds and malt consume 80–90% of the barley production in many Western countries. At the present time, very little barley is used in human foods except in the West Asia-North Africa region and until recently in the Pacific Rim countries, particularly Korea and Japan. Yet, historically, barley preceded wheat as a food grain in ancient Egypt and Nubia, and it has been consumed since then in many cultures. Only at the beginning of this century was barley replaced as a food grain by wheat because of the superior baking quality of wheat flour. Barley, grown in regions of the world from sub-Arctic to temperate, is a versatile cereal. It may be hulled, thin-hulled, or hull-less, two-rowed or six-rowed, have normal or high lysine levels, low or high amylose starch levels, and low or high levels of β-glucan, a major component of soluble dietary fiber implicated in hypocholesterolemia. Moreover, it does not contain any known antinutritional factors. In view of these properties, barley remains an underutilized cereal in human foods and in industrial applications, except for the malting and brewing industries.

This monograph contains 10 chapters, each written by internationally acclaimed experts in their respective fields. The editors suggested only broad guidelines to the authors, who developed their own chapters. The intention of the editors was to produce a volume that was broad in scope yet covered each topic in depth. In our opinion, these objectives have been largely met.

We are indebted to the authors for agreeing in the first place to write the chapters and for by and large meeting the various deadlines imposed on them, in spite of their busy schedules; to reviewers of the chapters; and finally to the American Association of Cereal Chemists for publishing the monograph.

A. W. MacGregor
R. S. Bhatty

CONTENTS

1. **Barley: Taxonomy, Origin, Distribution, Production, Genetics, and Breeding.** R. A. NILAN and S. E. ULLRICH, 1

Introduction, 1
Taxonomy, History, Origin, and Evolution, 2
  Taxonomy • History • Origin and Evolution
Adaptation, Distribution, and Production, 4
  Adaptation • Distribution • Production
Cytology, Genetics, Cytogenetics, 8
  Cytology • Genetics • Cytogenetics
Breeding, 18
  Male-Sterile-Facilitated Recurrent Selection • Doubled-Haploid Breeding •
  Mutation • Breeding • Hybrid Barley • Future Directions

2. **Formation of the Barley Grain—Morphology, Physiology, and Biochemistry.** C. M. DUFFUS and M. P. COCHRANE, 31

Introduction, 31
Embryo Development, 33
Carbohydrate Metabolism in the Developing Embryo, 34
Role of Nucellar Tissue in Grain Development, 34
Development of the Testa or Seed Coat, 37
Pericarp Development, 39
Pericarp Photosynthesis, 42
The Husk, 43
Endosperm Development, 43
  Starchy Endosperm • Aleurone
Nutrient Supply to the Developing Caryopsis, 56
  Sucrose Metabolism
Grain Catabolic Processes, 59
Overall Changes in Chemical Composition of Grains During Development and
Maturation, 61
  Sugars and Amino Acids • Starch, Protein, and Lipid • Mineral Elements •
  Composition of the Mature Grain
Environmental Effects on Grain Growth and Development, 65
Conclusions, 67

3. **Carbohydrates of the Barley Grain.** A. W. MacGREGOR and G. B. FINCHER, 73

Introduction, 73
Barley Starch, 74
  Amylose • Amylopectin • Starch Granules • Granule Size Distribution •
  Starch-Iodine • Interactions • Amylose Content of Barley Starch • Susceptibility
  of Starch Granules to Enzymatic Hydrolysis • Resistant Starch • Starch
  Gelatinization and Pasting
Cell Wall Polysaccharides, 96
  $(1\rightarrow3),(1\rightarrow4)$-$\beta$-Glucans • Arabinoxylans • Cellulose • Glucomannans •
  $(1\rightarrow3)$-β-Glucans
Other Carbohydrates, 116

4. **Barley Seed Proteins.** P. R. SHEWRY, **131**

Introduction, 131
Classification of Barley Seed Proteins, 131
Nonstorage Proteins, 132
  Albumins and Globulins • Glutelins and Residual Proteins • β-Amylase
  and Protein Z • Hordothionins • Endochitinases (Proteins C and T) • Protein
  Synthesis Inhibitors (Protein K) • Protease Inhibitors and Related Proteins •
  Aleurone-Specific Proteins • Miscellaneous Proteins of Known Function •
  Miscellaneous Proteins of Unknown Function
Storage Proteins, 158
  Globulin Storage Proteins • Prolamin Storage Proteins (Hordein)
Seed Protein Polymorphism in Varietal Identification and Fingerprinting, 181
Summary, 183

5. **Barley Lipids.** W. R. MORRISON, **199**

Introduction, 199
Methods of Analysis, 199
Lipids in the Whole Grain, 201
Distribution of Lipids in the Caryopsis, 204
  Nonstarch Lipids • Starch Lipids
Composition of Lipids, 214
  Fatty Acids in Nonstarch Lipids • Tocopherols • Fatty Acids in Starch Lipids
Enzymes Acting on Lipids, 220
  Lipase • Polar Lipid Acyl Hydrolase, Phospholipases-A and -B, and
  Lysophospholipase • Phospholipase-D • Lipoxygenase
Lipids in Developing Grain, 227
Changes in Lipids in Stored Grain, 228
Changes in Lipids in Germinating Barley, 229
Technological Aspects of Lipids, 232
  Interactions with Starch • Lipids in Brewing
Summary, 236

6. **Physiology and Biochemistry of Germination in Barley.**
    G. B. FINCHER and B. A. STONE, **247**

Introduction, 247
Hormone Action, 248
  Gibberellic Acid • Abscisic Acid
Aleurone Function During Germination, 251
  Morphological Changes • Biochemical Changes • Secretion of Enzymes •
  Role of Ca^{2+}
Scutellar Function During Germination, 256
  Morphological Changes • Biochemical Changes
Mobilization of Reserves in the Starchy Endosperm, 257
  Cell Walls • Starch • Reserve Proteins • Nucleic Acids
Structure and Regulation of Genes Encoding Hydrolytic Enzymes, 270
  Gene Structure • Regulation of Gene Expression at the Transcriptional Level
Protection of the Grain Against Microbial and Insect Attack, 273
  Enzymes • Enzyme Inhibitors • Thionins
Potential for Genetic Engineering, 280
  Malt Extract • Diastase Activity

7. **Malting Technology and the Uses of Malt.** C. W. BAMFORTH and
    A. H. P. BARCLAY, **297**

Introduction, 297

Biochemistry and Chemistry of Malting, 299
    Steeping • Germination • Biochemistry of Modification • Kilning
Properties of Barley with Regard to its Maltability, 311
    Viability • Dormancy • Water Sensitivity
Evaluation and Selection of Barley for Malting, 314
    Selection for Malting Quality in Breeding • Selection of Barley for
    Production Malting
Malting Technology, 315
    Barley Drying • Types of Storage • Steeping • Germination • Kilning
Uses for Malt, 332
    Brewing • Distilling • Vinegar • Other Food Uses

8. Nonmalting Uses of Barley. R. S. BHATTY, 355

Introduction, 355
Food Uses of Barley, 356
    Historical
Barley Food Products, 357
    Pearled Barley • Barley Milling • Barley Flour • Barley Bran
Malted and Germinated Barley Food Products, 364
Industrial (Nonmalting) Utilization of Barley, 366
Hypocholesterolemic Effects, 368
    Soluble Fiber • Animal and Human Feeding Experiments • Mechanisms
Feed Uses of Barley, 375
    Physical Factors
Chemical Factors, 378
    Protein • Lysine • Carbohydrates • Lipids • Polyphenols • Inhibitors
Barley for Poultry Feeding, 386
    Processing of Barley for Poultry Feed • Metabolizable Energy Content of Barley
    for Poultry • Barley for Laying Hens • Broiler Chicks • Mechanism of Action of
    β-Glucan
Barley for Swine Feeding, 393
    Processing Barley for Swine Feeds • β-Glucanase Treatment of Barley for Swine
    Feeds • Lysine Supplementation of Barley for Swine • Hull-less Barley for Swine
    Feeds
Barley for Ruminants, 400
Conclusions and Future Directions, 402

9. Potential Improvement of Barley Quality Through Genetic Engineering. K. J. KASHA, D. E. FALK, and A. ZIAUDDIN, 419

Introduction, 419
Potential Areas of Improvement for Malting, Brewing, Feed, and Food Uses, 420
    Comparison of Traits • Genetic Control of Quality Factors
Biotechnological Approaches to Genetic Modification of Barley, 424
    Molecular Technology • Plant Cell Cultures
Future Considerations, 431

10. Whole-Crop Utilization of Barley, Including Potential New Uses. P. B. PETERSEN and L. MUNCK, 437

Introduction, 437
Barley as an Industrial Raw Material, 440
Inventories to Ascertain the Potential Use of Barley and Other Cereals, 444
Dry and Wet Milling of Barley for Starch, 445
Utilization of Starch, 450

Utilization of Cereal Straw, **453**
   Chemical Composition • Botanical Components • Chemical Composition of
   Leaves and Internodes • Straw Milling and Fractionation • Uses of Mechanically
   Processed Fractions from Straw • Use of Straw Meal (Leaves) as Fodder • Use of
   Straw Meal for Energy
Realizing the Industrial Potential of Starch and Cellulose from Cereal Plants, **467**
Economic Considerations of the Use of Starch and Cellulose, **469**
Conclusion, **471**

Index, 475

CHAPTER 1

BARLEY: TAXONOMY, ORIGIN, DISTRIBUTION, PRODUCTION, GENETICS, AND BREEDING

R. A. NILAN
Department of Crop and Soil Sciences and
    Department of Genetics and Cell Biology
Washington State University
Pullman, WA 99164-6420

S. E. ULLRICH
Department of Crop and Soil Sciences
Washington State University
Pullman, WA 99164-6420

INTRODUCTION

Many important topics describing cultivated barley (*Hordeum vulgare* L.), hereafter referred to as barley, are covered in this chapter, including taxonomy, history, origin, genetics, cytology, cytogenetics, breeding, adaptation, production, and distribution. Most of these impinge, one way or another, upon the productivity, chemical composition, and end-use quality of the grain.

Each of these topics is important and warrants an individual chapter because over the past several years many books, monographs, and major reviews and hundreds of scientific articles have been written about each. However, for the purposes of this monograph, a general review of these topics should suffice as a background for readers who are primarily interested in barley chemistry and technology. This chapter provides basic information and major references, often review articles, from which interested readers can obtain more details about a particular topic. It certainly is not a comprehensive review for the specialist in any one of the topics described above.

Barley, a major world crop, ranks among the top 10 crops and is fourth among the cereals. Barley contributes significantly to the world's food supply as human food, malt products, and livestock feed. It also serves as an important experimental or model plant species for numerous studies in malting and brewing chemistry, plant breeding methodology, genetics, cytogenetics, restriction fragment length polymorphism genome mapping, mutagenesis, radiobiology, pathology (including the genetics of the pathogen and host and their

1

interrelationships), virology, physiology, and biotechnology (Hockett and Nilan, 1985; Hagberg, 1987).

Advances in molecular genetics, biotechnology, molecular evolution, and breeding of barley will certainly be of considerable value for advancing knowledge of the biology, chemistry, and biochemistry of barley grain. They will ultimately provide broader knowledge and greater variety of germ plasm that will lead to significant new breeding strategies and considerable trait improvements. These, in turn, will permit more rapid improvement of the various components that comprise end-use quality in livestock feed, human food, malt, and beer. Indeed, it is expected that the background provided in this chapter will give some hope to the barley chemist and technologist that such beneficial improvements in these areas of the barley grain are forthcoming.

TAXONOMY, HISTORY, ORIGIN, AND EVOLUTION

Many areas of barley research, including breeding, are influenced by barley taxonomy, origin, and evolution and by the relationships of these to those of other species and genera.

Taxonomy

Barley is a grass belonging to the family Poaceae, the tribe Triticeae, and the genus *Hordeum*. Taxonomic description and the details of morphology, ecology, and distribution of the various species of *Hordeum*, including cultivated barley, have been most recently described by Bothmer and Jacobsen (1985) and Bothmer et al (1987, 1991).

The chief taxonomic characteristic of *Hordeum* is its one-flowered spikelet (Bothmer and Jacobsen, 1985). Three spikelets alternate on opposite sides at each node of the flat rachis of the spike or head. Thus is formed a triplet of spikelets at each node—the central and the two laterals. Each spikelet is subtended by two glumes. When all three spikelets are fertile, the spike is described as six-rowed. When only the central spikelet is fertile, the spike is two-rowed.

Within each spikelet is a single floret consisting of a lemma, palea, the single female ovary and style, and three male stamens and anthers. Cultivated barley is self-pollinated with an extremely low occurrence of cross-pollination.

Cultivated barley (*H. vulgare*) is one of 31 *Hordeum* species tentatively separated into four sections. Among the 30 wild species, most are diploids ($2n = 14$), with about half being tetraploid ($2n = 28$) and hexaploid ($2n = 42$). Each of the three sections composed of wild species exhibits all three chromosome levels. Among the polyploids, at least four species are autoploids, while the rest are probably of allopolyploid or segmental allopolyploid origin.

Nearly three-fourths of the species are perennial (Bothmer and Jacobsen, 1985). Relationships or affinities among the species are studied to develop the taxonomy, understand evolution within the genus, and determine gene transfer potential among the species, especially between the cultivated and wild representatives. Meiotic chromosome pairing, chromosome architecture, as well as chromosome banding and isozyme- and DNA-variation patterns, are all being used to analyze species affinities (Bothmer et al, 1987).

H. vulgare comprises two subspecies and both cultivated and wild forms. All are closely related in terms of a number of biological factors and are interfertile. The cultivated forms are now considered the subspecies *vulgare* of *H. vulgare*, whereas the wild forms are described as the subspecies *spontaneum* of *H. vulgare*. The former is both two-rowed and six-rowed with nonbrittle rachises, whereas the latter is two-rowed with a brittle rachis.

History

Barley is among the most ancient of the cereal crops. Archeological studies have revealed two-rowed barley cultivation by about 8000 B.C. in Iran, with six-rowed barley appearing around 6000 B.C. (Bothmer and Jacobsen, 1985). However, other evidence indicates that barley in essentially the form we know it today existed and was used at least 17,000 years ago in the Nile River Valley of Egypt (Wendorf et al, 1979).

The original area of cultivation has been reported to be in the Fertile Crescent of the Middle East, in present day Lebanon, Iran, Iraq, and Turkey. This is also the most likely area of barley origin. There is now considerable evidence that barley was under cultivation in India and China considerably later than in the Middle East (Harlan, 1979). One of the best recent accounts of the history and prehistory of barley cultivation and distribution has been presented by Harlan (1979).

Origin and Evolution

Cultivated barley does not have a clearly traceable origin or path of descent. Since 1950, facts gathered from various disciplines, such as taxonomy and cytotaxonomy, archeology, history, ecology, geography, genetics, and cytogenetics, have shed considerable light on the evolution of cultivated and wild species of barley, on the origin of cultivated barley, and particularly on the roles of the often-proposed progenitors of cultivated barley, namely the two-rowed *H. vulgare spontaneum* and the six-rowed *H. vulgare agriocrithon*. The contributions of various disciplines to an understanding of the origin and evolution of cultivated barley have been analyzed in a thorough and elegant way by Harlan (1979) and to a lesser extent by Nilan (1964), Briggs (1978), and Bothmer and Jacobsen (1985). These contributions have emphasized that the time and place of origin and the evolution of cultivated barley are more obscure than previously supposed.

Most evidence suggests that the most recent and immediate ancestor of cultivated barley is the two-rowed wild *H. vulgare spontaneum*. The six-rowed forms are considered to be results of mutation and hybridization. Nevertheless, *H. v. spontaneum* is probably a transition between the true ancestor and cultivated barley, as the true progenitor of barley is earlier than the two-rowed *H. v. spontaneum* subspecies (Harlan, 1979). The nature of the "original barley" and its center of distribution, which could be its center of origin, are still unknown. Harlan (1979) concludes that a hypothetical progenitor for cultivated barley probably had a brittle rachis and was heterospiculate but had lateral florets less reduced than for *H. v. spontaneum*, as well as some other distinguishing traits.

Studies at the molecular level indicate considerable homology among barley, wheat, and rye (see below in this chapter and Fedak, 1985). These results must also be considered now in understanding the evolution of barley and possibly its origin.

ADAPTATION, DISTRIBUTION, AND PRODUCTION

From its apparent original center of cultivation in the Middle East, barley has spread around the world. A comprehensive review of the adaptation, distribution, and production of barley was presented by Poehlman (1985), who analyzed production of barley worldwide, with an emphasis on Africa, North America, South America, Asia, Europe, the former USSR, and Oceania.

Adaptation

Cultivated barley is adapted to and produced over a wider range of environmental conditions than any other cereal. It is grown farther toward the poles, into deserts, and at higher elevations than any other cereal and practically any other crop species. One of us (Ullrich) has observed barley growing at up to 4,200 m on the Altiplano and slopes of the Andes in Bolivia, at 65°N latitude in Alaska, on the fringe of the Sahara desert in Algeria, and near the equator in Ecuador and Kenya. According to Poehlman (1985), barley is grown as far north as 70°N latitude in Norway. Harlan (1979) describes barley production at 330 m below sea level near the Dead Sea.

Barley is a cool-season crop cultivated in the spring and summer at temperate latitudes and in the tropics at high elevations and in the winter at tropical and semitropical latitudes at low and medium elevations. It is relatively cold tolerant and is considered the most drought, alkali, and salt tolerant among the small-grain cereal-crop species, but it is not well adapted to acid and wet soil conditions (Poehlman, 1985). Barley's relatively early maturity and relatively low water use are major factors in its adaptation to drought and temperature extremes. Spring types are quite cold tolerant, but winter types are less winterhardy than wheat, rye, and triticale. In the driest areas, only barley and sometimes durum wheat extend to the limits of cultivation under temperate conditions.

Whereas barley survives and produces grain under extreme conditions, it grows best on well-drained, fertile loam soils under relatively cool temperatures (15–30°C) and moderate annual rainfall (500–1,000 mm). The highest commercial yields for barley tend to come from central and northern Europe (which exemplify the above conditions) at more than 10 t/ha under high-input conditions.

Distribution

The distribution of cultivated barley ultimately aligns with its adaptation in terms of both thriving and surviving. In 1989, the highest national average yields (over 5 t/ha) occurred under very favorable climatic and high management input conditions in West Germany, Belgium-Luxembourg, Switzerland, France, Ireland, the Netherlands, and Denmark. Under less favorable conditions, mainly due to suboptimum moisture and/or temperatures, country averages in 1989 ranged from 4.0 to 2.0 t/ha in Sweden, Poland, Italy, Norway, Finland, South Korea, Canada, the United States, and Spain. Yields of 2.0–0.3 t/ha, indicating poor to extremely poor growing conditions, occurred in 1989 in Australia, Turkey, India, Morocco, Ethiopia, Algeria, Bolivia, Tunisia, and Syria. The world average yield in 1989 was 2.3 t/ha based on nearly 170 million tonnes produced from about 75 million hectares (U.S. Feed Grains Council, 1990).

Production

The former USSR, due to its size and latitude range, was consistently the world's leading barley-producing country. The top 10 barley-producing countries, as estimated over the five-year period 1985–1989, are listed in Table 1. Whereas the giant USSR produced an average 50 million tonnes per year, which accounted for nearly 30% of the world's production, the 10th leading country was tiny Denmark, which produced an average of over 5 million tonnes per year and accounted for nearly 3% of world production. Barley produced in the former USSR and Denmark represented 25 and 85%, respectively, of each country's total cereal production (Poehlman, 1985). Interestingly, the 12 countries in the European Economic Community (EEC) produced almost as much barley as the USSR (48.4 vs. 50.5 million tonnes per year, 1985 -1989) but from less than half the area (12.4 vs. 29.5 million hectares per year, 1985–1989) (U.S. Feed Grains Council, 1990). The other top 10 countries are in North America (Canada and the United States), scattered across Europe (Germany, France, Spain, and the United Kingdom), and at

TABLE 1
Annual Barley Production Estimates[a] in the 10 Leading Barley-Producing Countries, Five-Year Averages, 1985–1989

Rank	Country	Production (1,000 t)	Area (1,000 ha)	Yield (t/ha)	World Production (%)
1	USSR	50.452	29.482	1.7	28.8
2	Canada	12,580	4,687	2.7	7.2
3	United States	10.524	4,007	2.6	6.0
4	France	10,320	1,991	5.2	5.9
5	Spain	9,716	4,283	2.3	5.5
6	W. Germany[b]	9,395	1,866	5.0	5.4
7	United Kingdom	9,149	1,858	4.9	5.2
8	Turkey	6,360	3,270	1.9	3.6
9	China	6,218	3,369	1.8	3.5
10	Denmark	5,050	1,058	4.8	2.9
	Top 10	129,756	55,871	2.3	74.0
	World	175,400	78,500	2.2	100.0

[a] Data from U.S. Feed Grains Council (1990).
[b] E. Germany had annual averages of 4,133 million tonnes from 889 million hectares (4.7 t/ha) for the same period. Therefore, the combined (East and West) German annual averages for the same period were 13,528 million tonnes from 2,755 million hectares (4.8 t/ha).

the eastern and western extremes in Asia (China and Turkey). Other major barley-producing countries within regions include Africa: Morocco, Algeria, Ethiopia; East Asia: South Korea, Japan; South and West Asia: India, Iran, Iraq, Syria; Europe: Poland, Czechoslovakia, Sweden, Romania; Oceania: Australia; and South America: Argentina, Brazil (U.S. Feed Grains Council, 1990). Other countries that produce relatively less but for which barley is important because it occupies greater than 25% of their cereal area and/or is the only cereal in a region (e.g., the high Andes) include North Africa: Tunisia, Libya; West Asia: Jordan, Cyprus; Europe: Benelux, Finland, Norway, Ireland, Switzerland; Oceania: New Zealand; and South America: Bolivia and Peru (Poehlman, 1985; U.S. Feed Grains Council, 1990).

Major barley-user nations tend to have considerable domestic production and/or are active in the import/export market. The top 10 importers and exporters of barley based on volume traded (tonnes per year) over the last five years are listed in Table 2. The leading exporters of barley have been France and Canada, whereas the leading importers have been Saudi Arabia and the former USSR. The USSR and Germany have been top 10 producers as well as top 10 importers, and two of the leading importers are leading exporters as well: Belgium-Luxembourg and Germany. The EEC countries collectively are both major exporters and importers, but the EEC as a unit exports nearly three times what it imports. Where major importing and exporting occur within the same country or countries, quality is usually the basis, with feed grade barley being exported and malting grade barley imported or vice versa.

The origin and distribution of cultivation (Wiebe, 1979; Poehlman, 1985) and production and marketing of barley in North America (Wilson, 1985) have been reviewed. Four distinct types of barley apparently are now grown in North America, and they originated from different areas around the world. The first, the Midwest type of malting barley, as illustrated by the six-rowed spring cultivars Morex and Bonanza, originally came from Manchuria (Northern China) and neighboring countries. This type is grown in the north central states and in the Prairie Provinces of Canada. The second, the Coast group, grown principally in the West (including California, Oregon, Idaho,

TABLE 2
Top 10 Exporters and Importers of Barley, Five-Year Averages, 1985–1989[a]

Rank	Exporters	Volume (million t/yr)	Importers	Volume (million t/yr)
1	*France	4.4	Saudi Arabia	5.9
2	Canada	4.3	USSR	3.1
3	*United Kingdom	3.1	Japan	1.3
4	Australia	2.1	*Belgium-Luxembourg	1.2
5	United States	2.1	*Italy	1.0
6	*W. Germany	1.4	E. Germany	1.0
7	*Denmark	1.1	*W. Germany	0.9
8	*Spain	1.0	*Netherlands	0.7
9	*Belgium-Luxembourg	0.7	Libya	0.6
10	*Ireland	0.3	Algeria	0.4
...	EEC[b]	12.2	EEC[b]	4.2

[a] Data from U.S. Feed Grains Council (1990).
[b] European Economic Community (12 countries); * = members.

Washington, and some of the intermountain states), is six-rowed with primarily a spring habit of growth and typified by the cultivar Steptoe. Sometimes varieties of this type are sown in the winter or fall. The Coast type originated from North Africa and was brought to North America via California by early Spaniards. Third, the two-rowed barleys, typified by Harrington and Klages, have European origin, and most of these are used for malting. They are grown in Alberta, Saskatchewan, and western Manitoba in Canada and in the Pacific Northwest and the intermountain states as far east as western North and South Dakota in the United States. A fourth group, winter barleys, probably originated from the Balkan-Caucasus region and from Korea. They are six-rowed (such as Kamiak and Schuyler), have a winter growth habit, and are grown principally in the southeastern and eastern states, the southern Great Plains, and the Pacific Northwest. More recently, another type of commercial livestock feed/human food barley has been emerging: hull-less or naked barley. These are spring two- and six-rowed types developed in western North America. Initial cultivars have included Scout, Tupper (Rossnagel et al, 1983, 1985), and Condor from Canada and Odyssey from the United States. Waxy (essentially 100% amylopectin starch) hull-less types are also being developed, especially for human food use. The hull-less trait is controlled by a single recessive gene (n) and is easily incorporated into adapted germ plasm. The waxy gene (wx) is also simply inherited and easily transferred.

Barley is the second ranking cereal after wheat in Canada and is grown mainly in the Prairie Provinces. In the five years from 1985 to 1989, the average annual Canadian barley production was 12.6 million tonnes from 4.7 million hectares (Table 1). Alberta, Saskatchewan, and Manitoba had 2.1, 1.4, and 0.7 million hectares, respectively, a total of 4.2 (90%) out of the annual average national total of 4.7 million hectares. These three provinces accounted for 88% (11.1 of 12.6 million tonnes) of the Canadian average annual barley production (Statistics Canada, 1989). Canada used an average of 8.4 million tonnes per year in the five years 1985–1989, 90% of it for feed and approximately 10% for malting and brewing. Canada exported 4.3 million tonnes per year over that same period (U.S. Feed Grains Council, 1990).

Barley is the fourth ranking cereal (after maize, wheat, and sorghum) in the United States. The five top-ranking barley-producing states are the northern tier states from Minnesota to Washington. The five states, in rank order by millions of tonnes, are North Dakota (2.1), Montana (1.5), Idaho (1.3), Minnesota (1.0), and Washington (0.6); they produced 75% of the total 8.8 million tonnes of barley produced (USDA-NASS, 1990) in 1989 in the United States. These five states had 77% of the total barley area in 1989. The states ranking sixth to 10th in production are all west of the Mississippi River and include, in order by millions of tonnes, South Dakota (0.4), California (0.3), Colorado (0.3), Oregon (0.3), and Utah (0.2). The top 10 states produced 90% of the barley in the United States in 1989 (USDA-NASS, 1990).

The United States used 9.1 million tonnes per year averaged over the five-year period from 1985 to 1989 (U.S. Feed Grains Council, 1990). During this same period, approximately 58% was used for feed and 40% was used for malting and brewing, with 2% used for food. The average value of barley as a raw agricultural commodity during the period 1983–1987 was U.S. $1.2

billion annually. With value-added from barley used in beer (U.S. $3 billion) and the U.S. federal excise taxes (U.S. $1.6 billion), the value rose to U.S. $5.6 billion dollars (Beer Institute, 1988); and with value-added for feed use (U.S. $2.4 billion; C. W. Newman, *personal communication*, 1989), the value rose to U.S. $8.2 billion annually. No figures are available for food use value-added.

CYTOLOGY, GENETICS, AND CYTOGENETICS

Barley is among the top half-dozen experimental organisms in genetic and cytogenetic analyses of flowering plants. The wide use of this important agricultural crop species in genetic studies is attributed to its diploid and self-fertile nature, ease of hybridization, and hundreds of easily classified heritable characters. Over 1,200 traits have been identified (Søgaard and von Wettstein-Knowles, 1987; von Wettstein-Knowles, 1990); many genes controlling these traits have been identified with the chromosomes; and at least 120 have been located to specific sites on the seven chromosome linkage maps (Tsuchiya, 1987; von Wettstein-Knowles, 1990). Many of the traits are of artificial mutant origin as a result of physical and chemical mutagen induction. There is no doubt that the immense number of induced mutations and mutants involving traits ranging from the plant to the molecular level have advanced the genetic analyses of barley.

Barley's intensive use in cytogenetics is attributable to its low number ($2n = 14$) of relatively large, distinct chromosomes, which allow detection of several kinds of chromosome aberrations or mutants. Many of these have arisen from physical and chemical mutagens and have played a major role in mapping, breeding, and analyzing the barley genome.

The cytology, genetics, and cytogenetics of barley, including mitosis; meiosis; gene nomenclature; genetics of traits; recombination and linkage data; mutagenesis; and the nature, behavior and uses of gene and chromosome mutants have been extensively reviewed and summarized in several major publications (Smith, 1951; Nilan, 1964, 1975; Briggs, 1978; Hockett and Nilan, 1985; Ramage, 1985). Much of the related research over the past 30 years has been described in the proceedings of the international barley genetics symposia (Lamberts et al, 1964; Nilan, 1971; Gaul, 1976; Whitehouse, 1981; Yasuda and Konishi, 1987). Information on cytology, genetics, and cytogenetics appears annually in the *Barley Genetics Newsletter* (beginning in 1971) and occasionally in the *Barley Newsletter* (beginning in 1954).

Thus, it is safe to say that the genetics, cytology, and cytogenetics of barley have been thoroughly reviewed, and every attempt has been made to maintain the literature in summary form for scientists working on different facets of this research over the past several years.

Cytology

Cultivated barley has seven pairs of chromosomes, whereas wild species occur with seven, 14, or 21 pairs. Their characteristics and behavior, in mitosis and meiosis, have been summarized (Nilan, 1964; Briggs, 1978; Ramage, 1985). The chromosomes can be easily distinguished in mitotic metaphase cells using root-tip squash techniques. Ideograms are readily produced, and the various distinguishing features leading to the standard karyotype are revealed. They are arabically numbered from one to seven, which also corresponds to the numbering of the linkage groups. The seven chromosomes are relatively large, measuring 6–8 μm in length, and are best characterized by total length, arm-length ratios (centromere placement), and secondary constrictions leading to satellites and tertiary constrictions. There are two satellite chromosomes, 6 and 7, with 6 having the longer and 7 the shorter satellite. The other chromosomes are best distinguished by length, with 1 being the longest and 5 the shortest. The chromosomes are also identified by Giemsa C and N banding patterns (Linde-Laursen, 1988). Bands are located mostly near the centromeres and secondary constrictions, with very few at the ends or in intercalary regions. The banding pattern of *H. v. spontaneum* is similar to that of cultivated barley. Variation in banding patterns in cultivated and wild barley species has been summarized (Søgaard and Wettstein-Knowles, 1987; Linde-Laursen, 1988). Sister-chromatid exchanges have been observed at metaphase in root-tip squashes (Ramage, 1985).

Meiotic chromosomes are best seen at diakinesis or metaphase I in squashes of microsporocytes. The analysis of chromosomes at the pachytene stage is quite difficult because of the clumped and knotted chromosome figures and the difficulty in distinguishing centromeres (Nilan, 1975).

Of particular interest to barley geneticists and breeders is the fact that chiasmata formation and crossing over are found near the ends of the chromosomes. This phenomenon leads to considerable differences between physical and genetic distances between loci and to problems in developing linkage maps. It is expected that the use of molecular markers (described later in this chapter) in gene mapping will reconcile genetic data and establish true physical distances between genes on each chromosome arm.

Genetics

As indicated above, the genetics of barley has been quite thoroughly studied, and major reviews are available. Only a brief summary is presented here. An up-to-date list of known genes, updated conventional linkage maps, and a summary of recent advances in molecular genetics, as well as molecular marker maps, have been published (Søgaard and Wettstein-Knowles, 1987; Melzer and Kleinhofs, 1987a,b; Wettstein-Knowles, 1989, 1990; Graner et al, 1991; Heun et al, 1991; Kleinhofs et al, 1993).

SOURCES OF VARIATION

Basic to all genetic and breeding studies is genetic variation. Fortunately, barley is rich in spontaneous and induced variants that have been the life blood of genetic and breeding progress. New sources of genetic variation are being transferred slowly to barley through interspecific and intergeneric hybridization.

Spontaneous Mutants. Genetic studies, commencing about 1890 when Mendel's laws were rediscovered and increasing in volume ever since, have revealed an extensive, natural variation in barley. This variation has been indispensable for a vast array of scientific studies conducted with barley and for barley improvement. Many of the spontaneous variants (mutants), land races, and cultivars that make up the natural germ plasm source for this variation are found in numerous collections (Moseman and Smith, 1985; Chapman, 1987; Knüpffer et al, 1987). These include those of the United States (25,000 entries), Canada (21,000 entries), Japan (12,000 entries), Nordic countries (14,000 entries), the former USSR (18,000 entries), International Center for Agricultural Research in the Dry Areas (ICARDA) (21,000 entries), and Germany (15,000 entries). Numerous special genetic stocks are maintained in the USDA Seed Storage Laboratory at Fort Collins, CO; in the Nordic Gene Bank in Sweden; and in smaller holdings in Japan and Germany. All collections have been analyzed frequently to determine the extent of variation and distribution of a number of important economic traits, such as pest resistance, early maturity, yield, and adaptation, as well as traits contributing to the chemical and physical characteristics of the grain that, in turn, determine livestock feed, human food, and malting and brewing quality. An interesting history of the analysis of various genes and spontaneous mutants, mainly determining plant characteristics, has been presented by Tsuchiya (1987).

Induced Mutants. Another important source of variation utilized in numerous basic and applied studies involving barley is contributed by induced mutants. Most of the reports published on barley mutagenesis and induced mutants have been listed in Briggs (1978), Konzak et al (1984), Hockett and Nilan (1985), and Nilan (1981a,b, 1987).

Induced mutants now constitute a large portion of the variation available for genetic, breeding, physiological, and biochemical studies. Since the early 1930s, when it was first discovered that radiation induced mutations in plants, barley has been a model plant for studying the genetic and cytological effects of a wide variety of mutagens (Lundqvist, 1991).

Barley is ideal for studying the genetic effects of mutagens because it is readily cultured in both field and greenhouse, and it permits the measurement of numerous biological end-points following a single mutagen treatment. These include easily measured growth patterns; characteristic, frequent, and easily scored chlorophyll-deficient seedling mutants; pollen mutants; chromosome aberrations or mutants in meiosis and mitosis; sterility; seedling growth; and DNA changes such as single- and double-strand breaks. Moreover, it permits the selection of a wide array of mutants at the molecular, cellular, and plant levels (Nilan, 1981b, 1987). The chlorophyll-deficient mutant assay (Constantin and Nilan, 1982b) and the chromosome aberration assays (Constantin and Nilan, 1982a) have been described in detail.

Several radiation types, including X- and γ-rays, neutrons, and UV light and numerous chemicals including some fungicides, herbicides, and insecticides are strongly to weakly mutagenic in barley (Nilan, 1981a, 1987). In general, frequencies of chlorophyll-deficient mutations as measured on an M_1-spike basis (an M_1-spike is the head of the barley plant raised from a mutagen-treated seed and containing M_2 seed) can be increased to 15–17% by X- and γ-rays and neutrons and to as high as 45–50% by a number of chemicals, including ethyl methanesulfonate and diethylsulfate. Frequencies up to 75–80% have been recorded following sodium azide treatment.

Sodium azide is the preferred chemical for mutation induction, as it is effective and efficient, inducing high frequencies of mutations and very few chromosome aberrations. Its metabolic conversion to the mutagenic agent (azidoalanine) and mode of action in barley and other organisms where it is mutagenic have been described (Kleinhofs et al, 1978; Owais and Kleinhofs, 1988). It is slightly, if at all, mutagenic in mammalian cells since azide is not converted to the mutagenic azidoalanine in these cells (Arenaz et al, 1989). This is fortunate since azide is the gas-generating chemical in automobile airbags and aeroplane escape chutes, and thus the production of this chemical and the subsequent exposure of humans to it is increasing enormously as airbags are becoming standard on many makes of automobiles.

It is clear from several studies that mutations induced by azide via azidoalanine are not chromosome rearrangements. Rather they appear to be DNA base changes. For example, K. Kristiansen and D. Wettstein (Carlsberg Laboratory, Copenhagen, *personal communication*) have determined that azide mutagenesis occurs within one of the genes, *Ant 18*, controlling the flavonoid biosynthetic pathway. The nature of the azide-induced mutations may be determined soon by DNA sequencing. No insertions or deletions within the gene have occurred in the mutations of *Ant 18*.

Induced mutants exist for just about every recognizable trait. For many traits, induced and spontaneous mutants (variants) appear to be similar. However, there are now several traits for which induced mutations have revealed complementation groups (loci) and alleles not found among the spontaneous genetic variance that has arisen in the recent evolutionary history of the barley species. Thus, the genetic variation induced and revealed for many traits has increased enormously (Nilan, 1981b).

A striking example involves the deposition of epicuticular waxes controlled by the *cer* (*eceriferum*) gene. Systematic allele testing among thousands of induced mutants has revealed 1,580 *eceriferum* mutants at 79 loci (Lundqvist, 1991). At some loci the number of induced alleles amounts to 40 or more, while at other loci the number is less than five. Spontaneous variation for this trait has revealed only six controlling loci.

Induced mutants have also extended the genetic variability and phenotypes of several other traits. The following indicates some of these traits with the number of loci in parenthesis: spike density, *ert* (*erectoides*) (26); male sterility, *msg* (34); flavonoid production, *ant* (27); desynaptic chromosomes, *des* (15); awn length, *lk* (17); maturity, *ea* (9); row number of spikelets, *V, I* (12); and shrunken endosperm, *seg* or *sex* (14) (Nilan, 1987; Wettstein-Knowles, 1989; Lundqvist, 1991). Analyses of thousands of induced chlorophyll-deficient mutants have revealed that probably 600-700 loci are involved in chlorophyll synthesis (Nilan, 1981b; Constantin and Nilan, 1982b). Known loci numbers (in parenthesis) revealed chiefly by induced mutants for the various chlorophyll-deficient mutants are: albino, *a, alb* (12); tigrina, *tig* (15); chlorina, *clo, f* (15); virides, *vir* (36); and xantha, *x, xan* (23) (Nilan, 1987; Lundqvist, 1991).

Induced mutants have also provided increased variation for probing and elucidating basic biochemical, physiological, developmental, and anatomical processes; the nature of mutations; and the structure of loci (Nilan, 1981b, 1987). Of particular interest for this review, they are broadening the available genetic basis and and increasing the understanding of a number of traits involved in grain quality and physical characteristics. Mutations affecting specific compounds or involved in selected biochemical pathways related to these characteristics have been identified and analyzed. According to Wettstein-Knowles (1989), seven complementation groups for the lysine content of seeds, 10 for esterases, and seven involved in nitrate assimilation have been identified.

Induced mutants have also been used widely to develop new cultivars—either directly or through crosses (see discussion of breeding below). Extensive collections of induced mutants and mutant cultivars are maintained, particularly in the Nordic Gene Bank (Sweden), Germany, Japan, and the USDA Seed Storage Laboratory at Fort Collins, CO (Chapman, 1987; Moseman and Smith, 1985).

Interspecific and Intergeneric Hybrids. In spite of the vast array of spontaneous and induced mutants, it is still not always possible to find needed variants of economic traits for barley breeding and the development of new cultivars. Therefore, related species and genera present another important source of variation. In attempts to utilize this variability, numerous interspecific and intergeneric hybrids have been created (Fedak, 1985, 1987).

Among the approximately 30 wild species of barley, very few have been screened for agronomic trait potential. Inherent problems, such as degree of crossability, sterility of hybrids, failure of chromosome doubling, and the separation of desirable from undesirable linked traits, make the use of wild species a very difficult method of gene transfer.

In transferring economic traits from wild to cultivated species, Bothmer et al (1987) have recognized three categories of gene pools, depending upon the degree of crossability. The primary gene pool consists of *H. v. spontaneum*, in which there are no crossing barriers with *H. v. vulgare*; the secondary gene pool consists of *H. bulbosum*, which has a rather high crossability with *H. vulgare*; and the tertiary gene pool consists of all other wild species, which appear to have literally no crossability with *H. vulgare* and in which gene transfer will be most difficult.

Some success has been achieved in transferring genes from wild species to cultivated barley, including successful cultivars developed from crosses involving interspecific hybrids (Fedak, 1985). Fedak (1985) and von Bothmer et al (1987) list numerous useful traits that exist in the wild barley species, such as resistance to certain diseases, winterhardiness, salt and drought tolerance, and unique lipid and protein composition.

Species of *Hordeum* and cultivars of *H. vulgare* have been crossed with other genera within the tribe Triticeae such as species and cultivars of *Triticum* (wheat), species and cultivars of *Secale* (rye), cultivars of *Triticale* (wheat-rye hybrid), and species of *Elymus* (wild-rye) and *Agropyron* (wheatgrass) (Fedak, 1985, 1987). These crosses have been made primarily to determine affinities among the genera of the Triticeae for an understanding of evolutionary pathways and to transfer traits such as drought tolerance, winterhardiness, straw strength, and disease and insect resistance into barley. Such transfers have not yet been achieved, although as Fedak (1985) indicates, breeders and geneticists have only begun to tap the potential of this source of variation.

A degree of homeology among the genera of the Triticeae has been found. For instance, barley chromosomes 1, 2, 3, 4, 5, 6, and 7 are homeologous to the wheat chromosomes 7, 2, 3, 4, 1, 6 and 5, respectively (Fedak, 1985).

Wheat-barley addition lines, where an individual barley chromosome pair has been added to the chromosome complement of wheat, have been developed;

their origin and breeding behavior are described by Ramage (1985) and Fedak (1985). Besides the various uses of these wheat-barley addition lines, they also permit the possibility of transferring barley characters to wheat. However, they cannot be used to transfer wheat characters into barley.

GENETIC ANALYSIS

Information about genetic analysis in barley has been well presented in several of the reviews listed in the introduction of this section. In the beginning of barley genetic studies, the most frequently detected and studied genetic characters were those that had been readily classified by visual inspection (Tsuchiya, 1987). Most of these characters were found to be controlled by single genes that usually segregated in 3:1 ratios. Later, multiple gene action was indicated for several characters such as plant height, straw strength, and yield. In recent years and with the help of induced mutants, genes controlling molecular and biochemical processes, including those leading to proteins contained in the grain, have been analyzed with increasing frequency (Melzer and Kleinhofs, 1987a,b; Shewry et al, 1987; Wettstein-Knowles, 1989).

Other forms of inheritance and gene expression have been found in barley. Xenia (the immediate effect of pollen on the embryo or endosperm) occurs for traits such as waxy endosperm and blue aleurone color. Maternal inheritance has been studied quite extensively and, according to Tsuchiya (1987), 21 lines of chlorophyll mutants, including chlorina, yellow stripe, and white stripe, have demonstrated maternal inheritance. Their gene control is obviously in the chloroplast.

The most recent lists of traits and nuclear genes in barley have been provided by Søgaard and Wettstein-Knowles (1987) and Wettstein-Knowles (1990), and the genetics of many of the traits have been summarized in Hockett and Nilan (1987), including those relating to kernel structure, biochemistry, and physiology. Most recent summaries of malting and nutritional quality, including some genetic information, are presented by Burger and LaBerge (1985) and Newman and McGuire (1985). Detailed information on the diseases (Kiesling, 1985) and insects (Starks and Webster, 1985) of barley have been published. The genetics of resistance to these and other pests has been summarized (Sharp, 1985).

MOLECULAR GENETICS

Genetic analysis at the molecular level has been relatively slow to develop in barley due to barley's relatively large genome size and complexity, limited cell culture capability, and lack of a transformation or transgenic system. Recently, however, this activity has been increased by use of improved cell and tissue culture techniques, including anther and microspore culture; induced genic and chromosome mutants; and rapidly advancing knowledge and technology in barley molecular biology. Progress in this area of barley genetics has been reviewed recently by Wettstein (1983, 1989), Melzer and Kleinhofs (1987a,b), Søgaard and Wettstein-Knowles (1987), and Wettstein-Knowles (1989). A comprehensive review of the biotechnology and molecular genetics of barley appears in Shewry (1992).

As in other higher plants, barley has its genetic information stored in three different genomes, namely, the chloroplast, mitochondrial, and nuclear genomes. Recent knowledge about the molecular genetics of these genomes is described in the above publications. The chloroplast genome is the most thoroughly characterized to date. It consists of 133 kilobase pairs with a total of 27 genes mapped. About 80% of the genome is cloned and extensively analyzed. Little is known about the mitochondrial genome, as analysis has only just begun (Yamaguchi and Tsutsumi, 1987). The nuclear genome is large, with a haploid nucleus value of 5.5 pg and approximately 5.5×10^9 base pairs. The number of functional genes is estimated to be about 50,000. Repeated sequences amount to about 75%, and nonrepeated sequences equal about 25%.

The technology required to fully understand the molecular genetics of barley traits includes gene cloning, genetic transformation with single genes, and transposon tagging of unknown genes. Gene cloning has been underway since about 1980, and many genes have now been cloned. Sixteen genomic and 47 cDNA clones have been described by Wettstein-Knowles (1990). However, transformation and transposon tagging are not yet developed in barley.

Genetic transformation of barley is forthcoming. Delivery systems for DNA have been developed, but regeneration of whole plants from transformed cells in culture has not yet been achieved at this writing. Nevertheless, research in this area is increasing rapidly, and success is a matter of time (Kleinhofs, 1985; Jensen, 1987; Wang et al, 1993). Protoplast fusions have been attempted to a limited extent. The *Agrobacterium* Ti-plasmid-mediated transformation, successful in some plant systems, is not successful in the cereals, including barley. Electroporation and DNA microinjection have been tried without success. The current, most promising approach focuses on microspore or embryoid cells from anther culture as the targets for bombardment with DNA-coated tungsten or gold particles. There are two or three genetic systems in barley that should lend themselves to a successful transformation. Transient expression of reporter genes in aleurone protoplasts has been achieved (Jensen, 1990).

Transposable elements have proven to be valuable tools for gene tagging or isolation in some species, such as maize and *Antirrhinum*, but not yet in barley. Indeed, transposable elements have not yet been detected in barley. Rohde et al (1987) have reviewed the prospects of transposon tagging in barley and have suggested certain genes that could serve as traps for transposable elements.

The molecular genetics of genes controlling barley seed proteins has been studied most extensively (Melzer and Kleinhofs, 1987b; Shewry et al, 1987; Khursheed and Rogers, 1988). These include the genes for hordeins, α-amylase, β-amylase, protein Z, α-amylase/subtilisin inhibitor, chymotrypsin inhibitors CI-1 and CI-2, antigen 1 B, and α-glucanase. The molecular genetics of other genes such as nitrate reductase, chlorophyll a/b protein, and ribosomal RNA has been reviewed (Melzer and Kleinhofs, 1987a).

Monoclonal antibodies constitute another powerful tool in plant molecular genetics. A monoclonal antibody is the specific product of a single cell from among the thousands making different antibodies against an antigen. They have been used in barley to characterize hordeins and identify their mutants (Ullrich et al, 1986a, 1987). Selection procedures are being developed to utilize immunological techniques for mutant selection and applied plant breeding (Rasmussen, 1985; Ullrich et al, 1987).

RECOMBINATION AND MAPPING

Recombination is the combination of genes different from those of the parents as a result of crossing over at meiosis. Studies of this important event have been numerous from the beginning of barley genetic studies in the early 1900s (Tsuchiya, 1987). These studies have intensified and, of course, have been the basis for the development of the conventional genetic linkage maps. There is no doubt that recombination and mapping studies in barley are as extensive as for any crop species except possibly maize and tomato. Over the past 50 years, reasonable genetic linkage maps have been constructed (Smith, 1951; Nilan, 1964; Søgaard and Wettstein-Knowles, 1987; Tsuchiya, 1987). The most recent have been prepared by Wettstein-Knowles (1990) and Kleinhofs et al (1993).

Although recombination is a most basic and important process in genetics, little is known about its control. Extensive studies are beginning to reveal that genetic variation for recombination exists in barley (Sall, 1989, 1990; Sall et al, 1990).

The various problems with conventional recombination and mapping procedures are well described by Tsuchiya (1987). As pointed out, locating genes on the chromosomes has been greatly aided on a physical basis by the use of a variety of induced chromosome mutants, as well as the chromosome banding techniques developed by Linde-Laursen (1988).

With all the efforts of the past 50 years in conventional recombination and linkage studies, at least 120 loci have been mapped to the seven chromosomes of barley (Wettstein-Knowles, 1990). This is only a fraction of the known genes (about 1,200), most of which have been assigned to a chromosome but not mapped. The mapped genes are not evenly distributed over the seven chromosomes, and there are arms or major chromosome segments within which few genes have been located. This is probably a result of the fact that chiasmata formation and crossing over are restricted to the proximal ends of the chromosomes. Thus, it is obvious that a saturated gene map of barley is most important for furthering classical and molecular genetics.

Restriction fragment length polymorphism (RFLP) has become a powerful and important tool in barley for constructing detailed linkage maps; identifying unknown genes and alleles, the magnitude of gene effects, and types of gene action; determining the location of trait loci; and facilitating genetic engineering (Nilan, 1990). Moreover, it will provide a greater understanding of the barley genome and its evolution and the genetic basis for the important economic traits for barley breeding.

Starting with the initial studies of Blake (1987) and Kleinhofs et al (1988), the North American Barley Genome Mapping Project has been initiated (Nilan, 1990). This is a major, cooperative, multiinstitutional project involving U.S. and Canadian scientists designed to develop a saturated "public" linkage map of barley using RFLPs. This project, involving nearly 50 scientists in more than 25 different laboratories in both countries, covers basic mapping and map construction through to the identification and location of genes controlling economic traits (Ullrich et al, 1993) and the development of new germ plasm and breeding strategies. Doubled haploids from the six-rowed cross Steptoe/ Morex and the two-rowed cross Harrington/TR306 are both mapped with RFLP markers and genetically analyzed for genes controlling economic traits such as yield, biotic and abiotic stress, malting, and quality for human food and livestock feed. A 295-point map has been developed from the Steptoe/ Morex cross (Kleinhofs et al, 1993). Linkages between RFLP and economic trait genes will determine the location of the qualitative and/or quantitative genes controlling the economic traits. Using the doubled haploids from a cross (Proctor/Nudinka), Heun et al (1991) have placed 144 RFLP markers on the barley linkage map. Other mapping-related studies have been published recently (Shin et al, 1990; Graner et al, 1991; Hayes et al, 1993). RFLP mapping and related projects are also progressing in Sweden, Denmark, Finland, Norway, England, the Netherlands, Germany, and Australia. It is expected that the maps constructed in these countries, from the Proctor/Nudinka cross and from the crosses of the U.S.-Canadian project, will be merged. In addition, the International Triticeae Mapping Initiative is under way, with one of its aims being to make RFLP maps of the genomes of wheat, rye, and barley to increase understanding of evolutionary relationships among these genera.

Cytogenetics

Because of the low number of relatively large chromosomes in barley, alterations in chromosome number and structure are easy to detect both at mitosis and meiosis and are readily isolated and maintained. Most of the chromosome mutants have been detected occasionally in natural populations. However, ionizing radiation and certain chemicals have increased the numbers and array of these mutants to where they have become very important tools for various studies in genetics, cytogenetics, and breeding. This section briefly reviews the alterations in chromosome number and structure. Their origins, descriptions, inheritance, behavior, and uses are described in more detail in Nilan (1964), Briggs (1978), and Ramage (1985).

ALTERATION IN CHROMOSOME NUMBER

Barley is a diploid with 14 chromosomes designated as $2n = 14$. Euploids contain cells with an exact multiple of the diploid number, designated as $2n = 21$, $2n = 28$, $2n = 56$, etc., for polyploids, or half of the diploid number, designated as $n = 7$, for haploids. Aneuploids contain cells with more or fewer chromosomes than the basic number such as $2n + 1$, $2n - 1$, etc.

Euploids. The euploids most frequently detected include haploids ($n = 7$), triploids ($2n = 21$), and autotetraploids ($2n = 28$).

Haploids are generated most readily through anther or pollen culture and by chromosome elimination in crosses between cultivated barley and *H. bulbosum* (Ramage, 1985). They also occur in relatively high frequency in progenies of plants possessing the haploid-initiator gene (*hap*) (Hagberg and Hagberg, 1987b,c). They are usually miniatures of the diploid parent and always are sterile. Their value lies in their fertile chromosome-doubled homozygous products, doubled haploids, which arise spontaneously or following colchicine treatment. Haploids are by far the most used of the euploids, being used with ever-increasing frequency in plant breeding and genetics research. Their new important uses are in the molecular marker genome mapping of barley and in doubled haploid breeding techniques.

Triploids, because of their unbalanced chromosome numbers, are usually partially fertile and are found only occasionally in nature. They are produced from crosses between triploids and autotetraploids, from plants carrying the triploid inducer gene (*tri*), or from an aneuploid (trisomic). They are sources of aneuploids and euploids (Ramage, 1985).

Autotetraploids have four sets of chromosomes, have thicker leaves and stems and are later maturing and shorter than diploid plants, and are partially sterile. They occur spontaneously and have been induced by treatments of heat and of various chemicals, especially colchicine. They are also found in the progenies of various aneuploids and triploids. About 160 autotetraploids have been isolated and are maintained in an appropriate collection (Ramage, 1985). Because of the partial sterility, no tetraploid cultivars have been developed. Nevertheless, improvements in fertility are being achieved through intercrossing different autotetraploids.

Aneuploids. Barley, being a diploid, can tolerate the addition of only one chromosome to the complement. Such a plant has the chromosome number $2n = 15$ and is called a trisomic. The extra chromosome may comprise various amounts and kinds of different chromosomes. Plants with addition of individual chromosomes above the trisomic number or subtractions of chromosomes below the diploid number do not survive, and thus plants with these numbers have not been collected.

Seven primary trisomics are possible in cultivated barley, and to date there are several sets of these trisomics with different genetic backgrounds, including *H. v. spontaneum*. Each primary trisomic can be easily distinguished from the other six. There is sufficient transmission of the extra chromosome through the female gametes to make them sufficiently fertile to be used in genetic and cytogenetic studies. They occur spontaneously in cultivated barley fields and also have been derived from translocations and triploids. Because each of the seven trisomic chromosomes can be readily distinguished genetically, the primary trisomics have been most effective in associating genes with chromosomes and have been most useful in developing the linkage maps of barley.

Special types of trisomics, the tertiary and balanced tertiary, have been collected in large numbers. They are used in assigning genes to chromosome segments, mapping translocation break points, and orienting linkage maps, and they have potential use in hybrid barley production (Ramage, 1985).

A telocentric chromosome is another special type of trisomic chromosome. It possesses a centromere and only one complete arm of a normal chromosome. Telotrisomics have been collected and studied intensively by Tsuchiya (1987), who has established a telocentric representative of each of the 14 arms of the seven chromosomes. There is good transmission of the telocentric trisomic, and thus the telotrisomic plants are relatively fertile. They have been useful in associating genes with chromosome arms and localizing the centromere in linkage maps (Ramage, 1985).

Acrosomic trisomics, or acrotrisomics, contain even less of a chromosome arm than the telotrisomics; the extra chromosome has a terminal deletion of one arm. Tsuchiya (1987) has collected and described several and has used them to determine the physical location of genes within a given chromosome arm.

ALTERATIONS IN CHROMOSOME STRUCTURE

Numerous variations in chromosome structure occur in barley; all arise from one or more chromosome breaks and different rejoining(s) within the chromosome (intrachromosomal) or between chromosomes (interchromosomal). The former type comprises inversions, deficiencies, and duplications, and the latter consists of chromosome interchanges or translocations.

An inversion results in a segment of genes in a reverse order. Their origin, characteristics, behavior, and uses have been described by Nilan (1964), Briggs (1978), and Ramage (1985). They occur spontaneously and have been induced. At least a half-dozen different inversions have been used regularly in a variety of cytogenetic and genetic studies.

The deficiency that involves the loss of a chromosome segment is rarely detected, probably due to the lack of adequate cytological resolution or genetic analysis. Nevertheless, deficiencies have been reported (Ramage, 1985).

Duplicated segments, or duplications, have been identified and collected. All have arisen in the progeny of translocation heterozygotes. In the short arms of chromosomes 6 and 7, over a dozen have been isolated, and their behavior and uses in barley genetics and breeding have been described (Hagberg and Hagberg, 1987a).

Translocations or interchanges involving an exchange of terminal segments between nonhomologous chromosomes have been most extensively studied because they are readily induced by a number of mutagens and are easy to detect. The literature is extensive. The characteristics of the translocations, their meiotic behavior, and their uses in a number of genetic, cytogenetic, and breeding studies have been summarized (Nilan, 1964; Briggs, 1978; Ramage, 1985). Recently Ramage (1985) indicated there are 602 translocations in the world collection, and these have been listed by Søgaard and Wettstein-Knowles (1987). Only 12 of these arose spontaneously; the remainder were induced. All have been classified as to the chromosomes involved, and, for many, the break points have been located on the chromosome arm.

Most homozygous translocations produce no specific effect on the phenotype, although about 30% of the plants with translocations exhibit reduced vigor and yield. There also has been some indication of "position effects" in translocation stocks, but no real proof of this phenomenon exists in barley.

BREEDING

The ongoing process of breeding has steadily improved barley productivity, adaptation, and quality since about 1900, when the first breeding programs were organized in North America. In Europe, organized barley breeding goes back into the 1800s. Considerable public and private investment has gone into barley cultivar development, with programs largely based in the public sector in North American and private sector in Europe. Barley breeding and barley breeders have contributed well beyond the art and science of cultivar development to such disciplines as genetics and other basic sciences that support applied breeding as well as to barley production and management. General breeding objectives have included increased yield; improved adaptation through stress resistance such as for drought, diseases, and insects; and improved quality, mainly malting and, more recently, nutritional or feed quality.

Major sources of germ plasm for barley breeders have been varied. They include major germ plasm collections such as the USDA National Small Grains Collection and Canada's Plant Gene Resources, the Nordic Barley Gene Bank (Sweden), and major collections held in Syria (ICARDA), Germany, Japan, and the former Soviet Union (Chapman, 1987). Another source is spontaneous and induced mutations directed with radiation or chemical mutagens (Nilan, 1981a,b, 1987) and more recently achieved through tissue culture and soma-clonal variation (Ullrich et al, 1991a). In addition, interspecific and intergeneric crosses (Fedak, 1985, 1987) and formal or informal germ plasm exchanges between breeders are sources of germ plasm. Considerable cooperation occurs among barley breeders around the world. Like other cereal breeders, they await the practical use of genetic transformation as a potential new germ plasm source. Genetic variation in barley and germ plasm sources were detailed previously in this chapter under "Sources of Variation."

Crossing the various germ plasm sources and subsequent recombinations form the basis for barley breeding and the development of pure-line cultivars of this self-pollinated crop species. Breeding methods or ways of handling germ plasm and crosses vary considerably among breeders. Although the pedigree method, with many modifications, has been the standard method over the years, bulk, backcross, and single-seed descent methods have also been extensively employed. More recently, or more uniquely, composite-cross and male-sterile-facilitated recurrent selection, doubled haploid, and mutation breeding have been important breeding methods. Excellent comprehensive reviews on barley breeding have been published (Anderson and Reinbergs, 1985; Poehlman, 1987). Presented below are the most unique and recent developments in barley breeding methodology.

Male-Sterile-Facilitated Recurrent Selection

Recurrent selection has traditionally been a primary method of breeding cross-pollinated crop species. Male-sterile-facilitated recurrent selection (MSFRS) in self-pollinated barley has evolved from composite-cross breeding technology. Whereas composite-cross breeding traditionally uses relatively large heterogeneous populations and natural and/or mass selection techniques, generally to accomplish long-term goals, MSFRS uses male sterility and more directed or selected mating to develop and exploit, through severe mass selection, heterozygous as well as heterogeneous populations to accomplish either short- or long-term goals (Eslick, 1977). Relatively rapid shifts in gene frequencies can result from intensive management of MSFRS populations. Linkage blocks may be broken and epistatic effects altered efficiently as a maximum amount of gene recombination occurs (Eslick, 1977). A major apparent advantage of MSFRS is its ability to place major genes for specific traits in "happy homes," i.e., the most desirable genetic backgrounds for maximum gene expression (Ramage, 1977). Additionally, major and minor genes for a trait (such as for stress resistance, e.g., to disease, drought) may be efficiently accumulated in individual genotypes (Eslick, 1977; Bockelman et al, 1981). MSFRS populations have been successfully developed for a number of traits, including short stiff straw, large seed, wide adaptation, drought resistance, winterhardiness, and resistance to various diseases (Ramage, 1981, and *personal communication*; Bockelman et al, 1981).

Cultivar releases from MSFRS populations have mainly been short-strawed, lodging-resistant six-rowed feed types adapted to irrigated production. Examples are the cultivars Columbia and Gus and various Westbred cultivars (Western Plant Breeders, Bozeman, MT). MSFRS populations, in addition to providing cultivars, may potentially provide parental material for conventional and hybrid cultivars, as well as diverse and extreme types for the study of traits and trait effects. MSFRS populations may be useful for developing both male and female parents for hybrid cultivars, since traits related to cross-pollination, such as high pollen number and large extruding stigmas, are favored in this open-pollinated breeding system. This is especially the case when seed is harvested separately from male-sterile plants that have been "naturally" cross-pollinated.

Doubled-Haploid Breeding

The major advantage of using the techniques of doubled haploids (DHs) in breeding is that the cultivar development process is accelerated. Single-seed descent is the more traditional acceleration method, whereby three to five generations are grown per year by advancing a single representative (seed) from each early-generation line (e.g., F_2–F_5). This is a relatively rapid method of obtaining nearly homozygous breeding lines. DHs are completely homozygous. Therefore, DHs developed from F_1 progeny of a cross produce "instant" homozygous breeding lines in one generation compared to the five to eight generations required to produce homozygous lines from segregation in conventional breeding programs. Selection occurs among homozygous lines instead of segregating plants, and subsequent evaluations occur with homozygous lines instead of segregating lines, which also improves the effectiveness and efficiency of the breeding process. The instant development of homozygous lines from an F_1 facilitates and accelerates genetic studies as well.

To be practically applied in a breeding program, a DH system must meet several requirements: 1) large numbers of DHs must be obtained from a given cross; 2) the system should not be too discriminatory of genotypes; 3) the DHs should represent a random sample of gametes; 4) as the system begins with haploid tissue, doubling of chromosomes should be effective and efficient; 5) the DHs should be genetically stable and agronomically productive; and 6) the system must be economically feasible to utilize. DH systems have been successfully used in barley breeding (Anderson and Reinbergs, 1985; Devaux, 1992; Pickering and Devaux, 1992).

There are several methods, theoretical and practical, for producing DHs. A method pioneered in barley involves chromosome elimination as the result of an interspecific cross with *H. bulbosum* (Kasha and Kao, 1970). Haploids of *H. vulgare* are produced as a result of elimination of *H. bulbosum* chromosomes from hybrid embryos in an in vitro embryo rescue culture. DH plants of *H. vulgare* are subsequently produced by doubling the chromosomes by chemical treatment of haploid seedlings with colchicine.

More recently, anther or microspore and ovule (unfertilized) culture techniques have been developed to produce haploid and DH barley plants (Friedt and Foroughi-Wehr, 1981; Foroughi-Wehr and Friedt, 1982). Anther culture currently seems the most viable of the gamete culture systems. Due to recent culture technique breakthroughs (Olsen, 1987; Hou et al, 1993), anther culture is now being used in applied plant breeding programs (cultivar development). Currently, the biggest drawback to anther culture seems to be the somewhat limited genotype response to culture and green plant regeneration. An advantage of anther culture over the *H. bulbosum* method is that the majority (65–85%) of the haploid regenerates undergo spontaneous chromosome doubling, making colchicine use unnecessary. Colchicine is difficult to handle and results in a reported 60–70% chromosome doubling success rate in the *H. bulbosum* system (Anderson and Reinbergs, 1985).

As reported earlier in this chapter, another haploid-producing system is described by Hagberg and Hagberg (1987c) and involves a haploid-inducing gene (*hap*). Currently this system is largely of theoretical interest as the *hap* gene must be transferred to adapted genotypes of interest, and most DHs are homozygous for the *hap* gene so that their progeny include many haploid-inducing plants. Therefore, to work for breeding purposes, a selection system facilitated by the *hap* gene marker must be developed. Such a system is described by Hagberg and Hagberg (1987b).

The *H. bulbosum* technique has been the most widely used DH-producing method. A number of countries around the world have adopted it, and commercial cultivars have been released in several countries from *H. bulbosum*-derived DH lines (Anderson and Reinbergs, 1985). DH breeding among the cereals began with barley. However, with the emergence of viable anther culture techniques, DH breeding is spreading to other cereals such as wheat, maize, and rice (Devaux, 1992). Due to relatively easier and cheaper application of anther culture vs. the *H. bulbosum* method, it is likely that anther culture will be the technique of choice in the future for barley DH breeding. Alternatively, the two methods may be used in combination.

DH methods can also be combined with recurrent selection methods including MSFRS. Kasha and Reinbergs (1976), Choo et al (1979), and Patel et al (1985) outlined DH recurrent-selection schemes that improve the efficiency of recurrent selection in terms of cycle time, evaluation of lines, and selection of parents for intercropping. A DH recurrent-selection scheme for winter barley, in which an off-season growing season is not feasible, was proposed by Hayes (1988) to accelerate development of winter barley cultivars.

Mutation Breeding

Mutation breeding is the use of mutants (primarily induced mutants) either directly as new cultivars or indirectly as parents in crosses with other genotypes. The ultimate goal of releasing a mutant as a new ("instant") cultivar is seldom achieved; thus, mutation breeding is most often a germ plasm-enhancement or parent-building strategy. Induced mutants enhance the genetic variability of a crop species and can easily be incorporated into conventional pedigree, bulk, backcross, or recurrent-selection breeding schemes. For some desirable traits, existing germ plasm sources may be inadequate or in poorly adapted genetic backgrounds (Konzak et al, 1984). New mutants can provide new genes at previously unknown loci, as well as new alleles at known loci, but in improved, adapted genetic backgrounds. Mutants are useful for genetic studies as well as for breeding purposes (Gustafsson and Lundqvist, 1981; Nilan, 1981a,b, 1987).

Induced mutants have been used throughout the world in barley breeding programs. They have led to the direct development of at least 75 cultivars and to the development of over 100 cultivars by using them in cross-breeding. For instance, the mutant varieties Diamont and Mari have been involved in 53 and 18 crossbred cultivars, respectively (Micke et al, 1988). Many of these mutant cultivars have had a considerable economic impact on the various major barley-growing regions of the world.

The first direct use of an induced mutant in North America was through the release of Luther, a diethyl sulfate-induced mutant in the winter cultivar Alpine with reduced plant height and increased lodging resistance (Muir and Nilan, 1967). Semidwarfism to condition lodging resistance has been a common target for induced mutagenesis. Many barley cultivars, especially in North America, Europe, and East Asia, carry semidwarf genes that trace to a number of induced (semidwarf and erectoides) mutants (Ullrich and Aydin, 1988; Ullrich et al, 1982).

Among other useful mutant traits that have been induced in barley are maturity, early and late; disease resistance, especially to powdery mildew (causal agent *Erysiphe graminis* f. sp. *hordei* Ém. Marchal), the most prevalent disease problem in Europe; male sterility; and a number of kernel quality traits (Anderson and Reinbergs, 1985). Several mutant kernel traits that affect end-use quality have been induced, including those for high protein content, high lysine content (Ullrich et al, 1984), lack of proanthocyanidin (Wettstein et al, 1985; Larsen et al, 1987), low and high β-glucan content, and waxy endosperm (Aastrup, 1983; Ullrich et al, 1986b; Nilan, 1987).

Mutations of qualitative traits are generally easier to select for than those of quantitative traits, due to their simple (single gene) vs. complex (multigene) inheritances, respectively. However, minor or modifier types of quantitative genes could be induced and accumulated in a population with repeated cycles of mutagenesis and selection, given sensitive screening methods. This type of procedure could be used, for example, to improve disease and environmental (e.g., drought) stress resistances, protein quantity and quality, and yield in MSFRS populations. General procedures for mutation breeding can be found in Anderson and Reinbergs (1985) and FAO/IAEA (1977).

Cell and tissue culture populations are other sources of mutations. Stable somaclonal variation in callus culture-derived plants has been demonstrated in a number of crops (Lörz et al, 1988), including barley (Ullrich et al, 1991a). The somaclonal variation reported has been attributed to a whole spectrum of genetic changes (Lee and Phillips, 1988; Lörz et al, 1988). However, much of the literature on cereal morphologic somaclonal variation reports data that were not genetically verified (Lörz et al, 1988). The literature also suggests that little somaclonal variation has been found in *Hordeum* (Karp et al, 1987; Lörz et al, 1988; Luckett et al, 1989; Pickering, 1989). Its diploid nature has been cited as a reason. However, if one approaches the evaluation of somaclonal variation as has been done traditionally with induced mutagenesis, one finds that considerable genetically stable somaclonal variation of seedling traits, (e.g., chlorophyll deficiency) was demonstrated in R_2 populations derived from immature embryo culture (Ullrich et al, 1991a). Somaclonal variation for agronomic traits (plant height, heading date) and malting quality traits (α-amylase, diastatic power, and protein content) have also been detected in barley (Ullrich et al, 1991b). However, the application of in vitro culture to generate somaclonal variation for barley improvement has yet to be demonstrated. The results of Ullrich et al (1991b) and those of Pickering (1989) related to increased resistance to scald (causal agent *Rhynchosporium secalis* (Oudem.) J. J. Davis) indicate positive potential. In addition, in vitro selection methods in callus culture may prove useful for traits such as herbicide and disease resistance (Wenzel, 1985).

Hybrid Barley

The development of hybrid barley systems has been the subject of serious research for over 30 years. However, other than one very limited production of commercial hybrid barley (Ramage, 1983), efforts to commercialize hybrid barley have largely failed. Since barley has perfect flowers and is self-pollinated, the development of an economically feasible system to produce hybrids is particularly difficult. Requirements include a practical system of inducing male sterility and/or fertility restoration, a high frequency of cross-pollination, and a high level of heterosis. The occurrence of genetic and cytoplasmic male sterility is no problem in barley. However, finding a feasible system to induce sterility and restore fertility for commercial hybrid seed production has been a problem. Heterosis studies have produced variable results in barley, but it seems that there probably is enough heterosis to justify the use of hybrid cultivars (Ramage, 1983). Hybrid barley cultivars, if developed, will probably be limited to use in relatively high-input production situations to justify the cost. Although considerable public and private research has been invested in hybrid barley development, sustained commercial application has yet to occur. Currently, perhaps the most promising hybrid system uses chemical hybridizing agents to induce male sterility in fertile female parents. This is being pursued primarily in the private sector in Europe (O. Laudoyer, Hybritech, France, *personal communication*).

Future Directions

Plant breeding has followed an evolutionary path. Breeding methodologies have evolved, as have selection techniques. Some of the more recent changes in barley breeding have been described above in this section. Some of the more recent advances in genetics yet to be applied to barley breeding have been described in other sections of this chapter. Plant breeding has been very successful in improving crops in the past with no convincing evidence that it will not continue to do so in the future. Yet molecular genetics and other "biotechnology" advances, such as in vitro techniques, have the potential to dramatically revolutionize plant breeding. A goal of the North American Barley

Genome Mapping Project, as described earlier in this chapter, is to improve barley by more directed breeding (Nilan, 1990, 1991). Many economically important traits (yield, stress resistance, quality) are quantitatively inherited with relatively low heritabilities, which makes them difficult to manipulate by conventional means. A saturated and merged RFLP, isozyme, and conventional genome map (Shin et al, 1990; Kleinhofs et al, 1993) and quantitative trait loci analyses (Lander and Botstein, 1989; Hayes et al, 1993; Ullrich et al, 1993) should provide much important new genetic information to allow for more directed breeding (Tanksley et al, 1989). Molecular-marker-assisted selection (e.g., with RFLPs) should make it possible to accumulate known individual genes for quantitative traits of interest in a single genotype.

On another but related front, given precise molecular genetic information, genetic transformation technology is advancing as described earlier in this chapter. Once a reliable, repeatable, and economically feasible transformation system is developed for barley, there will be great potential for improving barley with genes and traits heretofore unavailable to this crop plant.

Much promise and potential for barley breeding is expressed here. However, it should be noted that "conventional" breeding methods are proven and effective and that a balance of techniques will likely be important. Traditional, new, and emerging technologies should be compatible and necessary in the future.

LITERATURE CITED

AASTRUP, S. 1983. Selection and characterization of low β-glucan mutants from barley. Carlsberg Res. Commun. 48:307-316.

ANDERSON, M. K., and REINBERGS, E. 1985. Barley breeding. Pages 231-268 in: Barley. D. C. Rasmusson, ed. American Society of Agronomy, Madison, WI.

ARENAZ, P., HALLBERG, L., MANCILLAS, F., GUTIERREZ, G., and GARCIA, S. 1989. Sodium azide mutagenesis in mammals: Inability of mammalian cells to convert azide to a mutagenic intermediate. Mutat. Res. 227:63-67.

BEER INSTITUTE. 1988. The brewing industry in the United States. In: Brewer's Almanac 1988. The Institute, Washington, DC.

BLAKE, T. K. 1987. Strategies for restriction fragment length polymorphism analysis in barley. Pages 503-508 in: Barley Genetics V. Proc. 5th Int. Barley Genet. Symp. S. Yasuda and T. Konishi, eds. Sanyo Press, Okayama, Japan.

BOCKELMAN, H. E., SHARP, E. L., and ESLICK, R. F. 1981. Present status of recurrent selection populations for disease resistance. Barley Newsl. 24:85.

BOTHMER, R. VON, JACOBSEN, N., BADEN, C., JØRGENSEN, J. R. B., and LINDE-LAURSEN, I. 1991. An ecogeographical study of the genus *Hordeum*. Systematic and Ecogeographic Studies in Crop Genepools 7. Int. Board for Plant Genetic Resources, Rome.

BOTHMER, R. VON, and JACOBSEN, N. 1985. Origin, taxonomy, and related species. Pages 19-56 in: Barley. D. C. Rasmusson, ed. American Society of Agronomy, Madison, WI.

BOTHMER, R. VON, JORGENSEN, R. B., and LINDE-LAURSEN, I. 1987. Natural variation, phylogeny, and genetic resources in *Hordeum*. Pages 23-33 in: Barley Genetics V. Proc. 5th Int. Barley Genet. Symp. S. Yasuda and T. Konishi, eds. Sanyo Press, Okayama, Japan.

BRIGGS, D. E. 1978. Barley. Chapman and Hall Ltd., London. 612 pp.

BURGER, W. C., and LABERGE, D. E. 1985. Malting and brewing quality. Pages 367-401 in: Barley. D. C. Rasmusson, ed. American Society of Agronomy, Madison, WI.

CHAPMAN, C. G. D. 1987. Barley genetic resources, the status of collecting and conservation. Pages 43-49 in: Barley Genetics V. Proc. 5th Int. Barley Genet. Symp. S. Yasuda and T. Konishi, eds. Sanyo Press, Okayama, Japan.

CHOO, T. M., CHRISTIE, B. R., and REINBERGS, E. 1979. Doubled-haploids for estimating genetic variances and a scheme for population improvement in self-pollinating crops. Theor. Appl. Genet. 54:267-

271.
CONSTANTIN, M. J., and NILAN, R. A.
1982a. Chromosome aberration assays in
barley (*Hordeum vulgare*). Mutat. Res.
99:13-36.
CONSTANTIN, M. J., and NILAN, R. A.
1982b. The chlorophyll-deficient mutant
assay in barley (*Hordeum vulgare*). Mutat.
Res. 99:37-49.
DEVAUX, P. 1992. Haploidy in barley and
wheat improvement. Pages 139-151 in:
Reproductive Biology and Plant Breeding. Y.
DaHee, L. Dumas, and A. Gallais, eds.
Springer-Verlag, Berlin.
ESLICK, R. F. 1977. Male sterile facilitated
recurrent selection—Advantages and disad-
vantages. Pages 84-91 in: Barley, Vol. 2. Proc.
4th Regional Winter Cereals Workshop,
Amman, Jordan. S. Barghout, E. E. Sqori,
J. P. Srivastva, and G. Chancellor, eds.
ICARDA, Aleppo, Syria, and CIMMYT, El
Baton, Mexico.
FAO/IAEA. 1977. Manual on Mutation
Breeding, 2nd ed. Tech. Rep. Ser. 119. Int.
Atomic Energy Agency, Vienna.
FEDAK, G. 1985. Wide crosses in *Hordeum*.
Pages 155-186 in: Barley. D. C. Rasmusson,
ed. Am. Soc. Agron., Madison, WI.
FEDAK, G. 1987. Intergeneric hybrids in
Hordeum. Pages 301-310 in: Barley Genetics
V. Proc. 5th Int. Barley Genet. Symp. S.
Yasuda and T. Konishi, eds. Sanyo Press,
Okayama, Japan.
FOROUGHI-WEHR, B., and FRIEDT, W.
1982. Agronomic performance of andre-
genetic doubled-haploid lines of *H. vulgare*.
Pages 557-558 in: Plant Tissue Culture 1982.
Proc. 5th Int. Congr. Plant Tissue and Cell
Culture. A. Fujiwara, ed. Japanese Assoc.
for Plant Tissue Culture, Toyko.
FRIEDT, W., and FOROUGHI-WEHR, B.
1981. Anther culture of barley: Plant regener-
ation and agronomic performance of diploid
progenies. Pages 690-698 in: Barley Genetics
IV. Proc. 4th Int. Barley Genet. Symp.
R. N. H. Whitehouse, ed. Edinburgh Uni-
versity Press, Edinburgh.
GAUL, H., ed. 1976. Barley Genetics III. Proc.
3rd Int. Barley Genet. Symp. Verlag Karl
Theimig, Munich. 849 pp.
GRANER, A., JAHOOR, A.,
SCHONDELMAIER, J., SIEDLER, H.,
PILLEN, K., FISCHBECK, G., WENZEL,
G., and HERRMANN, R. G. 1991. Con-
struction of an RFLP map of barley. Theor.
Appl. Genet. 83:250-256.
GUSTAFSSON, A., and LUNDQVIST, U.
1981. Mutations and parallel variation. Pages
85-110 in: Inducted Mutations—A Tool in
Plant Research. Int. Atomic Energy Agency,
Vienna.
HAGBERG, A. 1987. Barley as a model crop
on plant genetic research. Pages 3-6 in: Barley
Genetics V. Proc. 5th Int. Barley Genet.
Symp. S. Yasuda and T. Konishi, eds. Sanyo
Press, Okayama, Japan.
HAGBERG, A., and HAGBERG, G. 1987a.
Some vigorous and productive duplications
in barley. Pages 423-426 in: Barley Genetics
V. Proc. 5th Int. Barley Genet. Symp. S.
Yasuda and T. Konishi, eds. Sanyo Press,
Okayama, Japan.
HAGBERG, A., and HAGBERG, G. 1987b.
Production of spontaneously doubled
haploids in barley using a breeding system
with marker genes and the "hap"-gene. Biol.
Zentralbl. 106:53-58.
HAGBERG, A., and HAGBERG, G. 1987c.
Spontaneously doubled haploids in *hap* gene
material. Pages 259-263 in: Barley Genetics
V. Proc. 5th Int. Barley Genet. Symp. S.
Yasuda and T. Konishi, eds. Sanyo Press,
Okayama, Japan.
HARLAN, J. R. 1979. On the origin of barley.
Pages 10-36 in: Barley: Origin, Botany,
Culture, Winter Hardiness, Genetics,
Utilization, Pests. Agric. Handb. 338. U.S.
Dept. Agric., Washington, DC.
HAYES, P. M. 1988. Winter and facultative
barley germplasm enhancement. Pages 244-
252 in: Winter Cereals and Food Legumes
in Mountainous Areas. Proc. Int. Conf. Inter-
national Center for Agricultural Research in
the Dry Areas, Aleppo, Syria.
HAYES, P. M., BLAKE, T. K., CHEN, T. H.
H., TRAGOONRUNG, S., CHEN, F., PAN,
A., and LIU, B. 1993. Quantitative trait loci
on barley (*Hordeum vulgare*) chromosome
7 associated with components of
winterhardiness. Genome 36:66-71.
HEUN, M., KENNEDY, A. E., ANDERSON,
J. A., LAPITAN, N. L. V., SORRELLS,
M. E., and TANKSLEY, S. D. 1991.
Construction of an RFLP map for barley
(*Hordeum vulgare* L.). Genome 34:437-447.
HOCKETT, E. A., and NILAN, R. A. 1985.
Genetics. Pages 187-230 in: Barley. D. C.
Rasmusson, ed. American Society of Agron-
omy, Madison, WI.
HOU, L., ULLRICH, S. E., KLEINHOFS, A.,
and STIFF, C. M. 1993. Improvement of
anther culture methods for doubled haploid
production in barley breeding. Plant Cell
Rep. In press.
JENSEN, C. J. 1987. Biotechnology: Barley cell
and tissue culture. Pages 493-501 in: Barley
Genetics V. Proc. 5th Int. Barley Genet.
Symp. S. Yasuda and T. Konishi, eds. Sanyo
Press, Okayama, Japan.
JENSEN, J. 1990. Transient gene expression

in barley protoplasts. MSc. thesis, Royal Veterinary and Agricultural University of Denmark, Copenhagen. 68 pp.

KARP, A., STEELE, S. H., PARMAR, S., JONES, M. G. K., SHEWRY, P. R., and BEIMAN, A. 1987. Relative stability among barley plants regenerated from cultured immature embryos. Genome 29:405-512.

KASHA, K. J., and KAO, K. N. 1970. High frequency haploid production in barley. Nature 225:874-876.

KASHA, K. J., and REINBERGS, E. 1976. Utilization of haploidy in barley. Pages 307-315 in: Barley Genetics III. Proc. 3rd Int. Barley Genet. Symp. H. Gaul, ed. Verlag Karl Theimig, Munich.

KHURSHEED, B., and ROGERS, J. C. 1988. Barley α-amylase genes. J. Biol. Chem. 263:18953-18960.

KIESLING, R. L. 1985. The diseases of barley. Pages 269-312 in: Barley. D. C. Rasmusson, ed. American Society of Agronomy, Madison, WI.

KLEINHOFS, A. 1985. Cereal transformation: Progress and prospects. Pages 261-272 in: Advances in Agricultural Biotechnology. Cereal Tissue and Cell Culture. S. W. J. Bright and M. G. K. Jones, eds. M. Nijhoff/ Dr. W. Junk, Dordrecht.

KLEINHOFS, A., OWAIS, W. M., and NILAN, R. A. 1978. Azide. Mutation Res. 55:165-195.

KLEINHOFS, A., CHAO, S., and SHARP, P. J. 1988. Mapping of nitrate reductase genes in barley and wheat. Pages 541-546 in: Proc. 7th Int. Wheat Genet. Symp., Vol. I. T. E. Miller and R. M. D. Koebner, eds. Agricultural and Food Research Council, Institute of Plant Science Research, Cambridge.

KLEINHOFS, A., KILIAN, A., SAGHAI MAROOF, M. A., BIYASHEV, R. M., HAYES, P., CHEN, F. Q., LAPITAN, N., FENWICK, A., BLAKE, T. K., KANAZIN, V., ANANIEV, E., DAHLEEN, L., KUDRNA, D., BOLLINGER, J., KNAPP, S. J., LIU, B., SORRELLS, M., HEUN, M., FRANCKOWIAK, J. D., HOFFMAN, D., SKADSEN, R., and STEFFENSON, B. J. 1993. A molecular, isozyme, morphological map of the barley (*Hordeum vulgare*) genome. Theor. Appl. Genet. In press.

KNÜPFFER, H., LEHMANN, C. O., and SCHOLTZ, F. 1987. Barley genetic resources in European genebanks: The European barley database. Pages 75-82 in: Barley Genetics V. Proc. 5th Int. Barley Genet. Symp. S. Yasuda and T. Konishi, eds. Sanyo Press, Okayama, Japan.

KONZAK, C. F., KLEINHOFS, A., and ULLRICH, S. E. 1984. Induced mutations

in seed-propagated crops. Pages 13-72 in: Plant Breeding Reviews, Vol. 2. J. Janick, ed. AVI, Westport, CT.

LAMBERTS, H., BROEKHUIZEN, S., DANTUMA, G., and LANGE, W., eds. 1964. Barley Genetics I. Proc. 1st Int. Barley Genet. Symp. Pudoc, Wageningen. 387 pp.

LANDER, E. S., and BOTSTEIN, D. 1989. Mapping Mendelian factors underlying quantitative traits using RFLP linkage maps. Genetics 121:185-199.

LARSEN, J., ULLRICH, S. E., INGVERSEN, J., NIELSEN, A. E., COCHRAN, J. S., and CLANCY, J. 1987. Breeding and malting behavior of two different proanthocyanidin-free barley gene sources. Pages 767 772 in: Barley Genetics V. Proc. 5th Int. Barley Genet. Symp. S. Yasuda and T. Konishi, eds. Sanyo Press, Okayama, Japan.

LEE, M., and PHILLIPS, R. L. 1988. The chromosomal basis of somaclonal variation. Annu. Rev. Plant Physiol. Plant Mol. Biol. 39:413-437.

LINDE-LAURSEN, I. 1988. Giemsa C-banding of barley chromosomes. V. Localization of breakpoints in 70 reciprocal translocations. Hereditas 108:65-76.

LÖRZ, H., GOBEL, H., and BROWN, P. 1988. Advances in tissue culture and progress towards genetic transformation of cereals. Plant Breed. 100:1-25.

LUCKETT, D. J., ROSE, D., and KNIGHT, E. 1989. Paucity of somaclonal variation from immature embryo culture of barley. Aust. J. Agric. Res. 40:1155-1159.

LUNDQVIST, U. 1991. The Swedish mutation research in barley with plant breeding aspects: A historical review. Pages 135-148 in: Plant Mutation Breeding for Crop Improvement. International Atomic Energy Agency, Food and Agriculture Organization of the United Nations, Vienna.

MELZER, J. M., and KLEINHOFS, A. 1987a. Molecular genetics of barley. Pages 481-491 in: Barley Genetics V. Proc. 5th Int. Barley Genet. Symp. S. Yasuda and T. Konishi, eds. Sanyo Press, Okayama, Japan.

MELZER, J. M., and KLEINHOFS, A. 1987b. Molecular genetics of barley and endosperm proteins. Barley Genet. Newsl. 17:13-25.

MICKE, A., DONINI, B., and MALUSZYNSKI, M. 1988. Induced mutations for crop improvement—A review. Trop. Agric. (Trinidad) 64:259-278.

MOSEMAN, J. G., and SMITH, D. H., Jr. 1985. Germplasm resources. Pages 57-72 in: Barley. D. C. Rasmusson, ed. American Society of Agronomy, Madison, WI.

MUIR, C. E., and NILAN, R. A. 1967. Registrations of Luther barley. Crop Sci.

7:278.

NEWMAN, C. W., and McGUIRE, C. F. 1985. Nutritional quality of barley. Pages 403-456 in: Barley. D. C. Rasmusson, ed. American Society of Agronomy, Madison, WI.

NILAN, R. A. 1964. The cytology and genetics of barley, 1951-1962. Monogr. Suppl. 3, Res. Stud. Vol. 32, No. 1. Washington State University Press, Pullman, WA. 278 pp.

NILAN, R. A. 1971. Barley Genetics II. Proc. 2nd Int. Barley Genet. Symp. Washington State University Press, Pullman, WA. 622 pp.

NILAN, R. A. 1975. Barley (*Hordeum vulgare*). Pages 93-110 in: Handbook of Genetics, Vol. 2. R. C. King, ed. Plenum Press, New York.

NILAN, R. A. 1981a. Recent advances in barley mutagenesis. Pages 823-831 in: Barley Genetics IV. Proc. 4th Int. Barley Genet. Symp. R. N. H. Whitehouse, ed. Edinburgh University Press, Edinburgh.

NILAN, R. A. 1981b. Induced gene and chromosome mutants. Phil. Trans. R. Soc. Lond. B. 292:457-466.

NILAN, R. A. 1987. Trends in barley mutagenesis. Pages 241-249 in: Barley Genetics V. Proc. 5th Int. Barley Genet. Symp. S. Yasuda and T. Konishi, eds. Sanyo Press, Okayama, Japan.

NILAN, R. A. 1990. The North American Barley Genome Mapping Project. Barley Newsl. 33:112.

OLSEN, F. L. 1987. Protocol and comments on growing barley for anther culture purpose and protocols and comments for barley anther tissue culture. EMBO Advanced Laboratory Course on DNA Transformation of Plant Protoplasts. Swiss Fed. Inst. Tech., Zurich. 49 pp.

OWAIS, W. M., and KLEINHOFS, A. 1988. Metabolic activation of the mutagen azide in biological systems. Mutat. Res. 97:313-323.

PATEL, J. D., REINBERGS, E., and FEJER, S. O. 1985. Recurrent selection in doubled haploid populations of barley (*Hordeum vulgare* L.). Can. J. Genet. Cytol. 27:172-177.

PICKERING, R. A. 1989. Plant regeneration and variants from calli derived from immature embryos of diploid barley (*Hordeum vulgare* L.) and *H. vulgare* L. × *H. bulbosum* L. crosses. Theor. Appl. Genet. 78:105-112.

PICKERING, R. A., and DEVAUX, P. 1992. Haploid production: Approaches and use in plant breeding. Pages 519-547 in: Barley: Genetics, Biochemistry, Molecular Biology and Biotechnology. P. R. Shewry, ed. C.A.B. International, Wallingford, U.K.

POEHLMAN, J. M. 1985. Adaptation and distribution. Pages 2-17 in: Barley. D. C. Rasmusson, ed. American Society of Agronomy, Madison, WI.

POEHLMAN, J. M. 1987. Breeding Field Crops, 3rd ed. AVI, Westport, CT. pp. 378-397.

RAMAGE, R. T. 1977. Male sterile facilitated recurrent selections and happy homes. Pages 92-98 in: Barley, Vol. 2. Proc. 4th Regional Winter Cereals Workshop. S. Barghout, E. E. Sqori, J. P. Srivastva, and G. Chancellor, eds. Amman, Jordan.

RAMAGE, R. T. 1981. Comments about the use of male sterile facilitated recurrent selection. Barley Newsl. 24:52-53.

RAMAGE, R. T. 1983. Heterosis and hybrid seed production in barley. Pages 71-93 in: Heterosis. Theor. Appl. Genet. Monogr., Vol. 6. R. Frankel, ed. Springer-Verlag, Berlin.

RAMAGE, R. T. 1985. Cytogenetics. Pages 127-154 in: Barley. D. C. Rasmusson, ed. American Society of Agronomy, Madison, WI.

RASMUSSEN, U. 1985. Immunological screening for specific protein content in barley seeds. Carlsberg Res. Commun. 50:83-93.

ROHDE, W., BARZEN, E., MAROCCO, A., SCHWARZ-SOMMER, Z., SAEDLER, H., and SALAMINI, F. 1987. Isolation of genes that could serve as traps for transposable elements in *Hordeum vulgare*. Pages 533-541 in: Barley Genetics V. Proc. 5th Int. Barley Genet. Symp. S. Yasuda and T. Konishi, eds. Sanyo Press, Okayama, Japan.

ROSSNAGEL, B. G., HARVEY, B. L., and BHATTY, R. S. 1983. Scout hulless barley. Can. J. Plant Sci. 63:751-752.

ROSSNAGEL, B. G., HARVEY, B. L., and BHATTY, R. S. 1985. Tupper hulless barley. Can. J. Plant Sci. 65:453-454.

SALL, T. 1989. Genetic variation for recombination in barley. Ph.D. thesis, The Swedish University of Agricultural Science, Uppsala.

SALL, T. 1990. Genetic control of recombination in barley. II. Variation in linkage between marker genes. Hereditas 112:171-178.

SALL, T., FLINK, J., and BENGTSSON, B. 1990. Genetic control of recombination in barley. I. Variation in recombination frequency measured with inversion heterozygotes. Hereditas 112:157-170.

SHARP, E. L. 1985. Breeding for pest resistance. Pages 313-333 in: Barley. D. C. Rasmusson, ed. American Society of Agronomy, Madison, WI.

SHEWRY, P. R. ed. 1992. Barley Genetics, Biochemistry, Molecular Biology and Biotechnology. C.A.B. International, Wallingford, U.K.

SHEWRY, P. R., WILLIAMSON, M. S.,

PARMAR, S., BURGESS, S. R., BUXTON, B., and KREIS, M. 1987. The biochemical and molecular genetics of barley seed proteins. Pages 433-443 in: Barley Genetics V. Proc. 5th Int. Barley Genet. Symp. S. Yasuda and T. Konishi, eds. Sanyo Press, Okayama, Japan.

SHIN, J. S., CHAO, S., CORPUZ, L., and BLAKE, T. 1990. A partial map of the barley genome incorporating restriction fragment length polymorphism, polymerase chain reaction, isozyme, and morphological marker loci. Genome 33:803-808.

SMITH, L. 1951. Cytology and genetics of barley. Bot. Rev. 17:1-51, 133-202, 285-355.

SØGAARD, B., and WETTSTEIN-KNOWLES, P. VON. 1987. Barley: Genes and chromosomes. Carlsberg Res. Commun. 52:123-196.

STARKS, K. J., and WEBSTER, J. A. 1985. Insects and related pests. Pages 337-365 in: Barley. D. C. Rasmusson, ed. American Society of Agronomy, Madison, WI.

STATISTICS CANADA. 1989. Field crop reporting series No. 8. Statistics Canada, Ottawa.

TANKSLEY, S. D., YOUNG, N. D., PATERSON, A. H., and BONERBALE, M. W. 1989. RFLP mapping in plant breeding: New tools for an old science. Biotechnology 7:257-265.

TSUCHIYA, T. 1987. Gene analysis and linkage studies in barley. Pages 175-187 in: Barley Genetics V. Proc. 5th Int. Barley Genet. Symp. S. Yasuda and T. Konishi, eds. Sanyo Press, Okayama, Japan.

ULLRICH, S. E., and AYDIN, A. 1988. Mutation breeding for semi-dwarfism in barley. Pages 135-144 in: Semi-dwarf Cereal Mutants and Their Use in Crossbreeding. III. IAEA/TECDOC/445. Int. Atomic Energy Agency, Vienna.

ULLRICH, S. E., NILAN, R. A., and BACALTCHUK, B. 1982. Evaluation and genetic analysis of semi-dwarf mutants. II. Barley. Pages 73-80 in: Semi-dwarf Cereal Mutants and Their Use in Crossbreeding. TEC/DOC/268. Int. Atomic Energy Agency, Vienna.

ULLRICH, S. E., KLEINHOFS, A., COON, C. N., and NILAN, R. A. 1984. Breeding for improved protein in barley. Pages 93-104 in: Cereal Grain Protein Improvement. STI/PUB/664. Int. Atomic Agency, Vienna.

ULLRICH, S. E., RASMUSSEN, U., HØYER-HANSEN, G., and BRANDT, A. 1986a. Monoclonal antibodies to hordein polypeptides. Carlsberg Res. Commun. 51:381-399.

ULLRICH, S. E., CLANCY, J. A., ESLICK, R. F., and LANCE, R. C. M. 1986b. β-

Glucan content and viscosity of waxy barley. J. Cereal Sci. 4:279-285.

ULLRICH, S. E., HØYER-HANSEN, G., and RASMUSSEN, U. 1987. Monoclonal antibodies in the characterization of hordeins and barley quality improvement. Pages 547-556 in: Barley Genetics V. Proc. 5th Int. Barley Genet. Symp. S. Yasuda and T. Konishi, eds. Sanyo Press, Okayama, Japan.

ULLRICH, S. E., KLEINHOFS, A., JONES, B. L., and JOHNSON, J. J. 1991a. Somaclonal variation in barley: Theoretical and practical implications. Pages 220-222 in: Barley Genetics VI, Vol. I. Proc. 6th Int. Barley Genet. Symp. L. Munck, ed. Munksgaard, Copenhagen.

ULLRICH, S. E., EDMISTON, J. M., KLEINHOFS, A., KUDRNA, D. A., and MAATOUGUI, M. E. H. 1991b. Evaluation of somaclonal variation in barley. Cereal Res. Comm. 19:245-260.

ULLRICH, S. E., HAYES, P. M., DYER, W. E., BLAKE, T. K., and CLANCY, J. A. 1993. Quantitative trait locus analysis of seed dormancy in 'Steptoe' barley. Pages 136-145 in: Preharvest Sprouting in Cereals 1992. M. K. Walker-Simmons and J. L. Ried, eds. Am. Assoc. Cereal Chem., St. Paul, MN.

U.S. FEED GRAINS COUNCIL. 1990. Grains data base report. The Council, Washington, DC.

USDA-NASS. 1990. Crop production 1989 summary. CrPr 2-1 (909). U.S. Dept. Agric., Natl. Agric. Statistics Serv., Washington, DC.

WANG, X., OLSEN, O., and KNUDSEN, S. 1993. Expression of the dihydroflavonol reductase gene in an anthocyanin-free barley mutant. Hereditas. In press.

WENDORF, F., SCHILD, R., HADIDI, N. E., CLOSE, A. E., KOBUSIEWICZ, M., WIECKOWSKA, H., ISSAWI, B., and HAAS, H. 1979. Use of barley in the Egyptian late paleolithic. Science 205:1341-1347.

WENZEL, G. 1985. Strategies in unconventional breeding for disease resistance. Annu. Rev. Phytopathol. 23:149-172.

WETTSTEIN, D. VON. 1983. Genetic engineering in the adaptation of plants to human needs. Experientia 39:687-783.

WETTSTEIN, D. VON. 1989. Perspectives for the genetic engineering of plants for agriculture horticulture and industry. Plant Mol. Biol. 13:313-317.

WETTSTEIN, D. VON, NILAN, R. A., AHRENST-LARSEN, B., ERDAL, K., INGVERSEN, J., JENDE-STRIDE, B., NYEGAARD KRISTIANSEN, K., LARSEN, J., OUTTRUP, H., and ULLRICH, S. E. 1985. Proanthocyanidin-free barley for brewing. Progress in breeding for high yield and research tool in polyphenol chemistry. Tech. Q. Master Brew. Assoc. Am. 22:41-52.

WETTSTEIN-KNOWLES, P. VON. 1989. Facets of the barley genome. Pflanzenzuechtung 16:107-124.

WETTSTEIN-KNOWLES, P. VON. 1990. Barley (*Hordeum vulgare*) 2N=14. Pages 125-134 in: Genetic Maps, Vol. 6. Locus Maps of Complex Genomes, 5th ed. S. J. O'Brien, ed. Cold Spring Harbor Laboratory Press, Cold Spring Harbor, NY.

WHITEHOUSE, R. N. H., ed. 1981. Barley Genetics IV. Proc. 4th Int. Barley Genet. Symp. Edinburgh University Press, Edinburgh.

WIEBE, G. A. 1979. Introduction of barley into the new world. Pages 2-9 in: Barley: Origin, Botany, Culture, Winter Hardiness, Genetics, Utilization. Pests Agric. Handb. 338. U.S. Dept. Agric., Washington, DC.

WILSON, W. W. 1985. Production and marketing in the United States and Canada. Pages 483-510 in: Barley. D. C. Rasmusson, ed. American Society of Agronomy, Madison, WI.

YAMAGUCHI, H., and TSUTSUMI, N. 1987. Molecular cloning of mitochondrial DNA in barley. Pages 525-532 in: Barley Genetics V. Proc. 5th Int. Barley Genet. Symp. S. Yasuda and T. Konishi, eds. Sanyo Press, Okayama, Japan.

YASUDA, S., and KONISHI, T., eds. 1987. Barley Genetics V. Proc. 5th Int. Barley Genet. Symp. Sanyo Press, Okayama, Japan.

CHAPTER 2

FORMATION OF THE BARLEY GRAIN— MORPHOLOGY, PHYSIOLOGY, AND BIOCHEMISTRY

C. M. DUFFUS
M. P. COCHRANE
Crop Science and Technology Department
The Scottish Agricultural College
Edinburgh EH9 3JG, Scotland

INTRODUCTION

Barley grain development starts when the vegetative apex is induced to become a reproductive organ, the first visible signs of this change being the appearance of double ridges on the apical meristem enclosed in leaf sheaths at the base of the plant. The differentiation of the apex is accompanied by the elongation of the main stem and the differentiation and growth of the flag leaf. Awns emerge at the base of the flag leaf blade, and eventually the flag leaf sheath splits to reveal the fully developed inflorescence. The stage of development reached by the inflorescence, or ear, at the time of its emergence from the leaf sheath depends on the cultivar and on environmental conditions. It is usually necessary to extract florets from leaf sheaths to determine the exact date of anthesis, i.e., the date on which pollen is first shed from the anthers (Merritt and Walker, 1969). The inflorescence is a terminal spike bearing three spikelets at each node of its axis, or rachis. In two-rowed barley, only the median spikelet is fertile, whereas in six-rowed barley, all three spikelets are fertile. The axis, or rachilla, of the wheat spikelet bears at least four florets, but on each spikelet of barley there is one floret only. In each floret, the carpel consists of parenchymatous tissue surrounding a single ovule made up of nucellar cells enclosed in two integuments. Before anthesis, intense mitotic activity occurs in the tissues at the base of the ovule and on the ventral side of the carpel, thus forming an elongated zone of attachment of the ovule to the ovary wall on the ventral side and positioning the micropyle at the lower end (Fig. 1). The maturation of the embryo sac is accompanied by the differentiation of a provascular strand in the zone of attachment (Savchenko and Petrova, 1963).

Pollen is shed from the anthers onto the two feathery stigmas of the carpel.

31

It germinates rapidly, and the pollen tube grows down the tissues of the style, makes its way through the degenerated cells of the outer integument and through the gap in the inner integument, i.e., the micropyle, and, within 40 min of pollination at 20°C, sperm nuclei enter the embryo sac (Bennett et al, 1975). The mature embryo sac before fertilization (Fig. 1) contains, at the micropylar end, the egg apparatus, consisting of a single egg cell and two synergids; in the center, a large vacuolated cell containing two fused polar nuclei; and at the chalazal end, up to 50 antipodal cells, which have a high degree of endopolyploidy. One male nucleus fuses with the egg nucleus to give a diploid zygote, and the other male nucleus fuses with the polar nuclei to form the triploid primary endosperm nucleus. The rate at which changes in grain morphology take place following pollination depends on the temperature at which the plants are growing. Pope (1943) reported that the temperature for optimal growth of both the endosperm and embryo of barley lies in the neighborhood of 30°C and that between 10 and 30°C the rate of growth, as measured by number of generations of cells in endosperm and embryo, doubled for every 10°C rise in temperature. Similar observations

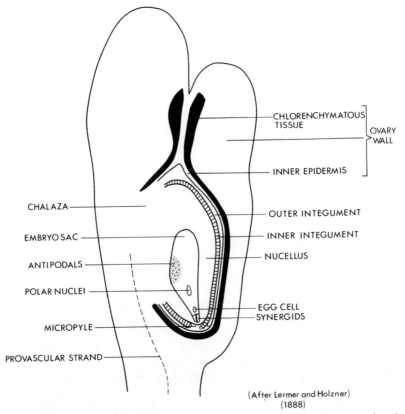

(After Lermer and Holzner)
(1888)

Fig. 1. Diagram representing a longitudinal section cut through a barley ovary just before fertilization. (Adapted from Lermer and Holzner, 1988)

made on wheat have shown that the time from pollination to the penetration of the embryo sac by the pollen tube at 20°C is twice that at 30°C, and the developmental processes in endosperms at 30°C proceed at one and a half to two times the rate of those in endosperms at 20°C (Hoshikawa, 1960, 1962).

EMBRYO DEVELOPMENT

Mitosis in the zygote occurs 18–30 hr after pollination, i.e., considerably later than in the primary endosperm nucleus. The cell cycle time remains constant over the first five days of grain development at 20°C, but, because the rate of embryo volume increase is much less than the rate of embryo cell number increase, the mean embryo cell volume decreases. Eventually the two rates become similar, and the volume of the embryo cell is then similar to that of other meristematic cells of the same species (Bennett et al, 1975). The development of the embryo of barley has been studied and illustrated in considerable detail by Lermer and Holzner (1888) and by Merry (1941). They observed that the scutellum and stem meristem began to differentiate eight to 10 days after pollination, and that a week later three leaf primordia could be recognized enclosed in the coleoptile. The differentiation of the primary root primordium about 10 days after pollination was followed by the differentiation of four pairs of seminal roots, all formed in front of the primary root and enclosed with it, inside the coleorhiza. From the 16th day, the epidermal cells of the dorsal side of the scutellum began to become narrower and also to elongate in a plane at right angles to the surface to form the scutellar epithelium. From 10 days onward, the vascular bundles of the scutellum could be distinguished as two strands of elongated cells, but, even in the mature embryo, phloem and xylem cells could not be distinguished. Swift and O'Brien (1970) showed that, in the mature wheat embryo, the entire vascular system of the scutellum is held in the provascular state and that there is no mature sieve tube connection between the scutellum, the coleoptile, and the first leaf until 18 hr after the beginning of imbibition. The position of the embryo inside the seed coat is such that the coleorhiza lies next to the micropyle. Up to the 20-cell stage of development, the embryo is attached to the nucellus at this point by the suspensor, but after that, the attachment is broken and the embryo lies in the free nuclear endosperm (Norstog, 1972). Later in embryo development, cells at the tip of the coleorhiza degenerate, leaving a mass of pectinaceous wall material filling the gap between the coleorhiza and the testa at the micropyle (Krauss, 1933). Collins (1918) referred to these cells as the embryonic appendage, a structure possibly derived from the suspensor, and he observed that pectinaceous material at the micropyle swelled rapidly when the grain came in contact with water. A considerable amount of starch is present in the developing embryo, but starch is rarely found in the mature embryo, in which the main storage materials are lipids, sucrose, and proteins. Cuticular layers are found on the epidermis at the apex of the coleoptile and on the epidermis of the concave surface of the scutellum next to the coleoptile, but not on the part of the scutellum that is covered by the tightly adhering germ aleurone layer (Krauss, 1933).

CARBOHYDRATE METABOLISM IN THE DEVELOPING EMBRYO

The critical threshold length for independent growth of immature barley embryos in culture lies between 0.20 and 0.30 mm (Cameron-Mills and Duffus, 1979). Such embryos are from grains aged seven to nine days after anthesis. Over the early stages of embryo development in vivo, the rate of carbohydrate accumulation is rapid, but as development proceeds, the rate of soluble protein accumulation exceeds that of total carbohydrate until final concentrations are similar (Duffus and Rosie, 1975). This contrasts with the developing endosperm, where protein, including storage protein, reaches no more than about 15% of the mature tissue. The enzymology of sucrose metabolism in the developing embryo differs somewhat from that in the endosperm. Invertase activity is present before sucrose synthase activity can be detected, and maximal rates of invertase activity slightly exceed those of sucrose synthase. However, when sucrose is taken up by immature embryos in vitro, most of it accumulates in a pool of free sucrose and only about 20% is used for macromolecular synthesis (Cameron-Mills and Duffus, 1979). The maintenance of a sucrose pool suggests that sucrose is protected in some way from degradation by sucrose-metabolizing enzymes, possibly by storage within vacuoles. The stability of the free sucrose pool, irrespective of the external sucrose concentration, and the specificity of the transport carrier for sucrose suggest that sucrose uptake by immature barley embryos is mediated by active transport. Presumably, this provides a mechanism whereby the developing embryo can compete effectively with the endosperm for available sucrose. By analogy with immature wheat embryos (Duffus and Binnie, 1990), there is a considerably higher concentration of sucrose in the barley embryo than in the associated endosperm. This would explain the existence of an energy-requiring system for sucrose uptake. The high levels of embryo sucrose may also play a role in the prevention of premature germination during the later phases of grain maturation since the sucrose pool may exert a desiccant effect, drawing water out of the cytosol, thus decreasing its water potential and preventing germination.

ROLE OF NUCELLAR TISSUE IN GRAIN DEVELOPMENT

At the time of fertilization, the embryo sac is embedded in the nucellus, which is attached to the surrounding integuments only at the chalaza (Fig. 1). The young embryo appears to derive its nourishment from the nucellus for a short period, as does the rapidly expanding endosperm. Within a few days, only the nucellar epidermis remains intact, and it is adpressed to the testa (Fig. 2a). Over the dorsal side of the embryo, nucellar tissue disappears completely. The cuticular layer on the outside of the nucellar epidermis adheres to the testa (Cochrane and Duffus, 1979; Freeman and Palmer, 1984) and was previously thought to be a testa cuticle (Krauss, 1933). The cytoplasm of the nucellar epidermis eventually degenerates (Fig. 2c), and by about halfway through grain development, i.e., just before cell wall thickening takes place in the aleurone, the nucellar epidermis is visible only as a layer of crushed cell wall (Tharp, 1935; Cochrane and Duffus, 1981, 1983b).

The nucellar cells in the crease region do not disintegrate, but instead, from about two days after fertilization, they undergo rapid cell division, followed by a differentiation sequence that apparently enables them to function in the transport of solutes into the endosperm and of water out of the endosperm. The structure thus formed is known as the nucellar projection (Fig. 3), and throughout the length of the crease it extends into the endosperm "deepest where the grain has the greatest circumference" (Collins, 1918). By 10 days after anthesis, in a developmental period of 60 days from anthesis to harvest-

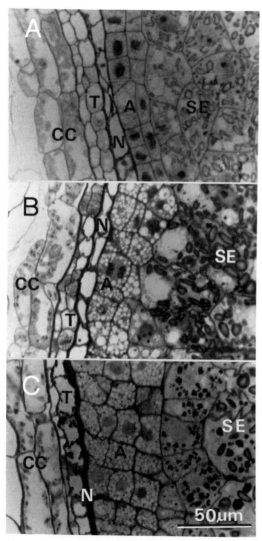

Fig. 2. Transverse sections of the lateral part or flank of three barley caryopses cut at midgrain. The sections illustrate the state of development of the cross cells (CC), testa (T), nucellus (N), aleurone (A), and starchy endosperm (SE) of grains that were fixed 15 (a), 23 (b), and 33 (c) "days" after anthesis on a developmental time scale of 60 "days" from anthesis to harvest-ripeness. (Reprinted, by permission, from Cochrane and Duffus, 1981; ©Macmillan Magazines Ltd.)

ripeness, the cells of the nucellar projection have elongated considerably in a plane at right angles to the long axis of the grain; two or three cell layers bordering the endosperm cavity have degenerated; and the cells immediately outside them have become thick-walled. As the caryopsis develops, the cells of the nucellar projection continue to elongate in a radial plane, and by 20 days after anthesis they have split into two lobes, thus enlarging the endosperm cavity. The cells at the edges of the lobes have very thick walls that stain for callose, whereas the cells in the core of the lobes have radial walls with the extensive outgrowths characteristic of transfer cells (Fig. 4). It therefore appears that these cells are the site of transfer of solutes from the symplast of the maternal tissue to the apoplast surrounding the filial tissue (Cochrane and Duffus, 1980; Felker et al, 1984a). If this is the case, then it is interesting to note that the transfer cells of the nucellar projection are separated from the transfer cells inside the crease aleurone (Fig. 4), not only by the endosperm cavity but also by the thick-walled cells that border the endosperm cavity. The endosperm cavity and the mucopolysaccharide it contains may function

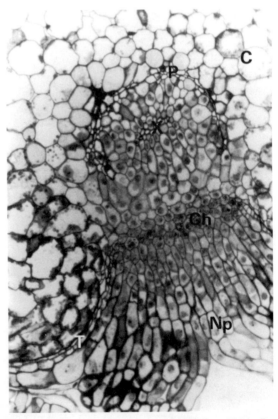

Fig. 3. Transverse section of the crease region at the middle of an 18-"day" caryopsis of barley cv. Midas fixed in a solution containing 2.5% glutaraldehyde and 1% caffeine. Np = nucellar projection. Ch = chalaza, T = testa, X = xylem, P = phloem, C = chlorenchyma. (Reprinted, by permission, from Cochrane, 1983)

in the temporary storage of solutes and water, in filtration, and in the control of the osmolarity of the solutions reaching the endosperm apoplast. There is as yet no experimental evidence for any of these proposed functions, but the fact that the endosperm cavity is surrounded by thick-walled cells that maintain its shape would seem to indicate that it is of some physiological significance during the grain-filling period.

The lumina of the cells of the nucellar projection are gradually blocked by massive wall thickening, but the innermost cells retain an apparently functional cytoplasm until the last few days of grain dehydration (Cochrane, 1983). At this stage of maturation, the endosperm cavity becomes very narrow and extends radially towards the center of the starchy endosperm, flanked by the cell wall material that forms the sheaf (Fig. 5). The massive wall thickening of the nucellar projection may thus serve not only to prevent further transport of solutes into the grain, but also to provide an efficient pathway for the exit of water from the endosperm.

DEVELOPMENT OF THE TESTA OR SEED COAT

Before fertilization, the ovule is surrounded, except at the micropyle, by two integuments, each of which is composed of two layers of cells (Fig. 1). After fertilization, the outer integument degenerates, and only the inner integument develops into the seed coat or testa. The two cell layers of the inner integument do not differentiate in the same way. Both increase in size initially by cell division, but early in grain development cell division in the

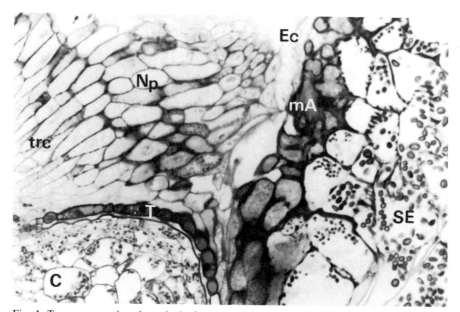

Fig. 4. Transverse section through the inner part of the crease region at the middle of a 25-"day" caryopsis of barley cv. Midas. C = chlorenchyma, T = testa, trc = transfer cells, Np = nucellar projection, Ec = endosperm cavity, mA = modified aleurone, SE = starchy endosperm. (Reprinted, with permission, from Cochrane and Duffus, 1982)

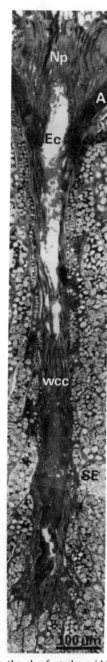

Fig. 5. Transverse section through the sheaf at the middle of a 50-"day" caryopsis of barley cv. Midas, fixed in glutaraldehyde; section stained in toluidine blue, pH 9.5. A = aleurone, Np = nucellar projection, Ec = endosperm cavity, SE = starch endosperm, wcc = walls of crushed cells. (Reprinted, by permission, from Cochrane, 1983)

outer layer ceases, and from then on this layer enlarges by cell expansion only (Tharp, 1935). Electron micrographs of caryopses about one-third of the way through development show that the cells of the outer layer have large nuclei, dense cytoplasm, and few vacuoles, whereas those of the inner layer have many vacuoles of all sizes and cytoplasm that is aggregated, leaving electron-lucent regions (Cochrane and Duffus, 1983b). The radial walls of these cells (Fig. 2b) are characteristically buckled (Krauss, 1933; Cochrane and Duffus, 1983b). The cuticular layers on either side of the testa are well developed, but they are not uniform in chemical composition, and Krauss (1933) therefore considered that they should be described as cuticular layers rather than as cuticles. The outer cuticular layer is formed by the outer layer of testa cells and is much thicker than the inner cuticular layer, which is formed from the nucellar epidermis. From an early stage of development, the inner cuticular layer adheres tightly to the innermost wall of the testa. As differentiation of the testa proceeds, thickening is laid down on the tangential walls of the inner cell layer, while the walls of the more elongate cells of the outer layer remain thin. Cell contents in the outer layer disappear (Fig. 2c), and eventually the cells are crushed (Tharp, 1935; Freeman and Palmer, 1984). Phenolic material is deposited in the vacuoles of the inner layer of cells, more accumulating in the cells surrounding the endosperm than in those surrounding the embryo, with particularly large deposits present in the testa cells adjoining the chalaza (Cochrane, 1983). In the mature grain, variations in the thickness of the outer cuticular layer have been observed. It is thickest over the apex of the endosperm, in the flanks of the crease near the chalaza, and on either side of the micropyle. It is thin over the embryo and very thin or nonexistent immediately over the micropyle (Tharp, 1935). In the mature grain, the cuticular layers appear slack and somewhat convoluted over the embryo but are taut over the endosperm.

PERICARP DEVELOPMENT

At anthesis, the ovary is just over 1 mm long. The ovary wall from which the pericarp is eventually formed, has an outer and inner epidermis separated by parenchymatous cells, of which the inner layers contain chloroplasts and the outer layers contain leucoplasts. Four vascular bundles are present at this stage (Kirby and Rymer, 1975; Lingle and Chevalier, 1985). Three of the bundles are composed of sieve tubes only, two being embedded in the lateral walls of the ovary (Cochrane and Duffus, 1983b) and the other, consisting of one or two sieve tubes, being on the dorsal side. The fourth bundle is much the largest and extends along the crease adjacent to the chalaza. It remains in the provascular state until anthesis and then differentiates rapidly into xylem and phloem as the ovary elongates. At the same time, the other three vascular bundles gradually become obliterated. Growth in the outer epidermis and in the nonchlorenchymatous cells in the ovary wall takes place mainly, if not entirely, by the elongation of cells in a plane parallel to the long axis of the ovary. The outer epidermis is covered by a cuticular layer. In the mature grain, this is quite thick over the endosperm but very thin over the embryo (Krauss, 1933; Cochrane and Duffus, 1983b). At the apex of the caryopsis, also known as the brush end, the epidermis bears many hairs, and among these on the ventral side there are a few stomata (Cochrane and Duffus, 1979). Early in development, the caryopsis appears whitish because the nonchlorenchymatous cells of the pericarp form a layer seven to eight cells thick, containing numerous small starch granules. By the time the caryopsis has reached its maximum length and rapid expansion of the endosperm is taking place, the starch has disappeared and the cell layers next to the chlorenchymatous cells have degenerated, leaving an air space inside the remaining cells of the pericarp, which are appropriately called the transparent layer. At this stage of development, small starch granules are often observed in the chlorenchymatous cells (Fig. 6). Later, when the endosperm has fully expanded and the grain begins to dry out, the transparent layer becomes tightly adpressed to the chlorenchymatous cells. The presence of an air space

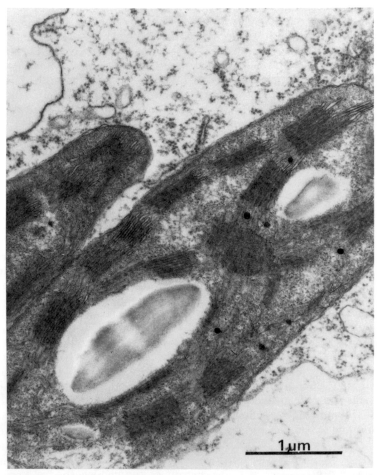

Fig. 6. Chloroplasts in a cell in the inner layer of cross cells of a 20-"day" caryopsis of cv. Julia. Transverse section cut at midgrain from tissue fixed in glutaraldehyde and postfixed in osmium tetroxide.

when the endosperm is respiring rapidly and the chlorenchymatous cells are photosynthesizing may have some physiological significance.

After fertilization, the chlorenchymatous cells of the ovary wall undergo a short period of cell division and then elongate in a plane at right angles to the long axis of the grain. These cells are known as cross cells, and around the developing starchy endosperm they form a compact tissue two or three cells thick (Fig. 2). However, over the part of the grain subsequently to be occupied by the embryo, these cells are larger and more rounded. Being more widely spaced, they form a tissue that resembles the spongy mesophyll of a leaf, just as the cross cells form a tissue that resembles palisade tissue. The inner epidermis of the ovary wall is also chlorenchymatous, but it undergoes no cell division. As the caryopsis expands, the cells elongate considerably in a plane parallel to the long axis of the grain. Over most of the testa surface they subsequently become crushed and are not visible in the mature grain, but over the embryo they remain as widely spaced, elongated cells that are known as tube cells.

On the ventral side of the grain in the crease (groove or furrow), the pattern of development of the pericarp is somewhat different from that described above. No degeneration of cells in the outer pericarp takes place, and the chlorenchymatous tissue is composed of many layers of cells, isodiametric in transverse section, lying on either side of the vascular bundle (Fig. 3). The testa is discontinuous at the crease, and the gap between the ends of the testa is occupied by the block of cells that make up the chalaza, or pigment strand. The pigmentation in the chalaza and the testa was identified as lipid by Krauss (1933) and Tharp (1935), but more recent work has established that phenolic material is accumulated in both tissues (Cochrane, 1983; Felker et al, 1984a; Lingle and Chevalier, 1985). From early in the development of the caryopsis, phenolic material can be detected in the contents of these cells. It is located in numerous small vacuoles that gradually fill and coalesce until, toward the end of the grain-filling period, most of the cell lumen is occupied by large tannin-filled vacuoles. At this stage of development, suberin is laid down in the secondary cell walls of the chalazal cells, thus effectively isolating the symplast of these cells from the surrounding apoplast. At about the same time, the primary cell wall becomes lignified. These changes in the cell wall have been interpreted as providing a means whereby assimilate can move inward only in the symplast, while the lignified layer provides a pathway that allows water but not sucrose to move from the endosperm cavity to the pericarp, thus eventually bringing about the dehydration of the endosperm. The suberized layer prevents this water from being drawn back into the symplast of the chalazal cells (Cochrane, 1983). In the final stages of grain maturation, massive wall thickening is laid down in the chalazal cells. They become crushed, and it appears that symplastic transport into the endosperm finally stops when the contents of the tannin vacuoles are released into the cytoplasm. The importance of the maternal tissues of the crease in the control of grain-filling has been established by Felker et al (1984a), using the *seg*1 mutant of barley cv. Betzes. This mutant has a shrunken endosperm with 35–55% of normal dry weight, even though the growth and net carbon exchange of the plant is normal, as is sucrose uptake and starch synthesis in the endosperm (Felker et al, 1983, 1984b). The *seg*1 mutant differs from the normal in having a shorter period of grain-filling. Light and electron microscope studies have shown abnormal development of the chalazal tissue, probably involving a breakdown in the compartmentation of tannins and an early precipitation of cytoplasmic proteins, thereby preventing any further symplastic transport of assimilates into the endosperm (Felker et al, 1984a).

The vascular bundle of the crease consists of a semicircle of phloem tissue separated by some parenchymatous cells from a core of xylem tissue. Between the xylem and the chalaza are thin-walled radially elongated cells with large nuclei and relatively dense cytoplasm (Fig. 3). These cells presumably function in the transport of solutes from the phloem to the endosperm, and they and the xylem parenchyma may also be responsible for bringing about the active removal of water from the endosperm during the last stages of grain maturation (Meredith and Jenkins, 1975; Cochrane, 1983). The relationship of the vascular tissue of the caryopsis to that of the rest of the plant must be considered in the context of the whole inflorescence. The grass inflorescence, as exemplified in wheat, is a spike, the axis of which is known as the rachis. Each lateral branch of the rachis is a rachilla bearing several florets that together make up a spikelet. In a spikelet, a floret is attached to the rachilla by a short peduncle. The barley spikelet is similar but is very much condensed and bears only one floret. The apical part of the rachilla is sterile and lies along the crease on the outside of the palea. The structure made up of the peduncle and the base of the rachilla is so short that the grain appears to be borne directly on the rachis. The vascular anatomy of the spikelet axis of barley has been investigated by Kirby and Rymer (1975). They observed a region of xylem discontinuity in the vascular tissue just below the base of the ovary. Further down the spikelet axis, at the level at which the vascular strands of the paleae join the vascular strands of the spikelet axis, they observed transfer cells. Both the zone of xylem discontinuity and the transfer cells may have an important function in controlling the water economy of the grain, and the transfer cells appear to make it possible for assimilate from the lemma and palea to enter the vascular tissue supplying the ovary. Deposition of pectic material in the vascular tissue of the rachis has been observed during the later stages of grain maturation. A more detailed investigation is needed to establish the role of this xylem blockage in the cessation of assimilate uptake and the dehydration of the grain (Cochrane, 1985).

PERICARP PHOTOSYNTHESIS

The chlorophyll-containing cells of the immature barley pericarp are capable of high rates of light-dependent oxygen evolution (Duffus and Rosie, 1973b; Nutbeam and Duffus, 1978), and there is evidence to suggest that these cells have some capacity for C_4 metabolism (Nutbeam and Duffus, 1976). In barley pericarps, for example, the first-formed product of photosynthesis is the C_4-acid malate, which is subsequently rapidly converted to sucrose. Successive removal of the husk (palea and lemma) and of the transparent layer of the pericarp resulted in marked increases in oxygen uptake in the dark by immature barley caryopses (Nutbeam and Duffus, 1978). This suggests that each of these layers may limit the influx of atmospheric oxygen. Similarly, in the light, successive removal of these layers results in increases in light-dependent oxygen evolution. Thus, it may be that these layers constitute a barrier to the efflux of oxygen from the photosynthesizing cells of the pericarp. Some of the oxygen generated by pericarp photosynthesis may therefore remain within the grain. The pericarp, then, may exert a controlling effect on endosperm biosynthetic processes by regulating the oxygen supply essential for endosperm respiratory processes. Immature, detached barley caryopses are capable of fixing externally supplied $^{14}CO_2$ in both light and dark and of transferring some of the labeled material to the endosperm and/or the embryo (Watson and Duffus, 1988). It may also be a function of the immature pericarp to act in the retrieval of internally derived carbon dioxide. This possibility has been investigated using ^{14}C-labeled caryopses obtained by incubating caryopses for 15 min in light in $^{14}CO_2$ and subjecting them to a 3-hr chase in either light or dark (Watson and Duffus, 1991). Since three times as much radiocarbon remained in the caryopses incubated in the light as in the dark, it may be concluded that photosynthesis in the pericarp green layer can prevent losses of internally produced carbon dioxide. Of the total amount of endosperm starch, around 2% could be derived from fixation of atmospheric carbon dioxide and 1% from fixation of internally derived carbon dioxide.

THE HUSK

In hull-less barley cultivars, the grain as harvested consists only of a one-seeded fruit or caryopsis, whereas in hulled barleys it consists of a caryopsis enclosed in the two flowering glumes that make up the hull, or husk. The ventral glume, or palea, is overlapped along its edges by the dorsal glume, or lemma, which, in most cultivars, terminates apically in a long awn. The glumes are more or less fully grown at anthesis, and recent evidence indicates that their thickness is determined by the growth conditions prevailing in the weeks before anthesis (Hamachi et al, 1989). Contact between the glumes and the pericarp is not established until grain-filling is almost complete. The glumes then adhere to the pericarp epidermis except over the embryo and at the brush end. It is thought that a cementing material produced by the pericarp early in development is responsible for the hull-caryopsis adherence (Gaines et al, 1985).

ENDOSPERM DEVELOPMENT

In plants growing at 20°C, the first division of the primary endosperm nucleus is complete about 7 hr after pollination, whereas mitosis in the zygote does not occur until 23 hr after pollination (Bennett et al, 1975). The endosperm is at first coenocytic but later becomes cellular. During the initial coenocytic phase of endosperm development, cell cycle time is as little as 4 hr and all divisions are synchronous. However, by 24 hr after pollination, a developmental gradient has been established and synchrony is observed only in groups of adjacent nuclei. Seventy-two hours after pollination, when about 2,000 endosperm nuclei have been formed, cell wall formation begins in the lower end of the embryo sac, and 24 hr later the endosperm is completely cellular. The mean nuclear doubling time increases considerably when cellularization takes place, and by five days after pollination synchronous divisions are no longer observed. The raw materials and energy required for this phase of rapid development of the endosperm are apparently derived from the breakdown of the starch-filled layer of nucellar cells surrounding the embryo sac and from the activities and ultimate degeneration of the antipodal cells (Bennett et al, 1975).

Following cellularization, cell division continues throughout the endosperm for a few days and then is confined to the peripheral layers. The exact timing of this change in the distribution of mitotic cells is difficult to establish, as is the duration of cell division in the endosperm. Total endosperm cell number, as estimated by counting the nuclei in tissue macerates, does not increase after the grain has reached a stage of development just less than halfway between anthesis and harvest-ripeness (Cochrane and Duffus, 1981; Kvaale and Olsen, 1986). However, early in grain development, some of the endosperm cells surrounding the embryo break down completely, and later others are reduced to a layer of crushed cell walls. In addition, as the grain matures, the cells bordering the endosperm cavity degenerate, leaving a zone of cell wall material that is known as the sheaf. Thus, accurate information on the duration of cell division in the endosperm cannot be obtained from estimates of the numbers of nuclei. The observation of mitotic profiles gives a more reliable indication of the length of time the outer layers of endosperm retain their ability to divide, and a systematic search of the whole endosperm is needed to find out whether peripheral layers at the apex and base remain mitotically active for longer than similar cells at midgrain. The peripheral cells undergoing mitosis are not typical meristematic cells but have, in fact, many of the characteristics of aleurone cells (Krauss, 1933; Cochrane and Duffus, 1982). They contain lipid bodies and many small vacuoles in which there appear to be single electron-dense deposits. The mature barley grain has two to four layers of aleurone cells, and so both daughter cells resulting from a mitotic division in the outermost layer are likely to continue to differentiate into aleurone cells, but a periclinal division occurring in the inner layer of partially differentiated aleurone may produce a daughter cell that undergoes dedifferentiation and simultaneously differentiates into a starchy endosperm cell. The cells at the center of the starchy endosperm are irregular in shape, presumably having been formed before cell division was localized in the peripheral layers (Fig. 7). Outside the irregular cells, except on the ventral side, there are several layers of prismatic cells, somewhat elongated in the radial axis and forming columns that indicate that they were derived from divisions in the peripheral layers. Between the prismatic cells and the aleurone is a layer of relatively small starchy endosperm cells. These, the last cells to differentiate into starchy endosperm, are known as the subaleurone.

After fertilization, nuclear divisions proceed much more slowly in the embryo than in the endosperm, and the embryo becomes embedded in endosperm cells that appear to have a haustorial function (Krauss, 1933). Early in the development of the embryo, the endosperm cells next to it are completely digested, but later, only the contents of the endosperm cells next to the scutellum of the embryo are digested (MacGregor and Dushnicky, 1989b), leaving cell walls that are crushed between the expanding embryo and the endosperm to form what is described as the intermediate layer or the depleted layer.

This layer separates the scutellum from the starchy endosperm in the mature grain (Fig. 8).

Starchy Endosperm

In the rest of the embryo sac, the endosperm cells are highly vacuolated except at the crease, where they have dense cytoplasm. Numerous starch granules are observed in endosperm cells within 24 hr of the start of cell wall formation (Bennett et al, 1975). Stereological analyses of wheat endosperm development have shown that increase in plastid number ceases several days before the end of cell division, which means that the outermost cells of the starchy endosperm have fewer amyloplasts than the inner cells (Briarty et al, 1979). For a number of cultivars of spring barley, a positive correlation was found between endosperm cell number and 1,000-grain weight (Cochrane and Duffus, 1983a), but observations on wheat indicate that the potential for accumulating starch may be more closely related to amyloplast number than to endosperm cell number (Gleadow et al, 1982; Chojecki et al, 1986).

Throughout the endosperm, plasmadesmata are very plentiful, indicating that symplastic pathways are available for solute movement. Hoshikawa (1984) has described cell wall morphology in all parts of the endosperm during the grain-filling phase of development. He interprets the undulations observed mainly in the anticlinal walls, as "modifications" that increase the surface area of the plasma membrane and facilitate more rapid transfer of solutes. Similar, but much less marked, cell-wall undulations can be seen in sections of developing barley grains grown in Scotland (Fig. 2) (Cochrane and Duffus, 1981; Cochrane and Duffus, 1983b). A possible explanation for the difference is that, at the higher temperatures at which the plants were grown in Japan, grain-filling did not keep pace with cell wall formation.

The starchy endosperm is not continuous throughout the center of the caryopsis but is divided by the endosperm cavity into two lobes (Fig. 7). At about the stage of development when dry matter accumulation ceases, the contents of the crease aleurone cells at mid-grain disappear, and the region

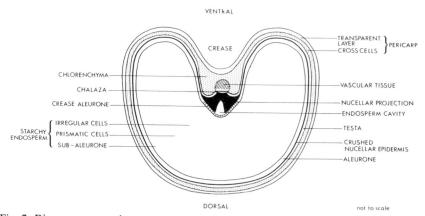

Fig. 7. Diagram representing a transverse section cut at midgrain through a barley caryopsis at the end of the grain-filling period.

previously identified as the endosperm cavity now appears as a core of cell wall material derived from the nucellar projection, the crease aleurone cells, and the neighboring starchy endosperm cells. Midway between the dorsal and ventral surfaces, this "sheaf" terminates in a structure resembling a delta, which is continuous with starchy endosperm cell walls in all directions (Fig. 5) (Cochrane, 1983). It is possible that this continuity between the endosperm cell walls and the maternal tissues provides a pathway for water loss from the endosperm during grain dehydration. The final phase of starchy endosperm development is characterized by rapid water loss and a considerable increase in the deposition of cell wall material, particularly the fraction described as "hemicellulose" (Coles, 1979).

During the first two weeks of endosperm development in grains that reach harvest-ripeness eight to nine weeks after anthesis, typically only one starch granule is initiated in each amyloplast. The granule is lenticular in shape and has a peripheral groove in or near which are located the tubuli of the amyloplast stroma (Buttrose, 1960). At maturity, these granules may be as

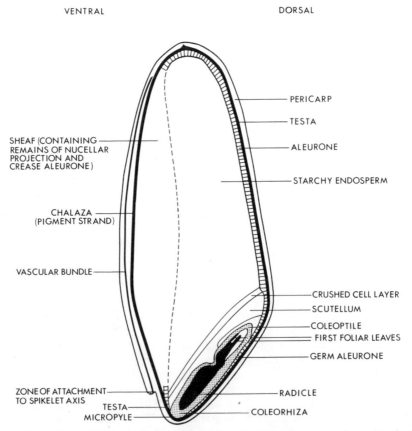

Fig. 8. Diagram representing a longitudinal section cut to bisect the crease of a mature barley caryopsis.

much as 35 μm in diameter. May and Buttrose (1959) reported that these large type-A granules cease to be initiated about two weeks after anthesis, at which time smaller, rounder type-B granules are first observed. B-type granules are initiated in the stroma of A-type amyloplasts and then released into the cytoplasm enclosed in a double membrane budded off from that of the parent amyloplast (Buttrose, 1960). In the mature starchy endosperm, although many cells contain large numbers of tightly packed polyhedral B-type granules, as much as 90% of the starch volume may be made up of A-type granules (May and Buttrose, 1959). In plants of cv. Triumph grown in a day temperature of 20°C and a night temperature of 15°C, the total number of starch granules per endosperm in mature grains was found to be 175×10^6, of which fewer than 5% were A-type. Elevated temperatures experienced by the plant just before anthesis induced a decrease in the numbers of both A- and B-type granules (MacLeod and Duffus, 1988a). The sizes of the granules were not affected.

Analyses of starch granules of a number of *Hordeum* species (Baum and Bailey, 1987) have shown that the bimodal distribution of granule size found in cultivated forms of barley is by no means characteristic of the genus as a whole. It was demonstrated in only six of the 39 species investigated.

The starch of mature endosperms contains about 25% amylose and 75% amylopectin. Banks et al (1973) showed that there is a steady increase in the amylose content of total starch during grain development; thus, it seems likely that amylopectin synthesis predominates at early stages of grain development. The increase in percentage amylose content might be caused by a steady change in the starch composition of all granules. On the other hand, it might be due to changes in relative numbers and/or changes in individual amylose contents of the A- and B-type starch granules. Early work (Williams and Duffus, 1977) suggested that the small or B-type granules had a higher percentage of amylopectin than the large or A-type granules throughout endosperm development but that by maturity no significant difference existed between the two populations. Other workers, including Stark and Yin (1986), have suggested that at maturity the large granules have a higher amylose content than the small ones. However, the determination of total and percentage amylose is not easy (Morrison and Laignelet, 1983) and may be confounded by such factors as starch solubilization and the presence in cereal starches of monoacyl lipids that complex with amylose, thus reducing its iodine-binding capacity and blue value.

McDonald et al (1991) estimated amylose in the presence and absence of starch lipids. They found that in cv. Glacier the percentage of amylose in A-granules was greater than that in B-granules throughout grain development, but in the mature grain the difference between the populations was small. However, in the isogenic line Glacier (high amylose), from 30 days after anthesis onwards, the percentage of amylose was higher in B-granules than in A-granules, and in the mature grain the amylose percentage was 39 in A-granules and 47 in B-granules.

STARCH SYNTHESIS AND DEPOSITION

The deposition of starch within endosperm amyloplasts commences within a few days of fertilization. Synthesis of the straight-chain component, amylose, or α-(1→4)-D-glucan, is catalyzed by the enzyme starch synthase. Amylopectin is then synthesized from α-(1→4)-D-glucan in a coordinated reaction involving starch synthase and branching enzyme. A debranching enzyme might also be required to produce primers for the starch synthase reaction. Since an isoenzyme of phosphorylase, present during early endosperm development in barley, is capable of unprimed synthesis of starch, this enzyme also may be capable of supplying primers for starch synthase (Baxter and Duffus, 1973b). This would be of particular advantage at the initial stages of development when little α-(1→4)-D-glucan has been synthesized.

The nucleotide sugars for the starch synthase reaction are derived from uridine diphosphate (UDP)-glucose via the pyrophosphorylase reaction (Fig. 9). Both UDP-glucose and adenosine diphosphate (ADP)-glucose pyrophosphorylases are present during the period of starch accumulation in barley endosperm. Pyrophosphorylase activity with both nucleotide sugars was similar during development, but the peak of activity with UDP-glucose occurred later in development than that with ADP-glucose (Baxter and Duffus, 1973a).

While it might be thought that UDP-glucose could be used by UDP-glucose-dependent starch synthase, this may not be the case since there is evidence (Delmer and Stone, 1988) that UDP-monosaccharides are used preferentially in the synthesis of structural polysaccharides such as β-D-glucan.

The starch synthases of immature barley endosperm are found in both the soluble form and bound to starch granules. In each case, activity is observed with UDP-glucose and ADP-glucose (Baxter and Duffus, 1973c). As development proceeds, however, starch synthase becomes increasingly granule-bound and activity is greatest when ADP-glucose is used as a donor.

Control of starch synthesis in developing cereal endosperms may be exerted by the permeability of the amyloplast inner membrane, as well as by the regulatory properties of the various enzymes involved. The form in which carbon enters the amyloplast has long been the subject of speculation, and hence the exact biochemical pathway whereby sucrose is converted to starch is still unknown. One of the problems is the difficulty in obtaining good yields of intact, undamaged, uncontaminated amyloplasts that can be used for transport studies. However, Keeling et al (1988) have shown that it is not necessary to prepare amyloplasts to investigate this problem, and experiments in which ^{13}C-labeled hexoses were supplied in vivo to wheat plants showed that a hexose phosphate is the most likely candidate for entry to the amyloplast. Previously it had been supposed, in the absence of any direct evidence and by analogy with chloroplasts, that carbon is transported into the amyloplast as triose phosphate (Duffus, 1987). Some of the enzyme-catalyzed reactions that could be involved in the conversion of sucrose to starch are shown in Fig. 9.

PROTEIN SYNTHESIS AND DEPOSITION

The deposition of storage protein begins several days after the formation of the first endosperm starch granules. In newly formed peripheral cells of the starchy endosperm, small deposits of storage protein are found in large vacuoles (Cameron-Mills and von Wettstein, 1980), while in older, more central starchy endosperm cells (Fig. 10), protein deposits may be enclosed in several concentric layers of membranes (Henderson, 1987). In the mature caryopsis, protein deposits are fused to form a matrix in which bounding membranes cannot be distinguished.

Protein is the major nitrogenous reserve of the barley grain, and, since many of the proteins in the endosperm have originally had a physiological role, there are very many different proteins in the mature grain. With such a variety of complex macromolecules, studying the deposition of individual proteins is difficult, and in practice it has proved preferable to study the deposition of groups of proteins with similar properties. Such groups were

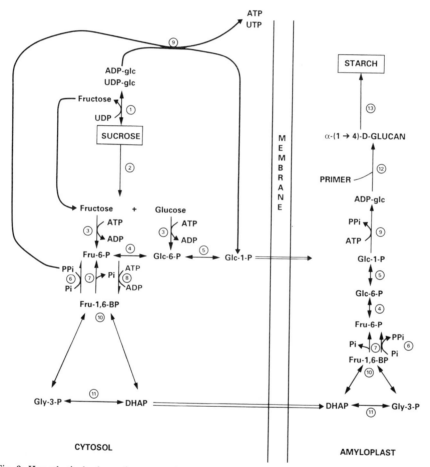

Fig. 9. Hypothetical scheme for conversion of sucrose to starch in developing barley endosperm. 1 = sucrose synthase, 2 = invertase, 3 = hexokinase, 4 = phosphohexose isomerase, 5 = phosphoglucomutase, 6 = PPi-dependent phosphofructokinase, 7 = fructose-1,6-bisphosphatase, 8 = adenosine triphosphate (ATP)-dependent phosphofructokinase, 9 = adenosine diphosphate (ADP)-glucose and uridine diphosphate (UDP)-glucose pyrophosphorylases, 10 = aldolase, 11 = triose phosphate isomerase, 12 = starch synthase, 13 = branching enzyme. UDP-glc = UDP-glucose, ADP-glc = ADP-glucose, Glc-6-P = glucose-6-phosphate, Glc-1-P = glucose-1-phosphate, Fru-1-P = fructose-1-phosphate, Fru-6-P = fructose-6-phosphate, Fru-1,6-BP = fructose-1,6-bisphosphate, Gly-3-P = glyceraldehyde-3-phosphate, DHAP = dihydroxyacetone phosphate, PPi = pyrophosphate, Pi = inorganic phosphate.

originally classified by Osborne (1895) on the basis of their solubility, and this is still the method in use today. There are four solubility groups, each highly heterogeneous and varying from species to species: albumins are soluble in water in neutral or slightly acidic conditions; globulins are soluble in salt solutions; glutelins are soluble in strong acid or alkali but insoluble in water, salt solutions, or ethanol; and prolamins are soluble in 60–70% alcohol but insoluble in water. A more complete extraction of prolamins is achieved using propan-1-ol (50% by volume) at 60°C in the presence of a reducing agent (Miflin and Shewry, 1979). These protein fractions exhibit considerable heterogeneity, and their characteristics depend very much on the extraction methods used.

The albumin fraction may include the soluble enzymatic proteins such as

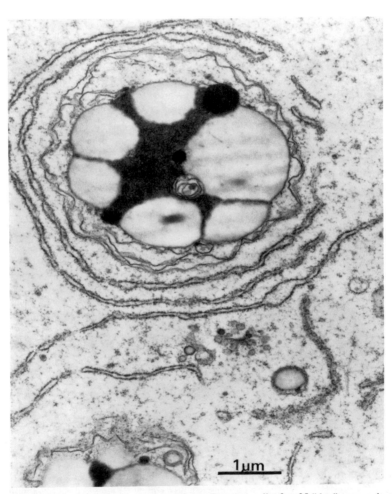

Fig. 10. Protein deposits in a central starchy endosperm cell of a 25-"day" caryopsis of cv. Midas. Transverse section cut at midgrain from tissue fixed in glutaraldehyde, and postfixed in osmium tetroxide.

sucrose synthase and the transaminases that are present in the developing grain (Duffus and Rosie, 1978; Chevalier and Lingle, 1983). Of the storage proteins (glutelins and prolamins), it is the prolamins (hordeins) that have attracted the most attention, since it is this class that appears to exert a key influence on many of the technological characteristics of the harvested grain. Three different groups of hordeins have been identified, all of them rich in proline and poor in basic amino acids. Hordeins account for 30% of the barley seed proteins (Fig. 11). Their effect on the technological characteristics of the harvested grain includes a lowering of nutritive value for nonruminant animals, since, unlike the salt-soluble and glutelin fractions, they are extremely deficient in lysine (containing less than 1%). Diets can be supplemented with lysine from external sources, but the deleterious effects of hordeins during the brewing process are less easily overcome. Hordeins may prevent the dissolution of starch during mashing, and this can cause loss of extract as well as filtration problems (Slack et al, 1979).

Changes in the endosperm protein fractions during grain development in barley cv. Bomi are shown in Fig. 11 (Brandt, 1976). As expected, the albumins dominated the early stages of development. The highest rates of accumulation of the hordeins and glutelins occurred after the major synthesis period of

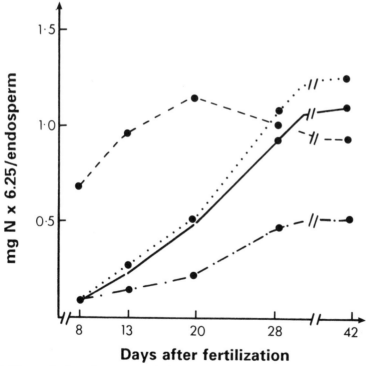

Days after fertilization

Fig. 11. Changes in the endosperm protein fractions during grain development in barley cultivar Bomi: albumins, including free amino acids (- - - - -), globulins (. – . – . – .), hordeins (——), and glutelins (............). (Reprinted, by permission, from Brandt, 1976)

the albumins was completed. Changes in the amount of hordein and its different components over the period of grain development in cv. Sundance have been described by Rahman et al (1984). Hordein was detectable in the endosperm by 18 days after anthesis, although it was not possible to recognize hordein polypeptides on sodium dodecyl sulfate-polyacrylamide gels at this stage. These were first observed at 22 days. From 22 days onward, changes were observed in the relative amounts of the different hordein fractions, with decreases in the proportion of B2, B3, and C1 polypeptides and an increase in the B1 polypeptide.

It has been shown (Cameron-Mills and Ingversen, 1978; Weber and Brandt, 1985) that hordein polypeptides are synthesized on the endoplasmic reticulum with cotranslational cleavage of the signal peptide and concomitant transport of the newly synthesized polypeptide into the lumen of the endoplasmic reticulum. More recently, the transcriptional and posttranscriptional regulation of hordein gene expression in developing barley endosperm has been investigated (Sørensen et al, 1989). The levels of the mRNAs encoding the hordeins and a major endosperm albumin were found to increase three- to fourfold from 8 to 25 days after anthesis and thereafter decrease. B and C hordein mRNAs were many times more abundant than any of the other mRNA species, and it was suggested that this was a consequence of posttranslational regulation. When the expression of hordein genes was investigated in a mutant that fails to synthesize the major storage polypeptides, it was shown that the reduced levels of mRNAs and storage protein in the mutant were probably a consequence of lower transcription activity of the genes encoding B and C hordeins and the major endosperm albumin (Sørensen et al, 1989).

LIPIDS

The lipid content of the mature barley grain is normally in the range of 2–4%. Much of this is present in the aleurone and embryo rather than in the starchy endosperm. The major class of lipid present is triglyceride. The free fatty acid fraction occupies a very small proportion of the total lipid (<2%), and the major fatty acids present are the unsaturated fatty acids, linoleic and oleic (Palmer, 1989). Other constituents of the lipid fraction include diacylgalactosylglycerides, di-O-acylphospholipids, and a unique class of lipids called the starch lipids. These are defined as those lipids that are present within the native starch granules (Morrison, 1988), and in barley, these are almost exclusively lysophospholipids. They are thought to exist as inclusion complexes of amylose.

The accumulation of lipids has been recorded for developing wheat caryopses (Skarsaune et al, 1970). It seems that esterification increases with maturation, and, when expressed as a percentage of total lipid, the glyceride levels increase markedly over the maturation period from a value of 10% to a final value of around 70% of total lipid.

It is likely that the high initial levels of polar lipid reflect the proliferation of cell membranes during the early stages of grain development. The relationship between amylose and lipid phosphorus content of A-type granules during endosperm development in barley has been investigated (McDonald et al, 1991). For each of four genotypes, a linear relationship was obtained between the total amylose content of the granules at each stage of development and the lipid phosphorus at the corresponding stage of development. From these results, it was concluded that A-type granule starches have a core of low-amylose, low-lipid starch and an outer shell of high-amylose, high-lipid starch. It is not known how these observations relate to the control of starch formation and deposition during endosperm development.

NONSTARCH POLYSACCHARIDES

The nonstarch polysaccharides found in mature grains include fructans, β-(1→4)-D-glucan (cellulose), (1→3),(1→4)-β-D-glucans (β-D-glucans), arabinoxylans, and glucomannans. The β-D-glucans are linear molecules with around 30% β-(1→3) and 70% β-(1→4) linkages randomly dispersed and are associated with firmly linked peptide sequences in the barley endosperm cell wall (Fleming and Kawakami, 1977; Forrest and Wainwright, 1977). Over 96% of total grain cellulose disappears following removal of the husk (MacLeod and Napier, 1959). This observation, together with analytical data of Fincher and Stone (1986), indicates that the barley endosperm cell wall contains very little cellulose. Differences are observed in the composition of the cell walls of the starchy endosperm and the aleurone. The cell walls of the starchy endosperm contain about 70% β-D-glucan and 20% arabinoxylan, whereas the aleurone cell walls contain about 26% β-D-glucan and 67% arabinoxylan. Both contain similar amounts of glucomannan and cellulose, i.e., between 2 and 4% of each polymer.

The cell walls of barley may interfere with the brewing process if they are insufficiently degraded during malting. For example, the presence of β-D-glucan or arabinoxylan interferes with beer filtration and increases the likelihood of haze formation in the finished product (Palmer, 1989). β-D-Glucans also cause feeding and digestive problems in domestic fowl (Hesselman et al, 1981). The content and solubility of β-D-glucan during grain development in barley has been described recently (Åman et al, 1989). Plants were grown in experimental plots in central Sweden near Uppsala (60°N). Total β-D-glucan content increased steadily over the developmental period, reaching a maximum value of about 6% of total grain dry weight just before harvest (Fig. 12). The rate of accumulation of the soluble fraction was greater than that of the insoluble fraction and reached a maximum value a few days earlier. Determination of the relative amounts of soluble and insoluble β-D-glucan depends on the method of extraction used. In this case, soluble mixed-linkage β-D-glucan was extracted with water for 2 hr at 38°C and was calculated as the difference between total and insoluble components. The content of soluble β-D-glucan was found to be about twice that of the insoluble fraction. It appeared from these results that most of the grain dry matter had been deposited before the majority of mixed-linkage β-D-glucan was synthesized.

The pattern of deposition of arabinoxylans in developing barley kernels has been reported by Cerning and Guilbot (1973); these apparently are synthesized early in development and before the β-D-glucans. Palmer (1989) has suggested that these early deposits of arabinoxylans may be located on the outside of the cell walls of the starchy endosperm cells. Arabinoxylans are also found in the aleurone, pericarp, and husk of the mature grain (Henry, 1988).

Aleurone

Shortly after cell division in the endosperm becomes confined to the outermost layers, the cells in these peripheral layers become distinguishable from those inside by their more or less cuboidal shape (Fig. 2a). Their dense cytoplasm contains numerous vacuoles and lipid bodies (Cameron-Mills and von Wettstein, 1980). Proplastids are present and also some small plastids containing starch granules. The vacuoles are electron-lucent, but many contain a single electron-dense globule. The subsequent stages of aleurone cell differ-

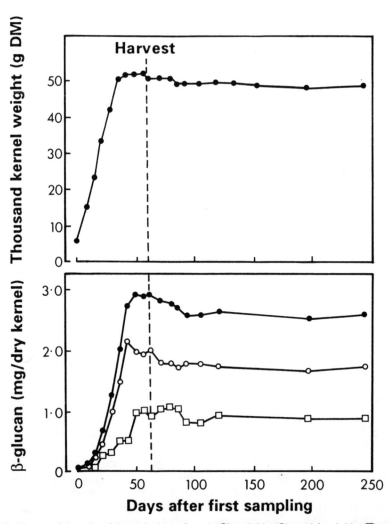

Fig. 12. Thousand-kernel weight and yield of total (●), soluble (○), and insoluble (□) mixed-linked β-glucan in two-rowed barley (cv. Golf) harvested at 10 different stages of kernel development in central Sweden. Broken line indicates the main harvest time. (Reprinted, by permission, from Åman et al, 1989)

entiation in barley have not been observed at the level of ultrastructure, but light micrographs show that no further thickening of the cell walls takes place until the grain is more than halfway through the developmental period from anthesis to harvest-ripeness and the nucellar epidermis has degenerated (Fig. 2c) (Cochrane and Duffus, 1981; Hoshikawa, 1984). Little, if any, increase in aleurone cell size takes place between the initial stages of differentiation and the onset of cell wall thickening. It appears that, as the volume of the starchy endosperm increases, the integrity of the aleurone layer is maintained by cell division rather than by cell expansion and that it is only when starchy endosperm has ceased to expand that wall thickening is laid down in the aleurone layer. It is after this stage that the vacuoles of aleurone cells become filled with protein. Thus, deposition of storage protein takes place much later in caryopsis development in the aleurone than in the starchy endosperm. The protein-containing vacuole of the mature aleurone cell is known as an aleurone grain. It contains two inclusions, globoids and crystalloids (Jacobsen et al, 1971). The globoids are composed of phytin, a substance made up of the calcium and magnesium salts of inositol hexaphosphoric acid. Each aleurone grain contains one to three globoids, those in the inner cell layer of the aleurone being larger than those in the outer cell layer. The crystalloids appear to be composed of densely packed proteins and polysaccharides. In mature aleurone cells, numerous lipid bodies surround the aleurone grains and there are no starch granules. Unlike the protein deposits of the starchy endosperm, the aleurone grain retains an intact membrane in the dry mature caryopsis, and the membrane is also evident in the imbibed seed, in which the aleurone grain acquires some of the functions of a lytic vacuole. The aleurone grain thus has many of the characteristics of the protein bodies of legume cotyledons. These tissues resemble aleurone in that they act as storage organs and also remain alive, in contrast to the starchy endosperm, which at maturity is essentially a nonliving tissue.

Early in its development, the embryo is embedded in endosperm cells, but as the embryo grows, some of these cells are digested. As a result, the convex face of the embryo scutellum lies adpressed to the intermediate layer of the starchy endosperm, and the rest of the embryo, except for the tip of the coleorhiza, is separated from the testa by a single layer of cells known as the germ aleurone (Mead, 1942) (Fig. 8). Germ aleurone cells are similar to aleurone cells but are flattened tangentially and at maturity contain no aleurone grains (Krauss, 1933). McFadden et al (1988) were able to demonstrate the presence of mRNA encoding for $(1\rightarrow3),(1\rightarrow4)$-$\beta$-glucanases in the aleurone over the scutellum of germinating barley grains.

When cellularization of the endosperm is complete, the outermost cells on the ventral side of the embryo sac differ from the other endosperm cells in having dense cytoplasm and in not undergoing mitosis. This layer of cells is continuous with the aleurone at the edges of the crease region and is known as crease or groove aleurone, although it has few if any of the characteristics of aleurone cells. By the time the caryopsis is 3.5–4 mm long, the crease aleurone cells have become radially elongate and the radial walls are massively and irregularly thickened with what appears to be callose (Cochrane and Duffus, 1980). The cytoplasm is extremely fragmented, thus greatly increasing the surface area of membrane available for movement of substances between the apoplast and the symplast. Another feature of these most unusual cells is their numerous and apparently very active dictyosomes. By the time the caryopsis is halfway through its developmental period, the cytoplasm is no longer fragmented, no callose can be detected, and the thick-walled irregular cells are separated by large regions of homogenous material. The function of the crease aleurone is a matter for speculation and may change as the caryopsis develops. Krauss (1933) considered that the mucilaginous material occupying the endosperm cavity was derived from the distended walls of the crease aleurone. The presence of numerous dictyosomes and the temporary storage of carbohydrate in the form of callose would support this hypothesis. However, the crease aleurone cells (Fig. 7) lie between the parental tissues that supply assimilates and the endosperm tissues that use them to synthesize storage compounds, and so it is likely that some of their modifications facilitate or even control the movement of solutes from the endosperm cavity to the cytoplasm of the endosperm cells. During the grain-filling phase of development, cells having wall ingrowths typical of transfer cells are found immediately inside the crease aleurone (Fig. 4). These cells may be the site of transfer of assimilate into the symplast of the endosperm. During the dehydration phase of grain maturation, the contents of the crease aleurone and neighboring cells degenerate, and their cell walls become crushed to form part of the sheaf.

NUTRIENT SUPPLY TO THE DEVELOPING CARYOPSIS

Much of the fixed carbon used in the biosynthesis of carbohydrate, lipid, and protein in the developing barley kernel is thought to be derived from photosynthesis occurring during the grain-filling period (Archbold, 1942; Thorne, 1966), although as we shall see, this can be supplemented by the mobilization of stored reserves. The tissues supplying photosynthetic assimilates for grain filling include the flag leaf, the stem immediately below the ear, and the ear itself (Thorne, 1965). In wheat, about 45–50% of flag leaf assimilates may be translocated to the ear, but the rate of photosynthesis varies depending on the demand for assimilate by the ear (King et al, 1967).

The contribution made by ear photosynthesis to kernel dry weight is influenced by plant growth conditions and cultivar. Furthermore, the results obtained also depend on the type of experiment used. For example, from shading experiments, the contribution to yield by barley ear photosynthesis has been shown to be between 15 and 39% (Thorne, 1963). It is likely, however, that these are underestimates, since removal of a photosynthetic source may be compensated for by increased contributions from other sources. These experiments did not take into account any respiration by the shaded organ. Fixation of radioactive carbon dioxide ($^{14}CO_2$) by different plant parts can also be used to determine the relative importance of different organs in the deposition of kernel storage material. Measurements obtained using this technique suggest that between 33 and 50% of the assimilates accumulated in barley kernels are supplied by CO_2 fixation in the ear (Birecka et al, 1964). An ingenious method of estimating the contribution of the barley ear to grain filling, which was thought to give a definitive result, was described by Frey-Wyssling and Buttrose (1959). The basis of the technique was the hypothesis that the reduction in grain weight following stem defoliation and shading at flowering depend on the number of grains developing per ear. They assumed that, under such competitive conditions, which do not exist in untreated plants, first, the total amount of kernel-filling material coming from non-ear parts is equal, no matter how many grains are developing, and, second, the quantity of kernel-filling material derived from photosynthetic products in any one floret is equal to that in any other floret. By comparing two treated plants differing in the number of florets per ear and with different final grain weights, they derived an equation from which the contribution of ear photosynthesis to grain yield could be determined. The results suggested that products of ear photosynthesis are fully used in grain development, and it was concluded that the maximum measured value of 76% for the contribution of the ear to grain dry weight could be a closer approximation to the true value than lower figures obtained using different techniques. All green parts of the inflorescence can contribute to ear photosynthesis (Carr and Wardlaw, 1965). For example, photosynthesis by developing wheat caryopses has been shown to account for 33–42% of gross ear photosynthesis. Rates were almost sufficient to balance the loss of carbon dioxide by dark respiration (Evans and Rawson, 1970). In barley, the net contribution by the caryopsis to starch formation in the grain from atmospheric carbon dioxide is around 2%. Other tissues of the ear that contribute to photosynthesis, and hence to assimilate supply, include the rachis, the glumes, the paleae, and the awns. Little is known of their individual contributions to grain storage material in barley. While it is generally agreed that much of the dry matter entering the developing grain is derived from photosynthesis occurring after ear emergence, there is good evidence that a significant part of the carbon found in mature barley grains is derived from stem reserves. This topic is reviewed in more detail by Hay and Walker (1989).

The contributions to grain yield of preanthesis reserves in the hot, dry year of 1976 and cool, wet year of 1977 in the United Kingdom are shown in Table 1 (Hay and Walker, 1989; Austin et al, 1980). Grain yields were much

TABLE 1
Grain Yields of Spring Barley Genotypes, Classified According to Height,
and the Calculated Contributions to Grain Yields from Assimilation
up to Five Days After Anthesis[a]

Year		Height to Base of Ear (cm)	Grain Yield (g/m²)	Contribution to Grain Yield from Assimilation During Period 18 Days Before Anthesis to Five Days After Anthesis	
				Amount (g/m²)	Percent
1976	Tall	45	318	173	54
	Single dwarf	36	296	180	61
	Double dwarf	30	291	178	61
1977	Tall	90	715	107	15
	Single dwarf	68	654	89	14
	Double dwarf	49	659	91	14

[a] Adapted from Austin et al (1980).

less in 1976 and contained considerably more material derived from preanthesis assimilates. After correction for assimilates produced in the five days after anthesis, the preanthesis contributions to yield were found to be 44 and 11% in 1976 and 1977, respectively. In similar experiments carried out in Mexico, Bidinger et al (1977) found that the preanthesis contribution to grain yield in barley was 12% in irrigated crops and 22% in droughted crops. There is also evidence from wheat to suggest that stem reserves of soluble carbohydrates may be accumulated postanthesis (Austin, 1980). That is, for 15–20 days after fertilization, the demand for assimilates by the developing grain is generally less than the capacity of the leaves to supply them. These reserves may then be translocated, when required, to supply the developing grain.

Mineral ions and nitrogen are also required by the developing grain. Much of the nitrogen entering the grain is derived from preanthesis reserves, but some can be accounted for by nitrogen taken up from the soil after anthesis (Russell, 1986). The timing of nitrogen uptake by the plant has a powerful influence on the suitability of the grain for malting. For example, late and/or heavy applications of nitrogen tend to produce grains with high nitrogen content that are unsuitable for malting.

The nutrients entering the developing barley grain have not so far been identified with any confidence. However, it is generally assumed that they include sucrose, amino acids, and mineral ions. The composition of peduncle sieve tube sap from wheat plants during grain filling has been reported by Fisher (1987). When samples were obtained using exuding aphid stylets, sucrose, amino acids, and potassium accounted for 75–90% of the total exudate osmolality. The predominant amino acid was glutamine. Alanine, asparagine, serine, threonine, and valine were next in importance. Since proline is one of the principal amino acids of cereal proteins, much metabolic transformation of amino acids probably occurs before their incorporation into grain protein. Transaminase activity was shown to reach a maximum in the barley endosperm about 40 days after anthesis in a 60-day developmental period (Duffus and Rosie, 1978). Using detached ears of wheat fed with ^{3}H-labeled amino acids for short periods, Donovan et al (1983) found that transport of glycine and valine into the grain is accompanied by extensive metabolism of both. At two-thirds maturity, the nitrogen content of the cell sap containing 25% amino acids (on a molar basis) was very similar to that reported for grains at the same stage of development. This indicates that amino acids are the predominant, if not the sole, source of nitrogen for the developing grain (Fisher, 1987).

Sucrose Metabolism

In barley, as in wheat, it appears (Felker et al, 1984b; Lingle and Chevalier, 1984) that sucrose is not metabolized during transfer from the phloem to the developing endosperm. This conclusion was reached by Lingle and Chevalier (1984) from results that showed that sucrose was the major labeled sugar in the endosperm after they fed uniformly labeled ^{14}C-sucrose (U-^{14}C-sucrose). However, the use of U-^{14}C-sucrose precluded determining whether sucrose was cleaved and resynthesized. In the work described by Felker et al (1984b), spikes of barley cv. Betzes were allowed to take up [fructose-U-^{14}C] sucrose 14 days after anthesis, and the radioactivity of endosperm sugars was examined during 3 hr of incubation. Since over 96% of the label of endosperm sugars was in sucrose, and since there was no randomization of label among the hexose moieties of sucrose, they concluded that hydrolysis of sucrose was not required for uptake into the developing barley endosperm.

Much of the sucrose entering the developing endosperm is presumably converted to starch, with some being used in the synthesis of structural polysaccharides and lipids. Some sucrose also enters the pathways of respiration, thus producing energy to drive grain biosynthetic processes. Another source of carbon may be carbon skeletons derived from amino acid metabolism. In barley it seems that incoming sucrose is first converted to UDP-glucose and fructose by UDP-dependent sucrose synthase (Baxter and Duffus, 1973a). While enzyme activity could be detected with ADP, the activity was very much less than that with UDP. Activity with ADP could not be detected until eight days after anthesis. Invertase activity in the immature endosperms was very low over the maturation period, and its presence may in fact be due to slight contamination of isolated endosperms by maternal tissues such as the pericarp. Similar results for invertase and UDP-dependent sucrose synthase were observed for developing barley endosperms by Chevalier and Lingle (1983). Thus, the major products of sucrose metabolism in immature barley endosperm appear to be UDP-glucose, ADP-glucose, and fructose. Baxter and Duffus (1973a) showed, however, that starch-bound ADP-glucose-dependent starch synthase may be responsible for the greater part of the starch-synthesizing activity of the developing barley endosperm. Thus, one would expect a major product of sucrose metabolism to be ADP-glucose and not UDP-glucose. It may be, then, that the UDP-glucose formed from the sucrose synthase reaction is first converted to glucose-1-phosphate and then to ADP-glucose via the enzyme ADP-glucose pyrophosphorylase. Fructose, formed also from the sucrose synthase reaction, may be converted (by the action of fructokinase, glucose-6-phosphate ketoisomerase, and phosphoglucomutase) to glucose-1-phosphate, and hence to starch. Any glucose could also be metabolized to glucose-1-phosphate by the action of hexokinase and phosphoglucomutase (Fig. 9). All these enzymes are present in the barley endosperm soon after anthesis (Baxter and Duffus, 1973a).

GRAIN CATABOLIC PROCESSES

It is assumed that the energy required for grain biosynthetic reactions is derived from processes of aerobic respiration (Duffus and Cochrane, 1982; Duffus, 1987). The developing barley grain, for example, is capable of significant rates of oxygen uptake, and there is evidence also for the presence of glycolytic, pentose phosphate pathway, and tricarboxylic acid cycle enzymes. The products of this activity include adenosine triphosphate (ATP), reduced nicotinamide adenine dinucleotide (NADH), and NADH phosphate (NADPH), which are used in the biosynthesis of polysaccharides, lipids, proteins, and other molecules. The developing barley grain also contains a number of enzymes usually associated with starch degradation. These include α- and β-amylases, phosphorylase, α-glucosidase, and debranching enzyme

(Duffus and Cochrane, 1982). Whether or not starch is the source of the sugars used as substrates for respiration is unknown. On the one hand, there is evidence that immature barley starch granules are not degraded by extracts from germinated barley grains (Williams and Duffus, 1977). On the other hand, there is evidence that digestion of cell contents, including starch, takes place in the endosperm cells next to the developing scutellum (MacGregor and Dushnicky, 1989b). It is probably more likely, however, that sucrose, or its soluble metabolites, is the direct source of substrates for respiration.

The presence of α-amylase activity in developing barley caryopses was reported by Duffus in 1969. More recently, MacGregor and Dushnicky (1989a) have shown that two groups of α-amylases are present in different parts of the caryopsis. The group designated α-amylase 1 is found in the pericarp early in grain development. Its activity falls rapidly, and by the time the transparent layer of the pericarp is devoid of starch, it is scarcely detectable. α-Amylase 1 is also synthesized in the germinating embryo (MacGregor and Marchylo, 1986). α-Amylase 2 is produced by the aleurone during early seedling growth. It is present in the starchy endosperm during embryo development and appears to be responsible for the breakdown of starch in the cells that form the intermediate or depleted layer in the mature grain (MacGregor and Dushnicky, 1989b). The α-amylase inhibitor (Mundy et al, 1983; Weselake et al, 1983) that is specific for α-amylase 2 increases steadily during grain development and is present in the mature grain in an amount (300–400 μg/g of dry weight) that varies little from one cultivar to another (Laurière et al, 1985).

β-Amylase activity has been shown to be present in intact barley kernels during development (LaBerge et al, 1971). This enzyme hydrolyzes α-(1→4)-glucan linkages in both amylose and amylopectin, with the successive release of maltose units from the nonreducing ends of the chains. The enzyme can exist in soluble form as well as in an insoluble or latent form. Both forms are present in developing barley grains (Duffus and Rosie, 1973a; Laurière et al, 1985). In the endosperm, activity of the soluble form is initially greater and appears earlier than the latent β-amylase activity. It may be, therefore, that β-amylase is first synthesized in the soluble form in endosperm, subsequently being converted to the latent form. Further studies (LaBerge and Marchylo, 1986) indicate that in addition to eight major β-amylase enzymes that can be separated by focusing techniques, barley may produce transient forms of malt enzymes during early kernel development. Enzymatic and immunochemical analysis of endosperm protein fractions separated on sucrose gradients suggests that β-amylase is not localized in protein bodies, but rather is synthesized as a cytosolic protein (Nishimura et al, 1987). Hara-Nishimura et al (1986) reported, from studies of starch granules isolated during the later stages of grain development, that there is a progressive association of β-amylase with starch granules during the desiccation phase of seed development.

Debranching enzyme is present early in caryopsis development in the free form, and, as with β-amylase, halfway through the developmental period the bound form appears. As the grain matures, progressively more of the enzyme is in the bound or insoluble form (Laurière et al, 1985). Several isoenzymes with α-glucosidase activity have been found at all stages of development of barley grains (Stark and Yin, 1987). α-Glucosidase is located mainly in the outer pericarp of developing kernels and the scutellum of germinating barley kernels (MacGregor and Lenoir, 1987).

OVERALL CHANGES IN CHEMICAL COMPOSITION OF GRAINS DURING DEVELOPMENT AND MATURATION

Sugars and Amino Acids

The substrates for starch and lipid biosynthesis and for grain respiratory processes are presumably derived from soluble carbohydrates. Similarly, the substrates for protein synthesis are derived from N-containing molecules, including amino acids, and C-containing respiratory intermediates. A fuller understanding of the mechanisms involved in the biosynthesis of grain storage reserves can therefore be gained from a knowledge of the concentrations of these metabolic intermediates in different tissues of the grain. However, while many determinations of sugars such as sucrose, glucose, and fructose have been reported, there are no recent reports covering all relevant intermediates for a defined grain tissue grown under controlled conditions.

The first comprehensive report was that of Harris and MacWilliam (1957), who found a rapid increase in both sucrose and fructosan early in grain development, followed by a sharp decrease in fructosan and a more gradual decrease in sucrose. Fructose, glucose, and maltose were present in small amounts in the young grain, but during grain maturation the amount per grain gradually fell to almost zero. Raffinose was not detected until about halfway through grain development, whereas glucodifructose was present in the early stages of grain development and scarcely detectable as the grain approached harvest-ripeness. Many of their results have subsequently been confirmed by other workers (Cerning and Guilbot, 1973; La Berge et al, 1973; Duffus, 1979; Chevalier and Lingle, 1983). Büttner et al (1985) found that 90% of the hexose units present in the grain when starch accumulation started were fructosyl. They detected raffinose only in the embryo.

Observations of events occurring during grain development are not easily compared. The rate of maturation depends on factors such as temperature, water supply, and genotype, and so age measured in days after anthesis is a true measure of development only for ears of one cultivar grown under a given set of conditions. This problem is overcome to some extent if sampling times are expressed in cumulative mean daily temperature from the time of anthesis (Cerning and Guilbot, 1973). In many studies, measurements made on extracts of intact caryopses, or kernels, are correlated with changes in particular tissues. Such comparisons are not tenable. One conclusion that we can reach from measurement of sugars is that sucrose levels are maintained throughout development and that sucrose supply does not appear to be a limiting factor in grain growth. Data from experiments in which [U-^{14}C]-sucrose was supplied to detached barley ears in liquid culture (Fig. 13) show that the label moved into the grains at all stages of development up to the final dehydration stage (Cochrane, 1985). Earlier work showed that, at this stage of maturation, the cytoplasm of the chalazal cells finally became disorganized, apparently as a result of the release of phenolic materials from the vacuoles (Cochrane, 1983).

Little is known of the changes that take place in the composition of the pool of N-containing substances during grain development in barley. However, Fisher and MacNicol (1986) determined the amino acid composition along the transport pathway during grain-filling in wheat and found that the proportions of amino acids in the endosperm cavity were generally similar to those in the sieve tube sap supplying the grain. On a mole percent basis, glutamine accounted for about half of the amino acids in the sieve tube sap. Fisher (1987) observed only minor changes in exudate amino acid composition except for the increasing preponderance of glutamine during the last few days of grain filling. Duffus and Rosie (1978) found significant amounts of ammonium ion and glutamate in the endosperm and in the testa/pericarp layer of developing barley caryopses over most of the developmental period, but by 50 days after anthesis, ammonium ion was undetectable and by 55 days after anthesis, glutamate was undetectable.

Starch, Protein, and Lipid

There are no reports of simultaneously determined overall changes in the major reserve materials of defined tissues of the barley grain during the developmental period using the same cultivar grown under the same environmental conditions. Consequently, a full understanding of the relationship between changes in composition of each substance and stage of grain development is difficult to achieve. Changes in dry weight, water content, starch, sugars, prolamin, and total N have been reported for cv. Bomi by Kreis and Doll (1980), but only for intact kernels. Variation in fresh and dry weight, moisture, and starch content in developing barley endosperms of cvs. Golden

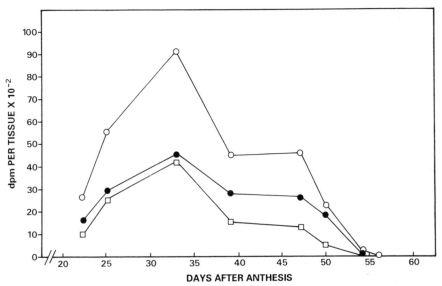

Fig. 13. Distribution of radioactivity (disintegrations per minute [dpm]) in grains from detached ears of barley cv. Midas, which had been allowed to take up (U-^{14}C)-sucrose for 4 hr at 17°C in the dark. O = caryopses, ● = outer layers, □ = endosperm. (Data from Cochrane, 1985)

Promise and Kym, grown under glasshouse conditions, are shown in Fig. 14. The results show that the final higher dry weight of cv. Kym, in comparison with that of cv. Golden Promise, is a function of both rate and duration of grain filling (Renwick and Duffus, 1987).

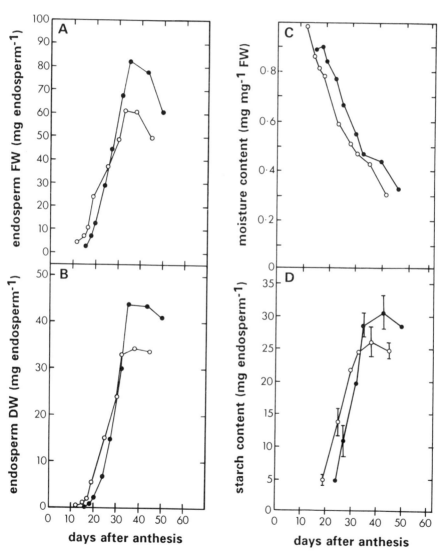

Fig. 14. Changes in fresh weight (A), dry weight (B), moisture content (C), and starch content (D) of developing barley endosperms grown under glasshouse conditions. ● = cv. Kym, ○ = cv. Golden Promise. DW = dry weight, FW = fresh weight. (Reprinted, by permission, from Renwick and Duffus, 1987)

Mineral Elements

Over the maturation period in barley cv. Julia, there is a steady accumulation of the essential major mineral elements nitrogen, phosphorus, potassium, calcium, magnesium, and sodium in the intact grain (Duffus and Rosie, 1976a). However, considerable variation from this pattern is observed within the different grain tissues. For example, at 15 days after anthesis, the pericarp was found to contain over half the total grain nitrogen and phosphorus, but by 40 days these values had fallen to 10% in both cases. At 40 days, over 90% of grain phosphorus and 70% of grain nitrogen were present in the endosperm. It may be that the observed gains in the endosperm and embryo are made at the expense of losses from the pericarp. In similar studies, changes in the amounts of the trace essential elements iron, zinc, manganese, and copper in intact grains, endosperm, testa/pericarp, and embryo have been recorded over the developmental period (Duffus and Rosie, 1976b). Accumulation of both iron and zinc was extremely rapid, and similar amounts of each were achieved by maturity (about 1 μg per grain). Accumulation of manganese and copper was much slower, reaching a final value of around 0.5 and 0.1 μg per grain, respectively. As with the major elements, variation from the overall pattern was seen within the different grain tissues. For example, throughout the early and middle stages of development, iron was distributed almost equally between the testa/pericarp and the endosperm, with a significant amount going to the embryo as it developed from 20 days after anthesis. By 55 days, only 15–20% of total iron was located in the pericarp and 7–8% was in the embryo. Duffus and Rosie (1976b) suggested that, as the pericarp loses photosynthetic activity, iron may no longer be required and supplies are directed almost exclusively to the endosperm.

Composition of the Mature Grain

At harvest-ripeness, the moisture content of the barley grain is about 15%. The dry matter is made up of approximately 80% carbohydrate, 10% protein, 3% lipid, and 2% minerals. The carbohydrate content of mature barley grains has been comprehensively reviewed by Henry (1988). Estimates of the starch content range from 51.5 to 72.1%, the range of values being accounted for in part by genetic and environmental effects and in part by differences in methods of estimation. Oligosaccharides, mainly fructans and raffinose, account for about 2% of grain dry weight, as does sucrose. Maltose, fructose, and glucose are present in very much smaller amounts. The embryo contains considerably higher concentrations of sugars than the endosperm. The β-D-glucan content of the barley grain varies with cultivar and environment but is usually between 3 and 6%. The proportion of arabinoxylans in the mature grain is reported to be approximately the same as that of β-glucans and at least twice that of cellulose. Most of the cellulose in the grain is located in the husk.

Protein from endosperms of harvest-ripe barley cv. Bomi was found by Brandt (1976) to be made up of approximately 30% hordein, 30% glutelin, and 10% globulin, the remaining 30% being composed of albumins and free amino acids. By including 2-mercaptoethanol in the extraction medium for hordein and glutelin, and extracting hordein at 60°C, Miflin and Shewry (1979) found that the endosperm proteins of cv. Bomi contained 59% hordein, 12% glutelin, and 11% of a combined albumin and globulin fraction.

In the living tissues of the mature grain, i.e., the aleurone and the embryo, the principal nonprotein storage materials are lipids. In aleurone cells, lipid droplets surround the aleurone grains, which contain a protein matrix rich in basic amino acids, embedded in which are deposits of both phytin and niacin (Fulcher et al, 1981). Phenolic substances are present in the testa (Cochrane and Duffus, 1983b) and in the chalazal cells at the crease (Cochrane, 1983). Arabinoxylans in both aleurone and starchy endosperm cell walls are esterified with ferulic acid (Henry, 1988).

ENVIRONMENTAL EFFECTS ON GRAIN GROWTH AND DEVELOPMENT

The rate and duration of grain growth and development, as well as final grain composition and quality, are influenced by prevailing environmental conditions.

In general, at elevated temperatures the rate of dry matter accumulation is increased but the duration of grain filling is reduced, and mature grain weights may be less than those at lower temperatures. For example, Ellis and Kirby (1980) have compared yield and its components in spring barleys grown in Scotland and Eastern England. Yield, as well as weight per grain, was greater in Scotland over two seasons. It was considered that the cooler temperatures in Scotland may have contributed to the increased dry weight per grain because at lower temperatures maturation was delayed and a longer period was available for grain-filling.

The effect of temperature on starch accumulation in developing barley endosperms has been described by MacLeod and Duffus (1988b). In one experiment, plants (cv. Triumph) were grown in a glasshouse (approximately 20/15°C) and transferred to environmentally controlled growth rooms at either 30/25°C or 20/15°C at two to three days preanthesis. The results confirm the observations above, i.e., that the duration of grain-filling was reduced and final grain starch content was significantly less at the higher temperatures. Further studies suggested that the reduction in starch deposition at higher temperature was not due to decreased sucrose levels, but rather to decreased activity of the sucrose cleavage enzyme, sucrose synthase. The observed decrease in starch content at elevated temperatures was accompanied by a decrease in endosperm volume, thus decreasing the space available for starch deposition. In addition, the numbers of A- and B-type starch granules initiated in the developing endosperm were reduced (Fig. 15). It seems, therefore, that one effect of elevated temperature on grain growth is to affect some mechanism involved in starch granule initiation in the developing endosperm (MacLeod and Duffus, 1988a). It may be that the endosperm cell division rate is increased by high temperature but plastid replication is not, or is less so.

Grain yield and quality in barley depend very much on fertilizer policy, and of all the variable inputs, nitrogen is the one that allows the greatest manipulation of the crop (Russell, 1986). A linear relationship between the rate of nitrogen applied and nitrogen concentration in the grain has been

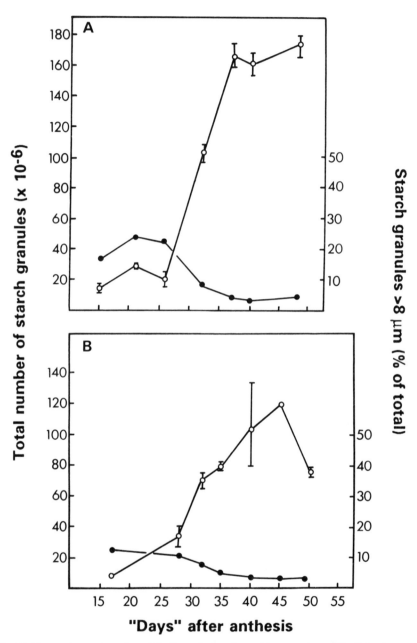

Fig. 15. Changes in total numbers (O) of starch granules and in percentages (●) of starch granules >8 μm (A-type) in endosperms during grain development at 20/15°C (A) and 30/25°C (B). Bars indicate the standard error of the mean. Age is expressed in "days" after anthesis using a developmental scale described by Cochrane and Duffus (1983). (Reprinted, by permission, from MacLeod and Duffus, 1988a)

seen in a large number of barley trials. In general, nitrogen application in barley increases yields but decreases protein quality, since the increased nitrogen content of the grain is due mainly to hordein (Giese et al, 1983; Corke and Atsmon, 1988). As we saw previously, this protein is of poor nutritive value and may also have an adverse effect on malting quality.

Sulfur application rates may also influence grain protein composition and quality (Rahman et al, 1983). For example, sulfur deficiency results in decreased accumulation of the "sulfur-rich" B-hordein polypeptides with little or no effect on the "sulfur-poor" C hordeins. How the relative rates of accumulation of the different hordein components in the endosperm are altered in response to nutrient availability is not known. Thus, while the farmer is powerless to manipulate such environmental variables as temperature and day length, there is clearly much scope for the manipulation of final grain weight and quality through the application of appropriate husbandry techniques.

CONCLUSIONS

The formation and development of a barley kernel have been shown to be the result of a closely integrated sequence of morphological and biochemical events. These commence when the vegetative apex is induced to become a reproductive organ and end when the grain has reached harvest-ripeness, i.e., in favorable conditions, has a moisture content of approximately 15%.

Much of the fixed carbon used in the biosynthesis of grain reserves appears to be derived from current photosynthesis. Sucrose supply does not appear to be a limiting factor in grain growth, and events in the developing grain itself may limit the extent and duration of grain filling.

While the precise details of the metabolic pathway leading from incoming sucrose, and perhaps amino acids, to starch deposition in the developing amyloplast are not clear, it seems that sucrose is first converted to UDP-glucose in the cytosol in a reaction catalyzed by UDP-dependent sucrose synthase. The molecule that transports carbon across the amyloplast membrane has not been identified with any certainty, but there is good evidence to suggest that it is a hexose phosphate. The mechanism whereby the relative proportions of amylose and amylopectin in starch are so closely controlled is unknown. The energy required for grain biosynthetic reactions is believed to come from aerobic respiration, some of the oxygen required being derived from photosynthesis in the cross cells of the pericarp.

The rate and duration of grain growth, as well as final grain composition and quality, are influenced by prevailing environmental conditions. These include such variables as temperature, day length, water supply, and the availability of soil minerals.

ACKNOWLEDGMENTS

We wish to thank Gemma Freeman for translating into English the paper by Luise Krauss (1933).

LITERATURE CITED

ÅMAN, P., GRAHAM, H., and TILLY, A.-C. 1989. Content and solubility of mixed-linked $(1\rightarrow3),(1\rightarrow4)$-$\beta$-D-glucan in barley and oats during kernel development and storage.

J. Cereal Sci. 10:45-50.

ARCHBOLD, H. K. 1942. Physiological studies in plant nutrition. XIII. Experiments with barley on defoliation and shading of the ear in relation to sugar metabolism. Ann. Bot. 6:487-531.

AUSTIN, R. B. 1980. Physiological limitations to cereal yields and ways of reducing them by breeding. Pages 3-19 in: Opportunities for Increasing Crop Yields. R. G. Hurd, P. V. Biscoe, and C. Dennis, eds. Association of Applied Biologists, London.

AUSTIN, R. B., MORGAN, C. L., FORD, M. A., and BLACKWELL, R. D. 1980. Contributions to grain yields from pre-anthesis assimilation in tall and dwarf barley phenotypes in two contrasting seasons. Ann. Bot. 45:309-319.

BANKS, W., GREENWOOD, C. T., and MUIR, D. D. 1973. Studies on the biosynthesis of starch granules, Part 5. Properties of starch components of normal barley, and barley with starch of high amylose content, during growth. Staerke 25:153-157.

BAUM, B. R., and BAILEY, L. G. 1987. A survey of endosperm starch granules in the genus *Hordeum*: A study using image analytic and numerical taxonomic techniques. Can. J. Bot. 65:1563-1569.

BAXTER, E. D., and DUFFUS, C. M. 1973a. Enzymes of carbohydrate metabolism in developing *Hordeum distichum* grain. Phytochemistry 12:1923-1928.

BAXTER, E. D., and DUFFUS, C. M. 1973b. Phosphorylase activity in relation to starch synthesis in developing *Hordeum distichum* grain. Phytochemistry 12:2321-2330.

BAXTER, E. D., and DUFFUS, C. M. 1973c. Starch synthetase: Comparison of UDPG and ADPG as glucosyl donors in immature barley endosperm. Planta 114:195-198.

BENNETT, M. D., SMITH, J. B., and BARCLAY, I. 1975. Early seed development in the Triticeae. Philos. Trans. R. Soc. Lond. B. 272:199-227.

BIDINGER, F., MUSGRAVE, R. B., and FISCHER, R. A. 1977. Contribution of stored pre-anthesis assimilate to grain yield in wheat and barley. Nature 270:431-433.

BIRECKA, H., SKUPINSKA, J., and BERNSTEIN, I. 1964. Photosynthesis, translocation and accumulation of assimilate in cereals during grain development. V. Contribution of products of current photosynthesis after heading to the accumulation of organic compounds in the grain of barley. Acta Soc. Bot. Pol. 33:601-618.

BRANDT, A. 1976. Endosperm protein formation during kernel development of wild type and a high-lysine barley mutant. Cereal Chem. 53:890-901.

BRIARTY, L. G., HUGHES, C. E., and EVERS, A. D. 1979. The developing endosperm of wheat—A stereological analysis. Ann. Bot. 44:641-658.

BÜTTNER, G., De FEKETE, M. A. R., and VIEWEG, G.H. 1985. Änderungen des Fructangehaltes in reifenden Gerstenkaryopsen. Angew. Bot. 59:171-177.

BUTTROSE, M. S. 1960. Submicroscopic development and structure of starch granules in cereal endosperms. J. Ultrastr. Res. 4:231-257.

CAMERON-MILLS, V., and DUFFUS, C. M. 1979. Sucrose transport in isolated immature barley embryos. Ann. Bot. 43:559-569.

CAMERON-MILLS, V., and INGVERSEN, J. 1978. In vitro synthesis and transport of barley endosperm proteins. Reconstitution of functional rough microsomes from polysomes and stripped microsomes. Carlsberg Res. Commun. 43:471-489.

CAMERON-MILLS, V., and VON WETTSTEIN, D. 1980. Protein body formation on the developing barley endosperm. Carlsberg Res. Commun. 45:577-594.

CARR, D. J., and WARDLAW, I. F. 1965. The supply of photosynthetic assimilates to the grain from the flag leaf and ear of wheat. Aust. J. Biol. Sci. 18:711-719.

CERNING, J., and GUILBOT, A. 1973. Changes in the carbohydrate composition during the development and maturation of wheat and barley kernels. Cereal Chem. 50:220-231.

CHEVALIER, P., and LINGLE, S. E. 1983. Sugar metabolism in developing kernels of wheat and barley. Crop Sci. 23:272-277.

CHOJECKI, A. J. S., GALE, M. D., and BAYLISS, M. N. 1986. The number and sizes of starch granules in the wheat endosperm and their association with grain weight. Ann. Bot. 58:819-831.

COCHRANE, M. P. 1983. Morphology of the crease region in relation to assimilate uptake and water loss during caryopsis development in barley and wheat. Aust. J. Plant Physiol. 10:473-491.

COCHRANE, M. P. 1985. Assimilate uptake and water loss in maturing barley grains. J. Exp. Bot. 36:770-782.

COCHRANE, M. P., and DUFFUS, C. M. 1979. Morphology and ultrastructure of immature cereal grains in relation to transport. Ann. Bot. 44:67-72.

COCHRANE, M. P., and DUFFUS, C. M. 1980. The nucellar projection and modified aleurone in the crease region of developing caryopses of barley (*Hordeum vulgare* L. var. *distichum*). Protoplasma 103:361-375.

COCHRANE, M. P., and DUFFUS, C. M. 1981. Endosperm cell number in barley. Nature 289:399-401.

COCHRANE, M. P., and DUFFUS, C. M. 1982. Opportunities for the regulation of grain development. Pages 167-178 in: Opportunities for Manipulation of Cereal Productivity. A. F. Hawkins and B. Jeffcoat, eds. Wessex Press, Wantage, Oxfordshire, U.K.

COCHRANE, M. P., and DUFFUS, C. M. 1983a. Endosperm cell number in cultivars of barley differing in grain weight. Ann. Appl. Biol. 102:177-181.

COCHRANE, M. P., and DUFFUS, C. M. 1983b. Observations on the development of the testa and pericarp in barley. Pages 154-161 in: Third International Symposium on Pre-Harvest Sprouting in Cereals. J. E. Kruger and D. E. LaBerge, eds. Westview Press, Boulder, CO.

COLES, G. 1979. Relationship of mixed-link beta-glucan accumulation to accumulation of free sugars and other glucans in the developing barley endosperm. Carlsberg Res. Commun. 44:439-453.

COLLINS, E. J. 1918. The structure of the integumentary system of the barley grain in relation to localized water absorption and semipermeability. Ann. Bot. 32:381-414.

CORKE, H., and ATSMON, D. 1988. Effect of nitrogen nutrition on endosperm protein synthesis in wild and cultivated barley grown in spike culture. Plant Physiol. 87:523-528.

DELMER, D. P., and STONE, B. A. 1988. Biosynthesis of plant cell walls. Pages 373-420 in: The Biochemistry of Plants. Vol. 14, Carbohydrates. J. Preiss, ed. Academic Press, New York.

DONOVAN, G. R., JENNER, C. F., LEE, J. W., and MARTIN, P. 1983. Longitudinal transport of sucrose and amino acids in the wheat grain. Aust. J. Plant Physiol. 10:31-42.

DUFFUS, C. M. 1969. Alpha-amylase activity in the developing barley grain and its dependence on gibberellic acid. Phytochemistry 8:1205-1209.

DUFFUS, C. M. 1979. Carbohydrate metabolism and cereal grain development. Pages 209-238 in: Recent Advances in the Biochemistry of Cereals. D. L. Laidman and R. G. Wyn Jones, eds. Academic Press, London.

DUFFUS, C. M. 1987. Physiological aspects of enzymes during grain development and germination. Pages 83-116 in: Enzymes and their Role in Cereal Technology. J. E. Kruger, D. Lineback, and C. E. Stauffer, eds. Am. Assoc. Cereal Chem., St. Paul, MN.

DUFFUS, C. M., and BINNIE, J. 1990. Sucrose relationships during wheat grain development. Plant Physiol. Biochem.

28:161-165.

DUFFUS, C. M., and COCHRANE, M. P. 1982. Carbohydrate metabolism during cereal grain development. Pages 43-66 in: The Physiology and Biochemistry of Seed Development, Dormancy and Germination. A. A. Khan, ed. Elsevier Biomedical Press, Amsterdam.

DUFFUS, C. M., and ROSIE, R. 1973a. Starch hydrolysing enzymes in the developing barley grain. Phytochemistry 109:153-160.

DUFFUS, C. M., and ROSIE, R. 1973b. Some enzyme activities associated with the chlorophyll-containing layers of the immature barley pericarp. Planta 114:219-226.

DUFFUS, C. M., and ROSIE, R. 1975. Biochemical changes during embryogeny in *Hordeum distichum*. Phytochemistry 14:319-323.

DUFFUS, C. M., and ROSIE, R. 1976a. Changes in mineral element composition of developing barley grain. J. Agric. Sci. 86:627-632.

DUFFUS, C. M., and ROSIE, R. 1976b. Changes in trace element composition of developing barley grain. J. Agric. Sci. 87:75-79.

DUFFUS, C. M., and ROSIE, R. 1978. Metabolism of ammonium ion and glutamate in relation to nitrogen supply and utilization during grain development in barley. Plant Physiol. 61:570-574.

ELLIS, R. P., and KIRBY, E. J. M. 1980. A comparison of spring barley grown in England and in Scotland. 2. Yield and its components. J. Agric. Sci., Camb. 95:111-115.

EVANS, L. T., and RAWSON, H. M. 1970. Photosynthesis and respiration by the flag leaf and components of the ear during grain development in wheat. Aust. J. Biol. Sci. 23:245-254.

FELKER, F. C., PETERSON, D. M., and NELSON, O. E. 1983. Growth characteristics, grain filling and assimilate transport in a shrunken endosperm mutant of barley. Plant Physiol. 72:679-684.

FELKER, F. C., PETERSON, D. M., and NELSON, O. E. 1984a. Development of tannin vacuoles in chalaza and seed coat of barley in relation to early chalazal necrosis in the *seg1* mutant. Planta 161:540-549.

FELKER, F. C., PETERSON, D. M., and NELSON, O. E. 1984b. [^{14}C] Sucrose uptake and labeling of starch in developing grains of normal and *seg1* barley. Plant Physiol. 74:43-46.

FINCHER, G. B., and STONE, B. A. 1986. Cell walls and their components in cereal grain technology. Pages 207-295 in: Recent

Advances in Cereal Science and Technology, Vol. 8. Y. Pomeranz, ed. Am. Assoc. Cereal Chem., St. Paul, MN.

FISHER, D. B. 1987. Changes in the concentration and composition of peduncle sieve tube sap during grain filling in normal and phosphate-deficient wheat plants. Aust. J. Plant Physiol. 14:147-156.

FISHER, D. B., and MacNICOL, P. K. 1986. Amino acid composition along the transport pathway during grain filling in wheat. Plant Physiol. 82:1019-1023.

FLEMING, M., and KAWAKAMI, K. 1977. Studies of the fine structure of β-D-glucans of barley extracted at different temperatures. Carbohydr. Res. 57:15-23.

FORREST, I. S., and WAINWRIGHT, T. 1977. The mode of binding of β-glucans and pentosans in barley endosperm cell walls. J. Inst. Brew. 83:279-286.

FREEMAN, P. L., and PALMER, G. H. 1984. The structure of the pericarp and testa of barley. J. Inst. Brew. 90:88-94.

FREY-WYSSLING, A., and BUTTROSE, M. S. 1959. Photosynthesis in the ear of barley. Nature 184:2031-2032.

FULCHER, R. G., O'BRIEN, T. P., and WONG, S. I. 1981. Microchemical detection of niacin, aromatic amine, and phytin reserves in cereal bran. Cereal Chem. 58:130-135.

GAINES, R. L., BECHTEL, D. B., and POMERANZ, Y. 1985. A microscopic study on the development of a layer in barley that causes hull-caryopsis adherence. Cereal Chem. 62:35-40.

GIESE, H., ANDERSEN, D., and DOLL, H. 1983. Synthesis of the major storage protein, hordein, in barley. Pulse labelling study of grain-filling in liquid cultured detached spikes. Planta 159:60-65.

GLEADOW, R. M., DALLING, M. J., and HALLORAN, G. M. 1982. Variation in endosperm characteristics and nitrogen content in six wheat lines. Aust. J. Plant Physiol. 9:539-551.

HAMACHI, Y., FURUSHO, M., and YOSHIDA, T. 1989. Husk development and the cause of underdevelopment of husks in malting barley. Jpn. J. Crop Sci. 58:507-512.

HARA-NISHIMURA, I., NISHIMURA, M., and DAUSSANT, J. 1986. Conversion of free beta-amylase to bound beta-amylase on starch granules in the barley endosperm during desiccation phase of seed development. Protoplasma 134:149-153.

HARRIS, G., and MacWILLIAM, I. C. 1957. Carbohydrates in malting and brewing. VI. Changes in the carbohydrate composition of barley on ripening and corresponding varia-

tions in nitrogenous constituents. J. Inst. Brew. 63:210-220.

HAY, R. K. M., and WALKER, A. J. 1989. An Introduction to the Physiology of Crop Yield. Longman, Harlow, England.

HENDERSON, J. 1987. Protein deposition in developing barley endosperm. Ph.D. thesis, University of Durham, UK.

HENRY, R. J. 1988. The carbohydrates of barley grains—A review. J. Inst. Brew. 94:71-78.

HESSELMAN, K., ELWINGER, K., NILSSON, M., and THOMKE, S. 1981. The effect of β-glucanase supplementation, stage of ripeness and storage treatment of barley in diets fed to broiler chicks. Poult. Sci. 60:2664-2671.

HOSHIKAWA, K. 1960. Influence of temperature upon the fertilization of wheat grown in various levels of nitrogen. Proc. Crop Sci. Soc. Jpn. 28:291-295.

HOSHIKAWA, K. 1962. Studies on the ripening of wheat, 4. The influence of temperature on endosperm formation. Proc. Crop Sci. Soc. Jpn. 30:228-231.

HOSHIKAWA, K. 1984. Development of endosperm tissue with special reference to translocation of reserves in cereals. II. Modification of cell shape in the developing endosperm parenchyma, aleurone and subaleurone of two-rowed barley. Jpn. J. Crop Sci. 53:64-70.

JACOBSEN, J. V., KNOX, R. B., and PYLIOTIS, N. A. 1971. The structure and composition of aleurone grains in the barley aleurone layer. Planta 101:189-209.

KEELING, P., WOOD, J. R., TYSON, R. H., and BRIDGES, I. C. 1988. Starch biosynthesis in developing wheat grain. Evidence against the direct involvement of triose phosphate in the metabolic pathway. Plant Physiol. 87:311-319.

KING, R. W., WARDLAW, I. F., and EVANS, L. T. 1967. Effect of assimilate utilization on photosynthetic rate in wheat. Planta 77:261-276.

KIRBY, E. J. M., and RYMER, J. L. 1975. The vascular anatomy of the barley spikelet. Ann. Bot. 39:205-211.

KRAUSS, L. 1933. Entwicklungsgeschichte der Fruchte von Hordeum, Triticum, Bromus, und Poa mit besonderer Berucksichtigung ihrer Samenschalen. Jahrb. Wiss. Bot. 77:733-808.

KREIS, M., and DOLL, H. 1980. Starch and prolamin level in single and double high-lysine barley mutants. Physiol. Plant. 48:139-143.

KVAALE, A., and OLSEN, O. A. 1986. Rates of cell division in developing barley endosperms. Ann. Bot. 57:829-833.

LABERGE, D. E., and MARCHYLO, B. A. 1986. Changes in beta-amylase enzymes during kernel development of barley and the effect of papain as an extractant. J. Am. Soc. Brew. Chem. 44:16-19.

LABERGE, D. E., MacGREGOR, A. W., and MEREDITH, W. O. S. 1971. Changes in alpha- and beta-amylase activities during the maturation of different barley cultivars. Can. J. Plant Sci. 51:469-477.

LABERGE, D. E., MacGREGOR, A. W., and MEREDITH, W. O. S. 1973. Changes in the free sugar content of barley kernels during maturation. J. Inst. Brew. 79:471-477.

LAURIÈRE, C., MAYER, C., RENARD, H., MacGREGOR, A., and DAUSSANT, J. 1985. Maturation du caryopse d'orge: Évolution des isoformes des α- et β-amylases, de l'enzyme débranchante, de l'inhibiteur d'α-amylases chez plusieurs variétés. Pages 675-682 in: Proc. Congr. Eur. Brew. Conv. 20th, Helsinki.

LERMER, Dr., and HOLZNER, G. 1888. Beiträge zur Kentniss der Gerste. R. Oldenbourg, Munich.

LINGLE, S. E., and CHEVALIER, P. 1984. Movement and metabolism of sucrose in developing barley kernels. Crop Sci. 24:315-319.

LINGLE, S. E., and CHEVALIER, P. 1985. Development of the vascular tissue of the wheat and barley caryopsis as related to the rate and duration of grain filling. Crop Sci. 25:123-128.

MacGREGOR, A. W., and DUSHNICKY, L. 1989a. α-Amylases in developing barley kernels—A reappraisal. J. Inst. Brew. 95:29-33.

MacGREGOR, A. W., and DUSHNICKY, L. 1989b. Starch degradation in endosperms of developing barley kernels. J. Inst. Brew. 95:321-325.

MacGREGOR, A. W., and LENOIR, C. 1987. Studies on α-glucosidase in barley and malt. J. Inst. Brew. 93:334-337.

MacGREGOR, A. W., and MARCHYLO, B. A. 1986. α-Amylase components in excised, incubated barley embryos. J. Inst. Brew. 92:159-161.

MacLEOD, A. M., and NAPIER, J. P. 1959. Cellulose distribution in barley. J. Inst. Brew. 65:188-196.

MacLEOD, L. C., and DUFFUS, C. M. 1988a. Temperature effects on starch granules in developing barley grains. J. Cereal Sci. 8:29-37.

MacLEOD, L. C., and DUFFUS, C. M. 1988b. Reduced starch content and sucrose synthase activity in developing endosperms of barley

plants grown at elevated temperatures. Aust. J. Plant Physiol. 15:367-375.

MAY, L. H., and BUTTROSE, M. S. 1959. Physiology of cereal grain. II. Starch granule formation in the developing barley kernel. Aust. J. Biol. Sci. 12:146-159.

McDONALD, A. M. L., STARK, J. R., MORRISON, W. R., and ELLIS, R. P. 1991. The composition of starch granules from developing barley genotypes. J. Cereal Sci. 13:93-112.

McFADDEN, G. I., AHLUWALIA, B., CLARKE, A. E., and FINCHER, G. B. 1988. Expression sites and developmental regulation of genes encoding (1→3, 1→4)-β-glucanases in germinated barley. Planta 173:500-508.

MEAD, H. W. 1942. Environmental relationships in a seed-borne disease of barley caused by *Helminthosporium sativum* Pammeel, King & Bakke. Can. J. Res. 20C:501-538.

MEREDITH, P., and JENKINS, L. D. 1975. Loss of moisture from developing and ripening cereal grains. N.Z. J. Sci. 18:501-509.

MERRITT, N. R., and WALKER, J. T. 1969. Development of starch and other components in normal and high amylose barleys. J. Inst. Brew. 75:156-164.

MERRY, J. 1941. Studies on the embryo of *Hordeum sativum*. 1. The development of the embryo. Bull. Torrey Bot. Club 68:585-598.

MIFLIN, B. J., and SHEWRY, P. R. 1979. The synthesis of proteins in normal and high lysine barley seeds. Pages 237-273 in: Recent Advances in the Biochemistry of Cereals. D. L. Laidman and R. G. Wyn Jones, eds. Academic Press, London.

MORRISON, W. R. 1988. Lipids in cereal starches: A review. J. Cereal Sci. 8:1-15.

MORRISON, W. R., and LAIGNELET, B. 1983. An improved colorimetric procedure for determining apparent and total amylose in cereal and other starches. J. Cereal Sci. 1:9-20.

MUNDY, J., SVENDSEN, I., and HEJGAARD, J. 1983. Barley α-amylase/subtilisin inhibitor. I. Isolation and characterization. Carlsberg Res. Commun. 48:81-90.

NISHIMURA, M., HARA-NISHIMURA, I., BUREAU, D., and DAUSSANT, J. 1987. Subcellular distribution of beta-amylase in developing barley endosperm. Plant Sci. 49:117-122.

NORSTOG, K. 1972. Early development of the barley embryo: Fine structure. Am. J. Bot. 59:123-132.

NUTBEAM, A. R., and DUFFUS, C. M. 1976. Evidence for C4 photosynthesis in barley pericarp tissue. Biochem. Biophys. Res. Commun. 70:1198-1203.

NUTBEAM, A. R., and DUFFUS, C. M. 1978. Oxygen exchange in the pericarp green layer of immature cereal grains. Plant Physiol. 62:360-362.

OSBORNE, T. B. 1895. The proteids of barley. J. Am. Chem. Soc. 17:539-567.

PALMER, G. H. 1989. Cereals in malting and brewing. Pages 61-242 in: Cereal Science and Technology. G. H. Palmer, ed. Aberdeen University Press, Aberdeen, Scotland.

POPE, M. N. 1943. The temperature factor in fertilization and growth of the barley ovule. J. Agric. Res. 66:389-402.

RAHMAN, S., KREIS, M., FORDE, B. G., SHEWRY, P. R., and MIFLIN, B. J. 1984. Hordein-gene expression during development of the barley (*Hordeum vulgare*) endosperm. Biochem. J. 223:315-322.

RAHMAN, S., SHEWRY, P. R., FORDE, B. G., KREIS, M., and MIFLIN, B. J. 1983. Nutritional control of storage-protein synthesis in developing grain of barley (*Hordeum vulgare* L.). Planta 159:366-372.

RENWICK, F., and DUFFUS, C. M. 1987. Factors affecting dry weight accumulation in developing barley endosperm. Physiol. Plant. 69:141-146.

RUSSELL, G. 1986. Fertilisers and Quality of Wheat and Barley. Proc. 253. Fertiliser Society, Greenhill House, London.

SAVCHENKO, M. I., and PETROVA, L. R. 1963. Morphology of the ovary of barley *Hordeum vulgare* L., and some special features in its development. Bot. J. USSR 48:1623-1638.

SKARSAUNE, S. K., YOUNGS, V. L., and GILLES, K. A. 1970. Changes in wheat lipids during seed maturation, II. Changes in lipid composition. Cereal Chem. 47:533-544.

SLACK, P. T., BAXTER, E. D., and WAINWRIGHT, T. 1979. Inhibition by hordein of starch degradation. J. Inst. Brew. 85:112-114.

SØRENSEN, M. B., CAMERON-MILLS, V., and BRANDT, A. 1989. Transcriptional and post-translational regulation of gene expression in developing barley endosperm. Mol. Gen. Genet. 217:195-201.

STARK, J. R., and YIN, X. S. 1986. The effect of physical damage on large and small barley starch granules. Starch/Staerke 38:369-374.

STARK, J. R., and YIN, X. S. 1987. Evidence for the presence of maltase and α-glucosidase isoenzymes in barley. J. Inst. Brew. 93:108-112.

SWIFT, J. G., and O'BRIEN, T. P. 1970. Vascularization of the scutellum of wheat. Aust. J. Bot. 18:45-53.

THARP, W. H. 1935. Developmental anatomy and relative permeability of barley seed coats. Bot. Gaz. 97:240-271.

THORNE, G. N. 1963. Varietal differences in photosynthesis of ears and leaves of barley. Ann. Bot. 27:155-174.

THORNE, G. N. 1965. Photosynthesis of ears and flag leaves of wheat and barley. Ann. Bot. 29:317-329.

THORNE, G. N. 1966. Physiological aspects of grain yield in cereals. Pages 88-105 in: The Growth of Cereals and Grasses. F. L. Milthorpe and J. D. Ivins, eds. Butterworth, London.

WATSON, P. A., and DUFFUS, C. M. 1988. Carbon dioxide fixation by detached cereal caryopses. Plant Physiol. 87:504-509.

WATSON, P. A., and DUFFUS, C. M. 1991. Light-dependent CO_2 retrieval in immature barley caryopses. J. Exp. Bot. 42:1013-1019.

WEBER, E., and BRANDT, A. 1985. Species specific signal peptide cleavage of plant storage protein precursors in the endoplasmic reticulum. Carlsberg Res. Commun. 50:299-308.

WESELAKE, R. J., MacGREGOR, A. W., and HILL, R. D. 1983. An endogenous α-amylase inhibitor in barley kernels. Plant Physiol. 72:809-812.

WILLIAMS, J. M., and DUFFUS, C. M. 1977. Separation and some properties of large and small amyloplasts throughout development in barley endosperm. Plant Physiol. 59:189-192.

CHAPTER 3

CARBOHYDRATES OF THE BARLEY GRAIN

A. W. MacGREGOR
Grain Research Laboratory
Canadian Grain Commission
Winnipeg, Manitoba
Canada R3C 3G8

G. B. FINCHER
Department of Plant Science
University of Adelaide, Waite Campus
Glen Osmond, South Australia
Australia 5064

INTRODUCTION

In plants, carbohydrates represent the major source of available energy, both in the form of simple carbohydrates for immediate energy release through oxidative pathways, and as complex polymeric molecules stored against future metabolic requirements. Another major role for carbohydrates in plants is in the maintenance of tissue structure. Thus, polysaccharides are major constituents of the walls that surround individual protoplasts and collectively provide the skeletal framework and intercellular cohesion necessary for growth and development. Tissue-specific differences are observed in both carbohydrate content and composition, depending on the function of individual tissues. In the case of barley, the principal end-uses involve mature grain, which is included as a major component in many stockfeed formulations and represents an important primary ingredient in the malting and brewing industries. Carbohydrates constitute about 80% by weight of barley grain. Starch is the most abundant single component, accounting for up to 65%, but polysaccharides of cell wall origin are also quantitatively important and may represent more than 10% of grain weight (Harris, 1962; Table 1). The cell walls of barley generally consist of cellulosic microfibrils that reinforce a matrix comprised mainly of arabinoxylans and $(1\rightarrow3),(1\rightarrow4)$-$\beta$-glucans. In some tissues, walls may be further strengthened through lignin deposition.

Because of their central role in barley grain utilization, research attention has been focussed on the properties of starch and on certain cell wall

73

$(1\rightarrow3),(1\rightarrow4)$-$\beta$-glucan fractions extracted from the starchy endosperm of mature grain. In animal nutrition, starch provides a valuable source of energy both for ruminants and for monogastric animals such as pigs and poultry. Cell wall polysaccharides can also be degraded or altered by microbial action in the prestomach fermentative sections of the ruminant's alimentary tract and in the lower alimentary tract of monogastric animals. Further, wall polysaccharides contribute to roughage or "dietary fiber" in human diets and are now considered to be nutritionally beneficial in promoting mobility of digesta through the alimentary tract. In the malting and brewing industries, degradation products from both starch and wall polysaccharides are central in providing substrates for the fermentative phase of the brewing process. However, in both the brewing and stockfeed industries, small starch granules and undegraded wall $(1\rightarrow3),(1\rightarrow4)$-$\beta$-glucans can cause serious problems, and this has led to close scrutiny of specific carbohydrate fractions of the grain.

In this chapter, levels and properties of the major carbohydrates of barley grain are considered, together with the genotypic and environmental factors that influence their development. Properties of the carbohydrates are related to their impact on the technology of barley grain utilization. The potential to overcome existing technical problems through a combination of traditional plant breeding and modern gene technology is also examined.

BARLEY STARCH

The average world production of barley over the 10-year period up to 1992 was 170 million tonnes (Canada Grains Council, 1992). At a conservative estimate, this translates into more than 100 MT of barley starch, a significant amount of a renewable resource. Despite such availability, relatively little research has been done on the functional properties of barley starch compared

TABLE 1
Chemical Composition of Barley Grain[a]

Component	Dry Weight (%)
Carbohydrates	78–83
Starch	63–65
Sucrose	1–2
Other sugars	1
Water-soluble polysaccharides	1–1.5
Alkali-soluble polysaccharides	8–10
Cellulose	4–5
Lipids	2–3
Protein	10–12
Albumins and globulins	3.5
Hordeins	3–4
Glutelins	3–4
Nucleic acids	0.2–0.3
Minerals	2
Others	5–6

[a]Data from Harris (1962).

to the research documented for wheat starch (important in the baking industry) and corn starch (important in the food industry). A major reason for this neglect, apart from the abundance and low cost of corn starch, is that a high proportion of barley is used for animal feed without processing. Only relatively small amounts of barley (15–20%) are subjected to sophisticated technological processing such as in the malting, fermentation, and food industries. Until recently, little attention has been paid to possible effects of starch functionality on the feeding quality of barley. This section discusses various chemical, physical, and functional properties of barley starch that are relevant to the end-use quality of barley and of barley-based products.

Total starch in cereal grains has proved to be surprisingly difficult to measure, mainly because of problems associated with starch extraction and the specificity of detection methods. The wide variation (48–72% of kernel dry weight) in reported levels of starch in barley grain (Bhatty et al, 1975; Henry, 1988c) can be attributed, in part, to these analytical difficulties. More reliable and precise methods are now available (Åman and Hesselman, 1984, Salomonsson et al, 1984), and recently reported values in the range of 58–64% are probably close to true values, although both genetic and environmental effects can cause significant variation (Åman et al, 1985; Morrison et al, 1986; Bach Knudsen et al, 1987; Henry, 1987b).

Amylose

Most barley starches, like those from other cereal grains, contain two major components, amylose and amylopectin. Amylose is the minor component of most cereal starches and consists of relatively long chains of α-(1→4)-linked D-glucose residues. Some properties of this polysaccharide are shown in Table 2. Amylose is often referred to as the linear component of starch, but this is incorrect. Although the extent of chain branching is much less than in amylopectin, it is not negligible, and so it would be more accurate to refer to amylose as having a low level of branching. Traditionally, the extent of branching in amylose has been determined by measuring the susceptibility

TABLE 2
Properties of Barley Starch Components

Property	Amylose	Amylopectin
Iodine affinity (mg I_2 bound/100 mg polysaccharide)	19.0–19.9[a–c]	0.33–1.5[a,b]
β-Amylolysis limit (% hydrolysis to maltose by β-amylase)	72–93[d,e]	57–58[a,e]
Limiting viscosity number [η] (ml/g)	240–390[d,f]	185–188[d,e]
Molecular weight (M_w) (weight average molecular weight)	1.17×10^6[f]	300×10^6[f]
Molecular weight (M_n) (number average molecular weight)	$19–26 \times 10^4$[c]	$3.6–4.1 \times 10^6$[c]
Average chain length (CL)	$\approx 1,800$[a,d]	21.7–25[a,e]
Internal chain length (ICL)	...	6.6[a,e]
External chain length (ECL)	...	15.1[a,e]

[a] Kano et al (1981).
[b] Banks et al (1971b).
[c] DeHaas and Goering (1972).
[d] Greenwood and Thomson (1959).
[e] Banks et al (1971a).
[f] Greenwood (1989).

of amylose to hydrolysis by the exoenzyme, β-amylase. Using this technique, Greenwood and Thomson (1959) showed that amylose extracted from barley starch at relatively low temperature (70°C) was almost completely linear. Successive extractions at higher temperatures yielded amylose samples of higher molecular weight and an increased degree of branching, as indicated by an increased resistance to β-amylolysis. Total amylose from barley with a β-amylolysis limit of 73% is, therefore, a mixture of linear and branched molecules. The extent of amylose branching depends on the origin of the amylose (Takeda et al, 1987) and increases with the molecular size of the amylose from a particular source (Greenwood and Thomson, 1959). Branching and molecular size also increase with increasing starch maturity (Banks et al, 1969). Amylose from mature barley is likely to be similar to that from mature wheat, which has an average of five side-chains per molecule (Takeda et al, 1984; 1987). These side-chains have not been characterized in barley amylose but range in size from four to more than 100 glucose residues in other amyloses (Takeda et al, 1984, 1990).

Amylose can be hydrolyzed completely to maltose by the combined actions of β-amylase and debranching enzymes such as isoamylase (Kjølberg and Manners, 1963) and pullulanase (Banks and Greenwood, 1966). This indicates that α-(1→6) linkages form the branch points in amylose as they do in amylopectin (Thompson and Wolfrom, 1951).

As is the case for most polysaccharides, barley amylose exhibits a wide distribution of molecular sizes but has an average degree of polymerization (DP) of 1,800 (Table 1). In neutral, aqueous solutions, the molecule exists as a random coil, but in the presence of certain complexing agents, it forms a helical structure with about six glucose residues per turn and the complexing agent bound within the helix (Banks and Greenwood, 1971). The iodine-amylose complex, with its characteristic blue color, is formed in this way, as are amylose-lipid complexes and complexes with polar organic molecules such as butanol and thymol. Under appropriate conditions, barley amylose binds iodine up to 19.0–19.5% of its weight (Greenwood and Thomson, 1959), which is similar to values reported for amyloses from a number of different sources (Takeda et al, 1984, 1987).

Amylose is unstable in aqueous solution, tending to precipitate (retrograde) in dilute solutions and to form gels in concentrated solutions. This instability is more marked in molecules of about DP 80; smaller and larger molecules appear to be more stable (Pfannemüller et al, 1971). It is thought that the conformational shape of amylose molecules of DP 80 must be conducive to the formation of intermolecular hydrogen bonding that allows aggregation and, ultimately, precipitation to occur. In larger molecules, more intramolecular bonding can occur, which helps to stabilize the amylose, whereas smaller molecules are inherently more soluble and stable in aqueous media (Pfannemüller and Ziegast, 1981).

Amylose can be isolated from dimethyl sulfoxide dispersions of potato starch by specific complexing with butanol at ambient temperature (Geddes et al, 1964), and it can be leached from aqueous suspensions of barley starch granules at temperatures of 70–90°C (Greenwood and Thomson, 1959). Separation of amylose from amylopectin under these mild conditions indicates that amylose is not covalently bound to amylopectin in the native starch granule.

Amylopectin

Amylopectin is the major component of most starches, and it, too, is composed of chains of α-(1→4)-linked glucose residues interconnected through α-(1→6) bonds. Unlike amylose, however, the unit chains in amylopectin are relatively small, and the 4–5% of interchain α-(1→6) linkages in the molecule leads to a highly branched, compact structure. Amylopectin, with a weight-average molecular weight of 10^6–10^8 (Table 2), is one of the largest known naturally occurring polymers. Because the average size of the unit chains is 20–25 glucose residues, an amylopectin molecule must contain several thousand of them. How these chains are organized within the molecule has been an intriguing problem in starch chemistry for over 50 years. The architecture of the amylopectin molecule has been the subject of numerous studies (Whelan, 1971; Manners, 1989; Hizukuri and Maehara, 1990), but variations on the cluster model first proposed by French (1972) and Nikuni (1975) appear to be the most widely accepted models at present. Recent advances in chromatographic techniques have allowed a much more detailed picture to emerge of the actual sizes and size distributions of the unit chains. One of the most recent amylopectin models in which this information has been utilized is that proposed by Hizukuri (1986); a portion of such a model is illustrated in Fig. 1. This is a variation on earlier models proposed by French (1972), Robin et al(1974), and Manners and Matheson (1981).

It is postulated that the amylopectin molecule contains three types of unit chains. There are A-chains, which are unbranched and are linked to the molecule through their reducing end-group; B-chains, which are joined to the molecule in the same way but carry one or more A-chains; and one C-chain, which carries the reducing end-group of the molecule. The unit chains do not occur randomly throughout the molecule but are thought to be concentrated in groups or clusters; hence the name for this type of model. Unit chains designated as A and B1 (Fig. 1) are confined within individual clusters, whereas B2-chains join two clusters, B3-chains join three clusters, etc. This type of structure has been deduced largely from analysis of the products obtained after complete enzymatic debranching of amylopectin. Support for this generalized picture of amylopectin has come from physicochemical studies on the molecule (Thurn and Burchard, 1985) and from analysis of the products formed during hydrolysis of amylopectin by amylases (Bertoft, 1989). The

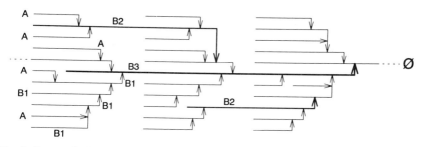

Fig. 1. Proposed cluster model of amylopectin. The different types of unit chains designated as A, B1, B2, and B3 are described in the text. Ø represents the reducing end of the single C chain in the molecule. (Reprinted, by permission, from Hizukuri, 1986)

following points are worth making about the general structure of amylopectin. In most amylopectin samples analyzed, there are more A-chains than B-chains, with the A-B ratio varying from 1 to 1.5, depending on the source of the amylopectin (Manners, 1989). The highly branched regions of amylopectin tend to limit the extent of molecular association among molecules. Therefore, amylopectin is less likely than amylose to retrograde and forms more stable solutions (Greenwood and Hourston, 1971). As a consequence, much higher concentrations of amylopectin are required to form gels compared to those required for gel formation with amylose (Zobel, 1988).

Traditionally, three different chain length measurements have been used to characterize the fine structure of a given sample of amylopectin (Table 1). The chain length is the number of glucose residues per nonreducing chain end; this is a measure, therefore, of the average length of unit chain within the molecule. The external chain length is a measure of the number of glucose residues in the exterior chains of the molecule, i.e., of all of the A-chains as well as of the outer segments of the B-chains. The interior chain length is a measure of the number of glucose residues per interior chain of the molecule (Manners, 1989). Such measurements give average results for these parameters but no indication of the range in size of the different unit chains. Crude as they may be, chain length measurements have been a valuable aid in determining differences in fine structure of amylopectins from different origins. More detailed information about the size distribution of unit chains can now be obtained with chromatographic methods of high resolution.

Barley amylopectin is a large molecule with a molecular mass of several million daltons based on light scattering (Banks et al, 1972) and polarographic measurements (DeHaas and Goering, 1972). Despite its large size, it has a relatively low viscosity in dilute solution compared to that of amylose, indicating that the molecule has a relatively compact conformation in aqueous solution.

The extensive branching in amylopectin restricts the extent of hydrolysis by β-amylase, so the β-amylolysis limits achieved are significantly lower than those observed with amylose. Also, iodine is unable to form stable complexes with amylopectin because of the short length of the unit chains; therefore, only small amounts of iodine are bound by amylopectin.

Debranched barley amylopectin has a trimodal distribution of unit chains (MacGregor and Morgan, 1984), as indicated by peaks 2, 3, and 4 in Fig. 2. Peak 1 is thought to consist of contaminating amylose in the amylopectin sample. Each peak represents a group of unit chains having a wide distribution of chain sizes. Group 4, the most abundant group, contains the shortest chains. These have an average chain length of 10–12 glucose residues and represent the A-chains shown in Fig. 1. The smallest unit chain found in barley amylopectin is maltohexaose (Kano et al, 1981), which probably represents the smallest A-chain in the molecule. Group 3 may contain some A-chains but is more likely to represent the B1-chains shown in Fig. 1. These have an average DP of 18–20 and would be confined within individual clusters of the amylopectin molecule. Group 2 contains chains of DP 40–50 and represents the B2- and perhaps B3-chains shown in Fig. 1. These chains would extend through more than one cluster.

Recent studies on debranched wheat amylopectin have revealed a polymodal distribution of unit chains, with as many as six groups (Hizukuri and Maehara, 1990). These groups varied in average DP from 11.4 to 1,600, but over 90% of the material was found in three groups of unit chains having DP values in the range 11.4–40. These correspond to the major unit chain groups present in barley amylopectin (Fig. 2). It is probable that barley amylopectin also contains small amounts of larger unit chains.

Barley amylopectin is similar to that from wheat and tapioca in having two groups of unit chains of short to intermediate length—many amylopectins have only one such group with an average size in the DP 16–20 range (Hizukuri, 1985). The weight proportion of short to long chains ([Peak 3 + 4]/Peak 2), illustrated in Fig. 2, has been used widely to characterize amylopectins from different sources. Values of 3.3–3.7 are similar to those found for other cereal amylopectins from A-type starches (see later) but are much higher than values reported for amylopectins from B-type starches such as potato and tulip (Hizukuri, 1985). Therefore, amylopectins from cereal starches, including barley, have shorter average chain lengths than do starches from other sources. This agrees with results obtained by the direct calculation of the average chain length of amylopectins from a variety of sources. Barley amylopectin, for

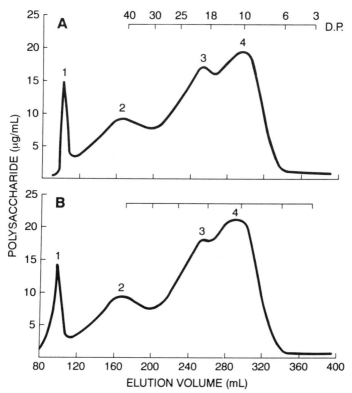

Fig. 2. Distribution of unit chains of debranched amylopectins from large starch granules (A) and small starch granules (B). Characteristics of the different peaks are described in the text. DP = degree of polymerization. (Reprinted, by permission, from MacGregor and Morgan, 1984)

example, has an average chain length of 22–25 (Table 1), whereas potato amylopectin has an average chain length of 34 (Hizukuri, 1985). The slower rate of retrogradation and of gel formation exhibited by amylopectins from barley and other cereal grains reflects this shorter chain length. Indeed, it is more difficult for intermolecular associations to occur in aqueous dispersions of cereal amylopectins because of their shorter chain segments (Kalichevsky et al, 1990). This is an example of how small changes in the fine structure of a macromolecule can have a significant effect on its functional properties.

Starch Granules

Starch exists in nature in the form of discrete granular bodies whose size and shape depend on their botanical origin. Barley starch consists of a mixture of large, lenticular granules 15–25 μm in diameter and smaller, irregularly shaped granules <10 μm in diameter (Fig. 3). In the mature kernel, the starch is present exclusively in the endosperm but is not distributed uniformly. The last cells in which starch synthesis occurs during kernel development are those around the endosperm periphery. Therefore, these cells, especially those in the subaleurone region, are filled, preferentially, with protein and not starch. In comparison, more centrally located cells are filled primarily with starch and contain lower levels of protein.

Purified starch granules contain low but varying levels of protein (0.25–0.56%), lipids (0.16–1.17%), and free fatty acids (0.03–0.09%) (Morrison

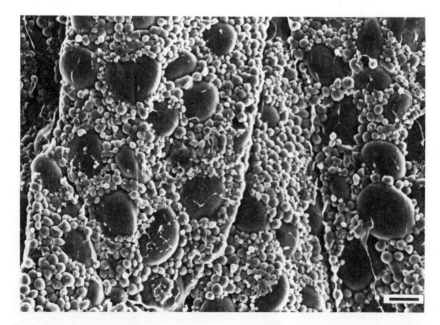

Fig. 3. Scanning electron micrograph of large and small starch granules in barley endosperm. Bar = 10 μm.

et al, 1986; McDonald and Stark, 1988). Protein was once considered an impurity in starch granules, but it is now recognized that small amounts are an integral part of the granule interior (Goldner and Boyer, 1989) and cannot be removed even with stringent starch purification methods (McDonald and Stark, 1988). Many of these proteins appear to be remnants of enzymes responsible for starch synthesis in the developing kernel. Starch lipids are discussed in detail in Chapter 5.

Starch from normal barley cultivars contains both amylose and amylopectin, and the precise way in which these two components are arranged within the starch granule remains an important and intriguing problem in starch chemistry. Current knowledge of granule architecture has been obtained through studies on starches from different origins, including barley. Some of the information obtained from studies on nonbarley cereal starches can be used with a high degree of confidence to develop ideas on the structure and morphology of barley starch granules.

Barley starch granules are birefringent and exhibit the characteristic "maltese cross" pattern when viewed under polarized light (Goering et al, 1973b). This indicates that there is a high degree of molecular orientation within the starch granule but not necessarily that the granule is crystalline (Banks and Greenwood, 1975). Evidence for starch crystallinity comes from X-ray diffraction techniques (Zobel, 1988), which yield diffraction patterns that, in general, are typical of the botanical source of the starch. Environmental conditions during the growing season, especially temperature, can affect the X-ray pattern of the resulting starch (Nikuni, 1978). Starch granules from barley exhibit the A-type X-ray pattern (Kang et al, 1985), which is typical of most cereal starches (Zobel, 1988). In general, starches from tubers give B-type patterns and starches from peas, beans, and tapioca tend to give a C-type pattern that is intermediate between A and B patterns. The parameters controlling the formation of these different types of starch are not well understood. However, from the work of Gidley (Gidley, 1987; Gidley and Bulpin, 1987) and Hizukuri (Hizukuri et al, 1983; Hizukuri, 1986), it appears that A-type starch is formed preferentially under conditions of higher crystallization temperature and polymer concentration and shorter unit chains in the amylopectin component (Biliaderis, 1991). Only a portion of the starch granule is crystalline, but it is difficult to determine accurately the relative proportions of highly ordered crystalline regions to less well-organized amorphous regions within the granule. Estimates of crystallinity for various cereal starches are in the range of 30–40% (Zobel, 1988), and starch granules from barley are likely to show a level of crystallinity in this range.

Amylopectin appears to be responsible for the crystallinity found in cereal starch granules (Kainuma and French, 1972). Waxy starches, which contain little or no amylose, from sources such as barley (Kang et al, 1985), rice (Nara, 1979), and corn (Nara, 1979; Fuwa et al, 1982) all show A-type X-ray diffraction patterns, indicating crystallinity. Amylose appears to have little effect on the crystallinity of barley starch.

It is possible that, in the starch granule, the outer chains of the amylopectin molecule, those forming the "clusters" (Fig. 1), are not linear but exist in the form of double helices (Imberty and Pérez, 1989). These double helices could pack together to form highly ordered, crystalline regions, whereas the regions of the molecule containing branch points would be amorphous. The picture of amylopectin that emerges is one containing alternating crystalline and amorphous regions, with the molecules aligned radially to the surface of the granule (Lineback, 1984). There is no obvious reason why these ideas, obtained from starches other than barley starch, cannot be applied equally well to the nature of amylopectin within barley starch granules.

At an ultrastructural level, as depicted by scanning electron microscopy, barley starch granules appear to have a relatively smooth outer surface. This is unlikely to be so at the molecular level. Much more likely is the picture of the granule having individual chains of amylose and amylopectin protruding from the granule surface as suggested by Stark and Yin (1986) and Lineback (1984). Barley starch granules, when highly degraded by α-amylase, exhibit an internal ring or shell structure (Fig. 4). These shells represent layers within the granule that differ in refractive index, density, crystallinity, and suscep- tibility to enzymatic hydrolysis (French, 1984). Their origin is not known, but it has been suggested that they represent different periods of starch synthesis; thus they have been called "growth rings." Layers that are more susceptible to enzymatic hydrolysis are thought to be more amorphous, whereas the crystalline, denser shells are more resistant to enzymatic attack. Similar shell structures have been observed in many other starches; in some, such as potato, this feature can be observed in the intact granule by optical microscopy (Banks et al, 1973c).

Outer regions of starch granules from normal barley are more resistant to enzymatic hydrolysis than inner core regions (Fig. 4), indicating a possible gradation of composition or physical structure through the granules. There is evidence that peripheral regions of cereal starch granules may contain higher concentrations of amylose than central regions (see Chapter 5), but the precise location and physical form of amylose in the granule are not known. It is unlikely that amylose, per se, would decrease the susceptibility of granules to enzymatic hydrolysis. Barley starch granules contain lipids, and there is some evidence that amylose exists as an amylose-lipid complex in the granule (Morrison, *personal communication*). Amylose in such a complex would be less susceptible than noncomplexed amylose to hydrolysis by α-amylase (Holm et al, 1983).

Granule Size Distribution

Starch granules from normal barley have a distinct bimodal size distribution (May and Buttrose, 1959; MacGregor et al, 1971) as shown in Fig. 3. The large and small granules are referred to as A- and B-type granules, respectively. Numerous values for granule size have been reported in the literature; some of these are documented in Table 2. These values were obtained using different methods; starches were isolated by various techniques; and many different barley cultivars grown under a range of environmental conditions were used. For example, barley grown at high ambient temperature (20° C) contains smaller A- and B-type granules and fewer B-granules than does grain grown at 10° C (Tester et al, 1991). In addition, a high proportion of the small granules are often lost during starch extraction and purification (McDonald and Stark, 1988). It should not be surprising, therefore, that the reported values show

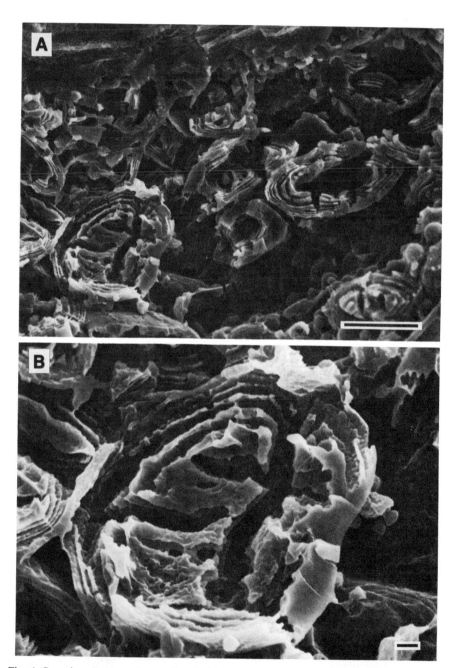

Fig. 4. Scanning electron micrographs of highly degraded starch granules in malt. A, interior of several granules showing concentric shells. Bar = 10 μm. B, closeup of granule interior, showing concentric shells and pattern of α-amylase hydrolysis within the granules. Bar = 1 μm.

wide variation for the granule size distribution of barley starch. In general, small granules (B-type) are taken to be those less than 6 μm in diameter (more often, 2–4 μm in diameter). These constitute 80–90% of the total number of starch granules but only 10–15% of the total starch weight, although levels as high as 30% have been reported (Goering et al, 1973b). Large granules (A-type) range in size from 10 to 30 μm but generally lie in the 15–20 μm range. They constitute a small proportion (10–20%) of the total number of starch granules but a high proportion (85–90%) of the total weight of starch. The small granules in barley constitute a lower proportion of the total granule population than do the small granules in either wheat or rye (Karlsson et al, 1983). Both A- and B-type granules from barley are smaller than the corresponding granules from wheat and rye (Karlsson et al, 1983; Soulaka and Morrison, 1985; Morrison and Scott, 1986).

In high-amylose barley starch, B-type granules are larger and A-type granules are smaller than the corresponding granule types in normal barley starch (Banks et al, 1973b; Morrison et al, 1986). In addition, the small-granule fraction constitutes a relatively high proportion of the total starch (Table 3). As a result, the granules in high-amylose starch have a more uniform size distribution (Merritt and Walker, 1969; Walker and Merritt, 1969), but this distribution is still bimodal.

TABLE 3
Size and Size Distribution of Barley Starch Granules

		Mean	Proportion of Total Starch		
Granule Type	Lines Analyzed	Diameter (μm)	Percent by Weight[a]	Percent by Number	Reference
Normal	1				May and Buttrose, 1959
Large		20	90	12	
Small		<6.7			
Normal	1				Banks et al, 1971a
Large		22			
Small		<4.6	5	75	
Normal	1				Bathgate and Palmer, 1972
Large		ca. 25	89	13	
Small		ca. 5			
Normal	26				Goering et al, 1973b
Large		20–40			
Small		3–5	6.2–30.6	84.6–97	
Normal	2				Evers et al, 1973
Large		>15	81–91		
Small		<10	5–11		
Normal	33				Mäkelä et al, 1982
Large		15–19.1	8.2–16		
Small		3.1–3.7			
Normal	1				Karlsson et al, 1983
Large		17			
Small		<7.6	13.0		
Normal	5				Kang et al, 1985
Large		13.6–30			
Small		6.0–6.1		90	

(*continued on next page*)

TABLE 3 (continued)

Granule Type	Lines Analyzed	Mean Diameter (μm)	Proportion of Total Starch		Reference
			Percent by Weight[a]	Percent by Number	
Normal	1				Naka et al, 1985
Large		15.4			
Small		4.3			
Normal (small)	8	2.9–3.6	4.6–15.1	80.7–90.8	Morrison et al, 1986
Normal (large)	1	>8	80–85	5	MacLeod and Duffus, 1988
Normal	2				McDonald et al, 1991
Large		11.0–12.3	91–92	8–15	
Small		2.5–2.6			
High-amylose	1				Banks et al, 1971a
Large		15			
Small		<4.6	10	85	
High-amylose	1				Goering et al, 1973b
Large		24			
Small		3	14.3	83	
High-amylose	4				Morrison et al, 1986
Large		11.1	50	8	
Small	4	3.9–4.4	29.2–46.3	90.4–93.8	
Waxy	2				Banks et al, 1970b
Large		22			
Small		3			
Waxy	2				Goering et al, 1973b
Large		20–25			
Small		4–5	10.2–26.3	89–97	
Waxy	9				Naka et al, 1985
Large		13.7–17.6			
Small		2.5–3.3			
Waxy	1				Kang et al, 1985
Large		14.0			
Small		6.7		80	
Waxy	8				Morrison et al, 1986
Large		10.3–13.6			
Small		2.1–3.1	3.5–13.6	72.4–90.2	

[a] In some publications, the weight percent is reported while in others the volume percent is used. These are equivalent (Morrison and Scott, 1986).

Granules from waxy barley starch also exhibit a bimodal size distribution (Table 3). Small granules appear to be similar in size to those in normal barley starch, but the large granules tend to be smaller. Again, although the large granules represent only a small proportion of the total number of granules, they constitute a high weight fraction of the total starch. The large-granule fraction, like that of high-amylose starch, appears to have fewer granules than normal barley starch in the 20–30 μm range (Goering et al, 1973b).

Starch-Iodine Interactions

Amylose complexes with polyiodide ion, I'_n ($n = 3\text{--}11$), to form a deep blue complex with an absorption maximum at 624 nm (Banks and Greenwood, 1975), whereas amylopectin reacts weakly with I'_n to give a red color with a maximum absorption at 529 nm (Banks et al, 1970a). Reported values of λ_{max} depend on the concentrations of both I_2 and KI. Various aspects of the amylose-iodine interaction have been used to characterize starches from different sources, including that from barley.

Determination of the "blue value" of a starch (Gilbert and Spragg, 1964) gives a measure of the absorbance of the starch-iodine complex; the higher the value, the more amylose is present in the starch or material under investigation. Published values for barley starch are shown in Table 4. Many of these results were probably subject to interference from starch lipids (Morrison and Laignelet, 1983) and so may err on the low side. Although the results are variable, it is clear that large granules generally give higher values than small granules, indicating that they contain a higher proportion of amylose. Waxy starches give low blue value readings, indicative of their reduced amylose content.

The iodine binding capacity or iodine affinity of a starch, defined as the weight of iodine (mg) bound per 100 mg of starch under controlled conditions, is also a measure of starch amylose content; again, a broad range of iodine affinity values has been reported for barley starch (Table 5). Small granules give lower values than large granules, indicative of less amylose in the small granules. Compared to normal starch, high-amylose starch gives higher values and waxy starch gives much lower values.

Values for the wavelength of maximum absorption of starch-iodine complexes are shown in Table 6. Absorption maxima for small-granule iodine complexes occur at lower wavelengths than those for the corresponding large-granule complexes, as would be expected from their slightly lower amylose content. Differences in starch preparation methods, experimental methodology,

TABLE 4
Barley Starch "Blue Values"[a]

Granule Type	Lines Analyzed	Blue Value	Reference
Normal	2	0.365–0.376	Harris and MacWilliam, 1958
Normal	12	0.344–0.367	Merritt and Walker, 1969
Normal	8	0.25–0.40	Slack and Wainwright, 1980
Normal	1		Bathgate and Palmer, 1972
Large		0.40	
Small		0.66	
Normal	5		Kang et al, 1985
Large		0.352–0.394	
Small		0.288–0.311	
Normal	1		Stark and Yin, 1986
Large		0.37	
Small		0.26	
Waxy	9		Naka et al, 1985
Large		0.102–0.193	
Small		0.072–0.154	

[a] The absorbance of a starch/iodine solution measured at 680 nm under standard conditions (Bourne et al, 1948).

and efficiency in lipid removal from the granules are more likely than intrinsic differences in starches to be responsible for the variation observed within a starch type.

Amylose Content of Barley Starch

Under controlled conditions, amylose binds 19.0–19.5 mg of iodine per 100 mg of amylose (Banks et al, 1971b). This is a general relationship that should apply to normal amylose from all cereal grains, including that from barley.

TABLE 5
Iodine Affinity of Barley Starch Granules[a]

Granule Type	Lines Analyzed	Iodine Affinity	Reference
Normal	2	5.6–5.76	Banks et al, 1971b
Normal	2	5.9–6.0	DeHaas and Goering, 1972
Normal	2	5.4–5.7	Goering et al, 1973a
Normal	1		Bathgate and Palmer, 1972
Large		4.98	
Small		8.25	
Normal	4		Goering and DeHaas, 1974
Large		5.4–6.1	
Small		4.3–5.7	
Normal	1		Stark and Yin, 1986
Large		4.4	
Small		3.55	
High amylose	1	8.2	Banks et al, 1971b
Waxy	8	0.1–2.6	Banks et al, 1970b
Waxy	2	0.35–0.7	Goering et al, 1973a
Waxy	1		Goering and DeHaas, 1974
Large		0	
Small		0.1	

[a] Milligrams of iodine bound per 100 mg of starch.

TABLE 6
Wavelength of Maximum Absorption (λ_{max}) for Barley Starch-Iodine Complexes

Granule Type	Lines Analyzed	λ_{max} (nm)	Reference
Normal	1	615	Kano, 1977
Normal	5		Kang et al, 1985
Large		594–597	
Small		580–590	
Normal	1		Stark and Yin, 1986
Large		620	
Small		614	
Waxy	9		Naka et al, 1985
Large		534–556	
Small		523–548	

Under similar conditions, amylopectin binds a negligible amount of iodine. Therefore, the amylose content of purified starch can be determined by measuring the iodine binding capacity (IBC) of the starch and assuming that the iodine is bound by the amylose fraction only. Lipids also form complexes with amylose and so prevent binding of iodine to the amylose. If starch is not defatted completely, amylose contents as determined by the IBC method may be underestimated by as much as 30% (Banks et al, 1971b; Morrison et al, 1986). Incomplete defatting of samples before IBC assays may explain some of the variation in the data reported in the literature (Table 7). The amylose content of starch has been determined also by debranching the starch completely and separating the high-molecular-weight amylose fraction from the low-molecular-weight unit chains of amylopectin by gel permeation chromatography. This method gives an estimate of the amylose content, but the values

TABLE 7
Amylose Content of Barley Starch

Granule Type	Lines Analyzed	Amylose Content (%)	Reference
Normal	2	25.2–26.1	Harris and MacWilliam, 1958
Normal	51	24–27.5	Merritt, 1967
Normal	12	23.7–26.2	Merritt and Walker, 1969
Normal	1	28	Banks et al, 1971a
Normal	13	26.2–34.0	Bhatty et al, 1975
Normal	20	23.1–35.1	Torp, 1980
Normal	15	25.3–30.1	Morrison et al, 1984
Normal	1	28.9	South and Morrison, 1990
Normal	2	28.3–28.5	McDonald et al, 1991
Normal Large Small	1	24.9 41.3	Bathgate and Palmer, 1972
Normal Large Small	3	28–30 28–30	Evers et al, 1973
Normal Large Small	1	23.6 20.4	MacGregor and Ballance, 1980
Normal Large Small	1	22.1 19.0	MacGregor and Morgan, 1984
Normal Large Small	1	22.6 18.2	Stark and Yin, 1986
High amylose	Glacier AC 38 (seven samples)	34.8–45.0	Merritt, 1967; Banks et al, 1971a, 1973a; Bhatty et al, 1975; Lorenz and Kulp, 1984; Morrison et al, 1984; McDonald et al, 1991

(continued on next page)

TABLE 7 (continued)

Granule Type	Lines Analyzed	Amylose Content (%)	Reference
High amylose	3	38.4–40.8	Morrison et al, 1984
High amylose	Glacier AC 38		Evers et al, 1973
Large	(one sample)	45	
Small		53	
High amylose	Glacier AC 38		Morrison et al, 1984
Large	(one sample)	37.4	
Small		47.9	
Waxy	8	0.4–13	Banks et al, 1970b
Waxy	2	10.3–13.6	Bhatty et al, 1975
Waxy	1	3.0	Lorenz and Kulp, 1984
Waxy	8	2.1–8.3	Morrison et al, 1984
Waxy	1		MacGregor and Ballance, 1980
Large		4.1	
Small		1.6	
Waxy	1		MacGregor and Morgan, 1984
Large		3.6	
Small		1.8	
Waxy	1		McDonald et al, 1991
Large		5.8	
Small		0	

are not identical to those of the IBC method (Sargeant, 1982; Tester et al, 1991).

Despite variation in reported values for amylose content, it is clear that when small and large granules are analyzed in the same study, the amylose content of small granules is almost always less than that of large granules. Therefore, the weight of evidence indicates that, within a given population of starch granules, small granules contain less amylose than do large granules.

Very few barley cultivars with high-amylose starch are available. Most research on this type of material has been done with Glacier AC 38, sometimes called Glacier Pentlandfield, or with lines derived from AC 38. Starch from Glacier AC 38 does contain increased levels of amylose (Table 7), and values as high as 50% have been reported (Morrison, 1987). Small granules from high-amylose barley starch contain more amylose than do large granules (McDonald et al, 1991, and Table 7), in contrast to granules from normal barley starch, as shown by the majority of studies.

Low but variable levels of amylose are present in waxy barley lines. The source of amylose in these lines has been the subject of some speculation but appears to be associated mainly with large granules. Indeed, small granules may not contain any amylose (McDonald et al, 1991). These results indicate that small amounts of amylose are an integral part of waxy starch and are not caused by contamination of waxy lines with small amounts of normal kernels. In the waxy lines, amylose synthesis is suppressed but, obviously, is not shut down completely.

Susceptibility of Starch Granules to Enzymatic Hydrolysis

Although several enzymes play a role in the hydrolysis of starch once it has been dispersed or solubilized, only two enzymes, α-amylase and glucoamylase, have the ability to hydrolyze and solubilize significant amounts of granular starch. α-Amylase is an endoenzyme that hydrolyzes α-(1→4) bonds in starch in a random manner, and glucoamylase is an exoenzyme that removes glucose residues in a stepwise manner from the nonreducing ends of starch molecules. Hydrolysis of starch granules by both α-amylase (Slack and Wainwright, 1980) and glucoamylase (Takahashi et al, 1985) is slow compared to the hydrolysis of solubilized starch by these enzymes. Other enzymes are able to hydrolyze solubilized starch and soluble starch products. β-Amylase is an endoenzyme that removes maltose residues in a stepwise manner from the nonreducing ends of starch molecules, and α-glucosidase hydrolyzes maltose preferentially. Limit dextrinase hydrolyzes α-(1→6) bonds in amylopectin and amylose and in the dextrins formed during the hydrolysis of these starch components by α- and β-amylases. All of these enzymes are required for the efficient hydrolysis of starch to small metabolizable carbohydrates.

Only the granule surface is available for initial stages of hydrolysis, so the effective starch concentration is relatively low. Under appropriate conditions, starch granules from a variety of sources adsorb and are subsequently hydrolyzed by α-amylases and glucoamylase (Sandstedt and Ueda, 1969; Takahashi et al, 1985). Malt α-amylase attacks large barley starch granules initially along the equatorial groove of the granule, followed by an apparently random attack on the granule surface (Fig. 5). This leads to the formation of numerous pinholes leading from the surface of the granule to the interior regions (Kiribuchi and Nakamura, 1973). Such hydrolysis exposes the layered nature of large granules because some of the concentric layers are hydrolyzed faster than others (Fig. 4). In addition, the granule interior is hydrolyzed preferentially over exterior regions, indicating a difference in the chemical or physical composition of these two areas of the granule.

Soluble products of α-amylolysis are a mixture of small, linear and larger, branched dextrins (MacGregor and Morgan, 1986). The rate of granule hydrolysis may be increased in the presence of other enzymes such as β-amylase and limit dextrinase (Maeda et al, 1978, 1979). These complementary enzymes presumably degrade the initial products of α-amylolysis to dextrins that are too small to act as competitive inhibitors for the α-amylase.

Small starch granules from barley are hydrolyzed faster than large granules by glucoamylase (Morrison et al, 1986) and α-amylases (MacGregor and Ballance, 1980; McHale, 1986), probably because of their significantly higher ratio of surface area to volume (Morrison et al, 1986). Although similar hydrolytic products are formed from large and small granules, the two granule types are degraded by different mechanisms. Degraded small granules exhibit roughened exterior surfaces rather than pinholes, indicating that hydrolysis takes place through surface erosion (Kiribuchi and Nakamura, 1973).

In general, starch granules from waxy maize (Fuwa et al, 1977), waxy rice (Evers and Juliano, 1976), and waxy sorghum (Tovar et al, 1977) are hydrolyzed by α-amylase and glucoamylase faster than their normal counterparts. Waxy starch from barley is also more susceptible than normal barley starch to degradation by α-amylase (Goering and Eslick, 1976) and glucoamylase (Fuwa, 1982). The isolated starch from one particular waxy barley cultivar (Washonupana) contained sufficient endogenous α-amylase that it was hydrolyzed extensively at 67–75° C (Goering and Eslick, 1976). This cultivar has been proposed as a good source of starch syrups (Goering et al, 1980). Surfaces of degraded waxy granules are greatly roughened, and α-amylolysis appears to proceed through the combined mechanism of surface erosion and pinhole formation (MacGregor and Ballance, 1980).

A barley mutant containing a different type of waxy starch has been described by DeHaas et al(1983). The granules of this material are small and polygonal in shape and, unlike other waxy starches, appear to be resistant to hydrolysis by α-amylase.

Little information has been published on the susceptibility of high-amylose barley starch to enzymatic degradation. Earlier reports claimed that high-amylose starches from barley (Merritt, 1969) and maize (Rogols and Meites, 1968) were hydrolyzed more quickly than the corresponding normal starches by α-amylases from several sources. This conclusion should be reevaluated in light of more recent reports claiming that high-amylose starch from barley is more resistant (Ellis, 1976) or equally resistant (Björck et al, 1990) to hydrolysis by amylases than normal starch and that high-amylose starch from

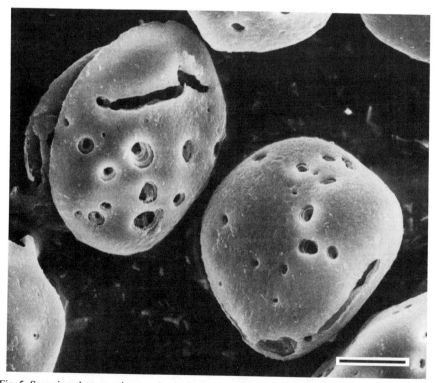

Fig. 5. Scanning electron micrograph of initial stages of hydrolysis of starch granules from barley by malt α-amylase. Bar = 5 μm.

maize is more resistant than normal maize starch to glucoamylase and a range of α-amylases (Fujita et al, 1989; Fuwa et al, 1977).

Variation in susceptibility of different types of barley starches to enzymatic degradation may affect starch digestibility by different classes of livestock.

Resistant Starch

During high-temperature processing, some starch may become resistant to subsequent enzymatic degradation. This form of starch has been called resistant starch (Englyst et al, 1982, 1983), and it has provoked much interest because it may not be susceptible to breakdown during the normal processes of digestion in humans (Anderson et al, 1981) and in monogastric animals (Wyatt and Horn, 1988). Most of the research on resistant starch has been done on wheat starch because of the larger quantities of wheat-based products used as human foods. A major form of the resistant wheat starch consists of retrograded amylose, and so prior solubilization of amylose is required for the formation of this material (Berry et al, 1988; Ring et al, 1988). However, a portion of the enzyme-resistant material may be in an amorphous form (Cairns et al, 1990).

Formation of resistant starch in barley products could be induced during industrial processes such as kilning, extrusion cooking, and pelleting. For example, the enzymatic susceptibility of malt starch may be lowered by increasing the severity of kilning (MacWilliam, 1972). The enzymatic susceptibility of starch can be reduced also through the formation of amylose-lipid complexes (Larsson and Miezis, 1979), starch-protein interactions (Holm et al, 1989), and heat-induced chemical modification of the starch (Theander and Westerlund, 1987; Østergård et al, 1989).

Starch Gelatinization and Pasting

When the temperature of a slurry of starch granules in an excess of water is increased to 100°C, a number of changes occur to the properties of the granules. Initially, the granules expand in volume slowly, but at a particular temperature they undergo rapid and irreversible swelling, thus increasing the viscosity of the slurry. This is accompanied or followed by disruption of the molecular order within the granules, as manifested by loss of birefringence; loss of granule crystallinity, as assessed by X-ray diffraction; an increase in the susceptibility of the granules to enzymatic degradation; a change in thermal properties of the granules, as measured by differential scanning calorimetry (DSC); and an increase in starch solubility (Atwell et al, 1988; Liu et al, 1991). Methods are available to measure each of these changes, but the results obtained with any one method apply to a specific event within this array of changes, and the changes do not all occur at the same temperature. The term "gelatinization" has been applied to all of these changes, and so it is not surprising that a wide range of gelatinization temperatures has been reported for any one starch, including that from barley (Table 8). Traditionally, loss of birefringence, as measured by polarized light microscopy, has been the major method for determining the temperature of gelatinization. More recently, DSC, which measures the temperature at which starch crystallites melt (Stevens and Elton, 1971) has been used widely for this measurement; most of the results shown in Table 8 have been obtained with either of these two methods. A third method is based on the ability of Congo red to stain damaged starch granules and tends to give higher values of gelatinization temperature. Results obtained by the two main methods should be comparable

TABLE 8
Gelatinization Temperature of Barley Starch

Granule Type	Lines Analyzed	Method Used[a]	Gelatinization Temperature (°C)	Reference
Normal	2	A	59–60	Banks et al, 1971a; Ellis, 1976
Normal	1	A	60.5	Lorenz and Kulp, 1984
Normal	8	A	<60	Slack and Wainwright, 1980
Normal	8	B	60–68	
Normal	1	C	59	Seog et al, 1988
Normal	1	C	56.6	South and Morrison, 1990
Normal	2	C	51.1–60.8[b]	Tester et al, 1991
Normal	1	C	56.5	Tester and Morrison, 1991a
Normal	1	B		Bathgate and Palmer, 1972
Large			59	
Small			61	
Normal	5	C		Kang et al, 1985
Large			58–63	
Small			57–64	
Normal	1	C		Naka et al, 1985
Large			63	
Small			63	
Normal (large)	1	A	52	Bathgate and Palmer, 1972
Normal	1	A		MacGregor and Ballance, 1980
Large			56.7	
Small			63.4	
High amylose	3	A	64–66	Banks et al, 1971a; Ellis, 1976; Lorenz and Kulp, 1984
High amylose	1	C	55.7–62.0[b]	Tester et al, 1991
Waxy	9	A	63.5–67.5	Banks et al, 1970b; Lorenz and Kulp, 1984
Waxy	1	C	57.6	Tester and Morrison, 1991a
Waxy	1	C	54.1–62.7[b]	Tester et al, 1991
Waxy	1	A		MacGregor and Ballance, 1980
Large			61.6	
Small			64.6	
Waxy (large)	5	C	62–65	Kang et al, 1985
Waxy (small)	5	C	64–65	Naka et al, 1985

[a] A = temperature at which 50% of the granules lose birefringence; B = temperature at which 50% of the granules are stained with Congo red; C = peak temperature of the granule endotherm determined by differential scanning calorimetry.
[b] Variation caused by barley growing conditions.

but not necessarily identical. Therefore, if meaningful comparisons are to be made of the gelatinization temperatures of different samples of starch (e.g., starches from different cultivars; large and small granules; normal, waxy and high-amylose starches), the samples must be analyzed by the same technique under identical conditions. Results shown in Table 8 should be interpreted with this in mind. It would be misleading, for example, to compare the gelatinization temperature of large starch granules with that of small granules determined by a different method or by a modification of the same method.

In a given sample of starch, the granules do not gelatinize at the same temperature. This is because the crystalline regions within a granule are composed of small crystallites, each having a slightly different degree of crystalline perfection. Each crystallite melts and becomes disorganized at a particular temperature, so the gelatinization temperature of an individual granule represents the sum of these individual events (Banks and Greenwood, 1975). Therefore, a starch sample gelatinizes over a range of temperatures. It is common to report the temperature at which 50% of the granules have lost their birefringence. By comparison, the onset, peak, and conclusion temperatures of DSC endotherms are recorded as a rule. Only the peak temperatures (Tp) are shown in Table 8, however.

Reported gelatinization temperatures for many bulk samples of normal starch lie in the range 56–62°C, but these values can be affected by both barley cultivar and growing conditions (Tester et al, 1991). High temperatures during the grain-filling period appear to increase the gelatinization temperature of the resulting starch. The reason for this is not clear, but the temperature prevailing during granule development may affect the structure of the amylopectin and amylose molecules, the way in which they pack within the granule, or the crystallinity of the individual crystallites within the granule. Moreover, since the granular structure exists in the form of various nonequilibrium crystals, it is amenable to annealing and mechanical deformation during isolation. Therefore, starch gelatinization data often reflect the thermal and mechanical history of the sample and may not represent properties of the granules within the kernel before extraction (Biliaderis, 1990).

Both high-amylose and waxy barley starches gelatinize at higher temperatures than normal granules and, in almost all studies, small granules appear to gelatinize at higher temperatures and over a wider range of temperature than the corresponding large granules (Table 8 and references cited therein).

If barley starch granules are maintained in aqueous suspension for several hours at temperatures just below their gelatinization temperature, then the gelatinization temperature is raised considerably but the gelatinization temperature range is narrowed markedly (Lorenz and Kulp, 1984; Tester et al, 1991). A similar effect has been observed with starches from wheat (Gough and Pybus, 1971) and rice (Tester and Morrison, 1991b). This effect has been called granule annealing. The process may be explained as follows. At temperatures slightly below the gelatinization temperature, the less perfect crystallites within the granule melt and then recrystallize to give more perfect crystallites with higher melting temperatures. The overall effect of this process is to increase the quality and uniformity of the crystallites within a starch sample, thus raising the temperature of gelatinization but reducing the temperature range required to achieve complete gelatinization (Banks and Greenwood, 1975).

The gelatinization temperature is an important characteristic of barley starch from a processing standpoint. It indicates the temperature at which the granules become more soluble and more susceptible to enzymatic hydrolysis—an important parameter for the mashing stage of brewing (see Chapter 7). Also, it indicates the temperature at which irreversible swelling of the granules commences. This swelling continues to increase as the temperature is raised through 80°C (Tester and Morrison, 1991a; Tester et al, 1991), long after all the granules have gelatinized. As the granules swell, rupture, and release their contents into the aqueous medium, there is a parallel increase in the viscosity of the starch suspension. Both the swelling power and viscosity-producing potential of barley starch have important implications for the use of barley flour and starch in the food industry.

The amylose and associated lipid content of a starch have a significant effect on its ability to swell (Table 9) when heated in excess water. Waxy barley starches, which contain low levels of both amylose and lipids, swell to a much greater extent than normal starches (Goering et al, 1973a), whereas high-amylose starches do not swell as much as normal starches (Morrison et al, 1986). It appears that the amylopectin fraction is responsible for the swelling power of a given starch. Amylose and lipids appear to restrict swelling of barley starch granules at temperatures below 60°C, but at higher temperatures, these granule components just dilute the amylopectin effect (Tester and Morrison, 1991a). Barley growing conditions also affect the swelling power of the resultant starch granules, with high temperatures at the grain-filling stage producing starch granules with decreased swelling ability (Tester et al, 1991).

The viscosity of starch pastes is an important property for the technological processing of cereal flours and starches. One of the most widely used methods for determining starch paste viscosity is the use of the Brabender Viscoamylograph (Swinkels, 1985). This methodology, in which the viscosity of a stirred aqueous suspension of starch granules is monitored continuously while the suspension is heated under controlled conditions, is used extensively for assessing quality features of wheat flour but has not found wide application for evaluating quality aspects of barley flour or starch. Major features measured by this technique are the temperature at which the viscosity of a starch granule suspension starts to increase (the pasting temperature), the temperature at

TABLE 9
Swelling Power of Barley Starch[a]

Starch Source	Swelling Factor[b] (at 70°C)
Compana	8.9
Waxy Compana	16.9
Hector	9.4
Waxy Hector	15.2
High-amylose Hector	4.1[c]
Glacier	8.4
High-amylose Glacier	5.3

[a] Data from Morrison et al, 1986.
[b] A measure of swelling power (Dengate et al, 1978).
[c] Average value for two samples grown in different years.

which the peak viscosity is achieved, the level of the peak viscosity, the stability of the paste viscosity, and the extent and rate of retrogradation of the starch (setback viscosity) when the suspension is cooled (Fig. 6).

There is considerable variation in the peak viscosities produced by starches from different barley cultivars (Goering et al, 1970; Munck, 1987). These must be caused by small variations in the chemical and physical properties of the granules. Much greater differences in the whole viscosity profile are observed when different types of barley starch are analyzed by this technique (Fig. 6). The two normal starches show rapid development of paste viscosity, fairly stable peak viscosities, and significant setback or retrogradation on cooling. Waxy starch has a different profile, however. It has a very high paste viscosity, characteristic of waxy starches, that is quite unstable, and there is very little retrogradation on cooling. In addition, the pasting temperature is considerably lower than that observed with the normal starches. High-amylose starch has a lower peak viscosity than that of its normal counterpart and exhibits significantly more retrogradation on cooling. These pasting characteristics of different types of barley starch may be useful for specific products within the food industry.

CELL WALL POLYSACCHARIDES

Plant cell walls consist of a reinforced, multicomponent matrix of noncovalently and covalently cross-linked polymers in which a network of cellulose microfibrils are embedded (Fincher and Stone, 1986; Fry, 1986). Although polysaccharides are the principal constituents of the wall, structural proteins, including glycine-rich proteins, threonine-rich glycoproteins, and hydroxy-

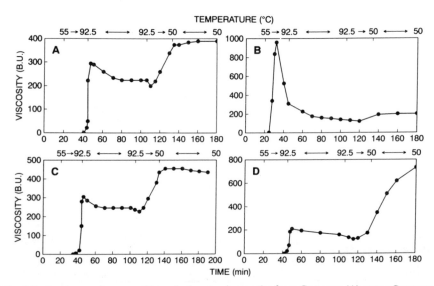

Fig. 6. Brabender amylograms of large barley starch granules from Compana (A), waxy Compana (B), Glacier (C), and high-amylose Glacier (D). (Reprinted, by permission, from Goering and DeHaas, 1974)

proline-rich glycoproteins, may form a second fibrillar network within the matrix phase (Cassab and Varner, 1988; Kieliszewski et al, 1990). Matrix-phase polysaccharides generally have extended conformations but do not aggregate into microfibrils because substituents on the polysaccharide back-bone or shape irregularities in the chain prevent ordered and stable molecular packing into a fibrillar form. During the deposition of secondary cell wall layers, the wall matrix of certain tissues may become encrusted with lignin, which is attached to matrix polysaccharides through covalent linkages (Iiyama et al, 1990).

The compositions of walls from selected tissues of barley grain are shown in Table 10, where it is clear that the major constituents are arabinoxylans and $(1\rightarrow3),(1\rightarrow4)$-$\beta$-glucans. In the starchy endosperm of mature barley grain, the matrix-phase arabinoxylans and $(1\rightarrow3),(1\rightarrow4)$-$\beta$-glucans represent up to 95% by weight of the walls (Table 10). The fibrillar, cellulosic phase thus constitutes a very small proportion of these unlignified walls, which reflects the requirement for rapid disintegration of the walls during endosperm mobilization in germinating grain. In contrast, the husk and other outer layers of barley grain consist of cell wall remnants in which the cellulose, silica, and lignin contents are high; heteroxylans are also present, but $(1\rightarrow3),(1\rightarrow4)$-$\beta$-glucan levels are low (Fincher and Stone, 1986; Henry, 1987a). Certain layers are also cutinized. The outer layers of the grain therefore provide physical support for the embryo and endosperm, can afford limited protection for the grain reserves against insect or microbial penetration, and remain largely intact during germination as a result of the refractory nature of their cellulose and lignin constituents. Walls of vegetative tissues of young barley seedlings have approximately 60% cellulose and may contain some lignin (Sakurai and Masuda, 1978; Kokubo et al, 1989), also reflecting the requirement of the walls to lend a higher degree of structural support to these tissues than is necessary in the starchy endosperm of the grain. Possible secondary roles

TABLE 10
Composition of Cell Walls from Barley

Tissue	Neutral Monosaccharide Composition of Total Polysaccharides, %					Pro-tein (%)	Phenolic Acids (%)	Major Polysaccharide Components[a]	References
	Ara	Xyl	Glx	Man	Gal				
Aleurone (mature grain)	24	47	26	2	2	16	1.2	71% Arabinoxylan 26% $(1\rightarrow3,1\rightarrow4)$-$\beta$-Glucan 2% Cellulose 2% Glucomannan 1% $(1\rightarrow3)$-β-Glucan	Bacic and Stone (1981a,b)
Starchy endosperm (mature grain)	11	11	75	3	0	5	0.05	75% $(1\rightarrow3,1\rightarrow4)$-$\beta$-Glucan 20% Arabinoxylan 2% Cellulose 2% Glucomannan	Fincher (1975, 1976); Ballance and Manners (1978)

[a]Values for polysaccharide components are estimated from compositional analyses presented in the references cited.

for wall polysaccharides include the potential, through their water-binding or gelation capacity, to help prevent desiccation of developing tissues under conditions of mild moisture stress (Fincher and Stone, 1986) or to provide a degree of cold-hardiness by interfering with ice crystal growth (Kindel et al, 1989).

$(1{\rightarrow}3),(1{\rightarrow}4)$-$\beta$-Glucans

STRUCTURE

The $(1{\rightarrow}3),(1{\rightarrow}4)$-$\beta$-glucans from barley grain consist of linear chains of β-glucosyl residues polymerized through both $(1{\rightarrow}3)$ and $(1{\rightarrow}4)$ linkages. It is not possible to assign a single structure to the barley $(1{\rightarrow}3),(1{\rightarrow}4)$-$\beta$-glucans because they are comprised of a family of polysaccharides that is heterogenous with respect to size, solubility, and molecular structure (Bacic and Stone, 1981b; Woodward and Fincher, 1983; Woodward et al, 1983a, 1988; Edney et al, 1991). Nevertheless, the fine structures of certain barley $(1{\rightarrow}3),(1{\rightarrow}4)$-$\beta$-glucan fractions, namely those extracted from barley flour or from endosperm cell wall preparations with water at 40 and 65°C, have been examined in considerable detail. Other fractions can be extracted at higher temperatures (Fleming and Kawakami, 1977), with alkali (Preece and MacKenzie, 1952; Preece and Hobkirk, 1953; Palmer and MacKenzie, 1986), or with chaotropic agents (Fincher, 1975).

The physical and chemical properties of one subpopulation of the $(1{\rightarrow}3,1{\rightarrow}4)$-$\beta$-glucan family, purified from 40°C water-soluble extracts of ethanol-inactivated barley flour by precipitation with 30% saturated ammonium sulfate, have been defined (Staudte et al, 1983; Woodward et al, 1983a,b). This fraction consists of $(1{\rightarrow}3),(1{\rightarrow}4)$-$\beta$-glucans with a degree of polymerization of up to 1,400 glucosyl residues and containing, on average, approximately 70% $(1{\rightarrow}4)$-linked β-glucosyl residues and 30% $(1{\rightarrow}3)$-linked residues (Table 11) (Woodward et al, 1983b). Traces of arabinose and xylose are present, together with approximately 1% protein (Woodward et al, 1983a), part of which may be covalently associated with the polysaccharide (Forrest, 1977). Along the polysaccharide chain, blocks of two or three contiguous $(1{\rightarrow}4)$-linked β-glucosyl residues are separated by single $(1{\rightarrow}3)$ linkages (Parrish et al, 1960; Woodward et al, 1983a), as shown below.

G3G4G4G4G3G4G4G3G4G4G3G4G4G4G3G4G4G3G4G4G3G4G4G3G—red

In this diagram, β-glucosyl residues are represented as G, $(1{\rightarrow}3)$- and $(1{\rightarrow}4)$-linkage positions are shown by *3* or *4*, *red* denotes the reducing end of the polysaccharide chain, and cellotriosyl and cellotetraosyl residues are bracketed. These structural features account for nearly 90% by weight of the polysaccharide (Table 11) (Woodward et al, 1983a) and indicate that the $(1{\rightarrow}4)$ and $(1{\rightarrow}3)$ linkages are not arranged at random. If this were so, one would expect significant levels of adjacent $(1{\rightarrow}3)$ linkages to be found. However, blocks of two or more adjacent $(1{\rightarrow}3)$ linkages are absent or constitute less than 0.2% (w/w) of this $(1{\rightarrow}3),(1{\rightarrow}4)$-$\beta$-glucan fraction (Luchsinger et al, 1965; Dais and Perlin, 1982; Woodward et al, 1983a) and could not be detected in total $(1{\rightarrow}3),(1{\rightarrow}4)$-

β-glucan fractions extracted from barley flour with perchloric acid (Edney et al, 1991). Other reports of much higher levels of adjacent (1→3) linkages in similar barley (1→3),(1→4)-β-glucan fractions (Fleming and Manners, 1966; Igarashi and Sakurai, 1966; Fleming and Kawakami, 1977) have been questioned on the grounds that incomplete acid hydrolysis during Smith degradation might lead to errors in the estimation of adjacent (1→3) linkages (Krusius and Finne, 1981; Woodward et al, 1983a). The question of contiguous (1→3) β-linkages in barley (1→3),(1→4)-β-glucans is of considerable importance in ascribing a functional role to the (1→3)-β-glucan endohydrolases that are found at high levels in the germinated grain. The (1→3)-β-glucanases cannot hydrolyze the single (1→3) β-linkages in (1→3),(1→4)-β-glucans but would be expected to hydrolyze a block of adjacent (1→3) linkages in the polysaccharides (Bathgate et al, 1974), should these be present, and thereby to release (1→3),(1→4)-β-glucan fragments from the cell wall. Although it remains a real possibility that adjacent (1→3)-β-glucosyl linkages exist in (1→3),(1→4)-β-glucans from other cereals (Moore and Stone, 1972; Kato and Nevins, 1986) or in other cell wall fractions from barley, there is as yet no compelling evidence to support their existence in barley (1→3),(1→4)-β-glucans.

At a higher organizational level, more than 90% of the 40°C water-soluble barley (1→3),(1→4)-β-glucan can be viewed as a copolymer of cellotriosyl and cellotetraosyl units linked by single (1→3) β-linkages (see diagram above). By treating the polymer as a two-state Markov chain and analyzing penultimate oligosaccharides (that is, oligosaccharides of DP 6–8, containing two adjacent units) released by the action of a specific (1→3),(1→4)-β-glucan endohydrolase (EC 3.2.1.73; Woodward and Fincher, 1982), the relative abundance of two

TABLE 11
Composition and Structure of Water-Soluble (1→3),(1→4)-β-Glucans from Barley Flour

Property	40°C-Soluble Fraction	65°C-Soluble Fraction
Monosaccharide composition, % w/w		
Glucose	98.3	100
Arabinose	1.1	0
Xylose	0.6	0
Linkage positions (% mol/mol)		
(1→3)-β-glucosyl	28	31
(1→4)-β-glucosyl	72	69
Protein (%N × 6.25)	1.2	2.6
Uronic acid, % w/w	0.1	3.3
Length of block of adjacent (1→4) linkages, % w/w		
1	4	4
2	56	60
3	32	30
4	5	5
5	1	1
6–7	<1	0
9 (precipitated material)[a]	7.4	7.0

[a]This material is precipitated during hydrolysis and represents a range of 6–14 adjacent (1→4) linkages. The values are not included in calculations of the lengths of blocks that remain in solution after hydrolysis with the (1→3),(1→4)-β-glucan by the (1→3),(1→4)-β-glucanase.

adjacent cellotriosyl, two adjacent cellotetraosyl, and adjacent cellotriosyl-cellotetraosyl residues could be estimated (Staudte et al, 1983). The Mathematical analysis of the results showed that the cellotriosyl and cellotetraosyl residues are arranged in an essentially independent or random fashion (Staudte et al, 1983), in contrast to the nonrandom arrangement of individual (1→3) and (1→4) β-linkages. Thus, these barley (1→3),(1→4)-β-glucans contain no strictly repeating linkage sequences.

Approximately 10% by weight of the 40°C water-soluble (1→3),(1→4)-β-glucan consists of longer blocks of up to 14 adjacent (1→4)-β-glucosyl residues (Table 11) (Luchsinger et al, 1965; Woodward et al, 1983a; Edney et al, 1991). The longer of these blocks are cellulosic in nature and therefore precipitate from solution when they are enzymatically excised from the soluble (1→3),(1→4)-β-glucan fraction with (1→3),(1→4)-β-glucan endohydrolases (Woodward et al, 1983a). The distribution of the longer blocks of adjacent (1→4) linkages along the polysaccharide chain has not been defined, but their importance as a determinant of molecular shape, and therefore of (1→3),(1→4)-β-glucan function, was clearly indicated in computer-assisted, theoretical conformational analyses that showed the blocks to be necessary to maintain the observed conformation of the polysaccharide (Buliga et al, 1986). The computer analysis also confirmed that adjacent (1→3) linkages do not exist in this (1→3),(1→4)-β-glucan fraction (Buliga et al, 1986).

Another barley (1→3),(1→4)-β-glucan preparation that has been subjected to detailed examination is the population extracted from barley flour with water in the temperature range of 40–65°C (Woodward et al, 1988). This fraction also contains about 70% (1→4) linkages and 30% (1→3) linkages (Table 11), but marginally fewer blocks of four or more adjacent (1→4) linkages are detected (Woodward et al, 1988). Similarly, "total" (1→3),(1→4)-β-glucan preparations extracted from barley flours with perchloric acid show a comparable overall ratio of (1→4) and (1→3) linkages but exhibit clear varietal differences in lengths of the blocks of adjacent (1→4) linkages (Edney et al, 1991).

SOLUTION BEHAVIOR

Many of the problems associated with barley (1→3),(1→4)-β-glucans in the stockfeed and malting and brewing industries are associated with the propensity of the polysaccharide to form aqueous solutions of high viscosity (Luchsinger, 1967; Forrest and Wainwright, 1977b; Woodward and Fincher, 1983; Bamforth, 1985). The precise definition of the chemical and physical properties of (1→3),(1→4)-β-glucans has provided an explanation for their behavior in solution and thereby offers an explanation for certain problems encountered in the commercial utilization of barley.

Published molecular weight values for water-soluble barley (1→3),(1→4)-β-glucans range from 20,000 to 40,000,000 (Fincher and Stone, 1986), but the values obtained depend on the method used for the estimation. Gel filtration chromatography generally leads to the overestimation of molecular weight of these asymmetrical polysaccharides. The more reliable average molecular weight values of 150,000–300,000, determined by sedimentation equilibrium ultracentrifugation or sedimentation velocity (Djurtoft and Rasmussen, 1955; Igarashi and Sakurai, 1965; Woodward et al, 1983b), correspond to degrees of polymerization of about 900–1,800. Physicochemical methods have been used to define, in some detail, the physical properties of the 40 and 65°C water-soluble (1→3),(1→4)-β-glucans from barley (Woodward et al, 1983b, 1988); some of these properties are shown in Table 12. The average molecular weight values indicate that the DPs of the (1→3),(1→4)-β-glucans are approximately 1,800 and 900 for the 40 and 65°C water-soluble fractions, respectively. Ballance and Manners (1978) also observed that the less-soluble fractions from isolated walls of the starchy endosperm had a lower degree of polymerization, although the absolute values they obtained by end-group analysis were significantly lower than those reported by Woodward et al (1983b, 1988).

The lower molecular weight of the 65°C fraction compared with the 40°C fraction is reflected in lower values for intrinsic viscosity and axial ratio (Table 12). In both cases the axial ratios, which give a measure of the length of the molecule in relation to its width, indicate that the polysaccharides are extremely asymmetrical, and further analyses of the data confirmed that the molecules assume the conformation of prolate ellipsoids (Woodward et al, 1983b). Given that the (1→3),(1→4)-β-glucans are not highly hydrated molecules, it can be concluded that the high intrinsic viscosities of the fractions (Table 12) are attributable mainly to their molecular asymmetry, in combination with their high molecular weight (Woodward et al, 1983b). This asymmetry was subsequently confirmed by theoretical conformation analysis (Buliga et al, 1986), and it has been concluded that, in aqueous media, the polysaccharide adopts an extended wormlike conformation that is sufficiently flexible to be stretched into a more linear form or compressed into an irregular kinked form (Woodward et al, 1983b; Buliga et al, 1986).

The fine structural features of the barley (1→3),(1→4)-β-glucans are of fundamental importance in explaining this conformation and the behavior of the polysaccharides in solution. Under normal conditions, one might expect a very long polysaccharide chain to be insoluble in water as a result of intermolecular aggregation, particularly where "cellulosic" (1→4)-glucosyl residues predominate. However, the apparently random distribution of the cellotriosyl and cellotetraosyl residues in the chain, together with the presence of 10% by weight of longer blocks of adjacent (1→4) linkages of variable length, results in the irregular spacing of the (1→3) linkages in the molecule (Staudte et al, 1983; Woodward et al, 1983a). Because a (1→3) linkage in a region of adjacent (1→4) linkages interrupts the extended, ribbonlike shape of the "cellulosic" (1→4)-β-glucosyl domains, and because these interruptions by the more flexible (1→3) linkages (Sundaralingam, 1968) lead to molecular kinks (Buliga et al, 1986) that are spaced at irregular intervals, the poly-

TABLE 12
Physical Properties of Water-Soluble Barley (1→3),(1→4)-β-Glucan

Property	40°C-Soluble Fraction	65°C-Soluble Fraction
Intrinsic viscosity (η, dl·g^{-1})	6.90	4.04
Degree of hydration	0.42	0.5
Weight average molecular weight	290,000	150,000
Axial ratio (a/b)	100	70

saccharide has an irregular shape overall, which reduces its tendency to pack into stable, regular molecular aggregates. The polysaccharides, therefore, remain relatively soluble in water, although their solubility can be reduced at low temperatures, particularly in the presence of ethanol. Solubility can also be reduced by artificially inducing molecular alignment in certain industrial centrifuges (Letters, 1977), and cast films of barley (1→3),(1→4)-β-glucans examined by X-ray analysis show diffraction patterns indicative of an ordered molecular aggregate (Tvaroska et al, 1983). Similarly, it has been proposed that the lower solubility of the 65°C (1→3),(1→4)-β-glucan fraction from barley flour, which in fact has a lower molecular weight than the 40°C water-soluble fraction but has fewer long blocks of adjacent (1→4) linkages, is determined not so much by the degree of polymerization or overall asymmetrical conformation, but rather by small differences in fine structure that permit the chains to align into more stable molecular aggregates (Woodward et al, 1988).

ORGANIZATION OF (1→3),(1→4)-β-GLUCAN IN CELL WALLS

Although the chemical and physical properties of some barley (1→3),(1→4)-β-glucan fractions have been described in detail, there is no definitive information on the molecular organization of the polysaccharide in cell walls, on the possible interactions between (1→3),(1→4)-β-glucans and other matrix phase polysaccharides, or on interactions with cellulosic microfibrils. These uncertainties apply to plant cell wall organization in general and have led to the proposal of several complex models involving both covalent and noncovalent cross-linking of constituent wall polymers (Fincher and Stone, 1986; Fry, 1986). Earlier views on the intermolecular associations involving (1→3),(1→4)-β-glucans in barley cell walls were influenced by observations that polysaccharides of plant cell wall origin can be induced to gel in vitro (Rees, 1972; Rees and Welsh, 1977; Fincher and Stone, 1986). In this model, it was suggested that noncovalent interactions between the "cellulosic" regions of the (1→3),(1→4)-β-glucan, where up to 14 adjacent (1→4)-β-glucosyl residues are clustered, could be stabilized by intermolecular hydrogen bonding to form "junction zones" over limited regions of the chains in a manner typical of molecular interactions in other polysaccharide gels (Fincher and Stone, 1986). Such a gellike matrix would satisfy the functional requirements for a wall in providing structural support for the cell, but it would also allow for apoplastic diffusion of water, sucrose, amino acids, ions, hormones, and other small molecules through the solvent-filled interstices of the gel. In addition, altered (1→3),(1→4)-β-glucan properties, particularly with respect to the number and length of the blocks of adjacent (1→4) linkages, would permit changes in viscoelastic properties of the gel, leading to an altered balance between rigidity and flexibility or an altered porosity that would be appropriate for the functional requirements of specific tissues at different stages of growth or development (Woodward et al, 1983a; Fincher and Stone, 1986). On this basis, it was suggested that the occurrence of longer blocks of (1→4) linkages, in greater abundance, might explain the relatively tight binding in the cell wall of the 65°C water-soluble (1→3),(1→4)-β-glucan in contrast to that of the 40°C water-soluble fraction (Woodward et al, 1983a). As mentioned earlier, however, this suggestion was not borne out by analyses of the fine structure of the 65°C water-soluble fraction, which contained fewer and slightly shorter blocks of adjacent (1→4) linkages (Woodward et al, 1988). This in itself does not preclude the possibility that noncovalent cross-linking of (1→3),(1→4)-β-glucans forms a gellike matrix in the wall, and the potential for junction zone formation between the blocks of (1→4) linkages in (1→3),(1→4)-β-glucans and cellulose microfibrils or unsubstituted regions of arabinoxylans has not yet been investigated.

Although the molecular organization of (1→3),(1→4)-β-glucans in barley cell walls remains undefined, some information suggests that the distribution of the polysaccharide across cell walls may not always be uniform. Thus, in the walls of barley aleurone cells, an inner, relatively thin layer can be clearly distinguished from a thicker, outer layer (Taiz and Jones, 1973; Bacic and Stone, 1981a), and there is increasing evidence that (1→3),(1→4)-β-glucans are enriched in the inner wall layer (Wood et al, 1983; Stone, 1984, 1985; Fincher, 1989).

EFFECTS ON END-USE QUALITY

Animal Nutrition. In general, vertebrates are unable to synthesize enzymes capable of hydrolyzing plant cell wall polysaccharides, such as barley (1→3),(1→4)-β-glucans or arabinoxylans, but herbivorous animals have evolved specialized compartments in their alimentary tract in which commensal microflora and microfauna can degrade the polysaccharides to simple carbohydrates and organic acids that, in turn, can be utilized by the host animal as an energy source (Bhatty, 1993). Although humans and other monogastric animals such as pigs and poultry have no such specialized regions in their alimentary tract, degradation and fermentation of cell wall polysaccharides does take place to some extent, by virtue of the action of microorganisms in the hindgut (Argenzio and Stevens, 1984).

Barley is extensively used in stockfeed formulations for pigs and poultry but is less digestible and yields less energy when fed to poultry than when fed to pigs or ruminants (Petersen, 1972). Further, this lowered nutritive value of poultry diets high in barley is correlated with sticky feces that adhere to the cages, carcasses, and eggs and thereby make hygienic handling of the products difficult (Burnett, 1966). Both problems are directly related to the (1→3),(1→4)-β-glucan content of the diet (Burnett, 1966). It has been suggested that the polysaccharide impairs digestion through its effect on viscosity of the gut contents; the high viscosity limits the diffusion and mixing not only of degradative enzymes, such as peptidases and α-amylases, but also of degradation products (Burnett, 1966; White et al, 1983). This results in lower digestibility and slower growth rates of the chickens. In the case of the sticky feces, it should be noted that (1→3),(1→4)-β-glucan is almost completely degraded by microbial action in the cecum of the chicken and that the high viscosity and high water-holding capacity of the feces are therefore not afforded by (1→3),(1→4)-β-glucan itself, but rather by the cecal microorganisms, together with associated mucopolysaccharides and other microbial products (Fincher and Stone, 1986). The undesirable characteristics of barley (1→3),(1→4)-β-glucans in diets for chickens can be partly overcome by the addition of hydrolytic enzymes (Gohl et al, 1978; Edney et al, 1989) or by pretreatment of the grain under conditions that induce the production of endogenous enzymes normally released during germination (Willingham et al, 1959; Adams and Naber, 1969).

In contrast to their undesirable effects in stockfeeds, barley $(1{\rightarrow}3),(1{\rightarrow}4)$-$\beta$-glucans have been recognized as important contributors to the "dietary fiber" component in human nutrition, a component that is considered to have salutary effects on the mobility of digesta through the alimentary tract (Fincher and Stone, 1986). Barley $(1{\rightarrow}3),(1{\rightarrow}4)$-$\beta$-glucans have also been implicated in other beneficial effects on blood glucose, blood cholesterol, hormone responses, colonic cancer, and micronutrient availability (Klopfenstein, 1988; Newman et al, 1989; Bengtsson et al, 1990; Bhatty, 1993), and these effects may ultimately lead to an expanding demand for barley grain in human diets (Petersen and Munck, 1993). The dietary potential of $(1{\rightarrow}3),(1{\rightarrow}4)$-$\beta$-glucans is discussed in detail in Chapters 8 and 10 of this monograph (Bhatty, 1993; Petersen and Munck, 1993).

Malting and Brewing. The $(1{\rightarrow}3),(1{\rightarrow}4)$-$\beta$-glucans extracted from malted barley or from ungerminated grain adjuncts such as barley, wheat, or rice are generally regarded as undesirable in the malting and brewing processes (Woodward and Fincher, 1983; Bamforth, 1985). First, high levels of $(1{\rightarrow}3),(1{\rightarrow}4)$-$\beta$-glucan in a malt sample indicate incomplete cell wall degradation and consequently diminished mobilization of starch and storage proteins. These result in lower malt extract values for the grain and hence in lower levels of available nutrients for fermentative growth by yeast during brewing (Bamforth and Barclay, 1993).

A second undesirable property of the $(1{\rightarrow}3),(1{\rightarrow}4)$-$\beta$-glucans is related to their tendency to form highly viscous aqueous solutions. A low degree of depolymerization of high-molecular-weight $(1{\rightarrow}3),(1{\rightarrow}4)$-$\beta$-glucans during malting, or the addition of cereal grain adjuncts containing undegraded $(1{\rightarrow}3),(1{\rightarrow}4)$-$\beta$-glucan with little or no $(1{\rightarrow}3),(1{\rightarrow}4)$-$\beta$-glucanase, can lead to viscous initial grain extracts. The viscosity, which is attributed to the high molecular weight and extreme asymmetry of the polysaccharides, can lead to filtration difficulties at various points in the brewing process (Bamforth and Barclay, 1993). Because the rate of beer filtration often limits the speed and hence the volume of production (Bathgate, 1983), the decreased rate of filtration and increased time required for filter maintenance are major problems in the brewery.

In a phenomenon also related to their molecular size and shape, undegraded or partially degraded $(1{\rightarrow}3),(1{\rightarrow}4)$-$\beta$-glucans in beer may precipitate at elevated ethanol concentrations, at low temperatures, or after treatment with certain industrial centrifuges, thus contributing to haze formation or to precipitates in the final product (Igarashi and Amaha, 1969; Letters, 1977; Woodward and Fincher, 1983; Bamforth, 1985; Yamashita et al, 1989). The $(1{\rightarrow}3),(1{\rightarrow}4)$-$\beta$-glucans, in association with polyphenolic compounds, proteins, and other polysaccharides, can be components of chill hazes, which form during beer storage (Bamforth, 1985). Thus, undegraded $(1{\rightarrow}3),(1{\rightarrow}4)$-$\beta$-glucans can have a detrimental effect on the stability of beer during storage.

Balanced against these problems are the observations that $(1{\rightarrow}3),(1{\rightarrow}4)$-$\beta$-glucans carried through the brewing process into the final beer can contribute positively to palate body, again through viscosity effects, and to foam stability (Luchsinger, 1967; Forrest and Wainwright, 1977b; Bamforth, 1985). Overall, however, undegraded $(1\rightarrow3),(1\rightarrow4)$-$\beta$-glucans from malt or from ungerminated cereal adjuncts are considered troublesome components in the brewing process. The problems caused by these $(1\rightarrow3),(1\rightarrow4)$-$\beta$-glucans have been tackled through the selection of grain varieties that produce well-modified malts containing high levels of $(1\rightarrow3),(1\rightarrow4)$-$\beta$-glucan endohydrolases, through the choice of kilning and mashing protocols that maximize the retention and activity of the same endogenous barley enzymes (Loi et al, 1987), by the careful estimation of permissible levels of adjuncts (Bourne and Pierce, 1970), or by the addition of exogenous β-glucan hydrolases.

LEVELS IN THE GRAIN

As a direct result of the recognition that $(1\rightarrow3),(1\rightarrow4)$-$\beta$-glucans adversely affect certain processes and quality parameters in the malting and brewing industries, together with their potential to decrease the growth rate of chickens fed diets rich in ungerminated barley grain or its products, very considerable efforts have been directed to the quantitation of $(1\rightarrow3),(1\rightarrow4)$-$\beta$-glucan levels in both feed and malting barley samples and in lines under development in barley breeding programs. The maintenance of low or manageable levels of the polysaccharide in ungerminated barleys has become a crucial selection criterion in breeding programs and has led to many analyses of the $(1\rightarrow3),(1\rightarrow4)$-$\beta$-glucan content of different barley varieties grown under various environmental conditions. Selected values are compared in Table 13. A number of methods have been used to estimate $(1\rightarrow3),(1\rightarrow4)$-$\beta$-glucan content. The most specific methods are based on the hydrolysis of the polysaccharide with purified $(1\rightarrow3),(1\rightarrow4)$-$\beta$-glucan endohydrolases (EC 3.2.1.73) that can hydrolyze only $(1\rightarrow3),(1\rightarrow4)$-$\beta$-glucans and have no activity on $(1\rightarrow3)$-β-glucan or $(1\rightarrow4)$-β-glucan (Anderson et al, 1978). The oligosaccharides released from the $(1\rightarrow3),(1\rightarrow4)$-$\beta$-glucan by enzymatic hydrolysis are extracted and quantitated

TABLE 13
Selected Estimates of Total $(1\rightarrow3),(1\rightarrow4)$-$\beta$-Glucan Contents in Barley Grain

Varieties and Harvest Location	Range (%, w/w)[a]	References
Australian and other malting varieties	3.64–6.44 (5.20)	Anderson et al, 1978
	4.03–5.26 (4.54)	Henry, 1985a
	3.80–4.81 (4.43)	McCleary and Glennie-Holmes, 1985
British malting varieties	6.13–10.70 (7.65)	Bamforth and Martin, 1981
	3.07–4.56 (3.75)	Gill et al, 1982
	3.33–4.03	Alexander and Fish, 1984
	3.03–5.04 (4.03)	Bourne and Wheeler, 1984
Canadian and western U.S. varieties	3.05–5.95 (4.40)	Edney et al, 1991
Finnish two-rowed varieties	3.5–5.3 (4.47)	Lehtonen and Aikasalo, 1987
Finnish six-rowed varieties	2.8–5.6 (4.4)	Lehtonen and Aikasalo, 1987
North American malting varieties	4.6–8.2 (6.5)	Prentice et al, 1980
North American feed varieties	5.1–7.2 (6.1)	Prentice et al, 1980
Scandinavian malting and other varieties	2.0–6.36 (4.5)	Aastrup, 1979a
	3.0–5.6 (4.4)	Åman and Graham, 1987

[a] Average in parentheses.

(Anderson et al, 1978; McCleary and Glennie-Holmes, 1985; Henry and Blakeney, 1986) using procedures that have been summarized and evaluated by Henry and Blakeney (1986) and Henry (1988a). To achieve accurate and reproducible results, the barley flour must be ground to a sufficiently small particle size and endogenous enzymes must be inactivated. Accessibility problems, in which the enzyme cannot penetrate the particles to hydrolyze the $(1\rightarrow3),(1\rightarrow4)$-$\beta$-glucan, might be anticipated in heavily lignified tissue such as the husk and other outer layers of the grain.

Another procedure for the estimation of $(1\rightarrow3),(1\rightarrow4)$-$\beta$-glucans is based on the specificity of their reaction with the dyes Calcofluor white and Congo red (Wood et al, 1983). The dyes can be used histochemically to show the location of $(1\rightarrow3),(1\rightarrow4)$-$\beta$-glucans in grain or malt sections (Aastrup and Erdal, 1980; Wood et al, 1983; MacGregor et al, 1989) or to detect $(1\rightarrow3),(1\rightarrow4)$-$\beta$-glucan in grain extracts (Wood et al, 1983). The formation of the Calcofluor-$(1\rightarrow3),(1\rightarrow4)$-$\beta$-glucan complex has been further developed to quantitate levels of the polysaccharide in barley grain samples (Jensen and Aastrup, 1981; Jørgensen and Aastrup, 1988) and in wort and beer (Manzanares et al, 1991). Near-infrared reflectance spectroscopy has been used to obtain good empirical correlations with water-soluble $(1\rightarrow3),(1\rightarrow4)$-$\beta$-glucan content and, subject to reliable calibration of the equipment, might prove useful in the rapid quantitation of $(1\rightarrow3),(1\rightarrow4)$-$\beta$-glucan levels in large numbers of barley samples (Allison et al, 1978). However, although near-infrared reflectance is used to determine moisture content and protein levels in grain, it has not found acceptance for routine estimation of $(1\rightarrow3),(1\rightarrow4)$-$\beta$-glucan content.

Total $(1\rightarrow3),(1\rightarrow4)$-$\beta$-glucan contents of barley grain range from 2 to 11% by weight of the grain, but they usually fall between 4 and 7% (Table 13). Most is found in the endosperm (Henry, 1987b), where there may be a relationship between wall thickness and $(1\rightarrow3),(1\rightarrow4)$-$\beta$-glucan content of the grain (Aastrup, 1983). In contrast, $(1\rightarrow3),(1\rightarrow4)$-$\beta$-glucan levels in the outer, maternal layers of the grain are low (Henry, 1987a). Glucose released from $(1\rightarrow3),(1\rightarrow4)$-$\beta$-glucan of endosperm walls is ultimately used as an energy source during germination and makes a significant contribution to total grain glucose available for seedling growth (Morrall and Briggs, 1978).

Despite their relatively small contribution to the total weight of the grain (Table 13), it is clear from the preceding sections of this chapter that $(1\rightarrow3),(1\rightarrow4)$-$\beta$-glucans can have a disproportionate impact on the technology of barley utilization and on the nutritional value of the grain. The values shown in Table 13 are influenced by both genotypic and environmental factors and, although the relative contributions of these factors cannot be precisely quantitated, there is general agreement that the genetic background of the barley is more important than environmental conditions as a determinant of the final $(1\rightarrow3),(1\rightarrow4)$-$\beta$-glucan content of the grain (Gill et al, 1982; Molina-Cano and Conde, 1982; Morgan et al, 1983; Henry, 1986; Stuart et al, 1988). Feed and six-rowed barleys may have slightly lower $(1\rightarrow3),(1\rightarrow4)$-$\beta$-glucan levels than malting and other two-rowed varieties (Table 13) (Prentice et al, 1980; Lehtonen and Aikasalo, 1987). Genetic analysis using random inbred lines produced by double haploids and single-seed descent suggests that $(1\rightarrow3),(1\rightarrow4)$-$\beta$-glucan content is controlled by a simple additive genetic system of three to five effective factors (Powell et al, 1989). Similarly, inheritance analysis using crosses with naturally occurring and mutant genotypes suggested that two or three dominant genes are responsible for $(1{\rightarrow}3),(1{\rightarrow}4)$-$\beta$-glucan levels (Greenberg, 1977), and potentially useful mutants have been described (Aastrup, 1983; Molina-Cano et al, 1989). However, our understanding of the development of $(1{\rightarrow}3),(1{\rightarrow}4)$-$\beta$-glucans in maturing grain is limited by the absence of information on the enzymatic products of these genetic factors. The $(1{\rightarrow}3),(1{\rightarrow}4)$-$\beta$-glucan synthases responsible for synthesis of the polysaccharides have not been purified or characterized. This represents a major gap in our knowledge of barley grain development and of the regulation of $(1{\rightarrow}3),(1{\rightarrow}4)$-$\beta$-glucan deposition. Recent reports in which β-glucan synthases from cotton and Italian ryegrass have been isolated and partially characterized (Delmer et al, 1991; Meikle et al, 1991) offer some encouragement for the study of barley $(1{\rightarrow}3),(1{\rightarrow}4)$-$\beta$-glucan synthases. Once the enzymes have been purified, it will be possible to isolate and characterize the corresponding genes and to devise strategies for the genetic manipulation of $(1{\rightarrow}3),(1{\rightarrow}4)$-$\beta$-glucan content using developing methods in gene technology.

The major environmental factor that influences $(1{\rightarrow}3),(1{\rightarrow}4)$-$\beta$-glucan levels appears to be the availability of water during grain maturation. Dry conditions before harvest result in high $(1{\rightarrow}3),(1{\rightarrow}4)$-$\beta$-glucan levels (Bendelow, 1975; Anderson et al, 1978), either because final grain-filling is adversely affected through the impairment of starch and protein deposition or because $(1{\rightarrow}3),(1{\rightarrow}4)$-$\beta$-glucan synthesis per se is enhanced in dry conditions. On the other hand, moist conditions cause a decrease in $(1{\rightarrow}3),(1{\rightarrow}4)$-$\beta$-glucan levels (Bendelow, 1975; Aastrup 1979b; Coles, 1979; Hesselman and Thomke, 1982; Stuart et al, 1988; Åman et al, 1989). In addition, one should remember that the $(1{\rightarrow}3),(1{\rightarrow}4)$-$\beta$-glucans of barley grain are members of a family of polysaccharides (Bathgate and Dalgliesh, 1975) and that their molecular size, fine structure, and solubility may also vary with the variety, the stage of kernel development, and the environmental conditions (Aastrup, 1979b; Smith et al, 1987; Åman et al, 1989).

Despite the widespread use of $(1{\rightarrow}3),(1{\rightarrow}4)$-$\beta$-glucan assays in barley breeding programs, $(1{\rightarrow}3),(1{\rightarrow}4)$-$\beta$-glucan levels in ungerminated barley are, in isolation, poor indicators of malting performance (Henry, 1988b; Stuart et al, 1988) (Table 14). Ultimately the most important direct indicator or determinant of malting performance, as measured by malt extract values, is the $(1{\rightarrow}3),(1{\rightarrow}4)$-$\beta$-glucan content of malt (Aastrup and Erdal, 1980; Bourne et al, 1982; Henry, 1988b; Stuart et al, 1988). Malt $(1{\rightarrow}3),(1{\rightarrow}4)$-$\beta$-glucan levels are, in turn,

TABLE 14
Linear Correlations (r) Between Barley Quality Parameters[a]

	Total β-Glucan	Malt β-Glucan	Percent Loss β-Glucan	β-Glucanase	Malt Extract
Total β-glucan	1.00	0.18	0.22	0.27	0.15
Malt β-glucan	...	1.00	−0.92[b]	−0.61	−0.74[b]
Percent loss β-glucan	...	...	1.00	0.72[b]	0.81[b]
β-Glucanase	...	...	...	1.00	0.85[b]
Malt extract	...	...	...	...	1.00

[a] Data from Stuart et al (1988).
[b] Significant to $P < 0.01$.

determined by a combination of initial levels in ungerminated grain and the capacity of the grain to produce (1→3),(1→4)-β-glucanases during the malting process (Stuart et al, 1988) (Table 14). Thus, the Australian malting variety Grimmett, which was bred for the higher rainfall areas of Queensland, has a high (1→3),(1→4)-β-glucan content, but through the development of high (1→3),(1→4)-β-glucanase levels during malting of Queensland-grown samples, a high proportion of the (1→3),(1→4)-β-glucan is degraded, low residual (1→3),(1→4)-β-glucan levels are detected in malt, and malt extract values are relatively high (Stuart et al, 1988). However, when Grimmett is grown in lower rainfall areas, (1→3),(1→4)-β-glucanase development is relatively slow, and malting performance is correspondingly poorer (Stuart et al, 1988).

In contrast to the considerable effort that has been directed to the breeding of barleys containing low (1→3),(1→4)-β-glucan levels, one might predict that increased consumption of barley in human diets as a result of its high dietary fiber content could lead to an increased demand in the future for barleys with high (1→3),(1→4)-β-glucan contents. An examination of the carbohydrate content of wild barley (*Hordeum spontaneum*) lines revealed (1→3),(1→4)-β-glucan contents ranging up to 13.2% (Henry and Brown, 1987). This may represent an important genetic resource for future barley breeding programs, since *H. spontaneum* is the progenitor of modern cultivated barleys and the two could be readily hybridized (Brown, 1983) to produce a high (1→3),(1→4)-β-glucan barley with acceptable agronomic characteristics.

Arabinoxylans

The other major noncellulosic polysaccharides of barley cell walls are the arabinoxylans. While these are particularly abundant in the walls of aleurone cells and in the starchy endosperm, they are also found in the husk (Aspinall and Ross, 1963) and presumably also in the wall remnants that make up the other maternal tissues surrounding the grain (Fincher and Stone, 1986). These polysaccharides consist predominantly of the pentoses arabinose and xylose and are therefore often referred to as pentosans. However, cereal arabinoxylans sometimes contain hexoses and hexuronic acids as minor constituents, and, if this is the case, they are more precisely referred to as heteroxylans (Fincher and Stone, 1986). In barley endosperm walls, the xylans contain very little, if any, hexuronic acid residues (Fincher, 1975; Bacic and Stone, 1981b), and we therefore refer to the polysaccharides there as arabinoxylans.

STRUCTURE
The arabinoxylans of barley walls, like the (1→3),(1→4)-β-glucans, consist of a family of polysaccharides in which individual members differ in molecular size, monosaccharide composition, structure, and solubility (Viëtor et al, 1992). Barley arabinoxylans generally have a (1→4)-β-xylopyranosyl backbone that carries single α-L-arabinofuranosyl residues, mostly through C(O)3 but also through C(O)2 of the xylosyl residues; some xylosyl residues can be doubly substituted (Fig. 7). Most arabinose is found as monomeric substituents, but a small proportion of oligomeric side-chains, consisting of two or more arabinosyl residues or an arabinosyl residue with a terminal xylosyl residue,

has been reported (Viëtor et al, 1992). Terminal galactosyl, glucosyl, and xylosyl residues can also be present but are usually quantitatively minor; glucurono-pyranosyl (and its 4-methyl ether) residues may constitute up to 4% by weight of the arabinoxylan from husk (Aspinall and Ferrier, 1957; Aspinall and Ross, 1963; Fincher, 1975; McNeil et al, 1975; Ballance and Manners, 1978; Bacic and Stone, 1981b; Ballance et al, 1986). Phenolic acids, principally ferulic acid but also *p*-coumaric acid, are covalently associated with arabinoxylans and constitute approximately 0.05% of walls in the starchy endosperm (Fincher, 1976; Viëtor et al, 1992) and 1.2% of aleurone walls (Bacic and Stone, 1981a). The insoluble, bound *p*-coumaric acid of barley grain is concentrated in the outer grain layers (Nordkvist et al, 1984), but it is not known whether this is always associated with heteroxylans. Ferulic acid residues are linked via ester linkages to C(O)5 atoms of arabinofuranosyl substituents (Gubler et al, 1985; Mueller-Harvey et al, 1986) (Fig. 8). In barley aleurone layers, arabin-oxylans appear to be distributed across both wall layers (Stone, 1985; Fincher, 1989), although autofluorescence attributed to ferulic acid appears to be more intense over the thin, inner cell wall layer (Gubler and Ashford, 1985). This implies that the degree of substitution of arabinoxylans with ferulic acid residues can vary, and that more highly feruloylated members of the polysaccharide family are concentrated in the inner layer of the aleurone wall. The functional significance of ferulic acid residues in barley arabinoxylans remains uncertain.

Barley arabinoxylan preparations vary widely with respect to the ratio of xylose to arabinose. In husk, ratios of approximately 9 are observed (Aspinall and Ferrier, 1957), whereas in arabinoxylans of the starchy endosperm or aleurone, ratios of 1–2.3 have been reported (Fincher, 1975; McNeil et al, 1975; Ballance and Manners, 1978; Bacic and Stone, 1981b; Ballance et al, 1986). Viëtor et al(1992) have fractionated the water-insoluble arabinoxylans from barley endosperm using ethanol precipitation and report xylose-arabinose ratios in the range of 0.8–3.4. Arabinoxylans extracted with water from barley

Region A

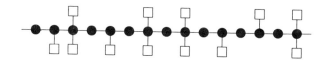

Region B

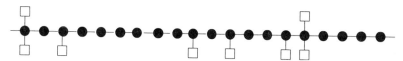

Fig. 7. Distribution patterns of arabinosyl residues along the backbone of barley arabinoxylans. Region A is more highly substituted than Region B, which is susceptible to hydrolysis by endoxylanases. ● = xylopyranosyl residues, □ = arabinofuranosyl residues. (Data from Viëtor, 1992, and Voragen et al, 1993)

aleurone walls are more highly substituted with arabinose (xylose-arabinose ratio of 1.4–1.5) than arabinoxylans that require alkali to render them soluble (xylose-arabinose ratio 2–4) (Bacic and Stone, 1981b), although in walls of the starchy endosperm, xylose-arabinose ratios are similar in arabinoxylans extracted with either water or alkali (Fincher, 1975; Ballance and Manners, 1978). Thus, while one would anticipate that a higher degree of arabinose substitution would increase the solubility of the xylan molecule (Perlin 1951a; Andrewartha et al, 1979), the observations outlined above on extracts from barley aleurone and starchy endosperm walls indicate that this is not always so and that other physical or chemical interactions affect the extractability of the arabinoxylans from the walls (Fincher and Stone, 1986). Similarly, no underlying patterns for the degree of arabinosylation of xylans from different tissues could be detected in a compilation of arabinoxylans from several cereal grains (Fincher and Stone, 1986). In some cases, arabinoxylans from outer lignified layers have relatively few arabinosyl substituents (Aspinall and Ferrier, 1957), but again this is not always observed (Fincher and Stone, 1986).

In addition to the importance of the degree of arabinosyl substitution, the distribution pattern of the arabinosyl residues along the xylan backbone has been identified as a significant determinant of arabinoxylan structure and properties (Ewald and Perlin, 1959; Goldschmid and Perlin, 1963; Ballance et al, 1986). Early work on the distribution of arabinosyl residues on arabin-oxylans from wheat endosperm walls indicates that the polysaccharides consist predominantly of highly substituted regions that are separated at intervals of approximately 20–25 xylosyl residues by domains containing two to five contiguous, unsubstituted xylosyl residues (Ewald and Perlin, 1959; Goldschmid and Perlin, 1963). More recent work on the water-insoluble arabinoxylan from barley endosperm, in which oligosaccharides released by

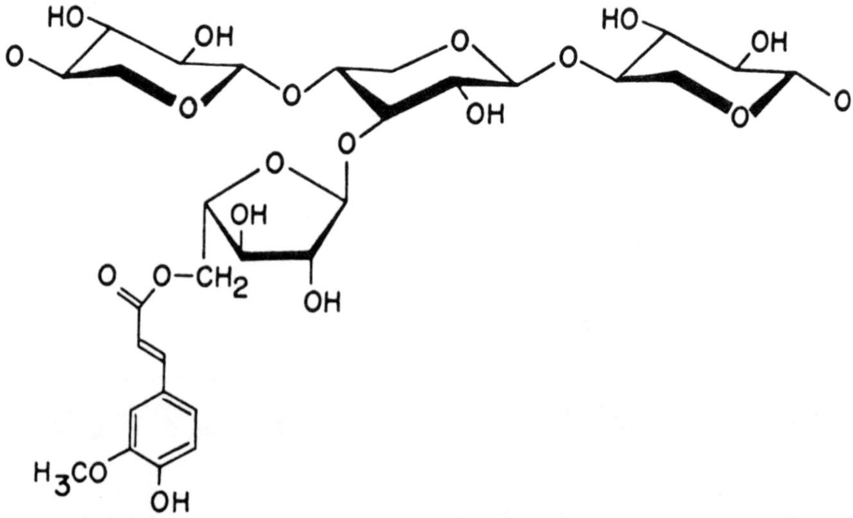

Fig. 8. Structure of part of the barley arabinoxylan chain, showing the substitution of the arabinosyl residue with a ferulic acid residue at C(O)5. (Reprinted, by permission, from Fincher and Stone, 1986)

specific enzymes have been characterized by methylation analysis, [1]H-nuclear magnetic resonance spectroscopy, and electrospray mass spectrometry, indicates that the distribution of arabinoxyl substituents along the xylan backbone is nonrandom (Viëtor, 1992; Viëtor et al, 1992; Voragen et al, 1993). Indeed, two distinct substitution patterns are found on these arabinoxylans (Fig. 1). In some regions, substituted xylosyl residues are clustered together and are often separated by single unsubstituted residues. Other regions, which are susceptible to hydrolysis by endoxylanases, contain relatively few arabinoxyl substituents (Viëtor, 1992; Voragen et al, 1993). The significance of these substitution patterns is not known, but they could clearly influence the physical properties of the molecules, and this would presumably be related to the functional requirements of the walls.

PHYSICAL PROPERTIES AND SOLUTION BEHAVIOR

The molecular weights of cereal arabinoxylans are generally lower than the those of the $(1\rightarrow3),(1\rightarrow4)$-$\beta$-glucans (Ballance et al, 1986; Fincher and Stone, 1986). Using sedimentation velocity techniques, Podrazky (1964) obtained a molecular weight of 58,800 for an arabinoxylan fraction extracted from barley flour with water. This corresponds to a degree of polymerization of about 445 and is on the same order of magnitude as values obtained for wheat arabinoxylans (Perlin 1951a; Morita et al, 1974; Andrewartha et al, 1979; Medcalf et al, 1968). Extremely high molecular weight values for barley endosperm cell wall arabinoxylans of up to 5×10^6, estimated by gel filtration chromatography (Bathgate et al, 1974; Forrest and Wainwright, 1977a), emphasize the difficulties in accurately measuring molecular weights of asymmetrical polysaccharides by this method (Fincher and Stone, 1986).

Although no detailed physicochemical analysis has been made of the arabinoxylans from barley walls, their compositional similarity to endosperm arabinoxylans from the closely related bread wheats (Bacic and Stone, 1981b) would indicate that their overall structure and conformation are likely to be similar. Cereal arabinoxylans generally form viscous solutions (Medcalf et al, 1968; Fincher and Stone, 1974; D'Applonia and MacArthur, 1975), which can be attributed to their molecular asymmetry. A water-soluble arabinoxylan from wheat flour exists in aqueous medium as a fully extended rod with an axial ratio (length to width) of approximately 140 (Andrewartha et al, 1979). An unsubstituted $(1\rightarrow4)$-β-xylan chain forms flexible, yet extended, threefold, left-handed helices (Settineri and Marchessault, 1965) that aggregate into highly insoluble complexes stabilized by intermolecular hydrogen bonding (Nieduszynski and Marchessault, 1972). Addition of arabinosyl substituents appears to stiffen the polysaccharide into a more extended conformation (Dea et al, 1973; Andrewartha et al, 1979) and increases its solubility by interfering with the ability of the $(1\rightarrow4)$-β-xylan chains to align themselves over extended regions. Conversely, chemical or enzymatic removal of arabinosyl substituents from arabinoxylans permits closer alignment of the molecules and eventually leads to the precipitation of insoluble aggregates from solution (Perlin, 1951b; Neukom et al, 1967; Andrewartha et al, 1979).

ORGANIZATION IN THE CELL WALL

The solubility properties of cereal arabinoxylans are similar to those of the $(1\rightarrow3),(1\rightarrow4)$-$\beta$-glucans but are achieved by different molecular strategies. Thus, while both polysaccharides have extended conformations, the large $(1\rightarrow3),(1\rightarrow4)$-$\beta$-glucans have a limited ability to form molecular aggregates because of the irregular spacing of the flexible "kinks" afforded by $(1\rightarrow3)$ β-linkages. In contrast, aggregation of the arabinoxylan molecules is limited by the steric hindrance imposed by the arabinosyl substituents that protrude from the xylan backbone. Nevertheless, both classes of wall polysaccharide possess structural features that might permit some intermolecular alignment over relatively short regions and hence have the potential to form junction zones that could enable gellike interactions in the matrix of the walls. Barley $(1\rightarrow3),(1\rightarrow4)$-$\beta$-glucans have "cellulosic" blocks of up to 14 adjacent $(1\rightarrow4)$-β-glucosyl residues, which have the potential to form junction zones, as discussed earlier. Unsubstituted regions of the $(1\rightarrow4)$-β-xylan backbone in arabinoxylans might also be expected to form intermolecular junction zones, stabilized by hydrogen bonding. Indeed, unsubstituted regions of arabinoxylans might form junction zones with cellulosic regions of $(1\rightarrow3),(1\rightarrow4)$-$\beta$-glucans or with cellulose itself to form multicomponent gels (Fincher and Stone, 1986). Taking this concept further, one could envisage that viscoelastic properties of the gels, and hence the resilience, strength, and porosity of the wall matrix, could be altered through changes in the degree and spatial arrangement of arabinosyl substitution along the xylan backbone.

These models for arabinoxylan organization in the cell walls are based on noncovalent interactions, but covalent cross-linking of wall polysaccharides is also possible (Fincher and Stone, 1986; Fry, 1986; Cassab and Varner, 1988; Fry and Miller, 1989). Ferulic acid is esterified to barley arabinoxylans (Gubler et al, 1985, and Fig. 8), and it has been observed that solutions of water-soluble arabinoxylans from wheat can form stiff gels in the presence of low concentrations of oxidizing agents (Geissman and Neukom, 1973; Crowe and Rasper, 1988; Izydorczyk et al, 1990). This has led to the suggestion that oxidative dimerization of ferulic acid residues on adjacent arabinoxylan chains could cross-link the polysaccharides into a firm gel (Markwalder and Neukom, 1976; Neukom and Markwalder, 1978). Whether or not this type of cross-linking actually occurs in barley cell walls remains uncertain, but the presence of ferulic acid residues on the arabinoxylan chains clearly provides some potential for covalent polysaccharide-polysaccharide or polysaccharide-protein interactions in the cell wall matrix (van Sumere et al, 1973; Fincher and Stone, 1986; Fry, 1986; Izydorczyk et al, 1990).

LEVELS IN THE GRAIN

In most arabinoxylan assays, the polysaccharides are first hydrolyzed to their constituent monosaccharides, usually in acid conditions. However, released arabinose and xylose are themselves subject to degradation in hot acid, and this represents a major source of error in analyses unless recoveries of the sugars are accurately determined and losses corrected for in the determinations (Harris et al, 1984). Released pentoses can subsequently be measured colorimetrically using orcinol (Southgate, 1991) or phloroglucinol (Douglas, 1981) as color reagents and can also be quantitated by gas-liquid chromatography of their alditol acetates (Harris et al, 1984). Other problems associated with arabinoxylan estimation in grain samples include an absence of information on the accessibility of both chemical and enzymatic agents to polysaccharides buried in particulate matter.

Estimates of arabinoxylan contents of barley grain range from 4 to 7% by weight. The arabinoxylans are concentrated in the outer, protective layers of the grain (Hashimoto et al, 1987). Henry (1987a) reported that only 22% of total barley arabinoxylan is found in the endosperm. In *H. spontaneum*, the progenitor of modern barleys, total arabinoxylan levels range from 4.2 to 9.9% by weight (Henry and Brown, 1987). In an examination of genotypic and environmental effects on arabinoxylan levels, Henry (1986) concluded that total arabinoxylan content and xylose-arabinose ratios varied somewhat with genotype but were influenced more by environmental factors. Small grains have a higher arabinoxylan content, presumably because most arabinoxylan is located in the outer layers of the grain, and small grains contain relatively less endosperm than larger grains. The higher concentration of arabinoxylans in maternal tissues, where $(1\rightarrow3),(1\rightarrow4)$-$\beta$-glucan content is relatively low, is further reflected in a higher ratio of arabinoxylans to $(1\rightarrow3),(1\rightarrow4)$-$\beta$-glucans in small grains (Henry, 1986).

There have been no comprehensive studies on the genetic basis for arabinoxylan levels in barley, nor is there information on the number of genes involved or their location in the genome. Xylan synthases, arabinosyl transferases, and other enzymes that might participate in the synthesis of the polysaccharide have not been characterized, nor have developmental patterns of the polysaccharide in the endosperm been studied. Again, purification of the synthases will clear the way for isolation of the corresponding genes, and detailed analyses of the genetics and regulation of arabinoxylan synthesis will be possible.

EFFECTS ON END-USE QUALITY

The effects of arabinoxylans on end-use quality of barley have not been afforded the same attention that has been directed to the $(1\rightarrow3),(1\rightarrow4)$-$\beta$-glucans, presumably because arabinoxylans are less abundant in the starchy endosperm. Arabinoxylans may constitute only about 1.5% by weight of barley endosperm (Henry, 1987a), but their ability to form highly viscous solutions can have a large impact on the technological utilization of barley. The arabinoxylans are more abundant in the outer grain layers, although their extraction from the highly lignified maternal tissues may not be easily effected with water.

Nevertheless, arabinoxylans are likely to make an important contribution to the viscosity of gut contents in chickens fed diets containing significant levels of barley flour (Bhatty et al, 1991) and will thereby adversely affect the digestibility of the feed and the growth rates. Indeed, nutritional studies with young chicks indicate that the principal antinutritive factor from rye grain is a water-soluble arabinoxylan (Fengler and Marquardt, 1988). The arabinoxylans would also be expected to undergo microbial conversion in the hind gut to form "sticky droppings." In human diets, the arabinoxylans are a major component of the "dietary fiber" afforded by barley grain or its products; other effects of arabinoxylans on human nutrition have not been investigated in detail (Klopfenstein, 1988; Bengtsson et al, 1990).

Although the extraction, filtration, and product stability problems commonly experienced in the malting and brewing industries are usually attributed to $(1\rightarrow3),(1\rightarrow4)$-$\beta$-glucans, undegraded arabinoxylans extracted from the malted grain would also contribute to extract viscosity, lowered filtration rates, and possibly the formation of certain types of beer hazes (Coote and Kirsop, 1976). The use of cereal adjuncts, such as wheat or rice, in which endosperm arabinoxylan concentrations are relatively higher than in barley, could exacerbate these potential problems. The total arabinoxylan contents of barley or of malted grain are poorly correlated with malt extract values (Henry, 1988b), presumably because the polysaccharide is most abundant in the husk, which is not extensively degraded during germination. However, levels of water-soluble arabinoxylan extracted from the endosperm of germinated barley may well reflect the degree of endosperm mobilization and hence malt extract values; they may also serve as useful indicators of potential problems later in the brewing process. Furthermore, the hydrolytic enzymes that depolymerize arabinoxylans during germination (Preece and MacDougall, 1958) generally develop much later than $(1\rightarrow3),(1\rightarrow4)$-$\beta$-glucanases and would not be present at high concentrations at the end of the germination period used in most commercial malting processes (Benjavongkulchai and Spencer 1989; Slade et al, 1989). One might anticipate, therefore, that degradation of arabinoxylans in most malts would be less advanced than degradation of $(1\rightarrow3),(1\rightarrow4)$-$\beta$-glucans.

Detailed analysis of the physical and solution properties of barley arabinoxylans and their degradation patterns during germination could prove to be of significant benefit in understanding and controlling the technological problems that are imposed by cell wall polysaccharides but that are more commonly attributed to the $(1\rightarrow3),(1\rightarrow4)$-$\beta$-glucans. The importance of barley arabinoxylans in industrial processes may well have been underestimated.

Cellulose

Cellulose is a $(1\rightarrow4)$-β-glucan containing up to several thousand β-glucopyranosyl residues linked through $(1\rightarrow4)$ β-linkages to form very long, linear chains. Cellulose chains have an extended, ribbonlike conformation in which hydrogen bonds between adjacent glucosyl residues render the molecule relatively inflexible (Gardner and Blackwell, 1974). Alignment and aggregation of individual cellulose chains result in the formation of crystalline microfibrils up to 25 nm in diameter. The microfibrils are stabilized by extensive intermolecular hydrogen bonding and lend considerable tensile strength to the cell walls (Fincher and Stone, 1986). In the walls of barley aleurone and starchy endosperm cells, cellulose microfibrils, which constitute only 2% of the walls (Table 10), are apparently embedded in a matrix of $(1\rightarrow3),(1\rightarrow4)$-$\beta$-glucan and arabinoxylan. Microfibrils are revealed after exhaustive extraction of matrix components with alkali and other extractants. The residual fibrillar material has been identified as cellulose on the basis of its monosaccharide composition and the predominance (more than 97%) of $(1\rightarrow4)$-β-glucosyl constituents (Fincher, 1975; Ballance and Manners, 1978; Bacic and Stone, 1981a). Related to the detection of cellulose in these walls is the observation that low levels of cellulases are found in germinated barley grain (Hoy et al, 1981; Manners et al, 1982).

Glucomannans

Glucomannans of plant cell walls usually consist of varying proportions of (1→4)-β-linked glucopyranosyl and mannopyranosyl residues arranged in linear chains, in which mannosyl residues are sometimes substituted with single α-D-galactopyranosyl residues (Whistler and Richards, 1970). Unsubstituted glucomannans crystallize into insoluble aggregates and can form noncovalent associations with crystalline cellulose in vitro (Chanzy et al, 1982). Similar associations might be expected at the interface of the microfibrils and the matrix phase in cell walls.

The presence of approximately 2% glucomannan in wall preparations from barley aleurone and starchy endosperm (Table 10) has been inferred from the detection of mannose in fractions extracted from the walls with concentrated alkali or in alkali-insoluble wall residues (Fincher, 1975; Ballance and Manners, 1978; Bacic and Stone, 1981a). However, the polysaccharide has not been purified from barley walls, and indeed the existence of glucomannans in barley remains to be demonstrated. Enzymes capable of depolymerizing glucomannans in germinated grains have not been reported.

(1→3)-β-Glucans

In higher plants, (1→3)-β-glucans are found in specialized cell walls and wall layers, or in discrete papillae that are deposited between the plasma membrane and the wall in response to wounding, infection, and physiological stresses (Stone, 1985). These polysaccharides form a triple helical conformation in the solid state and possibly also in solution (Marchessault and Deslandes, 1979; Bluhm et al, 1982), although in plant tissues they appear to be nonfibrillar (Stone, 1985). As yet, there are few grounds for considering them an integral structural component of cell walls in barley grain, but we deal with them in this section because of their chemical similarity to the wall (1→3),(1→4)-β-glucans and because they may be closely associated with wall surfaces in the starchy endosperm.

Small beadlike deposits of (1→3)-β-glucan on the inner cell wall have been detected throughout the starchy endosperm in several barley cultivars (Fulcher et al, 1977; MacGregor et al, 1989). Larger deposits, also associated with the inner surface of the walls and sometimes completely embedded in wall material, are concentrated in subaleurone regions of barley endosperm; their abundance varies among cultivars (Fulcher et al, 1977; Bacic and Stone, 1981a; Wood and Fulcher, 1984; MacGregor et al, 1989). The total (1→3)-β-glucan content of barley grain has been estimated at 1% (w/w) (Tiunova et al, 1988), although this is likely to vary considerably among varieties (MacGregor et al, 1989). Bacic and Stone (1981b) used a specific (1→3)-β-glucan exohydrolase to demonstrate that barley aleurone wall preparations contained approximately 1% (1→3)-β-glucan.

The deposits of (1→3)-β-glucan, often referred to as callose, have generally been detected histochemically in barley grain using the triarylmethane dye aniline blue (Currier, 1957) and confirmed by the removal of aniline blue fluorescence with (1→3)-β-glucanase treatment (Fulcher et al, 1977; Wood and Fulcher, 1984; MacGregor et al, 1989). The fluorochrome in commercial aniline blue dyes is 4,4'-[carbonylbis(benzene-4,1-diyl)bis(imino)] bisbenzensulfonic acid, which has a high, but not absolute, specificity for $(1\rightarrow3)$-β-glucans and their derivatives (Evans et al, 1984). The fluorochrome is a flexible molecule that is believed to bind specifically to the surface of a $(1\rightarrow3)$-β-glucan triple helix; it might also bind with lower affinity to conformationally regular $(1\rightarrow3),(1\rightarrow4)$-$\beta$-glucans such as lichenin (Evans et al, 1984). Monoclonal antibodies have now been raised against $(1\rightarrow3)$-β-glucans (Meikle et al, 1991) and may also be useful in studies on the location and quantitation of the polysaccharide in barley grain.

The origin and function of the $(1\rightarrow3)$-β-glucan deposits in barley endosperm are not known. Callosic material is deposited in the cell plate region of dividing plant cells and is seen in young walls, including those of developing wheat and barley endosperm (Morrison and O'Brien, 1976), but the beadlike appearance of the deposits in developing barley endosperm and their position on the inner surfaces of the walls (MacGregor et al, 1989) would argue against this $(1\rightarrow3)$-β-glucan simply representing the remnants of developmental material. Callose is also deposited in plant cells during wounding and can be induced during tissue sectioning for microscopy (Galway and McCully, 1987). It is unlikely, however, that the $(1\rightarrow3)$-β-glucans in the starchy endosperm of mature grain are sectioning artefacts, because the tissue is nonliving and therefore is presumably unable to effect $(1\rightarrow3)$-β-glucan synthesis. Some of the $(1\rightarrow3)$-β-glucan deposits in barley endosperm could arise as a result of physiological stress, particularly if periods of transient moisture stress occur during grain maturation or if the final drying of the grain causes plasmolysis at a stage when cells of the starchy endosperm are still capable of $(1\rightarrow3)$-β-glucan synthesis. Such an origin would be consistent with the location of the callose deposits on the inner surface of the walls (MacGregor et al, 1989). It is noteworthy that significant levels of $(1\rightarrow3)$-β-glucan endohydrolases are present in the endosperm of germinated barley (Manners and Wilson, 1974; Ballance et al, 1976; Høj et al, 1988, 1989; Ballance and Svendsen, 1988), but it is not clear whether these enzymes function solely to reclaim the $(1\rightarrow3)$-β-glucan deposits or whether they have additional roles during germination (Fincher, 1989).

OTHER CARBOHYDRATES

In addition to the polysaccharides discussed earlier in this chapter, a number of simple sugars and oligosaccharides are found in barley kernels (Table 15). These have been discussed in a review by Henry (1988c). Most of these carbohydrates are present in low levels and so are difficult to determine with high accuracy. This, undoubtedly, contributes to the variation observed in published results, but a genetic effect also occurs (MacLeod, 1952).

The simplest carbohydrates, glucose and fructose, are present in very low concentrations and are found mainly in the endosperm (MacLeod, 1952). The low levels of maltose sometimes found in barley appear to be present in endosperm regions adjacent to the embryo and aleurone (MacLeod, 1952). This suggests that the maltose may be formed through limited starch degradation caused by preharvest sprouting of the barley. It is debatable, therefore, whether or not sound, mature barley contains detectable amounts of maltose.

Small amounts of galactose and mannose have been detected in developing barley, but these monosaccharides are not present, in the free form, in sound, mature kernels (LaBerge et al, 1973).

Raffinose is a major oligosaccharide in barley and accounts for about 25% of the low-molecular-weight carbohydrates of the kernel (MacLeod, 1952). More than 80% of it is present in the embryo, and it is metabolized rapidly during early stages of germination (MacLeod, 1957).

Relatively large amounts of sucrose are also present in barley, and a high proportion (>80%) of this sugar is present in the embryo (MacLeod, 1952). Sucrose represents about 50% of simple barley carbohydrates in normal barley cultivars. High levels of sucrose (6.7%) have been reported in some "high sugar" barley lines (Åman and Newman, 1986), but possible technological applications for these lines have not yet been explored.

Fructans, or fructo-oligosaccharides, are nonreducing polymers of fructose that contain several fructosyl residues linked to a terminal glucose residue. If the fructosyl residues are linked through β-(2→6) bonds, the fructose polymers are called levans, but when the fructosyl residues are β-(2→1) linked, the polymers are called inulins. Very little is known about the structure and size distribution of the fructans in barley kernels. Those in barley leaves appear to be of the levan type (Haworth et al, 1937), and it is likely that the fructans in the grain would be similar. Fructans containing 10 fructosyl residues have been identified in barley kernels, but higher-molecular-weight fructans may well be present (MacLeod, 1953). Fructans of similar size have been reported in wheat flours (Nilsson et al, 1986). Further work is required to confirm the structure and size of the grain fructans.

Immature barley kernels contain high concentrations (20%) of fructans

TABLE 15
Low-Molecular-Weight Carbohydrates in Barley Kernels

Carbohydrate	Amount (%)	Reference
Glucose	0.02–0.11	Cerning-Beroard and Guilbot, 1975 MacLeod and Preece, 1954
Fructose	0.03–0.2	MacLeod and Preece, 1954 Åman et al, 1985 Henry, 1985b
Sucrose	0.74–1.9	Cerning-Beroard and Guilbot, 1975 Åman and Newman, 1986
Maltose	0.1	MacLeod, 1952
Glucodifructose	0.03–0.25	MacLeod, 1952 MacLeod and Preece, 1954
Raffinose	0.16–0.56	Hall et al, 1956 Henry, 1985b LaBerge et al, 1973
Fructans	0.3–0.78	Åman et al, 1985 MacLeod and Preece, 1954 Hall et al, 1956 Bach Knudson et al, 1987

(Cerning-Beroard and Guilbot, 1975), but these decrease rapidly as the kernels mature. Fructans, because of the relative ease by which they can be synthesized and hydrolyzed, may be used as a temporary energy store by the developing kernel. Fructan levels in mature kernels are comparable to those of sucrose and raffinose and, like those two carbohydrates, fructan appears to be concentrated in the embryo (MacLeod, 1952).

Some aspects of the biosynthesis of fructans in higher plants have been discussed in recent reviews (Pollock and Chatterton, 1988; Pollock and Cairns, 1991; Smeekens et al, 1991), but details of fructan biosynthesis in barley kernels remain unknown.

ACKNOWLEDGMENTS

GBF wishes to acknowledge the support of the Australian Research Council and the Grains Research and Development Corporation of Australia.

LITERATURE CITED

AASTRUP, S. 1979a. The relationship between the viscosity of an acid flour extract of barley and its β-glucan content. Carlsberg Res. Commun. 44:289-304.

AASTRUP, S. 1979b. The effect of rain on β-glucan content in barley grains. Carlsberg Res. Commun. 44:381-393.

AASTRUP, S. 1983. Selection and characterization of low β-glucan mutants in barley. Carlsberg Res. Commun. 48:307-316.

AASTRUP, S., and ERDAL, K. 1980. Quantitative determination of endosperm modification and its relationship to the content of 1,3:-1,4-β-glucans during malting of barley. Carlsberg Res. Commun. 45:369-379.

ADAMS, O. L., and NABER, E. C. 1969. Effect of physical and chemical treatment of grains on growth of and feed utilization by the chick. I. The effect of water and acid treatments of corn, wheat, barley and expanded or germinated grains on chick performance. Poult. Sci. 48:853-858.

ALEXANDER, H. P., and FISH, J. 1984. Total β-glucan content of 23 barley varieties from the 1983 harvest. J. Inst. Brew. 90:65-66.

ALLISON, M. J., COWE, I. A., and McHALE, R. 1978. The use of infra red reflectance for the rapid estimation of the soluble β-glucan content of barley. J. Inst. Brew. 84:153-155.

ÅMAN, P., and GRAHAM, H. 1987. Analysis of total insoluble mixed-linked (1→3),(1→4)-β-D-glucans in barley and oats. J. Agric. Food Chem. 35:704-709.

ÅMAN, P., and HESSELMAN, K. 1984. Analysis of starch and other main constituents of cereal grains. Swed. J. Agric. Res. 14:135-139.

ÅMAN, P., and NEWMAN, C. W. 1986. Chemical composition of some different types of barley grown in Montana, U.S.A. J. Cereal Sci. 4:133-141.

ÅMAN, P., HESSELMAN, K., and TILLY, A.-C. 1985. The variation in chemical composition of Swedish barleys. J. Cereal Sci. 3:73-77.

ÅMAN, P., GRAHAM, H., and TILLY, A.-C. 1989. Content and solubility of mixed (1→3),(1→4)-β-D-glucan in barley and oats during kernel development and storage. J. Cereal Sci. 10:45-50.

ANDERSON, I. H., LEVINE, A. S., and LEVITT, M. D. 1981. Incomplete absorption of the carbohydrate in all-purpose wheat flour. New Engl. J. Med. 304:891-892.

ANDERSON, M. A., COOK, J. A., and STONE, B. A. 1978. Enzymatic determination of 1,3:1,4-β-glucans in barley grain and other cereals. J. Inst. Brew. 84:233-239.

ANDREWARTHA, K., PHILLIPS, D. R., and STONE, B. A. 1979. Solution properties of wheat flour arabinoxylans and enzymically modified arabinoxylans. Carbohydr. Res. 77:191-204.

ARGENZIO, R. A., and STEVENS, C. E. 1984. The large bowel—Supplementary rumen. Proc. Nutr. Soc. 43:12-23.

ASPINALL, G. O., and FERRIER, R. J. 1957. The constitution of barley husk hemicellulose. J. Chem. Soc. pp. 4188-4194.

ASPINALL, G. O., and ROSS, K. M. 1963. The degradation of two periodate-oxidised arabinoxylans. J. Chem. Soc. pp. 1681-1686.

ATWELL, W. A., HOOD, L. F., LINEBACK, D. R., VARRIANO-MARSTON, E., and ZOBEL, H. F. 1988. The terminology and methodology associated with basic starch phenomena. Cereal Foods World 33:306, 308, 310-311.

BACH KNUDSEN, K. E., ÅMAN, P., and EGGUM, B. O. 1987. Nutritive value of Danish-grown barley varieties. I. carbohydrates and other major constituents. J. Cereal Sci. 6:173-186.

BACIC, A., and STONE, B. A. 1981a. Isolation and ultrastructure of aleurone cell walls from wheat and barley. Aust. J. Plant Physiol. 8:453-474.

BACIC, A., and STONE, B. A. 1981b. Chemistry and organization of aleurone cell wall components from wheat and barley. Aust. J. Plant Physiol. 8:475-495.

BALLANCE, G. M., and MANNERS, D. J. 1978. Structural analysis and enzymic solubilization of barley endosperm cell walls. Carbohydr. Res. 61:107-118.

BALLANCE, G. M., and SVENDSEN, I. 1988. Purification and amino acid sequence determination of an endo, 1,3-β-glucanase from barley. Carlsberg Res. Commun. 53:411-419.

BALLANCE, G. M., MEREDITH, W. O. S., and LaBERGE, D. E. 1976. Distribution and development of endo-β-glucanase activities in barley tissues during germination. Can. J. Plant Sci. 56:459-466.

BALLANCE, G. M., HALL, R. S., and MANNERS, D. J. 1986. Studies of some arabinoxylans from barley endosperm walls. Carbohydr. Res. 150:290-294.

BAMFORTH, C. W. 1985. Biochemical approaches to beer quality. J. Inst. Brew. 91:154-160.

BAMFORTH, C. W., and BARCLAY, A. H. P. 1993. Malting technology and the uses of malt. Pages 297-354 in: Barley: Chemistry and Technology. A. W. MacGregor and R. S. Bhatty, eds. Am. Assoc. Cereal Chem., St. Paul, MN.

BAMFORTH, C. W., and MARTIN, H. L. 1981. β-Glucan and β-glucan solubilase in malting and mashing. J. Inst. Brew. 87:365-372.

BANKS, W., and GREENWOOD, C. T. 1966. The fine structure of amylose: The action of pullulanase as evidence of branching. Arch. Biochem. Biophys. 117:674-675.

BANKS, W., and GREENWOOD, C. T. 1971. The conformation of amylose in dilute solution. Staerke 23:300-314.

BANKS, W., and GREENWOOD, C. T. 1975. Starch and Its Components. Edinburgh University Press, Edinburgh, Scotland.

BANKS, W., GREENWOOD, C. T., and SLOSS, J. 1969. Light-scattering studies on aqueous solutions of amylose and amylopectin. Carbohydr. Res. 11:399-406.

BANKS, W., GREENWOOD, C. T., and

KHAN, K. M. 1970a. The properties of synthetic amylopectin with long external-chains. Staerke 22:292-296.

BANKS, W., GREENWOOD, C. T., and WALKER, J. T. 1970b. Studies on the starches of barley genotypes: The waxy starch. Staerke 22:149-152.

BANKS, W., GREENWOOD, C. T., and WALKER, J. T. 1971a. Studies on the starches of barley genotypes. A comparison of the starches from normal and high-amylose barley. Staerke 23:12-15.

BANKS, W., GREENWOOD, C. T., and MUIR, D. D. 1971b. The characterization of starch and its components. Part 3. The technique of semi-micro, differential, potentiometric, iodine titration and the factors affecting it. Staerke 22:118-124.

BANKS, W., GEDDES, R., GREENWOOD, C. T., and JONES, I. G. 1972. Physico-chemical studies on starches. Part 63. The molecular size and shape of amylopectin. Staerke 24:245-251.

BANKS, W., GREENWOOD, C. T., and MUIR, D. D. 1973a. Studies on the biosynthesis of starch granules. Part 5. Properties of the starch components of normal barley and barley with starch of high amylose content during growth. Staerke 25:153-157.

BANKS, W., GREENWOOD, C. T., and MUIR, D. D. 1973b. Studies on the biosynthesis of starch granules. Part 6. Properties of the starch granules of normal barley and barley with starch of high amylose content during growth. Staerke 25:225-230.

BANKS, W., GREENWOOD, C. T., and MUIR, D. D. 1973c. Studies on the biosynthesis of starch granules. Part 7. Compound granules in potato starch. Staerke 25:331-335.

BATHGATE, G. N. 1983. The relationship between malt "friability" and wort viscosity. J. Inst. Brew. 89:416-419.

BATHGATE, G. N., and DALGLIESH, C. E. 1975. The diversity of barley and malt β-glucans. Proc. Am. Soc. Brew. Chem. 33:32-36.

BATHGATE, G. N., and PALMER, G. H. 1972. A reassessment of the chemical structure of barley and wheat starch granules. Staerke 24:336-341.

BATHGATE, G. N., PALMER, G. H., and WILSON, G. 1974. The action of endo-β-glucanases on barley and malt β-glucans. J. Inst. Brew. 80:278-285.

BENDELOW, V. M. 1975. Determination of non-starchy polysaccharides in barley breeding programmes. J. Inst. Brew. 81:127-130.

BENGTSSON, S., ÅMAN, P., GRAHAM, H., NEW, C. W., and NEWMAN, R. K. 1990.

Chemical studies on mixed-linked β-glucans in hull-less barley cultivars giving different hypocholesterolaemic responses in chickens. J. Sci. Food Agric. 52:435-445.

BENJAVONGKULCHAI, E., and SPENCER, M. S. 1989. Barley aleurone xylanase: Its biosynthesis and possible role. Can. J. Bot. 67:297-302.

BERRY, C. S., I'ANSON, K., MILES, M. J., MORRIS, V. J., and RUSSELL, P. L. 1988. Physical chemical characterisation of resistant starch from wheat. J. Cereal Sci. 8:203-206.

BERTOFT, E. 1989. Investigation of the fine structure of amylopectin using alpha- and beta-amylase. Carbohydr. Res. 189:195-207.

BHATTY, R. S. 1993. Non-malting uses of barley. Pages 355-417 in: Barley: Chemistry and Technology. A. W. MacGregor and R. S. Bhatty, eds. Am. Assoc. Cereal Chem., St. Paul, MN.

BHATTY, R. S., BERDAHL, J. D., and CHRISTISON, G. I. 1975. Chemical composition and digestible energy of barley. Can. J. Anim. Sci. 55:759-764.

BHATTY, R. S., MacGREGOR, A. W., and ROSSNAGEL, B. G. 1991. Total and acid-soluble β-glucan content of hulless barley and its relationship to acid-extract viscosity. Cereal Chem. 68:221-227.

BILIADERIS, C. G. 1990. Thermal analysis of food carbohydrates. Pages 168-220 in: Thermal Analysis of Foods. V. R. Harwalkar and C.-Y. Ma, eds. Elsevier Applied Science, London.

BILIADERIS, C. G. 1991. The structure and interactions of starch with food constituents. Can. J. Physiol. Pharmacol. 69:60-78.

BJØRCK, I., ELIASSON, A.-C., DREWS, A., GUDMUNDSSON, M., and KARLSSON, R. 1990. Some nutritional properties of starch and dietary fiber in barley genotypes containing different levels of amylose. Cereal Chem. 67:327-333.

BLUHM, T. L., DESLANDES, Y., MARCHESSAULT, R. H., PEREZ, S., and RINAUDO, M. 1982. Solid-state and solution conformation of scleroglucan. Carbohydr. Res. 100:117-130.

BOURNE, D. T., and PIERCE, J. S. 1970. β-Glucan and β-glucanase in brewing. J. Inst. Brew. 76:328-335.

BOURNE, D. T., and WHEELER, R. E. 1984. Environmental and varietal differences in total β-glucan contents of barley and the effectiveness of its breakdown under different malting conditions. J. Inst. Brew. 90:306-310.

BOURNE, D. T., POWLESLAND, T., and WHEELER, R. E. 1982. The relationship between total β-glucan of malt and malt quality. J. Inst. Brew. 88:371-375.

BOURNE, E. J., HAWORTH, N., MACEY, A., and PEAT, S. 1948. The amylolytic degradation of starch. A revision of the hypothesis of sensitisation. J. Chem. Soc. pp. 924-930.

BROWN, A. H. D. 1983. Barley. Pages 57-77 in: Isozymes in Plant Genetics and Breeding, Part B. S. D. Tanksley and T. J. Orton, eds. Elsevier, Amsterdam.

BULIGA, G. S., BRANT, D. A., and FINCHER, G. B. 1986. The sequence statistics and solution configuration of barley (1→3, 1→4)-β-D-glucan. Carbohydr. Res. 157:139-156.

BURNETT, G. S. 1966. Studies of viscosity as the probable factor involved in the improvement of certain barleys for chickens by enzyme supplementation. Br. Poult. Sci. 7:55-75.

CAIRNS, P., LELOUP, V., MILES, M. J., RING, S. G., and MORRIS, V. J. 1990. Resistant starch: An X-ray diffraction study into the effect of enzymatic hydrolysis on amylose gels in vitro. J. Cereal Sci. 12:203-206.

CANADA GRAINS COUNCIL. 1992. Canadian Grains Industry Statistical Handbook. The Council, Winnipeg, Manitoba. p. 48.

CASSAB, G. I., and VARNER, J. E. 1988. Cell wall proteins. Annu. Rev. Plant Physiol. Plant Mol. Biol. 39:321-353.

CERNING-BEROARD, J., and GUILBOT, A. 1975. Évolution de la composition glucidique des grains de céréals au cours de leur maturation: Maïs, blé, orge. Ann. Technol. Agric. 24:143-170.

CHANZY, H. D., GROSRENAUD, A., JOSELEAU, J. P., DUBE, M., and MARCHESSAULT, R. H. 1982. Crystallization behaviour of glucomannan. Biopolymers 21:301-319.

COLES, G. 1979. Relationship of mixed-link beta-glucan accumulation to accumulation of free sugars and other glucans in the developing barley endosperm. Carlsberg Res. Commun. 44:439-453.

COOTE, N., and KIRSOP, B. H. 1976. A haze consisting largely of pentosan. J. Inst. Brew. 82:34.

CROWE, N. L., and RASPER, V. F. 1988. The ability of chlorine and chlorine-related oxidants to induce oxidative gelation in wheat flour pentosans. J. Cereal Sci. 7:283-294.

CURRIER, H. B. 1957. Callose substance in plant cells. Am. J. Bot. 44:478-488.

D'APPOLONIA, B. L., and MacARTHUR, L. A. 1975. Comparison of starch, pentosans and sugars of some conventional height and semidwarf hard red spring wheat flours.

Cereal Chem. 52:230-239.

DAIS, P., and PERLIN, A. S. 1982. High-field, 13C-n.m.r. spectroscopy of β-D-glucans, amylopectin and glycogen. Carbohydr. Res. 100:103-116.

DEA, I. C. M., REES, D. A., BEVERIDGE, R. J., and RICHARDS, G. N. 1973. Aggregation with change of conformation in solutions of hemicellulose xylans. Carbohydr. Res. 29:363-372.

DeHAAS, B. W., and GOERING, K. J. 1972. Chemical structure of barley starches. 1. A study of the properties of the amylose and amylopectin from barley starches showing a wide variation in Brabender cooking viscosity curves. Staerke 24:145-149.

DeHAAS, B. W., GOERING, K. J., and ESLICK, R. F. 1983. Barley starch. VII. New barley starches with fragmented granules. Cereal Chem. 60:327-329.

DELMER, D. P., SOLOMON, M., and READ, S. M. 1991. Direct photolabeling with [³²P]UDP-glucose for identification of a subunit of cotton fiber callose synthase. Plant Physiol. 95:556-563.

DENGATE, H. N., BARUCH, D. W., and MEREDITH, P. 1978. The density of wheat starch granules: A tracer dilution procedure for determining the density of an immiscible dispersed phase. Staerke 30:80-84.

DJURTOFT, R., and RASMUSSEN, K. L. 1955. Studies on barley gum preparations including determination of the molecular weight. Pages 17-25 in: Proc. Congr. Eur. Brew. Conv., 5th, Baden-Baden.

DOUGLAS, S. G. 1981. A rapid method for the determination of pentosans in wheat flour. Food Chem. 7:139-145.

EDNEY, M. J., CAMPBELL, G. L., and CLASSEN, H. L. 1989. The effect of β-glucanase supplementation on nutrient digestibility and growth in broilers given diets containing barley, oat groats or wheat. Anim. Feed Sci. Technol. 25:193-200.

EDNEY, M. J., MARCHYLO, B. A., and MacGREGOR, A. W. 1991. Structure of total barley beta-glucan. J. Inst. Brew. 97:39-44.

ELLIS, R. P. 1976. The use of high amylose barley for the production of whisky malt. J. Inst. Brew. 82:280-281.

ENGLYST, H., WIGGINS, H. S., and CUMMINGS, J. H. 1982. Determination of the non-starch polysaccharides in plant foods by gas-liquid chromatography of constituent sugars as alditol acetates. Analyst 107:307-318.

ENGLYST, H. N., ANDERSON, V., and CUMMINGS, J. H. 1983. Starch and non-starch polysaccharides in some cereal foods.

J. Sci. Food Agric. 34:1434-1440.

EVANS, N. A., HOYNE, P. A., and STONE, B. A. 1984. Characteristics and specificity of the interaction of a fluorochrome from aniline blue (Sirofluor) with polysaccharides. Carbohydr. Polym. 4:215-230.

EVERS, A. D., and JULIANO, B. O. 1976. Varietal differences in surface ultrastructure of endosperm cells and starch granules of rice. Staerke 28:160-166.

EVERS, A. D., GREENWOOD, C. T., MUIR, D. D., and VENABLES, C. 1973. Studies on the biosynthesis of starch granules. Part 8. A comparison of the properties of the small and the large granules in mature cereal starches. Staerke 25:42-46.

EWALD, C. M., and PERLIN, A. S. 1959. The arrangement of branching in an arabino-xylan from wheat flour. Can. J. Chem. 37:1254-1259.

FENGLER, A. I., and MARQUARDT, R. R. 1988. Water-soluble pentosans from rye: II. Effects on rate of dialysis and on the retention of nutrients by the chick. Cereal Chem. 65:298-302.

FINCHER, G. B. 1975. Morphology and chemical composition of barley endosperm cell walls. J. Inst. Brew. 81:116-122.

FINCHER, G. B. 1976. Ferulic acid in barley cell walls: A fluorescence study. J. Inst. Brew. 82:347-349.

FINCHER, G. B. 1989. Molecular and cellular biology associated with endosperm mobilization in germinating cereal grains. Annu. Rev. Plant Physiol. Plant Mol. Biol. 40:305-346.

FINCHER, G. B., and STONE, B. A. 1974. Some chemical and morphological changes induced by gibberellic acid in embryo-free wheat grain. Aust. J. Plant Physiol. 1:297-311.

FINCHER, G. B., and STONE, B. A. 1986. Cell walls and their components in cereal grain technology. Pages 207-295 in: Advances in Cereal Science and Technology, Vol. 8. Y. Pomeranz, ed. Am. Assoc. Cereal Chem., St. Paul, MN.

FLEMING, M., and KAWAKAMI, K. 1977. Studies of the fine structure of β-D-glucans of barleys extracted at different temperatures. Carbohydr. Res. 57:15-23.

FLEMING, M., and MANNERS, D. J. 1966. A comparison of the fine-structure of lichenin and barley glucan. Biochem. J. 100:4P-5P.

FORREST, I. S. 1977. The role of protein in the structure of barley endosperm cell walls. Biochem. Soc. Trans. 5:1154-1156.

FORREST, I. S., and WAINWRIGHT, T. 1977a. The mode of binding of β-glucans and pentosans in barley endosperm cell walls.

J. Inst. Brew. 83:279-286.

FORREST, I. S., and WAINWRIGHT, T. 1977b. Differentiation between desirable and troublesome β-glucans. Pages 401-413 in: Proc. Congr. Eur. Brew. Conv., 16th, Amsterdam.

FRENCH, D. 1972. Fine structure of starch and its relationship to the organization of starch granules. Denpun Kagaku 19:8-25.

FRENCH, D. 1984. Organization of starch granules. Pages 183-247 in: Starch: Chemistry and Technology. R. L. Whistler, J. B. BeMiller, and E. F. Paschall, eds. Academic Press, Orlando, FL.

FRY, S. C. 1986. Cross-linking of matrix polymers in the growing cell walls of angiosperms. Annu. Rev. Plant Physiol. 37:165-186.

FRY, S. C., and MILLER, J. G. 1989. Toward a working model of the growing plant cell wall: Phenolic cross-linking reactions in the primary cell walls of dicotyledons. Pages 33-46 in: Plant Cell Wall Polymers: Biogenesis and Biodegradation. N. G. Lewis and M. G. Paice, eds. American Chemical Society, Washington, DC.

FUJITA, S., GLOVER, D. V., OKUNO, K., and FUWA, H. 1989. In vitro and in vivo digestion of high-amylose type starch granules. Starch/Staerke 41:221-224.

FULCHER, R. G., SETTERFIELD, G., McCULLY, M. E., and WOOD, P. J. 1977. Observations on the aleurone layer. II. Fluorescence microscopy of the aleurone-sub-aleurone junction with emphasis on possible β-1,3-glucan deposits in barley. Aust. J. Plant Physiol. 4:917-928.

FUWA, H. 1982. Enzymic degradation of starch granules. Denpun Kagaku 29:99-106.

FUWA, H., NAKAJIMA, M., HAMADA, A., and GLOVER, D. V. 1977. Comparative susceptibility to amylases of starches from different plant species and several single endosperm mutants and their double-mutant combinations with opaque-2 inbred Oh43 maize. Cereal Chem. 54:230-237.

FUWA, H., GLOVER, D. V., SUGIMOTO, Y., IKAWA, Y., and TAKAYA, T. 1982. Some properties of starches of opaque-2, sugary-2 opaque-2, and waxy opaque-2 mutants of two broad-based synthetic cultivars of maize. J. Nutr. Sci. Vitaminol. 28:127-138.

GALWAY, M. E., and McCULLY, M. E. 1987. The time course of the induction of callose in wounded pea roots. Protoplasma 139:77-91.

GARDNER, K. H., and BLACKWELL, J. 1974. The structure of native cellulose. Biopolymers 13:1975-2001.

GEDDES, R., GREENWOOD, C. T., MacGREGOR, A. W., PROCTER, A. R., and THOMSON, J. 1964. Observations on the isolation and subfractionation of amylose: The presence in amylose of a natural barrier to β-amylolysis. Makromol. Chem. 79:189-206.

GEISSMAN, T., and NEUKOM, H. 1973. Composition of the water soluble wheat flour pentosans and their oxidative gelation. Lebensm. Wiss. Technol. 6:59-62.

GIDLEY, M. J. 1987. Factors affecting the crystalline type (A-C) of native starches and model compounds: A rationalisation of observed effects in terms of polymorphic structures. Carbohydr. Res. 161:301-304.

GIDLEY, M. J., and BULPIN, P. V. 1987. Crystallization of malto-oligosaccharides as models of the crystalline forms of starch: Minimum chain-length requirement for the formation of double helices. Carbohydr. Res. 161:291-300.

GILBERT, G. A., and SPRAGG, S. P. 1964. Iodimetric determination of amylose. Pages 168-169 in: Methods in Carbohydrate Chemistry, Vol. IV. R. L. Whistler, ed. Academic Press, New York.

GILL, A. A., MORGAN, A. G., and SMITH, D. B. 1982. Total β-glucan content of some barley cultivars. J. Inst. Brew. 88:317-319.

GOERING, K. J., and DeHAAS, B. 1974. A comparison of the properties of large- and small-granule starch isolated from several isogenic lines of barley. Cereal Chem. 51:573-578.

GOERING, K. J., and ESLICK, R. F. 1976. Barley starch. VI. A self-liquefying waxy barley starch. Cereal Chem. 53:174-180.

GOERING, K. J., ESLICK, R., and DeHAAS, B. 1970. Barley starch. IV. A study of the cooking viscosity curves of twelve barley genotypes. Cereal Chem. 47:592-596.

GOERING, K. J., ESLICK, R., and DeHAAS, B. W. 1973a. Barley starch. V. A comparison of the properties of waxy Compana barley starch with the starches of its parents. Cereal Chem. 50:322-328.

GOERING, K. J., FRITTS, D. H., and ESLICK, R. F. 1973b. A study of starch granule size and distribution in 29 barley varieties. Staerke 25:297-302.

GOERING, K. J., DeHAAS, B. W., CHAPMAN, D. W., ESLICK, R. F., and GRAMERA, R. E. 1980. New process for production of ultra high maltose syrup from special genetically derived barley. Starch/Staerke 32:349-352.

GOHL, B., ALDEN, S., ELWINGER, K., and THOMKE, S. 1978. Influence of β-glucanase on feeding value of barley for poultry and moisture content of excreta. Br. Poult. Sci. 19:41-47.

GOLDNER, W. R., and BOYER, C. D. 1989. Starch granule-bound proteins and polypeptides: The influence of the waxy mutations. Starch/Staerke 41:250-254.

GOLDSCHMID, H. R., and PERLIN, A. S. 1963. Interbranch sequences in the wheat arabinoxylan. Selective enzymolysis studies. Can. J. Chem. 41:2272-2277.

GOUGH, B. M., and PYBUS, J. N. 1971. Effect on the gelatinization temperature of wheat starch granules of prolonged treatment with water at 50°C. Staerke 23:210-212.

GREENBERG, D. C. 1977. A diallel cross analysis of gum content in barley (*Hordeum vulgare*). Theor. Appl. Genet. 50:41-46.

GREENWOOD, C. T. 1989. Barley starches—Basic concepts. Pages 67-72 in: Alternative End Uses of Barley. D. H. B. Sparrow, R. C. M. Lance, and R. J. Henry, eds. Cereal Chemistry Division, Royal Australian Chemical Institute, Parkville, Victoria, Australia.

GREENWOOD, C. T., and HOURSTON, D. J. 1971. Some observations on the stability of amylose and amylopectin in aqueous solution. Staerke 23:344-347.

GREENWOOD, C. T., and THOMSON, J. 1959. A comparison of the starches from barley and malted barley. J. Inst. Brew. 65:346-353.

GUBLER, F., and ASHFORD, A. E. 1985. Release of ferulic acid esters from barley aleurone. I. Time course of gibberellic-acid-induced release from isolated layers. Aust. J. Plant Physiol. 12:297-305.

GUBLER, F., ASHFORD, A. E., BACIC, A., BLAKENEY, A. B., and STONE, B. A. 1985. Release of ferulic acid esters from barley aleurone. II. Characterization of the feruloyl compounds released in response to GA₃. Aust. J. Plant Physiol. 12:307-317.

HALL, R. D., HARRIS, G., and MacWILLIAM, I. C. 1956. Carbohydrates in malting and brewing. V. Further studies on the carbohydrates of barley, malt and wort. J. Inst. Brew. 62:232-238.

HARRIS, G. 1962. The structural chemistry of barley and malt. Pages 431-582 in: Barley and Malt. A. H. Cook, ed. Academic Press, London.

HARRIS, G., and MacWILLIAM, I. C. 1958. A note on the development of the starch of the ripening barley ear. Cereal Chem. 35:82-83.

HARRIS, P. J., HENRY, R. J., BLAKENEY, A. B., and STONE, B. A. 1984. An improved procedure for the methylation analysis of oligosaccharides and polysaccharides. Carbohydr. Res. 127:59-73.

HASHIMOTO, S., SHOGREN, M. D., BOLTE, L. C., and POMERANZ, Y. 1987. Cereal pentosans: Their estimation and significance. III. Pentosans in abraded grains and milling by-products. Cereal Chem. 64:39-41.

HAWORTH, W. N., HIRST, E. L., and LYNE, R. P. 1937. A water-soluble polysaccharide from barley leaves. Biochem. J. 31:786-788.

HENRY, R. J. 1985a. A comparative study of the total β-glucan contents of some Australian barleys. Aust. J. Exp. Agric. 25:424-427.

HENRY, R. J. 1985b. A comparison of the non-starch carbohydrates in cereal grains. J. Sci. Food Agric. 36:1243-1253.

HENRY, R. J. 1986. Genetic and environmental variation in the pentosan and β-glucan contents of barley, and their relation to malting quality. J. Cereal Sci. 4:269-277.

HENRY, R. J. 1987a. Pentosan and (1→3),-(1→4)-β-glucan concentrations in endosperm and whole grain of wheat, barley, oats and rye. J. Cereal Sci. 6:253-258.

HENRY, R. J. 1987b. Variation in the carbohydrate composition of barley. Pages 763-766 in: Barley Genetics V. Proc. 5th Int. Barley Genet. Symp. S. Yasuda and T. Konishi, eds. Sanyo Press, Okayama, Japan.

HENRY, R. J. 1988a. Evaluation of general methods for measurements of (1→3),(1→4)-β-glucans. J. Sci. Food Agric. 44:75-87.

HENRY, R. J. 1988b. Changes in β-glucan and other carbohydrate components of barley during malting. J. Sci. Food Agric. 42:333-341.

HENRY, R. J. 1988c. The carbohydrates of barley grains—A review. J. Inst. Brew. 94:71-78.

HENRY, R. J., and BLAKENEY, A. B. 1986. Determination of total β-glucan in malt. J. Inst. Brew. 92:354-356.

HENRY, R. J., and BROWN, A. H. D. 1987. Variation in the carbohydrate composition of wild barley (*Hordeum spontaneum*) grain. Plant Breed. 98:97-103.

HESSELMAN, K., and THOMKE, S. 1982. Influence of some factors on development of viscosity in the water-extract of barley. Swed. J. Agric. Res. 12:17-22.

HIZUKURI, S. 1985. Relationship between the distribution of the chain length of amylopectin and the crystalline structure of starch granules. Carbohydr. Res. 141:295-306.

HIZUKURI, S. 1986. Polymodal distribution of the chain lengths of amylopectins and its significance. Carbohydr. Res. 147:342-347.

HIZUKURI, S., and MAEHARA, Y. 1990. Fine structure of wheat amylopectin: The mode of A to B chain binding. Carbohydr. Res. 206:145-159.

HIZUKURI, S., KANEKO, T., and TAKEDA, Y. 1983. Measurement of the chain length of amylopectin and its relevance to the origin of crystalline polymorphism of starch granules. Biochim. Biophys. Acta 760:188-191.

HOLM, J., BJÖRCK, I., OSTROWSKA, S., ELIASSON, A.-C., ASP, N.-G., LARSSON, K., and LUNDQUIST, I. 1983. Digestibility of amylose lipid complexes in vitro and in vivo. Starch/Staerke 35:294-297.

HOLM, J., HAGANDER, B., BJÖRCK, I., ELIASSON, A.-C., and LUNDQUIST, I. 1989. The effect of various thermal processes on the glycaemic response to whole grain wheat products in humans and rats. J. Nutr. 119:1631-1638.

HOY, J. L., MacAULEY, B. J., and FINCHER, G. B. 1981. Cellulases of plant and microbial origin in germinating barley. J. Inst. Brew. 87:77-80.

HØJ, P. B., SLADE, A. M., WETTENHALL, R. E. H., and FINCHER, G. B. 1988. Isolation and characterization of a (1→3)-β-glucan endohydrolase from germinating barley (Hordeum vulgare): Amino acid sequence similarity with barley (1→3, 1→4)-β-glucanases. FEBS Lett. 230:67-71.

HØJ, P. B., HARTMAN, D. J., MORRICE, N. A., DOAN, D. N. P., and FINCHER, G. B. 1989. Purification of (1→3)-β-glucan endohydrolase isoenzyme II from germinated barley and determination of its primary structure from a cDNA clone. Plant Mol. Biol. 13:31-42.

IGARASHI, H., and AMAHA, M. 1969. Studies on frozen beer precipitates. II. Chemical structure of the β-glucan isolated from the precipitates. J. Inst. Brew. 75:292-299.

IGARASHI, O., and SAKURAI, Y. 1965. Studies on the non-starchy polysaccharides of the endosperm of naked barley. Part I. Preparation of the water soluble β-glucans from naked barley endosperm and their properties. Agric. Biol. Chem. 29:678-686.

IGARASHI, O., and SAKURAI, Y. 1966. Studies on the non-starchy polysaccharides of the endosperm of naked barley. Part II. The periodate oxidative degradation of F-1 β-glucan prepared from the endosperm of naked barley. Agric. Biol. Chem. 30:642-645.

IIYAMA, K., LAM, T. B. T., and STONE, B. A. 1990. Phenolic acid bridges between polysaccharides and lignin in wheat inter-nodes. Phytochemistry 29:733-737.

IMBERTY, A., and PÉREZ, S. 1989. Conformational analysis and molecular modelling of the branching point of amylopectin. Int. J. Biol. Macromol. 11:177-185.

IZYDORCZYK, M. S., BILIADERIS, C. G., and BUSHUK, W. 1990. Oxidative gelation studies of water-soluble pentosans from wheat. J. Cereal Sci. 11:153-169.

JENSEN, S. A., and AASTRUP, S. 1981. A fluorimetric method for measuring 1,3:1,4-β-glucan in beer, wort, malt and barley by use of calcofluor. Carlsberg Res. Commun. 46:87-95.

JØRGENSEN, K. G., and AASTRUP, S. 1988. Quantification of high molecular weight (1→3)(1→4)-β-D-glucan using calcofluor complex formation and flow injection analysis. II. Determination of total β-glucan content of barley and malt. Carlsberg Res. Commun. 53:287-296.

KAINUMA, K., and FRENCH, D. 1972. Naegeli amylodextrin and its relationship to starch granule structure. II. Role of water in crystallization of B-starch. Biopolymers 11:2241-2250.

KALICHEVSKY, M. T., ORFORD, P. D., and RING, S. G. 1990. The retrogradation and gelation of amylopectins from various botanical sources. Carbohydr. Res. 198:49-55.

KANG, M. Y., SUGIMOTO, Y., KATO, I., SAKAMOTO, S., and FUWA, H. 1985. Some properties of large and small starch granules of barley (Hordeum vulgare L.) endosperm. Agric. Biol. Chem. 49:1291-1297.

KANO, Y. 1977. Structural comparisons of the starches from barley and malt by the gel chromatographic method. Bull. Brew. Sci. 23:9-14.

KANO, Y., KUNITAKE, N., KARAKAWA, T., TANIGUCHI, H., and NAKAMURA, M. 1981. Structural changes in starch molecules during the malting of barley. Agric. Biol. Chem. 45:1969-1975.

KARLSSON, R., OLERED, R., and ELIASSON, A.-C. 1983. Changes in starch granule size distribution and starch gelatinization properties during development and maturation of wheat, barley and rye. Starch/Staerke 35:335-340.

KATO, Y., and NEVINS, D. J. 1986. Fine structure of (1→3),(1→4)-β-D-glucan from Zea shoot cell-walls. Carbohydr. Res. 147:69-85.

KIELISZEWSKI, M. J., LEYKAM, J. F., and LAMPORT, D. T. A. 1990. Structure of the threonine-rich extensin from Zea mays. Plant Physiol. 92:316-326.

KINDEL, P. K., LIAO, S.-Y., LISKE, M. R., and OLIEN, C. R. 1989. Arabinoxylans from rye and wheat seed that interact with ice. Carbohydr. Res. 187:173-185.

KIRIBUCHI, S., and NAKAMURA, M. 1973. Studies on germination of barley seeds. Part

3. Scanning electron microscopic observations of the starch granules isolated from the germinated barley. Denpun Kagaku 20:193-200.

KJØLBERG, O., and MANNERS, D. J. 1963. Studies on carbohydrate-metabolizing enzymes. 9. The action of isoamylase on amylose. Biochem. J. 86:258-262.

KLOPFENSTEIN, C. F. 1988. The role of cereal β-glucans in nutrition and health. Cereal Foods World 33:865-869.

KOKUBO, A., KURAISHI, S., and SAKURAI, N. 1989. Culm strength of barley. Plant Physiol. 91:876-882.

KRUSIUS, T., and FINNE, J. 1981. Use of the Smith degradation in the study of the branching pattern in the complex-type carbohydrate units of glycoproteins. Carbohydr. Res. 90:203-214.

LaBERGE, D. E., MacGREGOR, A. W., and MEREDITH, W. O. S. 1973. Changes in the free sugar content of barley kernels during maturation. J. Inst. Brew. 79:471-477.

LARSSON, K., and MIEZIS, Y. 1979. On the possibility of dietary fiber formation by interaction in the intestine between starch and lipids. Starch/Staerke 31:301-302.

LEHTONEN, M., and AIKASALO, R. 1987. β-Glucan in two- and six-rowed barley. Cereal Chem. 64:191-193.

LETTERS, R. 1977. Beta-glucans in brewing. Pages 211-224 in: Proc. Congr. Eur. Brew. Conf., 16th, Amsterdam.

LINEBACK, D. 1984. The starch granule: Organization and properties. Baker's Dig. 58:16-21.

LIU, H., LELIEVRE, J., and AYOUNG-CHEE, W. 1991. A study of starch gelatinization using differential scanning calorimetry, X-ray and birefringence measurements. Carbohydr. Res. 210:79-87.

LOI, L., BARTON, P. A., and FINCHER, G. B. 1987. Survival of barley (1→3, 1→4)-β-glucanase isoenzymes during kilning and mashing. J. Cereal Sci. 5:45-50.

LORENZ, K., and KULP, K. 1984. Steeping of barley starch. Effects on physicochemical properties and functional characteristics. Starch/Staerke 36:122-126.

LUCHSINGER, W. W. 1967. The role of barley and malt gums in brewing. Brew. Dig. 42:56-63.

LUCHSINGER, W. W., CHEN, S.-C., and RICHARDS, A. W. 1965. Mechanism of action of malt β-glucanases. 9. The structure of barley β-D-glucan and the specificity of A_{11}-endo-β-glucanase. Arch. Biochem. Biophys. 112:531-536.

MacGREGOR, A. W., and BALLANCE, D. L. 1980. Hydrolysis of large and small starch granules from normal and waxy barley cultivars by alpha-amylases from barley malt. Cereal Chem. 57:397-402.

MacGREGOR, A. W., and MORGAN, J. E. 1984. Structure of amylopectins isolated from large and small starch granules of normal and waxy barley. Cereal Chem. 61:222-228.

MacGREGOR, A. W., and MORGAN, J. E. 1986. Hydrolysis of barley starch granules by alpha-amylases from barley malt. Cereal Foods World 31:688-693.

MacGREGOR, A. W., LaBERGE, D. E., and MEREDITH, W. O. S. 1971. Changes in barley kernels during growth and maturation. Cereal Chem. 48:255-269.

MacGREGOR, A. W., BALLANCE, G. M., and DUSHNICKY, L. 1989. Fluorescence microscopy studies on (1,3)-β-D-glucan in barley endosperm. Food Microstr. 8:235-244.

MacLEOD, A. M. 1952. Studies on the free sugars of the barley grain. II. Distribution of the individual sugar fractions. J. Inst. Brew. 58:363-371.

MacLEOD, A. M. 1953. Studies on the free sugars of the barley grain. IV. Low-molecular fructosans. J. Inst. Brew. 59:462-469.

MacLEOD, A. M. 1957. Raffinose metabolism in germinating barley. New Phytol. 56:210-220.

MacLEOD, A. M., and PREECE, I. A. 1954. Studies on the free sugars of the barley grain. V. Comparison of sugars and fructosans with those of other cereals. J. Inst. Brew. 60:46-55.

MacLEOD, L. C., and DUFFUS, C. M. 1988. Temperature effects on starch granules in developing barley grains. J. Cereal Sci. 8:29-37.

MacWILLIAM, I. C. 1972. Effect of kilning on malt starch and on the dextrin content of resulting worts and beers. J. Inst. Brew. 78:76-81.

MAEDA, I., KIRIBUCHI, S., and NAKAMURA, M. 1978. Digestion of barley starch granules by the combined action of α- and β-amylases purified from barley and barley malt. Agric. Biol. Chem. 42:259-267.

MAEDA, I., JIMI, N., TANIGUCHI, H., and NAKAMURA, M. 1979. Purification of R-enzyme from malted barley and its role in in vitro digestion of barley starch granules. Denpun Kagaku 26:117-127.

MÄKELÄ, M. J., KORPELA, T., and LAAKSO, S. 1982. Studies of starch size and distribution in 33 barley varieties with a Celloscope. Starch/Staerke 34:329-334.

MANNERS, D. J. 1989. Recent developments in our understanding of amylopectin structure. Carbohydr. Polym. 11:87-112.

MANNERS, D. J., and MATHESON, N. K.

1981. The fine structure of amylopectin. Carbohydr. Res. 90:99-110.

MANNERS, D. J., and WILSON, G. 1974. Purification and properties of an endo-β-D-glucanase from malted barley. Carbohydr. Res. 37:9-22.

MANNERS, D. J., SEILER, A., and STURGEON, R. J. 1982. Observations on the endo-(1→4)-β-glucanase activity of extracts of barley. Carbohydr. Res. 100:435-440.

MANZANARES, P., NAVARRO, A., SENDRA, J. M., and CARBONELL, J. V. 1991. Selective determination of β-glucan in differing molecular size, using the calcofluor-fluorimetric flow-injection-analysis (FIA) method. J. Inst. Brew. 97:101-104.

MARCHESSAULT, R. H., and DESLANDES, Y. 1979. Fine structure of (1→3)-β-glucans: Curdlan and paramylon. Carbohydr. Res. 75:231-242.

MARKWALDER, H. U., and NEUKOM, H. 1976. Diferulic acid as a possible crosslink in hemicelluloses from wheat germ. Phytochemistry 15:836-837.

MAY, L. H., and BUTTROSE, M. S. 1959. Physiology of cereal grain. II. Starch granule formation in the developing barley kernel. Aust. J. Biol. Sci. 12:146-159.

McCLEARY, B. V., and GLENNIE-HOLMES, M. 1985. Enzymic quantification of (1→3)(1→4)-β-D-glucan in barley and malt. J. Inst. Brew. 91:285-295.

McDONALD, A. M. L., and STARK, J. R. 1988. A critical examination of procedures for the isolation of barley starch. J. Inst. Brew. 94:125-132.

McDONALD, A. M. L., STARK, J. R., MORRISON, W. R., and ELLIS, R. P. 1991. The composition of starch granules from developing barley genotypes. J. Cereal Sci. 13:93-112.

McHALE, R. H. 1986. Differential binding of concanavalin A to starch granules isolated from barley and maize. Starch/Staerke 38:413-417.

McNEIL, M., ALBERSHEIM, P., TAIZ, L., and JONES, R. L. 1975. The structure of plant cell walls. VII. Barley aleurone cells. Plant Physiol. 55:64-68.

MEDCALF, D. G., D'APPOLONIA, B. L., and GILLES, K. A. 1968. Comparison of chemical composition and properties between hard red spring and durum wheat endosperm pentosans. Cereal Chem. 45:539-549.

MEIKLE, P. J., NG, K. F., JOHNSON, E., HOOGENRAAD, N. J., and STONE, B. A. 1991. The β-glucan synthase from Lolium multiflorum. Detergent solubilization, purification using monoclonal antibodies and photoaffinity labelling with a novel photo-

reactive pyrimidine analogue of uridine 5'-diphosphoglucose. J. Biol. Chem. 266:22569-22581.

MERRITT, N. R. 1967. A new strain of barley with starch of high amylose content. J. Inst. Brew. 73:583-585.

MERRITT, N. R. 1969. The susceptibility of cereal starches to amylolysis during germination and maturation. J. Inst. Brew. 75:277-283.

MERRITT, N. R., and WALKER, J. T. 1969. Development of starch and other components in normal and high amylose barley. J. Inst. Brew. 75:156-164.

MOLINA-CANO, J. L., and CONDE, J. 1982. Genetic and environmental variation of gum content in barley. J. Inst. Brew. 88:30-33.

MOLINA-CANO, J. L., DE TOGORES, F. R., ROYO, C., and PEREZ, A. 1989. Fast germinating low β-glucan mutants induced in barley with improved malting quality and yield. Theor. Appl. Genet. 78:748-754.

MOORE, A. E., and STONE, B. A. 1972. A β-1,3-glucan hydrolase from Nicotiana glutinosa. II. Specificity, action pattern and inhibitor studies. Biochim. Biophys. Acta 258:248-264.

MORGAN, A. G., GILL, A. A., and SMITH, D. B. 1983. Some barley grain and green malt properties and their influence on malt hot-water extract. I. β-Glucan, β-glucan solubilase and endo-β-glucanase. J. Inst. Brew. 89:283-291.

MORITA, S.-I., ITO, T., and HIRANO, S. 1974. A gel-forming polysaccharide containing ferulic acid in protein-free form present in an aqueous extract of wheat flour. Int. J. Biochem. 5:201-205.

MORRALL, P., and BRIGGS, D. E. 1978. Changes in cell wall polysaccharides of germinating barley grains. Phytochemistry 17:1495-1502.

MORRISON, I. N., and O'BRIEN, T. P. 1976. Cytokinesis in the developing wheat grain; Division with and without a phragmoplast. Planta 130:57-67.

MORRISON, W. R. 1987. Lipids in wheat and barley starch granules. Pages 438-445 in: Cereals in a European Context. I. D. Morton, ed. Ellis Horwood Ltd., Chichester, U.K.

MORRISON, W. R., and LAIGNELET, B. 1983. An improved colorimetric procedure for determining apparent and total amylose in cereal and other starches. J. Cereal Sci. 1:9-20.

MORRISON, W. R., and SCOTT, D. C. 1986. Measurement of the dimensions of wheat starch granule populations using a Coulter Counter with 100-channel analyzer. J. Cereal Sci. 4:13-21.

MORRISON, W. R., MILLIGAN, T. P., and AZUDIN, M. N. 1984. A relationship between the amylose and lipid contents of starches from diploid cereals. J. Cereal Sci. 2:257-271.

MORRISON, W. R., SCOTT, D. C., and KARKALAS, J. 1986. Variation in the composition and physical properties of barley starches. Starch/Staerke 38:374-379.

MUELLER-HARVEY, I., HARTLEY, R. D., HARRIS, P. J., and CURZON, E. H. 1986. Linkage of p-coumaroyl and feruloyl groups to cell-wall polysaccharides of barley straw. Carbohydr. Res. 148:71-85.

MUNCK, L. 1987. Breeding for quality in barley. Experiences and perspectives. Pages 753-762 in: Barley Genetics V. Proc. 5th Int. Barley Genet. Symp. S. Yasuda and T. Konishi, eds. Sanyo Press, Okayama, Japan.

NAKA, M., SUGIMOTO, Y., SAKAMOTO, S., and FUWA, H. 1985. Some properties of large and small granules of waxy barley (*Hordeum vulgare* L.) endosperm starch. J. Nutr. Sci. Vitaminol. 31:423-429.

NARA, S. 1979. On the relationship between specific volume and crystallinity of starch. Starch/Staerke 31:73-75.

NEUKOM, H., and MARKWALDER, H. U. 1978. Oxidative gelation of wheat flour pentosans: A new way of cross-linking polymers. Cereal Foods World 23:374-376.

NEUKOM, H., PROVIDOLI, L., GREMLI, H., and HUI, P. A. 1967. Recent investigations on wheat flour pentosans. Cereal Chem. 44:238-244.

NEWMAN, R. K., NEWMAN, C. W., and GRAHAM, H. 1989. The hypocholesterolemic function of barley β-glucans. Cereal Foods World 34:883-886.

NIEDUSZYNSKI, I. A., and MARCHESSAULT, R. H. 1972. Structure of β,D(1→4)-xylan hydrate. Biopolymers 11:1335-1344.

NIKUNI, Z. 1975. Historical review of our studies on starch granules. Denpun Kagaku 22:78-92.

NIKUNI, Z. 1978. Studies on starch granules. Staerke 30:105-111.

NILSSON, U., DAHLQVIST, A., and NILSSON, B. 1986. Cereal fructosans: Part 2—Characterization and structure of wheat fructosans. Food Chem. 22:95-106.

NORDKVIST, E., SALOMONSSON, A.-C., and ÅMAN, P. 1984. Distribution of insoluble bound phenolic acids in barley grain. J. Sci. Food Agric. 35:657-661.

ØSTERGÅRD, K., BJÖRCK, I., and VAINIONPÄÄ, J. 1989. Effects of extrusion cooking on starch and dietary fibre in barley. Food Chem. 34:215-227.

PALMER, G. H., and MacKENZIE, C. I. 1986. Levels of alkali-soluble β-D-glucans in cereal grains. J. Inst. Brew. 92:461-462.

PARRISH, F. W., PERLIN, A. S., and REESE, E. T. 1960. Selective enzymolysis of poly-β-D-glucans, and the structure of the polymers. Can. J. Chem. 38:2094-2104.

PERLIN, A. S. 1951a. Isolation and composition of the soluble pentosans of wheat flours. Cereal Chem. 28:370-381.

PERLIN, A. S. 1951b. Structure of the soluble pentosans of wheat flours. Cereal Chem. 28:382-393.

PETERSEN, P. B., and MUNCK, L. 1993. Whole crop utilization of barley, including new potential uses. Pages 437-474 in: Barley: Chemistry and Technology. A. W. MacGregor and R. S. Bhatty, eds. Am. Assoc. Cereal Chem., St. Paul, MN.

PETERSEN, V. E. 1972. The properties and values of the various feed grains in poultry nutrition. Pages 67-75 in: Cereal Processing and Digestion. U.S. Feed Grains Council, London.

PFANNEMÜLLER, B., and ZIEGAST, G. 1981. Properties of aqueous amylose and amylose iodine solutions. Pages 529-548 in: Solution Properties of Polysaccharides. D. A. Brant, ed. American Chemical Society, Washington, DC.

PFANNEMÜLLER, B., MAYERHÖFER, H., and SCHULZ, R. C. 1971. Conformation of amylose in aqueous solution: Optical rotatory dispersion and circular dichroism of amylose iodine complexes and dependence on chain length of retrogradation of amylose. Biopolymers 10:243-261.

PODRAZKY, V. 1964. Some characteristics of cereal gums. Chem. Ind. (Lond.) pp. 712-713.

POLLOCK, C. J., and CAIRNS, A. J. 1991. Fructan metabolism in grasses and cereals. Annu. Rev. Plant Physiol. Plant Mol. Biol. 42:77-101.

POLLOCK, C. J., and CHATTERTON, N. J. 1988. Fructans. Pages 109-140 in: The Biochemistry of Plants. A Comprehensive Treatise, Vol. 14. J. Preiss, ed. Academic Press, San Diego.

POWELL, W., CALIGARI, P. D. S., SWANSTON, J. S., and JINKS, J. L. 1989. Genetic investigations into beta-glucan content in barley. Theor. Appl. Genet. 71:461-466.

PREECE, I. A., and HOBKIRK, R. 1953. Non-starchy polysaccharides of cereal grains. III. Higher molecular gums of common cereals. J. Inst. Brew. 59:385-392.

PREECE, I. A., and MacDOUGALL, M. 1958. Enzymic degradation of cereal hemicelluloses. II. Pattern of pentosan degradation.

J. Inst. Brew. 64:489-500.

PREECE, I. A., and MacKENZIE, K. G. 1952. Non-starchy polysaccharides of cereal grains. I. Fractionation of the barley gums. J. Inst. Brew. 58:353-362.

PRENTICE, N., BABLER, S., and FABER, S. 1980. Enzymic analysis of beta-D-glucans in cereal grains. Cereal Chem. 57:198-202.

REES, D. A. 1972. Shapely polysaccharides. Biochem. J. 126:257-273.

REES, D. A., and WELSH, E. J. 1977. Secondary and tertiary structure of polysaccharides in solution and gels. Angew. Chem. Int. Ed. Engl. 16:214-224.

RING, S. G., GEE, J. M., WHITTAM, M., ORFORD, P., and JOHNSON, I. T. 1988. Resistant starch: Its chemical form in foodstuffs and effect on digestibility in vitro. Food Chem. 28:97-109.

ROBIN, J. P., MERCIER, C., CHARBONNIERE, R., and GUILBOT, A. 1974. Lintnerized starches. Gel filtration and enzymatic studies of insoluble residues from prolonged acid treatment of potato starch. Cereal Chem. 51:389-406.

ROGOLS, S., and MEITES, S. 1968. The effect of starch species on alpha-amylase activity. Staerke 20:256-259.

SAKURAI, N., and MASUDA, Y. 1978. Auxin-induced changes in barley coleoptile cell wall composition. Plant Cell Physiol. 19:1217-1223.

SALOMONSSON, A.-C., THEANDER, O., and WESTERLUND, E. 1984. Chemical characterization of some Swedish cereal whole meal and bran fractions. Swed. J. Agric. Res. 14:111-117.

SANDSTEDT, R. M., and UEDA, S. 1969. α-Amylase adsorption on raw starch and its relation to raw starch digestion. Denpun Kagaku 17:215-228.

SARGEANT, J. G. 1982. Determination of amylose:amylopectin ratios of starches. Starch/Staerke 34:89-92.

SEOG, H.-M., PARK, Y.-K., NAM, Y.-J., KIM, J.-P., SOHN, T.-H., and YOON, H.-S. 1988. Physicochemical properties of starch granules isolated from naked barley seeds during germination. J. Korean Agric. Chem. Soc. 31:339-345.

SETTINERI, W. J., and MARCHESSAULT, R. H. 1965. Derivation of possible chain formations for poly-β-1,4-anhydroxylose. J. Polym. Sci. Part C 11:253-264.

SLACK, P. T., and WAINWRIGHT, T. 1980. Amylolysis of large starch granules from barleys in relation to their gelatinisation temperatures. J. Inst. Brew. 86:74-77.

SLADE, A. M., HØJ, P. B., MORRICE, N. A., and FINCHER, G. B. 1989. Purification and characterization of three (1→4)-β-D-xylan endohydrolases from germinated barley. Eur. J. Biochem. 185:533-539.

SMEEKENS, S., ANGENENT, G., EBSKAMP, M., and WEISBEEK, P. 1991. Molecular biology of fructan accumulation in plants. Biochem. Soc. Trans. 19:565-569.

SMITH, D. B., GILL, A. A., and AHLUWALIA, B. 1987. Cultivar differences in the concentration of β-D-glucans in developing and mature barley grains and their significance for malting quality. Aspects Appl. Biol. 15:105-113.

SOULAKA, A. B., and MORRISON, W. R. 1985. The amylose and lipid contents, dimensions, and gelatinisation characteristics of some wheat starches and their A- and B-granule fractions. J. Sci. Food Agric. 36:709-718.

SOUTH, J. B., and MORRISON, W. R. 1990. Isolation and analysis of starch from single kernels of wheat and barley. J. Cereal Sci. 12:43-51.

SOUTHGATE, D. A. T. 1991. Determination of Food Carbohydrates. Elsevier Science Publ., Barking, U.K.

STARK, J. R., and YIN, X. S. 1986. The effect of physical damage on large and small barley starch granules. starch/Staerke 38:369-374.

STAUDTE, R. G., WOODWARD, J. R., FINCHER, G. B., and STONE, B. A. 1983. Water-soluble (1→3),(1→4)-β-D-glucans from barley (*Hordeum vulgare*) endosperm. III. Distribution of cellotriosyl and cellotetraosyl residues. Carbohydr. Polym. 3:299-312.

STEVENS, D. J., and ELTON, G. A. H. 1971. Thermal properties of the starch/water system. Part 1. Measurement of heat of gelatinisation by differential scanning calorimetry. Staerke 23:8-11.

STONE, B. A. 1984. Noncellulosic β-glucans in cell walls. Pages 52-74 in: Structure, Function and Biosynthesis of Plant Cell Walls. W. M. Duggen and S. Bartnicki-Garcia, eds. Waverly Press, Baltimore.

STONE, B. A. 1985. Aleurone cell walls—Structure and nutritional significance. Pages 349-354 in: New Approaches to Research on Cereal Carbohydrates. R. D. Hill and L. Munck, eds. Elsevier Science Publ., Amsterdam.

STUART, I. M., LOI, L., and FINCHER, G. B. 1988. Varietal and environmental variations in (1→3, 1→4)-β-glucan levels and (1→3, 1→4)-β-glucanase potential in barley: Relationships to malting quality. J. Cereal Sci. 7:61-71.

SUNDARALINGAM, M. 1968. Some aspects of stereochemistry and hydrogen bonding of carbohydrates related to polysaccharide conformations. Biopolymers 5:189-213.

SWINKELS, J. J. M. 1985. Composition and properties of commercial native starches. Starch/Staerke 37:1-5.

TAIZ, L., and JONES, R. L. 1973. Plasmodesmata and an associated cell wall component in barley aleurone tissue. Am. J. Bot. 60:67-75.

TAKAHASHI, T., KATO, K., IKEGAMI, Y., and IRIE, M. 1985. Different behavior towards raw starch of three forms of glucoamylase from a *Rhizopus* sp. J. Biochem. 98:663-671.

TAKEDA, Y., SHIRASAKA, K., and HIZUKURI, S. 1984. Examination of the purity and structure of amylose by gelpermeation chromatography. Carbohydr. Res. 132:83-92.

TAKEDA, Y., HIZUKURI, S., TAKEDA, C., and SUZUKI, A. 1987. Structures of branched molecules of amyloses of various origins, and molar fractions of branched and unbranched molecules. Carbohydr. Res. 165:139-145.

TAKEDA, Y., SHITAOZONO, T., and HIZUKURI, S. 1990. Structures of subfractions of corn amylose. Carbohydr. Res. 199:207-214.

TESTER, R. F., and MORRISON, W. R. 1991a. Swelling and gelatinization of cereal starches. I. Effects of amylopectin, amylose, and lipids. Cereal Chem. 67:551-557.

TESTER, R. F., and MORRISON, W. R. 1991b. Swelling and gelatinization of cereal starches. II. Waxy rice starches. Cereal Chem. 67:558-563.

TESTER, R. F., SOUTH, J. B., MORRISON, W. R., and ELLIS, R. P. 1991. The effects of ambient temperature during the grain-filling period on the composition and properties of starch from four barley genotypes. J. Cereal Sci. 13:113-127.

THEANDER, O., and WESTERLUND, E. 1987. Studies on chemical modifications in heat-processed starch and wheat flour. Starch/Staerke 39:88-93.

THOMPSON, A., and WOLFROM, M. L. 1951. Degradation of amylopectin to panose. J. Am. Chem. Soc. 73:5849-5850.

THURN, A., and BURCHARD, W. 1985. Heterogeneity in branching of amylopectin. Carbohydr. Polym. 5:441-460.

TIUOVA, N. A., SOROVAEVA, A. V., MAZUR, N. S., ZAIKINA, I. V., KOBZEVA, N. Y., and USTINNIKOV, B. A. 1988. 1,3-β-Glucan—A nonstarch barley polysaccharide. Appl. Biochem. Microbiol. 24:175-180.

TORP, J. 1980. Variation in the concentration of major carbohydrates in the grain of some

spring barleys. J. Sci. Food Agric. 31:1354-1360.

TOVAR, D., LIANG, G. H., and CUNNINGHAM, B. A. 1977. Effect of the waxy gene on hydrolysis of sorghum starch. Crop Sci. 17:683-686.

TVAROSKA, I., OGAWA, K., DESLANDES, Y., and MARCHESSAULT, R. H. 1983. Crystalline conformation and structure of lichenan and barley β-glucan. Can. J. Chem. 61:1608-1616.

VAN SUMERE, C. F., DE POOTER, H., ALI, H., and DEGRAUW-VAN BUSSEL, M. 1973. *N*-Feruloylglycyl-L-phenylalanine: A sequence in barley proteins. Phytochemistry 12:407-411.

VIËTOR, R. J. 1992. Structural characteristics of arabinoxylans from barley, malt and wort. Ph.D. thesis, Wageningen Agricultural University, Netherlands.

VIËTOR, R. J., ANGELINO, S. A. G. F., and VORAGEN, A. G. J. 1993. Structural features of arabinoxylans from barley and malt cell wall material. J. Cereal Sci. 15:213-222.

VORAGEN, A. G. J., SCHOLS, H. A., and GRUPPEN, H. 1992. Structural studies of plant cell wall polysaccharides using enzymes. In: Proc. Int. Symp. Plant Polymeric Polysaccharides. F. Meuser and W. Seibel, eds. In press.

WALKER, J. T., and MERRITT, N. R. 1969. Genetic control of abnormal starch granules and high amylose content in a mutant of Glacier barley. Nature 221:482-483.

WHELAN, W. J. 1971. Enzymic explorations of the structures of starch and glycogen. Biochem. J. 122:609-622.

WHISTLER, R. L., and RICHARDS, E. L. 1970. Hemicelluloses. Pages 447-469 in: The Carbohydrates: Chemistry and Biochemistry, Vol. 2A. W. Pigman and D. Horton, eds. Academic Press, London.

WHITE, W. B., BIRD, H. R., SUNDE, M. L., and MARLETT, J. A. 1983. Viscosity of β-D-glucan as a factor in the enzymatic improvement of barley for chicks. Poult. Sci. 62:853-862.

WILLINGHAM, H. E., JENSEN, L. S., and McGINNIS, J. 1959. Studies on the role of enzyme supplements and water treatment for improving the nutritional value of barley. Poult. Sci. 38:539-544.

WOOD, P. J., and FULCHER, R. G. 1984. Specific interaction of aniline blue with (1→3)-β-D-glucan. Carbohydr. Polym. 4:49-72.

WOOD, P. J., FULCHER, R. G., and STONE, B. A. 1983. Studies on the specificity of interaction of cereal cell wall components with

Congo Red and Calcofluor. Specific detection and histochemistry of (1→3),(1→4)-β-glucan. J. Cereal Sci. 1:95-110.

WOODWARD, J. R., and FINCHER, G. B. 1982. Purification and chemical properties of two (1→3),(1→4)-β-glucan endohydrolases from germinating barley. Eur. J. Biochem. 121:663-669.

WOODWARD, J. R., and FINCHER, G. B. 1983. Water-soluble barley β-glucans. Fine structure, solution behaviour and organization in the cell wall. Brew. Dig. 58:28-32.

WOODWARD, J. R., PHILLIPS, D. R., and FINCHER, G. B. 1983a. Water-soluble (1→3),(1→4)-β-D-glucans from barley (*Hordeum vulgare*) endosperm. I. Physicochemical properties. Carbohydr. Polym. 3:143-156.

WOODWARD, J. R., FINCHER, G. B., and STONE, B. A. 1983b. Water-soluble (1→3),(1→4)-β-D-glucans from barley (*Hordeum vulgare*) endosperm. II. Fine structure. Carbohydr. Polym. 3:207-225.

WOODWARD, J. R., PHILLIPS, D. R., and FINCHER, G. B. 1988. Water-soluble (1→3),(1→4)-β-D-glucans from barley (*Hordeum vulgare*) endosperm. IV. Comparison of 40°C and 65°C soluble fractions. Carbohydr. Polym. 8:85-97.

WYATT, G. M., and HORN, N. 1988. Fermentation of resistant food starches by human and rat intestinal bacteria. J. Sci. Food Agric. 44:281-288.

YAMASHITA, H., FUJINO, S., AOYAGI, S., TSUMURA, Y., HAYASE, F., and KATO, H. 1989. Characterization and mechanisms of formation of frozen beer precipitates. J. Am. Soc. Brew. Chem. 47:77-81.

ZOBEL, H. F. 1988. Molecules to granules: A comprehensive starch review. Starch/Staerke 40:44-50.

CHAPTER 4

BARLEY SEED PROTEINS

P. R. SHEWRY
Department of Agricultural Sciences
University of Bristol
Agricultural and Food Research Council
Institute of Arable Crops Research
Long Ashton Research Station
Bristol, BS18 9AF, United Kingdom

INTRODUCTION

Proteins account for about 8–15% of the dry weight of the mature barley grain. Although they are quantitatively minor components compared with carbohydrates (starch alone accounts for about 70% of the dry weight), they have been studied in great detail. This is because their amount and composition influence the suitability and quality of the grain for its final end-uses. The quality for malting is negatively correlated with the total amount of hordein storage proteins and is also affected by the hordein composition, but it is positively correlated with the amounts of hydrolytic enzymes such as amylases and β-glucanase. Hordein also limits the nutritional quality of the grain for monogastric livestock (e.g., pigs and poultry), due to its low content of the essential amino acids lysine and threonine. These aspects of grain quality, discussed in detail elsewhere in this volume, have provided the stimulus for much of the work on barley seed proteins. Similarly, genetic variation in the suitability of barley for different purposes has led to the use of protein polymorphisms as markers for varietal identification and finger-printing.

This review aims to summarize current knowledge of the structure and synthesis of proteins present in the mature barley grain and to focus on work done over the last decade. Earlier work has been reviewed in several previous articles (for example, Djurtoft, 1961, and Shewry and Miflin, 1983), and changes that occur during malting are discussed in Chapter 7.

CLASSIFICATION OF BARLEY SEED PROTEINS

The classification of proteins into groups on the basis of their extraction and solubility in a series of solvents was pioneered by T. B. Osborne (Osborne,

1924) and has formed the basis for the modern study of cereal seed proteins. Four such groups were recognized. The albumins and globulins are soluble in water and dilute salt solutions, respectively, and the prolamins (called hordeins in barley) are soluble in alcohol-water mixtures. The final fraction, the glutelins, consists of all the proteins not extracted in the other solvents. Although glutelins are classically extracted with dilute acid or alkali, it is now more usual to use a detergent (e.g., sodium dodecyl sulfate [SDS]) and/or a chaotropic agent (e.g., urea), often in the presence of a reducing agent.

The advantages and limitations of the Osborne classifications have been discussed in detail previously (Miflin and Shewry 1977, 1979; Shewry et al, 1986) and will become apparent to the reader of this chapter. In this discussion, barley proteins are considered as two groups, defined according to function: nonstorage and storage. The latter includes only those that function solely for storage. These include members of two solubility groups: the major alcohol-soluble prolamins (hordeins) and the quantitatively minor globulins. The nonstorage group includes all the structural and metabolic proteins, some of which may accumulate in sufficient quantities to have a secondary storage role (e.g., β-amylase). In fact, all of the endosperm proteins can be considered to have a storage role in that they can be mobilized during germination to provide nutrients for the developing seedling.

NONSTORAGE PROTEINS

Electrophoretic analyses of albumin, globulin, and "true glutelin" (i.e., not contaminated by hordein) fractions show the presence of many components varying in relative molecular weight (M_r) (Figs. 1 and 2) and pI (Shewry et al, 1979b). Very few of these components, which can together account for half or more of the total grain protein, have been characterized in detail. I shall, therefore, initially summarize the characteristics of the three solubility fractions that make up the nonstorage proteins and then consider individual components in detail.

Albumins and Globulins

Major differences have been reported in the proportions of these two groups, which probably reflect the difficulties in ensuring reproducible extraction. Osborne (1895, 1924) appreciated that the presence of salts in all plant tissues made it impossible to prepare a true albumin fraction by direct extraction with water, and therefore he chose to extract total salt-soluble proteins and precipitate the globulins by dialysis against water. The albumins and globulins prepared in this way represented 2.8 and 18.1%, respectively, of the total seed proteins. More recently Rhodes and Gill (1980) used similar methods to show that the proportions of albumins and globulins varied from 8.5 to 12.5% and from 2.3 to 5.7%, respectively, of the total grain nitrogen in three cultivars containing 2.1–2.3% nitrogen. Other workers have used sequential extractions with water, followed by dilute saline (Brandt, 1976; Singh and Sastry, 1977).

Electrophoretic analyses of albumin and globulin fractions show many components that vary in their M_rs, from about 70,000 to below 10,000, with low-M_r components concentrated in the albumins (Fig. 2). The amino acid compositions determined by Folkes and Yemm (1956) are probably as accurate as any reported since and are on carefully prepared fractions (Table 1). They show that the albumins are similar in composition to a group of "protoplasmic" proteins prepared previously from leaves (Yemm and Folkes, 1953).

Difficulty in the reproducible preparation of "pure" (i.e., lacking cross-contamination) albumin and globulin fractions and increasing recognition that these fractions have little validity in terms of function have led most present-day workers to extract a combined salt-soluble protein fraction. The extraction of individual fractions is, however, still valuable as a first step in the purification of individual components.

Such salt-soluble protein preparations show the expected high degree of polymorphism on electrophoresis (Fig. 3) and have amino acid compositions similar to those of individual albumin and globulin fractions (Table 1).

The proportion of the total grain N extracted in the salt-soluble proteins varies inversely with the total N content of the grain. Bishop (1928) reported that the amount varied from 24 to 36% of the total nitrogen, and Kirkman et al (1982) reported 17–26%.

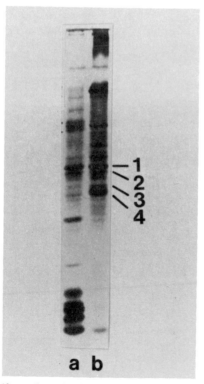

Fig. 1. Sodium dodecyl sulfate-polyacrylamide gel electrophoresis of salt-soluble proteins (track a) and glutelins (track b) from barley cv. Bomi. Band 1 is extracted as a salt-soluble protein when reduced, whereas bands 2 to 4 are contaminating hordeins. (Reprinted from Wilson et al, 1981, by permission of Oxford University Press)

The extractability of the salt-soluble proteins is determined by many factors, some of which are beyond the control of the experimenter. These include the fineness of grinding of the meal, the chemical composition of the extractant (molarity, pH, presence of a reducing agent), the temperature of extraction, and the physiological state of the grain, which may be affected by the storage conditions. These aspects have been discussed in detail by Djurtoft (1961) and Préaux and Lontie (1975).

However, not all of the salt-soluble nitrogen is present in proteins. Early work showed that about 40% of the extracted nitrogen was not precipitated by 5% trichloroacetic acid (Bishop, 1928) or retained on dialysis (Djurtoft, 1961), and we have reported similar values (40 and 30%, respectively) in a more recent study (Shewry et al, 1978a). These nonprotein components include peptides and free amino acids, although the latter probably account for only about 2% of the total grain amino acids (Bright et al, 1981).

Glutelins and Residual Proteins

Because the glutelin fraction contains proteins that have not been extracted in the previous fractions (albumins, globulins, prolamins), its total amount varies inversely with the efficiency of extraction. Furthermore, this contamination is often apparent in its protein pattern on electrophoresis and in its amino acid composition. There is no easy answer to the problem of incomplete extraction, as attempts to improve the extraction of previous

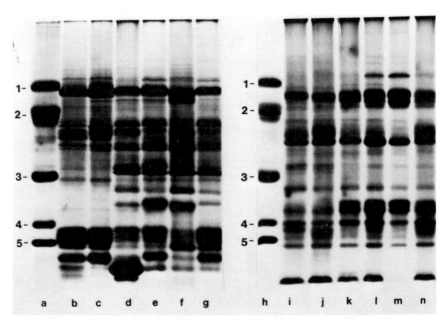

Fig. 2. Sodium dodecyl sulfate-polyacrylamide gel electrophoresis of albumin (b–g) and globulin (i–n) fractions from various cultivars of barley. Tracks a and h are M_r standards: 1, 66,000; 2, 45,000; 3, 24,000; 4, 18,400; 5, 14,300. (Reprinted from Rhodes and Gill, 1980, by permission of the Society of Chemical Industry)

fractions by using harsh conditions may render the true glutelins insoluble due to denaturation. The problem is further compounded by the innate low solubility of the glutelins, and the most effective classical solvents such as dilute alkali almost certainly cause partial degradation. Prolamin contamination is particularly a problem; early analyses of glutelin fractions prepared without prior extraction of prolamins in the presence of a reducing agent are practically worthless. These problems are exemplified by the study of Landry et al (1972), who showed that the glutelins could account for 7–38% of the total grain N and contain 9.4–14.1% proline (which gives a good indication of the degree of contamination with prolamins).

Although it may not be possible to prepare an undenatured glutelin fraction that is totally free of contaminating prolamins, the amounts of these contaminants can be reduced to a minimum, and they can be recognized by their mobility on SDS-polyacrylamide gel electrophoresis (PAGE) (Fig. 1). The nonprolamin components tend to have high molecular weights and give a high background on the stained gel, but some low-M_r components are also present. The amino acid compositions of such fractions (Table 1; Shewry and Miflin, 1983) tend to be similar to those of albumins and globulins, although

TABLE 1
Amino Acid Compositions (mol %) of Albumin, Globulin, and Glutelin Protein Fractions

Amino Acid	Albumins	Globulins	Protoplasmic Proteins	Salt-Soluble Proteins	Glutelins	Residual Proteins
Asp[a]	10.7	9.2	8.8	8.2	9.2	8.5
Thr	4.5	3.9	5.3	4.1	5.5	5.5
Ser	5.5	6.4	4.6	5.0	7.2	7.2
Glu[b]	9.6	11.4	10.6	13.9	12.7	11.8
Pro	5.6	4.4	5.2	8.4	6.1	6.5
Gly	9.0	17.5	9.2	9.6	8.9	10.7
Ala	9.6	1.1	11.0	7.9	9.1	10.1
Cys	2.0	4.3	1.2	5.3	1.2	1.2
Val	7.8	6.7	6.8	6.5	6.9	7.0
Met	1.9	1.5	1.6	1.7	1.4	1.4
Ile	5.5	3.6	6.0	3.3	4.1	4.0
Leu	7.6	7.4	8.0	7.1	8.7	7.8
Tyr	3.3	2.3	3.0	2.7	2.2	2.1
Phe	4.0	3.4	4.1	2.9	4.5	4.4
His	1.9	1.7	1.9	2.3	2.5	2.3
Lys	5.3	5.2	5.2	4.0	5.3	5.3
Arg	4.3	9.0	5.0	7.1	4.5	4.2
Trp	1.7	1.1	2.5	nd[c]	nd	nd
Percent amidation[d]	36	41	33	nd	nd	nd
Reference[e]	1	1	1	2	3	4

[a] Includes Asn.
[b] Includes Gln.
[c] Not determined.
[d] Amidation of Asp + Glu determined by mild hydrolysis.
[e] References: 1 = Recalculated from Folkes and Yemm (1956), 2 = Shewry et al (1979b), 3 = alcohol-insoluble reduced and alkylated glutelin fraction (Shewry et al 1978a; Shewry and Miflin, 1983), 4 = Shewry et al (1978a) and Shewry and Miflin (1983).

prolamin contamination may be reflected in increased proportions of proline and glutamate (which includes glutamine).

What are the "true" glutelin components? Very little is known, and few if any, have been characterized in detail. They are usually considered to be a mixture of bound enzymes and structural proteins (Wilson et al, 1981).

The insoluble residual proteins pose similar problems of contamination with denatured proteins from other groups and even greater problems of characterization. They account for about 10% of the total grain nitrogen and have an amino acid composition similar to that of glutelins. They probably include insoluble structural proteins, such as cell wall proteins.

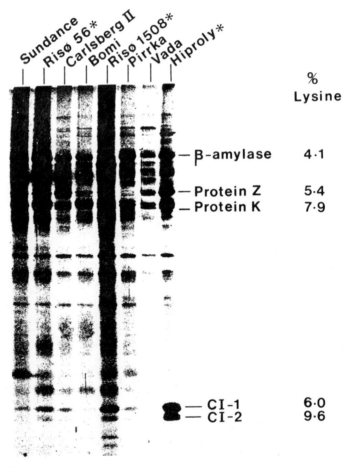

% Lysine

— β-amylase 4·1

— Protein Z 5·4
— Protein K 7·9

— CI-1 6·0
— CI-2 9·6

*high lysine mutants

Fig. 3. Sodium dodecyl sulfate-polyacrylamide gel electrophoresis of salt-soluble protein fractions from a range of barley lines, indicating high-lysine and basic proteins. Risø 56, Risø 1508, and Hiproly are high-lysine mutants. (Reprinted, by permission, from Shewry and Kreis, 1989)

β-Amylase and Protein Z

Although we now know that β-amylase and protein Z are not related structurally, they are similar in a number of their properties, including having high M_rs (about 40,000 for protein Z and 60,000 for β-amylase) and being present at elevated levels in the high-lysine line Hiproly. In addition, both occur in free and bound forms, and they may be associated to form heterodimers. Therefore, it is logical to consider these two proteins together.

β-Amylase—(1→4)-α-D-glucan maltohydrolase—is present in most, if not all, tissues of the barley plant (Shewry et al, 1988a), but it has been characterized in detail only from mature and germinating seed. Most genotypes of barley contain about 1 mg of β-amylase per gram of dry weight (corresponding to about 1% of the total seed proteins), but the amount is influenced by genetic and environmental factors. A substantial increase (about three- to fivefold) occurs in Hiproly, where it contributes to the increased lysine content of the whole seed (Hejgaard and Boisen, 1980). In contrast, the amount, whether determined as diastatic activity (Allison, 1978) or total protein (Shewry and Miflin 1985; Shewry et al, 1988a), is reduced in several high-lysine mutants of the Risø series, including Risø 1508 (Fig. 3). The differences in the amounts of β-amylase protein in Hiproly, Sundance (a normal-lysine cultivar), and Risø mutant 1508 are associated with differences in the abundance of β-amylase-related mRNAs (Kreis et al, 1987).

β-Amylase also behaves as a storage protein in that it is one of two major salt-soluble proteins that increase in amount in response to nitrogen nutrition (Giese and Hejgaard, 1984), although only a small increase occurs in the population of translatable mRNA (Giese and Hopp, 1984).

Analyses of β-amylase have shown a high degree of polymorphism, with the existence of isoenzymes varying in their pIs and charge characteristics and isoforms differing in their M_rs. Visuri and Nummi (1972) showed by sedimentation equilibrium ultracentrifugation that the form present in the mature grain had an M_r of 57,200 and that bands of about this size are present in reduced salt-soluble fractions from a range of genotypes (Shewry et al, 1988a) (Fig. 3). Western blotting, with an antibody raised against β-amylase from mature grain, showed a strong reaction with this band and a weaker reaction with a diffuse band of higher M_r (Fig. 4B). Isoelectric focusing showed two different patterns of isoenzymes in eight barley genotypes, with seven to nine major components with pIs of 5–6 (Shewry et al, 1988a). The relationship between these multiple components and the simple patterns of isoforms revealed by SDS-PAGE under reducing conditions is not known, but they could result at least partly from aggregation.

β-Amylase is present in the mature barley grain in two fractions, free and latent (Hejgaard, 1978). The free fraction is readily extractable with dilute saline but consists of a mixture of forms that may result in part from the formation of aggregates (stabilized by disulfide bonds) with itself and with other proteins such as protein Z (see below) (Nummi et al, 1965; Hejgaard and Carlsen, 1977; LaBerge and Marchylo, 1983). Disulfide bonding is probably also responsible for the properties of the bound form, which is extracted only in the presence of a reducing agent or by treatment with the proteolytic enzyme papain. SDS-PAGE of the free and bound fractions under reducing conditions shows that they consist of the same two isoforms (see above) in about the same proportions (Shewry et al, 1988a).

The free and bound forms both accumulate during seed development, mostly in the aleurone and starchy endosperm tissues. Immunochemical and enzymatic studies show that β-amylase is principally located in the cytosolic fraction, not in the protein bodies (Nishimura et al, 1987). There is also an increase in the proportion of bound enzyme during development, and Hara-Nishimura et al (1986) have suggested that the conversion of free β-amylase into the

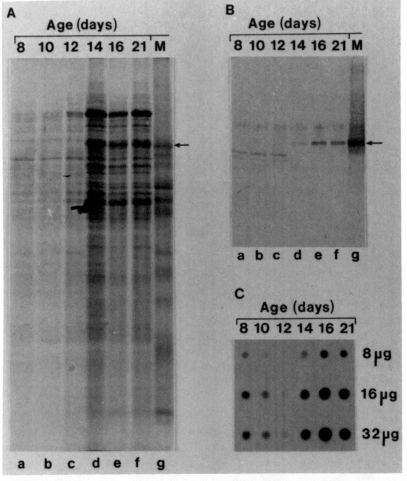

Fig. 4. β-Amylase protein and mRNA in developng seeds of barley cv. Sundance. A, analysis of total salt-soluble proteins by sodium dodecyl sulfate-polyacrylamide gel electrophoresis. Tracks a, b, and c are from whole caryopses at 8, 10, and 12 days after anthesis, respectively; d, e, and f are from isolated endosperms at 14, 16, and 21 days after anthesis, respectively; g is from mature grain. The arrow in g indicates the major β-amylase band present in mature grain. B, western blot analysis of the samples shown in A, using β-amylase antiserum. The arrow in g indicates the major β-amylase band present in mature grain. C, hybrid-dot analysis of the abundance of β-amylase mRNAs. (Reprinted, by permission, from Shewry et al, 1988a)

bound form occurs as a result of association with the periphery of starch granules during the desiccation phase of seed development.

Changes in the isoforms and isoenzymes of β-amylase also occur during seed development and germination. Shewry et al (1988a) showed that the β-amylase in young developing caryopses consisted of two low-M_r isoforms (and several isoenzymes) that were not observed in the older developing endosperms or in the mature grain (Fig. 4A and B). These were associated with a separate population of mRNAs (Fig. 4C) and may have corresponded to "green" β-amylase present in the pericarp and/or testa.

Recent work by Lundgard and Svensson (1986, 1987) has shown that lower-M_r isoforms may also occur in mature grain but that these result from partial proteolysis of the major ($M_r \approx 59,700$) isoform. Three such isoforms, of M_r 58,000, 56,000 and 54,000, were characterized, the conversion of the high-M_r isoform being catalyzed by malt enzymes. Although Shewry et al (1988a) failed to demonstrate significant amounts of these isoforms in the mature grain, they did demonstrate their appearance during germination or malting. This was associated with changes in the pattern of isoenzymes on isoelectric focusing.

Kreis et al (1987) reported the characterization of a cloned, full-length cDNA encoding a seed β-amylase from Hiproly. The protein consists of 535 amino acids, with a calculated molecular weight of 59,663 (Fig. 5). The N-terminal region was identical to a 12-residual cyanogen bromide peptide, indicating that β-amylase is synthesized as a mature protein. This is consistent with its deposition in the cytosol (Nishimura et al, 1987).

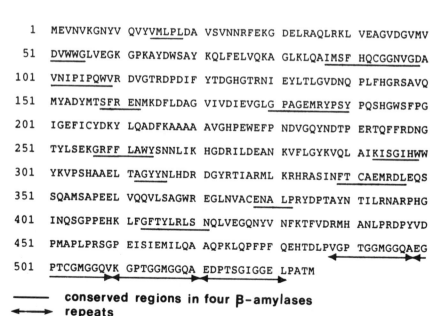

Fig. 5. Deduced amino acid sequence of a cDNA clone encoding β-amylase from barley endosperms (based on Kreis et al, 1987). The 12 underlined regions are conserved in β-amylases from four sources (Kitamoto et al, 1988). The arrows indicate four repeats of 11 residues.

The amino acid sequence is not related to those of any other barley proteins, but it does show homology with β-amylases from soybean (Mikami et al, 1988), *Bacillus polymyxa* (Kawazu et al, 1987), and *Clostridium thermosulforogenes* (Kitamoto et al, 1988). Kitamoto et al (1988) identified 12 regions that were reasonably well conserved in the four proteins (Fig. 5), which presumably include residues involved in the active site.

Four amino acid repeats of 11 residues, including five glycines, are present in the C-terminal region of the barley enzyme (Fig. 5). Lundgard and Svensson (1987) showed that the major low-M_r isoform produced by limited proteolysis (M_r 54,000) consisted of several components terminating between Gly 493 and Gln 497, within the first of these repeat blocks. They proposed that the other low-M_r isoforms (58,000 and 56,000) could have resulted from similar proteolytic processing within the other repeat blocks.

Analysis of β-amylase isoenzymes in developing and mature grains demonstrated that the phenotypes were controlled by co-dominant alleles at a single locus (Allison and Ellis, 1973) on the long arm of chromosome 4 (Ainsworth et al, 1987). Restriction-fragment analysis confirmed the presence of genes (probably two copies) on the long arm of chromosome 4 but also showed an additional (probably single copy) gene on the short arm of chromosome 2 (Kreis et al, 1988). These loci have been designated *Bmy1* and *Bmy2*, respectively (Nielsen et al, 1983; Kreis et al, 1988). It is not known whether the *Bmy2* gene is silent or expressed, either in vegetative tissues or in the developing endosperm, to give a quantitatively minor form.

Protein Z is one of the major grain albumins, being present at levels varying from about 0.2 mg/g in some "low-protein-Z cultivars" such as Pirrka to 1.5–2.5 mg/g in most commercially grown cultivars (Hejgaard, 1982). It resembles β-amylase in being increased (by about twofold) in Hiproly and derived lines, and its moderately high lysine content (about 5.3 mol%) (Hejgaard, 1982) contributes to their "high-lysine" phenotype (Hejgaard and Boisen, 1980). Hejgaard (1982) calculated that it could contribute up to 5% of the total lysine in normal barleys but more than 7% in some high-lysine lines.

Giese and Hejgaard (1984) showed that the amount of protein Z was increased at high levels of nitrogen nutrition, being similar to β-amylase and hordein in this respect. Subsequent studies showed that the amount of protein Z mRNA increased linearly with the amount of nitrogen fed to liquid-cultured detached spikes (Giese and Hopp, 1984).

Protein Z, like β-amylase, is present in free and bound (thiol- or papain-extractable) forms. The free form accounts for 20–30% of the total (Hejgaard, 1982) and includes heterodimers with β-amylase (Hejgaard, 1977; Hejgaard and Carlsen, 1977). It is very resistant to denaturation and proteolytic digestion during malting and germination, is the only well-defined protein of barley origin present in beer (where it is called antigen 1), and may contribute to foam stability and/or haze formation (Hejgaard, 1977; Hejgaard and Kaersgaard, 1983).

Protein Z purified from mature barley grain consists of four antigenically identical forms with M_rs of about 40,000 and pIs ranging from 5.56 to 5.8 (Hejgaard, 1982). Its amino acid composition is different from that of β-amylase, and the amino acid sequence (Fig. 6) shows no homology (Rasmussen et al, 1984; Hejgaard et al, 1985; Brandt et al, 1990). The amino acid sequence is, however, homologous with members of the α_1-antitrypsin family of protease inhibitors, which occur in animals (Hejgaard et al, 1985; Brandt et al, 1990). The homology between the C terminal 180 residues of protein Z and these proteins varies from 26 to 32% of residues in identical positions. Protein Z was partially cleaved by clostripain at a Met-Ser bond corresponding to the reactive sites of the inhibitors, suggesting a possible inhibitory role in barley. However, it did not inhibit a range of serine proteases (subtilisin, *Aspergillus* protease, pancreatic elastase, chymotrypsin, and trypsin) in in vitro assays. This does not, however, rule out a role in vivo, either in regulation of endogenous proteases or in protection from pathogens or pests.

Genetic analyses show that protein Z is encoded by a single locus (designated *Paz1*), which is in the center of chromosome 4 and loosely linked (48 cM) to the *Bmy1* locus (Nielsen et al, 1983, Hejgaard 1984). Southern blot analysis using a protein Z cDNA clone demonstrated that the protein was encoded by a small multigene family consisting of five to seven members (Rasmussen et al, 1984).

Hordothionins

Thionins were one of the first groups of cereal proteins to be purified, being isolated from wheat flour in the early 1940s (Balls et al, 1942). These were called purothionins. Although initially prepared from petroleum ether extracts and considered to be lipoproteins, they were subsequently shown to be identical to proteins present in the globulin fraction (Redman and Fisher, 1968; Hernández-Lucas et al, 1977); the association with lipids may be an artefact of extraction (Hernández-Lucas et al, 1977).

Thionins have since been purified from barley (Redman and Fisher, 1969), rye (Hernández-Lucas et al, 1978), and oats (Bekes and Lasztity, 1981). All are low-M_r ($\approx$5,000) proteins, rich in cysteine and basic residues.

Carbonero et al (1980) demonstrated that hordothionin (the thionin in barley seeds) is associated with protein bodies and estimated that it accounted for about 3–4% of the protein body fraction (compared to 50–60% of hordeins). More recent work from the same laboratory showed that it was possible to obtain protein bodies free of thionin by a brief treatment with the detergent Nonidet NP40 and suggested that hordothionin was extrinsically associated with the rough endoplasmic reticulum (ER) (Ponz et al, 1983). The amount

```
MATTLATDVR  LSIAHQTRFA  LRLRSAISSN  PERAAGNVAF  SPLSLHVALS   50
LITAGAAATR  DQLVAILGDG  GAGDAKELNA  LAEQVVQFVL  ANESSTGGPR  100
IAFANGIFVD  ASLSLKPSFE  ELAVCQYKAK  TQSVDFQHKT  LEAVGQVNSW  150
VEQVTTGLIK  QILPPGSVDN  TTKLILGNAL  YFKGAWDQKF  DESNTKCDSF  200
HLLDGSSIQT  QFMSSTKKQY  ISSSDNLKVL  KLPYAKGHDK  RQFSMYILLP  250
GAQDGLWSLA  KRLSTEPEFI  ENHIPKQTVE  VGRFQLPKFK  ISYQFEASSL  300
LRALGLQLPF  SEEADLSEMV  DSSQGLEISH  VFHKSFVEVN  EEGTEAGAAT  350
VAMGVAMSMP  LKVDLVDFVA  NHPFLFLIRE  DIAGVVVFVG  HVTNPLISA*  400
```

Fig. 6. Amino acid sequence of barley endosperm protein Z4 as deduced from the nucleotide sequence of the gene *Paz 1* (based on Brandt et al, 1990). A signal peptide does not appear to be present.

of hordothionin present in the high-lysine mutant Risø 1508 is about half of that in the parental line Bomi (Ponz et al, 1986).

Hordothionin consists of major (α-) and minor (β-) components (Redman and Fisher, 1969), both of which have been sequenced (Ozaki et al, 1980; Lecomte et al, 1982). In addition, cDNA clones for both proteins (Ponz et al, 1983, 1986; Hernández-Lucas et al, 1986) and a gene for α-hordothionin (Rodriguez-Palenzuela et al, 1988) have been isolated and characterized.

The mature α- and β-hordothionins consist of 45 residues, of which all except six are identical (Fig. 7). Both have N-terminal signal peptides of 18 residues. In addition, they are both synthesized as precursors, with C-terminal extensions of 64 residues. The role and fate of the C-terminal acidic proteins and the subcellular location of the processing event are not known (Ponz et al, 1986).

A further type of barley seed thionin, called γ-hordothionin, has recently been purified and characterized (Mendez et al, 1990). This is a single polypeptide chain of 47 residues, with a calculated molecular weight of 5,250. It has limited sequence homology with the α- and β-hordothionins and the corresponding purothionins of wheat (26–27% similarity) and inhibits translation in cell-free systems derived from mammals and other organisms. At least two related γ-purothionins are present in wheat (Colilla et al, 1990), and related proteins from sorghum are active as inhibitors of insect (locust and cockroach) α-amylases (Bloch and Richardson, 1991).

Until recently, the cereal grain thionins were little more than a curiosity. The situation has changed dramatically over the last few years, with interest

Signal

```
                                        18
α     M V C L L I L G L V L E [Q] V Q V E G
β     M V C L L I L G L V L E [H] V Q V E G
```

Mature Protein

```
α     K S C C R S T L G R N C Y N L C R V R G A Q K L C
β     K S C C R S T L G R N C Y N L C R V R G A Q K L C

                                                45
α     A [G V] C R C K L T S [S G] K C P [T G] F P K
β     A [N A] C R C K L T S [G L] K C P [S S] F P K
```

"Acidic Protein"

```
α     L A L V S N S D E P D T [V K] Y C N L G C R A S M C
β     L A L V S N S D E P D T [I D] Y C N L G C R A S M C

α     D Y M V N A A A D D E E M K L Y [L] E [N] C [S] D A C V
β     D Y M V N A A A D D E E M K L Y [V] E H C [G] D A C V

                                        64
α     N F C N G D [A] G L T S L T A
β     N F C N G D [V] G L T S L T A
```

Fig. 7. Amino acid sequences of α- and β-purothionins, based on Ponz et al (1986) and Hernandez-Lucas et al (1986).

centered on two topics: their relationships to proteins from other sources and their biological role.

Related proteins have been isolated from diverse sources: mistletoe leaves and stems (viscotoxins) (Samuelsson et al, 1968), seeds of the crucifer *Crambe abyssinica* (crambins) (Teeter et al, 1981), leaves and seeds of *Pyrularia pubera* (Santalaceae) (Vernon et al, 1985), and, more recently, leaves of barley (Bohlmann and Apel, 1987; Gausing, 1987; Bohlmann et al, 1988; Reimann-Philipp et al, 1989). Physiochemical studies have also shown that seed thionins from barley and wheat have conformations similar to those of crambin (Lecomte et al, 1982; Williams and Teeter, 1984).

Hordothionin contains eight cysteine residues, which probably form four disulfide bonds, as demonstrated for wheat purothionins (Hase et al, 1978; Lecomte et al, 1982). This high content of disulfide bonds has suggested a role in redox systems. Johnson et al (1987) demonstrated that wheat thioredoxin *h* can activate fructose-$(1\rightarrow6)$-bisphosphate by secondary thiol redox control via purothionin. In addition, purothionin also inhibited the activities of ribonucleotide reductases from *E. coli* and calf thymus with reduced thioredoxin as hydrogen donor, suggesting that purothionin competes with ribonucleotide reductase for reducing equivalents from thioredoxin. The authors suggested that inhibition of deoxyribonucleotide synthesis was a possible mechanism for the toxicity to cultured mammalian cells.

The well-documented toxicity of thionins to cultured mammalian cells, yeasts, and phytopathogenic bacteria (Garcia-Olmedo et al, 1982) suggests that they may form part of a defense mechanism against pests and pathogens. Carrasco et al (1981) showed that purothionins induced membrane leakiness in cultured mammalian cells, while Garcia-Olmedo et al (1983) demonstrated inhibition of cell-free protein synthesis using wheat germ and rabbit reticulocyte lysate systems. Purothionins also inhibit the activity of wheat α-amylase, although at relatively high concentrations (Jones and Meredith, 1982).

A role in crop protection is also indicated by recent studies of barley leaf thionins. Two subfractions of leaf thionins have been identified, an intracellular group present mainly within the vacuole (Reimann-Philipp et al, 1989) and an extracellular group present in cell walls (Bohlmann et al, 1988). The latter group is inhibitory to plant-pathogenic fungi, and its synthesis is induced by infection with pathogens (Bohlmann et al, 1988).

Endochitinases (Proteins C and T)

Hejgaard and Bjørn (1985) purified a basic protein of M_r 28,000 and pI 9.7, which was one of four major basic proteins that together accounted for up to 5% of the total salt-soluble proteins. This component, called C, was present at levels varying from about 0.09 to 0.60 mg/g of grain. Leah et al (1987) subsequently determined amino acid sequences of the protein N terminus (54 residues) and a cyanogen bromide fragment (40 residues), which showed strong homology with a bean endochitinase (Broglie et al, 1986) (Fig. 8). A major difference was that the bean endochitinase extended for 46 residues beyond the N terminus of the barley protein, and similar N-terminal extensions have since been demonstrated for endochitinases from other sources (Ary et al, 1989). This region of the bean enzyme is homologous to wheat germ agglutinin, leading to the suggestion that it is involved in the recognition of chitin rather than catalysis (Lucas et al, 1985). Nevertheless, the barley protein released soluble radioactivity from ^{3}H-labeled chitin polymer, indicating its ability to recognize, bind, and hydrolyze chitin. More recently, Leah et al (1991) isolated a full-length cDNA for endochitinase C, showing that it encodes a protein of 243 residues with a molecular weight of 25,933. However, the deduced protein sequence was not identical to that determined by direct sequencing (Leah et al, 1987), indicating the presence of isoforms. Leah et al (1991) also demonstrated that the purified protein inhibited the growth in vitro of *Trichoderma* and *Fusarium*, particularly in the presence of purified protein synthesis inhibitor and β-glucanase (see below). Protein C is encoded by structural genes on chromosome 1 (Hejgaard and Bjørn 1987).

Jacobsen et al (1990) subsequently isolated a second endochitinase, called T, which has an M_r of 33,000 and a pI of 9.8. A 23-residue sequence at the N terminus was related to the lectinlike sequence present in most other endochitinases, and a nine-residue sequence from a cyanogen bromide peptide was homologous with the cyanogen bromide fragment of endochitinase C

```
N-termini

                         10        20        30        40
Bean:       NH2- EQCGRQAGGALCPGGNCCSQFGWCGSTTDYCPGCQSQCGGP
Barley T: NH2- XQQGSQAGGATCPNXLCC

                         50        60        70        80
Bean:       SPAPTDLSALISRSTFDQMLKHRNDGACPAKGFYTYDAFIA
Barley C:   NH2- SVSSIVSRAQFDRMLLHRNDGATQAKGFYTYDAFVA

                         90       100
Bean:       AAKAYPSFGNTGDTATRK
Barley C:   AAAAFPGFGRTGSADARK


Cyanogen Bromide Peptides

                         10        20        30        40
Barley C: MTAQPPKPSSHAVIAGQWSPDGADRAAGRVPGFGVITNIIN
Barley T: MTAQAPKPS

Partial cDNA (probably T)


            10        20        30        40        50        60
HETTGGWATAPDGAFAWGYCFKQERGATSNYCTPSAQWPCAPGKSYYGRGPIQLSHNYNY

            70        80        90       100       110       120
GPAGRAIGVDLLRNPDLVATDPTVSFKTAMWFWMTAQAPKPSSHAVITGQWSPSGTDRAA
                                        ----P---------A-----D-A----
           130       140       150       160       170       178
GRVPGFGVITNIVNGGIECGHGQDSRVADRIGFYKRYCDILGVGYCNNLDCYSQRPFA*
            ------------I-

        * = stop codon.
```

Fig. 8. Partial amino acid sequences of barley endochitinases C and T, based on sequences reported by Leah et al (1987), Jacobsen et al (1990), and Swegle et al (1989). The N-terminal sequences are aligned with those of the bean endochitinase (Broglie et al, 1986), demonstrating that endochitinase T has homology with the lectinlike sequence present in most endochitinases.

(Fig. 8). The protein was closely similar, if not identical, to the product of a partial cDNA clone isolated from an aleurone cell library by Swegle et al (1989). This encoded 178 residues from the protein C terminus (Fig. 8) and gave a protein of M_r 36,000 on hybrid-selected translation. Southern blot analysis showed one to three hybridizing fragments located on chromosome 1.

Endochitinases C and T are both highly inhibitory to fungal growth. Roberts and Selitrennikoff (1986) initially identified endochitinase C as one of two barley proteins that actively inhibited the growth of *Trichoderma reesei* and showed that it also inhibited *Phycomyces, Alternaria*, and *Neurospora*. Jacobsen et al (1990) demonstrated that endochitinases C and T inhibited the growth of *T. viride*, and that both also exhibited low lysozyme activity, 10^4 lower than that of hen egg white lysozyme.

Both proteins are located in the starchy endosperm and aleurone but not in the embryo and accumulate relatively late in grain development (Jacobsen et al, 1990).

Protein Synthesis Inhibitors (Protein K)

The second antifungal protein isolated by Roberts and Selitrennikoff (1986) had an M_r of about 30,000 and was 20 times less active in inhibiting the growth of *T. reesei* than the endochitinase (protein C above). This protein inactivated fungal ribosomes and was probably identical to one of the protein synthesis inhibitors characterized by Asano et al (1984).

Asano et al (1984) demonstrated that barley seeds contain three closely related inhibitors of cell-free animal protein synthesis. These correspond to a major basic salt-soluble protein, called protein K, isolated subsequently by Hejgaard and Bjørn (1985). They demonstrated that protein K consisted of three immunologically identical components (Ka, Kb, and Kc) with pIs varying from 10.1 to 10.3 and the total amount ranging from 0.18 to 0.42 mg/g of grain.

Asano et al (1986) subsequently determined the complete amino acid sequence of the predominant component, called protein translation inhibitor II. It consisted of a single chain of 280 residues (Fig. 9A), with a calculated molecular weight of 29,836. It was homologous with the A-chain of ricin from castor bean, demonstrating that it belongs to a major family of ribosome-inactivating proteins (Stirpe and Barbieri, 1986).

Leah et al (1991) subsequently isolated a cDNA for an M_r 30,000 ribosome-inactivating protein from barley grain. This encoded a protein of 280 residues, which differed in six residues from the protein sequenced by Asano et al (1986). A purified preparation of the protein gave slight inhibition of the growth of *Trichoderma* and *Fusarium*, which was greatly increased in the presence of endochitinase (see above) and β-glucanase (see below). The cDNA also conferred resistance to the soilborne pathogen *Rhizoctonia solani* when transferred to tobacco plants under the control of a wound-inducible promoter (Logemann et al, 1992).

The ribosome-inactivating proteins are divided into two classes (Stirpe and Barbieri, 1986). Type 1 proteins, which include the barley toxin (and related proteins from wheat and rye [Reisbig and Bruland, 1983]), consist of single subunits of M_r about 30,000 that are toxic to animal cells only at concentrations exceeding 1–10μM. The type 2 proteins, such as ricin, consist of two polypeptide chains associated by disulfide bonds, of which one (the A-chain) is catalytic and related to the type 1 proteins and the second (the B-chain) is a galactose-binding lectin.

Asano et al (1986) studied the effects of the barley translation inhibitor II on various stages of protein synthesis using the rabbit reticulocyte lysate system. They concluded that it inhibited a reaction in the elongation cycle subsequent to binding of the amino acyl-tRNA but preceding the translocation. More recently Endo et al (1988) reported that the barley toxin inhibits hydrolysis of the N-glycosidic bond at adenine 4,324 of the 28S rRNA via an enzymatic reaction. This is similar to the mechanism of action of the ricin A-chain.

A. Barley Translation Inhibitor II

```
              10                    20
A A K M A K N V D K P L F T A T F N V Q
              30                    40
A S S A D Y A T F I A G I R N K L R N P
              50                    60
A H F S H N E P V L P P V E P N V P P S
              70                    80
R W F H V V L K A S P T S A G L T L A I
              90                   100
R A D N I Y L E G F K S S D G T W W E L
             110                   120
T P G L I P G A T Y V G F G G T Y R D I
             130                   140
L G D T D K L T N V A L G R Q Q L E D A
             150                   160
V T A L H G R T K A D K A S G P K Q Q Q
             170                   180
A R E A V T T L L L M V N E A T R F Q T
             190                   200
V S G F V A G L L H P K A V E K K S G K
             210                   220
I G N E M K A Q V N G W Q D L S A A L L
             230                   240
K T D V K P P P G K S P A K F T P I E K
             250                   260
M G V R T A E Q A A A T L G I L L F V E
             270                   280
V P G G L T V A K A L E L F H A S G G K
```

B. Barley α-Amylase/Subtilisin Inhibitor BASI

```
              10                    20
A D P P P V H D T D G H E L R A D A N Y
              30                    40
Y V L S A N R A H G G G L T M A P G H G
              50                    60
R H C P L F V S Q D P N G Q H D G F P V
              70                    80
R I T P Y G V A P S D K I I R L S T D V
              90                   100
R I S F R A Y T T C L Q S T E W H I D S
             110                   120
E L A A G R R H V I T G P V K D P S P S
             130                   140
G R E N A F R I E K Y H G A E V(S)E Y K
             150                   160
L M S C G D W C Q D L G V F R D L K G G
             170                   180
A W F L G A T E P Y H V V V F K K A P P
181
A
```

C. PAPI/Phospholipid Transfer Protein

```
              10                    20
L N C G Q V D S K M K P C L T Y V Q G G
              30                    40
P G P S G E C C N G V R D L H N Q A Q S
              50                    60
S G D R Q T V C N C L K G I A R G I H N
              70                    80
L N L N N A A S I P S K C N V N V P Y T
              90
I S P D I D C S R I Y
```

D. An "Aleurone Specific" Protein

```
              10                    20
M A M A M G M A M R K E A A V A V M M V
          ↓ 30 ↓                    40
M V V T L A A G A D A G A G A A C E P A
              50                    60
Q L A V C A S A I L G G T K P S G E C C
              70                    80
G N L R A Q Q G C L C Q Y V K D P N Y G
              90                   100
H Y V S S P H A R D T L N L C G I P V P
102
H C
```

Fig. 9. Amino acid sequences of barley seed proteins. A, barley translation inhibitor II (Asano et al, 1986); B, barley α-amylase/subtilisin inhibitor (BASI) (Svendsen et al, 1986); C, probable amylase/protease inhibitor (PAPI)/phospholipid transfer protein (Svensson et al, 1986); D, aleurone-specific protein, deduced from cDNA sequence (Jakobsen et al, 1989). The arrows in D indicate possible sites of signal peptide cleavage. The underlined residues in D are conserved in an albumin storage protein from sunflower (Allen et al, 1987).

The genetic control of barley protein synthesis inhibitor has not been determined, but the amounts of the protein and its mRNA are both increased about 2.5-fold in Hiproly (which has the high-lysine *lys1* gene) compared with the amounts in its normal-lysine sister line CI 4362 (Rasmussen et al, 1988).

Leah et al (1991) isolated a cDNA encoding a (1→3)-β-glucanase consisting of 306 residues with a molecular weight of 32,343. They also showed that the corresponding protein purified from barley grain inhibited the growth in vitro of *Trichoderma* and *Fusarium*, the activity being enchanced in the presence of endochitinase and ribosome-inhibiting protein (see above).

Protease Inhibitors and Related Proteins

Plant inhibitors of proteases are of widespread occurrence, especially in storage tissues such as tubers and seeds, and can be divided into families on the basis of their target enzymes (serine proteases, thiolproteases, metalloproteases, and acid proteases) and their amino acid sequences. In addition, related proteins, or even the same proteins, may display inhibitory activity against α-amylase enzymes from various sources. Plant protease inhibitors have been reviewed in detail (Garcia-Olmedo et al, 1987; Richardson, 1991); the following account is restricted to those present in barley grain. All so far characterized are inhibitors of serine proteases, although inhibitors of cysteine proteases have also been demonstrated in malted barley (Enari and Mikola, 1967), rice (Abe et al, 1988), and maize (Abe and Whitaker, 1988).

CHYMOTRYPTIC INHIBITORS CI-1 AND CI-2

These are among the most intensively studied inhibitors of plant origin, initially because of their role in high-lysine barleys, but more recently because their low-M_rs and absence of disulfide bonds make them attractive targets for protein engineering studies and the application of nuclear magnetic resonance (NMR) spectroscopy to study structure and folding.

Chymotryptic inhibitors I and II belong to the potato inhibitor 1 family of serine protease inhibitors, which also includes the wound-induced tomato inhibitor 2 (Graham et al, 1985) and eglin from the medicinal leech (Seemüller et al, 1980). Hejgaard and Boisen (1980) reported that two chymotryptic inhibitors, containing 9.5 and 11.5 g of lysine per 100 g of protein, were present in increased amounts in lines derived from Hiproly and contributed to the high-lysine phenotype. The total activities of chymotrypsin inhibitors in two normal lines of barley were 0.72 and 0.65 units per gram of grain compared to 4.33–5.57 units per gram in six lines derived from Hiproly, and the calculated amounts of inhibitors were 0.32–0.29 mg/g compared to 1.9–2.5 mg/g, respectively. In all lines, CI-1 was present at about three times the level of CI-2.

CI-1 and 2 were both purified at the Carlsberg Laboratory, and extensive or complete amino acid sequences were determined. Two forms of CI-2 (called SP11A and SP11B) were purified, with M_rs of 9,100 and 8,100, respectively (Jonassen, 1980a). These two proteins were immunologically related (Jonassen, 1980a) and together accounted for 37% of the difference between the protein lysine contents of Hiproly and the normal cultivar Bomi (Jonassen 1980b).

Subsequently, amino acid sequence analysis showed that SP11B was identical to SP11A, except that 8–11 residues were missing from the N terminus, presumably resulting from partial proteolysis (Svendsen et al, 1980a,b). Svendsen et al (1982) subsequently isolated three forms of CI-1, one of which was used for amino acid sequencing.

Isolation and nucleotide sequence analysis of cDNA clones (Williamson et al, 1987, 1988) has demonstrated that CI-1 and CI-2 both occur in two distinct forms (called A and B) that are closely homologous (Fig. 10). The amino acid sequences of CI-1A and CI-1B were consistent with the directly determined protein sequence, assuming that the purified protein consisted of a mixture of the two isoforms (Williamson et al, 1988). In contrast, the directly determined protein sequence of CI-2 corresponds almost exactly to that of the CI-2A isoform (Williamson et al, 1987). This suggests that CI-2A is the major isoform present in the grain. The mature CI-2A protein consists of 84 residues with an M_r of 9,380, while CI-1A and 1B both consist of 83 residues with M_rs of 8,790 and 8,960, respectively. These M_rs contrast with the mobilities of the proteins on SDS-PAGE, CI-1 being slower than CI-2 (Fig 3). The CI-1 mRNAs do not encode a signal peptide, and although a putative signal peptide is encoded by the CI-2A mRNAs, this contains a stop codon and is followed by a second ATG codon where the initiation of translation usually occurs. It is probable, therefore, that both CI-1 and CI-2 are synthesized as mature proteins. In the case of CI-1, synthesis also

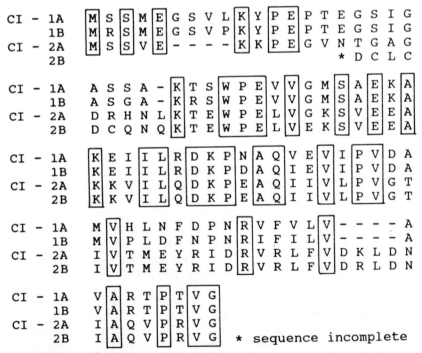

Fig. 10. Amino acid sequences of chrymotryptic inhibitors CI-1 and CI-2 of barley, based on cDNA sequences reported by Williamson et al (1987, 1988).

occurs on free polysomes (Williamson et al, 1988). It is rather surprising, therefore, that immunogold labeling clearly demonstrates the presence of CI-2 in protein bodies and in vesicles derived from the Golgi apparatus (Rasmussen et al, 1990). The mechanism involved in this deposition in the absence of a conventional signal peptide is not known.

Northern blotting using a CI-2 cDNA probe showed a major RNA transcript of about 550 nucleotides in developing endosperms but smaller amounts of a larger (about 840 bp) transcript in shoots and young leaves (Williamson et al, 1987). Hybridization to the latter transcript was eliminated by a high-stringency wash, indicating that it corresponded to the product of a related gene expressed specifically in the leaves and shoots. In contrast, the CI-1 probe hybridized to a 550-bp transcript in endosperm mRNA but did not hybridize to mRNAs from roots, leaves, or shoots (Williamson et al, 1988). Increases in CI-1 and CI-2 mRNAs occurred in developing endosperms of Hiproly relative to those in Sundance, and the amounts of CI-1 mRNAs were also increased in Risø 1508 and Risø 56 (Williamson et al, 1987, 1988). These reflect the increased amounts of CI-1 and CI-2 proteins in these three mutant high-lysine lines (Hejgaard and Boisen, 1980; Shewry and Miflin, 1985) (Fig. 3).

The structural genes for CI-1 and CI-2 were initially mapped to loci (called *Ica1* and *Ica2*, respectively) on the long arm of chromosome 5, using isoelectric focusing of wheat-barley addition lines (Hejgaard et al, 1984). Since an addition line with the long arm of chromosome 5 is not available, this conclusion was based on the absence of the proteins from wheat lines containing chromosomes 1–4, 6, and 7 of barley and a line with the short arm of chromosome 5 translocated to a wheat chromosome. This conclusion was supported by the increased amounts of both proteins present in a line of cv. Betzes trisomic for chromosome 5 (Hejgaard et al, 1984). However, more recent studies using a chromosome 5S addition line have shown that both loci are present on the short arm of chromosome 5 (Cannell et al, 1992). Southern blot analysis showed about three copies of CI-1-related genes and at least four copies of CI-2-related genes per haploid genome, with some polymorphism between cultivars (Shewry et al, 1987c; Williamson et al, 1987, 1988).

The three-dimensional structure of CI-2, alone and in complex with subtilisin, has been determined by X-ray crystallography and NMR spectroscopy (McPhalen et al, 1983, 1985; Clore et al, 1987a,b; Kjaer and Poulsen, 1987; Kjaer et al, 1987; McPhalen and James, 1987). The secondary structural elements are summarized in Fig. 11. The protein is a wedge-shaped disk of about $28 \times 27 \times 19$ Å with a single α-helix (3.6 turns) and four strands of β-sheet with a characteristic left-handed twist. The interface between the helix and sheet elements comprises the hydrophobic core of the protein.

Analysis of CI-2 peptides produced by limited hydrolysis by subtilisin and chymotrypsin identified the peptide bond Met[59]–Glu[60] as the reactive (inhibitory) site (Fig. 11) (Jonassen and Svendsen, 1982). This is located in a reactive loop region (Gly[54]–Tyr[61]) at the narrow edge of the wedge (Fig. 11). Campbell and co-workers have made detailed protein engineering studies of the reactive site, using expression of a CI-2 cDNA in *Eschericia coli* (Campbell, 1992). Changing Met[59] to Tyr reduced the rate of disassociation of the complex with chymotrypsin, resulting in stronger inhibition, and changing the same residue to lysine gave a new inhibitor of trypsin.

CI-1 has been studied in less detail than CI-2, but studies of Jonassen and Svendsen (1982) indicate that it has two reactive sites. The peptide bond Leu^{59}–Asp^{60} was reactive toward chymotrypsin and subtilisin, and Met^{30}–Ser^{31} to subtilisin only. Leu^{59}–Asp^{60} is in the same position within the protein as the reactive site (Met^{59}–Glu^{60}) in CI-2, but it differs in sequence. In addition, this bond is only present in the CI-1B subfamily, being replaced by Leu^{59}–Asn^{60} in CI-1A. This is probably also reactive, as Leu-Asp reactive sites are present in leech eglin and the tomato leaf inhibitor 1 (Campbell, 1992). The presence of two active sites for subtilisin and one for chymotrypsin is consistent with a previous report that CI-1 forms 1:2 and 1:1 complexes, respectively, with these two proteases (Mikola and Suolinna, 1971).

As with other protease inhibitors, the biological roles of CI-1 and CI-2 are not known, but they could form part of a wide-spectrum defense mechanism against fungal pathogens and insect pests.

CEREAL TRYPSIN/α-AMYLASE INHIBITOR FAMILY (CM PROTEINS)

This family consists of a number of components with M_rs ranging from about 9,000 to 16,000. Some, as individual subunits and/or as components of multisubunit holoproteins, are active as inhibitors of trypsin or insect α-amylase. Others have no known function. The best-characterized were initially defined as a group on the basis of their solubility in chloroform-methanol (CM) mixtures, and were called CM proteins (Salcedo et al, 1980). The presence of many related proteins has been demonstrated recently by cDNA cloning

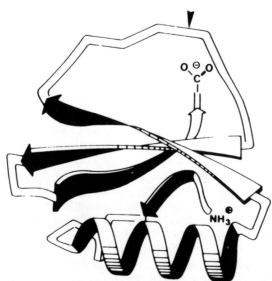

Fig. 11. The three-dimensional structure of chymotrypsin inhibitor CI-2. Large arrows denote β-strands; wide ribbons are α-helix; and narrow ribbons are turns or unclassified structures. The small arrow indicates the reactive (inhibitory) site. (Adapted, with permission, from McPhalen et al, 1985)

(Paz-Ares et al, 1986) and by separation of salt-soluble proteins by reversed-phase high-performance liquid chromatography (RP-HPLC) (Barber et al, 1988).

The individual subunits that have been characterized to date are listed in Table 2, and their partial or complete amino acid sequences are shown in Figs. 12 and 13. In all cases, the amino acid sequences can be divided into three regions, A, B, and C, which may have originated by triplication of a single ancestral domain (Kreis et al, 1985a,b; Kreis and Shewry, 1989). These are discussed in further detail below in the section on evolutionary relationships of hordeins. Although the individual sequences vary in detail, they are characterized by nine conserved cysteine residues, including characteristic Cys-Cys. and Cys-Arg-Cys. motifs in region B. CMd differs from the other subunits in the presence of an inserted sequence between regions A and B.

Sanchez-Monge et al (1986) reported that CMa, CMb, and CMd combine to form a tetrameric protein that inhibits α-amylase from larvae of the insect *Tenebrio molitor* but not the enzymes from human saliva or barley itself. These three subunits have, therefore, been called BTAI (barley tetrameric amylase inhibitor)-CMa, BTAI-CMb, and BTAI-CMd. Although CMa alone was also active against α-amylase (Barber et al, 1986), the activity was doubled when combined with CMb and CMd. Binary mixtures of CMa with CMb and CMd exhibited the same activity as CMa on its own, as did a binary

TABLE 2
Summary of the Properties of CM Proteins and Related Proteins
of the Cereal α-Amylase/Protease Inhibitor Family[a]

Protein[b]	cDNA/ gene	M_r	No. of Residues	Location of Genes	Inhibitory Activity	Subunit Interactions
BTAI-CMa	...	13,137[c]	119[d]	1	α-Amylase[e]	Tetrameric
BTAI-CMb/CMb*	...	14,000[c]	...	4	None	α-amylase inhibitor
BTAI-CMd	pCMd pUP38	16,032[d]	146[d]	4	None	
BTI-CMc	...	12,000[b]	...	1	Trypsin	
BTI-CMe	λCMe	13,305[f]	121[f]	3(*Itc1*)	Trypsin	
BDA1-1	...	...	...	6	α-Amylase[e]	Dimeric
CM44	pUP44	13,101	122[d]	...	...	Identical to BDA1-1?
CM13	pUP13	13,408	123[d]	...	...	Not known
CM23	pUP23	13,799	126[d]	...	...	Not known
S13	...	9,200[c]	?	?	?	
S14	...	14,100[c]	?	?	?	
S15	...	14,100[c]	?	?	?	Identical to BMAI-1?
BMAI-1 (14.5K allergen)	λAL-1	14,442[b]	132[d]	2	α-Amylase	Monomeric

[a] Data taken from Barber et al (1986, 1988, 1989); Halford et al (1988); Sanchez-Monge et al (1986, 1992); Paz-Ares et al (1986); Salcedo et al (1984); Hejgaard et al (1984); Lazaro et al (1988a,b); Odani et al (1983); Rodriguez-Palenzuela et al (1989); Mena et al (1992); Rasmussen and Johansson (1992).
[b] BTAI = barley tetrameric amylase inhibitor, BTI = barley trypsin inhibitor, BDAI = barley dimeric amylase inhibitor. CMb* (glycosylated form of CMb) is also a major grain allergen.
[c] By sodium dodecyl sulfate-polyacrylamide gel electrophoresis.
[d] Deduced from sequence of cDNA.
[e] From *Tenebrio molitor*.
[f] From directly determined protein sequence.

mixture of the two inactive subunits, CMb and CMd. The latter observations suggest that one of the two subunits undergoes a conformational change that confers activity. Two cDNA clones that encode CMd or closely related proteins have been characterized (pUP38 [Paz-Ares et al, 1986] and pCMd [Halford et al, 1988]) and one cDNA encoding CMa (Rasmussen and Johansson, 1992). A glycosylated form of CMb, called CMb*, is also a major grain allergen associated with baker's asthma (Sanchez-Monge et al, 1992).

A barley trypsin inhibitor was initially sequenced at the protein level by Odani et al (1983) and subsequently shown to be identical to CMe (Lazaro et al, 1985). Barber et al (1986) subsequently showed that CMc also inhibited trypsin. These two proteins have therefore been called BTI (barley trypsin inhibitor)-CMc and BTI-CMe. Both proteins are apparently active as single subunits, and the reactive (inhibitory) site in CMe has been identified as an Arg-Leu peptide bond at the C-terminal end of Region A (Fig. 12) (Odani et al, 1983). It is of interest that this site is absent from the characterized proteins that are not active as inhibitors of trypsin. A gene for CMe (γ-CMe) has been isolated and characterized (Rodriguez-Palenzuela et al, 1989). Moralejo et al (1993) have recently purified five genetic variants of CMe and shown differences in their inhibitory activities against trypsin from bovine pancreas and insect pests.

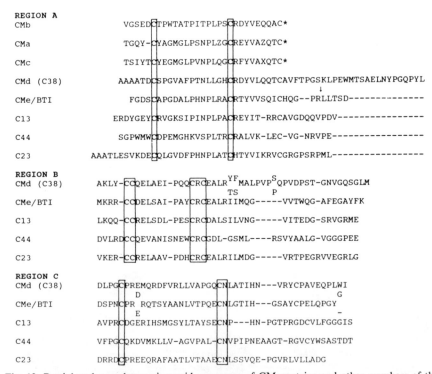

Fig. 12. Partial and complete amino acid sequences of CM proteins and other members of the cereal α-amylase/trypsin inhibitor family. Based on references listed in Table 2. Regions A–C are defined according to Kreis and co-workers (Kreis et al, 1985a,b; Kreis and Shewry, 1989).

Lazaro et al (1988b) prepared a crude fraction corresponding to dimeric α-amylase inhibitors by gel filtration and isolated a major component, called BDAI-1 (i.e., barley dimeric amylase inhibitor 1) by RP-HPLC. This subunit self-associated to form a dimer and exhibited activity against α-amylase from *T. molitor* but not from human saliva or mammalian pancreas. It was closely similar, or identical, to a protein (C44) encoded by a cloned cDNA (pUP-44) (Table 2, Fig. 13). BDAI-1 is encoded by the *Iad1* locus on chromosome 6 (Mena et al, 1992).

Barber et al (1989) demonstrated that an M_r 14,500 barley protein was a major immunogobulin E-binding component of sera from patients with baker's asthma. The purified protein was inhibitory to α-amylase from *T. molitor* but not human salivary glands, and N-terminal amino acid sequencing established that it was a member of the cereal trypsin/α-amylase inhibitor family. It appeared to be identical to a salt-soluble protein (S15) that had been purified previously by Barber et al (1988). Mena et al (1992) have recently shown that the 14.5K allergen is a glycosylated monomeric protein and have named it BMAI-1 (i.e., barley monomeric amylase inhibitor 1). It consists of 132 residues and is encoded by the *Iam1* locus on chromosome 2. Barber et al (1988) also isolated two proteins with closely related N-terminal amino acid sequences, S13 and S14 (Table 2). These proteins (S13, S14, S15, BMAI-1), together with BDAI-1/C44, appear to form a subfamily of inhibitors that are most closely related to the monomeric and dimeric α-amylase inhibitors of wheat (Garcia-Olmedo et al, 1987).

Two sequences deduced from cloned cDNAs have not yet been identified at the protein level, although both clearly belong to the cereal trypsin/α-amylase inhibitor family. These have been called C13 (Paz-Ares et al, 1986) and C23 (Lazaro et al, 1988a).

Paz-Ares et al (1983) showed that the CM proteins (CMa to CMd) are synthesized between 10 and 30 days after anthesis, with maximum activity between 15 and 20 days. They are all synthesized as precursors, with signal peptides of 20–30 residues (Paz-Ares et al, 1983, 1986; Halford et al, 1988;

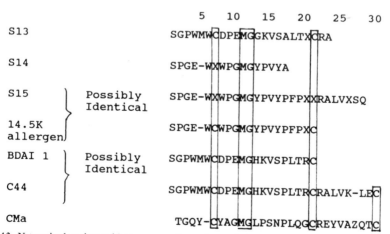

Fig. 13. N-terminal amino acid sequences of members of the cereal α-amylase/trypsin inhibitor family. Based on sequences reported by Barber et al (1986, 1988, 1989) and Lazaro et al (1988a).

Lazaro et al, 1988a; Rodriguez-Palenzuela et al, 1989). Subcellular fractionation procedures demonstrate that they are always present in the soluble fraction, indicating that they are transported from the ER either to the cytosol or to a labile particulate fraction (Paz-Ares et al, 1983). Since they have no known activity against endogenous enzymes, they are considered to have a role in protection of the seed against insect pests.

Genetic studies indicate that synthesis of CM proteins is controlled by a disperse multigene family, which has arisen by translocation and intrachromosomal duplication (Lazaro et al, 1985). Genes have so far been identified on chromosomes 1–4 and 6 (Table 2) (Salcedo et al, 1984; Nielsen and Hejgaard, 1985, Mena et al, 1992). Restriction fragment length polymorphism (RFLP) analyses show that the structural locus for CMe, designated *Itc1* (Hejgaard et al, 1984) or *CMe* (Rodriguez-Palenzuela et al, 1989), consists of only one or two copies per haploid genome (Rodriguez-Palenzuela et al, 1989).

The expression of the structural genes is also modulated by "regulatory" high-lysine genes, as summarized in Table 3. The most dramatic effect is of the *lys3a* gene of Risø mutant 1508, which reduces the amount of CMe to less than 2–3% of that in the normal-lysine parent line Bomi and the amount of the corresponding mRNA to about 1% (Rodriguez-Palenzuela et al, 1989).

PROBABLE AMYLASE/PROTEASE INHIBITOR

Mundy and Rogers (1986) characterized an aleurone-specific cDNA clone that encoded a protein of 117 residues. This corresponded to an abundant basic protein of M_r about 10,000, which was isolated and partially sequenced by Svensson et al (1986). These proteins may also have corresponded to the basic protein N that had been previously isolated by Hejgaard and Bjørn (1985).

Comparison of the deduced and directly determined amino acid sequences indicated that the mature protein consisted of 91 residues (Fig. 9C), from which a 26-residue signal peptide had been removed. It was called probable amylase/protease inhibitor (PAPI) because of sequence homology with the α-amylase inhibitor I-2 from finger millet (Campos and Richardson, 1984). In addition, a distant homology to Bowman-Birk type protease inhibitors was detected (Mundy and Rogers, 1986; Svensson et al, 1986). The purified protein did not exhibit detectable activity against a range of proteases and carbohydrases (including α-amylases), although UV spectroscopy showed the formation of a complex with porcine α-amylase (Svensson et al, 1986). A

TABLE 3
Changes in Amounts of CM Proteins a, b, and e in High-Lysine Mutants of Barley Compared to Those in Parental Lines of Risø Mutants and in a Normal-Lysine Sister Line (Cl 4362) of Hiproly[a]

Line[b]	Hiproly	Risø 1508	Risø 7	Risø 527	Risø 56
Mutant gene	*lys1*	*lys3a*		*lys6i*	*Hor2ca*
BTAI-CMa	↑	↑	↑	↓	↑
BTAI-CMb	↑	↑	↑	↓	↑
BTI-CMe	↓	↓	↑	↓	...

[a] ↑ increase, ↓ decrease, ... no change. Adapted from Lazaro et al (1985) to incorporate data from Rodriguez-Palenzuela et al (1989).
[b] BTAI = barley tetrameric amylase inhibitor, BTI = barley trypsin inhibitor.

related protein, which also lacked inhibitory activity, was also purified from rice seeds (Yu et al, 1988).

Bernhard and Somerville (1989) suggested that PAPI and related proteins have a different function, as phospholipid transfer proteins. This was based on sequence homology between PAPI and a lipid transfer protein from maize, which was about 52%. Breu et al (1989) subsequently demonstrated that PAPI was capable of transporting a significant proportion (about 7%) of the phosphatidylcholine from liposomes to potato mitochondria. They suggested that it functioned as a phospholipid transfer protein in vivo, although this remains to be demonstrated conclusively.

The structural gene for PAPI is probably located on chromosome 3 (Rasmussen, 1987).

BARLEY α-AMYLASE/SUBTILISIN INHIBITOR

Barley α-amylase/subtilisin inhibitor (BASI) has been studied intensively at the physiological, biochemical, and molecular levels. It first came to attention in 1983, when Mundy et al (1983) isolated an inhibitor of α-amylase-2 from germinating grain using glycogen precipitation of the enzyme/inhibitor complex. The purified protein corresponded to band-2, a protein reported by Rodaway (1978) to copurify with barley α-amylase. More surprisingly, the N-terminal amino acid sequence and other properties were identical to those of a specific inhibitor of subtilisin (Hejgaard et al, 1983), which had been isolated from mature barley grains by Yoshikawa et al (1976). Simultaneously Weselake et al (1983a,b) reported the isolation of the same protein from mature barley grains.

The mature BASI protein consists of 181 residues (Fig. 9B) with a molecular weight of 19,865 (Svendsen et al, 1986). Comparison of the directly determined amino acid sequence (Svendsen et al, 1986) with that encoded by a cloned cDNA (Leah and Mundy, 1989) indicates that it is synthesized as a precursor with a signal peptide of 22 residues. It is homologous with a subtilisin inhibitor of rice (Koide and Ikenaka, 1973) and belongs to the Kunitz family of serine protease inhibitors, which are widely distributed in legumes, most notably in soybean (Garcia-Olmedo et al, 1987).

Barley α-amylase consists of two groups of isoenzymes. The low-pI α-amylase-1 (or I) group is present in small amounts in both developing ("green" α-amylase) and germinating seeds, whereas the high-pI α-amylase-2 (or II) group is the major form synthesized by the aleurone layer during germination. BASI inhibits only α-amylase-2, giving rise to a change in electrophoretic mobility that initially resulted in the enzyme/inhibitor complex being defined as a third group of α-amylase isoenzymes, called α-amylase-3 (or III) (MacGregor and Ballance, 1980; Brown and Jacobsen, 1982). MacGregor, Hill, and co-workers reported detailed studies of the effects of the inhibitor on the hydrolysis of starch and the reaction products formed under various conditions (Weselake et al, 1983a,b, 1985; MacGregor et al, 1986), and Halayko et al (1986) showed that one molecule of α-amylase is complexed with two molecules of inhibitor.

The inhibition of subtilisin has been studied in less detail. Mundy et al (1983) showed that the presence of an equimolar amount of subtilisin did not affect the inhibition of α-amylase, indicating that the inhibitor is "double-headed," with separate inhibitory sites for the two enzymes. Yoshikawa et al (1976) suggested that a 1:1 complex with subtilisin was formed, but the inhibitory site does not appear to have been identified.

BASI is actively synthesized in developing barley grains (Laurière et al, 1985). Small amounts can be detected as early as one week after anthesis, followed by rapid accumulation up to about four weeks and a final level of about 60 μg per seed (Robertson and Hill, 1989). Synthesis is largely restricted to the starchy endosperm of the developing seed, with only trace amounts being detected in the embryo and aleurone (Mundy and Rogers, 1986; Mundy et al, 1986; Lecommandeur et al, 1987; Leah and Mundy, 1989). In contrast, synthesis occurs in the aleurone layer but not the starchy endosperm during germination (Leah and Mundy, 1989). Recent attention has focused on the hormonal and environmental control of BASI synthesis, by abscisic acid and dehydration stress in embryos (Robertson et al, 1989) and by gibberellic and abscisic acid in developing and mature aleurones (Mundy, 1984; Mundy and Rogers, 1986; Mundy et al, 1986; Leah and Mundy, 1989). The subcellular location of BASI has not been determined, but the presence of a signal sequence on newly synthesized protein indicates that it is initially transported into the lumen of the ER.

BASI is of particular interest because it is the only α-amylase inhibitor of barley that is active against endogenous enzyme. It has been suggested, therefore, that it has a regulatory role in vivo by modulating hydrolysis of starch during germination (Weselake et al, 1983b; Leah and Mundy, 1989). This is consistent with its activity against the germination-specific form of α-amylase and the antagonistic effects of abscisic and gibberellic acids on the amounts of the two proteins (BASI and α-amylase-2) and their respective mRNAs (Leah and Mundy, 1989). The strong inhibition of subtilisin may indicate a second role, in defense against invasion by pathogenic bacteria. In addition, Zawistowska et al (1988) showed that BASI can be used to improve the breadmaking quality of wheat flour supplemented with malted barley flour and suggested that it could be used to produce acceptable bread from flour with high levels of α-amylase activity.

BASI is controlled by the *Isa1* locus on chromosome 2 (Hejgaard et al, 1984), and RFLP analysis shows only one or two structural genes per haploid genome (Leah and Mundy, 1989). The expression of these genes is also modulated by mutant high-lysine genes, the amounts of BASI and its mRNA being increased in lines with the *lys3a* gene (Risø mutant 1508 and the derived line Piggy) and decreased in Hiproly, which has the *lys1* gene (Rasmussen et al, 1988; Leah and Mundy, 1989).

Aleurone-Specific Proteins

The aleurone and starchy endosperm tissues are both derived from the fusion of two polar nuclei and one male nucleus but are highly differentiated. Unlike the starchy endosperm cells, aleurone cells do not contain starch granules, and the major storage protein is a 7S globulin (see below) rather than hordein. In addition, the aleurone remains a living tissue throughout grain development and is active in the production of α-amylase and other hydrolytic enzymes during germination. Because the aleurone is, in quantitative terms, a minor tissue, most proteins purified from whole grain are derived from the starchy endosperm. Well-characterized aleurone-specific proteins are the 7S globulin (also present in the embyro) and PAPI (Mundy and Rogers, 1986) (see above). Jakobsen et al (1989) prepared a cDNA library using mRNA from aleurone cells at 20 days after anthesis and identified 11 groups of cDNAs expressed in aleurone but not in starchy endosperm. Seven groups were also expressed in the embryo, but four appeared to be aleurone-specific. They sequenced two of these, of which one corresponded to PAPI. The second had an open reading frame encoding a protein of 102 residues (M_r 10,400), including a putative signal peptide of about 20 residues. A region of 25 residues within the center of the putative mature protein showed limited homology with a 2S storage albumin from sunflower (Allen et al, 1987) (Fig. 9D). The function of this protein, and even whether it is present in the mature grain, is not known. The homology with the sunflower albumin suggests that it could be a minor storage protein of the cereal inhibitor superfamily (see above).

Miscellaneous Proteins of Known Function

LECTIN

Barley lectins have been neglected compared to the well-characterized wheat germ agglutinin (WGA). The purification of a lectin from barley was first reported by Foriers et al (1975, 1976) and Partridge et al (1976), but barley lectin has since been studied in more detail by Peumans and co-workers (Peumans et al, 1982a,b). Barley lectin resembles WGA in being a dimeric protein of two identical subunits of M_r 18,000 and in being located in the embryo. It also has the same sugar specificity (*N*-acetylglucosamine and oligomers of this) and can, in fact, exchange subunits with WGA in vitro to form active heterodimers (Peumans et al, 1982b). Its biological role is not known, but it could be involved in defense against pathogens and pests.

PEROXIDASE

Rasmussen et al (1991) have purified a peroxidase of M_r 37,000 and pI 8.5 from mature barley grain. They also isolated a cDNA clone that encoded the 158 C-terminal residues of the mature protein (established by comparison with tryptic peptides) and an extension of 22 residues that is apparently removed post-translationally. The latter could correspond to a vacuolar targeting sequence, as reported for vacuolar forms of endochitinase and β-glucanase (Linthorst et al, 1990; Payne et al, 1990). The protein and its mRNA were most abundant in the starchy endosperm, very low in the aleurone, and absent from the embryo. Its biological function is unknown, but it could play a role in protection against fungal pathogens.

LIPOXYGENASE

A lipoxygenase of M_r 90,000 and pI 5.2 has been purified (van Aarle et al, 1991). In addition, two M_r 63,000 bands are present; they appear to be breakdown products.

ASPARTIC PROTEASES

Two aspartic proteases have been purified (Sarkkinen et al, 1992). Both are heterodimers, one consisting of M_r 32,000 + M_r 16,000 subunits and the other of M_r 29,000 + M_r 11,000 subunits. Partial amino acid sequencing indicates that the smaller protein is derived from the larger one by post-translational cleavage, while amino acid sequence alignments and inhibition studies indicate a relationship to mammalian lysosomal cathepsin D.

Miscellaneous Proteins of Unknown Function

PROTEIN Q

Protein Q is a basic protein of M_r about 60,000, which is present at levels varying from 0.23 to 0.45 mg/g of grain (Hejgaard and Bjørn, 1985). It consists of three components, with pIs between 8.9 and 9.1 and closely similar amino acid compositions (notably 4.4 mol% lysine and 6.5 mol% arginine) (Hejgaard and Bjørn, 1985). Although its structural genes have been assigned to chromosome 2 (Rasmussen, 1987), protein Q has not been characterized in detail and its biological role is not known.

PROTEIN N

Hejgaard and Bjørn (1985) purified a low-M_r ($\approx$11,000) basic (pI $\approx$9.3) protein, present at a level of about 0.19–0.40 mg/g of grain. Although they noted that this component, called protein N, was similar in size to inhibitors of α-amylase and trypsin, it was not tested for inhibitor activity. The structural gene(s) has been assigned to chromosome 3 (Rasmussen, 1987). Leah et al (1987) suggested that protein N corresponded to PAPI.

PROTEINS S1–S4

Barber et al (1988) isolated and characterized 13 new salt-soluble proteins of barley by RP-HPLC. Although N-terminal amino acid sequencing allowed most of these to be assigned to recognized groups, four (S1–S4) appeared to be unrelated to any other barley proteins.

S1 had an M_r of about 21,000 and was rich in glycine ($\approx$22 mol%), glutamate + glutamine ($\approx$25 mol%), and arginine ($\approx$15 mol%). The N-terminal sequence was Ser-His-Asp-Gly-Gln.

S2, S3, and S4 had M_rs of about 5,200, 5,500, and 5,000, respectively, and had similar amino acid compositions, with about 20 mol% of basic residues. Short N-terminal sequences determined for S3 and S4 were about 33% identical and also showed limited sequence identity with part of the large subunit of ribulose bisphosphate carboxylase/oxygenase. The identities and functions of these proteins remain unknown.

STORAGE PROTEINS

Globulin Storage Proteins

7S GLOBULINS

The demonstration of 7S–8S globulins in barley and related cereals dates back to the 1940s (Quensel, 1942; Danielsson, 1949), but their precise identity and homology with 7S globulins from other species has only recently been established.

Quensel (1942) demonstrated that a γ-globulin with an $S_{20,w}$ value of 8.1 and a molecular weight of about 166,000 was present in extracts of whole grain, and Danielsson (1949) subsequently showed that this component alone occurred in the embryo. Although he did not analyze barley aleurone cells, he did show that the bran fraction of wheat contained a high concentration of γ-globulin. These early results, which have been reviewed in more detail by Djurtoft (1961) and Shewry and Miflin (1983), have been borne out by subsequent studies.

Burgess and Shewry (1986) showed that a total salt-soluble protein fraction from barley embryos contained major groups of bands with M_rs of between 40,000 and 60,000, with mobilities that were not affected by reduction and that reacted on western blotting with antiserum raised against 7S globulins from oat embryos (Burgess and Miflin, 1985). Major components with similar M_rs and properties were not observed in a fraction from whole endosperms.

Similar bands had previously been demonstrated in whole grain extracts by Robert et al (1985), who used a less specific antiserum raised against 3S + 7S globulins of oats. Weber and Manteuffel (1988) also showed similar bands in a globulin fraction from embryos, although, in contrast to the results of Burgess and Shewry (1986), they were also present in a fraction from endosperms.

Burgess and Shewry (1986) prepared a 7S fraction from mature barley embryos containing mainly bands of M_rs about 40,000 and 50,000 by sucrose density ultracentrifugation and determined the amino acid composition (Table 4). This was similar to that previously reported for the 7S globulin of oat embryos (Burgess et al, 1983).

More recently, Yupsanis et al (1990) have demonstrated that a closely similar or identical 7S globulin is the major salt-soluble protein in aleurone layers but is not present in the starchy endosperm tissue. They initially showed that total proteins from aleurone protoplasts from mature grain contained major bands with mobilities on SDS-PAGE similar to those in salt-soluble fractions from embryos. The protein purified from a crude aleurone fraction (prepared by pearling) gave a single sharp peak on RP-HPLC and consisted of major subunits of M_r about 50,000 and 40,000, with minor subunits of M_r 25,000 and 20,000 (Fig. 14). All except the M_r 20,000 subunit reacted with antibody raised against the 7S globulin of oat embryos, as did an M_r 70,000 subunit that was removed during the final purification step (immunoaffinity chromatography) (Fig. 14). Although Weber and Manteuffel (1988) reported that the 7S globulin from barley embryos bound to an affinity column of concanavalin A (a lectin), Yupsanis et al (1990) were unable to detect bound carbohydrate using a Schiff-Periodate gel stain.

The amino acid composition of the protein purified by Yupsanis et al (1990) was similar to that of the preparation from embryos (Table 4). The M_r 50,000, 40,000, and 25,000 subunits had similar or identical major N-terminal amino acid sequences, although heterogeneity was observed in all except the M_r 40,000 subunit. The major sequence also showed limited homology with sequences of 7S globulins from legumes (vicilins) and cotton seed (α'-globulins A and B) (Fig. 15). It is well established that the smaller subunits of vicilin arise from proteolysis of the M_r 50,000 subunits (Gatehouse et al, 1984), and similar processing could account for the subunit composition of the barley 7S globulins

(Fig. 16). If this is so, at least one additional subunit should also have been present, although its M_r ($\approx$10,000) may have been too low for it to be clearly resolved on the gel. The M_r of 166,000 demonstrated by Quensel (1942) is also consistent with the barley 7S globulins consisting of three M_r 50,000 subunits (or their products), similar to pea vicilin (Gatehouse et al, 1984).

By analogy with pea, the immunochemically related M_r 70,000 subunits could be similar to convicilin, which differs from vicilin subunits in an N-terminal extension of 121 residues. Since these subunits were separated from the other subunits during purification, they were presumably present in a separate holoprotein.

Although the subcellular location of the barley 7S globulin has not been determined, the related protein of oat embryos is located in protein bodies (Burgess and Miflin, 1985). The tissue specificity is also of interest, as the aleurone and starchy endosperm are triploid tissues derived from a separate fusion event to the diploid embryo.

12S GLOBULINS

The presence of 12S δ-globulin in barley was first demonstrated by Quensel (1942), but the amount was small and it was only reliably detected after preliminary fractionation of the preparation by salt-precipitation. He showed

TABLE 4
Comparison of Amino Acid Compositions (mol %) of the 7S Globulins
from Barley Aleurones and Embryos with Those Reported for 7S Globulins
from Oat Embryos and Legume Seeds

Amino Acid[a]	Barley		Oat Embryo	Pea		Bean Phaseolin
	Aleurone	Embryo		Vicilin	Convicilin	
Asp[b]	8.8	9.7	7.6	18.9	11.6	14.5
Thr	3.6	4.8	3.4	2.7	2.6	2.6
Ser	8.4	6.8	8.9	7.7	6.4	4.5
Glu[c]	14.9	13.7	15.8	19.2	22.1	19.9
Pro	4.2	4.7	4.3	2.0	5.5	2.6
Gly	13.6	10.8	12.5	4.8	5.9	3.3
Ala	7.3	9.9	7.0	4.1	4.2	3.5
Val	6.7	7.4	6.4	4.8	4.5	5.9
Cys[d]	0.4	1.2	1.3	0	0.1	0
Met	0.7	1.5	0.3	0	0.1	0.6
Ile	3.6	4.1	3.1	5.1	3.9	5.5
Leu	7.5	5.5	6.3	9.8	8.7	9.4
Tyr	1.6	2.0	2.3	1.9	2.6	3.4
Phe	3.9	3.5	4.6	4.7	3.3	7.8
Lys	5.2	6.3	4.4	8.1	8.2	7.6
His	1.7	2.2	2.8	1.6	2.2	3.6
Arg	7.9	5.9	9.0	4.6	8.2	5.4
Reference[e]	1	2	3	4	4	5

[a] Tryptophan was not determined.
[b] Includes Asn.
[c] Includes Gln.
[d] The low content of cysteine determined for the aleurone protein may result from partial loss during acid hydrolysis.
[e] References: 1 = Yupsansis et al (1990), 2 = Burgess and Shewry (1986), 3 = Burgess et al (1983), 4 = Croy et al (1980), 5 = Hall et al (1979).

that the δ-globulin had an $S_{20,w}$ value of 12.0 and an M_r of about 300,000. The characteristics of this component are still not known.

The major storage protein of oat endosperms is a 12S globulin related to the 11S legumins present in leguminous species (and to storage proteins present in many other families of flowering plants), but a protein of this type has not been demonstrated in barley. The oat globulin consists of pairs of subunits, of M_rs about 40,000 and 20,000, associated by interchain disulfide bond(s). Burgess and Shewry (1986) failed to detect subunits of this type in a total salt-soluble protein fraction of barley endosperms, and they observed no reaction with antiserum raised against the M_r 40,000 subunit of oat globulin.

However, studies of wheat demonstrate that leguminlike proteins are present,

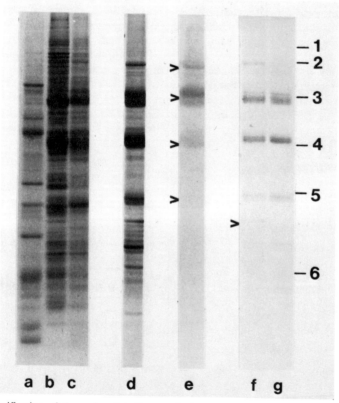

Fig. 14. Purification of the major globulin protein from barley aleurones. Tracks a, b, and c show sodium dodecyl sulfate-polyacrylamide gel electrophoresis (SDS-PAGE) separations of total salt-soluble proteins from starchy endosperms, embryos, and aleurone layers (prepared by pearling) respectively. Tracks d and e show SDS-PAGE and western blot analyses (the latter using antiserum raised to oat embryo 7S globulins) of the aleurone protein fraction precipitated between 55 and 75% saturation with ammonium sulfate. Tracks f and g show SDS-PAGE analyses of the 55–75% fraction separated by ion exchange chromatography on diethylaminoethyl Sephacel (track f) followed by immunoaffinity chromatography on a column prepared with antibody to the oat embryo 7S globulin (track g). The arrows in track e indicate immunoreactive bands. The arrow in track f indicates a minor component that is eliminated by immunoaffinity chromatography. 1–6 indicate M_r markers: 1, 130,000; 2, 75,000; 3, 50,000; 4, 39,000; 5, 27,000; 6, 17,000. (Based on Yupsanis et al, 1990; used by permission of Oxford University Press)

although differing in their detailed subunit structure (Singh and Shepherd, 1985; Singh et al, 1988). Singh and Shepherd (1985) showed that unreduced total seed protein fractions from wheat contained three minor bands of M_rs 150–160,000, which could be partially reduced to give subunit pairs of M_r 75,000 and 80,000 and completely reduced to give individual large (M_r 58,000 and 52,000) and small (M_r 22,000 and 23,000) subunits. The complexity of the protein pattern derived partly from the hexaploid constitution of bread wheat, pairs of large and small subunits being controlled by genes on chromosomes 1A and 1D. Partial amino acid sequences showed homology of the large and small subunits with the corresponding subunits of oat 12S globulins and with legumin-type proteins from a range of other species (Singh et al, 1988). However, they differ from legumins in having higher subunit M_rs and in their detailed subunit structures. Whereas legumins consist of six disulfide-bonded subunit pairs (M_r 40,000 + 20,000) associated by noncovalent forces, the triticins (as they have been named) of wheat consist of two disulfide-bonded subunit pairs (M_rs ≈55,000 + ≈20,000), which form a holoprotein stabilized by further disulfide bonds. Triticin is more soluble in salt solutions at 60°C than at the lower temperatures usually used for extraction and may account for 5–10% of the total endosperm protein (Singh and Shepherd, 1987; Singh et al, 1988). It also appears to be located in protein bodies in the developing endosperm (Payne et al, 1986; Singh and Shepherd, 1987), and

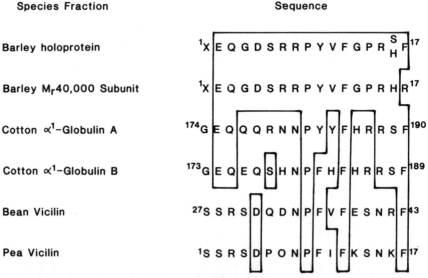

Fig. 15. Major N-terminal amino acid sequences determined for the barley holoprotein and M_r 40,000 group of subunits (Yupsanis et al, 1990) compared with sequences reported previously for α¹-globulins of cottonseed and for vicilins of field bean and peas. The numbering of the orignal authors is used. The α¹-globulin sequences are probably close to the N-termini of the mature proteins, whereas the N-termini of the mature vicilins are thought to correspond to residues 28 and 3 of the bean and pea proteins, respectively. The cottonseed α¹-globulin sequences are from Chlan et al (1986) and Dure (*unpublished*), and the vicilin sequences from Bassner et al (1987) (bean) and Watson et al (1988) (pea). (Reprinted from Yupsanis et al, 1990, by permission of Oxford University Press)

recent studies using immunogold labeling of tissue sections show that it is concentrated, if not wholly located, in densely staining granular inclusions within the starchy endosperm protein bodies (Bechtel et al, 1989).

Granular inclusions are also present in the protein bodies of barley starchy endosperms, and these do not react with antibodies raised against hordeins (Shewry, 1992). In addition, the protein bodies of the hordein-deficient mutant Risø 1508 consist largely of such material. Since barley is diploid, triticinlike proteins would be expected to consist of only one type each of large and small subunits. The demonstration of a molecular weight of about 300,000 for the 12S δ-globulin (Quensel, 1942) suggests that the holoprotein could consist of four subunit pairs.

Prolamin Storage Proteins (Hordein)

HORDEIN POLYMORPHISM AND GENETICS

The presence of substantial amounts of alcohol-soluble proteins in barley was first noted by Einhof (1806), with detailed analyses being reported by Osborne (1895) and Osborne and Clapp (1907).

It is now generally accepted that hordein consists of monomeric and polymeric proteins, the latter stabilized by interchain disulfide bonds. Some of the latter are not readily soluble in alcohol-water mixtures in the native state, but the individual subunits can be extracted in aqueous alcohols in the presence of a reducing agent such as 2-mercaptoethanol. The alcohol-soluble and insoluble fractions are called hordein I and hordein II, respectively

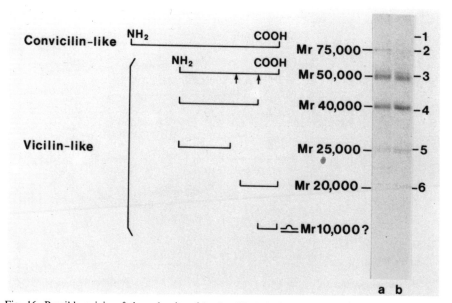

Fig. 16. Possible origin of the subunits of barley 7S globulin by post-translational processing of a single precursor polypeptide of M_r about 50,000 (based on pea vicilin; see Gatehouse et al, 1984).

(Shewry et al, 1978a). Together they account for about 35–55% of the total grain proteins, depending on the level of nitrogen nutrition.

Analysis of a total alcohol-soluble protein preparation by two-dimensional isoelectric focusing (2-D IEF)/SDS-PAGE (Fig. 17) shows a number of hordein polypeptides with M_rs varying from about 30,000 to 105,000. In addition, a number of low-M_r components are present, including low-molecular-weight hordeins and CM proteins.

The hordein polypeptides are classified into two major groups (B and C hordeins) and two minor groups (D and γ-type hordeins) (Figs. 17 and 18). Comparisons with wheat and rye show that these are members of three families that are recognized on the basis of their amino acid sequences and the chromosomal locations of their structural genes (Miflin et al, 1983; Shewry et al, 1986). The B hordeins and γ-type hordeins are sulfur (S)-rich prolamins, the C hordeins are S-poor prolamins, and D hordein is a high-molecular-weight (HMW) prolamin. The B and C hordeins account for about 70–80% and 10–20%, respectively, of the total fraction, with smaller amounts of D hordein (2-4%) and γ-hordeins (not precisely determined).

Genetic analyses show that all hordeins are encoded by structural genes on chromosome 5 (1H) of barley. The C hordeins and B hordeins are encoded by linked loci, designated *Hor1* and *Hor2*, respectively, on the short arm and D hordein by a loosely linked locus (*Hor3*) in the proximal region of the long arm (Fig. 19). The structural genes for γ-hordeins have not been

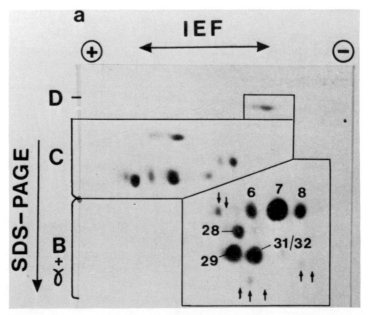

Fig. 17. Two-dimensional isoelectric focusing (IEF)/sodium dodecyl sulfate-polyacrylamide gel electrophoresis (SDS-PAGE) of total hordein from barley cv. Carlsberg II. B, C, D, and γ indicate the groups of hordein polypeptides. The arrows indicate the individual γ-hordeins. The major B hordein polypeptides are numbered according to Faulks et al (1981). (Modified from Kreis et al, 1983a)

conclusively identified but probably correspond to the *HrdF* (*Hor5*) locus, which is located distally to *Hor2* (Netsvetaev and Sozinov, 1982; Shewry and Parmar, 1987). In addition, a further locus, *HrdG* (*Hor4*), encodes B hordeinlike polypeptides in lines derived from the Russian cultivar Elgina (Netsvetaev and Sozinov, 1984; Shewry et al, 1988b). This is located between *Hor1* and the centromere (Fig. 19). The presence of additional loci encoding minor hordein-related polypeptides is indicated by the detailed studies of Sozinov and co-workers (Sozinov et al, 1979; Ladogina et al, 1987).

The B and C hordeins are highly polymorphic, both within and between genotypes (Fig. 20A). Faulks et al (1981) reported detailed analyses of B hordein fractions from eight commercial cultivars using quantitative 2-D IEF/SDS-PAGE and cyanogen bromide peptide mapping of single extracted polypeptides. A total of 47 major polypeptides were identified, with 10–16 present in each line. These varied in their M_rs (about 35,000–46,000), pIs (about 6.5–8.5), and contributions to the total fraction (about 1–44%). Comparison of their CNBr peptide maps allowed the individual polypeptides to be grouped into three classes, of which one (class III) was present in all cultivars. Most cultivars also contained class I or II polypeptides, but never both. Subsequent analyses of cloned cDNAs and genes (see below) have shown that class I/II and class

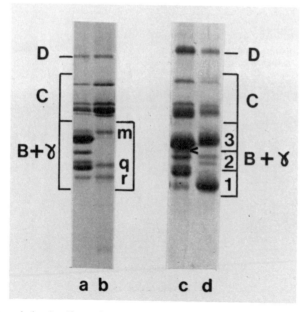

Fig. 18. Sodium dodecyl sulfate-polyacrylamide gel electrophoresis of total hordein from cv. Carlsberg II (a), Risø mutant 56 (b), line P12/3 (c), and cv. Bomi (d). All the proteins present in the B+ γ-hordein region of Risø 56 are γ-hordeins. These are labeled m, q, and r according to Kreis et al (1983a) and correspond to the γ_1, γ_2, and γ_3 hordeins of Rechinger et al (1983a). 1–3 indicate the major B hordein bands present in cv. Bomi and related genotypes (e.g., cvs. Sundance and Julia). The arrow in track c indicates a minor B hordein polypeptide encoded by the *Hor4* (*HrdG*) locus, which is present in P12/3 and in other lines derived from cv. Elgina. C and D indicate the C and D hordein polypeptides.

III polypeptides are the products of two subfamilies of mRNAs and genes at the *Hor2* locus. In addition, these subfamilies can be discriminated using specific monoclonal antibodies (Rechinger et al, 1993). The class I/II and class III subfamilies correspond to the B1 and B3 bands, respectively, in cultivars Bomi and Sundance, which are often used as experimental material.

A similar high degree of polymorphism is observed in the C hordeins, although in this case it has not been possible to classify the individual polypeptides into subfamilies. Shewry et al (1985a) mapped 34 major polypeptides in six cultivars, with M_rs of about 55,000–75,000, and four to 18 present in each cultivar.

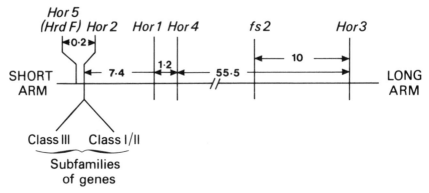

Fig. 19. Locations of structural loci for hordein storage proteins (*Hor1* to *Hor5*) on chromosome 5 of barley. The centromere is probably close to *fs₂*. The map distances in centimorgans are based on Jensen (1988). (Reprinted, by permission, from Shewry et al, 1990.

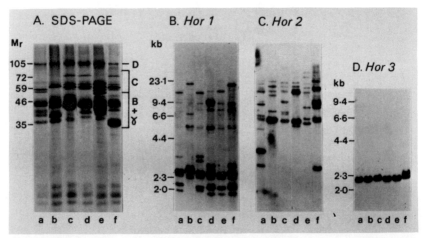

Fig. 20. Polymorphism in hordein polypeptides and genes. A, Sodium dodecyl sulfate-polyacrylamide gel electrophoresis (SDS-PAGE) analyses of total reduced and pyridylethylated hordein fractions from the cultivars Athos (a), Keg (b), Jupiter (c), Hoppel (d), Igri (e), and Sundance (f). B–D, total genomic DNAs from the same six cultivars, digested with *Hind*III and probed with cDNA clones related to C hordein (B), B hordein (C), and D hordein (D). (Reprinted, by permission, from Shewry, 1992, based on Bunce et al, 1986)

Restriction fragment analyses have shown that *Hor1* and *Hor2* are complex multigenic loci, with a high degree of polymorphism between genotypes and a total copy number of about 20–30 per haploid genome (Fig. 20B and C) (Shewry et al, 1985a; Bunce et al, 1986). In each case, the copy number is sufficiently high for each polypeptide to be encoded by at least one gene.

Sørensen (1989) has reported studies on the structure of the *Hor2* locus, using pulsed-field gel electrophoresis. This showed the maximum size at the locus to be about 360 kbp, with two fragment classes containing approximately equal numbers of genes. Although he was not able to establish whether these corresponded to the class I/II and class III subfamilies of genes, this appears likely in light of work reported by Shewry et al (1990). They identified a rare recombinant within the *Hor2* locus, and showed that recombination had occurred between the class I/II and class III subfamilies of genes. Linkage with the *HrdF* (*Hor5*) locus enabled the order of the two subfamilies of genes to be tentatively identified, with the class I/II genes closer to the centromere (Fig. 19). Although recombination within the *Hor1* and *Hor2* loci is assumed to have contributed to the high degree of polymorphism currently observed in B and C hordeins, this was the first intralocus recombination event to be identified in crosses.

D hordein is a single band with an M_r by SDS-PAGE of about 105,000 in European cultivars of barley, but some exotic lines have a band of lower M_r or two bands (Shewry and Miflin, 1982). It may be partially resolved into several components by IEF (Fig. 17), although RFLP analysis shows a single hybridizing fragment with one to two copies per haploid genome (Fig. 20D) (Bunce et al, 1986). The heterogeneity seen on 2-D IEF/SDS-PAGE may result from partial post-translational modification, which is believed to contribute to a similar degree of heterogeneity of the homologous HMW subunits of wheat glutenin.

γ-Type hordeins are minor components with M_rs by SDS-PAGE similar to those of B hordeins. They were initially purified from Risø mutant 56, a line in which B hordeins are absent due to deletion of the *Hor2* locus (Shewry et al, 1985b) (Fig. 18). They have been studied in detail only in this line, where they are separated by SDS-PAGE into three bands called $γ_1$, $γ_2$, and $γ_3$-hordeins (Rechinger et al 1993; V. Cameron-Mills, *personal communication*). These correspond to bands m, q, and r, respectively, in Fig. 18. Shewry and Parmar (1987) proposed that γ-hordein corresponded to the product of the *HrdF* (*Hor5*) locus, on the basis of SDS-PAGE analyses of lines that were isogenic at *Hor1* and *Hor2* but exhibited allelic variation at *HrdF* (*Hor5*). It appears to be encoded by a small multigene family, with limited polymorphism between cultivars (Cameron-Mills and Brandt, 1988; Shewry et al, 1990).

AMINO ACID COMPOSITIONS AND SEQUENCES

The amino acid compositions of total B, C, and D hordeins and of two γ-hordein subgroups (corresponding to $γ_1$, $γ_2$, and $γ_3$-hordeins from Risø mutant 56, see Fig. 18) are given in Table 5. Although all are rich in glutamate + glutamine and proline, the combined proportions of these range from about 40% in D hordein to 70% in C hordein. There are also differences in the proportions of other amino acids: C hordein is rich in phenylalanine (≈9 mol%) but deficient in sulfur-containing amino acids (notably no cysteine), whereas D hordein contains about 16 mol% glycine. We now know that these characteristic amino acid compositions result, to a large extent, from the presence of repetitive sequences that account for between 30 and almost 100% of the whole protein.

Our knowledge of the amino acid sequences of hordeins comes from direct sequencing of protein N termini (C, D, and γ-hordeins) and unordered peptides (B and C hordeins) and from the nucleotide sequences of incomplete (B, C, and D hordein) and full-length (B, C, and γ-hordeins) cloned DNAs.

The N termini of B hordeins are blocked to Edman degradation (Schmitt and Svendsen, 1980; Shewry et al, 1980b), so the first available amino acid sequences were derived from unordered peptides (Schmitt and Svendsen, 1980). More extensive sequences have been derived from cloned cDNAs and genes. Comparisons of the sequences of B hordeins encoded by a number of partial cDNAs and full-length genes (Fig. 21) show that they fall into two groups that differ particularly in their C-terminal sequences. These are typified by the proteins encoded by the partial cDNAs pB7 and pB11, which have been shown by hybrid release translation to encode B3 (class III) and B1 (class I/II) type polypeptides, respectively (Kreis et al, 1983b). The B1 type protein sequences include three derived from full-length genes. No complete sequence

TABLE 5
Amino Acid Compositions (mol %) of the Groups of Hordein Polypeptides
and of a Low-Molecular-Weight (LMW) Hordein

Amino Acid[a]	B	C	D	γ_3	$\gamma_1 + \gamma_2$	LMW
Asp[b]	1.4	1.0	1.3	2.9	2.8	2.0
Thr	2.1	1.0	8.1	3.1	2.1	7.5
Ser	4.7	4.6	9.7	5.5	5.7	7.4
Glu[c]	35.4	41.2	29.6	32.4	29.9	27.9
Pro	20.6	30.6	11.6	16.5	22.1	8.0
Gly	1.5	0.3	15.7	5.9	2.5	5.0
Ala	2.2	0.7	2.5	2.6	2.2	6.1
Cys	2.5	0	1.5	2.7	3.3	11.6
Val	5.6	1.0	4.5	3.7	5.5	4.8
Met	0.6	0.2	0.2	1.2	1.2	4.8
Ile	4.1	2.6	0.7	2.9	2.5	3.3
Leu	7.0	3.6	3.3	8.6	6.9	4.2
Tyr	2.5	2.3	3.9	1.7	2.1	2.6
Phe	4.8	8.8	1.4	4.7	6.1	2.2
His	2.1	1.1	3.4	2.0	1.6	0
Lys	0.5	0.2	1.1	1.6	1.2	0
Arg	2.4	0.8	1.5	2.0	2.5	2.7
Percent amidation of Asp + Glu	90	92	nd[d]	nd	nd	nd
References[e]	1	2	3	4	4	5

[a] Tryptophan was not determined.
[b] Includes Asn.
[c] Includes Gln.
[d] Not determined.
[e] References: 1 = Total B hordein from cv. Julia (Shewry et al, 1980b), 2 = total C hordein from cv. Julia (Shewry et al, 1980b), 3 = D hordein from Risφ mutant 1508 (Kreis et al, 1984), 4 = γ-hordein bands from Risφ 56 (Kreis et al, 1983b), 5 = M_r 22,000 component purified from Risφ 56 (Festenstein et al, 1987).

of a typical B3 hordein has been reported, but Carbajosa et al (1992) reported the sequences of two B hordein genes isolated by polymerase chain reaction (PCR) amplification of genomic DNA from the Russian cultivar Moskovsky 3. One gene encodes a B1 hordein protein but has an internal stop codon and is presumably a pseudogene. The second gene encodes a protein that differs from the B1 and B3 type hordeins shown in Fig. 21 in its C-terminal sequence. However, homology in its 3′-untranslated region indicates that it is more closely related to B3 hordein genes, and it could therefore encode a variant form of a B3 type hordein protein. The putative N termini of the B hordeins (shown in Figs. 21 and 22) were initially predicted by reference to rules for signal peptide structure (Forde et al, 1985a). This has since been confirmed for B1 hordein from cv. Bomi by radiosequencing of the in vitro-synthesized and processed polypeptide (Cameron-Mills and Madrid, 1989).

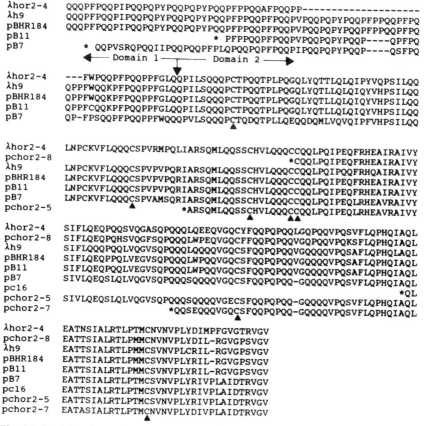

Fig. 21. Partial and complete amino acid sequences of individual B hordeins, deduced from the nucleotide sequences of clone cDNAs and genes (Forde et al, 1981, 1985a,b; Rasmussen et al, 1983; Brandt et al, 1985; Chernyshev et al, 1989). pB7, pc16, hor 2-5, and hor 2-7 are B3 (class III), and pB11, pBHR 184, λh9, hor 2-4, and hor 2-8 are B1 (class 1/11) polypeptides. * indicates last residue encoded by partial cDNA. Conserved cysteine residues are indicated by arrow heads.

Shewry et al (1985b) initially purified the γ-hordeins from Risø mutant 56 in two fractions corresponding to the $\gamma_1 + \gamma_2$ and γ_3 bands and showed that each had a single unique N-terminal sequence. Complete sequences of proteins corresponding to γ_2 and γ_3-hordeins have since been reported (Cameron-Mills and Brandt, 1988; V. Cameron-Mills, *personal communication*) and are aligned in Fig. 23.

B hordeins and γ-hordeins both consist of two structural domains: a repetitive N-terminal domain accounting for about a third to a half of the protein, and a nonrepetitive C-terminal domain. The repetitive domains extend to the N-termini of the mature B hordein proteins but are preceded by short

```
   B1 Hordein              γ2-Hordein              γ3-Hordein

NH2-¹ Q Q Q P F      NH2-¹ E M Q V N P S V Q V Q P    ¹I T T T T M Q F N
      P Q Q P I             T Q Q Q P Y P E             P S G L E L E R
      P Q Q P Q P Y         S Q Q P F I S Q             P Q Q L F
      P Q Q P Q P Y         S Q Q Q F P Q               P Q W Q P L
      P Q Q P F P           P Q Q P F P Q Q             P Q Q P P F
      P Q Q P F             P Q Q P F P Q               L Q Q E
      P Q Q P V             S Q Q Q C L Q Q             P E Q P Y
      P Q Q P Q P Y         P Q H Q F P Q               P Q Q Q P L
      P Q Q P F P           P T Q Q F P Q R             P Q Q Q P F
      P Q Q P F             P L L P F T H               P Q Q P Q L
      P Q Q P P F           P F L T F P D Q             P H Q H Q F
      W Q Q K P F           - L L - - P Q P             P Q Q L
      P Q Q P P F           P H Q S F P Q P             P Q Q Q F
      G L Q⁷⁹               P - Q S Y P Q P             P Q Q M P L Q
                            P L Q P F P Q P             P Q Q Q F
                            P Q Q K Y P E Q             P Q Q M P L⁹⁴
                            P Q Q P F P W Q¹³²
```

Fig. 22. Comparison of the sequences of the N-terminal regions and repetitive domains of B1 and γ-hordeins. Based on sequences reported by Forde et al (1985a), Cameron-Mills and Brandt (1988), and V. Cameron-Mills, *personal communication*.

```
γ2    ......¹EMQVNPSVQVQPTQQQPYPESQQPFISQSQQQFPQPQQQPFPQQPQQ
γ3    ¹ITTTTMQFNPSGLELERPQQLFPQW.QPLPQQPPFLQQEPEQPYPQ..QQ

γ2    PFPQSQ...QQCLQQPQHQFPQ..PTQQFPQRPLLPFTHPFLTFPDQLLP
γ3    PLPQQQPFPQQPQLPHQHQFPQQLPQQQFPQQ..MPL.QPQQQFPQQMPL

γ2    QPPHQSFPQPPQSYPQPPLQPFPQP.PQQKYPEQPQQPFPWQQPTIQLYL
γ3    QPQQQ..PQFPQ...QKPFGQYQQPLTQQPYPQ..QQPLAQQQPSIE..E

γ2    QQQLNPCKEFLLQQCRPV.......SLLSYIWSKIVQQSSCRVMQQQCCL
γ3    QHQLNLCKEFLLQQCTLDEKVPLLQSVISFLRPHISQQNSCQLKRQQCCQ

γ2    QLAQIPEQYKCTAIDSIVHAIFMQQGQRQGVQIVQQQPQPQQVGQCVLVQ
γ3    QLANINEQSRCPAIQTIVHAIVMQQQVQQQVGHGFVQSQLQQLGQGMPIQ

γ2    .....GQGVVQPQQLAQMEAIRTLVLQSVPSMCNFNVPPNCSTIKAPFVG
γ3    LQQQPGQAFVLPQQQAQFKVVGSLVIQTLPMLCNVHVPPYCS....PFGS

γ2    VVTGVGGQ²⁸⁶
γ3    MATGSGGQ²⁸⁹
```

Fig. 23. Alignment of the amino acid sequences of γ2 and γ3 hordeins. (Based on Cameron-Mills and Brandt, 1988, and on V. Cameron-Mills, *personal communication*)

nonrepetitive sequences in the γ-hordeins. In all cases, the repeats are rich in proline and glutamine, being based on the tetrapeptide PQQX (Fig. 22). Single cysteine residues are present in this domain in the γ₂-hordein and in the B1 hordein encoded by pB11.

The nonrepetitive domains contain most of the charged (basic and acidic) residues, and most of the cysteines: seven in the B1 and B3 hordeins, nine in γ₂-hordein, and eight in γ₃-hordein. This domain is also homologous in B and γ-hordeins, particularly in three conserved regions that were called A, B, and C by Kreis and coworkers (Kreis et al, 1985a,b; Kreis and Shewry, 1989). These are separated by less-conserved regions called I_1–I_4. The positions of these regions within B1 and γ₂-hordeins are shown in Fig. 24, and their sequences are aligned in Fig. 25.

The molecular weights of the B hordeins are between about 29,000 and 32,000, while the γ₂ and γ₃-hordeins have molecular weights of 32,600 and 33,200, respectively.

A number of N-terminal sequences of C hordein have been reported (Shewry and Miflin, 1983), showing a high degree of homology between individual components. They have a short, unique sequence of 12 residues, followed by several pentapeptides with the consensus sequence PQQPY (Fig. 26). Direct sequencing of unordered peptides showed the presence of tandem repeats based on the octapeptide PQQPFPQQ (Tatham et al, 1985a), while nucleotide sequencing of several partial cDNAs shows that similar repeats are also present close to the C terminus, with a short, unique C-terminal sequence of six residues

Bl Hordein

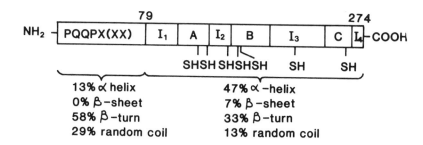

૪ –Hordein

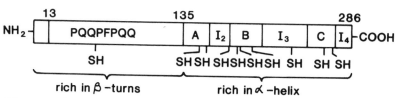

Fig. 24. Diagrammatical comparison of the structures of B1 hordein (Forde et al, 1985a) and γ₂-hordein (Cameron-Mills and Brandt, 1988). SH indicates cysteine residues. The three conserved regions A, B, and C are defined according to Kreis et al (1985a,b).

(Forde et al, 1985b; Rasmussen and Brandt, 1986). The latter contains a single methionine residue.

The proportions of glutamine, proline, and phenylalanine in the consensus repeat motif (4Q:3P:1F) are similar to their proportions in the whole protein (40:30:9 mol%), and Shewry et al (Shewry et al, 1987a; Shewry and Tatham, 1987) suggested that C hordein consisted almost entirely of repeated octapeptides. They also calculated that it consisted of about 440 residues, based on the M_rs (53,000–54,000) calculated by SDS-PAGE (for the major components), sedimentation equilibrium ultracentrifugation (52,500), and the intrinsic viscosity under denaturing conditions (54,300) (Shewry et al, 1980b; Field et al, 1986).

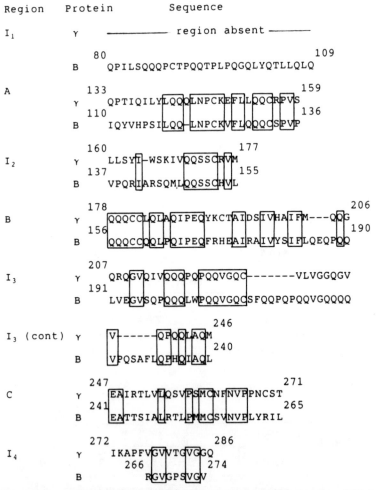

Fig. 25. Comparison of the amino acid sequences of the C-terminal domains of B1 hordein (Forde et al, 1985a) and γ_2-hordein (Cameron-Mills and Brandt, 1988). Regions I_1–I_4 and A–C are defined according to Kreis et al (1985a,b). The alignment is based on Cameron-Mills and Brandt (1988).

Entwistle (1988) isolated a C hordein gene, but the encoded protein has an "in frame" stop codon and also differs from the expressed proteins in its N-terminal and C-terminal sequences. In addition, the encoded protein (with "read through" of the stop codon) consists of only 327 residues. It does, however, show a highly repetitive structure, with about 40 repeats, most of which are based on the PQQPFPQQ motif.

More recently, Entwistle et al (1991) isolated a second C hordein gene encoding a protein with an N-terminal sequence identical to that determined directly and a C-terminal sequence similar to those encoded by the cloned

<u>Complete Gene</u>

NH$_2$-RQLNPSSQELQS
PQQSY
LQQPY
PQNPYL
PQKPFPV
QQPFHT
PQQYFPYL
PEELFPQ
YQIPTPLQ
PQQPFPQQ
PQQPLPR
PQQPFPWQ
PQQPFPQ
PQQPFPQ
PQEPIPQQ
PQQPFPQQ
PQQPFPQQ
PQQIIFQQ
PQQSYPVQ
PQQPFPQ
PQPVPQQR
PQQASPLQPQ
PQQASPLQ
PQQPFPQG
SEQII
PQQPFPLQ
PQPFPQQ
PQQPLPQ
PQQPFRQQ
AELIIPQQ
PQQPLPLQ
PHQPYTQQ
TIWSMV-cooh

<u>Protein N-Terminus</u>

NH$_2$-RQLNPSSQELQS
PQQSY
LQQPY
PQNPYL

<u>Chymotryptic Peptides</u>

XFXQQ	PNQQ
PQQPFPLQ	PQQIIPQQ
PQQPFPQQ	PQQPFPQQ
PQQI	PQQPFPQQ

<u>Partial cDNAs</u>

pchor1-3   pc919

	+Y
+FPQ	PQQPQPF
PQQPFPQQ	PQQPI
PQQPFPLQ	PQQPQPY
PQQPFPQQ	PQQPQPF
PQQPFPQ	SQQPI
PQQPFRQQ	PQQPQPY
AELIIPQQ	PQQPQPF
PQQPFPLQ	PQQPIPLQ
PHQPYTQQ	PHQPYTQQ
TIWSMV-cooh	TIWSMV-cooh

pcP387

+PQQSYPVQ
PQQPFPQ
PQPVPQQ
PQQASPLQ
PQQPFPQG
SEQII   pHvE-c251
PQQPFPLQ
PQPFPQQ   +PFPQQ
PQQPLPQ   PQQPLPQ
PQQPFRQQ   PQQPFRQQ
AELIIPQQ   AELIIPQQ
PQQPLPLQ   PQQPFPLQ
PHQPYTQQ   PHQPYTQQ
TIWSMV-cooh   TIWSMV-cooh

Fig. 26. Amino acid sequences of C hordein (Forde et al, 1985b; Tatham et al, 1985a; Rasmussen and Brandt, 1986; Entwistle et al, 1991).

cDNAs (Fig. 26). The remainder of the protein consists of repeats based on the PQQPFPQQ motif. Although the encoded protein is smaller (241 residues) than would be predicted based on the M_rs determined by physicochemical studies and by SDS-PAGE ($\approx$400 + residues), it appears to encode a typical C hordein protein.

The N-terminal amino acid sequence and amino acid composition of D hordein are similar to those of the HMW subunits of wheat glutenin (Shewry et al, 1988d, 1989), indicating that they have similar sequences. This is supported by the cross-hybridization behavior of their cDNAs (Forde et al, 1983). Comparison of the SDS-PAGE mobility of D hordein with those of HMW subunits suggests that the true M_r is probably below 80,000, not about 105,000, as indicated by comparison with globular standard proteins (Shewry and Miflin 1982).

The HMW subunits consist of 627–827 residues, with a central repetitive domain flanked by shorter nonrepetitive N-terminal domains (81–104 residues) and C-terminal domains (42 residues) (Shewry et al, 1989). The repetitive domains consist of tandem and interspersed copies based on three motifs: a hexapeptide (consensus PGQGQQ), a nonapeptide (GYYPTSP/LQQ), and a tripeptide (GQQ), the latter being present in only some subunits. The non-repetitive domains contain most or all of the cysteine residues, three or five at the N terminus and one at the C terminus.

Halford et al (1992) isolated a cDNA clone encoding the C-terminal part (441 residues) of a D hordein protein. The C-terminal domain of 42 residues is related to those of the HMW subunits of glutenin. The repeats consist of hexapeptides with the consensus sequence PGQGQQ in the N-terminal part and PHQGQQ in the C-terminal part of the domain. These are interspersed with 11 residue and tetrapeptide repeats. The former have the consensus sequence GYYPSXTSPQQ, being derived from the nonapeptides present in the wheat subunits by the addition of SX. The tetrapeptides are restricted to the C-terminal part of the domain and are based on the motif TTVS. This motif is unrelated to other repeat motifs present in prolamins.

EVOLUTIONARY RELATIONSHIPS OF HORDEINS

Comparisons of the amino acid sequences of hordeins indicate that they are structurally and evolutionarily related. This is most apparent in the repeat motifs of the S-rich and S-poor groups. These are all based on the PQQP tetrapeptide, and the consensus motif is identical in C and γ_2-hordeins (PQQPFPQQ). Also, regions related to the three conserved regions (A, B, and C) in the C-terminal domains of the S-rich hordeins are also present in the HMW subunits of wheat, with regions A and B in the N-terminal domain and region C in the C-terminal domain.

Kreis and co-workers demonstrated that sequences related to regions A–C were also present in a range of seed proteins from other species, including cereal inhibitors of α-amylase and trypsin, 2S storage albumins from dicotyledonous plants (oilseed rape, brazil nut, lupin, castor bean) and minor zeins (β- and γ-) of maize (see Kreis et al, 1985a,b; Kreis and Shewry, 1989). They also noted that regions A–C were homologous with each other, although at a low level of statistical significance, and proposed that all these proteins had evolved from a single ancestral protein of about 30 residues, with an initial triplication event giving rise to regions corresponding to A, B, and C. The major events leading to the S-rich, S-poor, and HMW hordeins have included the insertion and amplification of repetitive sequences and the deletion of most of the nonrepetitive sequences in C hordein. The fact that the related nonprolamin proteins (inhibitors and 2S albumins) are readily soluble in water indicates that these events are also responsible for conferring the characteristic solubility properties of prolamins.

CONFORMATIONS OF HORDEINS

Far-UV circular dichroism (cd) spectroscopy of B1 hordein dissolved in 50% (v/v) propan-1-ol at 20°C shows a spectrum typical of a protein rich in α-helix, and deconvolution using the method of Chen et al (1972) gives values of 28–30% α-helix, 8–10% β-sheet, and 60–62% aperiodic structure (random coil and β-turn). The distribution of these structures within the B1 hordein sequence (Fig. 27) can be predicted using the algorithm of Chou and Fasman (1978) (Tatham et al, 1990). This shows that the repetitive domain is rich in β-turns (about 58% of the total structure), with less random coil (29%) and little or no α-helix or β-sheet (13 and 0%, respectively). In contrast, the nonrepetitive domain is predicted to form 47% α-helix, 33% β-turns, 13% random coil, and 7% β-sheet. The predicted values for the whole protein (27–28% α-helix, 6–8% β-sheet, and 38–39% β-turn) (Shewry et al, 1987a) agree reasonably well with those determined by cd spectroscopy.

Preliminary cd studies of γ-hordeins showed spectra similar to those of other S-rich prolamins, indicating similar secondary structure contents (Tatham et al, 1990). The repetitive domain is again predicted to be rich in β-turns.

The conformation of C hordein has been studied in more detail. Structure prediction indicates that β-turns are the major, if not the only, secondary structure element. Two overlapping turns are predicted within the short N-terminal region, and four within the adjacent pentapeptides (Fig. 28). Two turns overlapping by one residue are predicted within the consensus octapep-

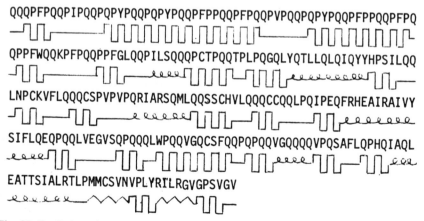

Fig. 27. Prediction of secondary structure of the B1 hordein sequence reported by Forde et al (1985a). ⟋⟍⟍ = α-helix, ⋀⋀⋀ = β-sheet, ⊓⊔⊓ = β-turn, —— = random coil. (Reprinted, by permission, from Tatham et al, 1990)

tides, one of which spans the junction between adjacent motifs (Fig. 28). Their precise distribution within the whole protein depends, of course, on the degree of conservation of the motifs.

Because C hordein contains no α-helix or β-sheet, it is possible to obtain direct confirmation of the presence of β-turns using cd spectroscopy. The far-UV cd spectrum of total C hordein dissolved in 70% (v/v) aqueous ethanol or 0.1M acetic acid at 20°C was consistent with the presence of β-turns, and heating the protein to 70°C or adding increasing concentrations of trifluoroethanol resulted in similar spectral changes, interpreted as indicating increases in turn content (Tatham et al, 1985a; Field et al, 1986). The increase in β-turn structure with increasing temperature (which would favor hydrophobic interactions) and decreasing hydrophobicity of the solvent (favoring hydrogen bonding) indicates that the β-turn-rich structure maximizes both hydrophobic interactions and hydrogen bonding.

Solid-state and solution ^{13}C-NMR spectroscopy showed that all the proline residues were in the *trans* configuration (Tatham et al, 1985b). This is consistent with their presence in β-turns, as a mixture of *cis* and *trans* configurations would be expected for other conformations.

Tatham et al (1987, 1989) have also reported detailed cd and Fourier-transform infrared comparisons of C hordein and a synthetic decapeptide based on the consensus repeat motif, using cryogenic solvents and temperatures down to −100°C. Analysis of the synthetic peptide indicated that a βI/III reverse-turn structure was present at room temperature. It was favored in solvents of low dielectric constant but was in equilibrium with a poly-L-proline II structure at low temperature. They suggested that the random-coil-like

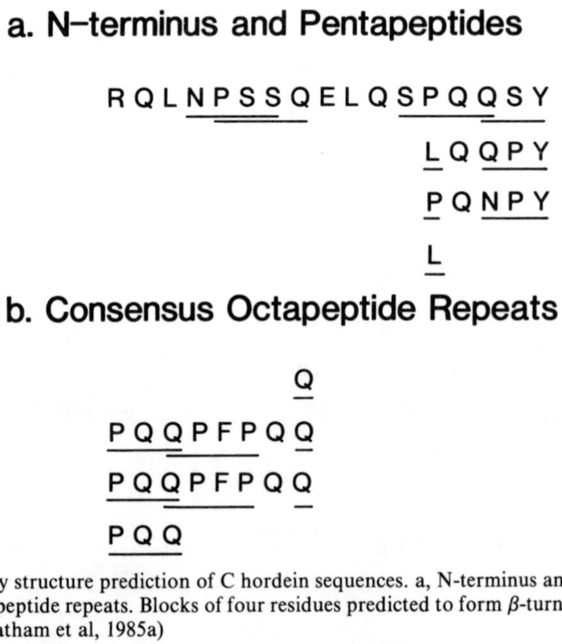

a. N–terminus and Pentapeptides

R Q L N P S S Q E L Q S P Q Q S Y

L Q Q P Y

P Q N P Y

L

b. Consensus Octapeptide Repeats

Q

P Q Q P F P Q Q

P Q Q P F P Q Q

P Q Q

Fig. 28. Secondary structure prediction of C hordein sequences. a, N-terminus and pentapeptides; b, consensus octapeptide repeats. Blocks of four residues predicted to form β-turns are underlined. (Adapted from Tatham et al, 1985a)

spectrum exhibited by the protein and peptide under certain conditions could result from a mixture of $\beta I/III$ reverse-turn and poly-L-proline II structures. Field et al (1986, 1987) determined the intrinsic viscosity of C hordein dissolved in a range of solvents and calculated the molecular dimensions. This indicated that the whole protein was an extended, semirigid rod, with dimensions of 282 × 19 Å in 0.1M acetic acid and 363 × 17.0 Å in 70% (v/v) aqueous ethanol (both at 30°C). The molecule was more extended in trifluoroethanol, with dimensions of 429 × 15.0 Å. The authors proposed that this rod-shaped structure resulted from the formation of a loose spiral structure based on β-turns. They also drew parallels with the β-spiral structure formed by a synthetic polypentapeptide based on elastin (Venkatachalam and Urry, 1981). This has 13.5 residues per turn, with a translation of 9.5 Å. Assuming that C hordein consists of about 440 residues, Field et al (1986) calculated that a β-spiral structure with dimensions similar to that formed by the elastin polypentapeptide would result in a molecule of about 294 × 17 Å, which is within the range determined experimentally. The presence of appreciable amounts of poly-L-proline II structure would result in a much more extended structure, which is not consistent with the hydrodynamic studies.

However, recent results from small-angle X-ray scattering in 0.1M acetic acid at 25°C (I'Anson et al, 1992) indicate that the C hordein is more extended, being a stiff coil (a so-called "worm-like" chain) with a length of about 700 Å. The shorter length calculated from the hydrodynamic data resulted from the assumption, now shown to be incorrect, that the molecule was rodlike rather than more highly extended.

Detailed analyses of the homologous HMW subunits of wheat glutenin, which are homologues of D hordein, have been reported (reviewed in Shewry et al, 1989). Whereas the nonrepetitive N- and C-terminal sequences are rich in α-helix, at least in trifluoroethanol, the repetitive sequences again form β-turns. The whole molecule is also rod-shaped, and scanning tunneling microscopy has provided direct visual evidence for a loose spiral structure with a diameter of about 20 Å (Miles et al, 1991). Thus, the repetitive domains of the HMW prolamins also appear to form a loose spiral structure based on repetitive β-turns, although the repeat motifs are different from that of the S-poor prolamins. Using structure prediction and cd spectroscopy of a synthetic peptide, Halford et al (1992) have demonstrated that the novel tetrapeptide repeat motif (TTVS) also forms β-turns.

DISULFIDE STRUCTURE AND POLYMER FORMATION

The site of disulfide bond formation in developing barley endosperms is not known, but it is most likely to occur in the lumen of the ER. The enzyme protein disulfide isomerase is known to be present within the ER lumen in various tissues (Freedman, 1989) and is associated with ER fractions in developing wheat endosperms (Roden et al, 1982). It also catalyzes disulfide bond formation in wheat prolamins (gliadins and glutenins) synthesized in vitro (Bulleid and Freedman, 1988a,b). It is possible, however, that exchange or rearrangement of disulfide bonds occurs during the later stages of transport and deposition.

C hordein contains no cysteine and is therefore unable to form disulfide bonds. In contrast, D hordein is always present in polymers stabilized by interchain disulfide bonds, although some intrachain disulfide bonds could also be present. Field et al (1983) showed that a substantial proportion of the S-rich prolamins of barley were present in disulfide-stabilized polymers. More recently, Rechinger and coworkers have found that all B hordeins, γ_1-hordein, and γ_2-hordein form interchain disulfide bonds, while γ_3-hordein forms only intrachain bonds (V. Cameron-Mills, *personal communication*). B and D hordeins may also form mixed polymers, as both are present in the gel protein fraction, which is associated with malting quality (Smith and Simpson 1983).

SYNTHESIS AND DEPOSITION OF HORDEINS

The synthesis of all four groups of hordeins is restricted to the starchy endosperm, where it occurs on microsomes bound to the ER (Brandt and Ingversen, 1976; Matthews and Miflin, 1980). Hordeins are synthesized with short (about 20-residue) signal peptides, which are cleaved as the protein is transported into the lumen of the ER. The hordein is ultimately deposited in membrane-bound protein bodies, but the precise mechanism of deposition and the origin of the protein body membrane are still uncertain. Whereas Miflin et al (1981) suggested that the protein was deposited directly within the lumen of the ER, other studies have shown the presence of protein deposits within vacuoles (Cameron-Mills and von Wettstein, 1980), indicating that the pathway of deposition may include transport in vesicles derived from the Golgi apparatus, as in wheat (Kim et al, 1988) and legumes (Chrispeels, 1984). It is possible that both pathways of deposition operate in barley, at the same or different stages of development. In particular, direct accumulation within the ER may become more important during the later stages of seed development, when the vacuolar pathway may be disrupted by accumulation of starch.

Hordein is synthesized in the developing starchy endosperm only from about 14 days postanthesis, when the endosperm has attained about 10% of its final dry weight (Shewry et al, 1979b; Rahman et al, 1982). It then accumulates rapidly to account for about 40% of the protein in the mature grain. The total amount of hordein synthesized, the proportions of the individual groups, and the ratio of class I/II to class III B hordeins are affected by a number of factors, including genotype, mineral nutrition (availability of N and S), and *trans*-acting mutant ("high-lysine") genes. These controls are outside the scope of the present chapter but are discussed in detail in recent reviews (Shewry et al, 1987b; Shewry, 1992).

HORDEIN GENE STRUCTURE AND EXPRESSION

Genes for B, C, and γ-hordeins have been isolated and characterized (Brandt et al, 1985; Forde et al, 1985a; Cameron-Mills and Brandt, 1988; Entwistle, 1988; Chernyshev et al, 1989; Entwistle et al, 1991; Rechinger et al, 1993), and the structures of one gene for each hordein group are summarized in Fig. 29.

The genes all have "TATA" boxes about 80–100 bp upstream of the ATG translation initiation codons (Fig. 30) and one or more putative polyadenylation signals (AATAAA) about 50–150 bp downstream of the stop codon (TAA or TGA). The B hordein genes also have "CATC" boxes about 60 bp upstream of the TATA boxes (Fig. 30), but these apparently are not present in the γ-hordein and C hordein genes. All five genes also have a conserved region of about 30 bp approximately 300 bp upstream of the ATG initiation codon. Forde et al (1985a) identified related sequences in the 5' upstream regions of other prolamin genes from wheat (α- and γ-gliadin) and maize (19k and 22k α-zeins) and suggested that these "-300 elements" have a role in the regulation of prolamin gene expression. It is of interest that a conserved "-300 element" is not present in the genes for the wheat HMW glutenin subunits. These are homologues of D hordein, which shows characteristic differences in regulation of expression from the other hordein groups (in particular, it is increased in the high-lysine line Risφ 1508; see Shewry et al [1987b] and Shewry [1992]).

Although the individual genes at the *Hor1* and *Hor2* loci are closely linked in genetic terms, all the genomic clones isolated so far have contained only single genes. Kreis et al (1983a) estimated that the minimum size of the *Hor2* locus was about 85 kb, based on the sizes and numbers of genomic fragments that were absent from a *Hor2* deletion mutant (Risφ 56). However, they estimated a total copy number of about 11–13 genes per haploid genome; more recent studies have suggested that this may be an underestimate (Bunce et al, 1986) (Fig. 20C) and that the minimum size estimate should be doubled (i.e., to 170 kbp). This estimate would also need to be increased if extensive regions of noncoding DNA or nonhordein genes are interspersed with the B hordein genes.

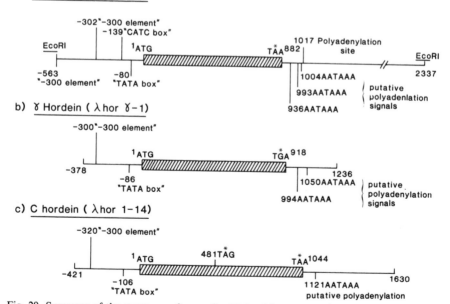

Fig. 29. Summary of the structures of genes for B1 hordein, γ2-hordein, and C hordein. Based on data in Forde et al (1985a), Entwistle (1988), and Cameron-Mills and Brandt (1988). (Reprinted, by permission, from Shewry, 1992)

An alternative approach to studying the size and organization of the *Hor2* locus was adopted by Sørensen (1989). Genomic DNA was digested with rare-cutting enzymes and separated by pulsed-field gel electrophoresis, and B hordein-related fragments were identified by southern blotting. This showed that two fragments of DNA, of about 160 and 200 kb, could together account for the whole *Hor2* locus. It is not known whether these correspond to the two subfamilies of B hordein genes.

Kreis and co-workers (Marris et al, 1988; Shewry et al, 1988c; Marris, 1990) have used two approaches to study the regulation of expression of the B1 hordein gene isolated by Forde et al (1985a). They initially transferred the entire 2.9-kb *Eco* R1 fragment containing the gene into tobacco using *Agrobacterium tumefaciens*. B1 hordein transcripts were detected in the seeds but not the leaves of the transgenic plants, but hordein protein could not be detected (Shewry et al, 1988c). They also made similar transgenic plants using only 549 bp of the immediate 5′ upstream region linked to the bacterial chloramphenicol acetyl transferase (CAT) gene (Marris et al, 1988). In this case, CAT enzyme activity was detected only in the endosperm of the developing seed, from about 15 days after pollination. It was not detected in any other seed (embryo, testa) or vegetative tissues. These results demonstrate that all the information required to specify the developmental and tissue specificity of

A. Putative "CATC" and "TATA" boxes

Gene Product	Clone		"CATC box"	"TATA box"
B1 hordein	pBHR184	-139	ACATCCAAACA	- 80 CTATAAATA
"	λhor 2-4	-140	GCATCCAAACA	- 80 CTATAAATA
"	λ r9	-139	ACATCCAAACA	- 80 CTATAAATA
γ hordein	λhor γ-1		not present	- 86 CTATAAAGA
C hordein	λhor 1-14		not present	-106 CTATAAATA

B "-300 elements"

Gene Product	Clone		"-300 element"
B1 hordein	pBHR184	-300	ACATG..TAAAGTGAATAAGG.TGAGTCATG
"	λhor 2-4	-303	ACATG..TAAAGTGAATAAGG.TGAGTCATG
"	λ r9	-300	ACATG..TAAAGTGAATAAGG.TGAGTCATG
γ-hordein	λhor γ-1	-300	AGATG..TAAAGTGAATAAGA.TGAGTCAGC
C hordein	λhor 1-14	-320	TAGTG..TAAAGTAAAAAAAA.TGACTCATC

Fig. 30. Conserved sequences in the 5′ upstream regions of genes for B1, γ₂, and C hordeins. Based on data in Brandt et al (1985), Forde et al (1985a), Cameron-Mills and Brandt (1988), Entwistle (1988) and Chernyshev et al (1989). (Reprinted, by permission, from Shewry, 1992)

expression are present in the 549 bp of 5′ sequence and are recognized in the developing endosperm of tobacco. Although the "-300 element" was present in this sequence, its role has not yet been demonstrated. Further attempts to dissect the promoter region using the β-glucuronidase reporter gene have given inconclusive results, due to the low levels of expression of many of the constructs (Marris, 1990).

The second approach adopted by Kreis and co-workers is the identification and characterization of "*trans*-acting" DNA-binding proteins in nuclei from developing endosperms. Kreis et al (1986) initially used a modified western blotting procedure to identify six major protein bands (with M_rs ranging from 37,600 to 200,000) that bound to the 5′ upstream sequence of the B1 hordein gene. Some of these were present only in nuclei from endosperms, including one (of $M_r \approx 120,000$) that also bound to a synthetic oligonucleotide based on the "-300 element" (Shewry et al, 1988c).

LOW-MOLECULAR-WEIGHT PROLAMINS

Aragoncillo et al (1981) showed that the chloroform/methanol (2:1) soluble fraction from barley endosperm contained two groups of proteins with M_rs below 25,000. The quantitatively major group was the CM proteins, which are discussed in detail above. The second group had low mobility on starch gel electrophoresis at low pH and gave a major band of M_r about 18,000 on SDS-PAGE.

Two individual components of this fraction have been purified, with M_rs by SDS-PAGE of about 16,500 (Salcedo et al, 1982) and 22,000 (Festenstein et al, 1987). These had similar amino acid compositions, with over 25% glutamate + glutamine, less than 10% proline, and little or no lysine or histidine (Table 5). Although their name (low-molecular-weight prolamin) implies a structural relationship to the hordeins, this remains to be established. An attempt to determine the N-terminal amino acid sequence of the M_r 22,000 component was unsuccessful, presumably due to N-terminal blocking (Festenstein et al, 1987).

SEED PROTEIN POLYMORPHISM IN VARIETAL IDENTIFICATION AND FINGERPRINTING

Polymorphism in seed protein patterns has been exploited in developing marker systems for use in plant breeding and grain trading.

This approach was pioneered by Frydenberg and co-workers, who studied the pattern of α-amylase isoenzymes in germinating grains (Frydenberg and Nielsen, 1965; Frydenberg et al, 1969). Only two allelic forms were present in European lines, but a third allele was present in Canadian cultivars (Fedak and Rajhathy, 1971; Fedak, 1974). Similarly, only two allelic forms of β-amylase are present in germinated seeds of European barleys (Anderson, 1982).

A number of other isoenzyme systems have been used to classify and identify barley varieties, but using leaf or root tissue rather than seeds (Nielsen, 1985). However, Nielsen (1985) did show that 66 barley cultivars from the Danish National list exhibited only two allelic forms of grain peroxidase and single allelic forms of dipeptidase and glucose-6-phosphate dehydrogenase (both from the mature embryo).

The B and C hordeins show a much higher degree of polymorphism and have consequently proved to be more useful as marker systems. Shewry et al (1978b, 1979a) examined 164 current and obsolete European varieties for polymorphism at the *Hor1* and *Hor2* loci using SDS-PAGE of reduced and alkylated total prolamins. They identified eight and 17 alleles at the *Hor1* and *Hor2* loci, respectively, and classified the varieties into 32 groups containing between one and 35 cultivars. The range of polymorphism is illustrated in Fig. 31. More complete lists of 17 *Hor1* and 24 *Hor2* alleles and of standard cultivars have been reported by Johansen and Shewry (1986).

Other studies have confirmed the value of hordeins as biochemical markers but have failed to result in a single widely accepted analytical system. This reflects the fact that no single electrophoretic system is capable of discriminating between all cultivars, and it is necessary to either use several systems or to combine electrophoretic data with other biochemical characters (e.g., isoenzymes) or with studies of grain morphology.

The range of electrophoretic procedures includes SDS-PAGE (Shewry et al, 1978b, 1979a; Montembault et al, 1983), electrophoresis at low pH (Autran and Scriban, 1977; van Lonkhuysen and Marseille, 1978; Schildbach and Burbidge, 1979; Marchylo and LaBerge, 1980; Cooke and Cliff, 1983), electrophoresis at pH 9 (Schildbach and Burbidge, 1979), isoelectric focusing (Scriban and Strobbel, 1979), and electrophoresis at low pH in polyacrylamide gradient gels (du Cros and Wrigley, 1979). A more recent approach uses HPLC with ion-exchange and reversed-phase columns (Marchylo and Kruger, 1984; Skerritt et al, 1986).

One attraction of using hordein polypeptides as markers is that the pattern is stable under a range of environmental conditions (although the precise proportions of the groups of polypeptides may vary) and is retained (despite

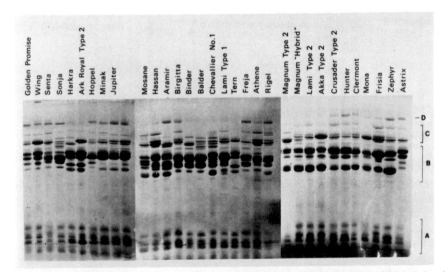

Fig. 31. Sodium dodecyl sulfate-polyacrylamide gel electrophoresis of reduced and pyridylethylated total hordein fractions from single seeds of a range of European cultivars of barley. (Reprinted from Shewry et al, 1978b, by permission of the Society of Chemical Industry)

some proteolysis) during malting and the early stages of germination (Shewry et al, 1980a). A disadvantage is that some cultivars, notably those bred before the use of electrophoresis, are mixtures of "biotypes" that differ in their hordein alleles (Shewry et al, 1981). More rigorous standards of varietal purity should have largely eliminated this problem.

Shewry et al (1979a) noted that the distribution of hordein polypeptide patterns in European cultivars was less random than would be expected for proteins with no selective advantage and that certain patterns had either increased or decreased in importance with time. They ascribed this to the linkage of the *Hor1* and *Hor2* loci to a number of loci controlling resistances to rusts and mildew (Jensen, 1988). In particular, a number of alleles at the *Mla* locus, which is located between *Hor1* and *Hor2*, have been introduced into breeding programs to confer resistance to particular strains of powdery mildew. Selection for these resistances has resulted in selection of specific hordein alleles by "hitch-hiking."

Although early work suggested that specific B hordein alleles were associated with good or poor malting quality (Baxter and Wainwright, 1979), this was not confirmed by subsequent studies (Shewry et al, 1980a; Riggs et al, 1983).

A further approach to cultivar identifications is by RFLP analysis, using probes related to B and C hordeins. Bunce et al (1986) reported that this could be used to discriminate between some cultivars with identical B and C hordein patterns by SDS-PAGE. More recently Hofstra et al (1989) reported that RFLP patterns are usually the same when protein patterns are identical but suggested that unique fingerprints for all cultivars could be obtained by choosing appropriate restriction enzymes and/or probes, including nonhordein probes such as glyceraldehyde-3-phosphate dehydrogenase and α-amylase. They also suggested that RFLP analysis could be especially valuable for analyses of malts, where protein digestion could render precise identification difficult. RFLP analysis clearly has a major role to play in the future but is currently too "high tech" and too expensive for routine use.

SUMMARY

Much of our knowledge of barley seed proteins derives from work carrried out over the past decade and has resulted, in particular, from the application of molecular cloning to isolate and characterize genes and/or cDNAs for individual proteins of interest. Much of the information is relevant to the quality of the crop (for food, feed, or industrial processing) or to its natural resistance to pests and pathogens. It should therefore provide a sound basis for future attempts to manipulate and improve the composition of the grain by genetic engineering. Although this is currently limited by our inability to transform the barley plant, progress in this area indicates that the production of improved barley varieties by genetic engineering may soon become a reality.

ACKNOWLEDGMENT

I am grateful to V. Cameron-Mills (Carlsberg Laboratory, Copenhagen) for providing information prior to publication.

184 / Barley: Chemistry and Technology

LITERATURE CITED

ABE, K., EMORI, Y., KONDO, H., ARAI, S., and SUZUKI, K. 1988. The NH$_2$-terminal 21 amino acid residues are not essential for the papain-inhibitory activity of oryzacystatin, a member of the cystatin superfamily. J. Biol. Chem. 263:7655-7659.

ABE, M., and WHITAKER, J. R. 1988. Purification and characterisation of a cysteine proteinase inhibitor from the endosperm of corn. Agric. Biol. Chem. 52:1583-1584.

AINSWORTH, C. C., MILLER, T. E., and GALE, M. D. 1987. α-Amylase and β-amylase homoeoloci in species related to wheat. Genet. Res. Camb. 49:93-103.

ALLEN, R. D., COHEN, E. A., VONDER HAAR, R. A., ADAMS, C. A., MA, D. P., NESSLER, C. L., and THOMAS, T. L. 1987. Sequence and expression of a gene encoding an albumin storage protein in sunflower. Mol. Gen. Genet. 210:211-218.

ALLISON, M. J. 1978. Amylase activity and endosperm hardness of high lysine barleys. J. Inst. Brew. 84:231-232.

ALLISON, M. J., and ELLIS, R. P. 1973. The inheritance of β-amylases in developing barley grain. Biochem. Genet. 10:165-173.

ANDERSON, H. J. 1982. Isoenzyme characters of 47 barley cultivars and their application in cultivar identification. Seed Sci. Technol. 10:405-413.

ARAGONCILLO, C., SANCHEZ-MONGE, R., and SALCEDO, G. 1981. Two groups of low molecular weight hydrophobic proteins from barley endosperm. J. Exp. Bot. 32:1279-1286.

ARY, M. B., RICHARDSON, M., and SHEWRY, P. R. 1989. Purification and characterisation of an insect α-amylase inhibitor/endochitinase from seeds of Jobs tears (Coix lachryma-jobi). Biochim. Biophys. Acta 993:260-266.

ASANO, K., SVENSSON, B., and POULSEN, F. M. 1984. Isolation and characterisation of inhibitors of animal cell-free protein synthesis from barley seeds. Carlsberg Res. Commun. 49:619-626.

ASANO, K., SVENSSON, B., SVENDSEN, I., POULSEN, F. M., and ROEPSTORFF, P. 1986. The complete primary structure of protein synthesis inhibitor II from barley seeds. Carlsberg Res. Commun. 51:129-141.

AUTRAN, J.-C., and SCRIBAN, R. 1977. Recherche sur la pureté variétale d'un malt. Pages 47-62 in: Proc. Congr. Eur. Brew. Conv. 16th, Amsterdam.

BALLS, A. K., HALE, W. S., and HARRIS, T. H. 1942. A crystalline protein obtained from a lipoprotein of wheat flour. Cereal Chem. 19:279-288.

BARBER, D., SANCHEZ-MONGE, R., MENDEZ, E., LAZARO, A., GARCIA-OLMEDO, F., and SALCEDO, G. 1986. New α-amylase and trypsin inhibitors among the CM-proteins of barley (Hordeum vulgare). Biochim. Biophys. Acta 869:115-118.

BARBER, D., LIMAS, G. G., GAVILANES, J. G., and MENDEZ, E. 1988. Isolation and characterisation of thirteen new salt-soluble proteins from barley by reversed-phase high-performance liquid chromatography. Planta 176:221-229.

BARBER, D., SANCHEZ-MONGE, R., GOMEZ, L., CARPIZO, J., ARMENTIA, A., LOPEZ-OTIN, C., JUAN, F., and SALCEDO, G. 1989. A barley flour inhibitor of insect α-amylase is a major allergen associated with baker's asthma disease. FEBS Lett. 248:119-122.

BASSÜNER, R., HAI, N. V., JUNG, R., SAALBACH, G., and MUNTZ, K. 1987. The primary structure of the predominating vicilin storage protein subunit from field bean seeds (Vicia faba L. var. minor cv. Fribo). Nucleic Acids Res. 15:9609.

BAXTER, E. D., and WAINWRIGHT, T. 1979. Hordein and malting quality. J. Am. Soc. Brew. Chem. Proc. 37:8-12.

BECHTEL, D. B., WILSON, J. D., and SHEWRY, P. R. 1989. Identification of legumin-like proteins in thin sections of developing wheat endosperms by immunocytochemical procedures. (Abstr.) Cereal Foods World 34:784.

BECHTEL, D. B., WILSON, J. D., and SHEWRY, P. R. 1991. Immunocytochemical localization of the wheat storage protein triticin in developing endosperm tissue. Cereal Chem. 68:573-577.

BEKES, F., and LASZTITY, R. 1981. Isolation and determination of amino acid sequence of avenothionin, a new purothionin analogue from oat. Cereal Chem. 58:360-361.

BERNHARD, W. R., and SOMERVILLE, C. R. 1989. Coidentity of putative amylase inhibitors from barley and finger millet with phospholipid transfer proteins inferred from amino acid sequence homology. Arch. Biochem. Biophys. 269:695-697.

BISHOP, L. R. 1928. The composition and quantitative estimation of barley proteins I. J. Inst. Brew. 34:101-118.

BLOCH, C., and RICHARDSON, M. 1991. A new family of small (5 kDa) protein inhibitors of insect α-amylases from seeds of sorghum (Sorghum bicolor (L) Moench) have sequence homologies with wheat γ-purothionins. FEBS Lett. 279:101-104.

BOHLMANN, H., and APEL, K. 1987. Isolation and characterisation of cDNAs coding for leaf-specific thionins closely related to the endosperm-specific hordothionin of barley (*Hordeum vulgare* L.). Mol. Gen. Genet. 207:446-454.

BOHLMANN, H., CLAUSEN, S., BEHNKE, S., GIESE, H., HILLER, C., REIMANN-PHILIPP, U., SCHRADER, G., BARKHOLT, V., and APEL, K. 1988. Leaf-specific thionins of barley—A novel class of cell wall proteins toxic to plant-pathogenic fungi and possibly involved in the defence mechanism of plants. EMBO J. 7:1559-1565.

BRANDT, A. 1976. Endosperm protein formation during kernel development of wild type and a high-lysine barley mutant. Cereal Chem. 53:890-901.

BRANDT, A., and INGVERSEN, J. 1976. In vitro synthesis of barley endosperm proteins on wild type and mutant templates. Carlsberg Res. Commun. 41:312-320.

BRANDT, A., MONTEMBAULT, A., CAMERON-MILLS, V., and RASMUSSEN, S. K. 1985. Primary structure of a B1 hordein gene from barley. Carlsberg Res. Commun. 50:333-345.

BRANDT, A., SVENDSEN, I., and HEJGAARD, J. 1990. A plant serpin gene. Structure, organisation and expression of the gene encoding barley protein Z₄. Eur. J. Biochem. 194:499-504.

BREU, V., GUERBETTE, F., KADER, J. C., KANNANGARA, C. G., SVENSSON, B., and VON WETTSTEIN-KNOWLES, P. 1989. 1A 10 kD barley basic protein transfers phosphatidylcholine from liposomes to mitochondria. Carlsberg Res. Commun. 54:81-84.

BRIGHT, S. W. J., MIFLIN, B. J., and ROGNES, S. E. 1981. Threonine accumulation in the seeds of a barley mutant with an altered aspartate kinase. Biochem. Genet. 20:229-243.

BROGLIE, K. E., GAYNOR, J. J., and BROGLIE, R. M. 1986. Ethylene-regulated gene expression: Molecular cloning of the genes encoding an endochitinase from *Phaseolus vulgaris*. Proc. Natl. Acad. Sci. USA 83:6820-6824.

BROWN, A. H. D., and JACOBSEN, J. V. 1982. Genetic basis and natural variation of α-amylase isozymes in barley. Genet. Res. Camb. 40:315-324.

BULLEID, N. J., and FREEDMAN, R. B. 1988a. Defective co-translational formation of disulphide bonds in protein disulphide-isomerase-deficient microsomes. Nature 335:649-651.

BULLEID, N. J., and FREEDMAN, R. B. 1988b. The transcription and translation in vitro of individual cereal storage-protein genes from wheat (*Triticum aestivum*, cv. Chinese Spring). Biochem. J. 254:805-810.

BUNCE, N. A. C., FORDE, B. G., KREIS, M., and SHEWRY, P. R. 1986. DNA restriction fragment length polymorphism at hordein loci: Application to identifying and fingerprinting barley cultivars. Seed Sci. Technol. 14:419-429.

BURGESS, S. R., and MIFLIN, B. J. 1985. The localisation of oat (*Avena sativa* L.) seed globulins in protein bodies. J. Exp. Bot. 36:945-954.

BURGESS, S. R., and SHEWRY, P. R. 1986. Identification of homologous globulins from embryos of wheat, barley, rye and oats. J. Exp. Bot. 37:1863-1871.

BURGESS, S. R., SHEWRY, P. R., MATLASHEWSKI, G. J., ALTOSAAR, I., and MIFLIN, yB. J. 1983. Characteristics of oat (*Avena sativa* L.) seed globulins. J. Exp. Bot. 34:1320-1332.

CAMERON-MILLS, V., and BRANDT, A. 1988. A γ-hordein gene. Plant Mol. Biol. 11:449-461.

CAMERON-MILLS, V., and MADRID, S. M. 1989. The signal peptide cleavage site of a B1 hordein determined by radiosequencing of the in vitro synthesised and processed polypeptide. Carlsberg Res. Commun. 54:181-182.

CAMERON-MILLS, V., and VON WETTSTEIN, D. 1980. Endosperm morphology and protein body formation in developing barley grain. Carlsberg Res. Commun. 45:577-594.

CAMPBELL, A. F. 1992. Protein engineering of the barley chymotrypsin inhibitor 2. In: Plant Protein Engineering. P. R. Shewry and S. Gutteridge, eds. Edward Arnold, Sevenoaks, U.K.

CAMPOS, F. A. P., and RICHARDSON, M. 1984. The complete amino acid sequence of the α-amylase inhibitor I-2 from seeds of ragi (Indian finger millet, *Eleusine coracana* Gaertn). FEBS Lett. 167:300-304.

CANNELL, M., KARP, A., ISAACS, P., and SHEWRY, P. R. 1992. Chromosomal assignment of genes in barley using telosomic wheat-barley addition lines. Genome 35:17-23.

CARBAJOSA, J. V., BERITASHVILI, D. R., KRAEV, A. S., and SKRYABIN, K. G. 1992. Conserved structure and organization of B hordein genes in the *Hor 2* locus of barley. Plant Mol. Biol. 18:453-458.

CARBONERO, P., GARCIA-OLMEDO, F., and HERNANDEZ-LUCAS, C. 1980. External association of hordothionin with protein bodies in mature barley. J. Agric. Food Chem. 28:399-402.

CARRASCO, L., VAZQUEZ, D., HERNANDEZ-LUCAS, C., CARBONERO, P., and GARCIA-OLMEDO, F. 1981. Thionins: Plant peptides that modify membrane permeability in cultured mammalian cells. Eur. J. Biochem. 116:185-189.

CHEN, Y. H., YANG, J. T., and MARTINEZ, H. M. 1972. Determination of secondary structures of proteins by circular dichroism and optical rotatory dispersion. Biochemistry 11:4120-4131.

CHERNYSHEV, A. K., DAVLETOVA, S. K., BASHKIROV, V. I., SHAKHMANOV, N. B., MEKHEDOV, S. L., and ANANIEV, E. V. 1989. Nucleotide sequence of B1 hordein gene of barley *Hordeum vulgare* L. Genetica 25:1349-1355.

CHLAN, C. C., PYLE, J. B., LEGOCKI, A. B., and DURE, L. III. 1986. Developmental biochemistry of cottonseed embryogenesis and germination. XVIII. cDNA and amino acid sequences of members of the storage protein families. Plant Mol. Biol. 7:475-489.

CHOU, P. Y., and FASMAN, G. D. 1978. Empirical predictions of protein conformations. Annu. Rev. Biochem. 47:251-276.

CHRISPEELS, M. J. 1984. Biosynthesis, processing and transport of storage proteins and lectins in cotyledons of developing legume seeds. Phil. Trans. R. Soc. London B. 304:309-322.

CLORE, G. M., GRONENBORN, A. M., KJAER, M., and POULSEN, F. M. 1987a. The determination of the three-dimensional structure of barley serine proteinase inhibitory 2 by nuclear magnetic resonance, distance geometry and restrained molecular dynamics. Protein Eng. 1:305-311.

CLORE, G. M., GRONENBORN, A. M., JAMES, M. N. G., KJAER, M., MCPHALEN, C. A., and POULSEN, F. M. 1987b. Comparison of the solution and X-ray structures of barley serine proteinase inhibitor 2. Protein Eng. 1:313-318.

COLILLA, F. J., ROCHER, A., and MENDEZ, E. 1990. γ-Purothionins: Amino acid sequence of two polypeptides of a new family of thionins from wheat endosperm. FEBS Lett. 270:191-194.

COOKE, R. J., and CLIFF, E. M. 1983. Barley cultivar characterisation by electrophoresis. I. A method for acid polyacrylamide gel electrophoresis of hordein proteins. J. Natl. Inst. Agric. Bot. 16:189-195.

CROY, R. R. D., GATEHOUSE, J. A., TYLER, M. E., and BOULTER, D. 1980. The purification and characterisation of a third

storage protein (convicilin) from the seeds of peas (*Pisum sativum* L.). Biochem. J. 191:509-516.

DANIELSSON, C. E. 1949. Seed globulins of the Gramineae and Leguminosae. Biochem. J. 44:387-400.

DJURTOFT, R. 1961. Salt-Soluble Proteins of Barley. Dansk Videnskabs Forlag, Copenhagen.

Du CROS, D. L., and WRIGLEY, C. W. 1979. Improved electrophoretic methods for identifying cereal varieties. J. Sci. Food Agric. 30:785-794.

EINHOF, H. 1806. Chemische Analyse der kleinen Gerste (*Hordeum vulgare*). Neues Allge. J. Chem. 6:62-98.

ENARI, T.-M., and MIKOLA, J. 1967. Characterisation of the soluble proteolytic enzymes of green malt. Pages 9-16 in: Proc. Congr. Eur. Brew. Conv. 11th, Madrid.

ENDO, Y., TSURUGI, K., and EBERT, R. F. 1988. The mechanism of action of barley toxin: A type 1 ribosome-inactivating protein with RNA N-glycosidase activity. Biochim. Biophys. Acta 954:224-226.

ENTWISTLE, J. 1988. Primary structure of a C-hordein gene from barley. Carlsberg Res. Commun. 53:247-258.

ENTWISTLE, J., KNUDSEN, S., MÜLLER, M., and CAMERON-MILLS, V. 1991. Amber codon suppression: The in vivo and in vitro analysis of two C-hordein genes from barley. Plant Mol. Biol. 17:1217-1231.

FAULKS, A. J., SHEWRY, P. R., and MIFLIN, B. J. 1981. The polymorphism and structural homology of storage polypeptides (hordein) coded by the *Hor 2* locus in barley (*Hordeum vulgare* L.). Biochem. Genet. 19:841-858.

FEDAK, G. 1974. Allozymes as aids to Canadian barley cultivar identification. Euphytica 23:166-173.

FEDAK, G., and RAJHATHY, T. 1971. Alpha amylase distribution and DDT response in Canadian barley cultivars. Can. J. Plant Sci. 51:353-359.

FESTENSTEIN, G. N., HAY, F. C., and SHEWRY, P. R. 1987. Immunochemical relationships of the prolamin storage proteins of barley, wheat, rye and oats. Biochim. Biophys. Acta 912:371-383.

FIELD, J. M., SHEWRY, P. R., and MIFLIN, B. J. 1983. Aggregation states of alcohol-soluble storage proteins of barley, rye, wheat and maize. J. Sci. Food Agric. 34:362-369.

FIELD, J. M., TATHAM, A. S., BAKER, A., and SHEWRY, P. R. 1986. The structure of C hordein. FEBS Lett. 200:76-80.

FIELD, J. M., TATHAM, A. S., and SHEWRY, P. R. 1987. The structure of a high molecular weight subunit of wheat gluten. Biochem. J. 247:215-221.

FOLKES, B. F., and YEMM, E. W. 1956. The amino acid content of the proteins of barley grain. Biochem. J. 62:4-11.

FORDE, B. G., KREIS, M., BAHRAMIAN, M. B., MATTHEWS, J. A., MIFLIN, B. J., THOMPSON, R. D., BARTELS, D., and FLAVELL, R. B. 1981. Molecular cloning and analysis of cDNA sequences derived from poly A+ RNA from barley endosperm: Identification of B hordein-related clones. Nucleic Acids Res. 9:6689-6707.

FORDE, J., FORDE, B. G., FRY, R., KREIS, M., SHEWRY, P. R., and MIFLIN, B. J. 1983. Identification of barley and wheat cDNA clones related to the high M_r polypeptides of wheat gluten. FEBS Lett. 162:360-366.

FORDE, B. G., HEYWORTH, A., PYWELL, J., and KREIS, M. 1985a. Nucleotide sequence of a B1 hordein gene and the identification of possible upstream regulatory elements in endosperm storage protein genes from barley, wheat and maize. Nucleic Acids Res. 13:7327-7339.

FORDE, B. G., KREIS, M., WILLIAMSON, M., FRY, R., PYWELL, J., SHEWRY, P. R., BUNCE, N., and MIFLIN, B. J. 1985b. Short tandem repeats shared by B- and C-hordein cDNAs suggest a common evolutionary origin for two groups of cereal storage protein genes. EMBO J. 4:9-15.

FORIERS, R., DE NEVE, R., and KANAREK, L. 1975. Specificity and partial purification of barley-germ agglutinin. Arch. Int. Physiol. Biochem. 83:362.

FORIERS, R., DE NEVE, R., and KANAREK, L. 1976. Purification of barley-germ agglutinin. Arch. Int. Physiol. Biochem. 84:617-618.

FREEDMAN, R. B. 1989. Protein disulfide isomerase: Multiple roles in the modification of nascent secretory proteins. Cell 57:1069-1072.

FRYDENBERG, O., and NIELSEN, G. 1965. Amylase isozymes in germinating barley seeds. Hereditas 54:123-139.

FRYDENBERG, O., NIELSEN, G., and SANDFAER, J. 1969. The inheritance and distribution of α-amylase types and DDT responses in barley. Z. Pflanzenzuecht. 61:210-215.

GARCIA-OLMEDO, F., CARBONERO, P., and JONES, B. L. 1982. Chromosomal locations of genes that control wheat endosperm proteins. Pages 1-47 in: Advances in Cereal Science and Technology, Vol. 5. Y. Pomeranz, ed. Am. Assoc. Cereal Chem., St. Paul, MN.

GARCIA-OLMEDO, F., CARBONERO, P., HERNANDEZ-LUCAS, C., PAZ-ARES, J., PONZ, F., VICENTE, O., and SIERRA, J. M. 1983. Inhibition of eucaryotic cell-free protein synthesis by thionins from wheat endosperm. Biochim. Biophys. Acta 740:52-56.

GARCIA-OLMEDO, F., SALCEDO, G., SANCHEZ-MONGE, R., GOMEZ, L., ROYO, J., and CARBONERO, P. 1987. Plant proteinaceous inhibitors of proteinases and α-amylases. Pages 275-334 in: Oxford Surveys of Plant Molecular and Cell Biology, Vol. 4. B. J. Miflin, ed. Oxford University Press, Oxford.

GATEHOUSE, J., CROY, R. R. D., and BOULTER, D. 1984. The synthesis and structure of pea storage proteins. CRC Crit. Rev. Plant Sci. 1:287-314.

GAUSING, K. 1987. Thionin genes specifically expressed in barley leaves. Planta 171:241-246.

GIESE, H., and HEJGAARD, J. 1984. Synthesis of salt-soluble proteins in barley. Pulse-labelling study of grain filling in liquid-cultured detached spikes. Planta 161:172-177.

GIESE, H., and HOPP, H. E. 1984. Influence of nitrogen nutrition on the amount of hordein, protein Z and β-amylase messenger RNA in developing endosperms of barley. Carlsberg Res. Commun. 49:365-383.

GRAHAM, J. S., PEARCE, G., MERRY-WEATHER, J., TITANI, K., ERICSSON, L., and RYAN, C. A. 1985. Wound-induced proteinase inhibitors from tomato leaves. J. Biol. Chem. 260:6555-6560.

HALAYKO, A. J., HILL, R. D., and SVENSSON, B. 1986. Characterisation of the interaction of barley α-amylase II with an endogenous α-amylase inhibitor from barley kernels. Biochem. Biophys. Acta 873:92-101.

HALFORD, N. G., MORRIS, N. A., URWIN, P., WILLIAMSON, M. S., KASARDA, D. D., LEW, E. J.-L., KREIS, M., and SHEWRY, P. R. 1988. Molecular cloning of the barley seed protein CMd: A varient member of the α-amylase/trypsin inhibitor family of cereals. Biochim. Biophys. Acta 950:435-440.

HALFORD, N. G., TATHAM, A. S., SUI, E., DARODA, L., DREYER, T., and SHEWRY, P. R. 1992. Identification of a novel β-turn rich repeat motif in the D hordeins of barley. Biochim. Biophys. Acta 1122:118-122.

HALL, T. C., SUN, S. M., MA, Y., McLEESTER, R. C., PYNE, J. W., BLISS, F. A., and BUCKBINDER, B. V. 1979. The major storage protein of french bean seeds:

Characterisation in vivo and translation in vitro. Pages 3-25 in: The Plant Seed; Development, Preservation and Germination. I. Rubenstein, E. Green, R. Phillips, and R. Gengenbach, eds. Academic Press, New York.

HARA-NISHIMURA, I., NISHIMURA, M., and DAUSSANT, J. 1986. Conversion of free β-amylase to bound β-amylase on starch granules in the barley endosperm during desiccation phase of seed development. Protoplasma 134:149-153.

HASE, T., MATSUBARA, H., and YOSHIZUMI, H. 1978. Disulfide bonds of purothionin, a lethal toxin for yeasts. J. Biochem. 83:1671-1678.

HEJGAARD, J. 1977. Origin of a dominant beer protein. Immunochemical identity with a β-amylase-associated protein from barley. J. Inst. Brew. 83:94-96.

HEJGAARD, J. 1978. "Free" and "bound" β-amylases during malting of barley. Characterisation of two-dimensional immunoelectrophoresis. J. Inst. Brew. 84:43-46.

HEJGAARD, J. 1982. Purification and properties of protein Z—A major albumin of barley endosperm. Physiol. Plant. 54:174-182.

HEJGAARD, J. 1984. Gene products of barley chromosomes 4 and 7 are precursors of the major antigenetic beer protein. J. Inst. Brew. 90:75-87.

HEJGAARD, J., and BOISEN, S. 1980. High lysine proteins in Hiproly barley breeding: Identification, nutritional signficance and new screening methods. Hereditas 93:311-320.

HEJGAARD, J., and BJØRN, S. E. 1985. Four major basic proteins of barley grain. Purification and partial characterisation. Physiol. Plant. 64:301-307.

HEJGAARD, J., and BJØRN, S. E. 1987. Chitinase locus (*Chil*) assigned to barley chromosome 1 (7H) by immunoblotting. Barley Genet. Newsl. 17:92-93.

HEJGAARD, J., and CARLSEN, S. 1977. Immunoelectrophoretic identification of a heterodimer β-amylase in extracts of barley grain. J. Sci. Food Agric. 28:900-904.

HEJGAARD, J., and KAERSGAARD, P. 1983. Purification and properties of the major antigenic beer protein of barley origin. J. Inst. Brew. 89:402-410.

HEJGAARD, J., SVENDSEN, I., and MUNDY, J. 1983. Barley α-amylase/subtilisin inhibitor. II. N-terminal amino acid sequence and homology with inhibitors of the soybean trypsin inhibitor (Kunitz) family. Carlsberg Res. Commun. 48:91-94.

HEJGAARD, J., BJØRN, S. E., and NIELSEN, G. 1984. Localisation to chromo-

somes of structural genes for the major protease inhibitors of barley grains. Theor. Appl. Genet. 68:127-130.

HEJGAARD, J., RASMUSSEN, S. K., BRANDT, A., and SVENDSEN, I. 1985. Sequence homology between barley endosperm protein Z and protease inhibitors of the α₁-antitrypsin family. FEBS Lett. 180:89-94.

HERNÁNDEZ-LUCAS, C., FERNÁNDEZ DE CALEYA, R., CARBONERO, P., and GARCIA-OLMEDO, F. 1977. Reconstitution of petroleum ether soluble wheat lipopurothionin by binding of digalactosyl diglyceride to the chloroform-soluble form. J. Agric. Food Chem. 25:1287-1289.

HERNÁNDEZ-LUCAS, C., CARBONERO, P., and GARCIA-OLMEDO, F. 1978. Identification and purification of a puro-thionin homologue from rye (*Secale cereale* L.). J. Agric. Food Chem. 26:794-796.

HERNÁNDEZ-LUCAS, C., ROYO, J., PAZ-ARES, J., PONZ, F., GARCIA-OLMEDO, F., and CARBONERO, P. 1986. Polyadenylation site heterogeneity in mRNA encoding the precursor of the barley toxin β-hordothion. FEBS Lett. 200:103-106.

HOFSTRA, H., HEIDEKAMP, F., LEBOUILLE, J. L. M., VAN MECHELEN, J., and KLOPPER, W. J. 1989. RFLP analysis as an alternative method for the identification of barley cultivars. Pages 179-185 in: Proc. Congr. Eur. Brew. Conv. 22nd, Zurich.

I'ANSON, K. J., MORRIS, V. J., SHEWRY, P. R., and TATHAM, A. S. 1992. Small angle X-ray scattering studies of the C hordeins of barley. Biochem. J. 287:183-185.

JACOBSEN, S., MIKKELSEN, J. D., and HEJGAARD, J. 1990. Characterisation of two antifungal endochitinases from barley grain. Physiol. Plant. 79:554-562.

JAKOBSEN, K., KLEMSDAL, S. S., AALEN, R. B., BOSNES, M., ALEXANDER, D., and OLSEN, O.-A. 1989. Barley aleurone cell development: Molecular cloning of aleurone-specific cDNAs from immature grains. Plant Mol. Biol. 12:285-293.

JENSEN, J. 1988. Co-ordinators report: Chromosome 5. Barley Genet. Newsl. 18:61-63.

JOHANSEN, H. B., and SHEWRY, P. R. 1986. Recommended designations for hordein alleles. Barley Genet. Newsl. 16:9-11.

JOHNSON, T. C., WADA, K., BUCHANAN, B. B., and HOLMGREN, A. 1987. Reduction of purothionin by the wheat seed thioredoxin system. Plant Physiol. 85:446-451.

JONASSEN, I. 1980a. Characteristics of Hiproly barley. I. Isolation and characterisation of two water-soluble high-lysine proteins. Carlsberg Res. Commun. 45:47-58.

JONASSEN, I. 1980b. Characteristics of Hiproly barley. II. Quantification of two proteins contributing to its high lysine content. Carlsberg Res. Commun. 45:59-68.

JONASSEN, I., and SVENDSEN, I. 1982. Identification of the reactive sites in two homologous serine proteinase inhibitors isolated from barley. Carlsberg Res. Commun. 47:199-203.

JONES, B. L., and MEREDITH, P. 1982. Inactivation of alpha-amylase activity by purothionins. Cereal Chem. 59:321.

KAWAZU, T., NAKANISHI, Y., UOZUMI, N., SASAKI, T., YAMAGATA, H., TSUKAGOSHI, N., and UDAKA, S. 1987. Cloning and nucleotide sequence of the gene coding for enzymatically active fragments of the *Bacillus polymyxa* β-amylase. J. Bacteriol. 169:1564-1570.

KIM, W. T., FRANCESCHI, V. R., KRISHNAN, H., and OKITA, T. W. 1988. Formation of wheat protein bodies: Involvement of the Golgi apparatus in gliadin transport. Planta 176:173-182.

KIRKMAN, M. A., SHEWRY, P. R., and MIFLIN, B. J. 1982. The effect of nitrogen nutrition on the lysine content and protein composition of barley seeds. J. Sci. Food Agric. 33:115-127.

KITAMOTO, N., YAMAGATA, H., KATO, T., TSUKAGOSHI, N., and UDAKA, S. 1988. Cloning and sequencing of the gene encoding thermophilic β-amylase of *Clostridium thermosulfurogenes*. J. Bacteriol. 170:5848-5854.

KJAER, M., and POULSEN, F. M. 1987. Secondary structure of barley serine proteinase inhibitor 2 determined by proton nuclear magnetic resonance spectroscopy. Carlsberg Res. Commun. 52:355-362.

KJAER, M., LUDVIGSEN, S., SØRENSEN, O. E., DENYS, L. A., KINDTLER, J., and POULSON, F. M. 1987. Sequence specific assignment of the proton nuclear magnetic resonance spectrum of barley serine proteinase inhibitor 2. Carlsberg Res. Commun. 52:327-354.

KOIDE, T., and IKENAKA, T. 1973. Studies on soybean trypsin inhibitors. 3. Amino-acid sequence of the carboxyl-terminal region and the complete amino acid sequence of soybean trypsin inhibitor (Kunitz). Eur. J. Biochem. 32:417-431.

KREIS, M., and SHEWRY, P. R. 1989. Unusual features of cereal seed protein structure and evolution. Bio-Essays 10:201-207.

KREIS, M., SHEWRY, P. R., FORDE, B. G.,

RAHMAN, S., and MIFLIN, B. J. 1983a. Molecular analysis of a mutation conferring the high lysine phenotype on the grain of barley (*Hordeum vulgare*). Cell 34:161-167.

KREIS, M., RAHMAN, S., FORDE, B. G., PYWELL, J., SHEWRY, P. R., and MIFLIN, B. J. 1983b. Sub-families of hordein mRNA encoded at the *Hor 2* locus of barley. Mol. Gen. Genet. 191:194-200.

KREIS, M., SHEWRY, P. R., FORDE, B. G., RAHMAN, S., BAHRAMIAN, M. B., and MIFLIN, B. J. 1984. Molecular analysis of the effects of the mutant *lys 3a* gene on the expression of *Hor* loci in developing endosperms of barley (*Hordeum vulgare*). Biochem. Genet. 22:231-255.

KREIS, M., FORDE, B. G., RAHMAN, S., MIFLIN, B. J., and SHEWRY, P. R. 1985a. Molecular evolution of the seed storage proteins of barley, rye and wheat. J. Mol. Biol. 183:499-502.

KREIS, M., SHEWRY, P. R., FORDE, B. G., FORDE, J., and MIFLIN, B. J. 1985b. Structure and evolution of seed storage proteins and their genes, with particular reference to those of wheat, barley and rye. Pages 253-317 in: Oxford Surveys of Plant Cell and Molecular Biology, Vol. 2. B. J. Miflin, ed. Oxford University Press, Oxford.

KREIS, M., WILLIAMSON, M. S., FORDE, J., SCHMUTZ, D., CLARK, J., BUXTON, B., PYWELL, J., MARRIS, C., HENDERSON, J., HARRIS, N., SHEWRY, P. R., FORDE, B. G., and MIFLIN, B. J. 1986. Differential gene expression in the developing barley endosperm. Phil. Trans. R. Soc. Lond. B. 314:355-365.

KREIS, M., WILLIAMSON, M., BUXTON, B., PYWELL, J., HEJGAARD, J., and SVENDSEN, I. 1987. Primary structure and differential expression of β-amylase in normal and mutant barleys. Eur. J. Biochem. 169:517-525.

KREIS, M., WILLIAMSON, M. S., SHEWRY, P. R., SHARP, P., and GALE, M. 1988. Identification of a second locus encoding β-amylase on chromosome 2 of barley. Genet. Res. Camb. 51:13-16.

LaBERGE, D. E., and MARCHYLO, B. A. 1983. Heterogeneity of the beta-amylase enzymes of barley. J. Am. Soc. Brew. Chem. 41:120-124.

LADOGINA, V., NETSVETAEV, P., POMORTSEV, A. A., OVCHINNIKOV, A. N., and SOZINOV, A. A. 1987. Two new glutelin-coding loci *GluA* and *GluB* on chromosome 5 of barley. Barley Genet. Newsl. 17:28-31.

LANDRY, J., MOUREAUX, T., and HUET, J. C. 1972. Extractabilité des Protéines du grain d'orge: Dissolution sélective et composition en acides amines des fraction isolées. Bios (Nancy) 7-8:281-292.

LAURIÈRE, C., MAYER, C., RENARD, H., MacGREGOR, A. W., and DAUSSANT, J. 1985. Maturation de caryopse d'orge: Évolution des isoformes des alpha- et béta-amylases, de l'enzyme débranchante, de l'inhibiteur d'alpha-amylases chez plusieurs variétés. Pages 675-682 in: Proc. Congr. Eur. Brew. Conv. 20th, Helsinki.

LAZARO, A., BARBER, D., SALCEDO, G., MENDEZ, E., and GARCIA-OLMEDO, F. 1985. Differential effects of high-lysine mutations on the accumulation of individual members of a group of proteins encoded by a disperse multigene family in the endosperm of barley (Hordeum vulgare L.). Eur. J. Biochem. 149:617-623.

LAZARO, A., RODRIGUEZ-PALENZUELA, P., MARANA, C., CARBONERO, P., and GARCIA-OLMEDO, F. 1988a. Signal peptide homology between the sweet protein thaumatin II and unrelated cereal α-amylase/trypsin inhibitors. FEBS Lett. 239:147-250.

LAZARO, A., SÁNCHEZ-MONGE, R., SALCEDO, G., PAZ-ARES, J., CARBONERO, P., and GARCIA-OLMEDO, F. 1988b. A dimeric inhibitor of α-amylase from barley. Cloning of the cDNA and identification of the protein. Eur. J. Biochem. 172:129-134.

LEAH, R., and MUNDY, J. 1989. The bifunctional α-amylase/subtilisin inhibitor of barley: Nucleotide sequence and patterns of seed-specific expression. Plant Mol. Biol. 12:673-682.

LEAH, R., MIKKELSEN, J. D., MUNDY, J., and SVENDSEN, I. 1987. Identification of a 28,000 dalton endochitinase in barley endosperm. Carlsberg Res. Commun. 52:31-37.

LEAH, R., TOMMERUP, H., SVENDSEN, I., and MUNDY, J. 1991. Biochemical and molecular characterization of three barley seed proteins with antifungal properties. J. Biol. Chem. 266:1464-1573.

LECOMMANDEUR, D., LAURIÈRE, C., and DAUSSANT, J. 1987. Alpha-amylase inhibitor in barley seeds: Localisation and quantification. Plant Physiol. Biochem. 25:711-715.

LECOMTE, J. T. J., JONES, B. L., and LLINAS, M. 1982. Proton magnetic resonance studies of barley and wheat thionins: Structural homology with crambin. Biochemistry 21:4843-4848.

LINTHORST, H. J. M., MELCHERS, L. S., MAYER, A., VAN ROEKEL, CORNELISSEN, B. J. C., and BOL, J. F. 1990. Analysis of gene families encoding acidic and basic β-1,3-glucanases of tobacco. Proc. Natl. Acad. Sci. USA 87:8756-8760.

LOGEMANN, J., JACK G., TOMMERUP, H., MUNDY, J., and SCHELL, J. 1992. Expression of a barley ribosome-inactivating protein leads to increased fungal protection in transgenic tobacco plants. Bio/Technology 10:305-308.

LUCAS, J., HENSCHEN, A., LOTTSPEICH, F., VOEGELI, U., and BOLLER, T. 1985. Amino terminal sequence of ethylene-induced bean leaf chitinase reveals similarities to sugar-binding domains of wheat germ agglutinin. FEBS Lett. 193:208-210.

LUNDGARD, R., and SVENSSON, B. 1986. Limited proteolysis in the carboxy-terminal region of barley β-amylase. Carlsberg Res. Commun. 51:487-491.

LUNDGARD, R., and SVENSSON, B. 1987. The four major forms of barley β-amylase. Purification, characterisation and structural relationship. Carlsberg Res. Commun. 52:313-326.

MacGREGOR, A. W., and BALLANCE, D. 1980. Quantitative determination of α-amylase enzymes in germinated barley after separation by isoelectricfocusing. J. Inst. Brew. 86:131-133.

MacGREGOR, A. W., WESELAKE, R. J., HILL, R. D., and MORGAN, J. E. 1986. Effect of an α-amylase inhibitor from barley kernels on the formation of products during the hydrolysis of amylase and starch granules by α-amylase II from malted barley. J. Cereal Sci. 4:125-132.

MARCHYLO, B. A., and KRUGER, J. E. 1984. Identification of Canadian barley cultivars by reversed-phase high-performance liquid chromatography. Cereal Chem. 61:295-301.

MARCHYLO, B. A., and LaBERGE, D. E. 1980. Barley cultivar identification by electrophoretic analysis of hordein proteins. Can. J. Plant Sci. 60:1343-1350.

MARRIS, C. 1990. Regulation of the expression of a seed-protein gene from barley in transgenic tobacco plants. Ph.D. thesis. Council for National Academic Awards, London.

MARRIS, C., GALLOIS, P., COPLEY, J., and KREIS, M. 1988. The 5'-flanking region of a barley B hordein gene controls tissue and development specific CAT expression in tobacco plants. Plant Mol. Biol. 10:359-366.

MATTHEWS, J. A., and MIFLIN, B. J. 1980. In vitro synthesis of barley storage proteins. Planta 149:262-268.

McPHALEN, C. A., and JAMES, M. N. G. 1987. Crystal and molecular structure of the serine proteinase inhibitor C1-2 from barley seeds. Biochemistry 26:261-269.

McPHALEN, C. A., EVANS, C., HAVAKAWA, K., JONASSEN, I., SVENDSEN, I., and JAMES, M. N. G. 1983. Preliminary crystallographic data for the serine protease inhibitor C1-2 from barley seeds. J. Mol. Biol. 168:445-447.

McPHALEN, C. A., SVENDSEN, I., JONASSEN, I., and JAMES, M. N. G. 1985. Crystal and molecular structure of chymotrypsin inhibitor 2 from barley seeds in complex with subtilisin Novo. Proc. Natl. Acad. Sci. USA 82:7242-7246.

MENA, M., SANCHEZ-MONGE, R., GOMEZ, L., SALCEDO, G., and CARBONERO, P. 1992. A major barley allergen associated with baker's asthma disease is a glycosylated monomeric inhibitor of insect α-amylase: cDNA cloning and chromosomal location of the gene. Plant Mol. Biol. 20:451-458.

MENDEZ, E., MORENO, A., COLILLA, F., PELAEZ, F., LIMAS, G. G., MENDEZ, R., SORIANO, F., SALINAS, M., and de HARO, C. 1990. Primary structure and inhibition of protein synthesis in eukaryotic cell-free system of a novel thionin, γ-hordothionin, from barley endosperm. Eur. J. Biochem. 194:533-539.

MIFLIN, B. J., and SHEWRY, P. R. 1977. An introduction to the extraction and characterisation of barley and maize proteins. Pages 13-25 in: Techniques for the Separation of Barley and Maize Proteins. B. J. Miflin and P. R. Shewry, eds. Commission of the European Communities, Luxembourg.

MIFLIN, B. J., and SHEWRY, P. R. 1979. The synthesis of proteins in normal and high lysine barley seeds. Pages 239-273 in: Recent Advances in the Biochemistry of Cereals. D. Laidman and R. G. Wyn Jones, eds. Academic Press, London.

MIFLIN, B. J., BURGESS, S. R., and SHEWRY, P. R. 1981. The development of protein bodies in the storage tissues of seeds. J. Exp. Bot. 32:119-219.

MIFLIN, B. J., FIELD, J. M., and SHEWRY, P. R. 1983. Cereal storage proteins and their effects on technological properties. Pages 255-319 in: Seed Proteins. J. Daussant, J. Mossé, and J. Vaughan, eds. Academic Press, London.

MIKAMI, B., MORITA, Y., and FUKAZAWA, C. 1988. Primary structure and function of β-amylase. Seikagaku 60:211-216. In Japanese.

MIKOLA, J., and SUOLINNA, E.-M. 1971. Purification and properties of an inhibitor of microbial alkaline proteinases from barley. Arch. Biochem. Biophys. 144:566-575.

MILES, M. J., CARR, H. J., McMASTER, T., BELTON, P. S., MORRIS, V. J., FIELD, J. M., SHEWRY, P. R., and TATHAM, A. S. 1991. Scanning tunnelling microscopy of a wheat seed protein shows a novel super-secondary structure. Proc. Natl. Acad. Sci. USA 88:68-71.

MONTEMBAULT, A., AUTRAN, J. C., and JOUDRIER, P. 1983. Varietal identification of barley and malt. J. Inst. Brew. 89:299-302.

MORALEJO, M. A, GARCIA-CASADO, G., SANCHEZ-MONGE, R., LOPEZ-OTIN, C., ROMAGOSA, I., MOLINA-CANO, J. L., and SALCEDO, G. 1993. Genetic variants of the trypsin inhibitor from barley endosperm show different inhibitory activities. Plant Sci. 89:23-29.

MUNDY, J. 1984. Hormonal regulation of α-amylase inhibitor synthesis in germinating barley. Carlsberg Res. Commun. 49:439-444.

MUNDY, J., and ROGERS, J. C. 1986. Selective expression of a probable amylase-protease inhibitor in barley aleurone cells: Comparison to the barley amylase-subtilisin inhibitor. Planta 169:51-63.

MUNDY, J., SVENDSEN, I., and HEJGAARD, J. 1983. Barley α-amylase/subtilisin inhibitor. I. Isolation and characterisation. Carlsberg Res. Commun. 48:81-90.

MUNDY, J., HEJGAARD, J., HANSEN, A., HALLGREN, L., JORGENSEN, K. G., and MUNCK, L. 1986. Differential synthesis in vitro of barley aleurone and starchy endosperm proteins. Plant Physiol. 81:630-636.

NETSVETAEV, V. P., and SOZINOV, A. A. 1982. Linkage studies of genes *Gle1* and *HrdF* in barley chromosome 5. Barley Genet. Newsl. 12:13-18.

NETSVETAEV, V. P., and SOZINOV, A. A. 1984. Location of a hordein G locus, *HrdG*, on chromosome 5 of barley. Barley Genet. Newslett. 14:4-6.

NIELSEN, G. 1985. The use of isozymes as probes to identify and label plant varieites and cultivars. Isozymes: Curr. Top. Biol. Med. Res. 12:1-32.

NIELSEN, G., and HEJGAARD, J. 1985. Linkage of a trypsin inhibitor locus *Itc1* and two esterase loci (*Est1* and *Est4*) with marker loci on barley chromosome 3. Barley Genet. Newslett. 15:16-18.

NIELSEN, G., JOHANSEN, H., JENSEN, J., and HEJGAARD, J. 1983. Localisation on barley chromosome 4 of genes coding for beta-amylase (*Bmy1*) and protein Z (*Paz1*). Barley Genet. Newslett. 13:55-57.

NISHIMURA, M., HARA-NISHIMURA, I., BUREAU, D., and DAUSSANT, J. 1987. Subcellular distribution of β-amylase in developing barley endosperm. Plant Sci. 49:117-122.

NUMMI, M., VILHUNEN, R., and ENARI, T.-M. 1965. β-Amylase of different molecular size in barley and malt. Pages 52-61 in: Proc. Congr. Eur. Brew. Conv., 10th, Stockholm.

ODANI, S., KOIDE, T., and ONO, T. 1983. The complete amino acid sequence of barley trypsin inhibitor. J. Biol. Chem. 258:7998-8003.

OSBORNE, T. B. 1895. The proteids of barley. J. Am. Chem. Soc. 17:539-567.

OSBORNE, T. B. 1924. The Vegetable Proteins. Longmans, Green & Co., London.

OSBORNE, T. B., and CLAPP, S. M. 1907. Hydrolysis of hordein. Am. J. Physiol. 19:117-124.

OZAKI, Y., WADA, K., HASE, T., MATSUBARA, H., NAKANISHI, T., and YOSHIZUMI, H. 1980. Amino acid sequence of a purothionin homolog from barley flour. J. Biochem. 87:549-555.

PARTRIDGE, J., SHANNON, L., and GUMPF, D. 1976. A barley lectin that binds free amino sugars. I. Purification and characterisation. Biochim. Biophys. Acta 451:470-483.

PAYNE, G., WARD, E., GAFFNEY, T., AHLGOY, P., MOYER, M., HARPER, A., MEINS, F., and RYALS, J. 1990. Evidence for a third structural class of β-glucanase in tobacco. Plant Mol. Biol. 16:797-808.

PAYNE, P. I., HOLT, L. M., BURGESS, S. R., and SHEWRY, P. R. 1986. Characterisation by two dimensional gel electrophoresis of the protein components of protein bodies, isolated from the developing endosperm of wheat (Triticum aestivum). J. Cereal Sci. 4:217-223.

PAZ-ARES, J., PONZ, F., ARAGONCILLO, C., HERNANDEZ-LUCAS, C., SALCEDO, G., CARBONERO, P., and GARCIA-OLMEDO, F. 1983. In vivo and in vitro synthesis of CM-proteins (A-hordeins) from barley (Hordeum vulgare L.). Planta 157:174-80.

PAZ-ARES, J., PONZ, F., RODRIGUEZ-PALENZUELA, P., LAZARO, A., HERNANDEZ-LUCAS, C., GARCIA-OLMEDO, F., and CARBONERO, P. 1986. Characterisation of cDNA clones of the family of trypsin/α-amylase inhibitors (CM-proteins) in barley (Hordeum vulgare L.). Theor. Appl. Genet. 71:842-846.

PEUMANS, W. J., STINISSEN, H. M., and CARLIER, A. R. 1982a. Isolation and partial characterisation of wheat-germ-agglutinin-like lectins from rye (Secale cereale) and barley (Hordeum vulgare) embryos. Biochem. J. 203:239-243.

PEUMANS, W. J., STINISSEN, H. M., and CARLIER, A. R. 1982b. Subunit exchange between lectins from different cereal species. Planta 154:568-572.

PONZ, F., PAZ-ARES, J., HERNANDEZ-LUCAS, C., CARBONERO, P., and GARCIA-OLMEDO, F. 1983. Synthesis and processing of thionin precursors in developing endosperm from barley (Hordeum vulgare L.). EMBO J. 2:1035-1040.

PONZ, F., PAZ-ARES, J., HERNANDEZ-LUCAS, C., GARCIA-OLMEDO, F., and CARBONERO, P. 1986. Cloning and nucleotide sequence of a cDNA encoding the precursor of the barley toxin α-hordothionin. Eur. J. Biochem. 156:131-135.

PRÉAUX, G., and LONTIE, R. 1975. The proteins of barley. Pages 89-111 in: The Chemistry and Biochemistry of Plant Proteins. J. B. Harborne and C. F. Van Sumere, eds. Academic Press, London.

QUENSEL, O. 1942. Untersuchungen über die Gerstenglobuline. Diss., Almqvist and Wiksell, Upsala, Sweden.

RAHMAN, S., SHEWRY, P. R., and MIFLIN, B. J. 1982. Differential protein accumulation during barley grain development. J. Exp. Bot. 33:717-728.

RASMUSSEN, S. K. 1987. Molecular analysis of four basic barley proteins appearing late in development. Page 138 in: Abstracts of the XIV International Botanical Congress. W. Greuter, B. Zimmer, and H.-D. Behnke, eds. Berlin.

RASMUSSEN, S. K., and BRANDT, A. 1986. Nucleotide sequences of cDNA clones for C-hordein polypeptides. Carlsberg Res. Commun. 51:371-379.

RASMUSSEN, S. K., and JOHANSSON, A. 1992. Nucleotide sequence of a cDNA coding for the barley seed protein CMa: An inhibitor of insect α-amylase. Plant Mol. Biol. 18:423-427.

RASMUSSEN, S. K., HOPP, H. E., and BRANDT, A. 1983. Nucleotide sequences of cDNA clones for B1 hordein polypeptides. Carlsberg Res. Commun. 48:187-199.

RASMUSSEN, S. K., HOPP, H. E., and BRANDT, A. 1984. A cDNA clone for protein Z, a major barley endosperm albumin. Carlsberg Res. Commun. 49:385-390.

RASMUSSEN, S. K., WELINDER, K. G., and HEJGAARD, J. 1991. cDNA cloning, characterisation and expression of an endosperm-specific barley peroxidase. Plant Mol. Biol. 16:317-327.

RASMUSSEN, U., WILLIAMSON, M. S., MUNDY, J., and KREIS, M. 1988. Differential effects of the hiproly lys1 gene on the developmental synthesis of (lysine-rich) proteins from barley endosperm. Plant Sci. 55:255-266.

RASMUSSEN, U., MUNCK, L., and ULLRICH, S. E. 1990. Immunogold localisation of chymotrypsin inhibitor-2, a lysine-rich protein, in developing barley endosperm. Planta 180:272-277.

RECHINGER, K. B., BOUGRI, O. V., and CAMERON-MILLS, V. 1993. Evolutionary relationship of the members of the sulphur-rich hordein family revealed by common antigenic determinants. Theor. Appl. Genet. 85:829-840.

REDMAN, D. G., and FISHER, N. 1968. Fractionation and comparison of puro-thionin and globulin components of wheat. J. Sci. Food Agric. 19:651-655.

REDMAN, D. G., and FISHER, N. 1969. Purothionin analogues from barley flour. J. Sci. Food Agric. 20:427-432.

REIMANN-PHILIPP, U., SCHRADER, G., MARTINOIA, E., BARKHOLT, V., and APEL, K. 1989. Intracellular thionins of barley. A second group of leaf thionins closely related to but distinct from cell wall-bound thionins. J. Biol. Chem. 264:8978-8984.

REISBIG, R. R., and BRULAND, O. 1983. The protein synthesis inhibitors from wheat, barley, and rye have identical antigenic determinants. Biochem. Biophys. Res. Commun. 114:190-196.

RHODES, A. P., and GILL, A. A. 1980. Fractionation and amino acid analysis of the salt-soluble protein fraction of normal and high lysine barleys. J. Sci. Food Agric. 31:467-473.

RICHARDSON, M. 1991. Seed storage proteins; The enzyme inhibitors. Pages 259-305 in: Methods in Plant Biochemistry, Vol. 5. L. J. Rogers, ed. Academic Press, New York.

RIGGS, T. J., SANADA, M., MORGAN, A. G., and SMITH, D. B. 1983. Use of acid gel electrophoresis in the characterisation of 'B' hordein protein in relation to malting quality and mildew resistance of barley. J. Sci. Food Agric. 34:576-586.

ROBERT, L. A., ADELI, K., and ALTOSAAR, I. 1985. Homology among 3S and 7S globulins from cereals and pea. Plant Physiol. 78:812-816.

ROBERTS, W. K., and SELITRENNIKOFF, C. P. 1986. Isolation and partial characterisation of two antifungal proteins from barley. Biochim. Biophys. Acta 880:161-170.

ROBERTSON, M., and HILL, R. D. 1989. Accumulation of an endogenous alpha-amylase inhibitor in barley during grain development. J. Cereal Sci. 9:237-246.

ROBERTSON, M., WALKER-SIMMONS, M., MUNRO, D., and HILL, R. D. 1989.

Induction of α-amylase inhibitor synthesis in barley embryos and young seedlings by abscisic acid and dehydration stress. Plant Physiol. 91:415-420.

RODAWAY, S. J. 1978. Composition of α-amylase from aleurone layers of grains of Himalaya barley. Phytochemistry 17:385-389.

RODEN, L. T., MIFLIN, B. J., and FREED-MAN, R. B. 1982. Protein disulphide-isomerase is located in the endoplasmic reticulum of developing wheat endosperm. FEBS Lett. 138:121-124.

RODRIGUEZ-PALENZUELA, P., PINTER-TORO, J. A., CARBONERO, P., and GARCIA-OLMEDO, F. 1988. Nucleotide sequence and endosperm-specific expression of the structural gene for the thionin α-hordothionin in barley (*Hordeum vulgare* L.). Gene 70:271-281.

RODRIGUEZ-PALENZUELA, P., ROYO, J., GOMEZ, L., SANCHEZ-MONGE, R., SALCEDO, G., MOLINA-CANO, J. L., GARCIA-OLMEDO, F., and CARBONERO, P. 1989. The gene for trypsin inhibitor CMe is regulated in *trans* by the *lys3a* locus in the endosperm of barley (*Hordeum vulgare* L.). Mol. Gen. Genet. 219:474-479.

SALCEDO, G., SANCHEZ-MONGE, R., ARGAMENTARIA, A., and ARAGONCILLO, C. 1980. The A-hordeins as a group of salt-soluble hydrophobic proteins. Plant Sci. Lett. 19:109-119.

SALCEDO, G., SANCHEZ-MONGE, R., ARGAMENTERIA, A., and ARAGONCILLO, C. 1982. Low molecular weight prolamins: Purification of a component from barley endosperm. J. Agric. Food Chem. 30:1155-1157.

SALCEDO, G., FRA-MON, P., MOLINA-CANO, J. L., ARAGONCILLO, C., and GARCIA-OLMEDA, F. 1984. Genetics of CM-proteins (A-hordeins) in barley. Theor. Appl. Genet. 68:53-59.

SAMUELSSON, G., SEGER, L., and OLSON, T. 1968. The amino acid sequence of oxidized viscotoxin A3 from the European mistletoe (*Viscum album* L. Loranthaceae). Acta Chem. Scand. 22:2626-2642.

SANCHEZ-MONGE, R., GOMEZ, L. GARCIA-OLMEDO, F., and SALCEDO, G. 1986. A tetrameric inhibitor of insect α-amylase from barley. FEBS Lett. 207:105-109.

SANCHEZ-MONGE, R., GOMEZ, L., BARBER, D., LOPEZ-OTIN, C., ARMENTIA, A., and SALCEDO, G. 1992. Wheat and barley allergens associated with baker's asthma. Biochem. J. 281:401-405.

SARKKINEN, P., KALKKINEN, N.,

TILGMANN, C., SIURO, J., KERVINEN, J., and MIKOLA, L. 1992. Aspartic proteinase from barley grains is related to mammalian lysosomal cathepsin D. Planta 186:317-323.

SCHILDBACH, R., and BURBIDGE, M. 1979. Identifizierung von Gerstensorten an Einzelkörnern durch Flachgel-Elektrophorese der Proteine und Aleuronfärbung. Monatsschr. Brau. 30th Nov. issue:470-480.

SCHMITT, J. M., and SVENDSEN, I. 1980. Amino acid sequences of hordein polypeptides. Carlsberg Res. Commun. 45:143-148.

SCRIBAN, R., and STROBBEL, B. 1979. Chemotaxonomic study of barley and malt by gel electrofocalization. Tech. Q. Master Brew. Assoc. Am. 16:28-32.

SEEMÜLLER, U., EULITZ, M., FRITZ, H., and STROBL, A. 1980. Structure of the Elastase-Cathepsin G. inhibitor of the leech Hirudo medicinalis. Hoppe-Syler's Z. Physiol. Chem. 3612:1841-1846.

SHEWRY, P. R. 1992. Barley seed storage proteins: Structure, synthesis and deposition. Pages 201-227 in: Nitrogen Metabolism of Plants. K. Mengel and D. J. Pilbeam, eds. Oxford University Press, Oxford, U.K.

SHEWRY, P. R., and KREIS, M. 1989. The development and composition of barley grain: Relationship to end use, and potential for manipulation. Pages 61-66 in: Alternative End Uses of Barley. D. H. B. Sparrow, R. C. M. Lance, and R. J. Henry, eds. Cereal Chem. Div., R. Aust. Chemical Inst., Parkville.

SHEWRY, P. R., and MIFLIN, B. J. 1982. Genes for the storage proteins of barley. Qual. Plant. Plant Foods Hum. Nutr. 31:251-267.

SHEWRY, P. R., and MIFLIN, B. J. 1983. Characterisation and synthesis of barley seed proteins. Pages 143-205 in: Seed Proteins: Genetics, Chemistry and Nutritive Value. W. Gottschalk and H. Muller, eds. Martinus Nijhoff, The Hague.

SHEWRY, P. R., and MIFLIN, B. J. 1985. Seed storage proteins of economically important cereals. Pages 1-83 in: Advances in Cereal Science and Technology, Vol. 7. Y. Pomeranz, ed. Am. Assoc. Cereal Chem, St Paul, MN.

SHEWRY, P. R., and PARMAR, S. 1987. The HrdF locus encodes γ-type hordeins. Barley Genet. Newslett. 17:32-34.

SHEWRY, P. R., and TATHAM, A. S. 1987. Recent advances in our understanding of cereal seed protein structure and functionality. Comments Agric. Food Chem. 1:71-93.

SHEWRY, P. R., HILL, J. M., PRATT, H. M., LEGGATT, M. M., and MIFLIN, B.

J. 1978a. An evaluation of techniques for the extraction and separation of hordein and glutelin from barley seed and a comparison of the protein composition of Bomi and Risø 1508. J. Exp. Bot. 29:677-692.

SHEWRY, P. R., PRATT, H. M., and MIFLIN, B. J. 1978b. The varietal identification of single seeds of barley by analysis of hordein polypeptides. J. Sci. Food Agric. 29:587-596.

SHEWRY, P. R, PRATT, H. M., FAULKS, A. J., PARMAR, S., and MIFLIN, B. J. 1979a. The storage protein (hordein) polypeptide pattern of barley (Hordein vulgare L.) in relation to varietal identification and disease resistance. J. Natl. Inst. Agric. Bot. (U.K.) 15:34-50.

SHEWRY, P. R., PRATT, H. M., LEGGATT, M. M., and MIFLIN, B. J. 1979b. Protein metabolism in developing endosperms of high-lysine and normal barley. Cereal Chem. 56:110-117.

SHEWRY, P. R., FAULKS, A. J., PARMAR, S., and MIFLIN, B. J. 1980a. Hordein polypeptide pattern in relation to malting quality and the varietal identification of malted grain. J. Inst. Brew. 86:138-141.

SHEWRY, P. R., FIELD, J. M., KIRKMAN, M. A., FAULKS, A. J., and MIFLIN, B. J. 1980b. The extraction, solubility and characterisation of two groups of barley storage polypeptides. J. Exp. Bot. 31:393-407.

SHEWRY, P. R., WOLFE, M. S., SLATER, S. E., PARMAR, S., FAULKS, A. J., and MIFLIN, B. J. 1981. Barley storage proteins in relation to varietal identification, malting quality and mildew resistance. Pages 596-603 in: Barley Genetics IV. Proc. 4th Int. Barley Genet. Symp. R. N. H. Whitehouse, ed. Edinburgh University Press, Edinburgh.

SHEWRY, P. R., BUNCE, N. A. C., KREIS, M., and FORDE, B. G. 1985a. Polymorphism at the Horl locus of barley (Hordeum vulgare L.). Biochem. Genet. 23:389-402.

SHEWRY, P. R., KREIS, M.; PARMAR, S., LEW, E. J.-L., and KASARDA, D. D. 1985b. Identification of γ-type hordeins in barley. FEBS Lett. 190:61-64.

SHEWRY, P. R., TATHAM, A. S., FORDE, J., KREIS, M., and MIFLIN, B. J. 1986. The classification and nomenclature of wheat gluten proteins: A reassessment. J. Cereal Sci. 4:97-106.

SHEWRY, P. R., FIELD, J. M., and TATHAM, A. S. 1987a. The structures of cereal seed storage proteins. Pages 421-437 in: Cereals in a European Context. I. D. Morton, ed. Ellis Horwood Ltd., Chichester, UK.

SHEWRY, P. R., WILLIAMSON, M. S., and

KREIS, M. 1987b. Effects of mutant genes on the synthesis of storage components in developing barley endosperms. Pages 95-118 in: Mutant Genes That Affect Plant Development. H. Thomas, ed. Cambridge University Press, Cambridge.

SHEWRY, P. R., WILLIAMSON, M. S., PARMAR, S., BURGESS, S. R., BUXTON, B., and KREIS, M. 1987c. The biochemical genetics of barley seed proteins. Pages 433-443 in: Barley Genetics V. Proc. 5th Int. Barley Genet. Symp. S. Yasuda and T. Konishi, eds. Sanyo Press, Okayama, Japan.

SHEWRY, P. R., PARMAR, S., BUXTON, B., GALE, M. D., LIU, C. J., HEJGAARD, J., and KREIS, M. 1988a. Multiple molecular forms of β-amylase in seeds and vegetative tissues of barley. Planta 176:127-134.

SHEWRY, P. R., PARMAR, S., FRANKLIN, J., and WHITE, R. 1988b. Mapping and biochemical analysis of *Hor4* (*HrdG*), a second locus encoding B hordein seed proteins in barley (*Hordeum vulgare* L.). Genet. Res. 51:5-12.

SHEWRY, P. R., TATHAM, A. S., FIELD, J. M., FORDE, B. G., CLARK, J., GALLOIS, P., MARRIS, C., HALFORD, N., FORDE, J., and KREIS, M. 1988c. The structure of barley and wheat prolamins and their genes. Biochem. Physiol. Pflanzen 183:117-127.

SHEWRY, P. R., TATHAM, A. S., PAPPIN, D. J., and KEEN, J. 1988d. N-terminal amino acid sequences show that D hordein of barley and high molecular weight (HMW) secalins of rye are homologous with HMW glutenin subunits of wheat. Cereal Chem. 65:510-511.

SHEWRY, P. R., HALFORD, N. G., and TATHAM, A. S. 1989. The high molecular weight subunits of wheat, barley and rye: Genetics, molecular biology, chemistry and role in wheat gluten structure and functionality. Pages 163-219 in: Oxford Surveys of Plant Molecular and Cell Biology, Vol. 6. B. J. Miflin, ed. Oxford University Press, Oxford.

SHEWRY, P. R., PARMAR, S., FRANKLIN, J., and BURGESS, S. R. 1990. Analysis of a rare recombination event within the multigenic *Hor2* locus of barley (*Hordeum vulgare* L.). Genet. Res. (Camb.) 55:171-176.

SINGH, N. K., and SHEPHERD, K. W. 1985. The structure and genetic control of a new class of disulphide-linked proteins in wheat endosperm. Theor. Appl. Genet. 71:79-92.

SINGH, N. K., and SHEPHERD, K. W. 1987. Solubility behaviour, synthesis, degradation and subcellular location of a new class of disulfide-linked proteins in wheat endosperm. Aust. J. Plant Physiol. 14:245-252.

SINGH, N. K., SHEPHERD, K. W., LANGRIDGE, P., GRUEN, L. C., SKERRITT, J. H., and WRIGLEY, C. W. 1988. Identification of legumin-like proteins in wheat. Plant Mol. Biol. 11:633-639.

SINGH, U., and SASTRY, L. V. S. 1977. Studies on the proteins of the mutants of barley grain. I. Extraction and electrophoretic characterization. Cereal Chem. 54:1-12.

SKERRITT, J. H., BATEY, I. L., and WRIGLEY, C. W. 1986. New approaches to barley variety identification and quality studies. Pages 59-62 in: Proc. 19th Conv. Inst. Brew. (Australia and New Zealand Section).

SMITH, D. B., and SIMPSON, P. A. 1983. Relationships of barley proteins soluble in sodium dodecyl sulphate to malting quality and varietal identification. J. Cereal Sci. 1:185-197.

SOZINOV, A. A., NETSVATAEV, V. P., GIGORYAN, E. M., and OBRAZTSOV, I. S. 1979. Mapping of the *Hrd* loci in barley (*Hordeum vulgare*). Soviet Gen. 14:1137-1147. (Translation of Genetika 14:1610-1619, 1978).

SØRENSEN, M. B. 1989. Mapping of the *Hor2* locus in barley by pulsed field gel electrophoresis. Carlsberg Res. Commun. 54:109-120.

STIRPE, F., and BARBIERI, L. 1986. Ribosome-inactivating proteins up to date. FEBS Lett. 195:1-8.

SVENDSEN, I., MARTIN, B., and JONASSEN, I. 1980a. Characteristics of hiproly barley. III. Amino acid sequences of two lysine rich proteins. Carlsberg Res. Commun. 45:79-85.

SVENDSEN, I., JONASSEN, I., HEJGAARD, J., and BOISEN, S. 1980b. Amino acid sequence homology between a serine protease inhibitor from barley and potato inhibitor I. Carlsberg Res. Commun. 45:389-395.

SVENDSEN, I., BOISEN, S., and HEJGAARD, J. 1982. Amino acid sequence of serine protease inhibitor Cl-1 from barley. Homology with barley inhibitor Cl-2, potato inhibitor 1 and leech eglin. Carlsberg Res. Commun. 47:45-53.

SVENDSEN, I. B., HEJGAARD, J., and MUNDY, J. 1986. Complete amino acid sequence of the α-amylase/subtilisin inhibitor from barley. Carlsberg Res. Commun. 51:43-50.

SVENSSON, B., ASANO, K., JOHASSEN, I., POULSEN, F. M., MUNDY, J., and SVENDSEN, I. B. 1986. A 10 kD barley seed protein homologous with an α-amylase inhibitor from Indian finger millet. Carlsberg Res. Commun. 51:493-500.

SWEGLE, M., HUANG, J. K., LEE, G., and MUTHUKRISHNAN, S. 1989. Identification of an endochitinase cDNA clone from barley aleurone cells. Plant Mol. Biol. 12:403-412.

TATHAM, A. S., DRAKE, A. F., and SHEWRY, P. R. 1985a. A conformational study of 'C' hordein, a glutamine and proline-rich cereal seed protein. Biochem. J. 226:557-562.

TATHAM, A. S., SHEWRY, P. R., and BELTON, P. S. 1985b. Carbon-13 NMR study of C hordein. Biochem. J. 232:617-620.

TATHAM, A. S., DRAKE, A. F., FIELD, J. M., and SHEWRY, P. R. 1987. The conformation of three synthetic peptides corresponding to the repeat motifs of two cereal prolamins. Pages 490-496 in: Proc. Int. Workshop on Gluten Proteins, 3rd. R. Lasztity and F. Bekes, eds. World Scientific, Singapore.

TATHAM, A. S., DRAKE, A. F., and SHEWRY, P. R. 1989. Conformational studies of a synthetic peptide corresponding to the repeat motif of C hordein. Biochem. J. 259:471-476.

TATHAM, A. S., SHEWRY, P. R., and BELTON, P. S. 1990. Structural studies of cereal prolamins, including wheat gluten. Pages 1-78 in: Advances in Cereal Science and Technology, Vol. 10. Y. Pomeranz, ed. Am. Assoc. Cereal Chem., St Paul, MN.

TEETER, M. M., MAZER, J. A., and L'ITALIAN, J. J. 1981. Primary structure of the hydrophobic plant protein crambin. Biochemistry 20:5437-5443.

VAN AARLE, P. G. M., DE BARSE, M. M. J., VELDINK, G. A, and VLIEGENTHART, J. F. G. 1991. Purification of a lipoxygenase from ungerminated barley. FEBS Lett. 280:159-162.

VAN LONKHUYSEN, H. J., and MARSEILLE, J. P. 1978. Schnellmethode zur Identifizierung von Weizensorten durch die St rkegel-Elektrophorese. Getreide Mehl Brot. 32:288-291.

VENKATACHALAM, C. M., and URRY, D. W. 1981. Development of a linear helical conformation from its cyclic correlate. β-Spiral model of the elasin polypentapeptide $(VPGVG)_n$. Macromolecules 14:1225-1231.

VERNON, L. P., EVETT, G. E., ZEIKUS, R. D., and GRAY, W. R. 1985. A toxic thionin from Pyrularia pubera: Purification, properties and amino acid sequence. Arch. Biochem. Biophys. 238:18-29.

VISURI, K., and NUMMI, M. 1972. Purification and characterisation of crystalline β-amylase from barley. Eur. J. Biochem. 28:555-565.

WATSON, M. D., LAMBERT, N., DELAUNEY, A., YARWOOD, J. N., CROY, R. R. D., GATEHOUSE, J. A., WRIGHT, D. J., and BOULTER, D. 1988. Isolation of a pea vicilin cDNA and expression in the yeast Saccharomyces cerevisiae. Biochem. J. 251:857-864.

WEBER, E., and MANTEUFFEL, R. 1988. Storage globulins in barley grains. Biochem. Physiol. Pflanzen. 183:153-158.

WESELAKE, R. J., MacGREGOR, A. W., and HILL, R. D. 1983a. An endogenous α-amylase inhibitor in barley kernels. Plant Physiol. 72:809-812.

WESELAKE, R. J., MacGREGOR, A. W., HILL, R. D., and DUCKWORTH, H. W. 1983b. Purification and characteristics of an endogenous α-amylase inhibitor from barley kernels. Plant Physiol. 73:1008-1012.

WESELAKE, R. J., MacGREGOR, A. W., and HILL, R. D. 1985. Effect of endogenous barley α-amylase inhibitor on hydrolysis of starch under various conditions. J. Cereal Sci. 3:249-259.

WILLIAMS, R. W., and TEETER, M. M. 1984. Raman spectroscopy of homologous plant toxins: Crambin and α- and β-purothionin secondary structures, disulfide conformation, and tyrosine environment. Biochemistry 23:6796-6802.

WILLIAMSON, M. S., FORDE, J., BUXTON, B., and KREIS, M. 1987. Nucleotide sequence of barley chymotrypsin inhibitor-2 (CI-2) and its expression in normal and high-lysine barley. Eur. J. Biochem. 165:99-106.

WILLIAMSON, M. S., FORDE, J., and KREIS, M. 1988. Molecular cloning of two isoinhibitor forms of chymotrypsin inhibitor 1 (CI-1) from barley endosperm and their expression in normal and mutant barleys. Plant Mol. Biol. 10:521-535.

WILSON, C. M., SHEWRY, P. R., FAULKS, A. J., and MIFLIN, B. J. 1981. The extraction and separation of barley glutelins and their relationship to other endosperm proteins. J. Exp. Bot. 32:1287-1293.

YEMM, E. W., and FOLKES, B. F. 1953. The amino acids of cytoplasmic and chloroplastic proteins of barley. Biochem. J. 55:700-706.

YOSHIKAWA, M., IWASAKI, T., FUJII, M., and OOGAKI, M. 1976. Isolation and some properties of a subtilisin inhibitor from barley. J. Biochem. 79:765-773.

YU, Y. G., CHUNG, C. H., FOWLER, A., and SUH, S. W. 1988. Amino acid sequence of a probable amylase/protease inhibitor from rice seeds. Arch. Biochem. Biophys. 265:466-475.

YUPSANIS, T., BURGESS, S. R., JACKSON, P. J., and SHEWRY, P. R. 1990. Characterisation of the major protein component from aleurone cells of barley (*Hordeum vulgare* L.). J. Exp. Bot. 41:385-392.

ZAWISTOWSKA, U., LANGSTAFF, J., and BUSHUK, W. 1988. Improving effect of a natural α-amylase inhibitor on the baking quality of wheat flour containing malted barley flour. J. Cereal Sci. 8:207-209.

CHAPTER 5

BARLEY LIPIDS

W. R. MORRISON
Department of Bioscience and Biotechnology
University of Strathclyde
Glasgow, Scotland

INTRODUCTION

There is a conspicuous lack of systematic and detailed information on the lipids in barley, and this author is not aware of any comprehensive review of the literature. Lack of interest in several areas has no doubt been caused by the need to focus attention on other features of more immediate importance in animal nutrition, malting, and brewing. However, lipids can be quite important in other less-obvious respects, and the pace and breadth of research may develop accordingly.

Fortunately, there are great similarities between barley and wheat, and there is much literature on wheat lipids, which has been reviewed extensively (Morrison, 1978a,b, 1988a, 1989c). The reader can therefore refer to this literature and to more general reviews on cereal lipids (Morrison, 1978a, 1984; Barnes, 1983a) to fill gaps and draw parallels, as has been done frequently in this chapter. Abbreviations for lipids used in the text are given in Table 1. The detailed structures of cereal lipids have been described in reviews by Morrison (1978a,b, 1983, 1984) and those of plant lipids in general textbooks (Harwood, 1980, 1986; Stumpf, 1987).

METHODS OF ANALYSIS

Quantitative information on lipids can be impaired by inadequate analytical methods; this is particularly true with lipids in cereals. The limitations and advantages of commonly used methods have been discussed at length (Morrison, 1978a, 1988a; Morrison et al, 1980), and only salient points are reiterated here.

Since the particle size and permeability of ground tissue can limit the effectiveness of solvent extraction methods, acid hydrolysis procedures are advisable for definitive lipid values. The lipid released by hydrolysis can be recovered by solvent extraction and weighed (AACC, 1983; Sanderson, 1986; AOAC, 1990), or the lipids can be converted to fatty acid methyl esters (FAME)

199

for quantification by gas chromatography, thereby eliminating problems caused by nonlipid artefacts (Morrison et al, 1975, 1980; Welch, 1977) and at the same time giving the fatty acid (FA) composition. Welch (1975, 1978) obtained excellent results by direct acid-catalyzed methanolysis of ground barley. The weights of FAs or FAME from individual lipid classes, or from the total lipids of various types of samples, can be converted to the weight of original lipid using appropriate conversion factors (Christie et al, 1970; Morrison et al, 1975, 1980; Weihrauch et al, 1977).

The terms "free" and "bound" have been used to describe, respectively, those lipids that can be extracted with nonpolar solvents and the remaining lipids that can be extracted only with polar solvents, which usually contain methanol, ethanol, propanol, or butanol. The proportions of free and bound lipids vary between tissues, and it should never be assumed that free lipids are the same as total lipids. The rationale for measuring free lipids in barley is not clear, because they have no recognized technological functions that are not shared with the bound lipids. In the manufacture of bread, cake,

TABLE 1
Abbreviations for Lipid Classes

Lipid	Abbreviation
Ceramide	CER
Diacylglycerol, diglyceride	DG
Digalactosyldiglyceride	DGDG
Digalactosylmonoglyceride	DGMG
Diphosphatidylglycerol	DPG
Esterified (acyl) sterylglycoside	ESG
Free (hexane/ether extractable)	F (prefix)
Fatty acid	FA
Fatty acid methyl ester	FAME
Free (unesterified) fatty acid	FFA
Glycolipids	GL
Hydrocarbon	HC
Lyso (monoacyl) prefix with any PL	L (prefix)
Monoacylglycerol, monoglyceride	MG
Monogalactosyldiglyceride	MGDG
Monogalactosylmonoglyceride	MGMG
N-acyllysophosphatidylethanolamine	NALPE
N-acylphosphatidylethanolamine	NAPE
Nonpolar lipids	NL
Phosphatidic acid	PA
Phosphatidyl methanol (artefact)	PMe
Phosphatidylcholine	PC
Phosphatidylethanolamine	PE
Phosphatidylglycerol	PG
Phosphatidylinositol	PI
Phosphatidylserine	PS
Phospholipids	PL
Polar lipids (GL + PL)	PoL
Sterol	S
Steryl ester	SE
Steryl glycoside	SG
Sulfolipid	SL
Triacylglycerol, triglyceride	TG

and biscuits/cookies, wheat flour free polar lipids probably function like surfactants (Morrison 1978a, 1989b).

In normal usage, the term *bound lipids* does not include starch lipids, which are located inside the starch granules and can be extracted efficiently only with hot alcohol-water mixtures (Morrison et al, 1975; Morrison and Coventry, 1985). The term *nonstarch lipids* was introduced to describe all lipids (free plus bound) other than those inside starch granules, and *starch surface lipids* to describe free fatty acids (FFA) and other monoacyl lipids (derived from the nonstarch lipids) that adsorb onto starch granules as artefacts during certain starch isolation procedures (Morrison, 1981). Special precautions must be taken when isolating starch for lipid analysis (Morrison, 1981, 1988a,b, 1992; Morrison et al, 1984, 1986; McDonald and Stark, 1988). In a few situations (e.g., white flour from wheat), it is possible to obtain good selective extractions of nonstarch lipids and starch lipids consecutively (Morrison et al, 1975), but more commonly, extraction of nonstarch lipids is incomplete because the solvents do not release all bound lipids or, alternatively, the nonstarch lipids include a variable proportion of starch lipids (mostly lysophospholipid [LPL]) because prolonged extraction with aqueous alcoholic solvents was used.

To date, the most satisfactory method for separating cereal lipid classes has been thin-layer chromatography (Morrison et al, 1980). Reversed-phase high-performance liquid chromatography has very limited applications for separating acyl lipids (Tweeten et al, 1981), but it is the preferred method for quantitative analysis of tocopherols (Thompson and Hatina, 1979; Barnes and Taylor, 1981; Barnes, 1983c; Hakkarainen et al, 1983a,b; Mueller-Mulot et al, 1983; Hakkarainen and Pehrson, 1987). Recently, good separations of wheat nonpolar lipids (NL), glycolipids (GL), and phospholipids (PL) on silica columns have been achieved by high-performance liquid chromatography, using complex ternary solvent elution systems (Christie and Morrison, 1988; Carr et al, 1989), but the method has not been used for barley lipids. Chromatography on silica-coated rods with flame ionization detection (Iatroscan) has been used to study the role of lipids in brewing (Byrne et al, 1983), but the rods can retain a "memory" of previous samples and give inaccurate results.

LIPIDS IN THE WHOLE GRAIN

The total lipid content of whole barley grain from diverse sources is given in Table 2. Numerous authors have reported values within these limits for one or two samples only, but they are not cited here. Hydrolysate lipid values include FA from starch lipids, but solvent-extracted lipid values include little or none of the starch lipids (starch lipid = ~1.6 × FA). As a general rule, lipid content does not vary much with grain protein content or edaphic variation, but it is significantly higher in Risø 1508 (Welch, 1978; Bhatty and Rossnagel, 1979, 1980), probably because mean kernel weight is much lower as a consequence of a reduction in starch synthesis. In normal six-rowed and two-rowed cultivars, there is little variation in total FA with grain size (De Man and Bruyneel, 1987; De Man and Vervenne, 1988).

The total lipids are comprised of 67–78% NL, 8–13% GL, and 14–21% PL (Price and Parsons, 1975; Zakryzhevskaya et al, 1978; Parsons and Price, 1979; Bhatty and Rossnagel, 1980; Lee et al, 1981; Bhatty, 1982; Shin and

Gray, 1983; Byrne et al, 1983), but these figures include little or none of the starch lipids. Similar proportions of NL, GL, and PL are found in wheat (Morrison, 1978a, 1988a).

The lipid classes comprising the NL, GL, and PL are given in Tables 3–5, but the data should be accepted with considerable reservations because, in the opinion of this reviewer, in several cases lipids have been misidentified, while others probably consist of at least two components, and (as noted above) they do not include starch lipids. The reader should compare whole barley lipids in these tables with the more complete data for wheat lipids given by Hargin and Morrison (1980) and Morrison (1988a). The sterols in the steryl ester and free sterol fractions consist of sitosterol (51–56%), campesterol (23–26%), and stigmasterol (12–16%) (Hughes and Goad, 1983).

The free and bound lipid contents of barley grain are given in Table 6. Comparable data are available for wheat (Morrison, 1978a). In three barley varieties, free lipids increased from 9 to 31 days after anthesis (DAA) and then declined slightly from 37 to 42 DAA (De Man and Cauberghe, 1988). The content and composition of these lipids change a little with postharvest drying and storage (Krikunova et al, 1981) but do not relate to germinative capacity (Skarsaune et al, 1972). Free lipids are mostly from aleurone and

TABLE 2
Total Lipid Contents of Barley Varieties

Type of Samples	Number of Samples	Range (%)	Mean (%)	Authors
Two-row	16	2.3–3.7[a]	2.8	Åman and Newman, 1986
Six-row	7	2.1–3.3[a]	2.7	Åman and Newman, 1986
Two-row	81	2.7–3.3[a]	3.0	Åman et al, 1985
Six-row	11	2.8–3.7[a]	3.3	Åman et al, 1985
Two-row	9	3.4–4.4[a]	3.9	Anness, 1984
Two-, six-row (spring/winter)	81	3.1–3.6[b]	3.4	DeMan and Bruyneel, 1987
Two-row	27	...	3.0[b]	DeMan and Vervenne, 1988
Six-row	27	...	2.8[b]	DeMan and Vervenne, 1988
Two-row	5	2.5–3.0[c]	2.7	Fedak and de la Roche, 1977
Six-row	13	2.5–3.1[c]	2.8	Fedak and de la Roche, 1977
Six-row (*Hordeum murinum* × *H. vulgaris*)	3	2.6–2.9[c]	...	Fedak and de la Roche, 1977
Two-row	3	2.1–2.3[a]	...	Gervais et al, 1987
Six-row	2	2.0–2.4[a]	...	Gervais et al, 1987
Three protein levels, six varieties	18	2.3–3.3[a]	2.9	Hernandez et al, 1967
Six-row	8	3.4–4.6[c]	3.9	Parsons and Price, 1974
Two-row	2	3.2–3.5[c]	...	Price and Parsons, 1974
Six-row	4	3.1–3.5[c]	...	Price and Parsons, 1974
Covered (2), naked (2)	4	3.1–3.5[c]	3.3	Shin et al, 1981
Mixed	3	2.1–3.4[c,d]	...	Shin and Gray, 1983
Mixed	6	2.5–3.0[a]	2.7	Skarsaune et al, 1972
Two-row	9	2.1–3.4[b]	2.6	Welch, 1978
Six-row	18	1.9–3.0[b]	2.4	Welch, 1978

[a]Lipid extracted after acid hydrolysis.
[b]Lipid expressed as fatty acid (FA); one value of 4.1% for Risø 1508 omitted from range (Welch, 1978); FA × 1.05 = triglyceride and (approximate) hydrolysate lipid.
[c]Lipid extracted with polar solvents.
[d]Values in paper are 1/10th of normal—this apparent error is corrected here.

TABLE 3
Composition of Nonpolar Lipids in Total Lipids of Barley, Malt, and Spent Grain[a,b]

Lipid Class	Barley, %								Malt, %					Spent Grain, %	
	A	B	C	D	F	G	H	I	B	D	E	F	G	E	H
SG	7	2	10	1	10	4	14	10	3	2	4	18	18	1	3
TG	86	95	56	88	55	70	73	52	91	85	64	38	58	61	56
FFA	3	4	9	5	20	5	6	9	4	8	6	28	1	11	22
S	3	2	8	...	6	4	...	9	2	...	...	4	6	...	...
DG															
1,2	...	...	6	...	4	...	...	7	...	...	...	7	...	...	...
1,2 + 1,3	1	...	...	4	...	8	7	...	...	4	2	...	7	5	14
1,3	...	...	7	...	5	...	...	9	...	...	...	5	...	...	...
MG	tr	...	...	1	...	9	...	...	...	1	1	...	8	5	...

[a] References:
A = Baikov et al (1979); 2.48% total lipid containing 5.6% PL; no GL reported; 7% unknown in NL.
B = Byrne et al (1983); 2.8% total lipid containing 7.7% NL, 11% GL, 12% PL in barley; 2.1% total lipid containing 75% NL, 13% GL, 12% PL in malt.
C = Shin and Gray (1983); average of similar data for three varieties; 4% unknown lipid in NL.
D = Anness (1984); averages for two barley varieties containing 4.2% hydrolysate lipid. Total extractable lipid contained ~8% GL and ~9% PL; composition of NL recalculated from FA data, hence lower values of SE.
E = Anness and Reed (1985a); 23% GL + PL in malt containing 3.2% lipid, 20% GL + PL in spent grains containing 9.4% lipid, composition of NL recalculated from FA data.
F = Shin et al (1986).
G = Holmberg and Sellmann-Persson (1967); 21% PL in barley lipid, 4% PL in malt lipid; 2% HC in NL.
H = Dawson et al (1987); 5% other lipid in NL.
I = Price and Parsons (1980); average values for two samples; 6% HC in SE; also three unknowns (4%); no MG reported.
[b] See Table 1 for definitions of abbreviations.

TABLE 4
Composition of Glycolipids in Total Lipids of Barley and Malt

Lipid Class[a]	Barley[b] (%)	Barley[c] (%)	Malt[c] (%)	Barley[d] (%)	Malt[d] (%)
ESG	14–15	...	...	0–3	0
MGDG	32–34	27–30	23–27	12–14	12–17
SG	3–4	18–24	23–28	...	...
CER 1	14–16	12–17	18–23	...	...
CER 2/MGMG	6–7	...	...	6–7	3–8
DGDG	22–25	32–39	27–32	40–42	33–35
SL	1–2	...	...	...	...
DGMG	...	...	...	35–37	46–47

[a] See Table 1 for definitions.
[b] From Shin and Gray (1983). Values for three varieties expressed as percent hexose recalculated to whole-lipid basis. One of CER components may be MGMG.
[c] From Lee et al (1981). Values for four varieties quantified by densitometry. Steryl glycoside and CER could include MGMG, other minor glycolipids such as 6-O-acylmonogalactosyl-glycerides, and even free sugars.
[d] From Anness (1984). Average fatty acid values for two varieties recalculated to whole-lipid basis.

germ, and the proportions of NL and polar lipids (PoL) reflect their origin (compare Tables 6 and 7).

Heating of grain tends to cause binding of some free lipids. This occurs in the so-called hydrothermal processes described by Russian workers (Fedorchenko and Baikov, 1974; Nechaev and Sandler, 1975; Grozdova and Potemkina, 1979) and in some grain-drying procedures, where it can cause low figures for fat content if inappropriate analytical methods are used (Connolly and Spillane, 1968).

DISTRIBUTION OF LIPIDS IN THE CARYOPSIS

Nonstarch Lipids

In cereals, lipids are stored in oil droplets or spherosomes bounded by a simple membrane. The principal core lipid is triacylglycerol (TG), and there are always small amounts of other NL such as steryl ester (SE), diacylglycerol (DG), monoacylglycerol (MG), and FFA. The PoL are located in the membrane and are predominantly phosphatidylcholine (PC), phosphatidylinositol (PI), and phosphatidylethanolamine (PE) (Morrison, 1978a, 1983, 1984, 1988a). Firn and Kende (1974) found PC (46%), PI (13%), PE (12%), phosphatidylglycerol (PG) (3%), and four minor PL in barley aleurone lipids, which were predominantly from spherosomes. The membrane proteins have been characterized from wheat aleurone spherosomes (Jelsema et al, 1977), wheat flour (Marion et al, 1989), and maize scutellum spherosomes (Qu et al, 1986),

TABLE 5
Composition of Phospholipids in Total Lipids of Barley and Malt[a]

Lipid Class	Barley[b] (%)	Barley[c] (%)	Barley[d] (%)	Barley[e] (%)	Barley[f] (%)	Malt[d] (%)	Malt[f] (%)
Unknown A	9–11	2	...	...	...	...	...
Unknown B	2–4	<1	...	...	...	...	...
Unknown C	...	...	...	4	...	...	9
PA	2–4	<1	...	...	...	...	...
PG	<2	2	...	9	15	...	17
PG	<2	<1	...	4	9	...	9
PE	10–12	9	4	11	14	5	4
PI	2–4	2	11	6	3	15	5
PS	<3	6	1	...	...	2	...
PC	54–60	51	70	44	39	70	31
LPC	4–7	28	14	22	19	8	15
LPE	<4	...	...	...	...	...	...

[a] See Table 1 for definitions of abbreviations.
[b] From Zakryzhevskaya et al (1978).
[c] From Parsons and Price (1979). Similar data as percent phosphorus for two varieties recalculated using conversion factors (Morrison et al, 1975) and averaged. Unknown A may be NAPE, unknown B may be DPG, DPG may be NALPE, and PS probably includes LPE.
[d] From Byrne et al (1983), no corrections for Iatroscan detector response to individual lipids applied.
[e] From Shin and Gray (1983). Similar data as percent phosphorus for three varieties recalculated, as above. Unknown C may be NALPE, and DPG is probably NAPE.
[f] From Lee et al (1981). Similar values for four varieties averaged. Unknown C could be PMe (artefact), DPG is probably NAPE, and PG may include NALPE.

and are presumably similar in barley. Spherosomes are concentrated in embryonic and aleurone tissue (Chapter 2) but disappear during senescence of pericarp (Morrison, 1988a). Some spherosomes have also been detected in the subaleurone starchy endosperm of wheat (Hargin et al, 1980) and have long been recognized in oat endosperm (Fulcher, 1986), so they may be expected in barley endosperm.

The ubiquitous structural lipids found in the membranes of all living plant tissues are PC and PE, with lesser amounts of other diacyl PL such as phosphatidylserine, PI, and PG. The *N*-acyl PL (*N*-acylphosphatidylethanolamine [NAPE] and *N*-acyllysophosphatidylethanolamine [NALPE]) and the major galactosylglycerides (monogalactosyldiglyceride [MGDG] and digalactosyldiglyceride [DGDG]) are almost exclusively in the starchy endosperm in wheat (Hargin and Morrison, 1980; Hargin et al, 1980) and may be located in amyloplast and other plastid membranes. Small amounts of these and other GL are found in all membranes, especially in actively metabolizing tissue (Morrison, 1985, 1988a).

Starch lipids, which are discussed at length later in this chapter, are invariably monoacyl lipids, and in barley they are comprised of lysophatidylcholine (LPC) and lysophosphatidylethanolamine (LPE), with small amounts of lysophosphatidylinositol (LPI), lysophosphatidylglycerol (LPG), and FFA. LPL (and other

TABLE 6
Free and Bound Lipid Contents of Barley Varieties

Type of Samples	Number of Samples	Total Lipids (%)	Nonpolar Lipids (%)	Glycolipids (%)	Phospholipids (%)
Free lipids					
cv. Hiproly, Risø 1508[a]	2	2.6, 4.2	71, 68	...	...
cv. Bonanza[b]	1	1.8	69	26	9
cv. Risø 1508[b]	1	3.9	75	7	18
Six varieties × three protein levels[c]	18	1.6–2.3	...	...	...
Covered[d]	2	1.7–1.8	76, 79	9, 13	12, 9
Naked[d]	2	2.0–2.1	87, 82	9, 14	3, 3
Mixed[e]	5	1.8–2.2	...	...	...
Mixed[f]	5	1.5–1.6	...	...	...
Indian varieties[g]	8	0.8 (mean)	73 (mean)	...	...
Four varieties × harvests[h]	6	1.9–2.6	...	...	...
Bound lipids					
Covered[d]	2	0.5–0.6	10	18, 8	80, 82
Naked[d]	2	0.5–0.6	25, 21	3, 7	70, 70
Mixed[f]	5	1.3–1.5	...	...	...
Indian varieties[g]	8	0.8 (mean)	55 (mean)	...	...
Four varieties × harvests[h]	6	0.7–0.8	...	...	...

[a] From Bhatty (1982).
[b] From Bhatty and Rossnagel (1980).
[c] From Hernandez et al (1967).
[d] From Kim and Shin (1982).
[e] From MacLeod and White (1961).
[f] From Pomeranz et al (1971).
[g] From Sukhija et al (1971).
[h] From Zakryzhevskaya and Samburova (1977).

monoacyl lipids) may also arise by partial lipolysis of diacyl PL and TG (see below), especially in tissue that has been milled and stored, and they cannot be distinguished from true starch lipids if found in lipids extracted from flour with very polar solvents.

The distribution of lipids in the principal anatomical parts of the barley grain (Tables 7 and 8) is similar to that in wheat (Morrison, 1978a, 1988a), but several points should be noted. Where petroleum ether, hexane, or diethyl ether was used as solvent, only free lipids would have been obtained, and higher values would have been recorded if bound lipids and starch lipids (in the case of endosperm only) had been included. The lipids in barley germ and its subfractions are very similar to those in wheat, but analyses of the lipid classes (Table 9) are less complete. The lipid content of the aleurone (a single result) is nearly three times that of wheat and is presumably comprised of similar lipid classes as embryonic tissue lipids. Finally, there is less PL but more GL in small kernels than in large kernels (De Man and Vervenne, 1988).

There appear to be no data for the lipids of the starchy endosperm free from bran and aleurone. The figures in Tables 7 and 8 for bran-endosperm fractions are undoubtedly low, for reasons given above, and do not include any of the starch lipids. The composition of the lipid classes has not been determined, but it should resemble that in wheat. The hull of one sample of Prilar Hulless barley has a remarkably high lipid content, with a high proportion of material identified as GL. Since this has an unusual FA

TABLE 7
Composition of Lipids in the Principal Parts of Barley Grain

| | Lipid Class (wt %) | | |
Tissue	Nonpolar Lipid (NL)	Glycolipid (GL)	Phospholipid (PL)
Whole grain[a,b]	75, 65	7, 26	18, 9
Whole meal[b,c]	69, 71	...	...
Whole grain[d]	73–75	6–7	19–20
Embryo[b,c]	87, 90	...	...
Bran-endosperm[b,c]	68, 65	...	...
Aleurone[e]	82	...	...
Coleorhiza[e]	74	4[g]	22[g]
Coleoptile[f]	67	6[g]	27[g]
Scutellum[f]	88	3[g]	8[g]
Hull[h]	76	18	6
Embryo[h]	76	6	18
Bran-endosperm[h]	64	13	23

[a] From Bhatty and Rossnagel (1980), two samples.
[b] Free (petroleum-extractable) lipids only. Similar values after acid hydrolysis except embryo = 15–18% lipid in tissue.
[c] From Bhatty (1982), first value for Risø barley, second value for Hiproly barley.
[d] From De Mann and Vervenne (1988).
[e] From Firn and Kende (1974).
[f] From Hølmer et al (1973).
[g] GL and PL analyses not reliable due to inadequate resolution of thin-layer chromatography system used; GL identified as esterified (acyl) sterylglycoside and PL as phosphatidylcholine + phosphatidylethanolamine.
[h] From Price and Parsons (1979).

composition (discussed below), the GL fraction may have little MGDG and DGDG, which are typical of endosperm nonstarch lipids.

The surface waxy lipid of decorticated barley (1–2 g/10 kg of grain) is concentrated in the testa region and is considered to have important functions in controlling entry of water and solutes into the caryopsis (Briggs, 1974, 1987). It is comprised of hydrocarbons, wax esters, TG, FFA, free alcohols, sterols, and 5-alkyl resorcinols. The hydrocarbons are mostly C_{21} to C_{36} (odd- and even-numbered chain lengths), similar to those in other cereals (Morrison, 1978a; Barnes, 1983a,c).

The lipid contents of milling fractions (Table 10) are consistent with the lipid contents of the various anatomical parts of the grain (Tables 7 and 8) and the proportions of these parts in the fractions. Sumner et al (1985) milled grain (3.0–3.3% total lipid) in several ways to obtain hull fractions

TABLE 8
Distribution of Lipids in the Principal Parts of Barley Grain

Tissue	Tissue in Grain (wt %)	Lipid in Tissue (wt %)	Lipid as Fraction of Total Lipid (%)
Whole grain[a]	100	2–4	100[b]
Embryo[a]	3–6	20–21[b]	28–37[b]
Endosperm[a]	88–97	1–3[b]	63–72[b]
Whole grain[c]	100	4.2, 2.6[b]	100[b]
Embryo[c]	5, 4	20.5, 21.4[b]	24, 33[b]
Bran-endosperm[c]	95, 96	3.4, 1.8[b]	76, 67[b]
Aleurone[d]	...	22–24	...
Coleorhiza[e]	...	17–23	...
Coleoptile[e]	...	15–30	...
Scutellum[e]	...	17–24	...
Whole grain[f]	100	3.2	100
Hull[f]	6.8	2.4	5.0
Embryo[f]	3.0	19.6	17.9
Bran-endosperm[f]	90.2	2.8	77.1

[a] From Bhatty and Rossnagel (1980).
[b] Free (petroleum-extractable) lipids only. Similar values after acid hydrolysis except embryo = 15–18% lipid in tissue.
[c] From Bhatty (1982), first value for Risø barley, second value for Hiproly barley.
[d] From Firn and Kende (1974).
[e] From Hølmer et al (1973).
[f] From Price and Parsons (1979).

TABLE 9
Composition of Lipids in Barley Embryonic Tissue[a]

Lipid Class	Coleorhiza (%)	Coleoptile (%)	Scutellum (%)
Steryl ester	7.1	5.3	1.1
Triglyceride	65.2	58.1	55.1
Free fatty acid	2.0	3.6	8.4
Esterified (acyl) sterylglycoside	4.1	5.8	12.3
Phosphatidylethanolamine	5.2	4.7	3.2
Phosphatidylcholine	16.4	22.5	5.5

[a] Adapted from Hølmer et al (1973).

(5.4–7.0% lipid), fines fractions (5.6–8.7% lipid), and pearled grain (0.7–1.9% lipid). Hull-less (naked) barley gave similar fines and pearled products. The free lipids in flour analyzed by Chun and Lee (1984) contained NL (93.6%), GL (3.9%), and PL (2.5%), whereas flour used by Bekes (1981) contained 83.1% NL. The composition of the NL (Table 11) is essentially the same as that of spherosomes, whereas the bound lipids are predominantly endosperm structural lipids (GL and PL, which were not analyzed).

Bekes (1981) studied the thionin lipoprotein complexes in barley, wheat, rye, and oats, isolated from the free lipid extracts of the cereal flours. The

TABLE 10
Free and Bound Lipid Contents of Some Barley Grain Fractions

Fraction	Free Lipid (%)	Bound Lipid (%)	Authors
Husk[a]	2.60	...	MacLeod and White (1961)
Husk-aleurone-embryo[a]	6.85	...	MacLeod and White (1961)
Embryo-aleurone[a]	6.74	...	MacLeod and White (1961)
Scutellum-aleurone-flour[a]	4.24	...	MacLeod and White (1961)
Flour-furrow[a]	2.02	...	MacLeod and White (1961)
Endosperm[a]	0.74	...	MacLeod and White (1961)
Milling fractions (6)[b]	1.2–3.3	...	Pomeranz et al (1970)
Milling fractions (13)[b]	1.1–2.8	0.4–1.3	Pomeranz et al (1971)
Husk[a]	0.6–1.2[c]	...	Skarsaune et al (1972)
Aleurone[a]	2.3–3.4[c]	...	Skarsaune et al (1972)
Endosperm[a]	0.3–0.6[c]	...	Skarsaune et al (1972)
Flour	1.67	...	Bekes (1981)
Decorticating fractions[d]	9.1–10.3	...	Bach Knudsen and Eggum (1984)
Flour	2.12	0.76	Chun and Lee (1984)
Meal flour, pearled grain	1.1–2.1	...	Bhatty (1986)

[a] Pearler fractions.
[b] Roller milling fractions.
[c] Values after various weeks postharvest storage.
[d] Bomi barley decorticated 6–20.6%; material sieved.

TABLE 11
Composition of Nonpolar Lipid Classes in Some Barley Fractions

Lipid Class[a]	Grain Free Lipids[b] (%)	Grain Bound Lipids[b] (%)	Flour Free Lipids[c] (%)	Flour Free Lipids[d] (%)	Flour Bound Lipids[d] (%)	Malt Free Lipids[e] (%)
SE, HC	4–8	1–6	3.4	7.4	0.8	4–5
TG	55–72	23–59	41.4	56.2	5.2	80–86
DG	4–8	2–7	20.6	6.0	8.4	7–8
S	2–4	3–7	2.1	6.0	5.2	...
FFA	4–7	4–20	8.7	14.9	5.2	3–7
MG	...	...	1.4	0.9	0.6	...
PoL	4–8	14–17	12.4	6.4	73.8	...
Unknown	4–11	3–17	2.1	0.9	...	...

[a] See Table 1 for definitions.
[b] From Zakryzhevskaya and Samburova (1977).
[c] From Bekes (1981).
[d] From Chun and Lee (1984).
[e] From O'Palka et al (1987); DG includes MG.

lipids associated with the thionins were similar in every case and in barley were comprised of SE (2.1%), steryl glycoside (2.4%), PE (29.3%), PC (24.5%), PI (11.5%), LPC (5.9%), LPE (3.2%), MGDG (5.4%), monogalactosylmono-glyceride (0.2%), and DGDG (16.5%). The natural function of thionins or lipopurothionins in cereals is not known, but they have an inhibitory effect on some yeasts and bacteria.

Diol lipids (in which a low-molecular-weight dihydric alcohol replaces glycerol) are associated with actively growing tissues (Bergelson, 1973). Noda and Umeda (1973) reported 72.5 μg of propane-1,2-diol and 74.9 μg of propane-1,3-diol (from lipids) per gram of milk-ripe barley, with lesser amounts of ethane-diol and butane-1,3-diol.

Starch Lipids

The starch granules in barley, as in other cereals, have lipids inside the granules in quantities generally proportional to amylose content (Morrison et al, 1984; Morrison, 1988b, 1993). In barley, wheat, rye, and triticale, the true starch lipids are almost exclusively LPL. According to Acker and Becker (1971), the lipids in one starch sample were comprised of LPC (62.4%), LPE (6.0%), LPI (3.1%), and FFA (4.4%). Wheat starch contains approximately twice as much LPG as LPI (Morrison et al, 1975, 1980; Morrison, 1978a,b; Hargin et al, 1980), and on reexamination of barley starches, their LPL may prove to be very similar. Since purified barley starch contains very little inorganic phosphate and hexose phosphate, total starch phosphorus content is a convenient measure of the total LPL. Factors that have been used to convert weight of phosphorus into weight of LPL are P × 16.5 (Morrison et al, 1975; Tester et al, 1991) and P × 16.39 (Morrison, 1988b). If an allowance is made for nonlipid phosphorus, the factor is (P − 2) × 16.16 (Tester and Morrison, 1992).

Most, if not all, of the FFA and other minor NL in barley starches are surface lipid artefacts; hence they vary with the quality of the purified starch. For example, Morrison et al (1984) reported FFA contents in the range of 200–525 mg/100 g of starch, but in samples prepared subsequently to minimize such artefacts, FFA contents were in the range of 28–92 mg/100 g of starch. It is also noteworthy that in both sets of samples, FFA contents were similar in waxy, normal, and high-amylose starches and were not related to amylose content (compare LPL, discussed below). The various NL reported by Goering et al (1975), although extracted with a solvent intended for starch lipids, were undoubtedly nonstarch lipids, and the FAME fraction was an additional artefact caused by methanolysis during the lipid extraction.

It has been known for some time that waxy cereal starches have little or no internal lipids and that high-amylose starches have more lipids than the normal starches from the same species (Acker and Becker, 1971; Becker and Acker, 1976; Morrison, 1978a); subsequent studies have shown a consistent relationship between amylose content and lipid content in the cereal starches (Morrison, 1988b; Tester and Morrison, 1992, 1993; Morrison et al, 1993b; Tester et al, 1993). It has been suggested that lipids probably have a regulatory function in the synthesis of amylose, but their precise role is not known (Morrison and Milligan, 1982; Morrison et al, 1984; Morrison, 1988b; Tester et al, 1991). In starches isolated from a collection of barley varieties, amylose and LPL contents were clearly segregated into three groups corresponding to waxy, normal, and high-amylose types (Table 12), and, although these parameters were superficially correlated in the full set of starches, there were no significant correlations within any of the three groups. Subsequent studies with starches grown in controlled conditions have shown highly significant correlations in waxy starches and in nonwaxy starches (Tester and Morrison, 1992, 1993; Morrison et al, 1993b; Tester et al, 1993).

McDonald et al (1991) studied changes in the amylose and lipid contents of A-type starch granules isolated from four barley genotypes. In every case, both parameters increased during the period of active starch biosynthesis, and amylose and LPL contents were linearly correlated (Fig. 1), as originally reported by Becker and Acker (1972). The barley starches showed the same pattern as in the A- and B-type starch granules isolated from developing wheat (Morrison and Gadan, 1987), which is consistent with the A-type granule having a core of low-amylose, low-lipid starch and outer layers (predominantly above and below the equatorial plane of the granule) of high-amylose, high-lipid starch (McDonald et al, 1991), as postulated for wheat (Fig. 2).

Another interesting observation arising from these studies is that the composition of the starch in the B-granules was always different from that of the A-granules at the same stages of barley grain development (days after anthesis). The most dramatic difference was in Waxy Oderbrucker, in which amylose content increased from 2 to 6% in the A-granules over the period 15–60 DAA, whereas it was apparently zero in the B-granules at all stages of grain development. It was found, subsequently, that amylose content had been underestimated and that waxy B-granules had less amylose and more lipids than the A-granules (Tester and Morrison, 1993). Since both types of granule are probably synthesized within the same amyloplasts, as in wheat (Parker, 1985), it would appear that at least one aspect of starch biochemistry (amylose content and the amylose-lipid relationship) is modified within the evaginations of the amyloplast, where the B-granules are synthesized

TABLE 12
Amylose and Lipid Contents of Barley Starches

Type	Cultivars/ Samples	Amylose (g/100 g)	Free Fatty Acids (mg/100 g)	Lysophospholipids (mg/100 g)
Waxy[a]	8/8	2.1–8.3	28–61[b]	158–460
Normal[a]	13/36	25.3–30.1	31–46[b]	630–984
High-amylose[a]	3/6	37.4–47.9	54–92[b]	997–1,216
Waxy[c]	12/12	1.7–7.4	...	120–569
Nonwaxy[c]	6/6	29.2–32.7	...	774–1,032
Risø mutants[d]	8/8	23.0–29.3	...	469–1,764
Waxy Hector[e]	1/4	2.9–4.9	...	278–527
Hector[e]	1/4	22.9–25.7	...	604–722

[a] Data from Morrison et al (1984, 1986).
[b] Excludes high values caused by surface lipid artefacts (see text).
[c] Data from Tester and Morrison (1992).
[d] Data from Tester et al (1993) for Bomi (normal) and seven Risø mutants.
[e] Data from Tester and Morrison (1993); samples from barleys at 20, 30, 40, and 50 days after anthesis.

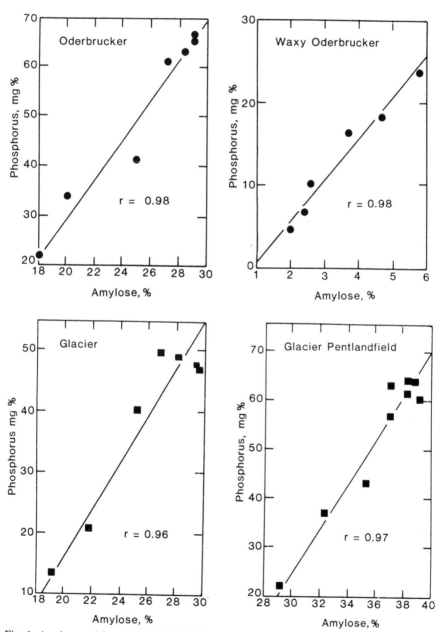

Fig. 1. Amylose and lysophospholipid (LPL) phosphorus (P) contents of large (A-type) starch granules isolated from Oderbrucker, Waxy Oderbrucker, Glacier, and Glacier (Pentlandfield) barleys at various stages of grain development. LPL = 16.5 × P. (Reprinted, by permission, from McDonald et al, 1991)

(McDonald et al, 1991). An alternative suggestion is that the outer layers of the A-granules are synthesized at the same time as the B-granules and have the same elevated amylose and lipid contents (Morrison, 1993).

Further evidence of the amylose-lipid relationship was seen in starches from single kernels of F_2 generation progeny exhibiting zero to three doses of high-amylose gene from Glacier (Pentlandfield) barley (Morrison, 1987); however, within each group there was considerable variation, particularly in lipid content.

These studies clearly demonstrate that the amylose-lipid relationship does apply to starches from barley grown under defined conditions, but the poor correlations within waxy, normal, and high-amylose groups (Morrison et al, 1984, discussed above) indicate that the relationship may be subject to appreciable genotypic variation and other disturbances.

In a recent study (Tester et al, 1991), starch was obtained from four barley genotypes grown at 10, 15, or 20°C in constant-environment chambers. In each genotype, gelatinization temperature, swelling behavior, and lipid content showed a strong response to growth temperature (Table 13). In Triumph and Golden Promise, amylose contents were not affected, although lipid contents did increase substantially with temperature. This independent effect of temperature on the lipids has not been demonstrated before, although it was indicated from previous studies of starch from Triumph barley grown at various locations in the United Kingdom (Morrison et al, 1986) and from six varieties of rice grown at 10 locations around the Mediterranean (Morrison and Nasir Azudin, 1987).

There is now good evidence from ^{13}C-nuclear magnetic resonance and differential scanning calorimetry experiments, supported by chemical studies, to show that the starch LPL occur as guest molecules in complexes with V-6 single-helix amylose (Morrison et al, 1993a,b). These complexes are present in the native granules and are not artefacts. Lipid-complexed amylose accounts for ~54% of the total amylose in waxy starches and ~21% in nonwaxy starches, the remainder being lipid-free (Morrison, 1993).

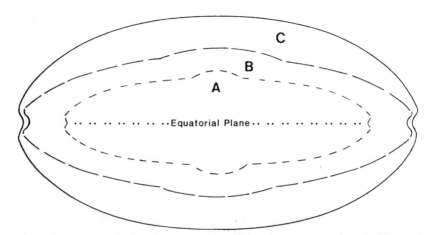

Fig. 2. Model of an A-type starch granule from wheat or barley, showing zones of increasing amylose and lipid (LPL) contents from A to C. A = low-amylose, low-lipid; B = intermediate-amylose, intermediate-lipid; C = high-amylose, high-lipid. (Adapted from Morrison, 1989a)

TABLE 13
Amylose and Lysophospholipid (LPL) Contents, Gelatinization Temperature (GT), and Swelling Factor (SF) at 80°C of Starches from Four Barley Genotypes Grown at a Constant Temperature of 10, 15, or 20°C[a]

	Waxy Oderbrucker			Triumph			Golden Promise			Glacier (Pentlandfield)		
	10°C	15°C	20°C	10°C	15°C	20°C	10°C	15°C	20°C	10°C	15°C	20°C
Amylose (g/100 g)[b]	3.6	2.3	5.1	28.2	27.7	27.5	28.0	27.4	28.0	54.7	40.0	40.9
LPL (mg/100 g)[b]	598	537	751	767	816	1,210	1,000	1,084	1,687	1,229	1,294	1,763
GT (°C)[b]	52.1	57.5	63.1	49.8	52.6	64.5	49.6	51.8	62.8	55.1	57.0	64.8
SF (amylopectin)[b]	15.6	17.8	14.3	14.0	13.2	10.1	12.5	10.8	5.9	8.9	10.0	4.4
Amylose (g/100 g)[c]	4.9	5.7	6.7	24.8	24.8	24.7	25.9	26.6	24.9	53.3	36.1	37.0
LPL (mg/100 g)[c]	333	459	482	662	912	825	815	1,129	1,087	865	1,251	1,040
GT (°C)[c]	54.1	61.6	62.7	52.1	60.8	59.6	51.1	58.3	59.8	55.7	62.0	61.7

[a] Data from Tester et al (1991).
[b] From experiment 1, using mercury vapor lamps for illumination.
[c] From experiment 2, using sodium vapor lamps for illumination.

COMPOSITION OF LIPIDS

Fatty Acids in Nonstarch Lipids

For some purposes, such as studies in animal nutrition, the component FAs in barley lipids are more important than the lipid classes since lipids are metabolized mostly as FFA and simple glycerides. The individual FAs in barley have not been fully characterized, but it is always assumed that the principal polyunsaturates are linoleic acid (9-*cis*, 12-*cis*-octadecadienoic acid, 18:2[*n*-6]) and linolenic acid (9-*cis*, 12-*cis*, 15-*cis*-octadecatrienoic acid, 18:3[*n*-3]) as in wheat and other cereals (Morrison, 1978a).

The FA composition of the total lipids and their major subdivisions in barley and malt are given in Table 14. The data are from authors who have analyzed several samples so that consistent patterns can be seen; data for single samples have not been included. Barley FAs are very similar to those in wheat except that they have more linolenic acid. Values tend to be higher for 16:0 and lower for 18:2 and 18:3 in larger barley kernels (De Man and Bruyneel, 1987). Different levels of nitrogen fertilization have only small effects on FA composition (De Man and Dondeyne, 1985). Roasting barley (for brewing) causes significant losses of 18:2 and 18:3 acids (Anness, 1984).

Similar data are given for the free lipids in Table 15 and the bound lipids in Table 16. As a general rule, storage lipids (mostly TG) and structural lipids in the caryopsis are not affected much by environmental temperature during grain filling; increased unsaturation in response to lower temperatures is most likely to be seen in actively growing tissue such as developing roots and shoots in the field, although not under the controlled conditions of malting.

The FA composition of the lipids in the principal parts of barley grain is given in Table 17 and of lipid classes of barley and malt in Table 18. Embryo lipids are notably richer in linolenate than starchy endosperm (nonstarch) lipids and aleurone lipids. Husk, hull, and bran lipids are not from dissected tissues; hence their compositions reflect the aleurone and germ lipids in their fractions. The surface lipids analyzed by Hareland and Madson (1989) and by Briggs (Table 18) were from typical pericarp material and have much higher levels of monoenoic acids and less polyunsaturated acids than the other lipids. Espelie et al (1979) reported that the components of barley seed coat lipids were alcohols (16:0–22:0; 1.4%), FFA (16:0 + 20:0; 0.9%), ω-hydroxy FFA (16:0 + 18:1; 12.8%), dihydroxy FFA (7,16-, 8,16-, 9,16-, and 10,16-isomers of 16:0; 16.2%), 9,10-epoxy, 18-hydroxyoctadecanoic acid (30.2%), and 9,10,18-trihydroxyoctadecanoic acid (9.6%)—these are typical cutin lipids, and there is some similarity to the wax esters described by Briggs (1974).

Not much information is available on the FA composition of individual lipid classes, and no complete analysis of the lipids in the whole grain or in any major tissue has been published. The reader should therefore compare the figures in Table 18 with the more comprehensive data for lipids in wheat (Morrison, 1988a) to obtain a better perspective. In addition, note that several sources of error appear to have impaired the results given by some authors. For example, TG is the major lipid class in the embryo, yet it is reported to have less linoleate and linolenate than embryo NL (Table 17). In other instances, published thin-layer chromatograms and FA compositions

TABLE 14
Fatty Acid Composition of Total Lipids, Total Nonpolar Lipids (NL), Total Glycolipids (GL),
and Total Phospholipids (PL) in Barley and Malt

Samples	Number	Fatty Acid, %					
		14:0	16:0	18:0	18:1	18:2	18:3
Total lipids							
Barley varieties[a]	9	...	20–21	1	10–14	56–59	6–9
Means			(20.7)	(0.8)	(12.7)	(57.9)	(7.9)
Malts[a]	7	...	20–23	<1	10–12	57–59	8–11
Six-, two-row (winter/spring) barleys × environments[b]	9(×6)	...	19–20	1	10	59–61	8
Six-, two-row (winter/spring) barleys[c]	81	<1	21–34	1	11–14	47–58	5–8
Six-row barleys[d]	27	...	21–22	1–2	13–14	57–58	6
Two-row barleys[d]	27	...	22	1	12–13	57–58	6–7
Six-, two-row barleys[e]	21	...	18–27	1	12–21	50–59	4–7
Means			(21.5)	(1.0)	(15.0)	(55.9)	(5.7)
Barleys (means)[f]	6	<1	24	2	12	56	6
Barleys (× protein)[g]	6(×3)	<1	24–25	1	12–14	53–56	4–6
Barleys[h]	4	<2	20	2	18	53	5
Malts[h]	4	2	31	3	11	48	4
Barleys[i]	3	<1	21–27	1–2	10–13	56–60	4–5
Barleys (winter/spring)[j]	2(×2)	...	21–24	1–2	9–13	58–59	5–8
Six-, two-row genotypes[k]	27	...	21–29	1	10–17	52–58	4–7
Means			(24.8)	(1.0)	(13.7)	(54.9)	(5.6)
Barley varieties[k]	23	...	24–28	1	10–14	54–57	5–7
Means			(25.9)	(0.9)	(12.0)	(55.5)	(5.7)
Malts[l]	...	<1	17–22	1	5–12	60–65	7–10
NL, GL, and PL							
Barley NL[h]	4	2	21	2	20	51	5
Malt NL[h]	4	3	33	3	13	45	4
Barley NL[i]	3	<1	21–28	1–2	11–15	54–60	4–5
Barley GL[i]	3	<1	18–22	1–2	6–7	65–69	4–5
Barley PL[i]	3	<1	27	2	8–9	59–61	2–3
Barley GL[m]	4	<1	20	1	8	66	5
Malt GL[m]	4	1	34	3	6	52	4
Barley PL[m]	4	<1	26	1	12	57	3
Malt PL[m]	4	1	38	3	9	46	3
Barley NL[n]	8	<1	23–39	1	15–20	48–52	3–6
Barley GL[n]	8	1	20–24	1–2	4–8	58–66	4–7
Barley PL[n]	8	1	31–37	<2	10–16	44–51	2–4
Barley NL[o]	6	<1	19–26	1	13–18	51–58	5–7
Barley GL[o]	6	1–2	21–26	2–4	4–9	56–65	4–6
Barley PL[o]	6	1–2	28–31	1–2	9–12	48–55	3–5

[a] From Anness (1984).
[b] From De Man (1985).
[c] From De Man and Bruyneel (1987).
[d] From De Man and Vervenne (1988).
[e] From Fedak and de la Roche (1977).
[f] From Hareland and Madson (1989).
[g] From Hernandez et al (1967).
[h] From Shin et al (1981).
[i] From Shin and Gray (1983).
[j] From Welch (1975).
[k] From Welch (1978).
[l] From Krauss et al (1972).
[m] From Lee et al (1981).
[n] From Parsons and Price (1974).
[o] From Price and Parsons (1974).

(compared with wheat lipids) strongly suggest that some lipids were misidentified; the more probable identities of these lipids (NAPE, the artefact phosphatidyl methanol [PMe], and NALPE) have been used in Table 18.

Tocopherols

For nutritional purposes, it is important to balance vitamin E intake with the amounts of polyunsaturated FAs and selenium in the diet. Barley is unique among cereals in having all eight naturally occurring tocopherols (Table 19). Their identities have been confirmed by gas chromatography-mass spectrometry (Govind Rao and Perkins, 1972). In the cereals, tocols are found exclusively in germ tissues (embryo, scutellum) and tocotrienols in the starchy endosperm and aleurone (Morrison et al, 1982; Barnes, 1983b), and the proportions of tocols and tocotrienols in products derived from the whole grain therefore depend on the relative amounts of these tissues in the particular fraction. Thus, dissected germ has no tocotrienols, whereas pearled barley mostly has the tocotrienols characteristic of the aleurone (Table 19). Qureshi et al (1986) found that α-T-3 isolated from barley inhibited cholesterol synthesis in vitro and in vivo (in chicks).

Total tocopherol contents in the range of 19–50 mg/kg of barley have been

TABLE 15
Fatty Acid Composition of Free Lipids in Barley Grain, Flour, and Malt

Sample, Lipids	Fatty Acid, %						
	14:0	16:0	18:0	18:1	18:2	18:3	Others
Flour, total[a]	tr	25	1	16	52	5	22:0 (1)
Nonpolar[a]	tr	25	1	16	51	5	
Glycolipids[a]	tr	21	1	7	63	5	
Phospholipids[a]	tr	25	1	10	59	4	
Grain, total[b]	tr	24–25	1–2	13	53–55	6	
Grain, total[c]	...	20	1	14	58	7	...
Grain, total[d]	tr	19–24	<2	15–17	54–59	3–6	20:0, 20:1 (tr)
Barley, total[e]	1	23	tr	17	52	5	20:0 (<1)
Nonpolar[e]	1	19	2	17	56	6	
Malt (7d), total[e]	tr	30	2	12	52	4	
Nonpolar[e]	1	25	1	15	51	5	16:1 (1.5), 20:0 (1)
Grain, total[f]	1–2	21–23	1–2	9–10	56–58	4–6	14:1, 16:1 (1)
Grain[g]	...	26	2	13	52	5	Not specified (2)
Grain[h]	1	19–20	1–5	12–14	44–58	6–8	
Grain[i]	...	17–22	1–2	16–20	53–59	3–7	
Meal[j]	...	21–24	1	10–15	57–60	4–5	
Flour[j]	...	21–25	1	10–15	57–59	4–5	
Pearled grain[j]	...	23–25	1–2	9–13	56–62	3	

[a] From Chun and Lee (1984). tr = trace.
[b] From Connolly and Spillane (1968).
[c] From De Man and Cauberghe (1988).
[d] From Demchenko et al (1969).
[e] From Shin et al (1986).
[f] From Skarsaune et al (1972).
[g] From Sukhija et al (1971).
[h] From Zakryzhevskaya and Samburova (1977).
[i] From Madazimov et al (1976).
[j] From Bhatty (1986).

TABLE 16
Fatty Acid Composition of Bound Lipids in Barley Grain and Malt

Sample, Lipids	Fatty Acid, %						
	14:0	16:0	18:0	18:1	18:2	18:3	Others
Flour, total[a]	tr	30	1	9	55	5	22:0 (<1)
Nonpolar lipids[a]	2	24	1	15	52	5	
Glycolipids[a]	tr	15	1	14	60	6	
Phospholipids[a]	tr	31	1	11	52	4	
Grain, total[b]	tr	33–34	1–2	9	51–52	4	
Grain, total[c]	24	1	8	62	4	...	
Barley, total[d]	1	29	2	7	58	3	16:1 (1)
Malt, total[d]	1	21	2	9	62	5	16:1 (<1)
Barley[e]	...	32	2	16	46	4	
Barley[f]	...	19–23	1–2	12–13	58–61	4–5	16:1 (<1)

[a] Chun and Lee (1984). tr = trace.
[b] From Connolly and Spillane (1968).
[c] From De Man and Cauberghe (1988).
[d] From Shin et al (1986).
[e] From Sukhija et al (1971).
[f] From Zakryshevskaya and Samburova (1977).

TABLE 17
Fatty Acid Composition of Lipids in Various Parts of the Barley Grain[a]

Anatomical Part	Lipid	Fatty Acid, %						
		14:0	16:0	18:0	18:1	18:2	18:3	Other
Embryo (dissected)	Total[b]	...	21–24	1	18	51–52	7–8	
	Total[c]	tr	19–22	<1	14–18	51–56	9–11	
	NL[d]	...	18	1	27	48	7*	
	GL[d]	1	19	3	17	43	17*	
	PL[d]	tr	18	tr	21*	54	6*	
Aleurone (fraction)	Total[e]	<1	20–21	1	12–15	55–58	6–7	14:1, 16:1 (1)
Endosperm (fraction)	Total[b]	...	19–22	2	22–23	51–53	2–4	
	Total[c]	...	22–23	1–2	11–19	53–60	3–4	
	Total[e]	...	22–23	2–3	9–11	59–62	3–5	14:0 (<1)
	NL[d]	...	19	1	26*	50*	3	16:1 (tr)
	GL[d]	...	19	2	12*	64	4	16:1 (<1)
	PL[d]	...	33*	2	16	41*	6*	16:1 (<1)
Husk	Total[e]	...	20–22	1–2	10–16	43–50	7–8	14:0 (3–6), 16:1 (2–4)
Hull	NL[d]	...	29	5	20	29	7	14:0 (4), 16:1 (2)
	GL[d]	...	40	4	13	20	16*	14:0 (4), 16:1 (tr)
	PL[d]	...	35	2	14	35	11	14:0 (1), 16:1 (1)
Bran	Total[f]	...	21	1	13	57	6	14:0 (1), 16:1 (tr)
Surface	Total[g]	...	25	1	3	9	4	14:0 (20), 16:1 (17)

[a] See Table 1 for definitions of abbreviations. tr = trace. * = average from wide range of values.
[b] From Bhatty (1982).
[c] From Bhatty and Rossnagel (1980).
[d] From Price and Parsons (1979).
[e] From Skarsaune et al (1972).
[f] From Weihrauch et al (1976).
[g] From Hareland and Madson (1989).

reported by Slover et al (1969), Slover (1971), Madsen et al (1973), and Barnes (1983b), but much higher levels (55–100 mg/kg) with considerable seasonal variation have been found in Swedish barleys (Hakkarainen et al, 1983a,b; Hakkarainen and Pehrson, 1987). Under good storage conditions, losses of tocopherols are about 5% per month, but they are much greater in damp stored grain unless stored in CO_2 or in other controlled conditions (Hakkarainen et al, 1983a,b; Työppönen and Hakkarainen, 1985). Losses of tocopherols are greater in stored moist grain treated with propionic acid than if the grain is dried (Madsen et al, 1973; Allen et al, 1974). Losses are also greatly accelerated by heating, and only 5% of the tocopherols survive 24 hr at 120°C (Työppönen and Hakkarainen, 1985). Considerable losses in food

TABLE 18
Fatty Acid Composition of Lipid Classes in Barley and Malt[a]

Lipid	Source	Fatty Acid, %							
		14:0	16:0	16:1	18:0	18:1	18:2	18:3	Other
SE[b]	Embryo	1–14	7–15	4–7	2–6	8–15	36–59	4–12	16:1 (<1), 17:1 (1–5), 20:1 (2–3) 22:0 (<1)
TG[b]	Embryo	1	19–24	1	1	14–18	47–52	7–12	20:1 (2), 22:1 (<1)
TG[c]	Barley	<1	17–21	...	1	19–23	53–55	4–5	
TG[d]	Barley	...	21	...	1	14	57	6	
TG[e]	Malt	tr	23	tr	2	7	61	7	12:0 (tr)
TG[f]	Testa	<1	21	1	<1	15	49	12	
DG[c]	Barley	<1	18–24	<1	2–3	12–14	53–62	4–5	
DG[e]	Malt	<1	30	1	5	11	46	6	12:0 (tr)
MG[e]	Malt	1	31	1	5	15	42	5	
FFA[c]	Barley	1	32–37	tr	2–4	7–9	46–52	1–4	
FFA[g]	Barley	1–2	30–34	1	2–4	10–13	46–49	3–5	
FFA[h]	Barley	...	24	...	2–4	8–12	42–59	6–14	
FFA[h]	Malt	...	30–35	...	2–5	4–6	50–56	4–5	
ESG[b]	Embryo	5–11	25–32	5–6	9–14	13–14	15–22	3–7	16:1 (1–3), 17:1 (3–4), 20:1, 20:2 (<3)
NAPE[i]	Barley	2	27	2	14	10	43	3	
PMe[i]	Barley	6	37	2	14	11	17	1	20:0 (3)
NALPE[i]	Barley	6	19	2	5	13	54	2	20:0 (tr)
PA[i]	Barley	7	36	3	15*	20	12	3	20:0 (5)*
PG[i]	Barley	5	35	2	12	26	17	2	20:0 (2)
PE[i]	Barley	1	21	1	6	17	52	2	20:0 (1)
PI[i]	Barley	3	23	1	4	24	44	1	20:0 (tr)
PS[i]	Barley	3	31	2	4	6	49	4	20:0 (3)
PC[i]	Barley	1	19	<1	2	19	55	4	20:0 (<1)
LPC[i]	Barley	1	27*	<1	2	13*	53	4	

[a]See Table 1 for definitions of abbreviations. tr = trace. * = average of individual values that were not close.
[b]From Hølmer et al (1973).
[c]From Price and Parsons (1980).
[d]From Peer and Leeson (1985).
[e]From Zürcher (1971).
[f]From Briggs (1974).
[g]From Connolly and Spillane (1968).
[h]From Narziss and Mueck (1986a).
[i]From Price and Parsons (1979). NAPE, PMe, and NALPE are given as unknown 1, unknown 2, and DPG in original paper but are probably misidentified. Values are averages for two barleys.

processing as a result of lipoxygenase activity and thermal treatment are also to be expected (Morrison, 1978a).

Several formulas have been' used to calculate the biopotency of the tocopherols relative to that of DL-α-tocopherol acetate (1 mg = 1 IU, biopotency = 1.00). For cereals, the most commonly used values are α-T = 1.49, β-T = 0.60, γ-T = 0.15, and δ-T = 0.37 (Bieri and McKenna, 1981). Beringer and Dompert (1976) gave the same biopotency to tocotrienols as to the corresponding tocol and suggested slightly different factors, namely α-T and α-T-3 = 1.49, β-T and β-T-3 = 0.4, γ-T and γ-T-3 = 0.2, and δ-T and δ-T-3 = 0.02. Hakkarainen et al (1984) measured the biopotency of tocopherols in barley oil fed in mixed rations to chicks and obtained the values α-T = 1.49, β-T = 0.60, γ-T = 0.15, δ-T-3 = 0.37, and total tocopherols = 0.37.

Fatty Acids in Starch Lipids

The FA composition of lipids associated with barley starch is given in Table 20. FFA, in the opinion of this author, are mostly or entirely surface lipid artefacts. The lipids isolated by Goering et al (1975) were comprised of roughly equal amounts of NL and PL, and there is no doubt that the NL were nonstarch lipid artefacts. This would explain the high level of 18:2 and low level of 16:0 in the FFA. On the other hand, the composition of the FFA isolated by Acker and Becker (1971) is more like that of total starch lipids, and they may not have been artefacts. However, monoacyl lipids with saturated FA tend to be absorbed more readily than those with unsaturated FA, so the

TABLE 19
Composition of Tocopherols in Barley (mg/kg)

	α-T	β-T	γ-T	δ-T	α-T-3	β-T-3	γ-T-3	δ-T-3
Whole grain[a]	2	0.4	0.3	0.1	11	3	2	
Whole grain[b]	4	3	0.5	0.1	13	7	2	
Whole grain[c]	4.6	0.2	0.7	0.2	13	2.7	8.4	0.7
Whole grain[d]	11.6	0.4	12.9	0.9	36.0	14.3	...	3.9
Whole grain[e]	11.7	0.6	4.9	0.9	49.3	9.6	14.0	3.8
Meal[f]	3	1	1	1	16	6	6	
Barley[g]	3	0.5	0.5	0.4	12.0	3.0	1.6	
Germ[b]	123–210	5	24–29	...	...	...	...	...
Pearled barley[i]	0.4	tr[j]	tr	...	5.1	3.2	1.2	
Pearled barley[i]	0.8	0.5	0.5	tr	6.7	4.8	2.3	

[a] From Slover et al (1969). Slover (1971) and Bauernfeind (1977) cite these values but give β-T = 4, δ-T = 1.
[b] From Slover (1971), collected data (five samples) from literature.
[c] From Barnes (1983b).
[d] From Hakkarainen et al (1983a). Data recalculated from percent composition and total of 80 mg of tocopherols per kilogram; γ-T-3 appears to be included in γ-T figure.
[e] From Hakkarainen and Pehrson (1987); mean values for six samples.
[f] From Piironen et al (1986).
[g] From Govind Rao and Perkins (1972). Data recalculated from average percent composition for two samples and total of 2.1 mg of tocopherols per 100 g. Identity of tocopherols in Soxhlet extracted oil verified by gas chromatography-mass spectrometry.
[h] From Barnes and Taylor (1981), Barnes (1982).
[i] From Bauernfeind (1977). Second entry given as barley was probably pearled barley.
[j] Trace.

composition of surface lipid artefacts (which may exist as guest molecules in amylose-lipid complexes) tends to be more like that of true starch lipids. The data given for LPC and for total starch lipids (which are >90% LPL) by Morrison et al (1984), De Man and Cauberghe (1988), and Tester et al (1991) are in excellent agreement and are typical for nonwaxy barley starch. FA composition changes in starch of developing grain (Becker and Acker, 1972; Tester and Morrison, 1993). In 12 waxy and six nonwaxy starches from mature grain, total saturated FA varied inversely with the lipid content of the starches (Tester and Morrison, 1992).

The figures given by Weihrauch et al (1976) are from food composition tables, and the source of their information is not given, but the figures are clearly atypical and indicate that the starch was contaminated with nonstarch lipids like that used by Goering et al (1975).

ENZYMES ACTING ON LIPIDS

Lipase

Triglyceride acyl hydrolase, or lipase (E.C. 3.1.1.3), acts at the oil-water interface to release long-chain FAs from TG (Brockerhoff and Jensen, 1974;

TABLE 20
Fatty Acid Composition (%) of Starch Lipids

Lipids[a]	14:0	16:0	18:0	18:1	18:2	18:3
FFA[b]	1.3	12.7	0	8.2	73.2	3.3
FFA[c]	1.7	45.9	3.0	9.0	33.6	4.5
FAME[b]	1.0	25.6	1.4	8.9	59.7	2.0
MG + DG[b]	tr[d]	34	4	25	31	tr
LPC[c]	0.5	44.3	...	3.8	45.6	4.1
Total lipids[e]	...	40.1	2.5	8.2	45.3	3.8
Total lipids[f]	...	48–62	2–4	3–5	30–42	1–3
Total lipids[g]	...	48–52	1–2	2–4	40–45	3–4
Total lipids[h]	...	68–70	2	3	24–26	1–2
Total lipids[i]	...	23	2	10	61	5
Total lipids[j]	...	34–38	3–5	9	43–47	5
Total lipids						
Waxy[k]	...	62–72	0–6	3–6	14–32	0–2
Nonwaxy[k]	...	47–56	1–6	2–4	36–44	2–4
Waxy Hector[l]	...	57–61	1	3–7	32–37	1–2
Hector[l]	...	44–54	1–2	3–5	38–42	2–8

[a] See Table 1 for definitions of abbreviations.
[b] Data for lipid classes (probably all artefacts) in one sample, from Goering et al (1975).
[c] Data for FFA and LPL in one sample, from Acker and Becker (1971).
[d] Trace.
[e] Data for one sample, from De Man and Cauberghe (1988).
[f] Data for 31 samples, from Morrison et al (1984).
[g] Data for nine nonwaxy starches, from Tester et al (1991).
[h] Data for three waxy starches, from Tester et al (1991).
[i] From Weihrauch et al (1976); data erroneous—see text.
[j] From De Man and Vervenne (1988).
[k] From Tester and Morrison (1992); total saturated FA of 12 waxy and six nonwaxy starches inversely correlated with total lipid content ($r = -0.974$) given in Table 12.
[l] From Tester and Morrison (1993); samples from barleys at 20, 30, 40, and 50 days after anthesis.

Galliard, 1983a; Morrison, 1988a). The enzyme should not be confused with esterases that hydrolyze water-soluble substrates such as triacetin, tributyrin, fluorescein dibutyrate, and 4-methylumbelliferonebutyrate. Unfortunately, many authors have used assays based on water-soluble substrates to study cereal lipases, and their results and conclusions are therefore open to question. Wheat esterase is more heat labile than wheat lipase (O'Conner and Harwood, 1992). However, lipase and esterase activities sometimes change in a similar manner (e.g., in germinating grain), so the general trends are not necessarily wrong. The most satisfactory assays for lipase in cereals are based on measurement of FFA liberated from natural TG or from added triolein (MacLeod and White, 1962; Drapron and Sclafani, 1969; Narziss and Sekin, 1974; Pryakhina et al, 1980; Matlashewski et al, 1982; Galliard, 1983b; O'Conner and Harwood, 1992).

At least two types of lipase must exist. Since TG in spherosomes of immature pericarp tissue disappears during grain ripening in the course of pericarp senescence, bran tissues must contain a lipase. In mature wheat, lipase activity is concentrated in the bran (Galliard, 1986; O'Conner et al, 1992), although one cannot exclude the presence of microbial lipases, which can also be very active (Galliard, 1983a). In other cereals, much lipase activity is associated with layers external to the starchy endosperm (Galliard, 1983a), and there is no reason why barley should be different. Wheat bran lipase and wheat germ lipase have different molecular weights, pH optima, and sensitivity to heat (O'Conner and Harwood, 1992). Lipase activity in barley is very similar to that in wheat and shows high specificity toward TG as substrate (O'Conner et al, 1992).

The second type of lipase is present in latent form bound to aleurone (and scutellar?) protein bodies. When the tissue is stimulated by gibberellic acid, the enzyme is readily released and is transferred to the spherosome membrane, where it hydrolyzes TG (Fernandez and Staehelin, 1987a,b). Thus, the protein body lipase should be relatively inactive in dormant grain but very active from the earliest stages of germination. MacLeod and White (1962), using a triolein assay, found most lipase activity to be in embryo- and aleurone-rich fractions of mature (nongerminating) grain. Lipase can hydrolyze TG dispersed on solid substrates at 0.15–0.20 water activity (Acker and Beutler, 1965), but maximum hydrolysis occurs at 0.8 water activity, corresponding to 17% moisture content (Drapron, 1972; Galliard, 1983a,b). Lipase is the enzyme normally responsible for losses of TG and increases in FFA in stored products, especially those that have been milled. The optimum pH for barley lipase is at near neutrality (Baxter, 1984). Narziss and Sekin (1974) reported an optimum temperature of 37°C at pH 8.0–8.5 in barley and at pH 7.5–8.0 in malt. Increases in FFA on parboiling barley are caused by lipase, which is progressively inactivated by the cooking and drying stages (Doronin and Zalesskaya, 1989).

Polar Lipid Acyl Hydrolase, Phospholipases-A and -B, and Lysophospholipase

Enzymes that hydrolyze acyl ester bonds of polar glycerolipids (Fig. 3) have been variously described as polar lipid acyl hydrolase (PLAH), lipid (or lipolytic) acyl hydrolase, monoglyceride lipase, galactolipase, phospholipase-A, phospholipase-B, and lysophospholipase (Galliard, 1983a,b; Morrison, 1978a, 1988a). Where the enzyme has been tested on a range of substrates, all polar glycerolipids exhibiting surfactant properties (i.e., capable of existing in the monodisperse state and as micellar dispersions in aqueous media) are hydrolzyed, but triglyceride is not a substrate (Galliard, 1978, 1983a).

In the case of barley, the identification of LPC and FFA in starch, and of LPC, FFA, and choline in malt and wort, led researchers to consider only phospholipases (Acker, 1985).

There are four ester bonds in PC (and other diacyl PL) that may be hydrolyzed. Phospholipase-D (see next section) hydrolyzes the phosphate-base ester bond giving (from PC) phosphatidic acid (PA) and free choline. Phospholipase-C hydrolyzes the other phosphate ester bond to give DG and the phosphate-base product, but its activity in barley and malt is insignificant (Acker, 1985).

Hydrolysis of the two acylester bonds could be attributed to an initial hydrolysis by a phopholipase-A (giving an LPL and FFA) followed by a lysophospholipase, or to the stepwise action of a single enzyme, phospholipase-B (Acker, 1985).

In wheat, the FA compositions of LPC and LPE from starch are very similar to those of the 1-position FA in PC and PE of the nonstarch lipids (Arunga and Morrison, 1971), which strongly indicates involvement of a specific phospholipase-A_2 in the synthesis of these starch lipids via the corresponding diacyl PL. The FA data for the same lipids in barley are very similar, although

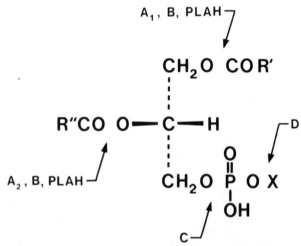

Fig. 3. Sites of enzymatic hydrolysis on a diacylglycerophospholipid. R' = 1-position fatty acid, R" = 2-position fatty acid. In lysophospholipids, R" is replaced by H, and, with isomerization, R' is distributed about 90% at the 1-position and about 10% at the 2-position. X = choline, ethanolamine, serine, glycerol, or N-acylethanolamine (Morrison, 1978a). Sites of attack are indicated by arrows. A_1, A_2, B, C, and D refer to corresponding phospholipases (see text). PLAH (polar lipid acyl hydrolase) hydrolyzes acyl ester bonds in all types of phospholipids, in galactosylglycerides (PO[OH]OX replaced by one to four galactosyl residues), and in diglycerides (PO[OH]OX replaced by H) and monoglycerides (R" also replaced by H).

less complete (Tables 18 and 20), and the same conclusions apply. However, no phospholipase-A_2 has been characterized in any cereal. It is worth noting that this enzyme gives equimolar amounts of LPL and FFA and that properly purified barley (and wheat) starches have almost no FFA, although there are LPL throughout the starch granules, so there must be a supplementary mechanism to remove the FFA or an alternative biosynthetic route to LPL. Rebmann and Acker (1973) suggested that phospholipase-B (below) produces starch LPL from diacyl PL, but there is no indication that this enzyme (which may be PLAH) exhibits the necessary positional specificity in the initial hydrolysis to account for the FA composition of the starch LPL. There would also need to be a special mechanism such as formation of amylose-lipid complexes to prevent complete hydrolysis of the LPL (Baisted, 1983). Baisted (1979) studied the incorporation of acetate-2-[^{14}C] and choline-Me-[^{14}C] into free (nonstarch) LPC and starch-bound LPC in developing barley but did not characterize the enzymes involved or address the points discussed above.

It is well established that there can be complete stepwise hydrolysis of PC via LPC to glycerylphosphorylcholine and FFA in germinating barley and malt, and this has been attributed to a phospholipase-B (Acker and Geyer, 1968a,b, 1969; Rebmann and Acker, 1973; Nolte et al, 1974). The enzyme preparations were not tested on substrates other than PC and PE, so it cannot be said that the enzyme is more specific than PLAH. Phospholipase-B is activated by FFA (Acker and Geyer, 1968b) and in this respect resembles potato PLAH (Galliard, 1978). The term phospholipase-B is generally obsolete in other areas of plant biochemistry.

A substantial part of the grain PL is in the starch granules. When the starch polysaccharides are degraded by amylases during germination, the starch LPL do not accumulate but are hydrolyzed (at a comparable rate) to water-soluble glycerophosphate esters and FFA (Baisted, 1983). The enzyme responsible was identified as lysophospholipase, which, for the reasons discussed above, may be PLAH. It has been characterized in soluble and particulate forms; the activity curve has an optimum at pH 8 and a lesser peak at pH 5; the enzyme is concentrated in aleurone and scutellar tissues (Baisted, 1981, 1983; Baisted and Stroud, 1982a,b; Fujikura and Baisted, 1983, 1985; Lundgard and Baisted, 1986); and activity increases in response to gibberellic acid (Baisted and Stroud, 1982b; Lundgard and Baisted, 1984).

Phospholipase-D

Phospholipase-D is present in developing barley and reaches peak activity when the grain is mature (Nolte et al, 1974). The enzyme hydrolyzes diacyl PL, and to a lesser extent LPL, at the phosphate-base ester bond, liberating free choline, ethanolamine (from PC and PE, respectively), and PA (Nolte and Acker, 1975a). The properties of the barley enzyme in vitro were determined by Nolte and Acker (1975b). The hydrolytic action of the enzyme is not considered important in malting and brewing compared with that of phospholipase-B. However, the enzyme also acts as a transferase in alcoholic solvents, forming PMe from any diacyl PL in chloroform-methanol-water extracting solvents and phosphatidyl butanol in water-saturated butanol (Galliard, 1983a; Acker, 1985). Unless precautions are taken to heat-inactivate the enzyme, these artefacts are likely to be formed (Morrison, 1988a) and are often misidentified (see footnotes to Tables 5 and 13; also Morrison et al, 1980).

Lipoxygenase

Lipoxygenase (LOX, E.C. 1.13.11.12) utilizes atmospheric oxygen to oxidize the cis-1, cis-4-pentadiene part of (n-6) and (n-3) polyunsaturated FAs (linoleate and linolenate in cereals) to hydroperoxides or hydroperoxy radicals as primary products. In cereals, these are largely converted to numerous nonvolatile and volatile products by enzymatic mechanisms, and to a lesser extent by nonenzymatic mechanisms. Free radicals generated by LOX can also initiate autoxidation, which is less specific and entirely nonenzymatic. Reviews on lipoxygenase have been published by Veldink et al (1977), Vliegenthart and Veldink (1977, 1980), Morrison (1978a, 1988a), Gardner (1980, 1988), Galliard and Chan (1980), and Galliard (1983a). Experimental work on this enzyme is full of pitfalls that can lead to erroneous conclusions (Gardner, 1980), and this may explain some of the discrepancies in the literature discussed below.

Lipoxygenases have been categorized in several ways according to their pH optima, substrate specificity, and oxidation mechanisms. According to Belitz and Grosch (1982), Type-1 LOX has optimum activity at near-neutral pH, acts only on free linoleic and linolenic acids (in cereals), produces very little volatiles, and has weak co-oxidation activity. By contrast, Type-2 LOX has optimum activity at neutral to alkaline pH, oxidizes free and esterified linoleate and linolenate, produces much more volatiles, and causes significant cooxidation of carotenoids, tocopherols, and proteins when these are present. LOX from ungerminated (quiescent) barley and the other cereals is all Type 1. Type-2 LOX is found in legumes, and the original soya enzyme (soya lipoxygenase-1, Theorell enzyme) is Type 2. The other soya isoenzymes (soya LOX-2 and LOX-3) are Type 1.

Lipoperoxidase is the name given to the enzyme that converts hydroperoxy acids into hydroxy acids, but this enzyme has never been separated from LOX in cereals and is considered to be the same enzyme (Gardner, 1980). Linoleate hydroperoxide isomerase (LHI), first described by Vick and Zimmerman (1968) and Zimmerman and Vick (1970), converts the dienoic hydroperoxides into monoenoic ketohydroxy acids (α-ketols). Other enzymes also described as isomerases give epoxyhydroxy acids. The mechanisms for these conversions have not been fully elucidated and may be partially enzymatic and partially nonenzymatic (Gardner, 1980). There is no hydroperoxide lyase in barley (Gardner, 1980; Lulai et al, 1981).

The optimum pH for barley LOX under assay conditions ranges from 6.0 to 7.98 (Table 21). Much of this variation can be attributed to differences in substrate concentration and other such factors. It is worth remembering that in vitro conditions may not be a particularly accurate guide to LOX behavior in vivo (including germination and malting). For example, wheat and soya LOX oxidation of various substrates in doughs is much greater than indicated by assays (Morrison and Panpaprai, 1975), and the kinetics of LOX adsorbed onto hydrophobic surfaces are not the same as in aqueous solutions with emulsified substrates (Wheeler and Wallace, 1978).

LOX is located almost exclusively in the embryonic tissues of quiescent barley (Franke and Frehse, 1953; Lulai and Baker, 1975; Yabuuchi and Amaha, 1975; Lulai et al, 1981), and activity increases on steeping and germination (Lulai and Baker, 1975; Yabuuchi, 1978; Baxter, 1982; Schwarz and Pyler, 1984; Von Ceumern and Hartfiel, 1984), with highest specific activities in rootlets and acrospire (Lulai and Baker, 1975; Lulai et al, 1981). A second LOX isoenzyme appears on germination (Yabuuchi, 1976) and is more active toward esterified substrates (discussed below); this may be Type 2.

LOX-1 (from quiescent barley) is more active toward free linoleic acid than free linolenic acid. Baxter (1982) and Fretzdorff and Joerdens (1986) observed no activity toward esterified substrates, but Lulai and Baker (1976), Heimann and Timm (1977a), and Yabuuchi (1976) reported low activity toward methyl linolate; Lulai and Baker (1976) were the only group to report oxidation of both methyl linoleate and trilinolein. LOX-2 from germinated barley embryos is much more active toward methyl linoleate and trilinolein (Yabuuchi, 1976) and may have been present in the barley used by Lulai and Baker. LOX activity in germinating barley is poorly correlated with activity in the original grain and is not affected by gibberellic acid (Schwarz and Pyler, 1984). There can be appreciable differences in LOX levels due to cultivar, location, and year-to-year variation (Schwarz and Pyler, 1984).

LOX in aqueous extracts is heat-stable up to 50°C but is rapidly inactivated at 65–70°C (Lulai and Baker, 1976; Fretzdorff and Joerdens, 1986), and none of the LOX in malt survives kilning (Lulai and Baker, 1975). Ca^{2+}, Mg^{2+}, CN^-, and ethylenediaminetetraacetic acid (EDTA) have little or no effect on barley LOX (Yabuuchi and Amaha, 1975; Lulai and Baker, 1976; Fretzdorff and Joerdens, 1986), but agents that attack thiols ($HgCl_2$, *p*-chloromercuribenzoate, *N*-ethylmaleimide, Cu^{2+}) and ascorbic acid are strongly inhibitory (Lulai and Baker, 1976). In complete disagreement, Yabuuchi and Amaha (1975) obtained no inhibition with $HgCl_2$, and Fretzdorff and Joerdens (1986) obtained only 30% inhibition. LOX is strongly inhibited by its own product, linoleate hydroperoxide (Yabuuchi and Amaha, 1975) if it is not removed by further metabolism.

Of the enzymes that metabolize the primary hydroperoxides, only LHI has

TABLE 21
Optimum pH for Barley Lipoxygenase Under Assay Conditions

pH	References
6.0	Fretzdorff and Joerdens (1986)
6.0	Lulai and Baker (1976)
6.5	Von Ceumern and Hartfiel (1984)
6.5	Führling (1975)
6.8	Franke and Frehse (1953)
7.0–7.5	Yabuuchi (1976)[a]
7.2–7.3	Heimann and Timm (1977a)[b]
7.5	Yabuuchi (1976)[c]
7.5	Yabuuchi and Amaha (1975)
7.75–7.80	Heimann and Timm (1977a)[d]

[a] Lipoxygenase-2 from germinated embryo.
[b] 0.25% linoleic acid in spectrophotometric assay medium.
[c] Lipoxyenase-1 from embryo of ungerminated grain.
[d] 0.1% linoleic acid in polarographic assay medium.

been characterized (Zimmerman and Vick, 1970; Lulai and Baker, 1975; Yabuuchi and Amaha, 1976; Lulai et al, 1981; Schwarz and Pyler, 1984). LHI is located in the embryo of quiescent grain but, unlike LOX, it is not water-soluble unless a detergent such as Tween is used. LHI activity increases in parallel with LOX activity on germination and is not affected by gibberellic acid (Lulai and Baker, 1975; Lulai et al, 1981; Schwarz and Pyler, 1984). However, it differs from LOX in that activity is concentrated in the rootlets and there is little in the embryo and acrospire (Lulai and Baker, 1975). Yabuuchi and Amaha (1976) found that LHI activity in embryos decreased with germination time; the contradiction might be explained if they had discarded rootlets, but this is not clear from their paper. LHI is slightly more heat-stable than LOX and can survive kilning (Lulai and Baker, 1975; Schwarz and Pyler, 1984). The enzyme is active from pH 5.5 to 9.0 and is little affected by 1 mM $CuSO_4$, KCN, EDTA, iodoacetamide, iodoacetate, and N-ethyl-maleimide but strongly inhibited by mercuric acetate (Yabuuchi and Amaha, 1976).

Most cereal LOXs exhibit a high degree of stereospecificity in hydrogen abstraction (at C-11 of linoleate) and in the configuration of the primary hydroperoxide, which is normally 9-D_s-LOOH (Morrison, 1978a, 1988a; Gardner, 1980). The 13-L_s-LOOH isomer is also formed by some isoenzymes, but under certain suboptimal conditions a near racemic mixture of D- and L-9-LOOH and 13-LOOH is formed and the products become very similar to those formed by autoxidation. The ratios of 9-LOOH and 13-LOOH reported for barley LOX (which include LOX-2 in germinated samples) are given in Table 22. Lulai et al (1981) have questioned the validity of some methods used to determine isomer ratios and to characterize products (below).

The nonvolatile products of linoleic acid (including LOOH) that have been identified in flour-water reaction systems are shown in Table 23. Quantities

TABLE 22
Linoleic Acid Hydroperoxide Isomers Formed by Barley Lipoxygenase

Test Material	pH	Isomer Ratio: 9-LOOH to 13-LOOH[a]	References
Seed	6.5	96:4	Führling (1975)
Seed	6.8	89:11	Graveland et al (1972)
Seed	7.0	90:10	Heimann and Timm (1977a)
Seed	7.75	70:30	Heimann and Timm (1977a)
Seed, mature	6.0	70:30	Lulai et al (1981)
Seed, five days[b]	6.0	41:59	Lulai et al (1981)
Embryo	7.5	90:10	Yabuuchi and Amaha (1975)
Embryo[c]	7.0	96:4	Yabuuchi (1976)
Embryo, three days[b]	7.0	75:25	Yabuuchi (1976)
Embryo, five days[b]	7.0	73:27	Yabuuchi (1976)
Embryo, seven days[b]	7.0	70:30	Yabuuchi (1976)
Embryo, LOX-1[d]	7.0	100:0	Yabuuchi (1976)
Embryo, LOX-2[e]	7.0	0:100	Yabuuchi (1976)

[a] See Table 23 for definitions.
[b] Period of germination.
[c] Ungerminated.
[d] LOX-1 from ungerminated embryo (type-1 LOX).
[e] LOX-2 from germinated embryo (type-2 LOX).

have been estimated from thin-layer chromatograms to decrease in the order C, A, G, E, B, D, F, in each case with isomers 1 and 2 in the same ratios as the 9- and 13-LOOH shown in Table 22 (Graveland et al, 1972). Lulai et al (1981) identified fewer products—quiescent barley LOX gave mostly α-ketol, whereas germinated barley LOX gave appreciable quantities of products A, C, and D (as in Table 23) and 11-hydroxy-12,-13-epoxy-9-*cis*-octadecenoic acid and 11-hydroxy-9-,10-epoxy-13-*cis*-octadecenoic acid (not identified by Graveland et al, 1972), which they attributed to the action of LHI. They did not consider that LOX-2 might affect the pattern of products.

LHI occurs as two isoenzymes (both with optimum activity at pH 6.5–6.8) that act at equal rates on 9-LOOH and 13-LOOH (Yabuuchi, 1978). The major products are α-ketols (A1→C1, A2→C2 in Table 23), but there are appreciable amounts of the corresponding γ-ketols.

The α-ketol from 9-LOOH (product C1) gives high yields of hexanal, a characteristic volatile from germinating barley (Yabuuchi, 1978). Heimann and Timm (1977b) identified hexanal, *trans*-2-heptenal, and *trans*-2-octenal in products formed by LHI from equimolar 9-LOOH and 13-LOOH. They showed subsequently (Heimann and Timm, 1977c) that 13-LOOH was the precursor of hexanal and *trans*-2-octenal, whereas 9-LOOH apparently did not yield any volatiles.

Trihydroxy acids (G1–G3 in Table 23) are very bitter-tasting substances (Biermann et al, 1980) and are thought (G1 and/or G2) to be the precursors of *trans*-2-nonenal, a substance contributing to stale cardboard off-flavor in beer.

LIPIDS IN DEVELOPING GRAIN

There is not much information on lipids in developing barley, but the pattern should be very similar to that in developing wheat (Morrison, 1978a, 1988a).

TABLE 23
Nonvolatile Products Formed by Barley Lipoxygenase from Linoleic Acid

Code	Product	Abbreviated
A1	9-hydroperoxy-10-*trans*-12-*cis*-octadecadienoic acid[a,b]	9-LOOH
A2	13-hydroperoxy-11-*trans*-9-*cis*-octadecadienoic acid[a,b]	13-LOOH
B1	9-hydroxy-10-*trans*-12-*cis*-octadecenoic acid[a]	9-LOH
B2	13-hydroxy-11-*trans*-9-*cis*-octadecenoic acid[a]	13-LOH
C1	9-hydroxy-10-oxo-12-*cis*-octadecenoic acid[a,b]	α-ketol
C2	13-hydroxy-12-oxo-9-*cis*-octadecenoic acid[a,b]	α-ketol
D1	9-hydroxy-12-oxo-10-*trans*-octadecenoic acid[a]	γ-ketol
D2	13-hydroxy-10-oxo-11-*trans*-octadecenoic acid[a,b]	γ-ketol
E1	9,10-dihydroxy-12-*cis*-octadecenoic acid[a]	L(OH)$_2$
E2	12,13-dihydroxy-9-*cis*-octadecenoic acid[a]	L(OH)$_2$
F1	9-oxo-12-,13-dihydroxy-10-*trans*-octadecenoic acid[a]	LO(OH)$_2$
F2	13-oxo-9-,10-dihydroxy-11-*trans*-octadecenoic acid[a]	LO(OH)$_2$
G1	9-,12-,13-trihydroxy-10-*trans*-octadecenoic acid[a]	L(OH)$_3$
G2	9-,10-,13-trihydroxy-11-*trans*-octadecenoic acid[a]	L(OH)$_3$
G3	9-,10-,11-trihydroxy-12-*trans*-octadecenoic acid[c]	L(OH)$_3$

[a] Reported by Graveland et al (1972).
[b] Reported by Lulai et al (1981).
[c] Reported by Esterbauer and Schauenstein (1977a,b).

Storage lipids in wheat increase throughout grain development, or decrease slightly during the late stages of ripening, while structural (nonstarch) lipids tend to stabilize at near maximum levels. Starch levels in wheat also increase with grain development, and starch lipids increase with starch amylose content (Morrison and Gadan, 1987).

In barley, the free lipids (which are mostly storage lipids in spherosomes), the structural nonstarch lipids, and the starch lipids were all found to increase up to about 24 DAA; then all categories decreased to grain maturity at 42 DAA (De Man and Cauberghe, 1988). The magnitude of the decreases is much greater than in wheat and suggests incomplete extraction of lipids as the grain dried out and became more difficult to analyze (Morrison, 1988a). MacGregor et al (1971) observed similar changes in total lipid content, and Nilsson et al (1967) noted that FFA content decreased with maturity, as in other cereals (Morrison, 1978a, 1988a). Zakryzhevskaya et al (1979) reported that TG increased from 28 to 54% of the total lipids as grain ripened.

Becker and Acker (1972), Baisted (1979), McDonald et al (1991), and Tester and Morrison (1993) all found that starch LPL increased up to grain maturity, in parallel with amylose content. Becker and Acker (1972) also reported that FFA content decreased from quite high levels at 10 DAA to minimum values at 30 and 53 DAA, but these particular lipids may have been surface lipid artefacts. Becker and Acker (1972) and Rebmann and Acker (1973) suggested that phospholipase-B hydrolyzed PC (a nonstarch lipid) to give LPC (a starch lipid). Baisted (1983) points out that synthesis of starch and its lipids is compartmentalized within the amyloplast, that there is no evidence for phospholipase-B within the amyloplast, and that the mode of synthesis of the starch lipids is still not known. One might add that if LPC is formed outside the amyloplast, it would need to cross the amyloplast membranes via a special transport mechanism because it is capable of disrupting the polar lipid bilayer of membranes and causing cell lysis (Galliard and Bowler, 1987).

In all lipid categories, FA composition shows a marked decrease in linolenate and an increase in linoleate at early stages of grain development, and thereafter FA composition remains fairly constant (Becker and Acker, 1972; De Man and Cauberghe, 1988; Tester and Morrison, 1993). This is the normal pattern in cereal lipids.

CHANGES IN LIPIDS IN STORED GRAIN

As a general rule, lipids are quite stable in sound stored grain, although there may be small long-term losses attributable to respiration. Safe storage conditions require optimized control of grain moisture content (water activity), equilibrium relative humidity, temperature, and oxygen content of the atmosphere (Morrison, 1978a, 1988a). Gamma-irradiation at levels used to preserve grain has negligible effects on lipid content and FA composition (El-Farra et al, 1977). Tocopherols in forage barley are best preserved by reducing the moisture content of the grain.

When grain is stored under adverse conditions (usually at a moisture content well above 14%), there is a much greater loss of lipids and also more active lipolysis, leading to increases in FFA—a common index of storage deterioration (Pomeranz, 1971; Takigawa and Ohyama, 1976; Morrison, 1978a, 1988a;

Galliard, 1983a). Grain quality and lipid deterioration are invariably worse under conditions that permit mold growth. Anaerobic storage of barley (17.5–24% moisture) is reported to prevent changes in fat content (Belcheva and Petrova, 1986).

According to McGee and Christensen (1970), increases in FFA are not seen until invasion of fungi is quite visible; hence FFA levels are not useful for predicting early invasion of fungi or storage stability.

Changes in the surface lipids of barley kernels on storage are of interest as a possible cause of decreased dormancy (Skarsaune et al, 1972; Briggs, 1974; Hareland and Madson, 1989). High levels of FFA and lipid peroxides have also been suggested as causes of disorders in pigs fed storage-deteriorated barley (Connolly and Spillane, 1968).

Skarsaune et al (1972) found changes in lipid content, lipid composition, and FA composition in whole grain, husk, endosperm (nonstarch), and aleurone that did not relate to a well-defined break in dormancy from two to four weeks postharvest. However, the lipids analyzed would include much more than any theoretical barrier to oxygen and water necessary to initiate germination, so the results of this study were inconclusive. Although Briggs (1974) did study the testa lipids as a possible impermeable barrier, he did not compare lipids from fresh and stored grain. Hareland and Madson (1989) compared the germinative capacity of grains before and after extraction of surface lipids with chloroform-methanol (1:1, by volume) and found that both water sensitivity and innate dormancy were reduced by this treatment. The FA composition of the total grain lipids changed little on storage at 20°C for up to 12 weeks, but there were losses of about two-thirds of the unsaturated FA (18:1, 18:2, and 18:3) in the surface lipids. Mysheva et al (1981) reported small increases in linoleate and small decreases in linolenate and palmitate in barley starch stored for three months at room temperature; linoleate content correlated with germinative vigor.

Connolly and Spillane (1968) found that total lipid content remained constant on storage for up to 14 days, but FFA content increased appreciably with storage time and with moisture content in the range 18–26%. On longer storage, there were decreases in free lipids with corresponding increases in bound lipids and substantial increases in lipid peroxides. As before, the extent of the changes increased with time and grain moisture content. McGee and Christensen (1970) also found some binding of free lipids (measured as petroleum-extractable FA) in grain stored for 30 days at 25°C and 13.7% moisture, but no growth of molds. However, although most kernels stored at 15.9% moisture became visibly contaminated with *Aspergillus glaucus*, free lipid content actually increased, with FA composition remaining reasonably constant. They concluded that measurement of FFA was of little value for judging storability or deterioration risk.

CHANGES IN LIPIDS IN GERMINATING BARLEY

There are two principal ways in which cereal lipids change on germination. First, storage lipids (spherosomes) are used as a source of metabolic energy and as a source of FAs from which new membrane lipids are made. Second, proliferation of membranes in actively metabolizing and growing tissue requires new structural lipids, which are mostly PL, synthesized from the pool of FAs. Taken alone, the literature on lipids in germinating barley does not give a particularly well-balanced perspective, but both aspects are well covered in more detail in general reviews of cereal lipids (Morrison, 1978a, 1988a; Clarke et al, 1983) and in the introductions to some research papers on lipids in germinating barley (Firn and Kende, 1974; Newman and Briggs, 1976; Fernandez and Staehelin, 1987a,b).

Hernandez et al (1967) studied six barley varieties, each at three protein levels, and found that total lipids (Table 2) and free lipids (Table 6) decreased by 10-50% on malting in each variety. In general, losses were greatest at intermediate protein levels ($\sim$14%) and least at high protein levels (15-16%). Anness (1984) reported lower lipid levels (as total FA) in commercial malts than in barleys and similar levels in experimental maltings.

In hydroponically sprouted barley, total lipids were lower after two days, then increased to a level slightly higher than the original level (up to seven days), which suggests that net synthesis had overtaken lipid oxidation for metabolic energy (Peer and Leeson, 1985).

Shin et al (1981) reported a decrease of only 12% (from an average of 3.3% to one of 2.9%) in total lipids of four Korean malting varieties. In a later study of changes over seven days of malting (Shin et al, 1986), free lipids decreased from 2.26 to 1.62%, bound lipids from 0.53 to 0.42%, and total lipids from 2.79 to 2.04% (all on a dry-weight basis)—relative decreases of 28, 21, and 27%, respectively. Mysheva et al (1981) reported decreases of 39-50% and 46-57% after seven and nine days of malting, respectively.

Krauss et al (1972) found that total FA decreased by at least 50% over eight days of malting, but levels of FFA, MG, and DG remained fairly constant. They attributed the loss of lipids to respiration and to incorporation of FA into lipids of the rootlets. Byrne et al (1983) showed that most decreases were in the TG fraction—total NL, GL, and PL were 2,167, 314, and 319 mg/100 g of barley and 1,735, 291, and 286 mg/100 g of malt, respectively. The compositions of NL, GL, and PL in malt are given in Tables 3-5.

MacLeod and White (1961) found that nearly all the (free) lipid in the embryo was consumed on germination, but this does not agree with the later and more detailed studies of Hølmer et al (1973), who found that the lipid content of the scutellum (Table 8) was little changed after five days of germination but that about half of the lipids in the coleorhiza and coleoptile were consumed.

Since much of the storage lipids survive malting, it is not surprising that the composition of the total NL in malt (Table 3) shows only moderate decreases in TG. The GL (Table 4) and PL (Table 5) are affected much less by malting. The NL of embryonic tissues (Table 9) show similar changes (Hølmer et al, 1973).

In the FAs of the total lipids (Table 14) and free lipids (Table 15), the general trend is for 16:0 to increase while 18:2 and 18:3 decrease, but the opposite trend is seen in the bound lipids (Table 16). The presence of conjugated dienoic FA and small decreases in 18:2 and 18:3 acids in malt within one day of flooring (Holmberg and Sellmann-Persson, 1967) indicate LOX activity.

Mobilization of spherosome lipids begins within 1 hr of steeping during the lag phase before the activity of induced enzymes such as α-amylase increases.

Gibberellic acid stimulates the transfer of inactive lipase from aleurone protein bodies to the spherosome membrane so that hydrolysis of TG can proceed (Fernandez and Staehelin, 1987a,b). The activity of lipase and other enzymes is stimulated by exposure of germinating barley to temperatures of 0°C or even −9°C (Abdurazakova and Arslanbekova, 1984). Newman and Briggs (1976) consider that some of the aleurone lipid is converted to sucrose for the growing embryo.

The distribution of "lipase" activity in sectioned germinated grains has been studied by following the release of fluorescein from fluorescein dibutyrate using microscopy (Gibbons, 1981; Jensen and Heltved, 1982). Fluorescence spreads from the scutellar region of the starchy endosperm in parallel with cell-wall breakdown (shown by the absence of fluorescence in cell-wall regions when stained with Calcofluor). In reality, this test is more likely following esterase activity, and one would expect to see true lipase activity concentrated much more in the aleurone and scutellum, where most of the substrate spherosomes are located.

In whole malt, lipase activity increases with germination time (Hernandez et al, 1967; Narziss and Sekin, 1974; Krikunova et al, 1982), and activity is enhanced by germinating at higher temperatures (12, 15, or 18°C) and at higher moisture contents (40, 44, or 48%) (Narziss and Sekin, 1974). Malt lipase activity varies during kilning at 50°C, and is greater in dry malt than in green malt. However, the enzyme is progressively inactivated if the malts are kilned at increasing temperatures from 70 to 100°C (Narziss and Sekin, 1974). According to Matlashewski et al (1982), barley, wheat, and rye flours have about 1/10th of the lipase activity of oat flour, and barley is anomalous in that lipase activity is less after two days of germination, whereas it is greater in the other cereals. This unexpected observation was not explained. Steryl ester hydrolase activity also increases and can account for higher levels of free sterols after eight days of germination (Hughes and Goad 1983). However, de novo synthesis of sitosterol has also been demonstrated in excised embryos (Lenton et al, 1975).

The development of new endoplasmic reticulum in aleurone cells shortly after imbibition indicates activation of phospholipid metabolic pathways. In the first few hours, gibberellic acid has no quantitative or qualitative effect on lipid synthesis, measured by ^{3}H-glycerol incorporation (Firn and Kende, 1974), but the hormone has been found to stimulate membrane development and phospholipid synthesis in isolated aleurone layers at later stages (Evins and Varner, 1971; Johnson and Kende, 1971; Koehler et al, 1972; Koehler and Varner, 1973; Ben-Tal, 1975). This apparently conflicting evidence has not been satisfactorily resolved (Firn and Kende, 1974; Clarke et al, 1983).

During germination, starch polysaccharides and LPL disappear at similar rates (Baisted, 1981; Fujikura and Baisted, 1983). Hydrolysis of the LPL is attributed to a lysophospholipase, which may be a more general polar lipid acyl hydrolase. The enzyme is found in the aleurone and starchy endosperm in germinating barley, and activity of the soluble and particulate forms is enhanced by gibberellic acid (Baisted and Stroud, 1982a,b; Fujikura and Baisted, 1983). The fates of the FFA and glycerophosphate ester products have not been determined.

TECHNOLOGICAL ASPECTS OF LIPIDS

Interactions with Starch

From the nutritional point of view, the fatty acyl moieties of the starch lipids (Table 20), which account for 20-27% of the total FA in the grain (De Man and Vervenne, 1988), are more relevant than the native LPL. These lipids, by analogy with wheat starch lipids (Morrison, 1978c), are exceptionally resistant to autoxidation. The segments of V-amylose complexed with LPL are also resistant to digestion in vitro with α-amylase and mineral acid (lintnerization), leaving an insoluble residue (Morrison et al, 1993a). However, the complex is digested in the lower gut (Holm et al, 1983), so both LPL and amylose should be available nutritionally.

It is commonly supposed that in native cereal starch granules the monoacyl lipids occur as guest molecules in inclusion complexes with single helix (V-type) amylose, but with older analytical methods this point could be neither proved nor disproved (Morrison and Milligan, 1982; Morrison, 1988a,b). There is always a possibility that complexes will form with FFA and LPL in any situation that permits even limited swelling of starch granules, or under conditions that permit starch granule annealing (Lorenz and Kulp, 1984). The existence of amylose-lipid complexes in native barley starches has now been proved beyond doubt using ^{13}C-nuclear magnetic resonance, differential scanning calorimetry, and various methods of chemical analysis (Morrison et al, 1993b). Lipid-saturated inclusion complexes of amylose with LPL contain 10.2% (Acker, 1977) to 12.5% lipid (Kugimiya and Donovan, 1981; Morrison et al, 1993b), whereas complexes with FFA contain 7-8% lipid depending on FA chain length and unsaturation (Karkalas and Raphaelides, 1986). Contrary to early reports, cis-polyunsaturated acids form complexes nearly as readily as saturated acids of the same chain length (Morrison, 1985; Karkalas and Raphaelides, 1986). In practice, cereal starches contain sufficient monoacyl lipids to form lipid-saturated complexes with about one-third of their amylose.

Lipids affect some of the technologically important properties of starch granules. Gelatinization, meaning disordering of crystallites, is a property of amylopectin that *appears* to be unaffected by starch lipids. There is some evidence that amylose complexed with LPL raises gelatinization temperature, while lipid-free amylose has the opposite effect (Morrison et al, 1993b). The associated process of granule swelling is considerably reduced when lipids are present (Tester and Morrison, 1990) by a mechanism that probably involves amylose-lipid inclusion complexes (Tester et al, 1991). Swelling at temperatures above the gelatinization range (approximately 45-70°C for normal barley starches) is a property of the intact amylopectin molecule, and starches with different amylose/amylopectin contents can be compared by recalculating swelling factors based on their amylopectin contents (Tester and Morrison, 1990). Using this approach, Tester et al (1991) obtained the results in Table 13, which show a strong negative correlation ($r = -0.987$, $P < 0.001$) between swelling at 80°C and lipid content for all 12 starches. The six starches from Triumph and Golden Promise gave a similar correlation ($r = -0.948$), which must be attributed to differences in their lipid contents since amylose contents were nearly identical. The overall correlation between swelling factor (SF) at 70°C and lipid content was also significant ($r = -0.936$, $P < 0.001$) at both 70 and at 80°C; an increment of 100 mg in lipid content caused a decrease of 1.0–1.2 in SF(amylopectin [AP]). When data from a previous study (Morrison et al, 1986) were similarly recalculated, SF(AP) at 70°C for 18 starches was negatively correlated with lipid content ($r = -0.936$, $P < 0.001$), and an increment of 100 mg of lipid caused a decrease of 1.7 in SF(AP). Latest studies (Morrison et al, 1993b) show that the situation may be more complicated, swelling being promoted by lipid-free amylose and inhibited nonlinearly by lipid-complexed amylose.

From these experiments it is easy to understand how native starch lipids can affect other technological properties of starches such as swelling, solubilization, and amylograph peak viscosity and setback, as reported in the literature (Morrison and Milligan, 1982). The effects of higher levels of starch lipids can be simulated by adding amylose-complexing monoacyl surfactants (e.g., distilled monoglyceride), but at present low-lipid effects can be obtained only by using suitable barley cultivars and by growing grain at lower temperatures. Surfactants have very little effect on the viscoelastic behavior of gelatinizing waxy barley starch (Eliasson, 1986) because the starch has little amylose and the surfactants do not complex with the amylopectin (Tester and Morrison, 1992).

Native starch lipids and added lipids (usually amylose-complexing surfactants) can modify many of the pasting and retrogradation properties of starches (Morrison and Milligan, 1982; Morrison, 1988a). The pasting properties of barley flour (measured with an amylograph) are affected by removal of free lipids. Comparatively small effects are obtained by adding free lipids, bound lipids, and NL or PoL fractions; the greatest changes are obtained with various FFA and some emulsifiers (Choi and Lee 1984).

Lipids in Brewing

Lipids derived from barley malt, and adjuncts if used, can affect the brewing process and beer properties in several ways. Variations in malt lipid composition are not important compared with differences in brewing procedures that determine the proportions of lipids entering the wort on mashing and the amounts of lipids removed at subsequent stages (MacWilliam, 1971; Krauss et al, 1972, 1975; Wainwright, 1981; Anness and Baxter, 1983; Byrne et al, 1983; Narziss and Mueck, 1986a,b).

Anness and Reed (1985a) determined the amounts of lipids at each stage in a pilot-scale brewery. Starting with malt (273 g of lipid, 3.1% by weight), wort contained 3.8 g of lipid; hopped wort received 3.2 g of lipid from hops, but 6.0 g was then removed in trub, leaving 0.5 g in the wort; and the finished beer contained only 0.1 g of lipid (0.03% of the original lipid). Most of the lipids were removed in spent grains, hot break, and cropped yeast. Similar material balances were obtained in commercial operations (Anness and Reed, 1985b).

Higher malt kilning temperatures (150–195°F) reduce the extractability of lipids (Witt and Sullivan, 1966), whereas higher mashing temperatures (50–68°C) increase the amounts of lipids in wort (Krauss et al, 1972, 1975). Squeezing the grains also increases the amount of lipids extracted, particularly

GL and PL (Anness and Baxter, 1983; Byrne et al, 1983). Over 20 classes of lipid have been identified in wort (Zürcher, 1971); some quantitative data are given in Table 24. The FA compositions of the total lipids and lipid classes in wort (Krauss et al, 1972, 1975; Anness and Reed, 1985a,b) are similar to those of the malt lipids (Tables 14–16). The lipids in beer consist of lower FFA (from yeast) and higher FFA (from malt) with very low levels of DG and MG (Jenkins, 1970; Jones et al, 1975; Krauss et al, 1975; Narziss and Mueck, 1986b; Narziss et al, 1986; DeVries, 1990) and PL (Kanimura, 1965; Silbereisen and Anthon, 1967; Acker, 1985). GL are less affected than NL and PL by brewing and comprise two-thirds of the lipids in a high-lipid beer (Byrne et al, 1983). The component long-chain FAs in beer lipids are much more saturated than in malt and wort (Zürcher, 1971; Krauss et al, 1972, 1975; Sandra and Verzele, 1975; Anness and Reed, 1985a,b; Narziss and Mueck, 1986b). Typical levels of total (free plus esterified) long-chain FAs in beer are 100–300 $\mu g/L$ in normal beers and up to 3,000 $\mu g/L$ in very high-lipid beers (Krauss et al, 1972, 1975; Sandra and Verzele, 1975; Anness and Reed, 1985a; Narziss et al, 1986; DeVries, 1990).

High levels of lipids can give unacceptable turbidity and cause problems if not removed (Narziss and Mueck, 1986a,b). The lipids in trub and haze material are very similar (Holmberg and Sellmann-Persson, 1967), consisting of partial glycerides and FFA (30 and 43%, respectively), sterols and steryl esters (14 and 9%), oxygenated compounds (32 and 27%), and phospholipids (22 and 18%). The oxygenated compounds were probably formed by LOX at an early stage of malting and would include precursors of off-flavors.

Another possible cause of turbidity and haze is formation of inclusion complexes between linear α-$(1\rightarrow4)$-glucan chains, derived from starch, and monoacyl lipids (Murtagh, 1974; Krueger and Strobl, 1984, 1985), similar to the amylose-lipid complexes discussed above. These complexes are resistant

TABLE 24
Compositions of Lipids in Worts and Beers

Lipid Class[a]	Grain Squeezings[b] (mg/L)	Hopped Wort[b] (mg/L)	Control Beer[b] (mg/L)	High-Lipid Beer[b] (mg/L)	Swedish Wort[c] (mg/L)	Sweet Wort[d] (mg/L)	Pitching Wort[d] (mg/L)	Beer[e] ($\mu g/L$)
SE	7	8	<1	3	2	1	tr[f]	...
TG	307	3	...	1	10	15	2	...
FFA	96	13	6	3	...	28	2	120–420
S	...	...	...	...	1	...	...	...
DG	...	...	...	...	1	3	<1	3–14
MG	...	...	...	...	6	2	<1	10–92
GL + PL	...	...	...	...	3	15	2	...
GL	236	29	4	30	...	...	...	...
PL	230	tr	3	3	...	...	...	...

[a] See Table 1 for definitions of abbreviations.
[b] From Byrne et al (1983). No DG resolved; PL in grain squeezings = PE, PI, PS, and PC (18, 12, 7, and 203 mg/L, respectively).
[c] From MacWilliam (1968).
[d] From Anness and Reed (1985a); lipids expressed as mg of FA per liter.
[e] From Krauss et al (1972, 1975).
[f] Trace.

to amylolytic digestion, but technological measures can prevent them from being transferred to beer. The inhibitory effects of lipids on the amylolysis of starch described by Wainwright (1981) seem exaggerated in view of more recent findings (Morrison, 1988a) and the results of Krueger and Strobl (1984).

Under oxygen-limiting conditions, hot-extracted worts, which have more lipids than normal, are beneficial to yeast growth and wort attenuation (Wainwright, 1981). This is probably because the wort lipids provide *cis*-unsaturated FA and sitosterol for the yeast (Taylor et al, 1979), which does not have sufficient oxygen for desaturase activity, and also explains why beer FAs have much less unsaturated FAs than wort (above). Added ^{14}C-labeled lipids have been recovered in the yeast structural lipids (Chen, 1980). However, wort lipids are not essential for oxygen-requiring yeast cells if ergosterol is supplied (David, 1974). It should also be noted that high levels of wort lipids (in trub) suppress ester formation by yeast and give beers with inferior flavor (Äyräpää and Lindström, 1973).

Scission products formed from oxidized lipids give volatiles responsible for stale off-flavors in beer. This problem is aggravated by conditions that favor LOX activity in malt, by retention of lipids in beer, by loading wort with oxygen before boiling, and by oxygen entrained during filling (Narziss and Mueck, 1986a,b). It is widely accepted that a trihydroxy FA (G2 in Table 23) is the precursor of the volatile *trans*-2-nonenal associated with cardboard flavor (Drost et al, 1971, 1974; Graveland et al, 1972; Stenroos et al, 1976; Esterbauer and Schauenstein, 1977a,b; Tressl et al, 1979; Yabuuchi and Yamashita, 1979; Barker et al, 1983). Numerous other secondary oxidation products, also formed from linoleic and linolenic acids, have been isolated from wort and beer (Drost et al, 1971; Tressl et al, 1979; Barker et al, 1983; Peppard et al, 1983), and they may be at least as important as causes of stale off-flavor. *Trans*-2-nonenal and 2-methylfurfural added to beer at 1 ppb gave no flavor individually, but they did give a characteristic off-flavor when added together (Drost et al, 1971), and the artificially high level of 250 ppb of *trans*-2-nonenal had no noticeable effect in lager beer (Peppard et al, 1983).

Wainwright (1981) also implicated oxygenated FAs formed by LOX as causes of increased viscosity and decreased rate and extent of wort run-off. His arguments are based on analogy with complexes thought to be formed between GL and gluten proteins in wheat flour doughs, but the quantities of GL and protein in dough are at least 100 times greater, and their effect, if any, is small. It is now thought that the GL behave as surfactants in dough (Morrison, 1989c).

Most of the lipids in beer are polar and therefore have surfactant properties that can affect foam stability or head retention, and they can also affect gushing (Hollemans et al, 1991). There is probably too little lipid in normal beers to have any effect (Blum, 1969; Krauss et al, 1972, 1975; Jones et al, 1975), but there is enough in high-lipid beers to cause a significant reduction in foam stability (Jenkins, 1970; Klopper, 1972; Krauss et al, 1972; Klopper et al, 1975; Roberts et al, 1978; Haboucha et al, 1981; Jackson, 1981; Byrne et al, 1983). GL introduced into hot-extracted worts and from grain squeezings are particularly detrimental (Byrne et al, 1983; Letters et al, 1986). Opinions are also divided on the extent to which FFA affect gushing (Wainwright, 1981). Saturated FFA at 5–20 ppm promote gushing on their own but have no effect if another promoter is present, whereas unsaturated FFA are powerful suppressants (Carrington et al, 1972).

SUMMARY

Lipids have received much less attention than other components of barley that are of more obvious practical importance, e.g., starch, amylases and cell-wall polysaccharides. Consequently, knowledge of lipid composition, functions, and technological properties is incomplete and often poorly understood. This chapter brings together most of the published information on barley lipids and, where necessary, draws parallels with wheat lipids to bridge certain gaps.

No comprehensive quantitative analysis of the numerous classes of lipids in barley has been published, but the exercise is probably not worth the effort because, as in wheat technology, components of groups of lipids (e.g., NL, PoL) have similar properties and each group behaves as a discrete entity. An obvious exception to this statement is FFA, generated by lipolytic enzymes from most lipid classes, the normal substrate for LOX, and the principal type of lipid from barley found in wort and beer.

There is a clear need to develop reliable standard methods for quantifying major groups of lipids, and obsolete methods should then be discarded. The methods should provide the correct information, but this may require supplementary research. For example, total lipids can be determined in various ways for nutritional purposes, but to what extent are spherosomes in intact aleurone cells, or LPL inside starch granules, in animal feed assimilated by ruminant and nonruminant species?

The distribution of lipids within the caryopsis is determined by the functions of the various tissues, as in all cereals, but considerable quantitative variation may occur due to factors that deserve further study. These factors include varietal differences and the interactions of variety or genotype with ambient temperature and other aspects of edaphic (site/environmental) variation during the grain-filling period. Postharvest changes mediated by the enzymes in stored or malting grain also deserve some attention.

The possible importance of lipids in technological situations is often not recognized. The problems here are threefold. The first is poor information on the nature of barley lipids, e.g., starch lipids are not oil (i.e., TG, spherosomes) as is sometimes said, but LPL, which have quite different properties. The second is the need for reliable analytical methods (mentioned above) to quantify lipids present at low levels in difficult materials such as wort and beer. Without such methods, progress will be seriously hindered. The third problem is a generally poor appreciation of the complex biochemical changes (e.g., those initiated by LOX) and physical interactions (e.g., with polysaccharides) in which lipids participate and which affect the organoleptic and rheological properties of diverse products. Literature on these topics relating specifically to barley is sparse, and the reader must therefore turn to the extensive general literature on lipids in cereals and other areas of food technology.

LITERATURE CITED

ABDURAZAKOVA, S. K., and ARSLANBEKOVA, I. G. 1984. Effect of germination temperature on the enzymic activity of barley during malting. Prikl. Biokhim. Mikrobiol. 20:115-118.

ACKER, L. 1977. The lipids of starch—An area of research between carbohydrates and lipids. Fette Seifen Anstrichm. 79:1-9.

ACKER, L. 1985. Phospholipases of cereals. Pages 85-104 in: Advances in Cereal Science and Technology, Vol. 7. Y. Pomeranz, ed. Am. Assoc. Cereal Chem., St. Paul, MN.

ACKER, L., and BECKER, G. 1971. New research on the lipids of cereal starches. II. The lipids of various types of starch and their binding to amylose. Staerke 23:419-424.

ACKER, L., and BEUTLER, H.-O. 1965. Enzymic fat splitting in low moisture foods. Fette Seifen Anstrichm. 67:430-433.

ACKER, L., and GEYER, J. 1968a. The role of phospholipase-B of malted barley in brewing. Brauwissenschaft 21:222-226.

ACKER, L., and GEYER, J. 1968b. Malt phospholipase-B. I. Substrate-activating factors. Z. Lebensm. Unters. Forsch. 137:231-237.

ACKER, L., and GEYER, J. 1969. Phospholipase-B of barley malt. II. Function of the enzyme. Z. Lebensm. Unters. Forsch. 140:269-275.

ALLEN, W. M., PARR, W. H., BRADLEY, R., SWANNACK, K., BARTON, C. R. Q., and TYLER, R. 1974. Loss of vitamin E in stored cereals in relation to a myopathy of yearling cattle. Vet. Rec. 94:373-375.

AMERICAN ASSOCIATION OF CEREAL CHEMISTS. 1983. Approved Methods of the AACC, 8th ed. Method 30-10, approved April 1961, revised October 1975 and October 1981. The Association, St. Paul, MN.

ÅMAN, P., HESSELMAN, K., and TILLY, A.-C. 1985. Variation in the chemical composition of Swedish barleys. J. Cereal Sci. 3:73-77.

ÅMAN, P., and NEWMAN, C. W. 1986. Chemical composition of some different types of barley grown in Montana, USA. J. Cereal Sci. 4:133-141.

ANNESS, B. J. 1984. Lipids of barley, malt and adjuncts. J. Inst. Brew. 99:315-318.

ANNESS, B. J., and BAXTER, E. D. 1983. The control of lipids and their oxidation products in malting and brewing. Pages 193-200 in: Proc. Congr. Eur. Brew. Conv. 19th, London.

ANNESS, B. J., and REED, R. J. R. 1985a. Lipids in the brewery—A material balance. J. Inst. Brew. 91:82-87.

ANNESS, B. J., and REED, R. J. R. 1985b.

Lipids in wort. J. Inst. Brew. 91:313-317.

ARUNGA, R. O., and MORRISON, W. R. 1971. Structural analysis of wheat flour glycerolipids. Lipids 6:768-776.

ASSOCIATION OF OFFICIAL ANALYTICAL CHEMISTS. 1990. Official Methods of Analysis, 15th ed. Method 922.06, page 780. The Association, Arlington, VA.

ÄYRÄPÄÄ, T., and LINDSTRÖM, I. 1973. Influence of long-chain fatty acids on the formation of esters by brewer's yeast. Pages 271-283 in: Proc. Congr. Eur. Brew. Conv. 14th, Salzburg.

BACH KNUDSEN, K. E., and EGGUM, B. O. 1984. The nutritive value of botanically defined mill fractions of barley. 3. The protein and energy value of pericarp, testa, germ, aleurone and endosperm-rich decorticated fractions of the variety Bomi. Z. Tierphysiol. Tierernaehr. Futtermittelkd. 51:130-148.

BAIKOV, V. G., PRYAKHINA, L. N., KATKOVA, O. N., KOROLEV, A. I., and NECHAEV, A. P. 1979. Effect of heating temperature during the "elementary layer" drying of barley grain on its lipid composition. Prikl. Biokhim. Mikrobiol. 15:123-128.

BAISTED, D. J. 1979. Lysophosphatidylcholine biosynthesis in developing barley. Phytochemistry 18:1293-1296.

BAISTED, D. J. 1981. Turnover of starch-bound lysophosphatidylcholine in germinating barley. Phytochemistry 20:985-988.

BAISTED, D. J. 1983. Starch lipids in barley and malt. Pages 93-110 in: Lipids in Cereal Technology. P. J. Barnes, ed. Academic Press, London.

BAISTED, D. J., and STROUD, F. 1982a. Soluble and particulate lysophospholipase in the aleurone and endosperm of germinating barley. Phytochemistry 21:29-31.

BAISTED, D. J., and STROUD, F. 1982b. Enhancement of gibberellic acid and asymmetric distribution of lysophospholipase in germinating barley. Phytochemistry 21:2619-2623.

BARKER, R. L., GRACEY, D. E. F., IRWIN, A. J., PIPASTS, P., and LEISKA, E. 1983. Liberation of staling aldehydes during storage of beer. J. Inst. Brew. 89:411-415.

BARNES, P. J. 1982. Composition of cereal germ preparations. Z. Lebensm. Unters. Forsch. 174:467-471.

BARNES, P. J., ed. 1983a. Lipids in Cereal Technology. Academic Press, London.

BARNES, P. J. 1983b. Nonsaponifiable lipids in cereals. Pages 33-55 in: Lipids in Cereal Technology. P. J. Barnes, ed. Academic

Press, London.

BARNES, P. J. 1983c. Cereal tocopherols. Pages 1095-1100 in: Developments in Food Science, Vol. 5B. Progress in Cereal Chemistry and Technology. J. Holas, ed. Elsevier, Amsterdam.

BARNES, P. J., and TAYLOR, P. W. 1981. α-Tocopherol in barley germ. Phytochemistry 20:1753-1754.

BAUERNFEIND, J. C. 1977. The tocopherol content of food and influencing factors. CRC Crit. Rev. Food Sci. Nutr. 8:337-382.

BAXTER, E. D. 1982. Lipoxidases in malting and mashing. J. Inst. Brew. 88:390-396.

BAXTER, E. D. 1984. Recognition of two lipases from barley and green malt. J. Inst. Brew. 90:277-281.

BECKER, G., and ACKER, L. 1972. Lipids of cereal starches and changes in them during the development of barley. Fette Seifen Anstrichm. 74:324-327.

BECKER, G., and ACKER, L. 1976. Die Lipide der Getreidestärken. M. Ulmann, ed. Paul Parey, Hamburg.

BEKES, F. 1981. Study of purothionin analogues of certain cereals. Acta Aliment. 10:343-356.

BELCHEVA, L., and PETROVA, I. 1986. Chemical composition changes in moist barley grain stored in anoxic conditions. Rastenievud. Nauki 23:6-10.

BELITZ, H.-D., and GROSCH, W. 1982. Lehrbuch der Lebensmittelchemie. Springer Verlag, Berlin.

BEN-TAL, Y. 1975. Activation of phosphorylcholine glyceride transferase by gibberellic acid in barley aleurone cells. Diss. Abstr. Int. B. 35(9):4345.

BERGELSON, L. D. 1973. Diol lipids—New types of naturally occurring lipid substances. Fette Seifen Anstrichm. 75:89-103.

BERINGER, H., and DOMPERT, W. U. 1976. Fatty acid and tocopherol pattern in oilseeds. Fette Seifen Anstrichm. 78:228-231.

BHATTY, R. S. 1982. Distribution of lipids in embryo and bran-endosperm fractions of Risø 1508 and Hiproly barley grains. Cereal Chem. 59:154-155.

BHATTY, R. S. 1986. Physicochemical and functional (breadmaking) properties of hull-less barley fractions. Cereal Chem. 63:31-35.

BHATTY, R. S., and ROSSNAGEL, B. G. 1979. Oil content of Risø 1508 barley. Cereal Chem. 56:586.

BHATTY, R. S., and ROSSNAGEL, B. G. 1980. Lipids and fatty acid composition of Risø 1508 and normal barley. Cereal Chem. 57:382-386.

BIERI, J. G., and McKENNA, M. C. 1981. Expressing dietary values for fat-soluble vitamins: Changes in concepts and terminology. Am. J. Clin. Nutr. 34:289-295.

BIERMANN, U,. WITTMAN, A., and GROSCH, W. 1980. Occurrence of bitter tasting hydroxy fatty acids in oats and wheat. Fette Seifen Anstrichm. 82:236-240.

BLUM, H. 1969. Lipids in malting and brewing—A review. Brew. Dig. 44(10):58, 60, 62-63.

BRIGGS, D. E. 1974. Hydrocarbons, phenols and sterols of the testa and pigment strand in the grain of Hordeum distichon. Phytochemistry 13:987-996.

BRIGGS, D. E. 1987. Endosperm breakdown and its regulation in germinating barley. Pages 456-464 in: Brewing Science, Vol. 3. J. R. A. Pollock, ed. Academic Press, London.

BROCKERHOFF, H., and JENSEN, R. G. 1974. Lipolytic Enzymes. Academic Press, New York.

BYRNE, H., LOUGHREY, M., and LETTERS, R. 1983. A novel technique for investigating the role of lipids in brewing. Pages 659-666 in: Proc. Congr. Eur. Brew. Conv. 19th, London.

CARR, N. O., DANIELS, N. W. R., and FRAZIER, P. J. 1989. Lipid complex formation in wheat flour doughs. Pages 151-172 in: Wheat End-Use Properties. H. Salovaara, ed. Univ. Helsinki, Lahti, Finland.

CARRINGTON, R., COLLETT, R. C., DUNKIN, I. R., and HALEK, G. 1972. Gushing promoters and suppressants in beer and hops. J. Inst. Brew. 78:243-254.

CHEN, E. C.-H. 1980. Utilisation of wort fatty acids by yeast during fermentation. J. Am. Soc. Brew. Chem. 38:148-153.

CHOI, I. S., and LEE, S. R. 1984. Effect of lipid composition on the amylograph characteristics of barley flour. Han'guk Sikp'um Kwahakhoechi 16:99-107.

CHRISTIE, W. W., and MORRISON, W. R. 1988. Separation of complex lipids of cereals by high-performance liquid chromatography with mass detection. J. Chromatogr. 436:510-513.

CHRISTIE, W. W., NOBLE, R. C., and MOORE, J. H. 1970. Determination of lipid classes by a gas-chromatographic procedure. Analyst 95:940-944.

CHUN, H. K., and LEE, S. R. 1984. Lipid composition of barley flour produced in Korea. Han'guk Sikp'um Kwahakhoechi 16:51-58.

CLARKE, N. A., WILKINSON, M. C., and LAIDMAN, D. L. 1983. Lipid metabolism in germinating cereals. Page 57-92 in: Lipids in Cereal Technology. P. J. Barnes, ed.

Academic Press, London.

CONNOLLY, J. F., and SPILLANE, T. A. 1968. Effects of storage, moisture content and high temperature on the lipids in barley. Ir. J. Agric. Res. 7:261-278.

DAVID, M. H. 1974. Absence of nutritional requirement for unsaturated fatty acids by brewers yeast in malt wort. J. Inst. Brew. 80:80-81.

DAWSON, K. R., EIDET, I., O'PALKA, J., and JACKSON, L. L. 1987. Barley neutral lipid changes during the fuel ethanol production process and product acceptability from the dried distillers grain. J. Food Sci. 52:1348-1352.

DE MAN, W. 1985. The effect of genotype and environment on the fatty acid content of barley (*Hordeum vulgare* L.) grains. Plant Cell Environ. 8:571-577.

DE MAN, W., and BRUYNEEL, P. 1987. Fatty acid content and composition in relation to grain-size in barley. Phytochemistry 26:1307-1310.

DE MAN, W., and CAUBERGHE, N. 1988. Changes of lipid composition in maturing barley kernels. Phytochemistry 27:1639-1642.

DE MAN, W., and DONDEYNE, P. 1985. Effect of nitrogen fertilisation on protein content, total fatty acid content and composition of barley (*Hordeum vulgare* L.) grains. J. Sci. Food Agric. 36:186-190.

DE MAN, W., and VERVENNE, B. 1988. Lipid composition of barley in relation to grain size. Phytochemistry 27:2037-2039.

DE VRIES, K. 1990. Determination of free fatty acids in wort and beer. J. Am. Soc. Brew. Chem. 48:13-17.

DEMCHENKO, A. I., OLIFSON, L. E., and NECHAEV, A. P. 1969. Chemical composition of barley oil. Maslo Zhir. Prom. 35:11-13.

DORONIN, A. F., and ZALESSKAYA, E. V. 1989. Lipids of parboiled pearl barley. Izv. Vyssh. Uchebn. Zaved. Pishch. Tekhnol. 3:44-47.

DRAPRON, R. 1972. Enzymic reactions in low-moisture systems. Ann. Technol. Agric. 21:487-499.

DRAPRON, R., and SCLAFANI, L. 1969. A method for the determination of lipolytic activity in solid or dough-consistency biological products. Ann. Technol. Agric. 18:5-16.

DROST, B. W., VAN EERDE, P., HOEKSTRA, S. F., and STRATING, J. 1971. Fatty acids and staling of beer. Pages 451-458 in: Proc. Congr. Eur. Brew. Conv. 13th, Estoril.

DROST, B. W., DUIDAM, J., HOEKSTRA, S. F., and STRATING, J. 1974. Role of individual compounds in beer staling. Tech.

Q. Master Brew. Assoc. Am. 11:127-134.

EL-FARRA, A. A., AHMED, E.-S. A., and ABDEL-MALEK, G. S. 1977. Some effects of gamma irradiation on the biochemical, storage and malt making properties of barley. Agric. Res. Rev. 55:87-100.

ELIASSON, A.-C. 1986. Viscoelastic behaviour during the gelatinization of starch. II. Effects of emulsifiers. J. Texture Stud. 17:357-375.

ESPELIE, K. E., DEAN, B. B., and KOLATTUKUDY, P. F. 1979. Composition of lipid-derived polymers from different anatomical regions of several plant species. Plant Physiol. 64:1089-1093.

ESTERBAUER, H., and SCHAUENSTEIN, E. 1977a. Isomeric trihydroxy acids in beer: Evidence for their presence and their quantitative measurement. Z. Lebensm. Unters. Forsch. 164:255-259.

ESTERBAUER, H., and SCHAUENSTEIN, E. 1977b. Formation of isomeric trihydroxy-octodecenoic acids by enzymic oxidation of linoleic acid by barley. Monatsh. Chem. 108:963-972.

EVINS, W. H., and VARNER, J. E. 1971. Hormone-controlled synthesis of endoplasmic reticulum in barley aleurone cells. Proc. Natl. Acad. Sci. USA 68:1631-1633.

FEDAK, G., and DE LA ROCHE, I. A. 1977. Lipid and fatty acid composition of barley kernels. Can. J. Plant Sci. 57:257-260.

FEDORCHENKO, S. F., and BAIKOV, V. G. 1974. Changes in the fatty acid composition of the lipids of pearled barley following hydrothermal treatment of barley. Vopr. Pitan. (5)70-73.

FERNANDEZ, D. E., and STAEHELIN, L. A. 1987a. Effect of gibberellic acid on lipid degradation in barley aleurone layers. Pages 323-334 in: Plant Growth Control. UCLA Symp. Mol. Cell. Biol., New Ser. 44, Mol. Biol.

FERNANDEZ, D. E., and STAEHELIN, L. A. 1987b. Does gibberellic acid induce the transfer of lipase from protein bodies to lipid bodies in barley aleurone cells? Plant Physiol. 85:487-496.

FIRN, R. D., and KENDE, H. 1974. Some effects of applied gibberellic acid on the synthesis and degradation of lipids in isolated barley aleurone layers. Plant Physiol. 54:911-915.

FRANKE, W., and FREHSE, H. 1953. Autoxidation of unsaturated fatty acids. VI. On the lipoxidase in Gramineae, in particular barley. Z. Physiol. Chem. 295:333-349.

FRETZDORFF, B., and JOERDENS, A. 1986. Comparative studies on substrate specificity, activation and inactivation of lipoxygenases in cereal extracts. Lebensm. Wiss. Technol. 19:437-442.

FÜHRLING, D. 1975. Lipoxygenase and linoleic acid hydroperoxide isomerase in barley (Hordeum vulgare). Ph.D. thesis, University of Berlin. (Cited in Gardner, 1988)

FUJIKURA, Y., and BAISTED, D. 1983. Changes in starch-bound lysophospholipids and lysophospholipase in germinating Glacier and Hi Amylose Glacier barley varieties. Phytochemistry 22:865-868.

FUJIKURA, Y., and BAISTED, D. 1985. Purification and characterization of a basic lysophospholipase in germinating barley. Arch. Biochem. Biophys. 243:570-578.

FULCHER, R. G. 1986. Morphological and chemical organization of the oat kernel. Pages 47-74 in: Oats: Chemistry and Technology. F. H. Webster, ed. Am. Assoc. Cereal Chem., St. Paul, MN.

GALLIARD, T. 1978. Lipolytic and lipoxygenase enzymes in plants and their action in wounded tissues. Pages 155-201 in: Biochemistry of Wounded Plant Storage Tissues. G. Kahl, ed. De Gruyter, Berlin.

GALLIARD, T. 1983a. Enzymic degradation of cereal lipids. Pages 111-148 in: Lipids in Cereal Technology. P. J. Barnes, ed. Academic Press, London.

GALLIARD, T. 1983b. Assays for lipid-degrading enzymes. Pages 403-408 in: Lipids in Cereal Technology. P. J. Barnes, ed. Academic Press, London.

GALLIARD, T. 1986. Hydrolytic and oxidative degradation of lipids during storage of wholemeal flour: Effects of bran and germ components. J. Cereal Sci. 4:179-192.

GALLIARD, T., and BOWLER, P. 1987. Morphology and composition of starch. Pages 55-78 in: Starch: Properties and Potential. T. Galliard, ed. John Wiley, Chichester, UK.

GALLIARD, T., and CHAN, H. W.-S. 1980. Lipoxygenases. Pages 131-161 in: The Biochemistry of Plants, Vol. 4. Lipids: Structure and Function. P. K. Stumpf, ed. Academic Press, New York.

GARDNER, H. W. 1980. Lipid enzymes: Lipases, lipoxygenases and "hydroperoxidases". Pages 447-504 in: Autoxidation in Food and Biological Systems. M. G. Simic and M. Karel, eds. Plenum Press, New York.

GARDNER, H. W. 1988. Lipoxygenase pathways in cereals. Pages 161-215 in: Advances in Cereal Science and Technology, Vol 9. Y. Pomeranz, ed. Am. Assoc. Cereal Chem., St. Paul, MN.

GERVAIS, P., ST. PIERRE, C. A., and LOISELLE, F. 1987. Comparisons of three spring cereals and of some of their cultivars

harvested for forage and grain. Can. J. Plant Sci. 67:137-145.

GIBBONS, G. C. 1981. On the relative role of the scutellum and aleurone in the production of hydrolases during germination of barley. Carlsberg Res. Commun. 46:215-225.

GOERING, K. J., JACKSON, L. L., and DE HAAS, B. W. 1975. Effect of some non-starch components in corn and barley starch granules on the viscosity of heated starch-water suspensions. Cereal Chem. 52:493-500.

GOVIND RAO, M. K., and PERKINS, E. G. 1972. Identification and estimation of tocopherols and tocotrienols in vegetable oils using gas chromatography-mass spectrometry. J. Agric. Food Chem. 20:240-245.

GRAVELAND, A., PESMAN, L., and VAN ERDE, P. 1972. Enzymatic oxidation of linoleic acid in barley suspensions. Tech. Q. Master Brew. Assoc. Am. 9:98-104.

GROZDOVA, E. A., and POTEMKINA, L. Y. 1979. Change in the lipid complex of barley during hydrothermal processing. Probl. Kachestva I Biol. Tsennosti Pishch. Produktov. L. pp. 163-168.

HABOUCHA, J., DEVREUX, A., and MASSCHELEIN, C. A. 1981. The lipids of wort and their effect on foam stability. Pages 451-459 in: Proc. Congr. Eur. Brew. Conv. 18th, Copenhagen.

HAKKARAINEN, J., and PEHRSON, B. 1987. Vitamin E and polyunsaturated fatty acids in Swedish feedstuffs for cattle. Acta Agric. Scand. 37:341-346.

HAKKARAINEN, R. V. J., TYÖPPÖNEN, J. T., and BENGTSSON, S. G. 1983a. Relative and quantitative changes in total vitamin E and isomer content of barley during conventional and airtight storage with special reference to annual variations. Acta Agric. Scand. 33:395-400.

HAKKARAINEN, R. V. J., TYOEPPOENEN, J. T., and BENGTSSON, S. G. 1983b. Changes in the content and composition of vitamin E in damp barley stored in airtight bins. J. Sci. Food Agric. 34:1029-1038.

HAKKARAINEN, R. V. J., TYOEPPOENEN, J. T., HASSAN, S., BENGTSSON, S. G., JÖNSSON, S. R. L., and LINDBERG, P. O. 1984. Biopotency of vitamin E in barley. Br. J. Nutr. 52:335-349.

HARELAND, G. A., and MADSON, M. A. 1989. Barley dormancy and fatty acid composition of lipids isolated from freshly harvested and stored kernels. J. Inst. Brew. 95:437-442.

HARGIN, K. D., and MORRISON, W. R. 1980. The distribution of acyl lipids in the germ, aleurone, starch and non-starch endosperm of four wheat varieties. J. Sci.

Food Agric. 31:877-888.

HARGIN, K. D., MORRISON, W. R., and FULCHER, R. G. 1980. Triglyceride deposits in the starchy endosperm of wheat. Cereal Chem. 57:320-325.

HARWOOD, J. L. 1980. Plant acyl lipids: Structure, distribution and function. Pages 1-55 in: The Biochemistry of Plants, Vol. 4. Lipids: Structure and Function. P. K. Stumpf, ed. Academic Press, New York.

HARWOOD, J. L. 1986. Lipid metabolism. Pages 485-525 in: The Lipid Handbook. F. D. Gunstone, J. L. Harwood, and F. B. Padley, eds. Chapman and Hall, London.

HEIMANN, W., and TIMM, U. 1977a. Characterisation of barley lipoxygenase. Z. Lebensm. Unters. Forsch. 165:5-6.

HEIMANN, W., and TIMM, U. 1977b. Enzymatic breakdown of linoleic acid hydroperoxides to volatile carbonyl compounds by barley isomerase. Z. Lebensm. Unters. Forsch. 165:7-11.

HEIMANN, W., and TIMM, U. 1977c. Volatile carbonyl compounds from the reaction of barley isomerase with linoleic acid. Their development from the 9- or 13-hydroperoxide isomers. Z. Lebensm. Unters. Forsch. 165:12-14.

HERNANDEZ, H. H., BANASIK, O. J., and GILLES, K. A. 1967. Changes in lipase activity and lipid content resulting from malting. Am. Soc. Brew Chem. Proc. pp. 24-31.

HOLLEMANS, M., TORRIES, T. R. J. M., BISPERINK, C. G. J., and RONTELTAP, A. D. 1991. The role of malt lipids in beer foam. Tech. Q. Master Brew. Assoc. Am. 28:168-173.

HOLM, J., BJÖRCK, I., OSTROWSKA, S., ELIASSON, A.-C., ASP, N., LARSSON, K., and LUNDQUIST, I. 1983. Digestibility of amylose-lipid complexes in vivo and in vitro. Starch/Staerke 35:294-297.

HOLMBERG, J., and SELLMANN-PERSSON, G. 1967. Degradation of lipids during malting. Pages 213-217 in: Proc. Congr. Eur. Brew. Conv. 11th, Madrid.

HØLMER, G., ORY, R. L., and HOY, C. E. 1973. Changes in lipid composition of germinating barley embryo. Lipids 8:277-283.

HUGHES, M. A., and GOAD, L. J. 1983. The hydrolysis of steryl esters during the germination of barley seed. Biochem. Soc. Trans. 11:588-589.

JACKSON, G. 1981. A technique for identifying foam damage by lipids. J. Inst. Brew. 87:242-243.

JELSEMA, C. L., MORRÉ, D. J., RUDDAT, M., and TURNER, C. 1977. Isolation and characterization of the lipid reserve bodies, spherosomes, from aleurone layers of wheat. Bot. Gaz. 138:138-149.

JENKINS, C. R. 1970. Some factors influencing head retention and yeast-head fermentation with special reference to commercial wort syrups. J. Inst. Brew. 76:481-485.

JENSEN, S. A., and HELTVED, F. 1982. Visualization of enzyme activity in germinating cereal seeds using a lipase-sensitive fluorochrome. Carlsberg Res. Commun. 47:297-303.

JOHNSON, K. D., and KENDE, H. 1971. Hormonal control of lecithin synthesis in barley aleurone cells and regulation of CDP-choline pathway by gibberellin. Proc. Natl. Acad. Sci. USA 68:2674-2677.

JONES, M. O., COPE, R., and RAINBOW, C. 1975. Changes in the free fatty acids and other lipids in worts during boiling and fermentation. Pages 669-681 in: Proc. Congr. Eur. Brew. Conv. 17th, Nice.

KANIMURA, M. 1965. β-Lysolecithin in brewing. Bull. Brew. Sci. 11:33-39.

KARKALAS, J., and RAPHAELIDES, S. 1986. Quantitative aspect of amylose-lipid interactions. Carbohydr. Res. 157:215-234.

KIM, H. K., and SHIN, H. S. 1982. Lipids and fatty acid composition of free and bound lipids in barley grain. Han'guk Sikp'um Kwahakhoechi 14:382-387.

KLOPPER, W. J. 1972. Recent research on foam stability (of beer). Fermentation 68:163-175.

KLOPPER, W. J., TUNING, B., and VERMIERE, H. A. 1975. Free fatty acids in wort and beer. Pages 659-667 in: Proc. Congr. Eur. Brew. Conv. 15th, Nice.

KOEHLER, D. E., and VARNER, J. E. 1973. Hormonal control of orthophosphate incorporation into phospholipids of barley aleurone layers. Plant Physiol. 52:208-214.

KOEHLER, D., JOHNSTON, K. D., VARNER, J. E., and KENDE, H. 1972. Differential effects of mannitol on gibberellin regulated phospholipid synthesis and enzyme activities of the CDP-choline pathway in barley aleurone cells. Planta 104:267-271.

KRAUSS, G., ZÜRCHER, C., and HOLSTEIN, H. 1972. The foam-destroying properties of some malt lipids and their fate during fermentation and brewing. Monatsschr. Brau. 25:113-123.

KRAUSS, G., FORCH, M., and HOLSTEIN, H. 1975. Fate of some malt lipids during fermentation and storage. Monatsschr. Brau. 28:229-237.

KRIKUNOVA, L. N., BAIKOV, V. G., and KALUNYANTS, K. A. 1981. Lipid composition during drying, postharvest ripening and malting of brewing barley. Izv. Vyssh.

Uchebn. Pischch. Tekhnol. (5)40-43.

KRIKUNOVA, L. N., KALUNYANTS, K. A., and BAIKOV, V. G. 1982. Change in lipase activity of brewing barley. Fermentn. Spirt. Promst. (5)30-31.

KRUEGER, E., and STROBL, M. L. 1984. Starch inclusion compounds and their importance in mashing. Monatsschr. Brau. 37:505-512.

KRUEGER, E., and STROBL, M. 1985. The significance of starch inclusion compounds for beer brewing. Pages 347-354 in: Proc. Congr. Eur. Brew. Conv. 20th, Helsinki.

KUGIMIYA, M., and DONOVAN, J. W. 1981. Calorimetric determination of the amylose content of starches based on formation and melting of the amylose-lysolecithin complex. J. Food Sci. 46:765-770, 777.

LEE, S.-Y., KIM, J.-S., and SHIN, H.-S. 1981. A comparative study of the lipid components of barley and malt. II. Composition of polar lipids. Han'guk Sikp'um Kwahakhoechi 13:37-42.

LENTON, J. R., GOAD, L. J., and GOODWIN, T. W. 1975. Sitosterol biosynthesis in Hordeum vulgare. Phytochemistry 14:1523-1528.

LETTERS, R., HURLEY, J. C., and HORAN, H. 1986. Wort lipids affecting beer foam. Monogr. Eur. Brew. Conv. 9:250-261.

LORENZ, K., and KULP, K. 1984. Steeping of barley starch. Effects on physicochemical properties and functional characteristics. Starch/Staerke 36:122-126.

LULAI, E. C., and BAKER, C. W. 1975. The alteration and distribution of lipoxygenase in malting barley and in finished malt. Proc. Am. Soc. Brew. Chem. 33:154-158.

LULAI, E. C., and BAKER, C. W. 1976. Physicochemical characterization of barley-lipoxygenase. Cereal Chem. 53:777-786.

LULAI, E. C., BAKER, C. W., and ZIMMERMAN, D. C. 1981. Metabolism of linoleic acid by barley lipoxygenase and hydroperoxide isomerase. Plant Physiol. 68:950-995.

LUNDGARD, R. P., and BAISTED, D. J. 1984. Characterization of the increased lysophospholipase activity in gibberellic acid-treated barley aleurone layers. Plant Physiol. 74:940-943.

LUNDGARD, R., and BAISTED, D. 1986. Secretion of a lipolytic protein aggregate by barley aleurone and its dissociation by starchy endosperm. Arch. Biochem. Biophys. 249:447-454.

MacGREGOR, A. W., LaBERGE, D. E., and MEREDITH, W. O. S. 1971. Changes in barley kernels during growth and maturation. Cereal Chem. 48:255-269.

MacLEOD, A. M., and WHITE, H. B. 1961. Lipid metabolism in germinating barley. I. The fats. J. Inst. Brew. 67:182-190.

MacLEOD, A. M., and WHITE, H. B. 1962. Lipid metabolism in germinating barley. II. Barley lipase. J. Inst. Brew. 68:487-495.

MacWILLIAM, I. C. 1968. Wort composition—A review. J. Inst. Brew. 74:38-54.

MacWILLIAM, I. C. 1971. Composition of brewing syrups—A review. J. Inst. Brew. 77:295-299.

MADAZIMOV, S. T., TUKHTAMURADOV, Z. T., and IBRAGIMOVA, K. I. 1976. Fatty acid composition of Uzbek barleys and changes during malting. Prikl. Biokhim. Mikrobiol. 12:734-740.

MADSEN, E., MORTENSEN, H. P., HJARDE, W., LEERBECK, E., and LETH, T. 1973. Vitamin E in barley treated with propionic acid with special reference to the feeding of bacon pigs. Acta Agric. Scand., Suppl. 1971(19):169-173.

MARION, D., LE ROUX, C., TELLIER, C., AKOKA, S., GALLANT, D., GUEGEN, J., POPINEAU, Y., and COMPOINT, J. P. 1989. Lipid-protein interactions in wheat gluten: A renewal. Abh. Akad. Wiss. DDR, Abt. Math., Naturwiss., Tech. 1N, Interact. Protein Syst., pp. 147-152. (Chem. Abstr. 113-07-057566)

MATLASHEWSKI, G. J., URQUHART, A. A., SAHASRABUDHE, M. R., and ALTOSAAR, I. 1982. Lipase activity in oat flour suspensions and soluble extracts. Cereal Chem. 59:418-422.

McDONALD, A. M. L., and STARK, J. R. 1988. A critical examination of procedures for the isolation of barley starch. J. Inst. Brew. 94:125-132.

McDONALD, A. M. L., STARK, J. R., MORRISON, W. R., and ELLIS, R. P. 1991. The composition of starch granules from developing barley genotypes. J. Cereal Sci. 13:93-112.

McGEE, D. C., and CHRISTENSEN, C. M. 1970. Storage fungi and fatty acids in seeds held thirty days at moisture contents of fourteen and sixteen per cent. Phytopathology 60:1775-1777.

MORRISON, W. R. 1978a. Cereal lipids. Pages 221-348 in: Advances in Cereal Science and Technology, Vol. 2. Y. Pomeranz, ed. Am. Assoc. Cereal Chem., St. Paul, MN.

MORRISON, W. R. 1978b. Wheat lipid composition. Cereal Chem. 55:548-558.

MORRISON, W. R. 1978c. The stability of wheat starch lipids in untreated and chlorine-treated cake flours. J. Sci. Food Agric. 29:365-371.

MORRISON, W. R. 1981. Starch lipids: A

reappraisal. Starch/Staerke 33:408-410.

MORRISON, W. R. 1983. Acyl lipids in cereals. Pages 11-32 in: Lipids in Cereal Technology. P. J. Barnes, ed. Academic Press, London.

MORRISON, W. R. 1984. Plant lipids. Pages 247-260 in: Research in Food Science and Nutrition, Vol. 5. Food Science and Technology: Present Status and Future Direction. J. V. McLoughlin and B. M. McKenna, eds. Boole Press, Dublin.

MORRISON, W. R. 1985. Lipids in cereal starches. Pages 61-70 in: New Approaches to Research on Cereal Carbohydrates. Progress in Biotechnology. 1. R. D. Hill and L. Munck, eds. Elsevier, Amsterdam.

MORRISON, W. R. 1987. Lipids in wheat and barley starch granules. Pages 438-445 in: Cereals in a European Context. I. D. Morton, ed. Ellis Horwood, Chichester.

MORRISON, W. R. 1988a. Lipids. Pages 373-439 in: Wheat: Chemistry and Technology, 3rd ed. Vol. 1. Y. Pomeranz, ed. Am. Assoc. Cereal Chem., St. Paul, MN.

MORRISON, W. R. 1988b. Lipids in cereal starches: A review. J. Cereal Sci. 8:1-15.

MORRISON, W. R. 1989a. Uniqueness of wheat starch. Pages 193-214 in: Wheat is Unique. Y. Pomeranz, ed. Am. Assoc. Cereal Chem., St. Paul, MN.

MORRISON, W. R. 1989b. Wheat lipids are unique. Pages 319-339 in: Wheat is Unique. Y. Pomeranz, ed. Am. Assoc. Cereal Chem., St. Paul, MN.

MORRISON, W. R. 1989c. Recent progress in the chemistry and functionality of flour lipids. Pages 131-149 in: Wheat End-Use Properties. H. Salovaara, ed. Univ. Helsinki, Lahti, Finland.

MORRISON, W. R. 1992. Analysis of cereal starches. Pages 199-215 in: Modern Methods of Plant Analysis, New Series. Vol. 14, Seed Analysis. H. F. Linskens and J. F. Jackson, eds. Springer-Verlag, Berlin.

MORRISON, W. R. 1993. Cereal starch granule development and composition. Pages 175-190 in: Seed Storage Compounds: Biosynthesis, Interactions and Manipulation. P. R. Shewry and A. K. Stobart, eds. Oxford Univ. Press, Oxford, UK.

MORRISON, W. R., and COVENTRY, A. M. 1985. Extraction of lipids from cereal starches with hot aqueous alcohols. Starch/Staerke 37:83-87.

MORRISON, W. R., and GADAN, H. 1987. The amylose and lipid contents of starch granules in developing wheat endosperm. J. Cereal Sci. 5:263-275.

MORRISON, W. R., and MILLIGAN, T. P. 1982. Lipids in maize starches. Pages 1-18 in: Maize: Recent Progress in Chemistry and Technology. G. E. Inglett, ed. Academic Press, New York.

MORRISON, W. R., and NASIR AZUDIN, M. 1987. Variation in the amylose and lipid contents and some physical properties of rice starches. J. Cereal Sci. 5:35-44.

MORRISON, W. R., and PANPAPRAI, R. 1975. Oxidation of free and esterified linoleic and linolenic acids in bread doughs by wheat and soya lipoxygenases. J. Sci. Food Agric. 26:1225-1236.

MORRISON, W. R., MANN, D. L., WONG, S., and COVENTRY, A. M. 1975. Selective extraction and quantitative analysis of nonstarch and starch lipids from wheat flour. J. Sci. Food Agric. 26:507-521.

MORRISON, W. R., TAN, S. L., and HARGIN, K. D. 1980. Methods for the quantitative analysis of lipids in cereal grains and similar tissues. J. Sci. Food Agric. 31:329-340.

MORRISON, W. R., COVENTRY, A. M., and BARNES, P. J. 1982. The distribution of acyl lipids and tocopherols in flour millstreams. J. Sci. Food Agric. 33:925-933.

MORRISON, W. R., MILLIGAN, T. P., and AZUDIN, M. N. 1984. A relationship between the amylose and lipid contents of starches from diploid cereals. J. Cereal Sci. 2:257-271.

MORRISON, W. R., SCOTT, D. C., and KARKALAS J. 1986. Variation in the composition and physical properties of barley starches. Starch/Staerke 38:374-379.

MORRISON, W. R., TESTER, R. F., GIDLEY, M. J., and KARKALAS, J. 1993a. Resistance to acid hydrolysis of lipid-complexed amylose and lipid-free amylose in lintnerized waxy and non-waxy barley starches. Carbohydr. Res. In press.

MORRISON, W. R., TESTER, R. F., SNAPE, C. E., LAW, R., and GIDLEY, M. J. 1993b. Swelling and gelatinization of cereal starches. IV. Some effects of lipid-complexed amylose and free amylose in waxy and normal barley starches. Cereal Chem. 70:385-391.

MUELLER-MULOT, W., ROHRER, G., OESTERHELT, G., SCHMIDT, K., ALLEMAN, L., and MAURER, R. 1983. Finding of α-, β- and γ-dehydrotocopherols in wheat germ oil by HPLC and GC-MS—A contribution to tocopherol analysis. Fette Seifen Anstrichm. 85:66-72.

MURTAGH, J. E. 1974. The significance of amylose-lipid complexes in distillery maize mashing. Brew. Distill. Int. 4:37-38.

MYSHEVA, E. D., KATKOVA, O. N., and KRIKUNOVA, L. N. 1981. Fatty acid composition of lipids during the postharvest ripening of brewing barley. Tr., Vses. Nauchno Issled. Inst. Zerna Prod. Ego Pererab. 96:62-68.

NARZISS, L., and MUECK, E. 1986a. The behaviour of long-chain free fatty acids during malting and their distribution in the malt grist. Monatsschr. Brau. 39:184-187.

NARZISS, L., and MUECK, E. 1986b. The influence of long-chain free fatty acids on the flavor stability of beer. Monatsschr. Brau. 39:296-230.

NARZISS, L., and SEKIN, Y. 1974. Lipase activity during the malting and brewing process. Monatsschr. Brau. 27:311-320.

NARZISS, L., MIEDANER, H., and MUECK, E. 1986. Determination of free fatty acids in malt, hops and hop products, wort and beer. Monatsschr. Brau. 39:109-114.

NECHAEV, A. P., and SANDLER, Z. Y. 1975. Grain lipids. In: Lipidy Zerna. Kolos, Moscow.

NEWMAN, J. C., and BRIGGS, D. E. 1976. Glyceride metabolism and gluconeogenesis in barley endosperm. Phytochemistry 15:1453-1458.

NILSSON, G., POLGAR, M. V., and WASS, L. 1967. The properties of ripening grain as regards its content of free fatty acids, fungi and succinate oxalase inhibitors. Acta Agric. Scand. 17:257-262.

NODA, M., and UMEDA, Y. 1973. Neutral diol lipids in plant seeds. Kyoto Furitsu Daigaku Gakujutsu Hokoku, Nogaku 25:53-60.

NOLTE, D., and ACKER, L. 1975a. Phospholipase D of cereals. Z. Lebensm. Unters. Forsch. 158:149-156.

NOLTE, D., and ACKER, L. 1975b. Phospholipase D—Occurrence and properties. Z. Lebensm. Unters. Forsch. 159:225-233.

NOLTE, D., REBMANN, H., and ACKER, L. 1974. Phosphatide-hydrolyzing enzymes in grain. Getreide Mehl Brot 28:189-191.

O'CONNER, J., and HARWOOD, J. L. 1992. Solubilization and purification of membrane-bound lipases from wheat flour. J. Cereal Sci. 16:141-152.

O'CONNER, J., PERRY, H. J., and HARWOOD, J. L. 1992. A comparison of lipase activity in various cereal grains. J. Cereal Sci. 16:153-163.

O'PALKA, J., EIDET, I., and JACKSON, L. L. 1987. Neutral lipids traced through the beverage alcohol production process. J. Food Sci. 52:515-516.

PARKER, M. L. 1985. The relationship between A-type and B-type starch granules in the developing endosperm of wheat. J. Cereal Sci. 3:271-278.

PARSONS, J. G., and PRICE, P. B. 1974.

Search for barley (Hordeum vulgare L.) with higher lipid content. Lipids 9:804-808.

PARSONS, J. G., and PRICE, P. B. 1979. Phospholipids of barley grain. J. Agric. Food Chem. 27:913-915.

PEER, D. J., and LEESON, S. 1985. Nutrient content of hydroponically sprouted barley. Anim. Feed Sci. Technol. 13:191-202.

PEPPARD, T. L., BUCKEE, G. K., and HALSEY, S. A. 1983. Relating flavor stability to different raw materials and brewing processes. Pages 549-556 in: Proc. Congr. Eur. Brew. Conv. 19th, London.

PIIRONEN, V., SYVÄOJA, E.-L., VARO, P., SALMINEN, K., and KOIVISTOINEN, P. 1986. Tocopherols and tocotrienols in cereal products from Finland. Cereal Chem. 63:78-81.

POMERANZ, Y. 1971. Biochemical and functional changes in stored cereal grains. CRC Crit. Rev. Food Sci. Technol. 4:45-80.

POMERANZ, Y., BURKHART, B. A., and MOON, L. C. 1970. Composition and utilization of milled barley products. II. Air-fractionated barley flours as adjunct in brewing. Am. Soc. Brewing Chem. Proc. pp. 47-55.

POMERANZ, Y., KE, H., and WARD, A. B. 1971. Composition and utilization of milled barley products. I. Gross composition of roller-milled and air-separated fractions. Cereal Chem. 48:47-58.

PRICE, P. B., and PARSONS, J. G. 1974. Lipids of six cultivated barley (Hordeum vulgare) varieties. Lipids 9:560-566.

PRICE, P. B., and PARSONS, J. G. 1975. Lipids of seven cereal grains. J. Am. Oil Chem. Soc. 52:490-493.

PRICE, P. B., and PARSONS, J. G. 1979. Distribution of lipids in embryonic axis, bran-endosperm and hull fractions of hulless barley and hulless oat grain. J. Agric. Food Chem. 27:813-815.

PRICE, P. B., and PARSONS, J. G. 1980. Neutral lipids of barley grain. J. Agric. Food Chem. 28:875-877.

PRYAKHINA, L. N., ROMANYUK, G. G., SOBINA, G. G., BAIKOV, V. G., and POPOV, M. B. 1980. New method for determining lipase activity of cereal grain crops. Izv. Vyssh. Uchebn. Zaved. Pishch. Tekhnol. 2:102-105.

QU, R., WANG, S.-M., LIN, Y.-H., VANCE, V. B., and HUANG, A. H. C. 1986. Characteristics and biosyntheses of membrane proteins of lipid bodies in the scutella of maize. Biochem. J. 235:57-65.

QURESHI, A. A., BURGER, W. C., PETERSON, D. M., and ELSON, C. E. 1986. The structure of an inhibitor of cholesterol biosynthesis isolated from barley. J. Biol. Chem. 261:10544-10550.

REBMANN, H., and ACKER, L. 1973. Activity of phospholipase B in barley during growth of the seed. Fette Seifen Anstrichm. 75:409-411.

ROBERTS, R. T., KEENEY, P. J., and WAINWRIGHT, T. 1978. The effects of lipids and related materials on beer foam. J. Inst. Brew. 84:9-12.

SANDERSON, P. 1986. A new method of analysis for the determination of crude oils and fats. Recent Adv. Anim. Nutr. 77-81.

SANDRA, P., and VERZELE, M. 1975. Analysis of long-chain fatty acids in beer. J. Inst. Brew. 81:302-306.

SCHWARZ, P. B., and PYLER, R. E. 1984. Lipoxygenase and hydroperoxide isomerase activity of malting barley. J. Am. Soc. Brew. Chem. 42:47-53.

SHIN, H. S., and GRAY, J. I. 1983. Lipids and fatty acid composition of barley grain. Han'guk Sikp'um Kwahakhoechi 15:195-201.

SHIN, H.-S., LEE, K.-H., and LEE, S.-Y. 1981. A comparative study of the lipid components of barley and malt. I. Composition of neutral lipids. Han'guk Sikp'um Kwahakhoechi 13:30-36.

SHIN, S. L., SONG, J. H., and KIM, K. S. 1986. Changes in free, bound and neutral lipids of malt during malting. Han'guk Nonghwa Hakhoechi 29:346-351.

SILBEREISEN, K., and ANTHON, H.-F. 1967. The choline phospholipids of barley malt, wort and spent grains and their influence on the head retention of beer. Monatsschr. Brau. 20:295-303.

SKARSAUNE, S. K., BANASIK, O. J., and WATSON, C. A. 1972. Lipids of post-harvest barley. Am. Soc. Brew. Chem. Proc. pp. 94-97.

SLOVER, H. T. 1971. Tocopherols in foods and fats. Lipids 6:291-296.

SLOVER, H. T., LEHMANN, J., and VALIS, R. J. 1969. Vitamin E in foods: Determination of tocols and tocotrienols. J. Am. Oil Chem. Soc. 46:417-420.

STENROOS, L., WANG, P., SIEBERT, K., and MEILGAARD, M. 1976. Origin and formation of 2-nonenal in heated beer. Tech. Q. Master Brew. Assoc. Am. 13:227-232.

STUMPF, P. K. 1987. Biochemistry of Plants, Vol. 9. Lipids: Structure and Function. Academic Press, New York.

SUKHIJA, P. S., MARWAHA, S. R., NARANG, A. S., and BHATIA, I. S. 1971. Tentative identification of various lipid components and fatty acid composition of barley (*Hordeum vulgare*) seed. Indian J. Agric. Sci. 41:782-785.

SUMNER, A. K., GEBRE-EGZIABHER, A., TYLER, R. T., and ROSSNAGEL, B. G. 1985. Composition and properties of pearled and fines fractions from hulled and hull-less barley. Cereal Chem. 62:112-116.

TAKIGAWA, A., and OHYAMA, Y. 1976. Changes in the fat of some milled grains during storage. Chikusan Shikenjo Kenkyu Hokoku 30:1-7.

TAYLOR, G. T., THURSTON, P. A., and KIRSOP, B. H. 1979. The influence of lipids derived from malt spent grains on yeast metabolism and fermentation. J. Inst. Brew. 85:219-227.

TESTER, R. F., and MORRISON, W. R. 1990. Swelling and gelatinization of cereal starches. I. Effects of amylopectin, amylose, and lipids. Cereal Chem. 67:551-557.

TESTER, R. F., and MORRISON, W. R. 1992. Swelling and gelatinization of cereal starches. III. Some properties of waxy and normal nonwaxy barley starches. Cereal Chem. 69:654-658.

TESTER, R. F., and MORRISON, W. R. 1993. Swelling and gelatinization of cereal starches. VI. Starches from Waxy Hector and Hector barleys at four stages of grain development. J. Cereal Sci. 17:11-18.

TESTER, R. F., SOUTH, J. B., MORRISON, W. R., and ELLIS, R. P. 1991. The effects of ambient temperature during the grain-filling period on the composition and properties of starch from four barley genotypes. J. Cereal Sci. 12:113-127.

TESTER, R. F., MORRISON, W. R., and SCHULMAN, A. H. 1993. Swelling and gelatinization of cereal starches. V. Risø mutants of Bomi and Carlsberg II cultivars. J. Cereal Sci. 17:1-9.

THOMPSON, J. N., and HATINA, G. 1979. Determination of tocopherols and tocotrienols in foods and tissues by high-performance liquid chromatography. J. Liquid Chromatogr. 2:327-344.

TRESSL, R., BAHRI, D., and SILWAR, R. 1979. Formation of aldehydes by oxidation of lipids and their importance as "off flavour" components in beer. Pages 27-41 in: Proc. Congr. Eur. Brew. Conv. 17th, Berlin.

TWEETEN, T. N., WETZEL, D. L., and CHUNG, O. K. 1981. Physicochemical characterization of galactosyldiglycerides and their quantitation in wheat flour lipids by high performance liquid chromatography. J. Am. Oil Chem. Soc. 58:664-672.

TYÖPPÖNEN, J. T., and HAKKARAINEN, R. V. J. 1985. Thermal stability of vitamin E in barley. Acta Agric. Scand. 35:136-138.

VELDINK, G. A., VLIEGENTHART, J. F. G., and BOLDINGH, J. 1977. Plant lipoxygenases. Prog. Chem. Fats Other Lipids 15:131-166.

VICK, B. A., and ZIMMERMAN, D. C. 1968. Properties of lipoxidase and hydroperoxide isomerase from flaxseed and their occurrence in other seeds. Proc. N. D. Acad. Sci. 22:29-33.

VLIEGENTHART, J. F. G., and VELDINK, G. A. 1977. On the mechanism of the reactions catalysed by plant lipoxygenases. Ann. Technol. Agric. 26:175-187.

VLIEGENTHART, J. F. G., and VELDINK, G. A. 1980. Lipoxygenase-catalyzed oxidation of linoleic acid. Pages 529-540 in: Autoxidation in Food and Biological Systems. M. G. Simic and M. Karel, eds. Plenum Press, New York.

VON CEUMERN, S., and HARTFIEL, W. 1984. Activity of lipoxygenase in cereals and possibilities of enzyme inhibition. Fette Seifen Anstrichm. 86:204-208.

WAINWRIGHT, T. 1981. Effect of barley and malt lipids on beer properties. Monogr. Eur. Brew. Conv. 6:118-128.

WEIHRAUCH, J. L., KINSELLA, J. E., and WATT, B. K. 1976. Comprehensive evaluation of fatty acids in foods. VI. Cereal products. J. Am. Diet. Assoc. 68:335-340.

WEIHRAUCH, J. L., POSATI, L. P., ERSON, B. A., and EXLER, J. 1977. Lipid conversion factors for calculating fatty acid contents of foods. J. Am. Oil Chem. Soc. 54:36-40.

WELCH, R. W. 1975. Fatty acid composition of grain from winter and spring sown oats, barley and wheat. J. Sci. Food Agric. 26:429-435.

WELCH, R. W. 1977. A micromethod for the estimation of oil content and composition in seed crops. J. Sci. Food Agric. 28:635-638.

WELCH, R. W. 1978. Genotypic variation in oil and protein in barley grain. J. Sci. Food Agric. 29:953-958.

WHEELER, E. L., and WALLACE, J. M. 1978. Kinetics of wheat germ lipoxygenase adsorbed onto hydrophobic surfaces. Phytochemistry 17:41-44.

WITT, P. R., Jr., and SULLIVAN, J. W. 1966. Wort and beer fatty acids as affected by malt processing conditions. Am. Soc. Brew. Chem. Proc. pp. 233-235.

YABUUCHI, S. 1976. Studies of lipid metabolizing enzymes in barley grains. III. Occurrence of a new lipoxygenase isoenzyme in germinating barley embryos. Agric. Biol. Chem. 10:1987-1992.

YABUUCHI, S. 1978. Hexanal production from linoleic acid in germinating barley grains via a linoleate hydroperoxide isomerase (studies of lipid metabolizing enzymes in barley grains, IV). Nippon Nogei Kagaku Kaishi 52:417-425.

YABUUCHI, S., and AMAHA, M. 1975. Partial purification and characterization of the lipoxidase from grains of Hordeum distichum. Phytochemistry 14:2569-2572.

YABUUCHI, S., and AMAHA, M. 1976. Partial purification and characterization of the linoleate hydroperoxide isomerase from the grains of Hordeum distichum. Phytochemistry 15:387-390.

YABUUCHI, S., and YAMASHITA, H. 1979. Gas chromatographic determination of trihydroxyoctadecenoic acids in beer. J. Inst. Brew. 85:216-218.

ZAKRYZHEVSKAYA, L. T., and SAMBUROVA, G. N. 1977. Composition of lipids in maritime varieties of barley grain. Izv. Vyssh. Uchebn. Zaved. Pishch. Tekhnol. (5)37-40.

ZAKRYZHEVSKAYA, L. T., NECHAEV, A. P., and SAMBUROVA, G. N. 1978. Neutral and polar lipids of barley grain of maritime varieties. Izv. Vyssh. Uchebn. Zaved. Pishch. Tekhnol. (1)33-36.

ZAKRYZHEVSKAYA, L. T., NECHAEV, A. P., and SAMBUROVA, G. N. 1979. Changes in barley lipids during ripening. Izv. Vyssh. Uchebn. Zaved. Pishch. Tekhnol. (6)14-16.

ZIMMERMAN, D. C., and VICK, B. A. 1970. Hydroperoxide isomerase found in flax, barley, wheat germ and maize. Plant Physiol. 46:445-453.

ZÜRCHER, C. 1971. Isolation of some lipids from malt and their quantitative determination in wort and beer. Monatsschr. Brau. 24:276-284.

CHAPTER 6

PHYSIOLOGY AND BIOCHEMISTRY OF GERMINATION IN BARLEY

G. B. FINCHER
Department of Plant Science
University of Adelaide, Waite Campus
Glen Osmond, South Australia 5064

B. A. STONE
Commonwealth Special Research Centre for Protein
 and Enzyme Technology and Department of Biochemistry
La Trobe University
Bundoora, Victoria, Australia 3083

INTRODUCTION

Barley grain is used extensively for the production of alcoholic beverages and as an important ingredient in many stockfeed formulations. Furthermore, claims that grain components exert beneficial effects on serum glucose and cholesterol levels, and on the absorption of other dietary components, could lead to a resurgence of barley utilization in human nutrition (Bhatty, 1993). The central importance of grain germination in the plant's life cycle and in the production of beer and whisky has attracted intense research interest into the physiology and biochemistry of the process. For the purposes of discussing germination physiology and biochemistry, we need only consider the structure and composition of barley grain in overview, with particular emphasis on the aleurone layer and starchy endosperm, the scutellum, and the outer, maternal layers of the grain (Briggs, 1987). The major importance of the outer layers is to provide the grain with strength and rigidity, together with a degree of protection against the penetration of insects and microorganisms. The structure and composition of barley grain have been described in detail elsewhere (Briggs, 1987; Duffus and Cochrane, 1993).

Germination of viable, nondormant barley grain is initiated by the uptake of water. Cuticularized layers in the husk, the pericarp, and the testa-nucellus act as barriers to the penetration of both water and solutes (Briggs, 1987), and most of the water that penetrates undamaged grain does so near the embryo, probably through the micropylar region (Reynolds and MacWilliam,

247

1966; Briggs, 1978). Water subsequently spreads through the grain, but at different rates in the various regions. Not unexpectedly, hydration of the central endosperm occurs relatively late in the uptake process, and mechanical damage to the grain can greatly accelerate the rate of water penetration (Sparrow, 1965; Freeman and Palmer, 1984; Briggs, 1987). Following the initiation of germination, hydrolytic enzymes, which are synthesized mainly in the aleurone and scutellum, are secreted into the nonliving starchy endosperm, where they catalyze the depolymerization of storage polymers. The degradation products move along a diffusion gradient generated by their active uptake into the epithelial layer of the scutellum. After absorption into the scutellum, they are translocated via a developing vascular system to the seedling, where they serve the immediate nutrient and energy needs of the enlarging and differentiating embryo in the period before the establishment of the photosynthetic leaf and absorptive root systems. Based on in vitro evidence, the synthesis and secretion of the hydrolases from these tissues appear to be controlled principally by the hormones gibberellic acid (GA) and abscisic acid (ABA).

Here, we examine the cellular and molecular events associated with germination of the barley grain. The depolymerization of starch, protein, and other reserves of the starchy endosperm requires the concerted action of numerous enzymes, and the degradation products must be transported from the endosperm to the developing embryo. The biochemical events that result in the conversion of aleurone and scutellar reserves into newly synthesized enzymes are considered in the context of de novo protein synthesis and the secretion of the enzymes via the cellular membrane system. Recent advances in our knowledge of hormone perception and the subsequent transduction of signals that lead to transcriptional activation of specific genes in the aleurone and scutellum are related to our increased understanding of the elements responsible for the regulation of barley genes encoding α-amylases and other hydrolytic enzymes. Finally, we examine emerging evidence for the existence of a broadly based defense system that is designed to protect the germinating grain against colonization and infection by a wide range of potentially pathogenic microorganisms.

HORMONE ACTION

Following imbibition of the grain, the germination process is activated. The initial cellular and molecular events in this process are undefined, but they result in the release of diffusible factors from the embryonic axis and possibly from other tissues, which stimulate target tissues elsewhere in the grain. In particular, aleurone cells respond to the factors by synthesizing and secreting hydrolytic enzymes into the starchy endosperm. Indeed, the observation that GA induces α-amylase secretion from barley aleurone cells (Paleg, 1960; Yomo, 1960), coupled with the development of a simple procedure for the isolation of viable aleurone layers that retain hormone sensitivity and an ability to secrete active enzymes (Chrispeels and Varner, 1967), has resulted in the widespread adoption of barley aleurone layers as a model experimental system for in vitro investigations of plant hormone action, the synthesis and secretion of hydrolytic enzymes, and the regulation of plant gene expression (Fincher, 1989; Jones and Jacobsen, 1991). In this section, we examine the role of GA in the induction of hydrolytic enzymes in germinating barley and consider potential roles for ABA in the process.

Gibberellic Acid

It is widely held that gibberellins released from the embryo are primarily responsible for the production of hydrolytic enzymes in barley aleurone cells. Secretion of α-amylase and other hydrolases from detached aleurone layers is greatly enhanced by exogenously applied GA (Paleg, 1960; Yomo, 1960; Chrispeels and Varner, 1967; Stuart et al, 1986). Isolated barley embryos release gibberellins (Radley, 1967), and levels of the hormone increase in the grain during the early stages of germination (Brookes and Martin, 1975). While there remains little doubt that GA plays a central regulatory role in the germination of barley grain, the exact site of synthesis of GA has not been defined, nor has the distribution of the hormone in the grain been established. The embryonic axis (MacLeod and Palmer, 1967), the scutellum (Radley, 1967), and even the aleurone (Atzorn and Weiler, 1983) have been suggested as possible sites of GA synthesis, although participation of the aleurone in GA synthesis has been disputed (Gilmour and MacMillan, 1984; Grosselindemann et al, 1991). The hormone might also be involved in grain development, so that residual GA in mature, dry grain could be an important source of GA in the germinating grain (Raynes and Briggs, 1985; Grosselindemann et al, 1991). Other observations that complicate our understanding of GA action include the variable sensitivities of grain samples to added hormone (Nicholls et al, 1986; Kusaba et al, 1991); this could be related to different levels of residual GA in the grain, to the requirement for specific chemical variants of GA (Gilmour and MacMillan, 1984; Pharis and King, 1985), or to other unknown factors relating to barley genotype and growth conditions. It is not clear whether specific GAs are synthesized in different tissues of the grain or whether target cells are differentially sensitive to the various chemical forms of GA. Barley aleurone does indeed respond to different GAs, as measured by enhanced secretion of α-amylase (Clutterbuck and Briggs, 1973). Using specific inhibitors of reactions in the GA biosynthetic pathway, Grosselindemann et al (1991) have concluded that de novo GA synthesis begins in the embryo 24 hr after imbibition but that the GA produced is not essential for enzyme induction in the aleurone. They further conclude that any signal from the embryo that causes α-amylase induction in the aleurone must originate either from stored GA precursors or by conversion of physiologically inactive GAs into an active form (Grosselindemann et al, 1991); this would be consistent with the very early appearance of α-amylase in imbibed grain. Thus, information on the important chemical variants of GA, their sites of synthesis in the grain, and their mode of action remains incomplete.

Much of our knowledge of GA action in the production of hydrolytic enzymes has been obtained through the incubation of isolated barley aleurone layers (Chrispeels and Varner, 1967) in solutions containing the hormone, followed by the measurement of α-amylase secreted into the medium surrounding the excised aleurone layers. While these in vitro experiments have provided us with valuable information on the induction of GA-sensitive genes and on the enhanced secretion of corresponding enzymes, they have also raised our awareness of the complexity of the induction processes and of our inability to confidently extrapolate the results back to the whole grain. For example, different α-amylase isoenzymes are differentially responsive to GA concentration (Huang et al, 1984; Nolan and Ho, 1988; Chandler and Jacobsen, 1991) and exhibit quite distinct developmental patterns in aleurone layers and intact germinated grain (Jacobsen and Higgins, 1982; Rogers, 1985; Deikman and Jones, 1986; Ho et al, 1987; Chandler and Jacobsen, 1991).

An important first step in the definition of the cellular and molecular mechanisms of GA action is to identify the factors involved in perception of the hormone by aleurone cells. Protein receptors of either plasma membrane or cytosolic origin would presumably mediate the action of the hormone, and various mechanisms for signal perception have been proposed (Fincher, 1989; Jones and Jacobsen, 1991). However, these suggestions are not supported by any experimental data, despite the considerable research effort that has been directed at other aspects of GA action in barley aleurone cells. Recent work by Hooley and his colleagues with oat aleurone offer some hope that GA receptors may soon be identified and characterized. In these experiments, GA immobilized on large, inert beads stimulated α-amylase synthesis in oat aleurone protoplasts (Hooley et al, 1991). Because the beads were too large to enter the cell, the results indicate that GA perception occurs at the protoplast surface and presumably involves a plasma membrane-bound receptor. Furthermore, anti-idiotypic antibodies raised against GA block GA action in oat aleurone protoplasts (Hooley et al, 1991) and could prove valuable as probes for GA receptors (Pain et al, 1988). Purification and characterization of the GA receptors from barley aleurone should now be possible.

The possibility that GA perception occurs at the surface of aleurone cells (Hooley et al, 1991) raises further questions regarding the subsequent transduction of the signal. In other eukaryotic systems, hormone binding to a cell surface receptor elicits a cascade of intracellular responses, mediated by second messenger molecules or activated enzymes, and culminating in altered patterns of gene expression. Several components of such a response have been identified in barley aleurone cells, including a requirement for Ca^{2+} in the GA response (Jones, 1985), GA-regulated Ca^{2+}-adenosine triphosphatases (ATPases) that pump Ca^{2+} across intracellular membranes (Bush et al, 1989; Bush and Jones, 1990), and genes encoding calmodulin (Zielinski, 1987). Furthermore, protein kinases, some of which are Ca^{2+}-dependent, are widely distributed in plants (Elliott and Kokke, 1987; Ranjeva and Boudet, 1987; Saluja et al, 1987; Lamb et al, 1989; Alderson et al, 1991), and cyclic adenosine 5'-monophosphate, putative G-proteins, and adenylate cyclase are also found (Lusini et al, 1991), although none of these has so far been isolated from barley.

It has been suggested that GA might exert its effects nonspecifically, stimulating the expression of all active genes in a cell rather than specific genes (Baulcombe et al, 1984). Thus, GA forms a complex with phosphatidylcholine, and the GA complex can increase membrane fluidity (Wood and Paleg, 1974). However, no good evidence has been presented to support a role for GA in changing membrane function in the aleurone of germinating barley. The mechanism of GA action clearly remains open to speculation, but the technologies are now available to define both the cellular and molecular strategies employed by the cell in the stimulus-response pathway that leads to gene activation. It should be pointed out that the scutellar epithelial layer secretes hydrolytic enzymes (Stuart et al, 1986; McFadden et al, 1988) and that the scutellum may also respond to GA (Stuart et al, 1986), or to other growth regulators, in a fashion analogous to the aleurone layer.

Abscisic Acid

Two distinct effects are observed when aleurone layers isolated from mature barley grain are treated with ABA. First, the hormone suppresses expression of genes encoding GA-inducible enzymes, including $(1 \rightarrow 3),(1 \rightarrow 4)$-$\beta$-glucanases (Mundy and Fincher, 1986), α-amylases (Jacobsen and Beach, 1985; Nolan and Ho, 1988), and endopeptidases (Koehler and Ho, 1990b). Second, ABA enhances the expression of several "ABA-specific" genes in barley aleurone layers (Lin and Ho, 1986). Although the ABA-inducible genes have not all been identified, they include a gene for an inhibitor of endogenous barley α-amylase (Weselake et al, 1985; Mundy and Rogers, 1986). These observations suggest that ABA might act to lower α-amylase activity not only by suppressing new synthesis of the enzyme through the inhibition of transcription of the corresponding genes, but also by inducing specific inhibitors for existing α-amylases in the cell (Jacobsen and Beach, 1985; Rogers, 1985; Deikman and Jones, 1986). The unidentified ABA-inducible genes might encode additional inhibitors of other key hydrolytic enzymes, and the overall effect of ABA may be to slow endosperm mobilization in response to environmental stresses (Fincher, 1989). The observation that dehydration of young barley seedlings significantly increases levels of mRNAs for ABA-inducible genes in the aleurone (Chandler et al, 1987; Chandler and Mosleth, 1990) lends some support for this possibility. Thus, ABA sensitivity may be retained in aleurone cells of mature and germinating grain to permit temporary suspension of endosperm mobilization in the face of transiently unfavorable environmental conditions.

· The mechanism of ABA action in barley aleurone cells is unknown, although the activity of the Ca^{2+}-dependent ATPase of the endoplasmic reticulum (ER) is significantly reduced by ABA, in contrast to its activation by GA (Jones and Jacobsen, 1991). Clearly it is too early to speculate as to the site of ABA perception and whether Ca^{2+} directly participates in signal transduction.

ALEURONE FUNCTION DURING GERMINATION

The respective functions of cells of the starchy endosperm and the aleurone stand in sharp contrast. In mature grain, the cells of the starchy endosperm are nonliving and function solely as reserves of carbohydrate, protein, lipid, and nucleic acids that await mobilization during germination. On the other hand, the aleurone cells of the mature grain remain alive, and on hormonal activation their contents undergo a remarkable sequence of morphological and biochemical changes. This results in their transformation from a dormant to a metabolically active tissue capable of synthesizing and secreting a diverse range of enzymatic proteins needed for the digestive depolymerization of the stored polymers in the starchy endosperm. The aleurone shares this role in endosperm digestion with the scutellar epithelium.

The aleurone component of the endosperm consists of a layer of cuboidal cells, three to four cells in thickness, overlying the surfaces of the starchy endosperm, except at the interface between the starchy endosperm and the scutellum (Briggs, 1987). Jacobsen et al (1985) estimated that there are 100,000 cells in the aleurone layer of a single barley grain. Details of the chemical composition of aleurone cell contents and their cell walls are given in Chapters 2 and 3 of this book (Duffus and Cochrane, 1993; MacGregor and Fincher, 1993). Ontogenetically, the aleurone cells arise from the same triploid fusion nucleus as the starchy endosperm cells. At maturity, the aleurone cells are characterized morphologically by their thick, bilayered walls and by their distinctive cellular contents, which include a large nucleus, mitochondria with poorly developed cristae, and many tightly packed, membrane-bound aleurone grains. The aleurone grains contain globoids, with phytin inclusions, and carbohydrate-rich inclusions or crystalloids (Jacobsen et al, 1971), and they are surrounded by membrane-bound spherosomes, or oleosomes. The spherosomes are also aligned along the plasma membrane (Paleg and Hyde, 1964; Gram, 1982a). The ER is not apparent, and no starch granules are present. The lateral walls of aleurone cells are penetrated by large plasmodesmatal canals (Haberlandt, 1890; Taiz and Jones, 1973).

Morphological Changes

The morphological changes in the protoplast and wall following activation of the aleurone have been recorded by light and electron microscopy (Paleg and Hyde, 1964; Van der Eb and Nieuwdorp, 1967; Jones, 1969a,b; Jones and Price, 1970; Buttrose, 1971; Vigil and Ruddat, 1973; Colborne et al, 1976; Obata, 1979; Jones, 1980; Gram, 1982a). Within 2 hr of GA treatment of isolated aleurone layers, the aleurone grains lose the spherical shape characteristic of water-imbibed cells and show a pronounced increase in volume (Jones, 1969a,b). Associated with the GA-induced changes is a proliferation of ER, followed by a change from single lamellae to stacks, and an increase in the number of membrane-associated ribosomes. Later, the ER further proliferates, the cisternae swell, and vesicles from both the ER and Golgi apparatus increase in abundance. These changes are accompanied by a reduction in the size of aleurone grains and a decrease in the number of spherosomes. Numerous plastids and some microbodies, together with extensive erosion of the outer wall layers, are apparent 20 hr after GA application (Jones, 1969a,b).

Gram (1982a) examined the changes in aleurone cells in malted barley. In sections cut through the grain in an area where active endosperm dissolution has occurred, the overlying aleurone shows distinct mitochondrial and rough ER profiles that are not obvious in the aleurone of resting grain. The aleurone grains are almost empty, but crystalloids are still present in many of them, and spherical microbodies appear in the cells. An occasional Golgi profile is observed, and the aleurone walls show dense inclusions in the outer wall layer but not in the more electron-dense inner layer. Spherosomes are still abundant but are now distributed at random. Secretory vesicles are not seen. At the same time, changes in aleurone cells at the distal end of the grain, where the endosperm is still only partially degraded, are not as advanced, although the aleurone grains are almost empty. In the enzyme secretion phase, but not in the synthesis phase, stacked rough ER is observed (Jones and Price, 1970; Vigil and Ruddat, 1973). After 8 hr spherosomes are dispersed, and at 24 hr the stacked rough ER is wound around mitochondria and the nucleus. Later, a large central vacuole forms. These observations are broadly in agreement with those made by Paleg and Hyde (1964) and Van der Eb and Nieuwdorp (1967), using germinating grains, and by Obata (1979), using embryoless half seeds.

Biochemical Changes

The morphological changes in aleurone cells during germination are accompanied by corresponding changes in their biochemical activities. Thus, increases in respiratory capacity and production of adenosine 5'-triphosphate associated with mitochondrial development and division are necessary for the synthesis of protein, RNA, and membrane lipids. The monomeric constituents of these newly synthesized polymers are obtained through mobilization of aleurone reserves of the mature grain. Proteolysis of the polypeptides stored in aleurone grains is presumably catalyzed by acid carboxypeptidases, acid and neutral aminopeptidases, and dipeptidases present in ungerminated grain (Mikola, 1987; Törmäkangas et al, 1991), although the specific roles of individual peptidases have not been established.

Phosphate required for nucleic acid and phospholipid synthesis is released from the phytin inclusions of aleurone grains by the action of phytases, some of which have been detected as acid phosphatases (Ory and Henningsen, 1969; Ashford and Jacobsen, 1974; Gabard and Jones, 1986). The acid phosphatase of mature aleurone is reported to be highly specific for phytate (Ory and Henningsen, 1969).

Lipases are primarily responsible for the release of fatty acids from triacylglycerol reserves in the spherosomes. It has been suggested that the enzymes are stored in the protein bodies of ungerminated barley aleurone cells and that GA induces their translocation to the spherosomes (Fernandez and Staehelin, 1987). Fatty acids released by lipase action provide precursors for the biosynthesis of phospholipids during cellular membrane proliferation. It is also possible that the fatty acids provide cellular energy through oxidative pathways or are required for glucose synthesis via the glyoxylate pathway following the depletion of soluble sugars that are stored initially in aleurone cells (Fincher, 1989). Enzymes of the glyoxylate pathway and glyoxysomes have been detected in barley aleurone (Jones, 1985).

Secretion of Enzymes

Following their synthesis in the rough ER of the aleurone, there is an intracellular movement of enzymes to the plasma membrane and secretion through the wall into the starchy endosperm. Several pathways have been considered for the transport of enzymes to the plasma membrane, including direct fusion of rough ER with the plasma membrane (Ashford and Gubler, 1984), transport via lysosomes (Gibson and Paleg, 1976), via rough ER-derived vesicles without the participation of any other organelle (Jones, 1969b; Vigil and Ruddat, 1973; Colborne et al, 1976; Pyliotis et al, 1979), or via the Golgi apparatus in Golgi-derived vesicles (Jones and Price, 1970; Fernandez and Staehelin, 1985; Heupke and Robinson, 1985; Gubler et al, 1986; Ashford and Gubler, 1987; Zingen-Sell et al, 1990). Although Chrispeels and Tague (1991) comment that "at the moment there is no credible evidence that proteins delivered to the 'extracellular matrix' do not pass through the Golgi complex," such evidence for secreted aleurone proteins has been difficult to obtain. The cytological profiles of actively metabolizing aleurone cells show very few Golgi complexes (Jones, 1969b; Chrispeels, 1976; Colborne et al, 1976; Gram, 1982a), and Golgi complexes have not been identified in sucrose gradients using typical Golgi marker enzymes (Locy and Kende, 1978), nor have radioactively labeled proteins been found in Golgi apparatus (Chen and Jones, 1974).

However, Fernandez and Staehelin (1985) used ultrarapid freezing techniques followed by freeze-fracture and freeze substitution to show that Golgi complexes are abundant in actively secreting aleurone cells and that there are numerous small vesicles associated with the edges of the Golgi cisternae. They found no evidence for the vesiculation of the ER that has been observed in chemically fixed sections (Jones, 1969b; Vigil and Ruddat, 1973; Colborne et al, 1976) and suggest that the evidence for direct participation of ER-derived vesicles in enzyme secretion is based on artefactual evidence. Further, they could find no evidence for direct fusion between ER cisternae and the plasma membrane.

The involvement of the Golgi apparatus is supported by direct immunocytochemical evidence using polyclonal α-amylase antibodies (Gubler et al, 1986; Zingen-Sell et al, 1990). These antibodies show that the α-amylases are located in both the ER and Golgi apparatus, but they do not indicate how the enzyme is transferred between the rough ER and the Golgi or between the Golgi and the plasma membrane. However, histochemical staining reactions for peroxidase suggest that the rough ER, the Golgi complex, and Golgi-derived vesicles are all involved in peroxidase secretion (Ashford and Gubler, 1987).

The final phase of secretion of enzymes from the aleurone is their apoplastic movement across the bilayered aleurone wall into the starchy endosperm. Several features of this passage are noteworthy. First, the walls of the aleurone cells are composed of polysaccharides that are chemically similar to those found in the starchy endosperm wall (Fincher, 1975; Bacic and Stone, 1981a,b; MacGregor and Fincher, 1993) and hence are potential substrates for wall-degrading polysaccharide hydrolases produced by the aleurone. Second, the pore sizes of plant walls are sufficiently small as to present a barrier to the release of secreted enzymes of the size found in the aleurone (Carpita et al, 1979; Tepfer and Taylor, 1981). These considerations lead to the conclusion that the aleurone walls must be modified to allow passage of the secreted enzymes. However, they must also retain their integrity as supporting structures for the turgid aleurone protoplasts. Available information suggests that the wall is structured to allow such modifications while retaining its supporting role.

During aleurone activation, the thick, outer aleurone wall layer is digested, presumably by polysaccharide hydrolases secreted from the aleurone, whereas the thin, inner wall layer remains intact (Taiz and Jones, 1970; Gram, 1982b; Gubler et al, 1987). When examined by electron microscopy, the thin, inner layer appears fibrillar and stains more intensely than the more electronlucent outer wall layer. A similar staining pattern is observed in a dark sleeve that is present around the plasmodesmatal canals (Taiz and Jones, 1973). Further evidence that the wall presents a barrier to enzyme secretion is shown histochemically by the accumulation of acid phosphatase (Ashford and Jacobsen, 1974), esterase (Pyliotis et al, 1979; Jones, 1987; Benjavongkulchai and Spencer, 1989), and peroxidase (Ashford and Gubler, 1984) in the walls of aleurone cells imbibed for 16 hr in the absence of GA. However, on GA treatment, the histochemical reactions characteristic of these enzymes are lost from the wall. The acid phosphatase in GA-stimulated aleurone is located both between the plasma membrane and the resistant wall layer and in the interstices of the resistant wall, but not in the outer wall layer (Jones, 1987). This suggests that GA treatment makes the inner wall layer permeable but that the wall is not completely digestible by the secreted polysaccharide hydrolases. Thus, selective wall hydrolysis appears to be a prerequisite for enzyme release.

The GA-induced wall hydrolysis begins in the middle lamella around groups of plasmodesmata and in patches spreading from the innermost region of the wall, especially at cell corners (Van der Eb and Nieuwdorp, 1967; Jones, 1972). In the multilayered barley aleurone, digestion begins first in the middle layer of cells and progresses until a system of connecting channels develops around the aleurone cells (Ashford and Gubler, 1984). Finally, only remnants of the outer wall are found, adjacent to the pericarp (Ashford and Jacobsen, 1974). During this process, both the feruloyl-arabinoxylan and the $(1\rightarrow3),(1\rightarrow4)$-$\beta$-glucan of the aleurone walls appear to be digested, although arabinoxylan degradation products can be detected before the appearance of released xylanase itself, while glucose is found later (Taiz and Honigman, 1976; Dashek and Chrispeels, 1977). Thus, there is some difficulty in reconciling the temporal appearance of endoxylanases, $(1\rightarrow3),(1\rightarrow4)$-$\beta$-glucanases, and their degradation products with the pattern of depolymerization of the wall polymers (Ashford and Gubler, 1984; Fincher, 1989).

Role of Ca^{2+}

Experiments with isolated aleurone layers show that exogenous Ca^{2+} stimulates the secretion of α-amylases, $(1\rightarrow3),(1\rightarrow4)$-$\beta$-glucanases, $(1\rightarrow3)$-β-glucanases, endopeptidases, nucleases, and acid phosphatases (Chrispeels and Varner, 1967; Jones and Jacobsen, 1983; Stuart et al, 1986; Jones et al, 1987). The Ca^{2+} is generally assumed to exert its influence at the intracellular transport level, although the mechanism of its action is unclear (Varner and Mense, 1972; Moll and Jones, 1982). Levels of Ca^{2+} in the cytosol are maintained homeostatically in the 200–350 nM range (Bush et al, 1988) but accumulate in the lumen of the ER at concentrations of up to 1 mM (Jones and Jacobsen, 1991) through the action of a specific Ca^{2+} transporter that is located on the ER membrane (Bush et al, 1989). This Ca^{2+} pump appears to be regulated by both GA and ABA in a manner that parallels the effects of the hormones on α-amylase secretion (Bush and Jones, 1990).

SCUTELLAR FUNCTION DURING GERMINATION

The scutellum is a diploid tissue comprising a mass of essentially spherical parenchymatous cells that cover the tissues of the embryonic axis; it has an epithelial layer on its abaxial surface, facing the proximal starchy endosperm (Smart and O'Brien, 1979). The scutellum is a highly specialized structure and functions both in the digestion of the adjacent starchy endosperm in the early stages of germination and in the absorption of the digestion products arising from enzymatic depolymerization of endosperm reserves.

Nieuwdorp and Buys (1964) and Gram (1982a) have made detailed examinations of the scutellum in mature and germinating grain. In mature, dormant seeds, the parenchyma cells have a distinct nucleus and are filled with large numbers of spherosomes, which surround the protein bodies and are aligned along the plasma membrane. The protein bodies are 2–4 μm in diameter, are bound by a single membrane, and contain inclusions that resemble the globoids of aleurone grains. Crystalloid inclusions are not observed. Small numbers of proamyloplasts (protoplastids) are also present, each with a double membrane and containing one or more small starch granules. The starch is concentrated in the cells of the basal third of the scutellum (Smart and O'Brien, 1979). Mitochondria are poorly developed, with few cristae. Little rough ER is visible, and no Golgi profiles are observed. The scutellar epithelium comprises a single layer of elongated cells, 30–40 μm long and 5–8 μm in diameter (Nieuwdorp, 1963; Gram, 1982a). The organelle profile of these cells is very similar in both number and distribution to that observed in the parenchymal cells. The middle lamella is clearly visible, and plasmodesmata are present in the lower ends of the cells.

Morphological Changes

In contrast to the aleurone, which is comprised of one cell type and does not differentiate during germination (Jones, 1985), the scutellum grows, differentiates, and becomes highly vascularized following imbibition of water (Negbi, 1984). Three days after the initiation of germination, the protein bodies of the parenchyma have been altered, and some appear to have been converted to vacuoles (Gram, 1982a). The spherosomes are no longer concentrated around the protein bodies, and their alignment along the plasma membrane is less pronounced. Mitochondria with well-developed cristae are clearly observed, as are rough ER and Golgi profiles. Amyloplasts are present in increased numbers and size. After seven days, amyloplasts containing starch granules of up to 4 μm in diameter are the most abundant organelles in the parenchyma cells. Spherosomes are still present but are decreased in number and are distributed randomly. The abundance of mitochondria, Golgi complexes, and rough ER does not change significantly between three and seven days (Gram, 1982a).

Changes also occur in the cells of the scutellar epithelium (Nieuwdorp and Buys, 1964; Gram, 1982a). Rough ER is apparent, and mitochondria showing distinct cristae are present in increased numbers. Protein bodies with degraded contents are seen, and the spherosomes are more randomly distributed. Amyloplasts are present in increased abundance but are smaller and less numerous than in the parenchyma. Well-defined Golgi complexes, mostly lying close to the plasma membrane, are apparent (Nieuwdorp and Buys, 1964; Gram, 1982a). During germination and early seedling growth, the scutellar epithelial cells elongate to approximately twice their original length (Nieuwdorp and Buys, 1964). In addition, the cells separate from one another laterally along the middle lamella region of the anticlinal wall (Nieuwdorp and Buys, 1964), and the plasma membrane takes on an undulating profile (Gram, 1982a). No detailed histochemical studies have been made on the scutellar epithelial walls, but, like the inner layer of aleurone walls, the relatively thin walls of the scutellar epithelium must be resistant to hydrolysis by, yet permeable to, the wall hydrolases that are secreted into the starchy endosperm. In any case, the separation of the epithelial cells provides a dramatic increase in the surface area of the cells, and the epithelium takes on the appearance of a papillary layer consistent with the absorptive function of the scutellum.

Biochemical Changes

As in the aleurone, the morphological changes in the scutellum and scutellar epithelium are accompanied by activation of metabolic pathways, but little specific information on these processes is available. During germination, proteolysis of storage proteins in the endosperm forms a pool of amino acids and short peptides (Higgins and Payne, 1981). The plasma membrane of the activated scutellum develops a peptide transport system with broad specificity, together with amino acid transport systems (Higgins and Payne, 1977, 1978a,b; Sopanen et al, 1978; Sopanen, 1979). These systems mediate the uptake of amino acids and peptides, against a concentration gradient, and result in their accumulation in the scutellar cells (Walker-Smith and Payne, 1983). The rate of peptide uptake reaches a maximum after about three days of germination. The concentration of peptides (2–4 mM) in the endosperm is very close to the K_m values for the peptide transport system and K_m values of embryo peptidases. The transport system has a pH optimum of 4, which is close to the ambient pH of the endosperm and the optimum pH for endosperm proteolysis. The system is dependent on the maintenance of a proton gradient and involves a dithiol-dependent transport protein (Walker-Smith and Payne, 1983).

MOBILIZATION OF RESERVES IN THE STARCHY ENDOSPERM

As a result of the central importance of endosperm mobilization in the malting and brewing industries, considerable attention has been paid to variations in endosperm dissolution between grain samples and to the three-dimensional patterns of modification within the grain (Briggs, 1987). Dissolution of the starchy endosperm in germinated barley grains begins in the region adjacent to the scutellum and proceeds from the proximal to the distal end of the grain in a front that is approximately parallel to the scutellar epithelium (Brown and Morris, 1890; Briggs and MacDonald, 1983). Because of the incline of the scutellum within the grain, modification of the starchy endosperm on the dorsal side of the grain appears more advanced than on the ventral side.

The dissolution patterns reflect temporally and spatially coordinated secretion of hydrolytic enzymes from the specialized tissues that surround the starchy endosperm. It is now clear that both the scutellum and aleurone participate in endosperm mobilization in barley. Enzymes secreted from the scutellar epithelium initially degrade the endosperm adjacent to the scutellum. As germination proceeds, the aleurone layer becomes the principal source of hydrolytic enzymes (Gibbons, 1981; McFadden et al, 1988), in a manner that may circumvent problems imposed by lengthening diffusion pathways between enzymes secreted from the scutellum and their substrates in the distal regions of the grain (Fincher, 1989). Thus, the relative contributions of the scutellum and the aleurone to total hydrolytic activity secreted into the starchy endosperm vary according to the particular enzyme and to the time after the initiation of germination. The scutellum appears to synthesize relatively high levels of $(1\rightarrow3),(1\rightarrow4)$-$\beta$-glucanases, particularly in the early stages of endosperm mobilization (McFadden et al, 1988). Stuart et al (1986) demonstrated that a single excised scutellum secreted, in vitro, approximately 40% of the $(1\rightarrow3),(1\rightarrow4)$-$\beta$-glucanase activity secreted by a single aleurone layer. The scutellum is also a major source of carboxypeptidase I (Mundy et al, 1985; Ranki et al, 1990). In contrast, levels of α-amylase secreted from the scutellum are significantly lower than those secreted from the aleurone (Ranki and Sopanen, 1984; Pogson et al, 1989; Ranki, 1990).

In this section we examine the depolymerization of the major reserve polymers of the starchy endosperm, together with the properties of the many hydrolytic enzymes that act in concert to effect the mobilization of grain reserves. It should be noted that the pH of the starchy endosperm is actively maintained at 5.0–5.2 in the germinated grain, probably by secretion of malic acid and other organic acids from the aleurone (Mikola and Virtanen, 1980). The pH optima of the hydrolytic enzymes are usually in the same range and distinguish enzymes involved in starchy endosperm mobilization from many of those that participate in intracellular metabolism in cells of the aleurone or scutellum; the latter enzymes generally have higher pH optima.

Cell Walls

The starch and protein reserves of the nonliving starchy endosperm cells are contained within walls that form a network throughout the tissue. The enzymes that hydrolyze the reserves are predominantly secreted from the aleurone or scutellum and therefore approach their substrates from outside the cells of the starchy endosperm. Furthermore, polypeptides and other large molecules do not move freely across walls (Carpita et al, 1979; Fincher and Stone, 1986), which therefore act as physical barriers between the enzymes and their substrates. Consequently, the removal of walls of starchy endosperm cells represents a crucial early event that is a prerequisite for successful germination of the grain. The walls of the starchy endosperm consist of approximately 75% $(1\rightarrow3),(1\rightarrow4)$-$\beta$-glucan and 20% arabinoxylan, with small amounts of cellulose, glucomannan, phenolic acids, and protein (Fincher, 1975, 1976; Ballance and Manners, 1978b). During germination, the walls are completely degraded in a biphasic process in which most of the wall is degraded by an initial front of hydrolytic enzymes, but in which wall remnants subsequently disappear more slowly (Selvig et al, 1986). The monosaccharides released from wall polysaccharides make a major contribution to the total energy released from the starchy endosperm for seedling development (Morall and Briggs, 1978). Most of our current knowledge on the hydrolytic enzymes that depolymerize wall components in germinating barley is restricted to the $(1\rightarrow3),(1\rightarrow4)$-$\beta$-glucanases, although some information on the enzymes that hydrolyze the arabinoxylans is also available.

$(1\rightarrow3),(1\rightarrow4)$-$\beta$-GLUCAN DEPOLYMERIZATION

The most important enzymes in the depolymerization of wall $(1\rightarrow3),(1\rightarrow4)$-$\beta$-glucan in the starchy endosperm of germinated barley are the $(1\rightarrow3),(1\rightarrow4)$-$\beta$-glucan 4-glucanohydrolases (EC 3.2.1.73). These enzymes catalyze the hydrolysis of $(1\rightarrow4)$-β-glucosyl linkages in $(1\rightarrow3),(1\rightarrow4)$-$\beta$-glucans only where the glucosyl residue involved is substituted at the C(O)3 position, as follows:

$$\downarrow \qquad\qquad \downarrow \qquad\qquad \downarrow$$
$$..... \text{ G 4 G 3 G 4 G 4 G 3 G 4 G 4 G 4 G 3 G 4 G } .....\text{red.}$$

In this diagram, the glucosyl residues are represented by G and the $(1\rightarrow3)$- and $(1\rightarrow4)$-β-linkages by 3 and 4, respectively; the reducing terminus (red) of the polysaccharide chain is indicated.

Thus, the enzymes have an absolute requirement for adjacent $(1\rightarrow3)$- and $(1\rightarrow4)$-β-linked glucosyl residues in their substrates. The polysaccharide structure shown above includes the major structural features of the $(1\rightarrow3),(1\rightarrow4)$-$\beta$-glucans from starchy endosperm walls (Staudte et al, 1983; Woodward et al, 1983; Edney et al, 1991). The $(1\rightarrow3),(1\rightarrow4)$-$\beta$-glucanases exhibit an endo-action pattern and release 3-*O*-β-cellobiosyl-D-glucose (G4G3G$_{red}$) and 3-*O*-β-cellotriosyl-D-glucose (G4G4G3G$_{red}$) as the major oligomeric products of hydrolysis (Woodward and Fincher, 1982b).

Much of the interest in barley $(1\rightarrow3),(1\rightarrow4)$-$\beta$-glucanases results from the recognition that residual wall material, in particular $(1\rightarrow3),(1\rightarrow4)$-$\beta$-glucans, can have serious and detrimental effects on the efficiency of the malting and brewing processes (Woodward and Fincher, 1983; Bamforth, 1985, 1993). High levels of $(1\rightarrow3),(1\rightarrow4)$-$\beta$-glucan in malt reflect incomplete wall breakdown and are associated with diminished mobilization of other storage polymers. This is manifested by lower malt extract values. Residual $(1\rightarrow3),(1\rightarrow4)$-$\beta$-glucan can also cause filtration difficulties in the brewing process and can contribute to certain hazes or precipitates that form in stored beer (Bamforth, 1993). Although total $(1\rightarrow3),(1\rightarrow4)$-$\beta$-glucan in ungerminated grain is not correlated with malt extract, residual $(1\rightarrow3),(1\rightarrow4)$-$\beta$-glucan in the malt is highly correlated, in a negative sense, with subsequent extract values (Bourne et al, 1982; Henry, 1986; Stuart et al, 1988). Low residual $(1\rightarrow3),(1\rightarrow4)$-$\beta$-glucan in malt is an indicator of the grain's capacity to rapidly synthesize high levels of $(1\rightarrow3),(1\rightarrow4)$-$\beta$-glucanases during malting and, as expected, $(1\rightarrow3),(1\rightarrow4)$-$\beta$-glucanase activity is positively correlated with malt extract values (Henry 1986; Stuart et al, 1988). Unfortunately, a high proportion of $(1\rightarrow3),(1\rightarrow4)$-$\beta$-glucanases in germinated grain, or green malt, is inactivated at the temperatures encountered during kilning or in the initial mashing steps of the brewing process (Woodward and Fincher, 1982b; Loi et al, 1987), and this has led to a considerable interest in the thermostability of the enzymes.

Two (1→3),(1→4)-β-glucan endohydrolases, designated isoenzymes EI and EII, have been purified to homogeneity from extracts of germinated barley and characterized (Woodward and Fincher, 1982a,b). Some of their properties are shown in Table 1. Although they exhibit essentially identical substrate specificities, pH optima, and action patterns (Woodward and Fincher, 1982b), the two (1→3),(1→4)-β-glucanase isoenzymes differ in their mobility during sodium dodecyl sulfate-polyacrylamide gel electrophoresis and have different isoelectric points and glycosylation patterns (Table 1). The complete amino acid sequences of the (1→3),(1→4)-β-glucanases have been deduced from the nucleotide sequences of corresponding cDNAs (Fincher et al, 1986; Slakeski et al, 1990) and show 91% positional identity. Because barley is predominantly self-fertilizing and plants of established varieties are essentially homozygous (Briggs, 1978), the differences in the amino acid sequences of the two (1→3),(1→4)-β-glucanase isoenzymes indicate that they represent the products of two separate genes (Woodward et al, 1982). This has been confirmed by southern blot analysis (Loi et al, 1988; Slakeski et al, 1990) and by isozyme analyses (MacLeod et al, 1991).

The high degree of positional identity in (1→3),(1→4)-β-glucanase amino acid sequences explains why polyclonal antibodies raised against either isoenzyme recognize both (Stuart and Fincher, 1983). The small but detectable difference in their electrophoretic mobility has allowed levels of the two isoenzymes to be independently evaluated by probing western blots of grain extracts with the polyclonal antibodies (Stuart and Fincher, 1983; Stuart et al, 1986). However, some polyclonal antibody preparations might also cross-react with related (1→3)-β-glucanases in grain extracts, and it is likely that the "isoenzyme EIII" detected by the antibodies in secretions of isolated barley scutella (Stuart et al, 1986) might in fact be a (1→3)-β-glucanase. As a result, specific monoclonal antibodies have subsequently been raised against the two purified (1→3),(1→4)-β-glucanases, and these discriminate between the isoenzymes in both enzyme-linked immunosorbant assays and western blot analyses,

TABLE 1
Properties of Barley (1→3),(1→4)-β-Glucanases[a]

Property	Isoenzyme EI	Isoenzyme EII
Isoelectric point	8.5	10.6
pH optimum	4.7	4.7
Apparent molecular weight[b]	30,000	32,000
Amino acids	306	306
Carbohydrate content, %	trace	4
N-Glycosylation sites	0	1
Thermal stability,[c] °C	≈37	≈45
Polyclonal antibodies	Cross react	Cross react
Monoclonal antibodies	Specific	Specific
Expression sites	Aleurone, scutellum, young leaves, young roots	Aleurone

[a] Values from Woodward and Fincher (1982a,b), Høj et al (1990), Slakeski et al (1990), Slakeski and Fincher (1992a).

[b] By sodium dodecyl sulfate-polyacrylamide gel electrophoresis.

[c] Temperature at which 50% of initial activity is retained after 15 min of incubation (Woodward and Fincher, 1982b).

despite the high degree of similarity in the primary structures of the isoenzymes (Høj et al, 1990).

Analysis of the cDNAs for the $(1\rightarrow3),(1\rightarrow4)$-β-glucanases reveals a single potential N-glycosylation site at Asn[190] in isoenzyme EII, a site not found in isoenzyme EI (Slakeski et al, 1990). This is consistent with the detection of 4% carbohydrate and approximately three N-acetylglucosamine residues in isoenzyme EII (Woodward and Fincher 1982a). Indeed, the carbohydrate on isoenzyme EII is responsible for its lower electrophoretic mobility and may contribute to its higher thermal stability; the carbohydrate is not a component of the epitope recognized by the specific monoclonal antibodies (Doan and Fincher, 1992).

The importance of $(1\rightarrow3),(1\rightarrow4)$-β-glucanase levels in the malting and brewing industries has provided incentives to study the developmental patterns of the enzymes in detail. In sound, ungerminated grain, $(1\rightarrow3),(1\rightarrow4)$-β-glucanase activity is very low or absent but, after a lag period of one to two days, rises steeply to a maximum five to six days after the initiation of germination (Ballance et al, 1976; Stuart and Fincher, 1983). Quantitative western transfer analyses indicate that in the malting variety Clipper, isoenzymes EI and EII develop in approximately equimolar proportions, with isoenzyme EI development slightly preceding that of isoenzyme EII (Stuart and Fincher, 1983). Considerable variation in this pattern is observed in different varieties and in grain produced under different environmental conditions (Henry, 1990).

The expression sites of the barley $(1\rightarrow3),(1\rightarrow4)$-β-glucanase isoenzymes have been investigated in excised aleurone layers and scutella by western blot analysis (Stuart et al, 1986). Isolated aleurone layers secrete isoenzyme EII, together with lower levels of isoenzyme EI. Isoenzyme EI is the predominant $(1\rightarrow3),(1\rightarrow4)$-β-glucanase secreted from isolated scutella (Stuart et al, 1986). Thus, in isolated tissue fragments, differential expression patterns are observed for the two isoenzymes, but care must be exercised in the extrapolation of in vitro results to the intact, germinated grain. A role for the scutellum in $(1\rightarrow3),(1\rightarrow4)$-β-glucanase synthesis in intact grain was subsequently confirmed by in situ hybridization experiments, in which sections of germinated grain were probed for $(1\rightarrow3),(1\rightarrow4)$-β-glucanase mRNA with a cDNA encoding barley $(1\rightarrow3),(1\rightarrow4)$-β-glucanase isoenzyme EII (Fincher et al, 1986; McFadden et al, 1988). In ungerminated grain, $(1\rightarrow3),(1\rightarrow4)$-β-glucanase mRNA is absent, but one day after the initiation of germination, very high levels of the $(1\rightarrow3),(1\rightarrow4)$-β-glucanase mRNA can be detected in the scutellar epithelium; at this stage no expression can be detected in the aleurone (McFadden et al, 1988). After day 1, $(1\rightarrow3),(1\rightarrow4)$-β-glucanase mRNA in the scutellar epithelium rapidly decreases, whereas levels in the aleurone increase progressively from the proximal to the distal end of the grain (McFadden et al, 1988). Specific isoenzyme EI and EII probes subsequently prepared from the 3' untranslated regions of near full-length cDNAs (Slakeski et al, 1990) have been used in northern blot analyses to confirm that isoenzyme EI mRNA predominates in scutella in intact, germinated barley, whereas both isoenzyme EI and EII mRNAs are present in the aleurone (Table 1; Slakeski and Fincher, 1992a). In addition, isoenzyme EI mRNA is detected in developing leaves and roots, where the enzyme may participate in wall metabolism during leaf differentiation (Slakeski et al, 1990; Slakeski and Fincher 1992a). Thus, while isoenzyme

EII appears to be "germination-specific" and its expression is detected principally in the aleurone cells, $(1\rightarrow3),(1\rightarrow4)$-$\beta$-glucanase isoenzyme EI is more widely distributed in the developing barley seedling (Table 1).

The $(1\rightarrow3),(1\rightarrow4)$-$\beta$-glucan endohydrolases depolymerize wall $(1\rightarrow3),(1\rightarrow4)$-$\beta$-glucans to oligosaccharides containing three, four, or more glucosyl residues (Woodward and Fincher, 1982b). There is increasing evidence for the presence of additional enzymes that may participate in the complete conversion of the polysaccharide to glucose. At the polysaccharide level, $(1\rightarrow3)$-β-glucan endohydrolases (EC 3.2.1.39) have been implicated in the initial degradation of $(1\rightarrow3),(1\rightarrow4)$-$\beta$-glucans (Ballance and Manners, 1978b), but as yet there is no compelling evidence that purified $(1\rightarrow3)$-β-glucanases can hydrolyze single $(1\rightarrow3)$-linkages in $(1\rightarrow3),(1\rightarrow4)$-$\beta$-glucans or that the polysaccharides themselves contain blocks of contiguous $(1\rightarrow3)$-linkages that could be hydrolyzed by the $(1\rightarrow3)$-β-glucanases (Fincher, 1989). Cellulases (EC 3.2.1.4) can hydrolyze the blocks of adjacent $(1\rightarrow4)$-linkages in barley $(1\rightarrow3),(1\rightarrow4)$-$\beta$-glucans, but cellulase levels in germinating grain are low and variable, with most of the activity attributable to commensal microorganisms on the surface of the grain (Hoy et al, 1981; Manners et al, 1982). Cellulases could nevertheless function to reclaim the low levels of cellulose found in starchy endosperm and aleurone walls (Fincher, 1975; Bacic and Stone, 1981a,b). A quite distinct enzyme, given the trivial name "β-glucan solubilase," has also been proposed as a possible participant in the initial release of $(1\rightarrow3),(1\rightarrow4)$-$\beta$-glucan from the walls (Bamforth et al, 1979; Bamforth and Martin, 1981). It was even suggested that the enzyme had associated carboxypeptidase activity (Bamforth et al, 1979). However, the enzyme has never been purified or satisfactorily characterized and may represent an artefact that originates from contaminating microorganisms (Yin et al, 1989).

Exo-β-glucanases that hydrolyze $(1\rightarrow3),(1\rightarrow4)$-$\beta$-glucans have been detected in extracts of germinated barley (Preece and Hoggan, 1957). Three exo-β-glucanases of M_r 67,000–70,000 purified from grain extracts hydrolyze $(1\rightarrow3),(1\rightarrow4)$-$\beta$-glucans, $(1\rightarrow3)$-β-glucans, or alkyl β-glucosides to release glucose as the sole product (J. Wang, P. B. Høj, and G. B. Fincher, unpublished). The enzymes are thought to be of plant origin rather than from associated microorganisms because the grain used in these experiments was germinated under rigorously aseptic conditions. The enzymes rapidly degrade the oligo-$(1\rightarrow3),(1\rightarrow4)$-$\beta$-glucosides that are released from wall $(1\rightarrow3),(1\rightarrow4)$-$\beta$-glucan by the $(1\rightarrow3),(1\rightarrow4)$-$\beta$-glucan endohydrolases and might therefore function to convert these oligosaccharides to glucose in a process designed to salvage glucose for use as an energy source by the developing seedling. However, whether the exo-β-glucanases are located in the grain or in associated vegetative tissues of the developing seedling has not been defined, nor has a physiological role for them in $(1\rightarrow3),(1\rightarrow4)$-$\beta$-glucan depolymerization been established. In addition, β-glucosidases have been reported in germinated barley (Manners and Marshall, 1969), but whether these represent a class of enzymes distinct from the exo-β-glucanases and can hydrolyze the tri- and tetrasaccharides released from $(1\rightarrow3),(1\rightarrow4)$-$\beta$-glucans remains to be demonstrated.

ARABINOXYLAN DEGRADATION

The depolymerization of wall arabinoxylans during endosperm mobilization is controlled by the concerted action of endo- and exoxylanases, α-arabino-furanosidase, and possibly xylobiase (or β-xylopyranosidase). Each of these enzymes has been detected in extracts of germinated barley (Preece and MacDougall, 1958). Analysis of the products released from arabinoxylan during the course of germination suggests that α-arabinofuranosidases first remove the arabinosyl side chains and allow exoxylanases to release xylose; the higher-molecular-weight oligoxylosides released by endoxylanase action are not detected until much later (Preece and MacDougall, 1958). Ferulic acid esterified to arabinoxylans of endosperm walls is recovered among the degradation products as feruloylated oligosaccharides (Gubler et al, 1985), suggesting that enzymes specific for the cleavage of the ester linkage are not present in the aleurone of germinating grain.

The only information available on individual isoenzymes that depolymerize arabinoxylans relates to the endoxylanases. Three $(1{\to}4)$-β-xylan endohydrolases (EC 3.2.1.8) of M_r 42,000 have been purified from extracts of grain germinated for five days (Slade et al, 1989). The enzymes are acidic proteins, with pI values of 5.2, are very labile in dilute solution, and are recovered from grain extracts in very low yields (Slade et al, 1989). The NH_2-terminal amino acid sequences of the three enzymes are identical, but, on the basis of their different behavior during purification procedures, Slade et al (1989) suggested that they represent the products of separate genes. The endoxylanases appear in aqueous extracts of germinating grain several days later than the $(1{\to}3),(1{\to}4)$-β-glucanases (Preece and MacDougall, 1958; Slade et al, 1989), and their importance in the initial degradation of the starchy endosperm walls has been questioned (Fincher, 1989). A possible explanation for the late appearance of the endoxylanases is that they mediate the degradation of aleurone walls, where they remain tightly bound until the outer wall layer is completely removed (Fincher, 1989; Slade et al, 1989). Following their release from the aleurone, the endoxylanases could be responsible for removal of wall remnants in the starchy endosperm that survive the first wave of hydrolytic enzymes (Selvig et al, 1986); the first wave presumably includes the $(1{\to}3),(1{\to}4)$-β-glucanases.

The three endoxylanases of M_r 42,000 and pI 5.2 characterized by Slade et al (1989) can be clearly distinguished from the xylanase of M_r 34,000 and pI 4.6 that has been purified from the medium surrounding GA-treated aleurone layers (Benjavongkulchai and Spencer, 1986). The latter enzyme could represent an additional endoxylanase or an exoxylanase, because both classes of xylan hydrolase are secreted from isolated barley aleurone layers in vitro (Taiz and Honigman, 1976; Dashek and Chrispeels, 1977). The xylanase described by Benjavongkulchai and Spencer (1986) is synthesized de novo, and its synthesis is enhanced by GA in the presence of Ca^{2+}. It can be detected within the aleurone cells soon after the addition of GA and Ca^{2+}, but it is not released into the medium until much later (Benjavongkulchai and Spencer, 1989). Again, this might indicate that xylan hydrolases are initially bound to the aleurone wall.

Arabinofuranosidases and exoxylanases have been detected in isolated aleurone layers (Taiz and Honigman, 1976; Dashek and Chrispeels, 1977) but have not been purified or characterized. A barley β-galactosidase, which exists in multiple isoforms, has been reported to have α-D-arabinofuranosidase activity (Simos and Georgatsos, 1988; Giannakouros et al, 1991), but whether this enzyme participates in the cleavage of the α-L-arabinofuranoside residues from arabinoxylans is unclear.

Starch

The insoluble starch granules stored in the starchy endosperm cells of barley grain, which generally contain about 75% amylopectin and 25% amylose (reviewed in Chapter 3, [MacGregor and Fincher, 1993]), are degraded to glucose and small oligosaccharides by the combined action of α-amylases, β-amylases, limit dextrinases (debranching enzyme), and α-glucosidases. Numerous morphological studies have shown that the surface of the large starch granules are initially degraded at discrete points, particularly along the equatorial axis, until large holes penetrating into the interior of the granule can be seen. The inner regions of the granule are progressively solubilized, leaving an outer shell that ultimately collapses and disappears (MacGregor and Ballance, 1980; MacGregor and Fincher, 1993). In contrast, small starch granules are degraded by more general surface erosion (MacGregor and Ballance, 1980). Although many of the enzymes that participate in amylopectin and amylose hydrolysis have been studied in detail, we are not yet able to match the sequence of events observed in morphological studies with the individual enzymes that clearly mediate in the dissolution of the granules. Here we consider the enzymatic properties and developmental patterns of hydrolases responsible for starch degradation in the germinating barley grain.

α-AMYLASES

α-Amylases (EC 3.2.1.1) are endohydrolases that cleave internal $(1\rightarrow4)$-α-glucosyl linkages of amylose or amylopectin in an essentially random fashion. They are unable to hydrolyze the $(1\rightarrow6)$-α-linkages at branch points in amylopectin and may vary in their ability to hydrolyze $(1\rightarrow4)$-α-linkages close to these branch points. The α-amylases synthesized in germinated barley grain are Ca^{2+} metalloproteins consisting of a single polypeptide chain of apparent M_r ~45,000; they can be classified into two groups on the basis of differences in their isoelectric points (Callis and Ho, 1983; Jacobsen and Chandler, 1987). Members of the low-pI, or AMY1, group have pIs of approximately 4.6, while the high-pI α-amylases (AMY2 group) have pI values of approximately 5.9 (MacGregor and MacGregor, 1987). An additional group of apparent pI 6.5 is actually comprised of high-pI isoforms complexed with an α-amylase inhibitor (MacGregor and MacGregor, 1987). The low- and high-pI isoforms differ in their sensitivity to sulfhydryl reagents, heavy metal ions, and low pH (Jacobsen and Chandler, 1987). Although the low- and high-pI isoforms have the same apparent substrate specificities and action patterns, members of the low-pI group degrade starch granules more rapidly than the high-pI isoenzymes (MacGregor and Ballance, 1980; MacGregor and Morgan, 1986). Whether this indicates that the two groups have different starch granule-binding affinities or that the two groups perform specialized functions in starch granule solubilization is not known. Nucleotide sequence analyses of cDNAs encoding the barley α-amylases show that the low-pI isoforms are approximately 11 amino acids longer than the high-pI isoforms and that amino acid sequence identities between the low- and high-pI enzymes are approximately 80% (Rogers and Milliman, 1984; Rogers, 1985). Within each group, amino acid sequence identities of 90–95% are observed (Chandler et al, 1984; Huang et al, 1984; Deikman and Jones, 1985; Rogers, 1985).

Distinct isoforms can also be detected within each α-amylase group, and a total of up to 12 α-amylase isoforms have been resolved by isoelectric focusing (Simon and Jones, 1988). In the low-pI group, four isoforms have been observed, but two of these result from posttranslational modification of the others and cannot be considered true genetic isoenzymes (Aoyagi et al, 1990). It is possible that hydrolases in the starchy endosperm could be susceptible to carboxypeptidase action and that some size heterogeneity could be generated without effect on enzyme activity. Thus, malt carboxypeptidase II has been implicated in the generation of different isoforms of the low-pI α-amylase through COOH-terminal processing (Søgaard et al, 1991). Several high-pI isoforms have also been resolved (Jacobsen et al, 1988; Aoyagi et al, 1990).

In germinating barley grain, the high-pI isoforms of α-amylase are far more abundant than the low-pI group and may constitute in excess of 90% of total α-amylase in malt (MacGregor et al, 1988). The two groups exhibit markedly different developmental patterns. High-pI forms appear first, increase to a maximum level, and then decline, whereas the low-pI isoforms appear later but accumulate over a longer period (Callis and Ho, 1983; Chandler and Jacobsen, 1991). In isolated aleurone layers treated with GA, different developmental patterns are observed, but the high-pI isoforms again predominate (Jacobsen and Higgins, 1982; Nolan and Ho, 1988).

Secretion of α-amylases from the scutellum in intact germinating barley grain represents a small proportion of the total α-amylase, which is synthesized principally in the aleurone layer (MacGregor et al, 1984; Ranki and Sopanen, 1984; Pogson et al, 1989; Chandler and Mosleth, 1990; Ranki, 1990). There is some suggestion that the low-pI isoforms predominate in barley embryos (MacGregor and Marchylo, 1986), although primer extension experiments indicate that mRNA for a high-pI α-amylase is also present in the scutellum, albeit in low abundance, where α-amylase mRNA levels peak one day after imbibition (Chandler and Mosleth, 1990).

β-AMYLASES

β-Amylases (EC 3.2.1.2) are exohydrolases that cleave the penultimate $(1\rightarrow4)$-α-linkage from the nonreducing termini of $(1\rightarrow4)$-α-glucans to release the disaccharide maltose. In theory, they should completely depolymerize unbranched or unsubstituted amylose molecules, but they are unable to bypass the $(1\rightarrow6)$-α-linked branch points in amylopectin. In ungerminated barley grain, β-amylase may account for 1–2% of total protein in the starchy endosperm, where most of the enzyme is located on the outer surface of starch granules (Hara-Nishimura et al, 1986; Laurière et al, 1986). Thus, in contrast to the majority of hydrolytic enzymes responsible for endosperm mobilization in barley, the β-amylases are synthesized exclusively in the starchy endosperm during grain maturation rather than in the aleurone or scutellum after the initiation of germination. Some of the β-amylase in ungerminated grain can be extracted with salt solutions, while some remains bound to other proteins through disulfide linkages (Hejgaard, 1978; Hara-Nishimura et al, 1986). Four major forms of barley β-amylase extracted in the presence of thiol reagents are single polypeptide chains of M_r 54,000–60,000, but the heterogeneity may be generated, in part at least, by limited proteolysis of the COOH-terminus. Their isoelectric points fall in the range 5.2–5.7 (Lundgard and Svensson, 1987). The complete primary structure of one member of a small family of barley β-amylases has been deduced from the nucleotide sequence of a full-length cDNA, which showed that the enzyme is synthesized in the mature form without an NH_2-terminal signal peptide (Kreis et al, 1987). The calculated molecular mass of the enzyme is 60,000, and the protein is characterized by four glycine-rich repeats, each of 11 amino acid residues, at the COOH-terminus; the repeat region might be involved in cross-linking β-amylase to other proteins on the surface of starch granules (Kreis et al, 1987).

During germination, the bound β-amylase is released and activated by the action of proteolytic enzymes (Sopanen and Laurière, 1989; Guerin et al, 1991). Barley β-amylases are unable to hydrolyze intact starch granules (Maeda et al, 1978), and this property is presumably important in preventing premature damage to starch in ungerminated grain. However, the β-amylases act synergistically with α-amylases to degrade the granules following secretion of the endohydrolases from the scutellum or aleurone (Maeda et al, 1978).

LIMIT DEXTRINASE

Limit dextrinase, or debranching enzyme (EC 3.2.1.41), hydrolyzes (1→6)-α-linkages in amylopectin or derived limit dextrins and increases the abundance of linear (1→4)-α-glucan chains that can be extensively depolymerized by the action of α-amylases and β-amylases. The limit dextrinase from germinated barley (Manners and Hardie, 1977) hydrolyzes the (1→6)-α-linkages of branched limit dextrins faster than those in large amylopectin molecules (MacGregor, 1987). In ungerminated grain, small amounts of limit dextrinase can be extracted in the presence of reducing agents or papain (Manners and Yellowlees, 1973; Yamada, 1981; Lenoir et al, 1984; McLeary, 1992). During germination, activity increases, but prolonged periods are required before maximum levels are obtained (Lee and Pyler, 1984; Longstaff and Bryce, 1993). The principal source of the enzyme in germinating barley appears to be the aleurone, based on indirect evidence that GA induces its de novo synthesis in embryoless half grains (Hardie, 1975), but there is also evidence that the enzyme is released from a bound form by the action of a cysteine peptidase (Longstaff and Bryce, 1993). Isoelectric focusing and gel electrophoresis indicate that several isoforms of limit dextrinase with pI values of 4.2–5.0 and M_r 80,000–104,000 are present in germinated grain (Lenoir et al, 1984; Sissons et al, 1992). Although purified limit dextrinase has no action on starch granules, it enhances the rate of granule dissolution when added to a mixture of α- and β-amylases (Maeda et al, 1978).

α-GLUCOSIDASE

α-Glucosidase (EC 3.2.1.20) releases glucose from a variety of α-glucosides and presumably functions in the final conversion of maltose and other small dextrins to glucose. The enzyme is found in the pericarp, aleurone, and embryo of ungerminated grain (Jorgensen, 1965; Watson and Novellie, 1974; MacGregor and Lenoir, 1987). After germination is initiated, rapid GA-induced synthesis of the enzyme is observed, and both the aleurone layer and embryo appear to be involved (Jorgensen, 1965; Clutterbuck and Briggs, 1973; Hardie, 1975; MacGregor and Lenoir, 1987).

Reserve Proteins

The reserve proteins of the starchy endosperm in mature barley grain are mobilized through the action of several endo- and exopeptidases (Rastogi and Oaks, 1986; Mikola, 1987). In barley, as in other temperate-zone cereals, carboxypeptidases are important components of the enzyme system that mediates storage protein mobilization (Winspear et al, 1984). There is no evidence for the presence of aminopeptidases in the starchy endosperm, but these enzymes may be involved in storage protein mobilization within the aleurone and scutellar cells (Mikola and Kolehmainen, 1972). Acting together, the endo- and exopeptidases that are secreted into the starchy endosperm during germination depolymerize storage proteins to a mixture of amino acids and short peptides. The endopeptidases are presumably important contributors to the initial solubilization of reserve proteins and provide short oligopeptide substrates for the carboxypeptidases. Many of the di- and tripeptide products of this process are resistant to further hydrolysis but can be rapidly transported into the scutellum (Sopanen et al, 1978; Payne and Walker-Smith, 1987), where they are finally converted to amino acids (Mikola, 1987). Additional functions of the endo- and exopeptidases may be to release or activate zymogen forms of β-amylase (Lungard and Svensson, 1987; Guerin et al, 1991) or carboxypeptidases (Doan and Fincher, 1988) or to participate in related reactions such as the COOH-terminal processing of α-amylase (Søgaard et al, 1991). In the following sections, the properties and developmental patterns of the major endo- and exopeptidases are compared.

CARBOXYPEPTIDASES

Five serine carboxypeptidases (EC 3.4.16.1) have been identified in germinating barley (Mikola, 1983). Each enzyme has a distinct preference for amino acids at or near the COOH-termini of the substrates, but their specificities are complementary and result in extensive degradation of most barley storage proteins (Mikola, 1983). Carboxypeptidases I–III hydrolyze, albeit at different rates, peptide bonds adjoining almost any COOH-terminal amino acid, including proline, but they will not hydrolyze a peptide if proline is at the penultimate position. However, carboxypeptidases IV and V do not have this restriction and will hydrolyze peptides with penultimate proline residues (Mikola, 1983). Carboxypeptidases I–III have been purified and their complete primary structures determined (Sørensen et al, 1986, 1987, 1989; Breddam and Sørensen, 1987). Carboxypeptidases I and II are dimeric proteins composed of two chains linked by disulfide bridges. The A-chains have 266 and 260 amino acid residues and the B-chains 148 and 159 amino acid residues for carboxypeptidases I and II, respectively, but sequence identity values between the two enzymes are only 30–40% (Sørensen et al, 1986, 1987). Nucleotide sequence analysis of a barley carboxypeptidase I cDNA, isolated from a scutellum cDNA library, demonstrated that the A- and B-chains of the enzyme originated from a single precursor polypeptide, encoded by a single mRNA (Doan and Fincher, 1988). In the primary translation product, a linker peptide of 55 amino acids joins the A- and B-chains, but this segment of the proenzyme is excised during maturation by endoproteolytic cleavage of peptide bonds on the COOH-terminal side of serine residues. This processing might be necessary to activate the zymogen form of the enzyme (Doan and Fincher, 1988). Although cDNAs corresponding to barley carboxypeptidase II have not been reported, it appears likely that the two chains originate in a similar fashion. In contrast to carboxypeptidases I and II, barley carboxypeptidase III consists of a single polypeptide chain of 411 amino acid residues, and again there is only limited sequence similarity with the other two enzymes (Sørensen et al, 1989). Sørensen et al (1989) suggest that carboxypeptidase III is also synthesized as an inactive zymogen that might be activated by NH_2- and COOH-terminal processing.

During germination, carboxypeptidase activity increases in the starchy endosperm. Carboxypeptidases I and III are absent in ungerminated grain but rise to high levels after the initiation of germination. Carboxypeptidases IV and V also increase, but carboxypeptidase II, which is relatively abundant in the resting grain, decreases during germination (Mikola, 1983). mRNA encoding carboxypeptidase I cannot be detected in ungerminated grain but rapidly appears in the scutellum during germination. Levels of the mRNA in the aleurone remain low during germination, suggesting that the scutellum is the principal source of the carboxypeptidase I that is detected in the starchy endosperm (Mundy et al, 1985; Ranki et al, 1990). In contrast, it now appears likely that barley carboxypeptidase III is secreted from the aleurone, where its expression may be enhanced by GA (Hammerton and Ho, 1986; H. Ranki, *personal communication*).

ENDOPEPTIDASES

At least four different endopeptidases, three of which are cysteine proteinases and the other a possible metalloproteinase, have been reported in GA-treated barley aleurone layers (Sundblom and Mikola, 1972). An aspartic endopeptidase has also been purified from ungerminated grain (Törmäkangas et al, 1991). A cysteine endopeptidase of M_r 37,000 identified in aleurone layer secretions was subsequently purified from embryoless half grains and characterized (Hammerton and Ho, 1986; Koehler and Ho, 1990a). The enzyme, designated EP-A, exists in three forms containing different but overlapping NH_2-terminal residues, suggestive of differential processing of a single polypeptide precursor (Koehler and Ho, 1988). A second cysteine endopeptidase of M_r 30,000, designated EP-B, has also been purified and exhibits 90% amino acid sequence similarity with EP-A in its NH_2-terminal region; both enzymes exist as a single polypeptide chain (Koehler and Ho, 1990a). Other cysteine endopeptidases of M_r ~30,000 have been purified from germinated barley (Poulle and Jones, 1988; Phillips and Wallace, 1989), and although their NH_2-terminal sequences have not been defined, they probably correspond to the EP-B enzyme purified by Koehler and Ho (1990a). In any case, the EP-A and EP-B enzymes constitute a major proportion of total endopeptidase secreted from barley aleurone, and EP-B appears to be most abundant (Koehler and Ho, 1988; Phillips and Wallace, 1989; Koehler and Ho, 1990a).

Nucleotide sequence analyses of cDNAs encoding two endopeptidase EP-B isoenzymes indicate that the enzyme is synthesized in precursor form and that maturation of the enzyme involves multiple processing events through which a segment of approximately 104 amino acids is cleaved from the NH_2-terminus of the proenzyme (Koehler and Ho, 1990b). The endopeptidases EP-A and EP-B differ from a putative cysteine endopeptidase, designated "aleurain," that was identified from mRNAs in GA-treated aleurone layers (Rogers et al, 1985). The molecular weight of aleurain, predicted from the sequence of the corresponding cDNA, is 37,000 (Rogers et al, 1985).

The levels of both mRNA and enzymatic protein corresponding to the secreted cysteine endopeptidases EP-A and EP-B in barley aleurone layers are enhanced by GA (Hammerton and Ho, 1986; Koehler and Ho, 1990b). However, endopeptidase EP-B responds to GA more quickly than endopeptidase EP-A and can be induced at 10-fold lower GA concentrations (Koehler and Ho, 1990b). Neither endopeptidase EP-A or EP-B is detected in the scutellum, although some aleurain may be present in this tissue (Koehler and Ho, 1990b). The major site of aleurain synthesis appears to be in the aleurone layer, but the enzyme may not be secreted into the starchy endosperm (Koehler and Ho, 1990a; Jones and Jacobsen, 1991). Instead, it could participate in the mobilization of internal storage proteins in aleurone cells to release amino acids for new enzyme synthesis.

The aspartic endopeptidase from ungerminated barley grain exists in two heterodimeric forms containing chains of 32,000 and 16,000, and 29,000 and 11,000, respectively (Törmäkangas et al, 1991). Nucleotide sequence analysis of a cDNA for the enzyme revealed that both forms are generated by progressive cross-linking and processing of a single polypeptide precursor (Törmäkangas et al, 1991). The precise tissue location of the enzyme in barley grain has not been reported (Törmäkangas et al, 1991).

Nucleic Acids

Significant levels of residual RNA and DNA remain in the nonliving cells of the starchy endosperm in mature barley grain (McFadden et al, 1988), and it comes as no surprise that an enzyme system has evolved to reclaim these nucleic acids during germination. In this process, nucleic acids are hydrolyzed by endonucleases to oligonucleotides and eventually to mononucleotides. The phosphate groups of the mononucleotides are removed by nucleotidases to form nucleosides, and the glycosidic linkages between nitrogen bases and the pentose residues are cleaved by nucleosidases to release free bases and pentose sugars. The GA-enhanced secretion of ribonucleases and deoxyribonucleases from isolated aleurone layers and in barley malt is well established (Chrispeels and Varner, 1967; Taiz and Starks, 1977; Lee and Pyler, 1985). Further, phosphodiesterases, 3'- and 5'-nucleotidases, phosphomonoesterases, and nucleosidases are detected in germinated grain (Lee and Pyler, 1985, 1986).

It has now been recognized that both ribonuclease and deoxyribonuclease activities, together with 3'-nucleotidase activity, are associated with a single glycosylated endonuclease of apparent M_r 35,000 (Brown and Ho, 1986). The enzyme has been purified and characterized, and it falls into the nuclease I (EC 3.1.30.2) classification (Brown and Ho, 1987). The nucleotides released by nuclease I are hydrolyzed to nucleosides by nucleotidases, some of which may correspond to acid phosphatases that are secreted from GA-treated aleurone layers (Ashford and Jacobsen, 1974; Lee and Pyler, 1985; Gabard and Jones, 1986). The resultant nucleosides are presumably hydrolyzed by a battery of nucleosidases. A specific adenosine nucleosidase purified from barley malt has a molecular weight of 120,000 and a pH optimum of 5.2 and is stable at elevated temperatures (Lee and Pyler, 1986). The tissue origin of the nucleosidases is not known, but the aleurone layer is likely to be involved in their synthesis.

STRUCTURE AND REGULATION OF GENES ENCODING HYDROLYTIC ENZYMES

During the germination of barley grain, different genes or sets of genes are progressively and differentially activated or deactivated in various tissues within the grain. The high level of spatial and temporal coordination of gene expression is demonstrated by the transcriptional activity of the two $(1\rightarrow3),(1\rightarrow4)$-$\beta$-glucanase genes (McFadden et al, 1988). Based on experiments with isolated barley aleurone layers, there is also evidence for a tightly programmed sequence of gene activation within individual cells (Nolan et al, 1987; Nolan and Ho, 1988). The mechanisms regulating tissue-specific and sequential expression of genes are not yet well defined, but it is becoming clear that a major point of regulation of gene expression in the aleurone cells is at the transcriptional level and that this control is often mediated by GA. Recent advances in the techniques of molecular genetics have led to the isolation of an increasing number of genes encoding hydrolytic enzymes that play central roles in the mobilization of starchy endosperm reserves. Specific nucleotide sequences, located in the promoter regions of the genes, are apparently related to the GA-responsiveness of those genes. The identification of these sequence elements will inevitably lead to the isolation and characterization of corresponding DNA-binding proteins that represent the final stage in the signal transduction pathway that begins with GA perception by the aleurone cells and ends with the activation of specific genes. However, gene expression is not complete until the transcribed mRNA is translated into a polypeptide that is subsequently directed to its correct cellular or extracellular destination in an active form. Thus, mRNA stability and turnover rates, translational efficiencies, posttranslational modifications, and cellular targeting must be considered as important complementary factors that may control the levels of active enzyme finally delivered into the starchy endosperm (Fincher, 1989).

Gene Structure

Although most attention has been directed toward the characterization of α-amylase genes, several other genes encoding hydrolytic enzymes that are important in the mobilization of endosperm reserves have also been isolated and analyzed. These genes, together with their corresponding cDNAs, are listed in Table 2. For each enzyme, the genes appear to be members of small gene families that presumably originated by duplications of common ancestral genes and subsequent translocation of some members to different chromosomes (Table 2). The barley genes listed in Table 2 exhibit structures typical of other plant genes. One notable property that appears to be restricted to GA-inducible genes in barley is the high content of the nucleotides G+C in coding regions for the mature enzyme. The high G+C content, which is typically greater than 65% in these exons, is attributable to the extreme bias toward the use of G+C in the third base position of codons. The apparent conservation of this pattern of codon usage in barley α-amylases, $(1\rightarrow3),(1\rightarrow4)$-β-glucanases, and endopeptidases (Rogers and Milliman, 1984; Koehler and Ho, 1990b; Slakeski et al, 1990) suggests a functional role that might be related to mRNA stability or translational efficiency (Fincher, 1989).

Functional analyses of the promoter of a high-pI α-amylase gene have identified a TAACAAA sequence motif that is an absolute requirement for the GA-induction of the genes (Jacobsen and Gubler, 1991; Skriver et al, 1991), together with a TATCCAC motif that may modulate the level of the GA response (J. V. Jacobsen and F. Gubler, *personal communication*).

Regulation of Gene Expression at the Transcriptional Level

The experimental convenience of incubating isolated aleurone layers with different hormones has led to many in vitro studies on the hormonal effects on specific mRNA synthesis in barley aleurone. Levels of mRNA for $(1\rightarrow3),(1\rightarrow4)$-β-glucanases, α-amylases, endopeptidases, and other unidentified proteins are greatly enhanced by GA treatment (Chandler et al, 1984; Mundy and Fincher, 1986; Koehler and Ho, 1990a; Slakeski and Fincher, 1992b), and although the Ca^{2+} ion affects the levels of α-amylase that are finally secreted from the cell, it does not affect α-amylase mRNA levels (Deikman and Jones, 1985, 1986). In nuclei from GA-treated aleurone protoplasts, the abundance of α-amylase transcripts increases several-fold over those of untreated controls, although total RNA transcription actually decreases with GA treatment (Jacobsen and Beach, 1985). These results are indicative of GA-enhanced expression of the genes at the transcriptional level. This conclusion is made in the absence of detailed information on the turnover rates of specific mRNAs because the effects of mRNA processing, transport, and stability on total mRNA levels have not yet been evaluated.

The availability of isoenzyme-specific oligonucleotide or cDNA probes has allowed the abundance of mRNAs for individual isoforms to be estimated. For α-amylase, mRNA encoding the low-pI isoforms can be detected in the absence of GA and increases approximately 20-fold after treatment with low concentrations of the hormone. In contrast, the high-pI mRNAs cannot be detected in untreated aleurone layers but increase up to 100-fold over 16 hr after treatment with relatively high concentrations of GA and then decrease again to low levels. Thus, the induction patterns and GA-sensitivity of α-amylase gene transcription vary between the low-pI and high-pI gene families (Rogers, 1985; Jacobsen and Chandler, 1987; Nolan and Ho, 1988). The earlier transcription of low-pI α-amylase genes may reflect a lower hormone concentration threshold for these genes (Jones and Jacobsen, 1991). Similarly, transcription of genes for the cysteine endopeptidase isoenzyme EP-B is more sensitive to GA and increases more rapidly than that for isoenzyme EP-A

TABLE 2
Genes and cDNA Clones for Hydrolytic Enzymes Involved in Endosperm Mobilization in Barley

Enzyme	Isoform	Type of Clone	GA Induction[a]	Gene Location	Genes per Haploid Genome[b]	References
(1→3),(1→4)-β-Glucanase	Isoenzyme EI	Genomic	Yes (?)	Chromosome 5, long arm	1	Loi et al (1988), Slakeski et al (1990), Litts et al (1990)
		cDNA				Slakeski et al (1990)
	Isoenzyme EII	Genomic	Yes	Chromosome 1, long arm	1	Slakeski et al (1990), Wolf (1991), Stuart et al (1986)
		cDNA				Fincher et al (1986), Jackson et al (1986), Slakeski et al (1990), MacLeod et al (1991)
α-Amylase	Low pI	Genomic	Yes	Chromosome 1	≈3	Whittier et al (1987), Knox et al (1987), Muthukrishnan et al (1984)
		cDNA				Rogers and Milliman (1983)
	High pI	Genomic	Yes	Chromosome 6	≈5	Knox et al (1987), Khursheed and Rogers (1988, 1989), Rahmatullah et al (1989), Brown and Jacobsen (1982)
		cDNA				Rogers (1985), Chandler et al (1984), Huang et al (1984), Deikman and Jones (1985)
β-Amylase		cDNA	No	Chromosome 2, short arm	≈3	Kreis et al (1987)
		cDNA		Chromosome 4, long arm		Kreis et al (1988)
Carboxypeptidase	I	cDNA	No (?)	Chromosome 3	1	Doan and Fincher (1988), Devos et al (1992)
Endopeptidase	Thiol endopeptidase EP-B	cDNA	Yes		4 (or 5)	Koehler and Ho (1990a)
	Aspartate endopeptidase	cDNA	?			Törmäkangas et al (1991)

[a] A question mark indicates some doubt as to whether the genes are GA-regulated in barley aleurone during germination.
[b] In some instances, this might include pseudogenes.

(Koehler and Ho, 1990b). Specific cDNA probes that discriminate between barley $(1\rightarrow3),(1\rightarrow4)$-$\beta$-glucanase isoenzymes EI and EII are also available (Slakeski et al, 1990), and although levels of isoenzyme EII mRNA are strongly enhanced by treating the aleurone layers with GA, no induction of isoenzyme EI gene transcription is detected (Slakeski and Fincher, 1992b). However, isoenzyme EI mRNA levels are relatively high in untreated control aleurone layers (Slakeski and Fincher, 1992b). The effects of GA concentration and the time course of induction of individual $(1\rightarrow3),(1\rightarrow4)$-$\beta$-glucanase mRNAs have not yet been examined.

It may be concluded, therefore, that members of different gene families are differentially responsive to GA and that the developmental patterns of individual isoenzymes can vary significantly. This serves to underline the complex nature of GA action on gene transcription in barley aleurone.

PROTECTION OF THE GRAIN AGAINST MICROBIAL AND INSECT ATTACK

Because of their high content of starch and storage proteins, barley grains should represent an attractive source of nutrients for insects and microbial pathogens. The vulnerability of the grain to insect and pathogen attack would be expected to increase during germination, when amino acids, fermentable sugars, nitrogenous bases, and other degradation products of reserve polymers accumulate in the starchy endosperm. It is not surprising, therefore, that barley has evolved efficient mechanical and molecular strategies to counter pathogen invasion in the grain.

A wide range of bacteria, yeasts, and filamentous fungi colonize the surface of mature barley grains both in the field and during storage (Gyllang et al, 1981; Petters et al, 1988). Microflora associated with the grain can cause gushing or undesirable flavors in beer and can produce harmful mycotoxins (Gjertsen et al, 1963; Gyllang and Martinson, 1976; Flannigan et al, 1984), but they seldom interfere with germination. Germination of grain in moist soil exposes the grain to an additional spectrum of microorganisms under conditions favorable for microbial growth. Penetration of microorganisms is usually arrested by the cuticularized layers and highly lignified walls of the surface layers of the grain. Microbial growth appears to extend to the testa-nucellar cuticle, which acts as a barrier to further penetration (Briggs, 1987). However, these mechanical barriers to microbial invasion may be weakened when grains crack during drying or harvesting or when surface layers soften at the high moisture contents required for germination.

In general, plants elicit a variety of proactive and reactive defense mechanisms against penetration by potentially pathogenic microorganisms. Several components of plant-pathogen interactive systems have been detected in ungerminated and germinating barley grain. These include the presence of "pathogenesis-related" (PR) proteins, peptide toxins, inhibitors of hydrolytic enzymes of exogenous origin, and inhibitors of protein synthesis. There is an increasing body of indirect evidence that barley may dedicate a significant proportion of its total energy reserves to such defense strategies. It has been reported that over 10% of total proteins in barley grain are toxic or inhibitory toward pathogens and that the albumin and globulin fractions of endosperm proteins consist predominantly of toxic thionins and enzyme inhibitors that have been implicated in defense of the grain (Garcia-Olmedo et al, 1992). Selected antimicrobial agents and other protective factors that have been identified in dormant barley grain are shown in Table 3. However, it should be noted that direct evidence that these components actually provide any degree of protection against microbial attack is generally lacking.

Enzymes

When plants are challenged with viruses, viroids, fungi, or bacteria, a group of soluble PR proteins, which includes $(1\rightarrow3)$-β-glucanases and endochitinases, is synthesized (Boller, 1987; Dixon and Lamb, 1990). These enzymes are present in germinated barley grain and can act synergistically to inhibit fungal growth in vitro (Leah et al, 1991).

$(1\rightarrow3)$-β-GLUCANASES

Relatively high levels of $(1\rightarrow3)$-β-glucan endohydrolase (EC 3.2.1.39) activity are found in the embryo of mature barley grain, and activity increases markedly during germination (Manners and Wilson, 1974; Ballance et al, 1976). Isolated aleurone layers also secrete the enzyme in response to GA (Taiz and Jones, 1970). Three $(1\rightarrow3)$-β-glucanases have been purified from extracts of germinated barley. They are designated isoenzyme GI (Høj et al, 1988), isoenzyme GII (Ballance and Svendsen, 1988; Høj et al, 1989; MacGregor and Ballance, 1991), and isoenzyme GIII (Wang et al, 1992; Hrmova and Fincher, 1993), and differences in their amino acid sequences indicate that they are the products of separate genes. The $(1\rightarrow3)$-β-glucanases all exhibit action patterns typical of polysaccharide endohydrolases, releasing laminaribiose and laminaritriose as the major final products from laminarin, as follows:

$$\downarrow \qquad \downarrow \qquad \downarrow$$
$$\ldots\ldots \text{G 3 G 3 G 3 G 3 G 3 G 3 G 3 G 3} \ldots\ldots \text{ red}$$

In this diagram, arrows indicate the hydrolysis of $(1\rightarrow3)$-β-linkages between glucosyl residues (G), and "red" indicates the reducing terminus of the polysaccharide. The $(1\rightarrow3)$-β-glucanases are unable to hydrolyze the single $(1\rightarrow3)$-β-linkages that are found in $(1\rightarrow3),(1\rightarrow4)$-$\beta$-glucans (Høj et al, 1988, 1989).

More recently, southern blot analysis of genomic DNA has shown that the $(1\rightarrow3)$-β-glucanases in barley are encoded by a small gene family of approximately six genes; cDNA and genomic clones for each of these genes have now been characterized (Høj et al, 1989; Xu et al, 1992). The properties of the genes and their corresponding enzymes, designated isoenzymes GI-GVI, are compared in Table 4. Amino acid sequences deduced from the cDNAs and isolated genes reveal positional identities ranging from 44–78%, and their catalytic amino acids are conserved (Chen et al, 1993). The sequence similarities, together with an extreme bias toward the use of G and C in the third base position of codons and the insertion of a single intron in the signal peptide coding region, provide strong evidence that the genes share a common evolutionary origin (Xu et al, 1992). Furthermore, similar structural features in the two genes that encode the barley $(1\rightarrow3),(1\rightarrow4)$-$\beta$-glucanases suggest that

TABLE 3
Potential Protective Factors in Barley Grain

Factor	Isoforms	Molecular Weight	Location	Possible Target	References
Enzymes	(1→3)-β-Glucanases (isoenzymes GII and GIV?)	32,000	Aleurone, embryo	Fungal cell walls	Ballance et al (1976), Ballance and Svendsen (1988), Høj et al (1988, 1989), Xu et al (1992)
	Endochitinases	28,000 33,000	Embryo, endosperm	Fungal cell walls	Leah et al (1987), Roberts and Selitrennikoff (1988), Jacobsen et al (1990)
Ribosome inactivating factor	Translation inhibitor II	30,000		Fungal and animal protein synthesis	Roberts and Selitrennikoff (1986), Asano et al (1984, 1986)
Inhibitors	α-Amylase/subtilisin inhibitor (BASI)	20,000	Endosperm	Barley high-pI α-amylase, microbial α-amylases, or peptidases?	Yoshikawa et al (1976), Mundy et al (1983), Weselake et al (1983a,b), Svendsen et al (1986), Halayko et al (1986)
	Trypsin/α-amylase inhibitors (more than 20 forms)	12,000–16,000	Endosperm	Insect and microbial α-amylases and peptidases	Mikola and Suolinna (1969), Odani et al (1983), Shewry et al (1984), Garcia-Olmedo et al (1992)
	Chymotrypsin inhibitors CL-1, CL-2	9,000	Endosperm	Chymotrypsin, subtilisin	Svendsen et al (1982), Williamson et al (1987, 1988)
Thionins	Type II thionins— α, β isoforms	5,000	Endosperm	Microorganisms?	Garcia-Olmeda et al (1992)

TABLE 4
Properties of Barley (1→3)-β-Glucanase Isoenzymes and Genes[a]

Property	Isoenzyme					
	G1	GII[b]	GIII	GIV	GV	GVI
Amino acids	310	306	305	327	312	315
Molecular weight[c]	33,000	32,300	32,400	35,000	34,000	32,900
Isoelectric point	8.6	9.5	9.8	10.7	7.5	4.6
N-Glycosylation sites	1	0	5	1	1	1
Codon bias in gene, %[d] (amino acid number)	(67)		(75 132 133 259 296)	(317)	(119)	(26)
	99.4	98.1	87.6	90.4	91.2	94.5
Transcription sites	Young roots, young leaves	Aleurone	Young roots, young leaves, shoots	Aleurone	Young roots, young leaves	Not known

[a] From Xu et al (1992).
[b] From Høj et al (1989).
[c] Excluding carbohydrate.
[d] Percentage of codons in the coding region of the mature enzyme that have G or C in the wobble base position.

the two classes of β-glucan endohydrolase originate from a single "super-gene" family and that these related, yet quite distinct, substrate specificities have evolved from a common ancestral enzyme. Indeed, when the amino acid sequences are compared using the algorithms of Hein (1990), the phylogenetic relationships of the (1→3)- and (1→3),(1→4)-β-glucanases from barley are clearly apparent (Xu et al, 1992; Fig. 1).

Specific oligonucleotide and DNA probes have enabled the transcription sites of individual (1→3)-β-glucanases to be assessed. The enzymes appear to be expressed in young roots and young leaves and in the aleurone of germinated grain (Table 4). However, mRNAs encoding isoenzymes GII and GIV were detected only in the aleurone. It appears, therefore, that (1→3)-β-glucanase isoenzyme GII is the major isoform found in germinating barley grain (Ballance and Svendsen, 1988; Høj et al, 1989; Xu et al, 1992) and that isoenzymes GI (Høj et al, 1988) and GIII (Wang et al, 1992) originate in vegetative tissues of the developing seedling.

The functional significance of (1→3)-β-glucanases in germinated barley grain is not yet clear. Endogenous (1→3)-β-glucan levels in the grain are normally low and are restricted to small callosic deposits scattered throughout the starchy endosperm (Fulcher et al, 1977; MacGregor et al, 1989). Although the (1→3)-β-glucanases could presumably reclaim the glucose associated with these deposits for seedling growth, the apparently low abundance of the polysac-

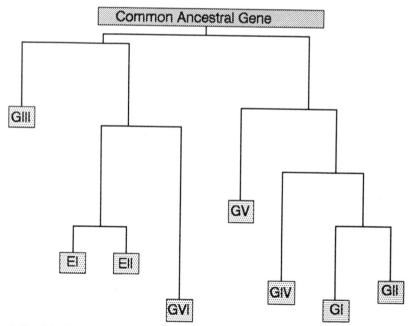

Fig. 1. Possible phylogenetic tree for the barley (1→3)- and (1→3),(1→4)-β-glucanase gene family reconstructed using the algorithms of Hein (1990). Vertical branch lengths are proportional to the number of sequence changes that have occurred. The (1→3),(1→4)-β-glucanase isoenzymes are designated EI and EII and the (1→3)-β-glucanases GI to GVI. (Adapted from Xu et al 1992)

charide is not commensurate with the high levels of the enzyme. The specific activity of $(1\rightarrow3)$-β-glucanase in unpurified extracts of germinated barley grain may exceed that of the $(1\rightarrow3),(1\rightarrow4)$-$\beta$-glucanases by a factor of 10-fold (Hrmova and Fincher, 1993). It should be reemphasized that purified $(1\rightarrow3)$-β-glucanases cannot hydrolyze the $(1\rightarrow3),(1\rightarrow4)$-$\beta$-glucans of the starchy endosperm walls (Høj et al, 1988; 1989). Earlier reports suggested that contiguous $(1\rightarrow3)$-β-linked glucosyl residues might be present in wall $(1\rightarrow3),(1\rightarrow4)$-$\beta$-glucan of the starchy endosperm and that the $(1\rightarrow3)$-β-glucanases might participate in the initial degradation of the walls during germination (Ballance and Manners, 1978a). However, there is as yet no strong evidence for the existence of contiguous $(1\rightarrow3)$-linkages in barley $(1\rightarrow3),(1\rightarrow4)$-$\beta$-glucans (Woodward et al, 1983) or that $(1\rightarrow3)$-β-glucanases function to release wall $(1\rightarrow3),(1\rightarrow4)$-$\beta$-glucans.

As a result of the apparent paucity of endogenous substrate, coupled with the general ability of $(1\rightarrow3)$-β-glucanases to hydrolyze the $(1\rightarrow3)$- and $(1\rightarrow3),(1\rightarrow6)$-$\beta$-glucans that are major constituents in walls of common fungal pathogens of the Basidiomycetes, Ascomycetes, and Oomycetes (Wessels and Sietsma, 1981), it has been speculated that the enzymes could constitute one component of barley's defenses against invading microorganisms (Fincher, 1989). The $(1\rightarrow3)$-β-glucanases might degrade hyphal walls directly and cause lysis of the fungal cells (Mauch et al, 1988; Leah et al, 1991), or oligosaccharides released by the enzyme from wall $(1\rightarrow3),(1\rightarrow6)$-$\beta$-glucans could elicit further reactions in a defense cascade (Boller, 1987). However, the synthesis of $(1\rightarrow3)$-β-glucanases in grain germinated under strictly sterile conditions (Høj et al, 1988, 1989) indicates that pathogen invasion is not prerequisite for synthesis. Rather, proactive expression of the enzymes in advance of microbial attack could represent a form of insurance against penetration of microorganisms into the starchy endosperm of germinating grain. The only evidence in support of a role for $(1\rightarrow3)$-β-glucanases in these defense strategies comes from observed increases in $(1\rightarrow3)$-β-glucanase gene expression when barley leaves are infected with the powdery mildew fungus, *Erisiphe graminis* (Jutidamrongphan et al, 1991; Xu et al, 1992). While such a function of the $(1\rightarrow3)$-β-glucanases in the germinating grain appears plausible, there are no reports of $(1\rightarrow3)$-β-glucanase induction by pathogens or corresponding elicitors in the grain, nor has any correlation been established between $(1\rightarrow3)$-β-glucanase gene expression and disease resistance.

ENDOCHITINASES

Endochitinases (EC 3.2.1.14) of M_r 28,000 and 33,000 have been reported in the aleurone, embryo, and starchy endosperm of ungerminated barley (Roberts and Selitrennikoff, 1986; Leah et al, 1987; Roberts and Selitrennikoff, 1988; Jacobsen et al, 1990). The higher-molecular-weight isoform differs from the lower-molecular-weight form by the presence of an NH_2-terminal extension, but the properties of the two isoenzymes are similar (Jacobsen et al, 1990). Again, there is no chitin substrate for the enzymes in the barley grain, but chitin is a major wall constituent of many pathogenic fungi (Wessels and Sietsma, 1981), and chitinases are commonly detected among PR proteins (Legrand et al, 1987; Vogeli-Lange et al, 1988). Furthermore, chitinases are potent inhibitors of fungal growth (Schlumbaum et al, 1986; Roberts and

Selitrennikoff, 1988; Jacobsen et al, 1990; Leah et al, 1991) and cause lysis of fungal walls that increases synergistically in the presence of $(1\rightarrow3)$-β-glucanases (Boller, 1987; Leah et al, 1991). Chitinases can also depolymerize peptidoglycans of bacterial cell walls, which have polysaccharide backbones with structural features similar to those of chitin. Taken together, these observations point to a likely role for chitinases in the protection of the barley grain against fungal or bacterial infection, although the effects of pathogen attack on chitinase levels have not been examined.

Enzyme Inhibitors

Barley grain contains several families of proteinaceous inhibitors of hydrolytic enzymes, including inhibitors of α-amylase, trypsin, chymotrypsin, and subtilisin.

The barley α-amylase/subtilisin inhibitor (BASI) is a bifunctional protein of M_r 20,000 that inhibits the high-pI α-amylases of barley as well as subtilisin, a bacterial peptidase (Yoshikawa et al, 1976; Mundy et al, 1983; Weselake et al, 1983a,b; Halayko et al, 1986; Svendsen et al, 1986). It is now recognized that this α-amylase/subtilisin inhibitor is homologous with the "Kunitz" family of soybean trypsin inhibitors (Kunitz, 1947). The protein accumulates in the developing endosperm in parallel with storage protein deposition (Giese and Hejgaard, 1984). Levels of the BASI inhibitor in embryoless half grains are elevated following treatment with ABA (Mundy, 1984). This implies that it may play a physiological role in the regulation of α-amylase activity in the germinating grain, particularly in periods of transient environmental stress where ABA levels rise and endosperm dissolution is temporarily suspended (Chandler et al, 1987); such a function remains to be unequivocally demonstrated.

A protein of M_r 10,000 purified from ungerminated barley grain was also thought to be an inhibitor of α-amylases and/or peptidases and was designated the "probable amylase/protease inhibitor" (Svensson et al, 1986). The protein shows some homology with the Bowman-Birk group of bifunctional inhibitors (Birk, 1985; Mundy and Rogers, 1986). However, it does not inhibit α-amylases or peptidases from a variety of organisms (Svensson et al, 1986), and it has now been identified as a lipid transfer protein (Breu et al, 1989).

Two chymotrypsin inhibitors, designated CI-1 and CI-2, have been identified in barley grain (Svendsen et al, 1982). The proteins have M_r values of approximately 9,000, inhibit chymotrypsin and subtilisin but not trypsin, and have been classified with the potato inhibitor I group (Svendsen et al, 1982; Williamson et al, 1987, 1988). There are about three copies of the CI-1 gene per haploid genome (Williamson et al, 1988), whereas CI-2 inhibitors are encoded by a small gene family of four to six members (Williamson et al, 1987); one of the CI-2 genes has been cloned and characterized (Peterson et al, 1991).

Other important inhibitors in barley grain are detected among the chloroform-methanol-soluble proteins. These include inhibitors of trypsin and other serine proteases, together with inhibitors of exogenous α-amylases. Their apparent M_r values range from 12 to 16 kD. Trypsin inhibitors were first identified in barley by Mikola and Suolinna (1969), and their sequence homology with the exogenous α-amylase inhibitors was recognized by Odani et al (1983). The α-amylase inhibitors exist in monomeric, dimeric, and tetrameric forms (Shewry et al, 1984; Barber et al, 1986; Sanchez-Monge et al, 1986) and show different activities against a range of eukaryotic α-amylases (Garcia-Olmedo et al, 1992). The α-amylase/trypsin inhibitor family is encoded by more than 20 genes that are dispersed over several chromosomes (Garcia-Olmedo et al, 1992). The genes are expressed in the developing endosperm before the majority of the reserve proteins and starch are deposited (Kirsi, 1973; Paz-Ares et al, 1983), but they disappear abruptly after the initiation of germination (Kirsi and Mikola, 1971; Pace et al, 1978). These observations suggest that this class of inhibitors may participate in the protection of developing and mature grain rather than germinating grain, possibly against attack by insects. Another interesting property of this group is that it contains the major barley allergens associated with baker's asthma (Sanchez-Monge et al, 1992).

Thionins

Barley thionins are small polypeptides of M_r ~5,000 and have three or four disulfide bridges. Multiple isoforms of the proteins have been identified and classified into three structural types (Gausing, 1987; Bohlmann et al, 1988; Garcia-Olmedo et al, 1992). The type I thionins are endosperm-specific and accumulate in protein bodies in the developing endosperm (Ponz et al, 1983). Analyses of cDNAs and genomic clones indicate that the protein is synthesized as a precursor containing a signal peptide, the thionin domain, and a relatively long COOH-terminal acidic peptide domain (Ponz et al, 1986; Rodriguez-Palenzuela et al, 1988). Type II thionins have been isolated from leaves, while the third type, designated type V and showing considerable sequence divergence, is found in cereal endosperm (Garcia-Olmedo et al, 1992). Thionins are toxic to plant-pathogenic microorganisms, and types I and II are about equally effective (Bohlmann et al, 1988; Garcia-Olmedo et al, 1992). Fungal infection of barley leaves induces expression of the leaf-specific type II thionins (Bohlmann et al, 1988). Although this can be taken as evidence for a general defense role, the true in vivo function of the thionins in barley grain is as yet unclear.

POTENTIAL FOR GENETIC ENGINEERING

Germination physiology and biochemistry are central to the utilization of barley grain in the malting and brewing industries. Criteria for barley quality demanded by these industries include large grain size, short dormancy period, specific grain protein levels, rapid development of amylolytic enzymes, high malt extract values, and low $(1\rightarrow3),(1\rightarrow4)$-$\beta$-glucan content. Of these, malt extract, which is the percentage of malted grain that can be extracted with hot water, is a particularly important and widely used indicator of barley quality, because higher extract values result in more nutrients being available for fermentative growth by yeast during the brewing process (Bamforth, 1993). Similarly, rapid development of amylolytic enzymes leads to rapid release of maltose and glucose from starch for the fermentation steps in brewing.

Amylolytic enzyme levels are expressed as "diastatic power," a measure of the combined levels of α-amylases, β-amylases, limit dextrinases, and α-glucosidases in the malted barley (Chapter 7 [Bamforth, 1993]).

Spectacular advances in molecular genetics and recent successes in the genetic engineering of dicotyledonous plants have raised expectations that barley might also be engineered to improve quality characteristics important for its commercial utilization in the malting and brewing industries. Improvement of any agriculturally important plant through gene technology requires the identification of genes that impart desirable phenotypic properties to the plant, a thorough understanding of the regulation of expression of the gene, isolation of the gene (or genes) and its in vitro manipulation, reintroduction and appropriate expression of the manipulated genetic material in the plant, and field trials to demonstrate that the genetic manipulation has indeed resulted in an improved phenotype. Clearly, this can be a long process and none of the steps can be classified as trivial. Although transgenic barley plants have not yet been reported, potentially useful genetic material has been identified and isolated, and considerable effort is being directed toward the regeneration of fertile barley plants from single transformed cells. Here, we briefly discuss the potential held by modern gene technology for the improvement of malt extract and diastatic power, quality characteristics that are closely related to grain biochemistry and physiology.

Malt Extract

The ability of barley grain to rapidly synthesize enzymes that hydrolyze the cell walls of the starchy endosperm is an important determinant of malt extract values because the walls act as barriers to the free diffusion of starch- and protein-degrading enzymes during germination. Inadequate degradation of the walls will therefore result in diminished solubilization of starch and protein and attendant decreases in malt extract values. The major component of walls in the starchy endosperm is $(1\rightarrow3),(1\rightarrow4)$-$\beta$-glucan (Fincher, 1975), and although total $(1\rightarrow3),(1\rightarrow4)$-$\beta$-glucan content in ungerminated barley grain is not correlated with malt extract (Henry, 1986; Loi et al, 1988), $(1\rightarrow3),(1\rightarrow4)$-$\beta$-glucanase levels are highly correlated with this important quality parameter (Bourne et al, 1982; Henry, 1986; Loi et al, 1988). This reflects the importance of $(1\rightarrow3),(1\rightarrow4)$-$\beta$-glucanase development in degrading the walls of the starchy endosperm in the germinating grain.

The identification of $(1\rightarrow3),(1\rightarrow4)$-$\beta$-glucanases as important determinants of malting quality, coupled with detailed information on their expression patterns (Stuart et al, 1986; McFadden et al, 1988; Slakeski and Fincher, 1992a,b) and the availability of genes for both isoenzymes (Litts et al, 1990; Slakeski et al, 1990; Wolf, 1991), might now be applied to the generation of barley varieties with improved malting performance as a result of enhanced $(1\rightarrow3),(1\rightarrow4)$-$\beta$-glucanase levels. This might be achieved simply by increasing the copy number of the $(1\rightarrow3),(1\rightarrow4)$-$\beta$-glucanase genes or by altering the gene promoters to enhance expression levels. The latter possibility might involve manipulation of the existing promoter, although this would require information on the *cis*-acting sequence elements responsible for the regulation of $(1\rightarrow3),(1\rightarrow4)$-$\beta$-glucanase gene expression (Wolf, 1992) and the *trans*-acting protein factors that participate in transcription. Alternatively, the $(1\rightarrow3),(1\rightarrow4)$-$\beta$-glucanase gene promoters could be replaced in toto by more powerful promoters that would direct transcription in an appropriate tissue-specific and temporal fashion; the high-pI α-amylase promoter (Knox et al, 1987; Khursheed and Rogers, 1988; Rahmatullah et al, 1989) would be a prime candidate for this approach.

Enhanced $(1\rightarrow3),(1\rightarrow4)$-$\beta$-glucanase activity might also be achieved by engineering increased thermostability into the enzymes. The two $(1\rightarrow3),(1\rightarrow4)$-$\beta$-glucanase isoenzymes are unstable at elevated temperatures, both in a highly purified form and in extracts of malted grain (Woodward and Fincher, 1982b; Loi et al, 1987). Thus, more than 60% of the $(1\rightarrow3),(1\rightarrow4)$-$\beta$-glucanase in the germinated grain is inactivated during commercial kilning processes, and much of the remaining activity is rapidly lost in simulated mashes at 55°C (Loi et al, 1987). If the thermostabilities of the $(1\rightarrow3),(1\rightarrow4)$-$\beta$-glucanases could be improved, either through random mutagenesis or site-directed alteration at the DNA level, losses of activity incurred during kilning and mashing could be partially overcome and the enzymes would be able to hydrolyze residual $(1\rightarrow3),(1\rightarrow4)$-$\beta$-glucans in malt extracts during mashing. Considerable success has been realized in the genetic engineering of thermostable $(1\rightarrow3),(1\rightarrow4)$-$\beta$-glucanases of bacterial origin, through domain interchange and the generation of hybrid enzymes (Olsen et al, 1991), and the stability of barley $(1\rightarrow3),(1\rightarrow4)$-$\beta$-glucanase isoenzyme EI has been improved by engineering an N-glycosylation site into the protein (Doan and Fincher, 1992).

The in vitro manipulation of cDNAs or genes encoding barley $(1\rightarrow3),(1\rightarrow4)$-$\beta$-glucanases is technically feasible, but the current constraint on genetic engineering of barley lies in our inability to routinely regenerate fertile transgenic plants. Foreign or manipulated DNA can be integrated into the barley genome in a stable form (Lazzeri et al, 1991) and fertile plants can be regenerated from single protoplasts (Jahne et al, 1991a,b), but these two steps, which are critical in the overall process of producing transgenic barley plants, have not yet been successfully combined. Nevertheless, it is likely that the regeneration of transgenic barley will be possible in the immediate future.

Diastase Activity

The ability of grain extracts to rapidly convert both granular and soluble starch to the fermentable sugars maltose and glucose represents another important quality parameter that could be amenable to manipulation by in vitro gene technology. Diastase activity reflects the concerted action of several enzymes, although it is not clear which enzymes are the most important and which might be present in limiting concentrations in the germinating grain. The α-amylases are primarily responsible for the initial depolymerization of amylose and amylopectin to smaller oligosaccharides, and genes encoding both the low- and high-pI isoforms have been cloned (Table 2). The rate of α-amylase expression could be increased by increasing gene copy number or by inserting additional copies of the TAACAAA and TATCCAC sequence elements that are involved in the GA-responsiveness of the high-pI α-amylase gene promoter (Skriver et al, 1991; Jacobsen and Gubler, 1991). It must be remembered that the barley α-amylases are encoded by a multigene family and that manipulation of one member of the family may have little overall effect on α-amylase levels in the germinating grain.

Another target for genetic manipulation, particularly for the production of low-calorie beers, is the limit dextrinase gene. This enzyme is crucially important in the cleavage of (1→6) linkages in amylopectin, because the branched limit dextrins containing (1→4)-α and (1→6)-α linkages are not fermentable by yeast during the brewing process. However, development of the enzyme during germination occurs relatively late, and maximal levels are not obtained until many days after α-amylase activity peaks (Lee and Pyler, 1984). Isolation of limit dextrinase genes would theoretically permit in vitro manipulation of the promoter region to accelerate expression in the germinating grain. Again, the improvement of diastatic power by manipulations of this kind are subject to the practical constraints associated with barley transformation and regeneration.

ACKNOWLEDGMENTS

The support of the Australian Research Council and the Grains Research and Development Corporation of Australia is gratefully acknowledged.

LITERATURE CITED

ALDERSON, A., SABELLI, P. A., DICKINSON, J. R., COLE, D., RICHARDSON, M., KREIS, M., SHEWRY, P. R., and HALFORD, N. G. 1991. Complementation of snf1, a mutation affecting global regulation of carbon metabolism in yeast, by a plant protein kinase cDNA. Proc. Natl. Acad. Sci. USA. 88:8602-8605.

AOYAGI, K., STICHER, L., WU, M., and JONES, R. L. 1990. The expression of barley α-amylase genes in *Xenopus laevis* oocytes. Planta 180:333-340.

ASANO, K., SVENSSON, B., and POULSEN, F. M. 1984. Isolation and characterization of inhibitors of animal cell-free protein synthesis from barley seeds. Carlsberg Res. Commun. 49:619-626.

ASANO, K., SVENSSON, B., POULSEN, F. M., NYGARD, O., and NILSSON, L. 1986. Influence of a protein synthesis inhibitor from barley seeds upon different steps of animal-free protein synthesis. Carlsberg Res. Commun. 51:75-81.

ASHFORD, A. E., and GUBLER, F. 1984. Mobilization of polysaccharide reserves from endosperm. Pages 117-162 in: Seed Physiology, Vol. 2. D. Murray, ed. Academic Press, New York.

ASHFORD, A. E., and GUBLER, F. 1987. The pathway of secretion of enzymes from isolated barley aleurone layers. Pages 512-521 in: Fourth International Symposium on Pre-Harvest Sprouting in Cereals. D. J. Mares, ed. Westview Press, Boulder, CO.

ASHFORD, A. E., and JACOBSEN, J. V. 1974. Cytochemical localization of phosphatase in barley aleurone cells: The pathway of gibberellic-acid-induced enzyme release. Planta 120:81-105.

ATZORN, R., and WEILER, E. W. 1983. The role of endogenous gibberellins in the formation of α-amylase by aleurone layers of germinating barley caryopses. Planta 159:289-299.

BACIC, A., and STONE, B. A. 1981a. Isolation and ultrastructure of aleurone cell walls from wheat and barley. Aust. J. Plant Physiol. 8:453-474.

BACIC, A., and STONE, B. A. 1981b. Chemistry and organization of aleurone cell wall components from wheat and barley. Aust. J. Plant Physiol. 8:475-495.

BALLANCE, G. M., and MANNERS, D. J. 1978a. Partial purification and properties of an endo-1,3-β-D-glucanase from germinated rye. Phytochemistry 17:1539-1543.

BALLANCE, G. M., and MANNERS, D. J. 1978b. Structural analysis and enzymic solubilization of barley endosperm cell walls. Carbohydr. Res. 61:107-118.

BALLANCE, G. M., and SVENDSEN, I. 1988. Purification and amino acid sequence determination of an endo-1,3-β-glucanase from barley. Carlsberg Res. Commun. 53:411-419.

BALLANCE, G. M., MEREDITH, W. O. S., and LABERGE, D. E. 1976. Distribution and development of endo-β-glucanase activities in barley tissues during germination. Can. J.

Plant Sci. 56:459-466.

BAMFORTH, C. W. 1985. Biochemical approaches to beer quality. J. Inst. Brew. 91:154-160.

BAMFORTH, C. W. 1993. Malting technology and the uses of malt. Pages 297-354 in: Barley: Chemistry and Technology. A. W. MacGregor and R. S Bhatty, eds. Am. Assoc. Cereal Chem., St. Paul, MN.

BAMFORTH, C. W., and MARTIN, H. L. 1981. β-Glucan and β-glucan solubilase in malting and mashing. J. Inst. Brew. 87:365-371.

BAMFORTH, C. W., MARTIN, H. L., and WAINWRIGHT, T. 1979. A role for carboxypeptidase in the solubilization of barley β-glucan. J. Inst. Brew. 85:334-338.

BARBER, D., SANCHEZ-MONGE, R., MENDEZ, E., LAZARO, A., GARCIA-OLMEDO, F., and SALCEDO, G. 1986. New α-amylase and trypsin inhibitors among the CM-proteins of barley (*Hordeum vulgare*). Biochim. Biophys. Acta 869:115-118.

BAULCOMBE, D., LAZARUS, C., MARTIENSSEN, R. 1984. Gibberellins and gene control in cereal aleurone cells. J. Embryol. Exp. Morphol. Suppl. 83:119-135.

BENJAVONGKULCHAI, E., and SPENCER, M. S. 1986. Purification and characterization of barley-aleurone xylanase. Planta 169:415-419.

BENJAVONGKULCHAI, E., and SPENCER, M. S. 1989. Barley aleurone xylanase: Its biosynthesis and possible role. Can. J. Bot. 67:297-302.

BHATTY, R. S. 1993. Non-malting uses of barley. Pages 355-417 in: Barley: Chemistry and Technology. A. W. MacGregor and R. S. Bhatty, eds. Am. Assoc. Cereal Chem., St. Paul, MN.

BIRK, Y. 1985. The Bowman-Birk inhibitor. Trypsin and chymotrypsin-inhibitor from soybeans. Int. J. Peptide Protein Res. 25:113-131.

BOHLMANN, H., CLAUSEN, S., BEHNKE, S., GIESE, H., HILLER, C., REIMAN-PHILIPP, U., SCHRADER, G., BARKHOLT, V., and APEL, K. 1988. Leaf-specific thionins of barley—A novel class of cell wall proteins toxic to plant-pathogenic fungi and possibly involved in the defense mechanism of plants. EMBO J. 7:1559-1565.

BOLLER, T. 1987. Hydrolytic enzymes in plant disease resistance. Pages 385-413 in: Plant-Microbe Interactions: Molecular and Genetic Perspectives, Vol. 2. T. Kosuge and E. W. Nester, eds. Macmillan, New York.

BOURNE, D. T., POWLESLAND, T., and WHEELER, R. E. 1982. The relationship

between total β-glucan of malt and malt quality. J. Inst. Brew. 88:371-375.

BREDDAM, K., and SØRENSEN, S. B. 1987. Isolation of carboxypeptidase III from malted barley by affinity chromatography. Carlsberg Res. Commun. 52:275-283.

BREU, V., GUERBETTE, F., KADER, J.-C., KANNANGARA, C. G., SVENSSON, B., and VON WETTSTEIN-KNOWLES, P. 1989. A 10 kD barley basic protein transfers phosphatidylcholine from liposomes to mitochondria. Carlsberg Res. Commun. 54:81-85.

BRIGGS, D. E. 1978. Barley. Chapman and Hall, London.

BRIGGS, D. E. 1987. Endosperm breakdown and its regulation in germinating barley. Pages 441-532 in: Brewing Science, Vol. 3. J. R. H. Pollock, ed. Academic Press, London.

BRIGGS, D. E., and MacDONALD, J. 1983. Patterns of modification in malting barley. J. Inst. Brew. 89:260-273.

BROOKES, P. A., and MARTIN, P. A. 1975. The determination and utilization of gibberellic acid in germinating barley. J. Inst. Brew. 81:357-363.

BROWN, A. H. D., and JACOBSEN J. V. 1982. Genetic basis and natural variation of α-amylase isoenzymes in barley. Genet. Res. 40:315-324.

BROWN, H. T., and MORRIS, G. H. 1890. Researches on the germination of some of the Gramineae. J. Chem. Soc. 57:458-528.

BROWN, P. H., and HO, T.-H. D. 1986. Barley aleurone layers secrete a nuclease in response to gibberellic acid. Plant Physiol. 82:801-806.

BROWN, P. H., and HO, T.-H. D. 1987. Biochemical properties and hormonal regulation of barley nuclease. Eur. J. Biochem. 168:357-364.

BUSH, D. S., and JONES, R. L. 1990. Hormonal regulation of Ca^{++} transport in microsomal vesicles isolated from barley aleurone layers. Pages 60-66 in: Calcium in Plant Growth and Development. R. T. Leonard and P. K. Hepler, eds. American Society of Plant Physiologists, Bethesda, MD.

BUSH, D. S., BISWAS, A. K., and JONES, R. L. 1988. Measurement of cytoplasmic Ca^{2+} and H^+ in barley aleurone protoplasts. Plant Cell Tissue Organ Cult. 12:159-162.

BUSH, D. S., BISWAS, A. K., and JONES, R. L. 1989. Gibberellic-acid-stimulated Ca^{2+} accumulation in endoplasmic reticulum of barley aleurone: Ca^{2+} transport and steady state levels. Planta 178:411-420.

BUTTROSE, M. S. 1971. Ultrastructure of barley aleurone cells as shown by freeze-etching. Planta 96:13-26.

CALLIS, J., and HO, T.-H. D. 1983. Multiple forms of the gibberellin-induced α-amylase from the aleurone layers of barley seeds. Arch. Biochem. Biophys. 224:224-234.

CARPITA, N., SABULARSE, D., MONTEZINOS, D., and DELMER, D. P. 1979. Determination of the pore size of cell walls of living plant cells. Science 205:11-17.

CHANDLER, P. M., and JACOBSEN, J. V. 1991. Primer extension studies on α-amylase mRNAs in barley aleurone. II. Hormonal regulation of expression. Plant Mol. Biol. 16:637-645.

CHANDLER, P. M., and MOSLETH, E. 1990. Do gibberellins play an in vivo role in controlling alpha-amylase gene expression? Pages 100-109 in: Fifth International Symposium on Pre-Harvest Sprouting in Cereals. K. Ringlund, E. Mosleth, and D. Mares, eds. Westview Press, Boulder, CO.

CHANDLER, P. M., ZWAR, J. A., JACOBSEN, J. V., HIGGINS, T. J. V., INGLIS, A. S. 1984. The effects of gibberellic acid and abscisic acid on α-amylase mRNA levels in barley aleurone layers studied using an α-amylase cDNA clone. Plant Mol. Biol. 3:407-418.

CHANDLER, P. M., ARIFFIN, Z., HUIET, L., JACOBSEN, J. V., and ZWAR, J. 1987. Molecular biology of expression of alpha-amylase and other genes following grain germination. Pages 295-303 in: Fourth International Symposium on Pre-Harvest Sprouting in Cereals. D. J. Mares, ed. Westview Press, Boulder, CO.

CHEN, L., FINCHER, G. B., and HØJ, P. B. 1993. Evolution of polysaccharide hydrolase substrate specificity. Catalytic amino acids are conserved in barley 1,3-1,4- and 1,3-β-glucanases. J. Biol. Chem. In press.

CHEN, R.-F., and JONES, R. L. 1974. Studies on the release of barley aleurone cell proteins: Kinetics of labelling. Planta 119:193-206.

CHRISPEELS, M. J. 1976. Biosynthesis, intracellular transport, and secretion of extracellular macromolecules. Annu. Rev. Plant Physiol. 27:19-38.

CHRISPEELS, M. J., and TAGUE, B. W. 1991. Protein sorting in the secretory system of plant cells. Int. Rev. Cytol. 125:1-45.

CHRISPEELS, M. J., and VARNER, J. E. 1967. Gibberellic acid-enhanced synthesis and release of α-amylase and ribonuclease by isolated barley aleurone layers. Plant Physiol. 42:398-406.

CLUTTERBUCK, V. J., and BRIGGS, D. E. 1973. Enzyme formation and release by isolated barley aleurone layers. Phytochemistry 12:537-546.

COLBORNE, A. J., MORRIS, G., and

LAIDMAN, D. L. 1976. The formation of endoplasmic reticulum in the aleurone cells of germinating wheat: An ultrastructural study. J. Exp. Bot. 27:759-767.

DASHEK, W. V., and CHRISPEELS, M. J. 1977. Gibberellic-acid-induced synthesis and release of cell wall degrading endoxylanase by isolated aleurone layers of barley. Planta 134:251-256.

DEIKMAN, J., and JONES, R. L. 1985. Control of α-amylase accumulation by gibberellic acid and calcium in barley aleurone layers. Plant Physiol. 78:192-198.

DEIKMAN, J., and JONES, R. L. 1986. Regulation of the accumulation of mRNA for α-amylase isoenzymes in barley aleurone. Plant Physiol. 80:672-675.

DEVOS, K. M., ATKINSON, M. D., CHINOY, C. N., LIU, C. J., and GALE, M. D. 1992. RFLP based genetic map of the homoeologous group 3 chromosomes of wheat and rye. Theor. Appl. Genet. 83:931-939.

DIXON, R. A., and LAMB, C. J. 1990. Molecular communication in interactions between plants and microbial pathogens. Annu. Rev. Plant Physiol. Plant Mol. Biol. 41:339-367.

DOAN, D. N. P., and FINCHER, G. B. 1988. The A- and B-chains of carboxypeptidase I from germinated barley originate from a single precursor polypeptide. J. Biol. Chem. 263:11106-11110.

DOAN, D. N. P., and FINCHER, G. B. 1992. Differences in thermostabilities of barley (1→3,1→4)-β-glucanases are only partly determined by N-glycosylation. FEBS Lett. 309:265-271.

DUFFUS, C. M., and COCHRANE, M. P. 1993. Development, structure and composition of the barley kernel. Pages 31-72 in: Barley: Chemistry and Technology. A. W. MacGregor and R. S. Bhatty, eds. Am. Assoc. Cereal Chem., St. Paul, MN.

EDNEY, M. J., MARCHYLO, B. A., and MacGREGOR, A. W. 1991. Structure of total barley beta-glucan. J. Inst. Brew. 97:39-44.

ELLIOTT, D. C., and KOKKE, Y. S. 1987. Partial-purification and properties of a protein kinase-C type enzyme from plants. Phytochemistry 26:2929-2935.

FERNANDEZ, D. E., and STAEHELIN, L. A. 1985. Structural organization of ultrarapidly frozen barley aleurone cells actively involved in protein secretion. Planta 165:455-468.

FERNANDEZ, D. E., and STAEHELIN, L. A. 1987. Does gibberellic acid induce the transfer of lipase from protein bodies to lipid bodies in barley aleurone cells? Plant Physiol.

85:487-496.

FINCHER, G. B. 1975. Morphology and chemical composition of barley endosperm cell walls. J. Inst. Brew. 81:116-122.

FINCHER, G. B. 1976. Ferulic acid in barley cell walls: A fluorescence study. J. Inst. Brew. 82:347-349.

FINCHER, G. B. 1989. Molecular and cellular biology associated with endosperm mobilization in germinating cereal grains. Annu. Rev. Plant Physiol. Plant Mol. Biol. 40:305-346.

FINCHER, G. B., and STONE, B. A. 1986. Cell walls and their components in cereal grain technology. Pages 207-295 in: Advances in Cereal Science and Technology, Vol. 8. Y. Pomeranz, ed. Am. Assoc. Cereal Chem., St. Paul, MN.

FINCHER, G. B., LOCK, P. A., MORGAN, M. M., LINGELBACH, K., WETTENHALL, R. E. H., BRANDT, A., and THOMSEN, K.-K. 1986. Primary structure of a $(1\rightarrow3,1\rightarrow4)$-$\beta$-glucan 4-glucanohydrolase from barley aleurone. Proc. Natl. Acad. Sci. USA 83:2081-2085.

FLANNIGAN, B., DAY, S. W., DOUGLAS, P. E., and McFARLANE, G. B. 1984. Growth of mycotoxin-producing fungi associated with malting of barley. Pages 52-60 in: Toxigenic Fungi—Their Toxins and Health Hazards. H. Kurata and Y. Ueno, eds. Kodansha/Elsevier, Tokyo.

FREEMAN, P. L., and PALMER, G. H. 1984. The influence of the pericarp and testa on the direct passage of gibberellic acid into the aleurone of normal and abraded barleys. J. Inst. Brew. 90:95-104.

FULCHER, R. G., SETTERFIELD, G., McCULLY, M. E., and WOOD, P. J. 1977. Observations on the aleurone layer. II. Fluorescence microscopy of the aleurone-subaleurone junction with emphasis on possible β-1,3-glucan deposits in barley. Aust. J. Plant Physiol. 4:917-928.

GABARD, K. A., and JONES, R. L. 1986. Localization of phytase and acid phosphatase isoenzymes in aleurone layers of barley. Physiol. Plant. 67:182-192.

GARCIA-OLMEDO, F., SALCEDO, G., SANCHEZ-MONGE, R., HERNANDEZ-LUCAS, C., CARMONA, M. J., LOPEZ-FANDO, J. J., FERNANDEZ, J. A., GOMEZ, L., ROYO, J., GARCIA-MAROTO, F., CASTAGNARO, A., and CARBONERO, P. 1992. Trypsin/α-amylase inhibitors and thionins: Possible defence proteins from barley. Pages 335-350 in: Barley: Genetics, Molecular Biology and Biotechnology. P. R. Shewry, ed. CAB International, Oxon.

GAUSING, K. 1987. Thionin genes specifically expressed in barley leaves. Planta 171:241-246.

GIANNAKOUROS, T., KARAGIORGOS, A., and SIMOS, G. 1991. Expression of β-galactosidase multiple forms during barley (Hordeum vulgare) seed germination. Separation and characterization of enzyme isoforms. Physiol. Plant 82:413-418.

GIBBONS, G. C. 1981. On the relative role of the scutellum and aleurone in the production of hydrolases during germination of barley. Carlsberg Res. Commun. 46:215-225.

GIBSON, R. A., and PALEG, L. G. 1976. Purification of gibberellic acid-induced lysosomes from wheat aleurone cells. J. Cell Sci. 22:413-425.

GIESE, H., and HEJGAARD, J. 1984. Synthesis of salt-soluble proteins in barley. Pulse-labelling study of grain filling in liquid-cultured detached spikes. Planta 161:172-177.

GILMOUR, S. J., and MacMILLAN, J. 1984. Effect of inhibitors of gibberellin biosynthesis on the induction of α-amylase in embryoless caryopses of Hordeum vulgare cv. Himalaya. Planta 162:89-90.

GJERTSEN, P., TROLLE, B., and ANDERSEN, K. 1963. Weathered barley as a contributory cause of gushing in beer. Pages 320-341 in: Proc. Congr. Eur. Brew. Conv., 9th, Brussels.

GRAM, N. H. 1982a. The ultrastructure of germinating barley seeds. I. Changes in the scutellum and the aleurone layer in Nordal barley. Carlsberg Res. Commun. 47:143-162.

GRAM, N. H. 1982b. The ultrastructure of germinating barley seeds. II. Breakdown of starch granules and cell walls of the endosperm in three barley varieties. Carlsberg Res. Commun. 47:173-185.

GROSSELINDEMANN, E., GRAEBE, J. E., STÖCK, D., and HEDDEN, P. 1991. ent-Kaurene biosynthesis in germinating barley (Hordeum vulgare L., cv. Himalaya) caryopses and its relation to α-amylase production. Plant Physiol. 96:1099-1104.

GUBLER, F., ASHFORD, A. E., BACIC, A., BLAKENEY, A. B., and STONE, B. A. 1985. Release of ferulic acid esters from barley aleurone. II. Characterization of the feruloyl compounds released in response to GA$_3$. Aust. J. Plant Physiol. 12:307-317.

GUBLER, F., JACOBSEN, J. V., and ASHFORD, A. E. 1986. Involvement of the Golgi apparatus in the secretion of α-amylase from gibberellin-treated barley aleurone cells. Planta 168:447-452.

GUBLER, F., ASHFORD, A. E., and JACOBSEN, J. V. 1987. The release of α-amylase through gibberellin-treated barley aleurone cell walls. Planta 172:155-161.

GUERIN, J. R., LANCE, R. C. M., and WALLACE, W. 1991. Release and activation of barley beta-amylase by malt endopeptidases. J. Cereal Sci. 15:5-14.

GYLLANG, H., and MARTINSON, E. 1976. Studies on the mycoflora of malt. J. Inst. Brew. 82:350-352.

GYLLANG, H., KJELLEN, K., HAIKARA, A., and SIGSGAARD, P. 1981. Evaluation of fungal contaminations of barley and malt. J. Inst. Brew. 87:248-251.

HABERLANDT, G. 1890. Die kleberschicht des gras-endosperms als diastase ausscheidendes drusen-gewebe. Ber. Dtsch. Bot. Ges. 8:40-48.

HALAYKO, A. J., HILL, R. D., and SVENSSON, B. 1986. Characterization of the interaction of barley α-amylase inhibitor from barley kernels. Biochim. Biophys. Acta 873:92-101.

HAMMERTON, R. W., and HO, T.-H. D. 1986. Hormonal regulation of the development of protease and carboxypeptidase activities in barley aleurone layers. Plant Physiol. 80:692-697.

HARA-NISHIMURA, J., NISHIMURA, M., and DAUSSANT, J. 1986. Conversion of free β-amylase to bound β-amylase on starch granules in the barley endosperm during the desiccation phase of seed development. Protoplasma 134:149-153.

HARDIE, D. G. 1975. Control of carbohydrase formation by gibberellic acid in barley endosperm. Phytochemistry 14:1719-1722.

HEIN, J. 1990. Unified approach to alignment and phylogenies. Methods Enzymol. 183:626-645.

HEJGAARD, J. 1978. "Free" and "bound" β-amylase during malting of barley. Characterization by two-dimensional immunoelectrophoresis. J. Inst. Brew. 84:43-46.

HENRY, R. J. 1986. Genetic and environmental variation in the pentosan and β-glucan contents of barley, and their relation to malting quality. J. Cereal Sci. 4:269-277.

HENRY, R. J. 1990. Qualitative analysis of barley (1→3,1→4)-β-glucanase isoenzymes by high performance liquid chromatography. J. Cereal Sci. 12:187-192.

HEUPKE, H.-J., and ROBINSON, D. G. 1985. Intracellular transport of α-amylase in barley aleurone cells: Evidence for the participation of the Golgi apparatus. Eur. J. Cell Biol. 39:265-272.

HIGGINS, C. F., and PAYNE, J. W. 1977. Peptide transport by germinating barley embryos. Planta 134:205-206.

HIGGINS, C. F., and PAYNE, J. W. 1978a. Peptide transport by germinating barley embryos: Uptake of physiological di- and oligopeptides. Planta 138:211-215.

HIGGINS, C. F., and PAYNE, J. W. 1978b. Peptide transport by germinating barley embryos: Evidence for a single common carrier for di- and oligopeptides. Planta 138:217-221.

HIGGINS, C. F., and PAYNE, J. W. 1981. The peptide pools of germinating barley grains: Relation to hydrolysis and transport of storage proteins. Plant Physiol. 67:785-792.

HO, T.-H. D., NOLAN, R. C., LIN, L.-S., BRODL, M. R., and BROWN, P. H. 1987. Regulation of gene expression in barley aleurone layers. Pages 35-49 in: Molecular Biology of Plant Growth Control. J. E. Fox and M. Jacobs, eds. Liss, New York.

HØJ, P. B., SLADE, A. M., WETTENHALL, R. E. H., and FINCHER, G. B. 1988. Isolation and characterization of a (1→3)-β-glucan endohydrolase from germinating barley (*Hordeum vulgare*): Amino-acid sequence similarity with barley (1→3,1→4)-β-glucanases. FEBS Lett. 230:67-71.

HØJ, P. B., HARTMAN, D. J., MORRICE, N. A., DOAN, D. N. P., and FINCHER, G. B. 1989. Purification of (1→3)-β-glucan endohydrolase isoenzyme II from germinated barley and determination of its primary structure from a cDNA clone. Plant Mol. Biol. 13:31-42.

HØJ, P. B., HOOGENRAAD, N., HARTMAN, D. J., YANNAKENA, H., and FINCHER, G. B. 1990. Identification of individual (1→3,1→4)-β-D-glucanase isoenzymes in extracts of germinated barley using specific monoclonal antibodies. J. Cereal Sci. 11:261-268.

HOOLEY, R., BEALE, M. H., and SMITH, S. J. 1991. Gibberellin perception at the plasma membrane of *Avena fatua* aleurone protoplasts. Planta 183:274-280.

HOY, J. L., MACAULEY, B. J., and FINCHER, G. B. 1981. Cellulases of plant and microbial origin in germinating barley. J. Inst. Brew. 87:77-80.

HRMOVA, M., and FINCHER, G. B. 1993. Purification and properties of three (1→3)-β-D-glucanase isoenzymes from young leaves of barley (*Hordeum vulgare*). Biochem. J. 289:453-461.

HUANG, J.-K., SWEGLE, M., DANDEKAR, A. M., and MUTHUKRISHNAN, S. 1984. Expression and regulation of α-amylase gene family in barley aleurones. J. Mol. Appl. Genet. 2:579-588.

JACKSON, E. A., BALLANCE, G. M., and THOMSEN, K. K. 1986. Construction of a yeast vector directing the synthesis and secretion of barley (1→3,1→4)-β-glucanase.

Carlsberg Res. Commun. 51:445-458.

JACOBSEN, J. V., and BEACH, L. R. 1985. Control of transcription of α-amylase and rRNA genes in barley aleurone protoplasts by gibberellin and abscisic acid. Nature 316:275-277.

JACOBSEN, J. V., and CHANDLER, P. M. 1987. Gibberellin and abscisic acid in germinating cereals. Pages 164-193 in: Plant Hormones and Their Role in Plant Growth and Development. P. J. Davies, ed. Martinus Nijhoff, Dordrecht.

JACOBSEN, J. V., and GUBLER, F. 1992. Hormonal control of gene expression. Pages 116-127 in: Progress in Plant Growth Regulation. C. M. Karssen, C. L. van Loon, and D. Vreugdenhil, eds. Kluwer-Academic Publishers, Dordrecht, Netherlands.

JACOBSEN, J. V., and HIGGINS, T. J. V. 1982. Characterization of the α-amylases synthesized by aleurone layers of Himalaya barley in response to gibberellic acid. Plant Physiol. 70:1647-1653.

JACOBSEN, J. V., KNOX, R. B., and PYLIOTIS, N. A. 1971. The structure and composition of aleurone grains in the barley aleurone layer. Planta 101:189-209.

JACOBSEN, J. V., ZWAR, J. A., and CHANDLER, P. M. 1985. Gibberellic acid-responsive protoplasts from mature aleurone of Himalaya barley. Planta 163:430-439.

JACOBSEN, J. V., BUSH, D. S., STICHER, L., and JONES, R. L. 1988. Evidence for precursor forms of the low isoelectric point α-amylase isozymes secreted by barley aleurone cells. Plant Physiol. 88:1168-1174.

JACOBSEN, S., MIKKELSEN, J. D., and HEJGAARD, J. 1990. Characterization of two antifungal endochitinases from barley grain. Physiol. Plant. 79:554-562.

JAHNE, A., LAZZERI, P. A., JAGER-GUSSEN, M., and LORZ, H. 1991a. Plant regeneration from embryogenic cell suspensions derived from anther cultures of barley (*Hordeum vulgare* L.). Theor. Appl. Genet. 82:74-80.

JAHNE, A., LAZZERI, P. A., and LORZ, H. 1991b. Regeneration of fertile plants from protoplasts derived from embryogenic cell suspensions of barley (*Hordeum vulgare* L.). Plant Cell Rep. 10:1-6.

JONES, R. L. 1969a. Gibberellic acid and the fine structure of barley aleurone cells. I. Changes during the lag-phase of α-amylase synthesis. Planta 87:119-133.

JONES, R. L. 1969b. Gibberellic acid and the fine structure of barley aleurone cells. II. Changes during the synthesis and secretion of α-amylase. Planta 88:73-86.

JONES, R. L. 1972. Fractionation of the enzymes of the barley aleurone layer. Evidence for a soluble mode of enzyme release. Planta 103:95-109.

JONES, R. L. 1980. Quantitative and qualitative changes in the endoplasmic reticulum of barley aleurone layers. Planta 150:70-81.

JONES, R. L. 1985. Protein synthesis and secretion by the barley aleurone: A perspective. Isr. J. Bot. 34:377-395.

JONES, R. L. 1987. Localization of ATPase in the endoplasmic reticulum and Golgi apparatus of barley aleurone. Protoplasma 138:73-88.

JONES, R. L., and JACOBSEN, J. V. 1983. Calcium regulation of the secretion of α-amylase isoenzymes and other proteins from barley aleurone layers. Planta 158:1-9.

JONES, R. L., and JACOBSEN, J. V. 1991. Regulation of synthesis and transport of secreted proteins in cereal aleurone. Int. Rev. Cytol. 126:49-88.

JONES, R. L., and PRICE, J. M. 1970. Gibberellic acid and the fine structure of barley aleurone cells. III. Vacuolation of the aleurone cell during the phase of ribonuclease release. Planta 94:191-202.

JONES, R. L., BUSH, D. S., STICHER, L., SIMON, P., and JACOBSEN, J. V. 1987. Intracellular transport and secretion of barley aleurone α-amylase. Pages 325-340 in: Plant Membranes: Structure, Function, Biogenesis. C. Leaver and H. Sze, eds. Liss, New York.

JORGENSEN, O. B. 1965. Barley malt α-glucosidase. VI. Localisation and development during barley germination. Acta Chem. Scand. 19:1014-1015.

JUTIDAMRONGPHAN, W., ANDERSEN, J. B., MacKINNON, G., MANNERS, J. M., SIMPSON, R. S., and SCOTT, K. J. 1991. Induction of β-1,3-glucanase in barley in response to infection by fungal pathogens. Mol. Plant-Microbe Interact. 4:234-238.

KHURSHEED, B., and ROGERS, J. C. 1988. Barley α-amylase genes. J. Biol. Chem. 263:18953-18960.

KHURSHEED, B., and ROGERS, J. C. 1989. Barley α-amylase genes and the thiol protease gene aleurain: Use of a single poly (A) addition signal associated with a conserved pentanucleotide at the cleavage site. Proc. Natl. Acad. Sci. USA 86:3987-3991.

KIRSI, M. 1973. Formation of proteinase inhibitors in developing barley grains. Physiol. Plant. 29:141-144.

KIRSI, M., and MIKOLA, J. 1971. Occurrence of proteolytic inhibitors in various tissues of barley. Planta 96:281-291.

KNOX, C. A. P., SONTHAYANON, B., CHANDRA, G. R., and MUTHUKRISHNAN, S. 1987. Structure and organization of two divergent α-amylase genes from barley. Plant Mol. Biol. 9:3-17.

KOEHLER, S., and HO, T.-H. D. 1988. Purification and characterization of gibberellic acid-induced cysteine endoproteases in barley aleurone layers. Plant Physiol. 87:95-103.

KOEHLER, S., and HO, T.-H. D. 1990a. A major gibberellic acid induced barley aleurone cysteine proteinase which digests hordein: Purification and characterization. Plant Physiol. 94:251-258.

KOEHLER, S., and HO, T.-H. D. 1990b. Hormonal regulation, processing, and secretion of cysteine proteinases in barley aleurone layers. Plant Cell 2:769-783.

KREIS, M., WILLIAMSON, M., BUXTON, B., PYWELL, J., HEJGAARD, J., and SVENDSEN, I. 1987. Primary structure and differential expression of β-amylase in normal and mutant barleys. Eur. J. Biochem. 169:517-525.

KREIS, M., WILLIAMSON, M., SHEWRY, P. R., SHARP, P., and GALE, M. D. 1988. Identification of a second locus encoding β-amylase on chromosome 2 of barley. Genet. Res. 51:13-16.

KUNITZ, M. 1947. Crystalline soybean trypsin inhibitor. 2. General properties. J. Gen. Physiol. 30:291-307.

KUSABA, M., KOBAYASHI, O., YAMAGUCHI, I., TAKAHASHI, N., and TAKEDA, G. 1991. Effects of gibberellin on genetic variations in α-amylase production in germinating barley seeds. J. Cereal Sci. 14:151-160.

LAMB, C. J., LAWTON, M. A., DRON, M., and DIXON, R. A. 1989. Signals and transduction mechanisms for activation of plant defenses against microbial attack. Cell 56:215-224.

LAURIERE, C., LAURIERE, M., and DAUSSANT, J. 1986. Immunohistochemical localization of β-amylase in resting barley seeds. Physiol. Plant. 67:383-388.

LAZZERI, P. A., BRETTSCHNEIDER, R., LUHRS, R., and LORZ, H. 1991. Stable transformation of barley via PEG-induced direct DNA uptake into protoplasts. Theor. Appl. Genet. 81:437-444.

LEAH, R., MIKKELSEN, J. D., MUNDY, J., and SVENDSEN, I. 1987. Identification of a 28,000 dalton endochitinase in barley endosperm. Carlsberg Res. Commun. 52:31-37.

LEAH, R., TOMMERUP, H., SVENDSEN, I., and MUNDY, J. 1991. Biochemical and molecular characterization of three barley seed proteins with antifungal properties. J. Biol. Chem. 266:1564-1573.

LEE, W. J., and PYLER, R. E. 1984. Barley malt limit dextrinase: Varietal, environmental and malting effects. J. Am. Soc. Brew. Chem. 42:11-17.

LEE, W. J., and PYLER, R. E. 1985. Nucleic acid degrading enzymes of barley malt. I. Nucleases and phosphatases. J. Am. Soc. Brew. Chem. 43:1-6.

LEE, W. J., and PYLER, R. E 1986. Nucleic acid degrading enzymes of barley malt. III. Adenosine nucleosidase from malted barley. J. Am. Soc. Brew. Chem. 44:86-90.

LEGRAND, M., KAUFFMAN, S., GEOFFROY, P., and FRITIG, B. 1987. Biological function of pathogenesis-related proteins: Four tobacco pathogenesis-related proteins are chitinases. Proc. Natl. Acad. Sci. USA 84:6750-6754.

LENOIR, P., MacGREGOR, A. W., MOLL, M., and DAUSSANT, J. 1984. Identification of debranching enzymes from barley and malt by isoelectric focussing. C.R. Acad. Sci. Ser. 3. 298:243-248.

LIN, L.-S., and HO, T.-H. D. 1986. Mode of action of abscisic acid in barley aleurone layers. Plant Physiol. 82:289-297.

LITTS, J. C., SIMMONS, C. R., KARRER, E. E., HUANG, N., and RODRIGUEZ, R. L. 1990. The isolation and characterization of a barley 1,3-1,4-β-glucanase gene. Eur. J. Biochem. 194:831-838.

LOCY, R., and KENDE, H. 1978. The mode of secretion of α-amylase in barley aleurone layers. Planta 143:89-99.

LOI, L., BARTON, P. A., and FINCHER, G. B. 1987. Survival of barley (1→3,1→4)-β-glucanase isoenzymes during kilning and mashing. J. Cereal Sci. 5:45-50.

LOI, L., AHLUWALIA, B., and FINCHER, G. B. 1988. Chromosomal location of genes encoding barley (1→3,1→4)-β-glucan 4-glucanohydrolases. Plant Physiol. 87:300-302.

LONGSTAFF, M. A., and BRYCE, J. H. 1993. Development of limit dextrinase in germinated barley (*Hordeum vulgare* L.). Evidence of proteolytic activation. Plant Physiol. 101:881-889.

LUNDGARD, R., and SVENSSON, B. 1987. The four major forms of barley β-amylase. Purification, characterization and structural relationship. Carlsberg Res. Commun. 52:313-326.

LUSINI, P., TRABALIZINI, L., FRANCHI, G. G., BOLAVINI, L., and MARTELLI, P. 1991. Adenylate cyclase in roots of *Ricinus communis*; stimulation by GTP and Mn^{2+}. Phytochemistry 30:109-111.

MacGREGOR, A. W. 1987. α-Amylase, limit dextrinase, and α-glucosidase enzymes in barley and malt. CRC Crit. Rev. Biotechnol. 5:117-128.

MacGREGOR, A. W., and BALLANCE, D. L. 1980. Hydrolysis of large and small starch granules from normal and waxy barley cultivars by alpha-amylases from barley malt. Cereal Chem. 57:397-402.

MacGREGOR, A. W., and FINCHER, G. B. 1993. Carbohydrates of the barley grain. Pages 73-130 in: Barley: Chemistry and Technology. A. W. MacGregor and R. S. Bhatty, eds. Am. Assoc. Cereal Chem., St. Paul, MN.

MacGREGOR, A. W., and LENOIR, C. 1987. Studies on α-glucosidase in barley and malt. J. Inst. Brew. 93:334-337.

MacGREGOR, A. W., and MARCHYLO, B. A. 1986. α-Amylase components in excised, incubated barley embryos. J. Inst. Brew. 92:159-161.

MacGREGOR, A. W., and MORGAN, J. E. 1986. Hydrolysis of barley starch granules by alpha-amylases from barley malt. Cereal Foods World 31:688-693.

MacGREGOR, A. W., MacDOUGALL, F. H., MAYER, C., and DAUSSANT, J. 1984. Changes in levels of α-amylase components in barley tissues during germination and early seedling growth. Plant Physiol. 75:203-206.

MacGREGOR, A. W., MARCHYLO, B. A., and KRUGER, J. E. 1988. Multiple α-amylase components in germinated cereal grains determined by isoelectric focusing and chromatofocusing. Cereal Chem. 65:326-333.

MacGREGOR, A. W., BALLANCE, G. M., and DUSHNICKY, L. 1989. Fluorescence microscopy studies on (1,3)-β-D-glucan in barley endosperm. Food Microstr. 8:235-244.

MacGREGOR, E. A., and BALLANCE, G. M. 1991. Possible secondary structure in plant and yeast β-glucanase. Biochem. J. 274:41-43.

MacGREGOR, E. A., and MacGREGOR, A. W. 1987. Studies of cereal α-amylases using cloned DNA. CRC Crit. Rev. Biotechnol. 5:129-142.

MacLEOD, A. M., and PALMER, G. H. 1967. Gibberellin from barley embryos. Nature 216:1342-1343.

MacLEOD, L. C., LANCE, R. C. M., and BROWN, A. H. D. 1991. Chromosomal mapping of the Glb 1 locus encoding (1→3,1→4)-β-D-glucan 4-glucanohydrolase EI in barley. J. Cereal Sci. 13:291-298.

MAEDA, I., KIRIBUCHI, S., and NAKAMURA, M. 1978. Digestion of barley starch granules by the combined action of α- and β-amylases purified from barley and barley malt. Agric. Biol. Chem. 42:259-267.

MANNERS, D. J., and HARDIE, D. G. 1977. Studies on debranching enzymes. VI. The starch-debranching enzyme system of germinated barley. Tech. Q. Master Brew.

Assoc. Am. 14:120-125.

MANNERS, D. J., and MARSHALL, J. J. 1969. Studies on carbohydrate metabolizing enzymes. XXII. The β-glucanase system of malted barley. J. Inst. Brew. 75:550-561.

MANNERS, D. J., and WILSON, G. 1974. Purification and properties of an endo-β-D-glucanase from malted barley. Carbohydr. Res. 37:9-22.

MANNERS, D. J., and YELLOWLEES, D. 1973. Studies on debranching enzymes. I. The limit dextrinase activity of extracts of certain higher plants and commercial malts. J. Inst. Brew. 79:377-385.

MANNERS, D. J., SEILER, A., and STURGEON, R. J. 1982. Observations on the endo-(1→4)-β-glucanase activity of extracts of barley. Carbohydr. Res. 100:435-440.

MAUCH, F., HADWIGER, L. A., and BOLLER, T. 1988. Antifungal hydrolases in pea tissue. I. Purification and characterization of two chitinases and two β-1,3-glucanases differentially regulated during development and in response to fungal infection. Plant Physiol. 87:325-333.

McLEARY, B. V. 1992. Measurement of the content of limit dextrinase in cereal flours. Carbohydr. Res. 227:257-268.

McFADDEN, G. I., AHLUWALIA, B., CLARKE, A. E., and FINCHER, G. B. 1988. Expression sites and developmental regulation of genes encoding (1→3,1→4)-β-glucanases in germinated barley. Planta 173:500-508.

MIKOLA, J. 1983. Proteinases, peptidases, and inhibitors of endogenous proteinases in germinating seeds. Pages 35-52 in: Seed Proteins. J. Daussant, J. Moss, and J. Vaughan, eds. Academic Press, London.

MIKOLA, J. 1987. Proteinases and peptidases in germinating cereal grains. Pages 463-473 in: Fourth International Symposium on Pre-Harvest Sprouting in Cereals. D. J. Mares, ed. Westview Press, Boulder, CO.

MIKOLA, J., and KOLEHMAINEN, L. 1972. Localization and activity of various peptidases in germinating barley. Planta 104:167-177.

MIKOLA, J., and SOULINNA, E. M. 1969. Purification and properties of a trypsin inhibitor from barley. Eur. J. Biochem. 9:555-560.

MIKOLA, J., and VIRTANEN, M. 1980. Secretion of L-malic acid by barley aleurone layers. Plant Physiol. 65(Suppl.):142.

MOLL, B. A., and JONES, R. L. 1982. α-Amylase secretion by single barley aleurone layers. Plant Physiol. 70:1149-1155.

MORRALL, P., and BRIGGS, D. E. 1978. Changes in cell wall polysaccharides of germinating barley grains. Phytochemistry 17:1495-1502.

MUNDY, J. 1984. Hormonal regulation of α-amylase inhibitor synthesis in germinating barley. Carlsberg Res. Commun. 49:439-444.

MUNDY, J., and FINCHER, G. B. 1986. Effects of gibberellic acid and abscisic acid on levels of translatable mRNA for (1→3,1→4)-β-glucanase in barley aleurone. FEBS Lett. 198:349-352.

MUNDY, J., and ROGERS, J. C. 1986. Selective expression of a probable amylase/protease inhibitor in barley aleurone cell in comparison to the barley amylase/subtilisin inhibitor. Planta 169:51-63.

MUNDY, J., SVENDSEN, I., and HEJGAARD, J. 1983. Barley α-amylase/subtilisin inhibitor. I. Isolation and characterization. Carlsberg Res. Commun. 48:81-90.

MUNDY, J., BRANDT, A., and FINCHER, G. B. 1985. Messenger RNAs from the scutellum and aleurone of germinating barley encode (1→3,1→4)-β-D-glucanase, α-amylase and carboxypeptidase. Plant Physiol. 79:867-871.

MUTHUKRISHNAN, S., GILL, B. S., SWEGLE, M., and CHANDRA, G. R. 1984. Structural genes for barley α-amylases are located on chromosomes-1 and -6. J. Biol. Chem. 259:13637-13639.

NEGBI, M. 1984. The structure and function of the scutellum of the Gramineae. Bot. J. Linean Soc. 88:205-222.

NICHOLLS, P. B., MacGREGOR, A. W., and MARCHYLO, B. A. 1986. Production of α-amylase isozymes in barley caryopses in the absence of embryos and exogenous gibberellic acid. Aust. J. Plant Physiol. 13:239-247.

NIEUWDORP, P. J. 1963. Electron microscopic structure of the epithelial cells of the scutellum of barley. I. The structure of the epithelial cells before germination. Acta Bot. Neerl. 12:295-301.

NIEUWDORP, P. J., and BUYS, M. C. 1964. Electron microscopic structure of the epithelial cells of the scutellum of barley. II. Cytology of the cells during germination. Acta Bot. Neerl. 13:599-565.

NOLAN, R. C., and HO, T.-H. D. 1988. Hormonal regulation of gene expression in barley aleurone layers. Planta 174:551-560.

NOLAN, R. C., LIN, L.-S., and HO, T.-H. D. 1987. The effect of abscisic acid on the differential expression of α-amylase isozymes in barley aleurone layers. Plant Mol. Biol. 8:13-22.

OBATA, T. 1979. Fine structural changes in barley aleurone cells during gibberellic acid-induced enzyme secretion. Ann. Bot. 44:333-337.

ODANI, S., KOIDE, T., and ONO, T. 1983. The complete amino acid sequence of barley trypsin inhibitor. J. Biol. Chem. 258:7998-8003.

OLSEN, O., BORISS, R., SIMON, O., and THOMSEN, K. K. 1991. Hybrid *Bacillus* (1→3,1→4)-β-glucanases: Engineering thermostable enzymes by construction of hybrid genes. Mol. Gen. Genet. 225:177-185.

ORY, R. L., and HENNINGSEN, K. W. 1969. Enzymes associated with protein bodies isolated from ungerminated barley seeds. Plant Physiol. 44:1488-1498.

PACE, W., PARLAMENTI, R., UR RAB, A., SILANO, V., and VITTOZZI, L. 1978. Protein α-amylase inhibitors from wheat flour. Cereal Chem. 55:244-254.

PAIN, D., KANWAR, Y. S., and BLOBEL, G. 1988. Identification of a receptor for protein import into chloroplasts and its localization to envelope contact zones. Nature (London) 331:232-237.

PALEG, L. 1960. Physiological effects of gibberellic acid. II. On starch hydrolyzing enzymes of barley endosperm. Plant Physiol. 35:902-906.

PALEG, L., and HYDE, B. 1964. Physiological effects of gibberellic acid. VII. Electron microscopy of barley aleurone cells. Plant Physiol. 39:673-680.

PAYNE, J. W., and WALKER-SMITH, D. J. 1987. Isolation and identification of proteins from the peptide-transport carrier in the scutellum of germinating barley (*Hordeum vulgare* L.) embryos. Planta 170:263-271.

PAZ-ARES, J., PONZ, F., ARAGONCILLO, C., HERNANDEZ-LUCAS, C., SALCEDO, G., CARBONERO, P., and GARCIA-OLMEDO, F. 1983. In vivo and in vitro synthesis of CM-proteins (A-hordeins) from barley (*Hordeum vulgare* L.). Planta 157:74-80.

PETERSON, D. M., FORDE, J., WILLIAMSON, M., RHODE, W., and KREIS, M. 1991. Nucleotide sequence of a chymotrypsin inhibitor-2 gene of barley (*Hordeum vulgare*). Plant Physiol. 96:1389-1390.

PETTERS, H. J., FLANNIGAN, B., and AUSTIN, B. 1988. Quantitative and qualitative studies of the microflora of barley malt production. J. Appl. Bacteriol. 65:279-297.

PHARIS, R. P., and KING, R. W. 1985. Gibberellins and reproductive development in seed plants. Annu. Rev. Plant Physiol. 36:517-568.

PHILLIPS, H. A., and WALLACE, W. 1989. A cysteine endopeptidase from barley malt which degrades hordein. Phytochemistry 28:3285-3290.

POGSON, B. J., ASHFORD, A. E., and

GUBLER, F. 1989. Immunofluorescence localization of α-amylase in the scutellum, germ aleurone and "normal" aleurone of germinated barley grains. Protoplasma 151:128-136.

PONZ, F., PAZ-ARES, J., HERNANDEZ-LUCAS, C., CARBONERO, P., and GARCIA-OLMEDO, F. 1983. Synthesis and processing of thionin precursors in developing endosperm from barley (Hordeum vulgare L.). EMBO J. 2:1035-1040.

PONZ, F., PAZ-ARES, J., HERNANDEZ-LUCAS, C., GARCIA-OLMEDO, F., and CARBONERO, P. 1986. Cloning and nucleotide sequence of a cDNA encoding the precursor of the barley toxin α-hordothionin. Eur. J. Biochem. 156:131-135.

POULLE, M., and JONES, B. L. 1988. A proteinase from germinating barley. Plant Physiol. 88:1454-1460.

PREECE, I. A., and HOGGAN, J. 1957. Carbohydrate modification during malting. Pages 72-83 in: Proc. Congr. Eur. Brew. Conv., 6th, Copenhagen.

PREECE, I. A., and MacDOUGALL, M. 1958. Enzymic degradation of cereal hemicelluloses. II. Pattern of pentosan degradation. J. Inst. Brew. 64:489-500.

PYLIOTIS, N. A., ASHFORD, A. E., WHITECROSS, M. J., and JACOBSEN, J. V. 1979. Localization of gibberellic acid-induced acid phosphatase activity in the endoplasmic reticulum of barley aleurone cells with the electron microscope. Planta 147:134-140.

RADLEY, M. 1967. Site of production of gibberellin-like substances in germinating barley embryos. Planta 75:16-71.

RAHMATULLAH, R. J., HUANG, J.-K., CLARK, K. L., REECK, G. R., CHANDRA, G. R., and MUTHUKRISHNAN, S. 1989. Nucleotide and predicted amino acid sequences of two different genes for high-pI α-amylases from barley. Plant Mol. Biol. 12:119-121.

RANJEVA, R., and BOUDET, A. M. 1987. Phosphorylation of proteins in plants: Regulatory effects and potential involvement in stimulus/response coupling. Annu. Rev. Plant Physiol. 38:73-93.

RANKI, H. 1990. Secretion of α-amylase by the epithelium of barley scutellum. J. Inst. Brew. 96:307-309.

RANKI, H., and SOPANEN, T. 1984. Secretion of α-amylase by the aleurone layer and the scutellum of germinating barley grain. Plant Physiol. 75:710-715.

RANKI, H., SOPANEN, T., and VOUTILAINEN, R. 1990. Localization of carboxypeptidase I in germinating barley grain. Plant Physiol.

93:1449-1452.

RASTOGI, V., and OAKS, A. 1986. Hydrolysis of storage proteins in barley endosperms. Analysis of soluble products. Plant Physiol. 81:901-906.

RAYNES, J. G., and BRIGGS, D. E. 1985. Genotype and the production of α-amylase in barley grains germinated in the presence and absence of gibberellic acid. J. Cereal Sci. 3:55-65.

REYNOLDS, T., and MacWILLIAM, I. C. 1966. Water uptake and enzymic activity during steeping of barley. J. Inst. Brew. 72:166-170.

ROBERTS, W. K., and SELITRENNIKOFF, C. P. 1986. Isolation and partial characterization of two antifungal proteins from barley. Biochim. Biophys. Acta 880:161-170.

ROBERTS, W. K., and SELITRENNIKOFF, C. P. 1988. Plant and bacterial chitinases differ in antifungal activity. J. Gen. Microbiol. 134:169-176.

RODRIGUEZ-PALENZUELA, P., PINTOR-TORO, J. A., CARBONERO, P., and GARCIA-OLMEDO, F. 1988. Nucleotide sequence and endosperm-specific expression of the structural gene for the toxin α-hordothionin in barley (Hordeum vulgare L.). Gene 70:271-281.

ROGERS, J. C. 1985. Two barley α-amylase gene families are regulated differently in aleurone cells. J. Biol. Chem. 260:3731-3738.

ROGERS, J. C., and MILLIMAN, C. 1983. Isolation and sequence analysis of a barley α-amylase cDNA clone. J. Biol. Chem. 258:8169-8174.

ROGERS, J. C., and MILLIMAN, C. 1984. Coordinate increase in major transcripts from the high pI α-amylase multigene family in barley aleurone cells stimulated with gibberellic acid. J. Biol. Chem. 259:12234-12240.

ROGERS, J. C., DEAN, D., and HECK, G. R. 1985. Aleurain: A barley thiol protease closely related to mammalian cathepsin H. Proc. Natl. Acad. Sci. USA 82:6512-6516.

SALUJA, D., BERRY, M., and SACHAR, R. C. 1987. Inorganic phosphate mimics the specific action of gibberellic acid in regulating the activity of monophenolase in embryo-less half-seeds of wheat. Phytochemistry 26:611-614.

SANCHEZ-MONGE, R., GOMEZ, L., GARCIA-OLMEDO, F., and SALCEDO, G. 1986. A tetrameric inhibitor of insect α-amylase from barley. FEBS Lett. 207:105-109.

SANCHEZ-MONGE, R., GOMEZ, L., BARBER, D., LOPEZ-OTIN, C., ARMENTIA, A., and SALCEDO, G. 1992. Wheat and barley allergens associated with baker's asthma:

Glycosylated subunits of the α-amylase inhibitors family have enhanced IgE-binding capacity. Biochem. J. 281:401-405.

SCHLUMBAUM, A., MAUCH, F., VOGELI, U., and BOLLER, T. 1986. Plant chitinases are potent inhibitors of fungal growth. Nature 324:365-367.

SELVIG, A., AARNES, H., and LIE, S. 1986. Cell wall degradation in endosperm of barley during germination. J. Inst. Brew. 92:185-187.

SHEWRY, P. R., LAFIANDRA, D., SALCEDO, G., ARAGONCILLO, A., GARCIA-OLMEDO, F., LEW, E. J.-L., DIETLER, M. D., and KASARDA, D. D. 1984. N-terminal amino acid sequences of chloroform/methanol-soluble proteins and albumins from endosperm of wheat, barley and related species. FEBS Lett. 175:359-363.

SIMON, P., and JONES, R. L. 1988. Synthesis and secretion of catalytically active barley α-amylase isoforms by *Xenopus* oocytes injected with barley mRNAs. Eur. J. Cell Biol. 47:213-221.

SIMOS, G., and GEORGATSOS, J. G. 1988. Lactose hydrolysing β-glycosidases of barley meal. Biochim. Biophys. Acta 967:17-24.

SISSONS, M. J., LANCE, R. C. M., and SPARROW, D. H. B. 1992. Studies on limit dextrinase in barley. 1. Purification of malt limit dextrinase and production of monospecific antibodies. J. Cereal Sci. 16:107-116.

SKRIVER, K., OLSEN, F. L., ROGERS, J. C., and MUNDY, J. 1991. *Cis*-acting DNA elements responsive to gibberellin and its antagonist abscisic acid. Proc. Natl. Acad. Sci. USA 88:7266-7270.

SLADE, A. M., HØJ, P. B., MORRICE, N. A., and FINCHER, G. B. 1989. Purification and characterization of three (1→4)-β-D-xylan endohydrolases from germinated barley. Eur. J. Biochem. 185:533-539.

SLAKESKI, N., and FINCHER, G. B. 1992a. Developmental regulation of (1→3,1→4)-β-glucanase gene expression in barley. I. Tissue-specific expression of individual isoenzymes. Plant Physiol. 99:1226-1231.

SLAKESKI, N., and FINCHER, G. B. 1992b. Barley (1→3,1→4)-β-glucanase isoenzyme EI gene expression is mediated by auxin and gibberellic acid. FEBS Lett. 306:98-102.

SLAKESKI, N., BAULCOMBE, D. C., DEVOS, K. M., AHLUWALIA, B., DOAN, D. N. P., and FINCHER, G. B. 1990. Structure and tissue-specific regulation of genes encoding barley (1→3,1→4)-β-glucan endohydrolases. Mol. Gen. Genet. 224:437-449.

SMART, M. G., and O'BRIEN, T. P. 1979. Observations on the scutellum. I. Overall development during germination in four grasses. Aust. J. Bot. 27:391-401.

SØGAARD, M., OLSEN, F. L., and SVENSSON, B. 1991. C-terminal processing of barley α-amylase 1 in malt, aleurone protoplasts, and yeast. Proc. Natl. Acad. Sci. USA 88:8140-8144.

SOPANEN, T. 1979. Development of peptide transport activity in barley scutellum during germination. Plant Physiol. 64:570-574.

SOPANEN, T., and LAURIERE, C. 1989. Release and activity of bound β-amylase in a germinating barley grain. Plant Physiol. 89:244-249.

SOPANEN, T., BURSTON, D., TAYLOR, E., and MATHEWS, D. M. 1978. Uptake of glycylglycine by the scutellum of germinating barley grain. Plant Physiol. 61:630-633.

SØRENSEN, S. B., BREDDAM, K., and SVENDSEN, I. 1986. Primary structure of carboxypeptidase I from malted barley. Carlsberg Res. Commun. 51:475-485.

SØRENSEN, S. B., SVENDSEN, I., and BREDDAM, K. 1987. Primary structure of carboxypeptidase II from malted barley. Carlsberg Res. Commun. 52:285-295.

SØRENSEN, S. B., SVENDSEN, I., and BREDDAM, K. 1989. Primary structure of carboxypeptidase III from malted barley. Carlsberg Res. Commun. 54:193-202.

SPARROW, D. H. B. 1965. Effect of gibberellic acid on the malting of intact and crushed barley. J. Inst. Brew. 71:523-529.

STAUDTE, R. G., WOODWARD, J. R., FINCHER, G. B., and STONE, B. A. 1983. Water-soluble (1→3),(1→4)-β-D-glucans from barley (*Hordeum vulgare*) endosperm. III. Distribution of cellotriosyl and cellotetraosyl residues. Carbohydr. Polym. 3:299-312.

STUART, I. M., and FINCHER, G. B. 1983. Immunological determination of (1→3),(1→4)-β-D-glucan endohydrolase development in germinating barley (*Hordeum vulgare*). FEBS Lett. 155:201-204.

STUART, I. M., LOI, L., and FINCHER, G. B. 1986. Development of (1→3),(1→4)-β-D-glucan endohydrolase isoenzymes in isolated scutella and aleurone layers of barley (*Hordeum vulgare*). Plant Physiol. 80:310-314.

STUART, I. M., LOI, L., and FINCHER, G. B. 1988. Varietal and environmental variations in (1→3,1→4)-β-glucan levels and (1→3,1→4)-β-glucanase potential in barley: Relationships to malting quality. J. Cereal Sci. 7:61-71.

SUNDBLOM, N.-O., and MIKOLA, J. 1972. On the nature of the proteinases secreted by the aleurone layer of barley grain. Physiol. Plant. 27:281-284.

SVENDSEN, I., BOISEN, S., and HEJGAARD, J. 1982. Amino acid sequence of serine protease inhibitor CI-1 from barley. Homology with barley inhibitor CI-2, potato inhibitor I, and leech eglin. Carlsberg Res. Commun. 47:45-53.

SVENDSEN, I., HEJGAARD, J., and MUNDY, J. 1986. Complete amino acid sequence of the α-amylase/subtilisin inhibitor from barley. Carlsberg Res. Commun. 51:43-50.

SVENSSON, B., ASANO, K., JONASSEN, I., POULSEN, F. M., MUNDY, J., and SVENDSEN, I. 1986. A 10 kd seed protein homologous with an α-amylase inhibitor from Indian finger millet. Carlsberg Res. Commun. 51:493-500.

TAIZ, L., and HONIGMAN, W. A. 1976. Production of cell wall hydrolyzing enzymes by barley aleurone layers in response to gibberellic acid. Plant Physiol. 58:380-386.

TAIZ, L., and JONES, R. L. 1970. Gibberellic acid β-1,3-glucanase and the cell walls of barley aleurone layers. Planta 92:73-84.

TAIZ, L., and JONES, R. L. 1973. Plasmodesmata and an associated cell wall component in barley aleurone tissue. Am. J. Bot. 60:67-75.

TAIZ, L., and STARKS, J. E. 1977. Gibberellic acid enhancement of DNA turnover in barley aleurone cells. Plant Physiol. 60:182-189.

TEPFER, M., and TAYLOR, I. E. P. 1981. The permeability of plant cell walls as measured by gel filtration chromatography. Science 213:761-763.

TÖRMÄKANGAS, K., RUNEBERG-ROOS, P., KERVINEN, J., SARKKINEN, P., MIKOLA, L., TILGMANN, C., KALKKINEN, N., and SAARMA, M. 1991. Structure and putative processing of barley aspartic proteinases. Pages 114-166 in: Barley Genetics VI, Vol. 1. Proc. 6th Int. Barley Genet. Symp. L. Munck, ed. Munksgaard. Int. Publ., Copenhagen.

VAN DER EB, A. A., and NIEUWDORP, P. J. 1967. Electron microscopic structure of the aleuron [sic] cells of barley during germination. Acta Bot. Neerl. 15:690-699.

VARNER, J. E., and MENSE, R. M. 1972. Characteristics of the process of enzyme release from secretory plant cells. Plant Physiol. 49:187-189.

VIGIL, E. L., and RUDDAT, M. 1973. Effect of gibberellic acid and actinomycin D on the formation and distribution of rough endoplasmic reticulum in barley aleurone cells. Plant Physiol. 51:549-558.

VOGELI-LANGE, R., HANSEN-GEHRI, A., BOLLER, T., and MEINS, F. 1988. Induction of the defense-related glucanohydrolases. β-1,3-glucanase and chitinase, by tobacco mosaic virus infection of tobacco

leaves. Plant Sci. 54:171-176.

WALKER SMITH, D. J., and PAYNE, J. W. 1983. Peptide uptake in germinating barley embryos involves a dithiol-dependent transport protein. FEBS Lett. 160:25-30

WANG, J., XU, P., and FINCHER, G. B. 1992. Purification, characterization and gene structure of (1→3)-β-glucanase isoenzyme GIII from barley (Hordeum vulgare). Eur. J. Biochem. 209:103-109.

WATSON, T. G., and NOVELLIE, L. 1974. Extraction of Sorghum vulgare and Hordeum vulgare α-glucosidase. Phytochemistry 13:1037-1041.

WESELAKE, R. J., MacGREGOR, A. W., and HILL, R. D. 1983a. An endogenous α-amylase inhibitor in barley kernels. Plant Physiol. 72:809-812.

WESELAKE, R. J., MacGREGOR, A. W., HILL, R. D., and DUCKWORTH, H. W. 1983b. Purification and characteristics of an endogenous α-amylase inhibitor from barley kernels. Plant Physiol. 73:1008-1012.

WESELAKE, R. J., MacGREGOR, A. W., and HILL, R. D. 1985. Endogenous alpha-amylase inhibitor in various cereals. Cereal Chem. 62:120-123.

WESSELS, J. G. H., and SIETSMA, J. H. 1981. Fungal cell walls: A survey. Pages 352-394 in: Encyclopedia of Plant Physiology Plant Carbohydrates II, Vol. 13B (NS). W. Tanner and F. A. Loewus, eds. Springer-Verlag, Berlin.

WHITTIER, R. F., DEAN, D. A., and ROGERS, J. C. 1987. Nucleotide sequence analysis of alpha-amylase and thiol protease genes that are hormonally regulated in barley aleurone cells. Nucleic Acids Res. 15:2515-2135.

WILLIAMSON, M. S., FORDE, J., BUXTON, B., and KREIS, M. 1987. Nucleotide sequence of barley chymotrypsin inhibitor 2 (Cl-2) and its expression in normal and high-lysine barley. Eur. J. Biochem. 165:99-106.

WILLIAMSON, M. S., FORDE, J., and KREIS, M. 1988. Molecular cloning of two isoinhibitor forms of chymotrypsin inhibitor 1 (CI-1) from barley endosperm and their expression in normal and mutant barleys. Plant Mol. Biol. 10:521-535.

WINSPEAR, M. J., PRESTON, K. R., RASTOGI, V., and OAKS, A. 1984. Comparisons of peptide hydrolase activities in cereals. Plant Physiol. 75:480-482.

WOLF, N. 1991. Complete nucleotide sequence of a Hordeum vulgare gene encoding (1→3,1→4)-β-glucanase isoenzyme II. Plant Physiol. 96:1382-1384.

WOLF, N. 1992. Structure of the genes

encoding *Hordeum vulgare* (1→3,1→4)-β-glucanase isoenzymes I and II and functional analysis of their promoters in barley aleurone protoplasts. Mol. Gen. Genet. 234:33-42.

WOOD, A., and PALEG, L. G. 1974. Alteration of liposomal membrane fluidity by gibberellic acid. Aust. J. Plant Physiol. 1:31-40.

WOODWARD, J. R., and FINCHER, G. B. 1982a. Purification and chemical properties of two 1,3;1,4-β-glucan endohydrolases from germinating barley. Eur. J. Biochem. 121:663-669.

WOODWARD, J. R., and FINCHER, G. B. 1982b. Substrate specificities and kinetic properties of two (1→3),(1→4)-β-D-glucan endo-hydrolases from germinating barley (*Hordeum vulgare*). Carbohydr. Res. 106:111-122.

WOODWARD, J. R., and FINCHER, G. B. 1983. Water-soluble barley β-glucans. Fine structure, solution behaviour and organization in the cell wall. Brew. Dig. 58:28-32.

WOODWARD, J. R., MORGAN, F. J., and FINCHER, G. B. 1982. Amino acid sequence homology in two 1,3;1,4-β-glucan endohydrolases from germinating barley (*Hordeum vulgare*). FEBS Lett. 138:198-200.

WOODWARD, J. R., FINCHER, G. B., and STONE, B. A. 1983. Water-soluble (1→3),(1→4)-β-D-glucans from barley (*Hor-*

deum vulgare) endosperm. II. Fine structure. Carbohydr. Polym. 3:207-225.

XU, P., WANG, J., and FINCHER, G. B. 1992. Evolution and differential expression of the (1→3)-β-glucan endohydrolase-encoding gene family in barley, *Hordeum vulgare*. Gene 120:157-165.

YAMADA, J. 1981. Purification of oat debranching enzyme and occurrence of inactive debranching enzyme in cereals. Agric. Biol. Chem. 45:1013-1015.

YIN, X. S., MacGREGOR, A. W., and CLEAR, R. M. 1989. Field fungi and β-glucan solubilase in barley kernels. J. Inst. Brew. 95:195-198.

YOMO, H. 1960. Studies on the amylase-activating substance. IV. Amylase-activating activity of gibberellin. Hakko Kyokaishi 18:600-603.

YOSHIKAWA, M., IWASAKI, T., FUJII, M., and OOGAKI, M. 1976. Isolation and some properties of a subtilisin inhibitor from barley. J. Biochem. 79:765-773.

ZIELINSKI, R. E. 1987. Calmodulin mRNA in barley (*Hordeum vulgare* L.). Plant Physiol. 84:937-943.

ZINGEN-SELL, I., HILLMER, S., ROBINSON, D. G., and JONES, R. L. 1990. Localization of α-amylase isozymes within the endomembrane system of barley aleurone. Protoplasma 154:16-24.

CHAPTER 7

MALTING TECHNOLOGY AND THE USES OF MALT

C. W. BAMFORTH
BRF International
Nutfield, Surrey, RH1 4HY
England

A. H. P. BARCLAY
Bass Maltings Ltd.
Alloa, FK10 1NU
Scotland

INTRODUCTION

Malt is germinated barley. Other cereals, such as sorghum or wheat, can be malted, but these processes are less common and, clearly, it would be inappropriate to discuss them in a monograph on barley.

Barley malt has long been used to impart distinctive flavors and colors to a variety of foodstuffs (Table 1). The most extensive use for barley malt worldwide, however, is as a source of fermentable sugars for alcoholic fermentations, principally to produce beer and whisky. Some 10% of the barley crop (Table 2) is devoted, after malting, to the production of beer. The characteristic properties of many beers (for example, their color, foam, and some of the flavor notes) are a direct consequence of the major complement of malted barley used in their production. Indeed, the use of barley malt has profound implications for traditional techniques of beer production, in that brewers have taken advantage of the husk as a filter medium through which the fermentable extract (wort) is separated before the addition of yeast (see below).

The malting operation is similar irrespective of the foodstuff for which the malt is intended. The process commences with the steeping of barley in water to achieve a moisture level sufficient to activate metabolism in the embryonic and aleurone tissues, leading in turn to the development of hydrolytic enzymes. Moisture uptake into the starchy endosperm is also critical before the food reserves of that tissue can be mobilized through the action of the enzymes. The enzymes migrate through the starchy endosperm, progressing from the embryo (proximal) end of the kernel to the distal end. In this mobilization phase, generally referred to as "modification," the cell walls and protein matrix of the starchy endosperm are degraded, exposing the starch granules and rendering the grain friable and readily milled. After a period of germination sufficient to achieve even modification, the "green

TABLE 1
Food Uses for Malt[a]

Foodstuff	Use of Malt				
	Color	Enzyme	Flavor	Sweetness	Nutrition
Biscuits and crackers	x	x	x	x	x
Bread	x	x	x	x	x
Breakfast cereal			x	x	x
Cakes	x		x	x	
Coffee alternative	x		x		
Confectionery	x		x	x	x
Desserts	x		x		
Gravy	x				
Ice cream	x		x		
Infant food		x ·	x	x	x
Malted food drinks		x	x	x	x
Meat products	x				
Mincemeat	x				
Pickles	x				
Preserves	x				
Sauces	x		x	x	
Soft drinks	x		x	x	x
Soups	x				
Stock cubes	x				
Type of malt product used	Soluble extract	Soluble extract or flour	Soluble extract, flour, flake	Soluble extract	Soluble extract, flour, flake

[a] Adapted from Turner (1986).

TABLE 2
Production and Uses of Barley

Area	Production[a] (million t)	Uses	Amount[b] (million t)
USSR	48.4	Malt and human use	52.1
Germany	13.5	Feed and other	136.5
Canada	12.5		
United States	10.7		
France	10.2		
United Kingdom	9.6		
Spain	8.5		
China	6.4		
Turkey	6.1		
Denmark	5.3		
Australia	3.9		
Poland	3.9		
Other	34.3		
Total	173.3		

[a] Mean production 1981–1990. (Data from Canada Grains Council, 1991)
[b] World barley consumption and trade 1987–1988. (Data from Lawrence, 1988)

malt" is kilned to arrest germination and stabilize the malt by lowering moisture levels, typically to less than 5%. In the process, undesirable raw flavors are removed and pleasant "malty" notes are introduced. The kilning process is also responsible for developing the color of malt. Kilning, however, must be carefully regulated to ensure survival of enzymes that will be crucial in the brewery or distillery to hydrolyze the malt starch into fermentable sugars or that are the key components of enzymatic malt extracts.

Malt used in nonfermented foodstuffs is most frequently employed to provide specific flavor, color, or bulking characteristics, in which case enzyme survival is not important.

The uses for malt and the types of malt required in each case are discussed later. First let us consider the biochemistry of malting in some detail.

BIOCHEMISTRY AND CHEMISTRY OF MALTING

Steeping

In many respects, the steeping operation is the most critical stage in malting. To produce a homogeneous malt, it is necessary to achieve an even moisture content across the grain bed. Steeping conditions must take into consideration the nature of the barley (for example, variety, kernel size, protein content, and physiological condition). Barleys differ in the moisture content that they require in order to germinate. None will germinate below approximately 30% moisture, whereas the most intransigent batches may require a final moisture approaching 50% to achieve uniform germination. Most barleys require a steeping regime that takes them to 42–46% moisture.

In dried barley, the concentration of water in the embryo is very similar to that of the grain as a whole. At the commencement of steeping, the embryo and husk absorb water far more rapidly than does the starchy endosperm. It seems that water uptake is regulated by the embryo, although the mechanism by which it does this is unknown. However, treatments that damage the embryo certainly interfere with this regulatory function, to the detriment of malting performance. Palmer (1989) cites the pumping of barley in pneumatic malting systems as being one possible way in which such damage may occur, because excessive hydrostatic pressures can kill the embryo (Yoshida et al, 1979).

Radioisotope tracing and electron microscopy studies have firmly established that those barleys that are easiest to malt take up water most efficiently (Proudlove et al, 1990).

Several factors influence the rate of water uptake. The so-called steeliness/mealiness character of the starchy endosperm appears to be of particular importance (Palmer and Harvey, 1977). Mealy endosperms, characteristic of good malting barleys, have a relatively open structure containing many cracks, and the starch granules are relatively loosely packed in the protein matrix. Water diffuses more readily through such an open structure than it does through a steely endosperm, which has tight protein-starch packing.

Thin kernels absorb water more rapidly than do larger ones. For example, kernels that screen between 2.2 and 2.5 mm absorb water about 33% faster than do larger berries (Bathgate, 1989).

Water temperature is also relevant: moisture uptake is more rapid at elevated temperatures (Macey, 1977).

Access of water is restricted by the nonpermeable covering layers of the kernel, notably the pericarp (Briggs, 1987). In the intact kernel, water enters principally in the embryo region, although Axcell et al (1983) used auto-radiography to show that moisture can also penetrate slowly at the distal end of the kernel and possibly also in the ventral region. This has been supported by studies of iodine staining of endosperm as detected by scanning electron microscopy (Davies, 1989, 1991).

Physical damage to the pericarp layer of barley permits water uptake at additional sites. Such abrasion or scarification treatments have been used to facilitate more rapid and even steeping, thereby accelerating modification (Palmer, 1989).

Besides water, barley requires a supply of oxygen to support respiration. Oxygen access is inhibited if the grain is submerged in water for prolonged periods, a phenomenon that dictates the use in modern malting regimes of steeps interrupted by air rest periods. Additionally, steep water may be aerated or oxygenated (e.g., Cantrell et al, 1981; French and McRuer, 1990).

Air rests serve the added role of removing carbon dioxide and ethanol, which may inhibit germination. These substances are produced as a result of respiratory metabolism in the embryo and aleurone tissues, as well as through the action of microorganisms populating surface tissues.

A typical steeping regime may involve an initial steep to 32–38% moisture, with more water-sensitive barleys achieving a lower level. The start of germination is promoted by an air rest of 10–20 hr, followed by a second steep to raise moisture to 40–42%. Emergence of the root tip (chitting) is encouraged with a second air rest of 10–15 hr, before the final steep. The entire steeping operation in modern malting plants is likely to cover 48–52 hr.

Germination

Modification of barley commences at the proximal end of the grain, adjacent to the scutellum. The rate of modification depends on: 1) the rate at which moisture distributes through the starchy endosperm, 2) the rate of synthesis of hydrolytic enzymes, 3) the extent of release of these enzymes into the starchy endosperm, and 4) structural features of the starchy endosperm that determine its resistance to digestion. These features are not wholly understood. Although the degree of mealiness influences the rate of water uptake, barleys showing similar moisture uptake capabilities can nevertheless display widely differing tendencies to modify. These differences may be related to the structure of the starchy endosperm cell walls, perhaps in terms of the degree of cross-linking of β-glucans, pentosans, and protein (Palmer, 1975; Smith et al, 1980). Alternatively, differences in protein structure may have a role to play (Gothard et al, 1978).

It has been suggested that the rate of modification of different samples of barley is principally determined by their content of cell wall β-glucan and (especially) their ability to synthesize β-glucanase. High rates of modification correlate with low β-glucan and high β-glucanase levels (Henry, 1989). Conversely, Masak and Basarova (1991) concluded that less readily modified ("feed") barleys develop levels of β-glucanase similar to those in readily modifiable ("malting") barleys but that the β-glucans in the former break down more slowly.

Other than regulating water relations, the most important role for the embryo is in controlling enzyme production. The embryo is capable of producing gibberellins, which stimulate enzyme synthesis by the aleurone layer (MacLeod et al, 1964; MacLeod and Palmer, 1966, 1967). Radley (1967, 1969) proposed that these hormones are produced by the scutellum. However, barley grains with damaged axes but fully functional scutella are incapable of gibberellin production (MacLeod and Palmer, 1967), pointing to the embryonic axis as being the principal site of hormone production.

Gibberellin production by germinating embryos is at its maximum after the first two days of germination (Cohen and Paleg, 1967). Clearly, this is a critical period for malting practice, and sound embryo functioning at this stage is crucial if homogeneous malt is to be obtained.

It is claimed that the gibberellins migrate via vascular tissue preferentially to the aleurone cells on the dorsal side of the kernel, there to trigger enzyme production (Palmer, 1972). The route seems to be from the axis, through the scutellum, to the scutellar-dorsal aleurone junction, the first point at which enzyme synthesis is induced.

Malting-grade barleys may produce more gibberellin than do feed-grade barleys (Proudlove and Muller, 1989). Also, aleurones from different varieties may have different susceptibilities to gibberellins (Palmer, 1988). The ability of barleys to develop hydrolytic enzymes may depend both on the extent to which those barleys can synthesize gibberellin and on their "responsiveness to gibberellin" (Kusaba et al, 1991).

It seems certain, however, that other hormones also have a role to play. Auxins may support the action of gibberellins (MacLeod and Palmer, 1969), whereas levels of abscisic acid in barley were shown to relate to the degree of dormancy (Goldbach and Michael, 1975). Certainly, added abscisic acid blocks the germination of barley, antagonizing all events promoted by gibberellins (Jacobsen and Chandler, 1987). Cytokinins, however, may release barley from dormancy (unpublished work of Palmer and Taylor, cited in Palmer, 1989). Ethylene can counter the contrary effect of abscisic acid in the presence of high concentrations of gibberellin (Jacobsen, 1973) and can suppress rootlet growth (Briggs, 1978). More recently, it has been reported that certain analogs of abscisic acid resemble gibberellic acid in promoting α-amylase and β-amylase activities and cell wall modification but do not promote nitrogen modification to the same extent as does gibberellic acid (Li et al, 1991).

It has been suggested that calcium ions influence the synthesis (Deikman and Jones, 1986) and release (Moll and Jones, 1982) of α-amylase and other enzymes. Abscisic acid promotes, whereas gibberellic acid suppresses, the synthesis of an α-amylase inhibitor in barley (Mundy, 1984). The transcription of α-amylase is believed to be repressed by abscisic acid (Nolan et al, 1987). Abscisic acid reduces the amount of mRNA for $(1 \rightarrow 3),(1 \rightarrow 4)$-β-glucanase in barley aleurone cells, whereas gibberellic acid and calcium elevate it (Mundy and Fincher, 1986; Litts et al, 1990). Skriver et al (1991) have defined gibberellin- and abscisic acid-responsive sites in aleurone, which should form the basis not only for improved understanding of hormonal control of enzyme synthesis, but also for an appreciation of how exogenous genes introduced into barley may be effectively expressed when required.

It is now firmly established that the aleurone cells are capable of synthesizing most of the hydrolytic enzymes necessary for dissolution of the starchy endosperm (with the notable exception of β-amylase, Table 3). Nevertheless, it is still not unequivocally established whether the aleurone tissue is responsible for synthesizing all these hydrolases during the steeping and germination of barley, or whether the scutellar epithelium itself can elaborate enzymes, at least in the earliest stages of germination.

The scutellum certainly functions in the uptake of degradation products from the starchy endosperm. Many workers have suggested that, additionally, it synthesizes hydrolytic enzymes involved in producing these degradation products from the storage macromolecules. Briggs (1987) has summarized a detailed argument in support of this concept. Palmer (1989) presents the converse opinion, stressing that the scutellar preparations employed in the studies reviewed by Briggs were contaminated with aleurone tissue.

Since the observation of Mundy and Munck (1985) that there is far less mRNA encoding α-amylase in the scutellum than in the aleurone, it has seemed increasingly probable that Palmer's theories are correct. Further, it has been clearly demonstrated that the poor modification of certain barleys is a direct function of the inefficient response of their aleurone cells to gibberellin (Sole et al, 1987; Palmer, 1988). Nevertheless, it has also been suggested that aleurone cells are capable of enzyme synthesis in the absence of gibberellin and that the huskless variety Himalaya, most extensively used in fundamental investigations, possesses an aleurone quite unlike others in its over-dependence on gibberellins for enzyme synthesis (Fincher, 1989).

Fincher (1989) maintains that arguments for aleurone contamination as the source of enzyme synthesis in scutellar preparations can be discounted on account of evidence from hybridization histochemistry (see Chapter 6 of this monograph). He insists that, early in modification, enzyme synthesis occurs in the scutellum and that, once the proximal starchy endosperm is mobilized, modification is continued by enzymes secreted from the aleurone (McFadden et al, 1988; Ranki, 1990).

TABLE 3
Principal Hydrolytic Enzymes Produced by Barley Aleurone

Enzyme	Gibberellic Acid Dependent	Reference
Endo-(1→3),(1→4)-β-glucanase (isoenzyme II)	Yes	Stuart et al (1986)
Endo-(1→3)-β-glucanase	Yes	Taiz and Jones (1970)
Endo-(1→4)-β-xylanase	Yes	Taiz and Honigman (1976)
Endopeptidase	Yes	Hammerton and Ho (1986)
Carboxypeptidase	No	Hammerton and Ho (1986)
α-Amylases (types I and II)	Yes	Jones and Jacobsen (1983) Jones and Carbonell (1984) Carbonell and Jones (1984)
α-Amylase (type III)	Yes	Jacobsen and Higgins (1982)
Limit dextrinase	Yes	Hardie (1975)
Nuclease	Yes	Brown and Ho (1986)

With regard to the aleurone cells, it has been suggested that the first role of enzymes synthesized therein is in the hydrolysis of aleurone cell walls, thereby enabling release of further enzymes into the starchy endosperm (Palmer et al, 1985). It is suggested that the extent to which these enzymes are released from the aleurone cells determines modification potential, as opposed to the absolute level of enzyme synthesis.

Biochemistry of Modification

The starchy endosperm of barley consists of a mass of dead cells, incapable of enzyme synthesis. Such cells have relatively thin walls surrounding a protein matrix in which large and small starch granules are embedded. Since enzyme synthesis occurs in the aleurone (and perhaps the scutellum) and the enzymes subsequently migrate into the endosperm to effect hydrolysis, it would be entirely logical for enzyme development to follow the sequence: cell wall degrading enzymes, then proteases, then amylases. This certainly appears to be the case (MacLeod et al, 1964).

CELL WALLS

The starchy endosperm cell walls of barley comprise approximately 75% $(1{\rightarrow}3),(1{\rightarrow}4)$-$\beta$-D-glucan, 20% arabinoxylan (pentosan), and 5% protein, together with minor proportions of cellulose, mannan, and perhaps low-molecular-weight phenolics such as ferulic acid (Fincher and Stone, 1986). The structure of these walls is discussed in Chapter 3. It is sufficient here to stress that they are unusual in their high content of mixed-linkage β-glucan and that there remains a serious lack of understanding of how the various polymers are linked together in the walls. Such information might prove particularly valuable to the maltster in terms of optimizing the digestion of these wholly troublesome entities during processing.

This ignorance over cell wall structure is reflected in a controversy surrounding the mechanism by which the walls are degraded during germination. It is generally agreed that two types of activity are involved in cell wall mobilization: initial attack by a ("cytoclastic") enzyme(s), which "loosens" their structure and releases the polymers, chiefly β-glucans, into solution ready for subsequent "cytolysis," primarily by β-glucanases (see Bamforth, 1982 for a review).

The controversy resides in the precise nature of the enzymes involved in the initial solubilization.

Four different systems have been proposed:

1. Endo-$(1{\rightarrow}3)$-β-glucanase (EC 3.2.1.39), which is not present in significant quantities in raw barley but is developed to high levels during germination, acts preferentially on sections of β-glucan with contiguous β-$(1{\rightarrow}3)$ linkages between the glucosyl moieties (Bathgate et al, 1974). Nonetheless, it is now understood that long sequences of β-$(1{\rightarrow}3)$ links do not occur in the polymer from barley endosperm walls (Woodward et al, 1983). Furthermore, it is quite evident that β-glucan solubilization is possible as soon as barley is wetted and before any additional enzyme development has occurred (Martin and Bamforth, 1980). Endo-$(1{\rightarrow}3)$-β-glucanase may function in the opening of aleurone cell walls (see above), thereby serving a critical role in the release

of other hydrolases into the starchy endosperm during germination (Palmer et al, 1985). Conversely, the enzyme may have a role in protecting grain against pathogenic attack (Høj et al, 1989). The isolation of this enzyme from grain germinated under sterile conditions would indicate a constitutive development for this function. It should also be noted that there are deposits of $(1\rightarrow3)$-β-glucan in barley (Fulcher et al, 1977; MacGregor et al, 1989), which may be the substrate for the enzyme in question.

2. Carboxypeptidase (EC 3.4.12.1) may act in an esterolytic mode to split glucan-peptide bonds responsible for cell wall integrity (Bamforth, 1981). It has been shown that protein is an integral feature of the starchy endosperm cell walls of barley, covalently linked to β-glucan (Forrest and Wainwright, 1977) and that such walls may be separated by proteases (MacLeod and McCorquodale, 1958; Palmer, 1975) and esterases (unpublished work cited by Palmer, 1989). Furthermore, the dissolution of the walls by alkali or hydrazine (Palmer, 1971; Forrest and Wainwright, 1977) is also in keeping with a carbohydrate-protein association. A detailed study pointed very much in the direction of carboxypeptidase acting as a "β-glucan solubilase" (Bamforth, 1985). Solubilase, like carboxypeptidase, is unusual in being present in high activity in the starchy endosperm of raw grain. The glucan-releasing and carboxypeptidase functions copurify, and carboxypeptidase and solubilase have similar high heat-resistance, a property in keeping with observations on β-glucan release in brewery mashes (e.g., Aastrup and Erdal, 1987). Evidence that esterase action is involved in β-glucan solubilization is, however, circumstantial. Most carboxypeptidases display not only peptidase activity but also esterase activity. Esterolytic activity and β-glucan solubilase activity in barley display pH responses that are similar but are at variance with the proteolytic activity of carboxypeptidase (Bamforth, 1981). Furthermore, solubilase and esterase activities are similar in inhibitor-activator specificity.

Brunswick et al (1988) showed that purified endo-barley-β-glucanases (see below) are capable of solubilizing at most half of the β-glucan in purified endosperm cell walls. The remainder could be solubilized by crude malt enzyme, and the authors inferred that the balance was due to solubilase. In view of the fact that proteinase K (EC 3.4.21.14, from *Tritirachium album*) failed to influence β-glucan solubilization, they concluded that protein degradation was not an a priori requirement for this event. However, this is not an argument against a role for carboxypeptidase as the solubilizing agent. It is plausible that individual amino acids or short peptide chains (or indeed other acidic contributors to ester formation) are involved in cross-linking β-glucans. There is no reason why they should be susceptible to action by proteinase K. Similar conclusions to those of Brunswick et al (1988) were drawn by McCleary (1988), again using proteinase K. He concluded that the ability of β-glucanase to totally degrade soluble and insoluble β-glucan to glucose rules out peptide attachment. Again it is difficult to rule out the possibility that the limited degree of esterification necessary to cross-link β-glucans will not be detectable in this system. However, doubts will understandably remain until such time as β-glucan-peptide ester bonding is unequivocally demonstrated in the endosperm cell walls and it is shown that these bonds are ruptured by the enzyme in question.

If, indeed, β-glucan solubilase is already present in raw grain, it might be expected that it would be able to commence its action once the water activity of the starchy endosperm has reached a critical minimum level. Indeed, solubilase seems to be concentrated toward the embryo end of the kernel (Bamforth and Martin, 1981), where moisture uptake occurs fastest in unscarified grain. It would be relevant to ascertain whether cell wall dissolution commences in response to the achievement of a suitable moisture level in the endosperm and before significant release of endo-barley-β-glucanase from the aleurone, or, conversely, whether cell wall degradation requires the direct synergy of both enzymes.

3. Endo-(1→4)-β-glucanase (EC 3.2.1.4) produced by microorganisms thriving on the surface of the barley kernel (Yin and MacGregor, 1988, 1989; Yin et al, 1989; MacGregor and Yin, 1990) can also solubilize β-glucan. This is entirely plausible—indeed enzyme secretion by malt-borne microorganisms (Høj et al, 1981; Petters et al, 1988) demands further analysis for the role that it plays in determining malt performance, for example, in brewing (van Waesberghe, 1991). However, the conditions employed by Yin and MacGregor are at variance with those under which β-glucan solubilization phenomena are known to occur in brewing mashes (Bamforth, 1989), and furthermore it seems unlikely that enzymes produced by surface-growing organisms have a function in cell wall modification during germination.

4. Phospholipase (EC 3.1.1.32) acting on plasmodesmata that are believed to be present in the walls is the fourth candidate (Palmer, 1987).

Although there may be disagreement regarding the solubilizing system, there is universal agreement that the subsequent hydrolysis of released β-glucan is effected by endo-(1→3),(1→4)-β-glucanases (endo-barley-β-glucanases, EC 3.2.1.73), which are specific for (1→4)-β bonds adjacent to (1→3)-β linkages.

Two such enzymes have been demonstrated in malt, differing in molecular weight and isoelectric point but acting by closely similar mechanisms (Woodward and Fincher, 1982a, 1982b; Woodward et al, 1982). It seems that one isozyme (EI) is secreted by the scutellum and may act early in germination; isozyme EII (which is glycosylated) is secreted by the aleurone in response to gibberellic acid and calcium (Stuart et al, 1986). The two endo-barley-β-glucanases have 92% positive commonality in their primary amino acid sequences (Slakeski et al, 1990). Interestingly, endo-(1→3)-β-glucanase probably arises from the same ancestral gene as both of these enzymes (Ballance and Svendsen, 1988; Høj et al, 1989). Slakeski and Fincher (1992) demonstrated the presence in untreated aleurone layers of mRNAs for both isozymes of endo-barley-β-glucanase but found that gibberellic acid promoted the synthesis of isozyme II only. Abscisic acid reduced the level of enzyme expressed, apparently by reducing the amount of mRNA present. Indole acetic acid had the converse effect.

The endo-barley-β-glucanases produce tri- and tetrasaccharides, which may be further degraded to glucose by exo-β-glucanases (EC 3.2.1.74; Fincher, 1989) and β-glucosidases (EC 3.2.1.21, Craig and Stark, 1985). Endo-β-glucanases can also catalyze the transfer of glucose residues between oligosaccharides to produce insoluble products that form the core of precipitates in frozen beer (Yamashita et al, 1987).

Raw barley contains substantial quantities of β-glucan solubilase but is essentially devoid of endo-barley-β-glucanases (Bamforth and Martin, 1983).

During malting, both enzymes increase in activity, and the mobilization of the cell walls ensues. Gibberellic acid appears to stimulate the synthesis of both solubilase (Bamforth and Martin, 1981) and endo-barley-β-glucanase (Stuart et al, 1986).

Although pentosan (arabinoxylan) comprises one-fifth of the cell walls of barley starchy endosperm (Fincher, 1975), only recently have detailed studies commenced on the enzymes responsible for its degradation during modification. Three endo-$(1\rightarrow4)$-β-xylanases (EC 3.2.1.8) have been purified from malt by Slade et al (1989). These enzymes increase in activity during germination several days later than do the endo-barley-β-glucanases, so Slade et al (1989) question whether pentosan degradation is a necessary precursor to proteolysis and amylolysis. In common with the endo-barley-β-glucanases, endoxylanases may function in the release of enzymes from the aleurone. This would, however, need to be reconciled with the observation that endoxylanases are found in the medium surrounding isolated aleurone layers later than are other hydrolases (Taiz and Honigman, 1976).

Enzymes capable of cleaving arabinosyl side chains from a xylan backbone and of cleaving xylobiose from the latter exocatalytically have been shown to be secreted from aleurone cells in response to gibberellic acid before endoxylanase (Preece and MacDougall, 1958; Taiz and Honigman, 1976). It appears that the presence of arabinosyl residues substituting at the C2 position of xylosyl residues profoundly inhibits endoxylanase activity (Vietor et al, 1991).

PROTEIN

It has been estimated that about 50% of the total grain protein may be mobilized during the malting of barley (Barrett and Kirsop, 1971). The extent of this proteolysis, in conjunction with that of cell wall degradation, depends upon the precise steeping and germination conditions employed.

Protein degradation commences with the endopeptidases (proteases) that generate peptides, upon which the exopeptidases (carboxypeptidases) act to release amino acids. Aminopeptidases have been reported in barley malt but, as they have a relatively high pH optimum, are found only in the embryo and aleurone, and do not increase in activity during germination, it is not believed that they play a significant role in malting.

The endopeptidases (EC 3.4.21) are less well understood than are the other major enzymes in barley malt. It is known that there are two categories of endopeptidase (Enari and Sopanen, 1986): the cysteine (sulfhydryl)-dependent enzymes, which account for about 90% of the total activity, and the metal-dependent endopeptidases. Phillips and Wallace (1989) have characterized in some detail a hordein-degrading enzyme that accounts for 66% of the protease in green malt. The enzyme has properties similar to those described previously by Baxter (1976) and by Poulle and Jones (1988). The endopeptidases are synthesized de novo during germination in response to gibberellin (Hammerton and Ho, 1986). Activity may also increase during germination due to the disappearance of specific inhibitors (Enari and Mikola, 1967). In common with the endo-barley-β-glucanases, the endopeptidases are heat-labile (Kringstad and Kilhovd, 1957).

It has long been recognized (Baxter, 1976) that the use of "unnatural" substrates for assaying endopeptidases is likely to lead researchers to incorrect conclusions regarding the relevance of some enzyme fractions. Wrobel and Jones (1992) have stressed that the malt endopeptidases most often studied, and which are most active at around pH 3.8, are least likely to be important during malting and malt extraction processes. It seems that there is much still to do in the characterization of proteases in barley malt.

The carboxypeptidases (EC 3.4.12.2) are present at high levels in raw barley (see solubilase above) and increase further during germination. They are heat-resistant (Narziss and Lintz, 1975). Five of these enzymes have been demonstrated in barley. They differ in substrate specificity, molecular size, and the stage at which they are developed in the malting process, although the feature of most relevance to the maltster (and brewer) is that high activities are present at all stages from barley to finished malt (Breddam et al, 1983; Breddam, 1985; Breddam and Sorensen, 1987). However, it has been suggested recently that carboxypeptidase I, the major component of this family of enzymes, is absent from raw barley and is synthesized during germination, primarily in the scutellum (Ranki et al, 1990).

STARCH

Four categories of starch-degrading enzymes are developed in germinating barley (MacGregor, 1987).

α-Amylase. In common with the degradation of protein, there is an initial attack by an endoenzyme to release smaller units, which form the substrates for succeeding exoenzymes. In the case of starch, the initial attack is by the α-amylases (EC 3.2.1.1), which attack α-$(1{\rightarrow}4)$ linkages in amylose and amylopectin, although not linkages in the latter that are adjacent to α-$(1{\rightarrow}6)$ bonds. There is no detectable α-amylase in sound ungerminated barley, it being synthesized during germination. There are two major active groups of α-amylase, distinguished by their isoelectric points (MacGregor et al, 1988). In both categories, several isoforms of slightly differing isoelectric points may form as a result of a deamidase activity in aleurone (Sticker and Jones, 1991).

The major category is so-called Group III (pI 6.4–6.6), which consists of a complex between α-amylase II (pI 6.0–6.4) and a barley α-amylase-subtilisin inhibitor molecule of low molecular weight (Mundy et al, 1983; Weselake et al, 1983). This inhibitor is cleaved from the α-amylase by heating to 70°C for 15 min (Munck et al, 1985) or by increasing ionic strength (Hill and MacGregor, 1988).

α-Amylase I (pI 4.8–5.0) contributes just 1–2% of the total activity in malt. It has kinetic properties similar to those of α-amylase II, although α-amylase I does seem to degrade starch granules more rapidly (MacGregor and Morgan, 1986). α-Amylase is, indeed, the only enzyme in malt capable of hydrolyzing, and hence solubilizing, intact starch granules. It effects a rapid release of dextrins containing at least six glucosyl residues (MacGregor, 1978).

α-Amylase is extremely heat-resistant, especially in the presence of stabilizing calcium ions, which also form a part of the structure of the enzyme (Bush et al, 1989).

Because it is an endoenzyme, α-amylase rapidly solubilizes starch to yield smaller fragments, thereby reducing the viscosity of starch solutions, a key event in brewers' mashes (see below).

β-Amylase. β-Amylase (EC 3.2.1.2) is an exoenzyme that releases maltose by hydrolyzing from the nonreducing ends of the dextrins generated by α-amylase, halting at the α-(1→6) side chains of amylopectin. Like the carboxy-peptidases, β-amylase is present in the starchy endosperm of raw barley, both in a soluble form and in an essentially inert form through its association via disufide bridges with protein Z (Hejgaard, 1978). The link between these two proteins is severed through the action of reducing agents or, in vivo, probably via proteolytic enzymes (Shinke and Mugibayashi, 1971; Hejgaard and Carlsen, 1977; Lundgard and Svenssen, 1987; Guerin et al, 1992). Such activation of β-amylase occurs during germination (Sopanen and Laurière, 1989), during which time α-amylase is synthesized de novo in response to gibberellins. Whereas α-amylase is stable, β-amylase is comparatively sensitive to heat (Piendl, 1973).

Limit Dextrinase. Limit dextrinase ("R" enzyme; EC 3.2.1.10) is responsible for hydrolyzing the α-(1→6) side chains in the amylopectin fraction of starch (Harris et al, 1957). This enzyme is one of the last to be synthesized during the germination of barley (Lee and Pyler, 1984). Furthermore, it has long been believed to be rapidly lost during anything other than moderate heating, although recent evidence suggests that perhaps the enzyme is more tolerant to heat than was hitherto believed (Daussant et al, 1987). The enzyme appears to be firmly bound to other grain components, which may limit its accessibility to substrate (Longstaff and Bryce, 1991). The enzyme can be solubilized by cysteine, dithiothreitol, and papain, and it is suggested that they all act via the reducing action of their thiol groups (Longstaff and Bryce, 1991). The bound form is released during germination (Serre and Laurière, 1989).

α-Glucosidases. Malt contains α-glucosidases (EC 3.2.1.20) (Jørgensen, 1965; Clutterbuck and Briggs, 1973), which have the least well-characterized activities in the amylolytic complex. These enzymes are located also in the pericarp tissue of developing barley kernels (MacGregor and Lenoir, 1987). A recent report suggests that this activity may have a significant function in degrading starch granules (Sun and Henson, 1990).

Whereas extensive degradation of cell wall materials is required during malting, as is adequate solubilization of protein, it is invariably desirable to have minimum conversion of starch. Certainly in the case of malts that will be employed as a source of fermentable material for brewing and distilling, high starch contents are essential.

The small starch granules tend to be preferentially degraded during germination. If they survive to malt, their high gelatinization temperature and consequent greater resistance to amylolytic attack (as compared to that of large granules) mean that they can cause problems in brewing (see below).

LIPIDS

Lipids constitute about 3% of the dry weight of barley (Anness and Reed, 1985). Barley develops lipases (EC 3.1.1.3) that are capable of splitting fatty acids from glycerol, but these enzymes are poorly characterized (Baxter, 1984).

Barley also contains lipoxygenases (EC 1.13.11.12) and hydroperoxide isomerases, which together are capable of oxidizing unsaturated fatty acids, leading ultimately to products such as *trans*-2-nonenal, causative staling agents (Baxter, 1982; van Aarle et al, 1991). Unsaturated fatty acids may also be oxidized nonenzymatically by oxygen radicals (Bamforth and Parsons, 1985). Barley contains various enzymes that may have a role to play in eliminating oxygen radicals. Superoxide dimutases (EC 1.15.1.1.) eliminate superoxide O^-_2, by forming ground-state oxygen (the least reactive form) and hydrogen peroxide, H_2O_2 (Bamforth, 1983):

$$2H^+ + O^-_2 + O^-_2 \rightarrow O_2 + H_2O_2$$

Peroxide, which is even more reactive than superoxide, is subsequently eliminated by catalase (EC 1.11.1.6):

$$H_2O_2 \rightarrow H_2O + \tfrac{1}{2}O_2$$

The two enzymes, acting sequentially, are capable of keeping oxygen in its least reactive state. Catalase in barley is very heat-sensitive (Narziss and Sekin, 1974). By contrast, the nonspecific peroxidases (EC.1.11.1.7) in barley are very active and stable and are probably very important in eliminating peroxide by reacting it, perhaps with polyphenols (Bamforth et al, 1991):

$$H_2O_2 + RH_2 \rightarrow 2H_2O + R$$

OTHER ENZYMES

Such peroxidases are likely to be more important in oxidizing polyphenol than is polyphenol oxidase (EC 1.14.18.1), which is in high activity in raw barley but extensively lost during malting (Clarkson et al, 1992). The extent to which polyphenol oxidation occurs during malting is uncertain, but the process probably is important in any malt extraction process, in terms of determining the extent to which tanning reactions occur.

A range of enzymes (nucleases, phosphatases, nucleotidases, and nucleoside deaminases) capable of degrading nucleic acids and their constituents are present in malt (Lee and Pyler, 1985, 1986). The activity of these enzymes may influence the level of flavor-enhancing nucleotides derivable from malt.

Phytase (EC 3.1.3.26) regulates phosphate release from the phytic acid (inositol phosphate) store of barley (Lee, 1990).

Various β-galactosidase (EC 3.2.1.23) isoforms are located in barley (Giannakouros et al, 1991).

An endochitinase (EC 3.2.1.14) present in the aleurone and starchy endosperm of barley probably serves, like endo-$(1 \rightarrow 3)$-β-glucanase, as a protectant against invasive microbes (Leah et al, 1987; Jacobsen et al, 1990). Thaumatinlike proteins with antifungal activity have been reported (Hejgaard et al, 1991). A study is warranted of the role that these types of protein have in determining the activity of fungi on the surface of grain, particularly as such organisms are increasingly believed to contribute to the measured enzyme potential of malt.

Kilning

Through the controlled drying of green malt, the maltster is able to 1) arrest modification and render malt stable for storage, 2) ensure survival of enzymes, where appropriate, for subsequent employment in processing, and 3) introduce desirable flavor and color characteristics, which may be especially necessary for those malts to be used as flavorants and colorants.

The basic principles of kilning are that drying should commence at a relatively low temperature to ensure survival of the most heat-sensitive enzymes (endo-barley-β-glucanases, endopeptidase, limit dextrinase), followed by a progressive increase of temperature to effect flavor and color changes and complete drying within the limited turnover time available (typically less than 24 hr) in most reasonably sized kilns. Bourne et al (1976) demonstrated the influence of temperature and malt moisture content on the stability of endo-barley-β-glucanase. This, with other enzymes, is more tolerant of heat at lower moisture contents.

Drying of a malt for subsequent use in the production of lager-type beers may commence at, say, 50°C, with the final temperature unlikely to exceed 75°C. At low temperatures, modification continues; thus, regimes of kiln loading must be carefully monitored with respect to heterogeneities that they may introduce (Munck et al, 1981; Anderson et al, 1989). Comparable kiln cycles are employed in the production of malt destined for distilleries, save for the imparting of specific flavor characters in some instances by the intro-duction of peat smoke from secondary burners.

Malts destined for ale-type beers may reach a curing temperature of 110°C, whereas especially flavorsome and darker colored malts can reach much higher temperatures (Table 4). Clearly, the latter malts do not retain (or indeed require) active enzymes, and so the initial drying phase may commence at a relatively high temperature.

Principal among the changes occurring during kilning is the browning or Maillard reaction (Hodge, 1953). The interaction of reducing sugars and amino acids produces reductones, which in turn can be converted by polymerization to the colorful melanoidins or, by alternative routes, to the heterocyclic pyrazines, thiophenes, pyrrolles, and furans (Fig. 1). The oxygen heterocyclics are responsible for toffee or caramel flavors (for example, in crystal malt). The pyrazines afford the roasted, coffeelike flavors typical of more intensely kilned malts.

Other key flavor changes involved in kilning are the disappearance of "grassy" notes due to *cis*-3-hexen-1-ol, *trans*-2-hexenel, *trans*-2-*cis*-6-nonodienal, and 1-hexanol and the appearance of malty (isovaleraldehyde) character (Seaton,

TABLE 4
Colored Malts

Type	Color (°EBC)	Production Regime
Cara pils	15–30	Green malt; surface moisture dried off at 50°C for 5 min; stewing over 40 min; temperature increased to 100°C; curing 100–120°C for <1 hr
Crystal	75–300	As for Cara pils, but first curing is for <2 hr at 135°C
Chocolate	500–1,200	Roasting of lager malt, temperature rising from 75 to 150°C over 1 hr; temperature then allowed to rise up to 220°C
Black	1,200–1,400	Comparable to chocolate, but with more intense roasting

1987; Moir, 1989). Isovaleraldehyde is formed in the Strecker degradation reactions between leucine and α-diketones or reductones.

Kilning also has a profound role to play in the regulation of levels of heat-labile S-methylmethionine (Fig. 2), which decomposes to dimethyl sulfide, a major flavor attribute of lager-type beers (Anness and Bamforth, 1982).

Furthermore, during kilning, possibly carcinogenic nitrosamines, including *N*-nitrosodimethylamine (Fig. 3), can be produced unless palliative procedures are employed, such as indirect firing, burning sulfur on the kilns, and maintenance of atmospheres low in oxides of nitrogen (Hardwick et al, 1981; Wainwright, 1986).

PROPERTIES OF BARLEY WITH REGARD TO ITS MALTABILITY

The properties demanded of malts destined for different purposes are described later. However, the production of malt for whichever purpose is dependent upon barley having high viability, low dormancy, low water sensitivity, and high vigor.

The maltster will certainly specify that the grain being purchased must be above a certain minimum viability. Methods for assessing the extent of dormancy, water-sensitivity, and vigor are also needed to enable better control of the process. The maltster may also seek assurance concerning the variety

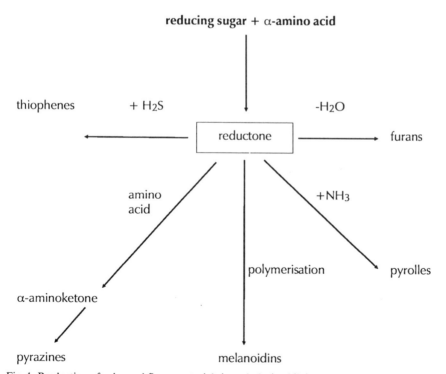

Fig. 1. Production of color and flavor materials in malt during kilning.

of barley delivered, for barley varieties differ widely in their malting potential. Although a variety can be identified visually by inspecting grain morphology, biochemical methods based on analysis of protein banding after sodium dodecyl sulfate-polyacrylamide gel electrophoresis are also being used. Recent developments have led to systems whereby up to two dozen samples can be analyzed in 1 hr (Vasconcelos et al, 1991).

Germination. Promoted by factors stimulating acrospire and rootlet growth. Blocked by rootlet inhibitors.

$$\text{Methionine} \xrightarrow{\text{methylation}} (CH_3)_2\overset{(+)}{S} \, CH_2CH_2CH(NH_2)CO_2H$$

S-methyl methionine (SMM)
in acrospire and rootlets

Kilning. Degradation enhanced at high temperatures.

$$\text{SMM} \xrightarrow{\text{heat}} \text{homoserine} + (CH_3)_2S \text{ dimethyl sulfide} + (CH_3)_2 \text{ SO dimethyl sulfoxide}$$

Malt. Level of SMM surviving into malt dictated by quantity produced in germination and extent of decomposition on kiln.

SMM surviving into malt breaks down in brewhouse and proportion not volatilized survives into beer. Supplemented by dimethyl sulfide produced by enzymatic reduction of dimethyl sulfoxide by yeast.

Fig. 2. S-methyl methionine as a precursor of dimethyl sulfide.

Germination. Production of hordenine stimulated by factors promoting germination.

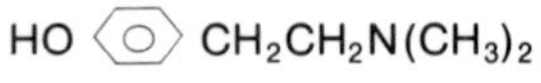

$$HO \langle O \rangle CH_2CH_2N(CH_3)_2$$

Kilning. NDMA formation promoted by presence of NO_x (oxides of nitrogen).

$$\text{Hordenine} \xrightarrow{NO_x} (CH_3)_2N{\rightarrow}O$$

nitrosodimethylamine (NDMA)

Malt. Level of NDMA in malt depends on quantity of precursors formed during germination and extent of nitrosation on kilning. Therefore, enhanced hydrostatic pressure in steeping and use of rootlet inhibitors, such as bromate, suppress NDMA, as does avoidance of high NO_x contact with malt (e.g., indirect kilning).

Fig. 3. The principal source of nitrosamine in malt.

Viability

The viability of barley can be reduced in various ways—for example, through injudicious storage of grain at excessive moisture contents for prolonged periods and by subjecting grain to excessive temperatures during drying. Viability can be assessed as germinative capacity (GC), by a test that measures the percentage of kernels germinating in the presence of hydrogen peroxide over a three-day period (Institute of Brewing, 1991). Typically, a maltster may demand a GC for barley in excess of 96%. However, this would still permit the presence of 4% dead, unmodifiable kernels in a sample, a level at which substantial processing difficulties could ensue, for example, in brewing (see below).

A more rapid assessment of viability used by the production maltster for immediate screening of deliveries of barley to the maltings is by the tetrazolium test, in which viable embryos are stained red (Mackay, 1972). This method, however, can be unreliable in that it provides "false positive" scores, with grain of poor vigor still staining positive. The test is also highly subjective. However, it is possible to perform quantitative tetrazolium-type reactions on samples of milled barley; the level of formazin produced per unit of dry matter affords an index of viability (Pitz, 1991). The same author reviews and proposes methods for assessing pregermination in barley.

Dormancy

Viable grain may not be capable of immediate germination, i.e., it is dormant. Plainly, dormant barley is unsuitable for malting for the same reasons as is nonviable grain. Dormancy in barley while it is "on the ear" is crucial to preventing pregermination, a phenomenon that leads to premature enzyme development, subsequent killing of grain if dried, and lack of homogeneity in malting.

Dried barley normally emerges from a dormant condition relatively rapidly (in less than three months). Varieties grown in cooler climates, such as Triumph in northern regions of the United Kingdom, are especially prone to dormancy, breakage of which is accelerated by warm storage of dried grain, for example at 30°C (Palmer and Taylor, 1980; Rijs et al, 1989). Storage of barley is, of course, costly, and the maltster ordinarily prefers to minimize the holding of stock where feasible.

Dormancy is assessed by the difference between the GC value and the germinative energy (GE) score. The latter is the percentage of kernels that germinate over three days on filter paper soaked in 4 ml of water. Again, the maltster is looking for a GE value of greater than 96% before a barley is ready for malting.

The biochemistry underlying dormancy is ill-understood (Briggs, 1990). Roberts and Smith (1977) proposed that it is related to the absence of a functional pentose phosphate pathway in dormant barley. Factors that alleviate the dormant state, for example, warm storage or oxidizing conditions, seem to induce the pentose phosphate pathway. Alternatively, oxidizing conditions may remove inhibitors of germination (Crabb and Kirsop, 1970). Doran has demonstrated that dormant samples of the variety Triumph contain more abscisic acid than do mature samples (cited in Brookes, 1992). Furthermore, during germination there is a fall in levels of glutathione, and so it is believed that there is a role for thiols in regulation of dormancy.

Nondormant, viable grain may still not germinate rapidly—it lacks vigor (Aastrup et al, 1989). Over a three- to nine-month storage period, the ability to produce enzymes in response to gibberellic acid increases (Crabb, 1971). It has been suggested that monitoring of levels of embryonic glyceraldehyde 3-phosphate dehydrogenase might serve a useful role in assessing vigor (Bourne and Wheeler, 1985; Kitamura et al, 1990). Rijs and Bang-Olsen (1991) propose the germination index (GI) as a measure of vigor. The GI is basically the average rapidity with which the kernels in a GE test germinate. These authors also define a second new term, germination homogeneity, a measure of uniformity in the rate at which grain germinates in a sample. High GI and germination homogeneity (i.e., rapid and even germination, respectively) are clearly necessary if a barley is to be rapidly and efficiently converted to a homogeneous malt.

Water Sensitivity

Nongermination can be induced if barley encounters excessive levels of moisture, a phenomenon called water sensitivity (Essery et al, 1956). The extent of this condition is estimated by doubling the amount of water in the GE test. The demonstration of water sensitivity led to the concept of interrupted steeping, whereby successive steeps of barley are separated by periods of drainage ("air rests").

Major and Roberts (1968) suggested that a major cause of the phenomenon is the presence of microorganisms on the surface of the grain, which compete with the embryo for available oxygen. Such a conclusion has been reinforced recently (Kelly and Briggs, 1992).

EVALUATION AND SELECTION OF BARLEY FOR MALTING

This can be discussed in two separate contexts: first, the identification of those barley lines in a breeding program that are likely to malt well and, second, the analysis of barley at the point of purchase by the maltster.

Selection for Malting Quality in Breeding

Although any viable barley can be malted, top quality malts as demanded, for example, by the brewer or distiller, are produced from those varieties capable within short malting times of ready and even modification with high yields of fermentable extract. These are the "malting grade" varieties, as opposed to the "feed grade" varieties. The methods required for prediction of malting quality in breeding programs are diverse (Orive et al, 1991; Bamforth and Proudlove, 1992; Sage, 1992). The preferred requirements in such methods are rapidity, simplicity, use of few kernels, and, of course, the ability to differentiate barleys of malting quality as reliably as possible. Proposed methods include the use of near-infrared reflectance spectroscopy, milling energy, and the rate at which moisture is taken up by grain (Davies, 1992).

Selection of Barley for Production Malting

Barley is purchased by the maltster according to strict specifications. Apart from freedom from foreign matter, infection, infestation, odor and taint, specifications typically include the following factors.

1. Variety. All batches of grain should be of a single cultivar to preclude differences in performance during malting, leading to heterogeneous malt.

2. Moisture. In the United Kingdom, the specification typically is 16%, with progressive price reductions for higher moistures up to 21%. Lower moisture contents might be anticipated in other countries.

3. Size. For two-rowed barley, the specification may typically be >60% retained on a 2.8-mm sieve and >85% retained on a 2.5-mm sieve, with freedom from excess screenings (>3% retained on a 2.0-mm sieve) and from extraneous matter. The weight of a thousand kernels is a useful index of mean kernel size.

4. Protein content. The barley should have a low protein content, especially when it is targeted for brewing and distilling. For a given kernel size, the more protein that is present, the less starch (and therefore potential fermentable sugar) that is available. The grower can expect an increasing premium for batches of progressively lower nitrogen content. Typical N levels preferred for two-rowed malting barley in Europe may be 1.5–1.7%. For six-rowed malting barley in North America, preferred N levels would, more typically, be 1.8–2.0%.

5. Modification potential. The grain should be capable of ready and even modification, with the generation of sufficient enzymes to mobilize the endosperm. This requires that the grain should have high viability (GC >96%), low dormancy (GE >96%), high vigor, and a starchy endosperm that is amenable to degradation.

Barley from storage is analyzed for GC, GE, and water sensitivity to predict the steeping and germination conditions that are needed to deal with it. For example, water sensitivity data afford a useful indication of the necessary steep-air-rest regime. The maltster also relies upon microscale water uptake, steeping, and germination trials.

MALTING TECHNOLOGY

Commercial malting operations involve four basic stages: barley intake, drying, and storage; steeping; germination; and kilning.

The maltster may be producing malts destined for a range of uses (see below). Irrespective of the nature of the malt being produced, it is incumbent upon the maltster to operate an effective production, in terms of product quality and process cost. Regarding the latter, apart from minimizing energy usage, labor costs, and effluent demands, it is important to maximize yields (i.e., malt produced per unit input of barley). To produce quality malts, it is impossible at present to avoid a degree of embryo development. Clearly, the more this "malting loss" occurs, the greater is the call on endosperm reserves and the less malt is obtained.

It is not within the scope of this chapter to debate the rationale behind the selection of malting sites with respect to the availability of convenient barley supplies, a source of water, strategic location for sales and distribution, and reliable effluent disposal. Rather, the authors restrict themselves to broad consideration of types of equipment and the processes that they are designed to effect. The discussion begins with barley reception and drying (Fig. 4).

Barley Drying

Drying enhances the storage properties of barley. It is necessary only in those climates, for example, in the United Kingdom, where barley would otherwise be put into storage at a moisture content in excess of 16%. At higher moistures, barley is prone to spoilage; this is indicated by a rise in grain temperature ("wet grain heating") due to respiration by grain and field fungi, such as *Alternaria, Helminthosporium*, and *Fusarium*. Grain under 15% moisture can also be subjected to heating ("dry grain heating") by insect infestation. Although temperatures reached (38–42°C) are lower than for wet grain heating (50–52°C), the grain is still subject to viability loss.

All dryers demand a high-flux supply of clean ambient air, a source of heat, and a means for cooling grain after drying.

Drying is generally performed at temperatures below 55°C, although the grain is unlikely to rise above 30°C, due to latent heat of evaporation. High airflows (20–30 m^3 min^{-1} t^{-1}) are used, with accurate temperature control.

Although many types of dryers may be found on farms, they generally suffer from inadequate capacity, inefficiency, and inferior temperature control and airflow. As a consequence, the maltster often takes responsibility for grain drying. This may be done in either batch dryers or continuous-flow dryers, which are either direct-fired or indirect-fired, depending on how heat is transferred to the grain. With direct-firing, combustion products pass into the grain with the heated air, whereas in indirect-fired systems the air passes through a heat exchanger. The combustion gases are vented to atmosphere without encountering the grain.

Direct-fired systems are cheaper and are more economical, as they avoid transferred heat losses and the plant tends to be relatively simple. However they present some risk of fire by straw or dust ignition in the burner.

The size of the dryer is dictated by the required throughput, extraction rate, and properties of the ambient air.

Continuous dryers are customarily modular, built with extra modules added where increased throughput is required. They can be either vertical or horizontal. In vertical systems, grain enters at the top and falls by gravity through a drying section in which moisture is removed by warm, dry air. Such air is either blown or sucked through the dryer. The latter is preferred as the dryer is under negative pressure and, in this way, dust emission is reduced. Grain is progressively dried as it descends. Once it reaches the bottom quarter of the dryer, ambient air is used for cooling before the grain is discharged. Typically, grain may take about 4 hr to pass through the dryer.

In horizontal dryers, grain normally passes, on a slightly inclined mesh conveyor, through a current of warm air. The speed of the conveyor dictates the rate of discharge.

Although vertical dryers are normally run continuously, they may also be used batchwise for smaller quantities of grain. The entire column has warm

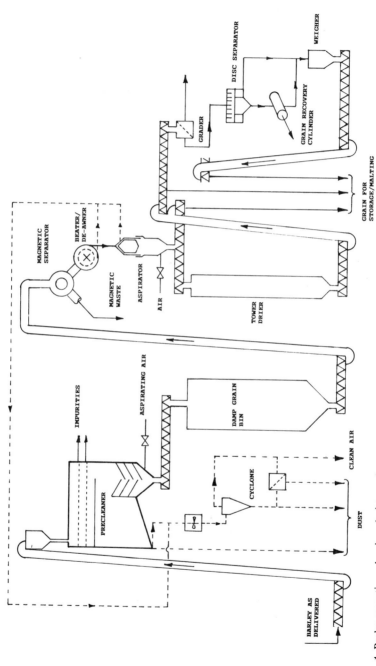

Fig. 4. Barley reception, cleaning, drying, and storage.

air passed through it. Once drying is complete, heating is stopped and the whole column is cooled before emptying.

Batch drying may also be performed in a malt kiln during the harvest period. Green barley is loaded to a greater depth than green malt, since much less moisture needs to be removed.

A typical continuous drying operation begins with barley at intake being tested and the analysis being compared either with a prepurchase sample or with the specification cited in the contract. Only if the analysis is acceptable will the barley be passed for intake. The load may be bulked with other loads according to commonality of moisture and nitrogen content, kernel size, and, of course, variety.

The grain is passed through a precleaner and weigher en route to predrying holding bins. Dust is removed from the precleaner by aspirating air.

Grain is then carried by conveyor, via a magnetic separator to remove metallic objects, to the dryer. The "air on" temperature must be suitable for the barley being dried. Samples are drawn, typically at 2-hr intervals, from the dryer for moisture testing. If discharge moisture is higher than target, the rate of throughput is reduced.

On discharge, the grain is either conveyed directly to storage or is afforded further cleaning and passage to a grader, which removes small kernels and dust and may separate the grain into various size fractions.

Half kernels and other seeds can be removed in a half-kernel separator. The barley is then weighed for weight comparison with the quantity of "green" barley taken into the operation.

The barley may be treated with insecticide, depending on the estimated length of storage or on restrictions enforced by the intended use for the barley after malting.

Sturdy storage is clearly critical to long-term grain stockholding. Stores must exclude rodents and birds and should keep out rain and air drafts. There must be controlled ventilation (airflow up to 10 m^3 min^{-1} t^{-1}).

The duration of storage is dictated by the barley moisture content. In the climate of the United Kingdom, for example, barley with a moisture content of >18% would likely be dried as soon as possible; with 16–18% moisture, it would be given short storage with ventilation; at 14–16%, medium storage with ventilation; at 12–14%, long storage with ventilation; and at <12%, long storage without ventilation.

Drying reduces the activity of storage fungi such as *Penicillium* and *Aspergillus*. It also induces temporary dormancy, but germination recovers in a few weeks. Recovery can be accelerated by transferring the grain to storage at 25–35°C and holding it at this temperature for a few weeks. The grain is then cooled by ventilation to ambient temperature. This is a useful technique for breaking dormancy for early steeping after harvest or for particularly dormant barley varieties. The treatment does, however, reduce the long-term viability of the barley and is suitable only for short-term storage.

Airflow in ventilation may either be upward (blowing) or downward (sucking). Blowing is preferable in flat storage, because air is then more evenly distributed and cooling is more even and rapid. Furthermore, the warmest regions shift to the top of the bulk and can be more readily detected by probes.

In silos it is better to suck air downward. Silos are usually free-standing and outdoors, with the grain in close proximity to a cold metal roof. When warm air, blown upward, hits the roof, it is cooled and condensation drains back into the bulk.

Anoxic or low oxygen conditions benefit storage, as they eliminate the need to use pesticides (Baxter and Dawe, 1990). The practicalities of using such conditions depend on the type of storage. It would be easier to maintain low-oxygen conditions in bins or silos than in flat storage.

Types of Storage

Commercial barley storage systems are either: 1) flat stores for bulk quantities of 10,000–30,000 t, 2) circular, flat-bottomed, steel bins for up to 5,000 t, 3) square or round hopper-bottomed steel bins for up to 750 t, or 4) reinforced concrete silos. The last type can be prohibitively expensive to construct nowadays and will not be discussed further.

FLAT STORAGE

This has become increasingly popular in recent years. Flat stores are cheaper to construct than are silos and are useful for large quantities of individual varieties. Grain is conveyed to a depth of up to 6 m on the floor of a large steel- or concrete-framed shed with load-bearing corrugated steel side walls. The floor may be internally ducted for aeration and for emptying conveyors. Cables suspended from the roof support are used for monitoring grain temperature.

Partitions can be employed to separate varieties. However, the demands on such systems to withstand considerable horizontal pressures make them very costly.

Obviously if a problem is encountered in a bulk store of this type (for example, water seepage through fabric damage or localized insect heating), there are serious logistical difficulties in moving large tonnages before the troublesome area can be reached.

FLAT-BOTTOMED, CIRCULAR STORAGE BINS

These are more expensive to construct than is flat storage. They have concrete circular bases and central discharge hoppers. The base may also be ducted with steel perforated covers for aeration by externally mounted fans. Grain removal may be via a screw conveyor cast into the base or a chain conveyor, mounted in an underground duct. The latter is more expensive, the duct needing to be large enough to enable access for maintenance. Bin sides are corrugated galvanized steel sheets bolted to vertical posts. The roof is of steel segments with an angle slightly greater than the angle of repose of the barley.

Bins are filled by overhead conveyor. A sweep auger inside the bin removes the last of the barley after the angle of repose has been reached. Such bins must be emptied symmetrically through the central spout, as any discharge via the side walls causes uneven pressure on these walls, leading to distortion and possible collapse.

Pendant cables suspended from the roof again provide the means for temperature monitoring. If a hot spot is detected, the barley can be moved easily and treated with insecticide as necessary. Conveyor sequencing is generally automatic and, thus, labor needs are minimized.

HOPPERED BINS

These bins can be corrugated, flat-sided, and either square or rectangular, and bins can be joined together to make up silo blocks. Capacities in excess of 750 t are too expensive in view of the necessary support steelwork and hopper diameter. The hopper allows self-emptying by gravity. Such silos are used for specific purposes, such as storage of screenings or for rapid outloading of small quantities of barley.

Steeping

The major objective of steeping is to increase the moisture content of barley from 11–12% to 43–46% within 48–72 hr. The moisture content at casting from the steep to germination is such as to ensure rapid and even modification, while minimizing embryo growth and respiration (malting loss). Lower-quality barleys of higher nitrogen content possessing steely endosperms may need to be steeped to 46–48% moisture, whereas low-nitrogen barleys of high malting grade may give good results at a moisture level of 42–43%. At under 32% moisture, grain will not germinate, while at about 35% moisture, it will germinate vigorously but is unlikely to modify adequately.

Water sensitivity in barley is overcome by interrupting steeps with air rests. In former times, grain could not be processed until profound dormancy had been overcome and water sensitivity had been minimized. However, to achieve the necessary water content, water-sensitive grain can be steeped initially to 33–37% moisture over 6–16 hr, air-rested for 12–24 hr, and then rewet for a further 10–20 hr to take the moisture to 43–45%.

In the air rest period, the grain takes up the film of moisture that coats it. Air is sucked downward through the bed to help disturb this film, to introduce oxygen, and to encourage carbon dioxide elimination. Blowing air into the base of the steeps is avoided, as compressors heat air, leading to localized grain drying and possibly contamination with oil fumes. Alternatively, the grain may be mixed and aerated in steeps using a rouser. This is both costly and inefficient.

Steeps are aerated to maintain grain viability and to ensure rapid and even germination during transfer from the steep (casting). As steeping induces respiration, the temperature of the grain must be controlled. A supply of oxygen is required, and carbon dioxide must be removed to avoid damage to the kernels. Prolonged anaerobiosis and the accumulation of ethanol produced by the embryo impair germination and will kill the grain if precautions are not taken.

A range of alternative steeping procedures include traditional steeping, steeping with air rest periods, spray steeping, flush steeping, resteeping, and hot water steeping.

In traditional floor maltings, steeping involved submerging grain in water for two to three days, until the moisture content reached 42–45%. The water was changed up to three times and, after the final drain, the barley was left for 8–10 hr before casting.

The use of air rests is now normal (see above). This technique affords more homogeneous products.

In spray steeping, grain is steeped to 35% moisture, and, after an air rest, sufficient water is sprayed on it to renew the surface moisture film. Spraying is repeated at intervals until the required final moisture content is reached. This method minimizes water usage and effluent, and the grain is well-aerated. However, even spraying of a large bulk of grain is problematic, with the attendant risk of uneven modification.

Flush steeping is a compromise between steeping with air rests and spray steeping. After an initial steep to 35% moisture, the grain is air-rested for about 12 hr before water is restored as a 5-min flush. Further air rests and flushes follow, until the required final moisture is obtained. The method provides good control of steep temperature, and excellent aeration and rapid water uptake are achieved. However, water usage is high and considerable effluent is produced.

In resteeping, barley is taken to 40% moisture and germinated for up to three days before the roots are killed by resteeping anaerobically for 24 hr. The grain is returned to the germination box before kilning. Malting losses are reduced, and the high moisture contents of over 50% ensure rapid modification. However, kilning costs are high, and separate equipment for resteeping is needed. Furthermore, ensuring complete root kill is difficult. The method is valuable when the use of additives, such as bromate (see below), is forbidden.

The use of hot water (e.g., 40°C) for relatively short steeping periods (perhaps one wet steep of 8 hr) rapidly hydrates grain but also damages the embryo. Rootlet growth is reduced, but gibberellic acid must be added to promote even modification. The heating of large quantities of steep water is expensive.

STEEPING VESSELS

Modern steep tanks are usually either conical-bottomed, ventilated conical-bottomed, or ventilated flat-bottomed.

Conical-bottomed steeps are self-emptying, either wet or dry, and do not require specialized filling or emptying equipment. However, as grain in the lower layers is subject to extremes of pressure and because it is difficult to provide even treatment to the whole batch, such vessels are rarely larger than 40–50 t in capacity.

To improve the extraction of carbon dioxide and the aeration of grain, ventilated conical steeps were introduced (Fig. 5). These vessels suffer the same capacity limitations as do nonventilated vessels.

Recently, large flat-bottomed ventilated steeping vessels have emerged. Typical batch sizes are 150–250 t. They have the advantages of a uniform bed depth, excellent aeration, and efficient carbon dioxide extraction. However, it is necessary to fill the plenum chamber below the perforated base plates during steeping. In a 200-t steep, this additional water requirement amounts to about 17,500 gal per wet, which is 30% more than in a conical steep. Water and effluent costs are clearly elevated. Cleaning below the perforated floor is also problematic. In recent designs, the floor can be raised and lowered through 0.5–2.0 m using hydraulic rams. Flat-bottomed steeps typically have a rotary loader-discharger (*giracleur*), with emptying at the side of the vessel. Central emptying is preferable where high discharge rates are required.

Steeping vessels are normally fabricated from steel, preferably stainless. Cost constraints often dictate the use of mild steel with an epoxy internal finish. Flat-bottomed steeps have perforated floors of galvanized or stainless steel.

During filling of steeps, the delivery spout is surrounded by water sprays to dampen the falling grain, thus reducing the dust hazard. Overflow pipes and baskets are provided to enable light grains and other low-density particles to be skimmed off by overflow. The skimmings are dried and sold as animal feed pellets.

Water used during steeping is either from a borehole, in which case it is relatively constant in temperature (14–16°C) or, more commonly, from the local city supply. Maltings may need to heat incoming water at low winter temperatures to around 18°C or, conversely, chill it from high summer temperatures.

ADDITIVES

Several additives have been employed during steeping or during transfer to germination to facilitate malting. These include hypochlorite, alkalis,

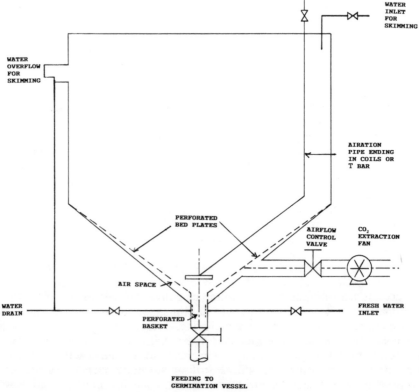

Fig. 5. A ventilated conical steeping vessel.

formaldehyde, hydrogen peroxide, gibberellic acid, bromate, and ammonium persulfate.

Hypochlorite, Alkalis (Calcium or Sodium Hydroxide or Sodium Carbonate), and Formaldehyde. These reduce the population of microorganisms on the grain. Such organisms compete with the barley embryo for available oxygen. However such treatments introduce a risk of killing the grain and imparting off-flavors to malt.

Hydrogen Peroxide. This additive can be used to help release barley from dormancy.

Use of the above substances is rare in modern malting operations. The following, however, are widely used, if permitted.

Gibberellic Acid. Gibberellic acid (GA₃), isolated industrially from culture filtrates of the fungus *Gibberella fujikuroi,* can be used to augment the kernel's own supply of gibberellin. GA₃ may be used to help break dormancy, to accelerate germination, perhaps by two or three days, and to stimulate the production of enzymes.

GA₃ at 0.1–0.5 ppm is commonly sprayed onto grain on casting from steep tank to germination vessel. Response to added GA₃ is highly dose-dependent, and barley varieties respond to different extents. The use of GA₃ may be coupled with abrasion or scarification of the grain, facilitating access of the hormone to aleurone cells in the distal regions of the kernel.

GA₃ may be used to promote modification of barley after the embryo is damaged or killed by techniques such as hot water steeping (see above). If excessive GA₃ is used, then malts may be over-modified, yielding too high levels of sugars and soluble nitrogenous substances during germination. These cross-link during kilning to cause excessive color development.

Potassium Bromate. This may be used in conjunction with GA₃. Bromate inhibits respiration in the embryo, thereby reducing heat generation in the grain bed and relieving refrigeration loads. Bromate also reduces rootlet growth, thereby reducing malting loss. As a result, the volume occupied by green malt during germination is reduced and capacity is increased. Bromate also inhibits proteolytic enzymes and lessens the production of soluble nitrogenous material (Melcher and Varner, 1971).

Potassium bromate is sprayed onto steeped barley at levels of between 30 and 200 ppm. Bromate suppresses the formation of the dimethyl sulfide precursor, S-methyl methionine (SMM, see Fig. 2). Brewers vary in the extent to which they require dimethyl sulfide in their beers. The use of bromate in malting is advantageous if low levels of SMM are required but is avoided if SMM needs to be present.

Ammonium Persulfate. Ammonium persulfate (APS; Wainwright et al, 1986) inhibits rootlet growth in a manner comparable to that of bromate at rates between 125 and 500 ppm. The inhibition of SMM production, however, is less marked with APS than with bromate. Unfortunately, APS has corrosive properties.

The importance of restricting embryo development during malting has become particularly acute since maltsters came to appreciate that acrospire and rootlet tissues are sources of precursor materials, which can yield possibly carcinogenic substances, such as nitrosamines (Fig. 3), during malting or later in processing. Recently the ultimate source of one such substance, ethyl carbamate in grain-based spirits, was traced to a cyanogenic glycoside produced in the barley acrospire (Cook et al, 1990). The glycoside is extracted into worts (see below) and is hydrolyzed during fermentation by a yeast β-glucosidase, to yield a cyanohydrin that breaks down to hydrogen cyanide on distillation. Cyanide reacts with ethanol to yield ethyl carbamate. Clearly, a comparatively unique set of conditions is needed for the formation of ethyl carbamate. Most beers seem to be free from ethyl carbamate (Canas et al, 1989).

Germination

Germination is generally targeted to generate the maximum available extractable material by promoting endosperm modification through the development, distribution, and action of enzymes. The process is controlled by maintaining moisture levels within the grain, supplying oxygen, removing carbon dioxide, and eliminating excess heat formed by respiration. Furthermore, the grain is turned mechanically to prevent rootlet matting.

In traditional floor malting, germination is performed at 13–16°C over eight to ten days. Temperature control of the "piece" is by thinning out (cooling) or bulking up (warming), either being achieved by human labor.

In modern pneumatic maltings, temperature is controlled by mixing fresh ambient air with recirculated air from the germination room. In warmer periods, the ambient air may have to be chilled by refrigeration. In some maltings, the amount of air and, in turn, the temperature of the germinating grain is controlled by adjusting the fan speed.

Temperature control in pneumatic (mechanical) maltings is generally programmed in advance, typically over the range 16–20°C. Germination trials at 25°C or higher have been unproductive. Fully mature grain, uniformly steeped and then cast at between 12 and 25°C, germinates faster as the temperature is increased, producing roots faster and, in the early stages, producing enzymes more quickly. However, the rate of formation of enzymes such as α-amylase falls away, such that grain germinating at lower temperatures ultimately contains higher levels of enzyme. By commencing germination at a relatively high temperature, and then reducing the temperature, an enhanced enzyme formation rate can be sustained. As a result, malt of the desired quality is produced more rapidly, and malting loss is reduced. Long, cool germination cycles maximize fermentability and also minimize malting loss (Bathgate et al, 1978).

During germination, moisture is transferred from the green malt to the surrounding air. To sustain its growth, the embryo withdraws moisture from the starchy endosperm, causing a progressive drying (0.5% per day) of the endosperm and therefore interference with modification. Spraying can be employed to restore moisture, but this increases the malting loss without necessarily boosting modification. A preferred means of reducing loss is to humidify the air passing through the bed via a series of spray nozzles or spinning disks. Spinning disks can prove troublesome, as their associated electrics may be interfered with by high moisture levels over long periods.

About 4% of the initial barley dry matter is lost to embryo respiration during germination, although the extent of respiration is greatly influenced by malting conditions. Steep aeration, additions of GA_3, increased germination temperatures, and high moisture levels all cause vigorous germination and enhanced rates of respiration.

Heat is also a product of respiration, demanding for its dissipation the use of large volumes of attemperated air during germination. Air is also required as a source of oxygen to promote metabolism and to remove high concentrations of inhibitory carbon dioxide.

Grain must be "turned," to prevent matting of the developing rootlets. Such matting restricts airflow, apart from making it arduous to move or convey the grain.

Turning of the grain is done by shovel in floor maltings but mechanically in modern facilities (see below). Turning typically is done every 8–12 hr and immediately before kilning.

Traditionally, the progress of modification is followed by visually noting the extent of acrospire growth and by assessing the ease with which the endosperm is rubbed out between finger and thumb. When the acrospire is three-quarters the length of the grain and the whole endosperm is easily rubbed out, the "green malt" is ready to kiln. It is important to inspect several kernels, as they modify at different rates. The progress of modification can also be followed by using more sophisticated and objective analyses (discussed below).

During germination, grain moisture content is preferably monitored daily and bed temperature continuously.

Three methods are commonly employed for transfer of grain from steep to germination: 1) by gravity through a chute, 2) mechanically by conveyor, and 3) by pumping a barley-water mixture.

In single-vessel designs, the grain, of course, remains in situ.

In floor maltings, the steeped barley is spread out on large waterproof floors and allowed to germinate at a depth of 75–100 mm. Floors are usually long, low rooms, one above another. Although such maltings are said to provide an enhanced extract, the difficulty of controlling grain temperature and the low outputs, high fabrication costs, and high labor demands have led to their rapid decline and replacement by pneumatic plants.

Initially, mechanical maltings employed rectangular germination vessels (Saladin boxes, Fig. 6). This design was soon surpassed by the drum, with improved control but high unit cost and size restrictions.

Rectangular vessels suffer from uneven air distribution when the length-to-width ratio exceeds approximately 8:1. This, along with box width restrictions to accommodate turner design, imposes a capacity limitation of about 200–250 t. These boxes, fabricated of brick or concrete, feature (Fig. 6): a plenum chamber to allow the passage of attemperated and humidified air; a perforated floor, preferably stainless steel, to allow air to pass through the bed; an air conditioning unit to supply humidified air under pressure into the plenum chamber; a turning mechanism, such as a helical screw; an air inlet and outlet; conveying equipment to and from the box; and a system for emptying the box, either a tipping floor, a "stripper," or dual-purpose turning and stripping machines.

Circular germination vessels (Fig. 7) have been developed that allow improved air distribution and, therefore, capacities of over 500 t. The first circular vessels employed vertical turners located on radial rotating booms.

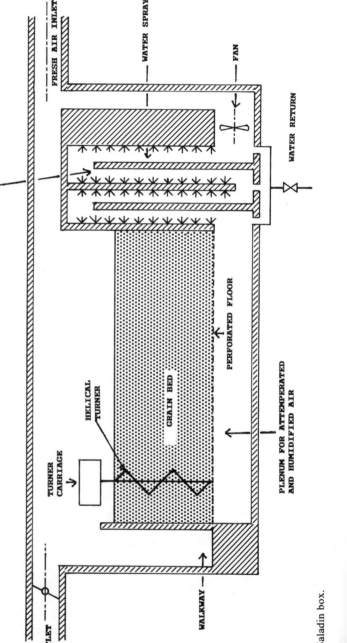

Fig. 6. A Saladin box.

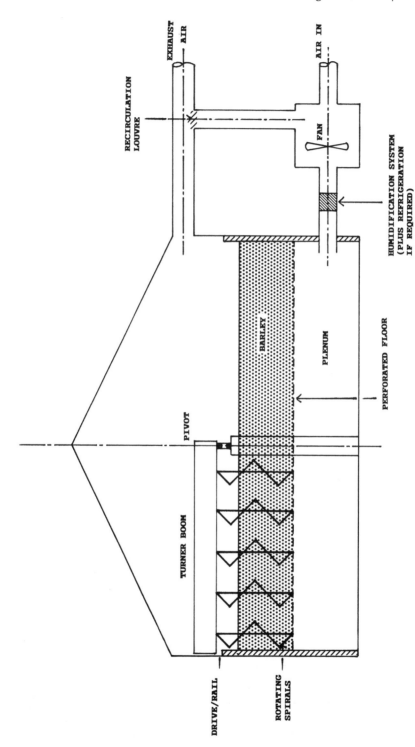

Fig. 7. A circular germination vessel.

Recent designs feature rotating floors, with a fixed turner boom.

Modern circular germination vessels are of steel or concrete, or a combination of both, often with glass-reinforced plastic roofing. The rate of air passage through the bed is normally $0.15–0.20$ m^3 sec^{-1} t^{-1} of barley. Germination in such vessels is typically monitored by microprocessor control.

It is possible to design boxes, generally circular, that can be used to dry barley and also perform steeping, germination, and kilning. Such equipment is relatively cheap and simple to build and operate and clearly circumvents the need to transfer grain between steeping, germination, and kilning. Combined germination and kilning vessels have the advantage that bacteria and fungi, which develop in hospitable conditions caused by high air humidity emerging through the grain bed, are largely destroyed by the heat of kilning, leaving a dry, readily removed residue. However, compromises need to be made in the engineering design of these combined systems. It is self-evident that the structure must resist wide ranges in temperature. After a kilning cycle, the structure (particularly if concrete) must cool before another steep can be performed. Such systems use increased quantities of water and, as a result, are normally employed where water and effluent charges are low. Another disadvantage is that furrows left on the grain by turning during germination cause air-channeling in the kilning phase, and, as a result, drying is uneven.

Tower maltings, with circular germination vessels vertically stacked, have several advantages. They economize on ground space, allow very efficient distribution of services, and enable relatively easy recovery of heat. Most towers feature steeping vessels on top, with each level operated as a separate compartment. Kilns are either at the base of the tower or in a separate building.

Drum plants comprise elongated horizontal metal cylinders, supported on rollers, in which grain is mixed, leveled, and turned by rotation on the long axis. Drums are limited in size, typically holding some 30–50 t. Drums are usually constructed of mild steel and, in common with Saladin boxes, feature a perforated floor, an air-conditioning unit, an air inlet and outlet, and a grain transfer mechanism to and from the drum, as well as a turning mechanism to accommodate loading, emptying, and turning of green malt during germination.

Continuous helical blades may be fitted, extending from the end to the middle of the drum, allowing easy loading and discharging. As drum plants are self-contained, they don't have the same humidity problems as other designs.

Several semicontinuous or continuous plants have been described. One of the most successful is the Ostertag "Wanderhaufen" or moving piece system, which extends the open-ended malting box principle. Steeped barley is deposited in one end of the box and a turner passes the grain sequentially down the "street." At intervals, new loads are leveled at the start. Finished green malt is off-loaded to kilning. Grain is normally turned and advanced twice or three times per day. Mixing is said to be minimal (less than 5%) and each turner serves a number of streets. The Lausmann system is comparable, but grain is moved along a street divided into compartments by raising the floor of a full compartment, while lowering the adjacent floor of an empty compartment. Simultaneously, the turner takes green malt from the top of the box being emptied, depositing it in the box being filled.

Kilning

Traditionally, kilning was in natural-draft kilns with "pagoda"-shaped chimneys. Malt beds were shallow, about 30–50 cm, with low airflows and, therefore, long kilning times. Temperature control was poor. Modern deep-bed, forced-draft kilns have excellent airflow and temperature control, permitting accurate scheduling for the controlled production of different types of malt.

Kiln drying is divided into four merging phases: 1) free drying down to approximately 23% moisture; 2) an intermediate stage, to 12% moisture; 3) the bound water stage, from 12 to 6% moisture; and 4) curing, in which the moisture is typically taken to 2–3%.

During free drying, the flow of air (5,000–6,000 m^3 min^{-1} t^{-1}) at an air-on temperature of 50–60°C causes unrestricted removal of water. Once the moisture content approaches 23%, the decreased ability of water to reach the surface of the grain and the fact that residual moisture is bound, both restrict evaporation. The air-off temperature above the bed suddenly starts to increase in the kiln; "break point" has been reached.

Naturally, the relative humidity of air emerging from the bed starts to drop. Therefore, the air-on temperature can be increased, and the airflow may be reduced to maximize this relative humidity. When moisture content reaches approximately 12%, all the water in the kernel is said to be "bound." The air-on temperature is further increased and the fan speed reduced more, and, as the relative humidity of the air declines, some of the air can be recirculated. When the moisture content approaches 6%, the malt can be "cured." The air-on temperature is increased to within the range 80–110°C, depending on the type of malt required, and further air recirculation may be performed.

As stated earlier, it is important that early in kilning the air-on temperature be maintained as low as practical, as excessive heat, when the grain is wet, results in heat inactivation of enzymes. However, with regard to energy conservation, the highest efficiency is attained with high air-on temperatures.

Rootlets boost the rate of drying, presumably by affording increased surface area for evaporation. Malt is more readily dried than is barley because the water is less firmly bound to grain components.

Kilns vary greatly in design, but most modern kilns are deep-bed. Such kilns, whether circular or rectangular, have become increasingly popular because of their simplicity, relative cheapness, and low fuel costs.

With the adoption of larger batch sizes, there has been a drift from rectangular brick kilns toward circular kilns. These give good air distribution, improved process control, and, therefore, greater product consistency. Corrosion-resistant steel is likely to be used to counteract the effects of sulfur, burnt on the kiln as an antinitrosamine palliative or bleaching agent.

Modern deep-bed kilns feature the following: 1) a source of heat for warming incoming air; 2) a fan to push or pull this air through the grain bed; 3) a plenum to distribute air evenly under the grain bed; 4) a wedge-wire floor permitting air to pass through the grain bed; 5) temperature monitoring for process control, which is automated and preprogrammed in modern operations; 6) an energy conservation system, usually heat exchanger and recirculation; 7) conveyors to and from the kiln; and 8) a kiln loading and stripping system.

Green malt is transferred onto a wedge-wire floor to a depth enabling efficient drying, balancing the initial capital cost against the higher fuel and electrical demands of deeper beds. The optimum bed depth of a kiln is of the order of 350–500 kg of malt per square meter of floor area, which equates to a bed depth of 0.85–1.2 m. Modern automatic or semiautomatic stripper-loaders provide level beds of uniform compaction.

On traditional kilns with a shallow grain bed and regular turning, malt dries relatively evenly. In an unturned, deeply loaded kiln, hot air forced into the grain bed from below shifts the drying zone progressively upward. The flow and temperature of air are regulated such that the emerging air is 90–95% saturated. (Heating air is costly; thus, the air emerging from the bed should be as saturated as possible.) Although drying occurs throughout the bed, there is clearly a degree of unevenness through it.

The majority of commercial kilns are still direct-fired, the products of combustion passing through the bed of grain before being passed to exhaust. New kilns invariably use indirect firing. Conducting fluid, hot water, or steam, heated via a boiler, is employed as a medium and circulated through a heater battery to raise air to the necessary temperature. Indirect firing is principally used as a means for minimizing nitrosamine levels. These systems are more costly to operate in terms of fuel consumption than are direct-fired systems.

Small, specialized drum kilns are used for the production of colored malts. These are, typically, gas-fired with a perforated deck, as in germination drums. Mechanically turned, they may have sprinkler bars inside for quenching the grain in the event of overheating. These drums are also fitted with a "scrubber" or an "afterburner" to remove the organic residues generated in the combustion gases.

Kilning is by far the most energy-demanding stage of malting, consuming at least 75% of the energy input. A traditional kiln employs 4.75 GJ to dry 1 t of malt from 45 to 3% moisture. By the introduction of heat recovery systems, this usage has been reduced to about 2.32–2.85 GJ per tonne.

Heat recovery systems are most commonly simple glass-tube air-to-air heat exchangers, but run-around coil systems or heat recovery units combined with heat pumps are used.

Considerable energy savings may be achieved by employing adjacent kilns (Fig. 8). By staggering the cycles of the two kilns, hot air with low relative humidity, recovered from the kiln furthest into its program, is used to commence the drying of green malt on the second kiln.

At the end of kilning, the heat supply is switched off, and malt is cooled in situ before being stripped in a stream of ambient air. Malt must be cooled before storage, to arrest color formation and to stabilize enzyme levels. To avoid excessive cooling of the kiln before loading with the next batch of green malt, dried malt needs to be stripped to buffer bins rapidly. From these bins, the malt is either screened or transferred directly to storage. During transfer to storage, it is customary to recover a representative sample of the malt for analysis using a "trickle" sampler.

Screening ("malt dressing") includes mechanical removal of dried rootlets (culms); aspiration of dust, loose husk, and half kernels; and removal of large contaminating matter.

After screening, the malt is binned for storage or blending. Storage is mostly

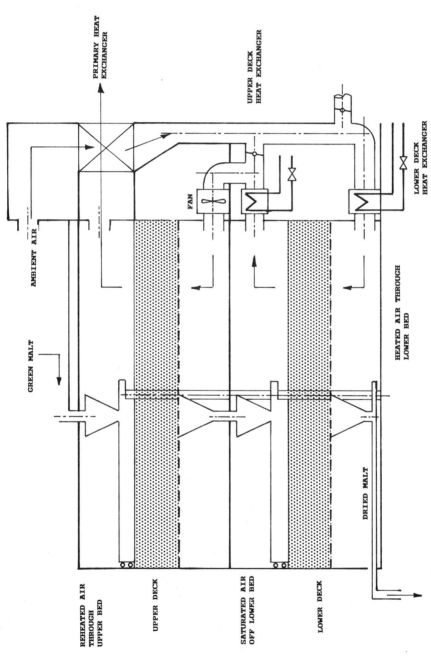

Fig. 8. A double-deck kiln.

in steel or concrete hopper-bottomed bins or silos. These may be cylindroconical or flat-sided with pyramid bottoms. Both are self-emptying. Storage may also be in flat-bottomed silos, with auger discharge. However, such silos demand manual sweeping to remove debris. They are usually built in blocks, sharing internal walls.

Malt is stored for a period, typically four weeks, before being despatched to the customer. Why malt for brewing performs better after this storage period is still unclear but may relate to the equalization of moisture through the grain. SMM levels are, however, reduced with prolonged storage.

After storage, the malt is cleaned a final time before transfer to an outloading bin.

Wherever possible, malt movement after kilning is minimized to avoid damage. Good housekeeping is essential to avoid infestation by insects (saw-toothed grain beetle, confused flour beetle, khapra beetle) and rodents and moisture uptake. The latter leads to unstable "slack malt" (malt above specification in moisture).

Malt culms and dust are collected via a dust extraction unit and sold, after pelletization, along with any barley dust, as animal feedstuff.

USES FOR MALT

Malt is used in various food processes such as brewing, distilling, and vinegar production. Each is discussed below, emphasizing the effects that malt properties have on processing and product quality and on the manner by which malt is analyzed and specified for each function.

Brewing

The brewer is concerned with providing beers of high, consistent quality with maximum process efficiency.

A schematic representation of the fundamental brewing process is given in Fig. 9.

Malt is milled in order that water (liquor) may gain access to grain particles in the mashing phase. Mashing is fundamentally an extension of the malting process, wherein enzymolysis of substrate molecules takes place. Milled malt is mixed thoroughly with two to four volumes of hot water. Mashing is geared, principally, to the controlled hydrolysis of starch to the required degree of sugar formation. The amylolytic enzymes involved are better able to act upon gelatinized starch, hence mashing "conversion" temperatures typically reach 65°C, at which temperature most malt starch is gelatinized. However, the enzymes that hydrolyze proteins and residual cell walls are relatively heat-labile and, if substantial hydrolysis of these substances is required in mashing, e.g., if the malt is relatively under-modified, mashing is likely to be started at a relatively low temperature, e.g., 45–50°C, before being increased to a temperature capable of effecting gelatinization. During mashing, soluble substances (sugars, amino acids, and peptides) produced in malting and mashing are extracted into the liquid fraction ("sweet wort"), which is then separated from the residual solid particles (spent grains).

Although various separation methods exist, the most common is lautering, in which grain particles (chiefly husk-derived) form a filter medium through which wort is run off, with careful application of raking and pressure differentials to optimize flow. Additional water (sparge) is used to ensure efficient leaching of wort from solid particles. The rate of liquid flow from grains is a critical determinant of brewhouse turnover: the more quickly wort can be separated in high yield from spent grains, the more brews can be performed per unit time.

Malt may be supplemented with solid adjuncts such as flaked, torrefied or roasted barley, wheat flour, rice, or maize grits. Rice and maize grits must be cooked before extraction, as their starch granules have higher gelatinization temperatures than do those from barley. Adjuncts are either used on the basis of cost savings (relative to malt) or to impart specific flavor or color characteristics to beer. The starch in adjuncts is converted to fermentable carbohydrates using enzymes present in malt.

The sweet wort is boiled with hops and, perhaps, with sugars as additional sources of fermentable carbohydrate. Polyphenols extracted from the hops

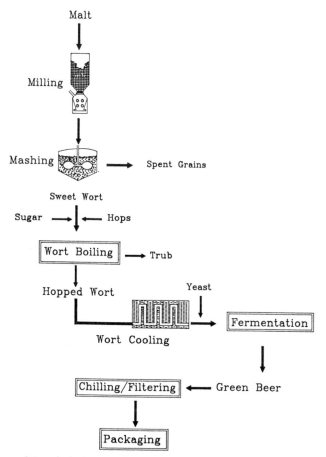

Fig. 9. Scheme of the principal stages of the brewing process.

(and also from malt) help precipitate proteinaceous substances in wort that might otherwise drop from solution in the finished beer, giving unacceptable hazes. Hops also provide the typical bitter and aromatic characteristics to beer. Boiling of wort inactivates all enzymes, as well as effecting sterilization.

Once again a solid-liquid separation stage ensues, with the bright hopped wort being separated from the insoluble "trub." Cooled wort is subsequently aerated or oxygenated and pitched with yeast (*Saccharomyces cerevisiae*), which converts fermentable sugars to alcohol and produces various flavor components, such as esters. After fermentation (which may be at temperatures between 8 and 20°C), a series of maturation and stabilization stages is generally performed, before the finished beer is packaged into various container types (bottles, cans, or kegs).

Barley needs to be malted before brewing to enable the synthesis of enzymes that 1) soften the grain, rendering it more readily milled; 2) remove polymeric substances that hinder wort separation from spent grains due to their high viscosity and contribution to "fines" that block the filter bed (Barrett et al, 1973); 3) convert starch to fermentable sugars during mashing; 4) generate the other nutrients demanded by yeast for efficient fermentation (for example, amino acids and nucleic acid degradation products); 5) eliminate proteins that jeopardize beer handling (such as filtration) and product quality (for example, formation of haze).

The brewer places an increasing number of specifications on malt, not all of which are necessarily mutually compatible (Aastrup et al, 1991). These specifications relate to the contribution that malt makes to process performance and product quality, and it is instructive to discuss the specifications systematically on this basis. Table 5 lists a typical selection of specifications that may be used.

Many of the procedures employed are recommended methods, either of the Institute of Brewing (IOB, 1991), the American Society of Brewing Chemists (ASBC, 1976), or the European Brewery Convention (EBC, 1987). There are many similarities in the methodology, with the most significant variations relating to localized brewing conditions, typical of a given country. For example, malts employed for ale brewing in the traditional isothermal mash tuns of the United Kingdom are relatively well-modified, and the methodology laid down in the *Recommended Methods of Analysis* of the Institute of Brewing (IOB, 1991) reflects this. A single, high-temperature mash is used, for example, in the hot water extract test (see below). By contrast, continental lager malts customarily are less well-modified and demand more complex mashing conditions at a range of (increasing) temperatures. The small-scale mashes used to establish analytical parameters on such malts reflect these conditions— hence the EBC Congress mash employs a system of temperature increases.

Differences, however, are comparatively subtle for the most part and are not highlighted here. The critical need is for methods that are standardized to form the basis of commercial transactions between maltster and brewer.

HOT WATER EXTRACT

Hot water extract (HWE) is an index of the total extractable material that is likely to be obtained from a given malt. High values clearly indicate the availability from a malt of large amounts of potentially fermentable carbo-

TABLE 5
Typical Malt Analyses[a]

	Ale Malt—U.K. (IOB Analysis)	Lager Malt—U.K. (IOB Analysis)	Lager Malt—Pilsen (EBC Analysis)	Lager Malt—U.S. (ASBC Analysis) From Six-Rowed Barley	Lager Malt—U.S. (ASBC Analysis) From Two-Rowed Barley	Distilling Malt—U.K. (IOB Analysis)
Moisture, %	2.7	4.3	4.3	4.0	3.9	4.5–5.0
Hot water extract (coarse)						
1°/kg	307	307	...	...	...	300–310
Percent (db)	...	...	80.4	78.1	79.3	...
Fine-coarse difference						
1°/kg	4	4	...	...	...	4–8
Percent (db)	...	...	1.5	1.5	1.6	...
Color (°)	5	2.5	3.1	1.85	1.75	...
Diastatic power						
°IOB	42	>65	...	...	...	...
°Windisch-Kolbach	...	...	230	...	...	...
°Lintner	...	...	...	155	156	...
α-Amylase, dextrinizing units	...	...	...	45.1	49.0	...
Cold water extract, %	18.5	18	...	...	...	...
Total nitrogen						
Percent	1.56	1.55	1.74	...	...	<1.65
As protein (% × 6.25)	...	...	...	12.6	11.9	...
Soluble nitrogen ratio	39.7	39.3	...	43.0	43.9	38–42
Kolbach index	...	...	40	...	...	...
Friability, %	...	...	88	...	...	...
Fermentability, %	...	...	...	...	...	86–87
Peatiness, arbitrary phenol units	...	...	...	...	...	1–55
Nitrosamines (NDMA,[b] ppb)	...	...	...	...	...	<1.0
Reference	S. M. Sole, 1991[c]	S. M. Sole, 1991[c]	Aastrup et al, 1991	Pyler and Thomas, 1991		Bathgate, 1989

[a] Analyses by Institute of Brewing (IOB, 1991), European Brewery Convention (EBC, 1987), and American Society of Brewing Chemists (ASBC, 1976).
[b] Nitrosodimethylamine.
[c] Personal communication.

hydrate. The parameter is determined from closely controlled small-scale mashes of malt milled relatively coarsely and is quoted on the basis of the specific gravity of the resultant wort (so-called "coarse-grind HWE"). In view of the fact that the milling systems employed (generally disc mills) act by a different principle than those used more widely on a production scale and, also, because it is difficult to recreate full-scale systems for separating wort from spent grains, the HWE figure tends to give little information about how a given malt will behave in a brewhouse. However, this value is regarded as an essential yardstick by which the extract potentially available from a malt can be quantified, and no malt specification will omit it.

If the malt is milled particularly finely to maximize extractability of soluble substances during laboratory mashing, the resultant HWE is called the "fine-grind HWE." Many brewers view the extract difference obtained between the two grinds as reflecting the extent of modification of a malt, as a well-modified sample will more readily mill to finer particles even at coarse mill settings. Thus, the smaller the difference between the coarse and fine ground HWEs, the greater the degree of modification.

MODIFICATION

This "coarse-fine difference" is a relatively simple index of modification. There have been several other suggestions as to how modification might be estimated, thereby providing a valuable guide for selection of the milling conditions necessary to deal with that malt in the brewhouse. Appropriate milling would yield the best distribution of particle sizes for extraction and subsequent wort run-off. In practice, brewers are reluctant to adjust mill settings too frequently. A measure of modification is nevertheless important, as it predicts how a malt is likely to perform in the brewhouse in terms of extract yield and rate of wort separation.

Bourne and Wheeler (1982) built upon the coarse-fine difference test by proposing a "fine-concentrated difference" index. The most significant variation in their HWE methodology was to perform a more concentrated coarse-grind mash, with a liquor-to-grist ratio closer to that used in most breweries as opposed to the unrealistically dilute, well-mixed systems employed in the recommended method. Bourne and co-workers demonstrated that the fine-concentrated difference indeed correlated with extract yield in a commercial-type brewhouse operation. Equally, it was shown that the index correlated closely with the total quantity of β-glucan remaining in the malt (Bourne et al, 1982; Bourne and Wheeler, 1984).

This is not surprising, as such residual material (reflecting unmodified regions in a malt batch) can increase viscosity and thus slow down the flow of wort from spent grains and can form aggregates with other mash components (e.g., small starch granules, lipids, protein) to form sludges that interfere with liquid flow, much as clay retains water.

(Indeed, undegraded β-glucans, if they survive into beer, impede filtration and can cause hazes and sediments. See Bamforth [1982] for a full review.)

Modern brewhouses are equipped to deal with such problems, provided malt is uniformly under-modified; consistency in the degree of modification being critical. Adjustments can be made to processing conditions to deal with homogeneous malts of various degrees of modification. Mill settings, mash temperatures, and thickness and degree of mixing can all be adjusted (Bamforth, 1986). However, evenly and well-modified grain of low residual β-glucan content is preferred.

The fine-concentrated difference is, however, a relatively lengthy measurement to take, and it would be more logical, in any event, to monitor β-glucan directly. Bourne and Wheeler (1984) used the enzymatic procedure of Martin and Bamforth (1981), which employs fungal cellulase to convert hydrazine-solubilized β-glucan to glucose, which is then measured (see also Bamforth and Quain, 1989). Although the extraction and hydrolysis is comprehensive, this procedure is also too protracted for routine analytical use, certainly for routine checking of malt at delivery.

Ahluwalia and Ellis (1984) shortened the procedure by replacing hydrazinolysis with peracetic acid solubilization. Other methods rely upon the direct reaction of malt samples with enzymes (e.g., McCleary and Glennie-Holmes, 1985) or with the fluorochrome Calcofluor (Wood et al, 1983). This latter agent is relatively specific for β-linked glucan and is most commonly used to stain sanded longitudinal sections of malt (Munck et al, 1981). Areas of endosperm that stain with Calcofluor contain unconverted β-glucan (of a molecular weight $>10,000$). Such sanded block techniques (usually 100 kernels are used) afford rapid indication of overall modification and the extent to which grossly under-modified kernels are present (homogeneity). The above methods (enzymatic and staining) for measuring β-glucan have been compared by Ullrich et al (1991), whose results serve to indicate that widely differing levels are recorded by the various procedures. For example, a cellulase-based procedure based on that of Martin and Bamforth (1981) affords substantially higher β-glucan results than does the McCleary and Glennie-Holmes (1985) method. Ullrich et al (1991) concluded that the former type of procedure provides the most thorough means for measuring total β-glucan in barley, whereas the Calcofluor method, which measures only the higher-molecular-weight β-glucans, which are most problematic in brewing, is perhaps the best suited to malt analysis. It is clearly necessary for the maltster and/or brewer to adhere to a procedure that affords useful information in terms of process performance, realizing that it may not give an absolute value for "β-glucan" per se.

The "mirror-image" of the calcofluor procedure involves staining sanded kernels with methylene blue (Kringstad, 1969; van Eerde, 1983). In this case, modified portions accept the dye.

Quantification of these staining procedures is difficult. For this reason, many laboratories resort to the use of procedures that determine the hardness of malt by calibrated devices. Modification results in a softening of grain, rendering it more friable. Accordingly, hardness is an inverse index of modification. Most common in recent years has been the use of the Friabilimeter (Chapon et al, 1980), in which malt is "ground" between a rubber roller and metal sieve. The percentage of the malt that is "powdered" is an indicator of friability, ergo modification. A subsequent sieving of the unmilled residues through a 2.2-mm mesh sieve indicates the proportion of grossly under-modified kernels (Baxter and O'Farrell, 1983). Such kernels, if present in a malt entering the commercial brewhouse, do not mill adequately and, as unmodified kernels are rich in β-glucan, they may cause the type of problem referred to earlier.

High levels of grossly under-modified kernels are likely to be a direct result of some source of unevenness in the original barley or in the malting process used to process it (see above).

Other indices of modification include wort viscosity (the viscosity of the wort produced in the coarse-grind HWE test, which indicates soluble high-molecular-weight gums) and the cold water extract test. The latter test is dependent upon malt being extracted in ammoniacal solution, which is of a pH precluding enzyme action. The specific gravity of the resultant "mash" is a reflection of substances solubilized during malting per se.

A further measure of modification is the 70°C mash viscosity (Bourne et al, 1976). At this temperature, endo-barley-β-glucanase is inactivated but β-glucan solubilase survives to release residual β-glucan into solution. At this high temperature, gum extraction is increased, and viscosity differences between "good" and "bad" malts are exaggerated.

A recent proposal is the adaptation of the Hagberg falling number method, developed originally to determine the α-amylase activity of wheat flour, to afford rapid prediction of overall malt quality (Best and Muller, 1991). The falling number correlates well with friability.

SOLUBLE NITROGEN RATIO

This is a further index of modification, only in this instance it is a measure of the extent of protein conversion, as opposed to cell wall modification.

The total nitrogen content of malt is generally comparable to that of the barley from which it is derived, which is not surprising as the value is based on a total N measurement by Kjeldahl digestion. Although extensive protein modification is likely to have occurred during malting, the absolute level of N is unlikely to diminish significantly. Total N is likely to be specified in malt for brewing simply as confirmation that a low-nitrogen, high-extract (i.e., high-starch) barley has been employed.

Total soluble nitrogen is the level of Kjeldahl N present in a wort produced by a standard laboratory mash (whether IOB, EBC, or ASBC). Clearly, the more extensive the proteolysis that has taken place during malting, the more nitrogenous substances that will have been solubilized. Solubilization also takes place in the laboratory mash—the more so at lower temperatures. Practically, this total soluble nitrogen is related on a percentage basis in a ratio with total nitrogen to yield the soluble nitrogen ratio (SNR). When derived in an EBC Congress mash, this ratio is called the Kolbach index. Brewers demand an SNR sufficiently high to indicate that protein modification has been achieved and that high-molecular-weight protein material will not be extracted into wort, with the risk of carryover to form hazes in beer. Such protein may also cross-link via sulfhydryl bridges to retard wort flow in wort separation systems (Baxter and Wainwright, 1979). Furthermore, proteins embed starch granules and must be removed to enable gelatinization of starch and hydrolysis of the starch by amylases (Slack et al, 1979). The so-called "gel proteins" (Moonen et al, 1987), which are capable of causing cross-linking of polymers in the brewer's grain bed, thereby restricting wort separation, may constitute a part of malt specifications in the future. Excessively high SNRs predict over-modification with attendant risks of malt shattering on the mill and poor foam stability in the finished beer.

There is, as yet, no definite evidence that the proteins responsible for haze formation (which they produce in beer by cross-linking with oxidized polyphenols originating in barley and hops) are different from those contributing to foam. Procedures have been proposed in an attempt to afford more information about the types of proteinaceous material in wort (e.g., Hickman and Buckee, 1982). These methods invariably fractionate polypeptides according to size, whereas it seems that the relative hydrophobicity of a polypeptide is more important in determining its foam potential (Slack and Bamforth, 1983). As yet no predictive tests have been standardized for measuring foam polypeptides in wort. Haze potential in wort can be predicted from saturated ammonium sulfate precipitation limits. Small, progressively increasing aliquots of ammonium sulfate solution are added to the wort (or beer), and the haze resulting after each addition is measured. The more precipitable proteins (those most likely to come out of solution in the finished beer as a haze) are salted out at lower concentrations. Thus, the lower the salt concentration needed to trigger a haze increase, the less the predicted stability of the wort. Equivalent "titration" may also be performed by adding tannic acid to wort.

FREE AMINO NITROGEN

Yeast requires a minimum level of assimilable low-molecular-weight nitrogenous substances (amino acids and some peptides) to support its metabolism. Such free amino nitrogen (FAN) is estimated in laboratory worts by reaction with ninhydrin. Excessive levels are undesirable, as they lessen the microbiological stability of the finished beer. Because the level of amino acids in wort determines the extent to which yeast will produce flavor substances, such as esters, higher alcohols, vicinal diketones, and sulfur-containing compounds (MacDonald et al, 1984), it is critical that their level be controlled.

FERMENTABILITY

It is not usual for specifications to be placed upon individual amino acids. Neither is it the case that given sugars are specified, although this may become more common with the availability of high-performance liquid chromatographic techniques. Rather, the malt specification is likely to include "fermentability" as a parameter. This is determined from small-scale forced fermentations of laboratory worts by a "standard" yeast, measuring the extent to which the yeast is able to decrease specific gravity. The value is generally more relevant to the distiller, whose principal target is maximum alcohol yield. For beer, nevertheless, it is necessary to achieve a consistent degree of "attenuation" (that is, the limit to which fermentation proceeds). Brewers generally demand a residual level of unfermentable carbohydrate in beer, believing that this makes a meaningful contribution to the mouthfeel of the product. The fermentability figure, accordingly, is relevant, if often unreliable. It must also be borne in mind that the level of FAN in wort influences the extent of fermentation by yeast, as does any factor that influences the extent to which the yeast flocculates.

FILTRATION RATE

The rate at which wort can be separated from spent grains is a principal determinant of the perceived quality of a malt for mashing. If wort "run off" in a commercial brewhouse is slow, then grains must be discharged before full extract potential is realized or else the wort separation stage must be prolonged. Either way, brewhouse efficiency is reduced. Thus, any information that forecasts "brewhouse performance" is valuable to the brewer. Although wort viscosity, modification, fine-concentrated extract difference, and β-glucan level give useful information, none correlates absolutely with brewhouse performance. It is certainly difficult to reproduce commercial wort separation in a laboratory. Various small-scale wort separation devices have been proposed, with a view to using them to forecast how a malt will behave on a commercial scale (for example, Webster and Portno, 1981). None seems to have achieved widespread acceptance. Many brewers merely look to the rate at which wort separates from grains in a filter funnel filtration after the standard laboratory mash. Certainly this simple technique, although greatly influenced by seemingly trivial factors such as filter paper grade, can pick out malts that are likely to be especially problematic.

MOISTURE

The water content of malt is of major relevance in terms of establishing the price of that malt. It is determined by oven drying, as for barley. Excessive moisture content is undesirable from the aspect of decreased storage potential ("slack malt"). The moisture content, allied to other information (e.g., color, enzyme content), also indicates the severity with which malt has been kilned.

COLOR

The color of malt contributes significantly to that of the beer derived from it, although oxidation of polyphenols during mashing and wort boiling also contributes to beer color. Furthermore, the melanoidin-type reactions occurring in kilning can also occur during wort boiling. The color of malt relates to its amino acid and sugar content (and hence to modification). High levels of these substances, at high temperatures, combine to produce high colors. Color can be determined in laboratory worts either by comparison with standard colored disks or by spectrophotometric measurement at 430 or 530 nm.

Determination of color is, of course, the principal analysis made on roasted malts, which are employed as a grist ingredient for darker beers.

ENZYMES

The measurement of specific enzymes is seldom relevant when parameters such as modification, HWE, and viscosity are fully documented. These latter values are, after all, "functional" measures that directly relate to enzyme content. Enzyme measurements do, however, serve a confirmatory role and are certainly relevant if nonenzymatic adjuncts such as roasted barley, flaked maize, or wheat flour are used as significant proportions of the grist. Then the malt needs to provide sufficient enzymes to deal with the polymers in these adjuncts (unless exogenous enzymes can also be employed).

The starch-degrading enzyme complex is reported from two measurements, diastatic power (DP) and α-amylase, reported in dextrinizing units (DU). The former gives an overall measure of α-amylase and β-amylase activity and is determined from the release of reducing sugars from a buffered starch solution. Once again, it is of greater relevance to the distiller, particularly grain distillers (see below), than to the brewer. DU are determined by measuring the hydrolysis of β-limit dextrins (resistant to β-amylase) formed by the hydrolysis of starch by β-amylase. Thus, the difference between DP and DU relates to β-amylase. Few, if any, malt specifications contain any direct reference to a measure of limit dextrinase. Simple colorimetric assays for α-amylase, β-amylase, and limit dextrinase have recently been developed (McCleary and Sheehan, 1987; McCleary and Codd, 1989), but these have not yet been adopted as recommended methods.

Endo-barley-β-glucanase in malt extracts can be assessed from the decrease in viscosity of a standard β-glucan solution (Bathgate, 1979), from the zone clearing in complexes of β-glucan and Congo red (Martin and Bamforth, 1983), or by dye release from standard dyed β-glucan (McCleary and Shameer, 1987). As endo-barley-β-glucanase is rapidly destroyed in most mashes (Scott, 1972), its inclusion in many malt specifications is of little relevance, save as an indication of the severity to which a malt has been kilned. Survival of all enzymes is, of course, higher at lower temperatures. Accordingly, mashing may commence at a relatively low temperature, for example 50°C, to enable endoproteases and β-glucanases to act. In these circumstances, specification for such enzymes is warranted.

BARLEY VARIETY

Many brewers are conservative about the barley varieties that they are prepared to use as malt. Even though new barleys have clearly demonstrated an acceptable malting quality, there is a reluctance to use varieties with which the brewer is not familiar. Often these decisions are made on the basis of no firm scientific foundation, although it is indeed sometimes the case that a malt with ostensibly good analysis, but from a "problematic" variety, does not "behave well" in a brewery.

This serves to highlight that the breadth of analytical techniques available to predict brewing quality is still inadequate or, at least, insufficiently informative.

Presently, varietal specifications are generally established on a "trust" basis between maltster and brewer. Electrophoretic discrimination of varieties in malts is less straightforward than for their parent barleys.

FLAVOR

Gross flavor differences in malt, resulting perhaps from infestation, can be qualitatively screened organoleptically.

Most of the flavor notes characteristic of beers originate in hops or as a result of yeast metabolism of wort. The majority of those from malt develop in kilning (see above), but virtually none are, as yet, specified in any malt analysis. Astringency and perhaps body in beer may be due to polyphenols (tannins) originating in the husk of barley (Eastmond and Gardner, 1974).

One compound that is well-documented and specified is SMM. Upon heating, SMM is degraded into dimethyl sulfide, a significant contributor to lager flavor (Fig. 2). Therefore, lager malts are likely to have a specification for SMM.

NITROSAMINES

Maximum levels in malt for these potentially carcinogenic substances are generally specified (see above). Typically, malts should contain less than 5 ppb nitrosodimethylamine.

POTENTIAL FUTURE ANALYSES

It would be logical for brewers to specify the tolerable level of small starch granules in malt, in view of the fact that they can impede wort separation by cross-linking with other polymers (Barrett et al, 1973). Small granules are less digestible in mashes than are large granules due to their higher gelatinization temperatures (Ellis, 1976). Even so, the small granules are preferentially degraded during malting (Bathgate and Palmer, 1973). As they contribute only 10% of the total starch content by weight, it may be desirable for them to be degraded during germination. It must be remembered, though, that this will contribute to malting loss.

In view of the fact that processing aids such as GA_3 are not permissible in certain markets, there is likely to be an increased requirement for methods that detect such agents (Donhauser et al, 1990).

Observations that husk-derived polysaccharides can influence the flocculation behavior of yeast (Herrera and Axcell, 1991) might, in the future, lead to tests on malt that indicate the extent to which a malt will influence fermentation in this way.

Distilling

There are various types of whisky—the Scottish malt and grain whiskies, Irish whiskey, rye in Canada, and bourbon in the United States of America. All of them contain a proportion of malt.

Unlike the case for most beers, a high yield of fermentable sugar is the basic requirement in the production of whisky in order to maximize alcohol levels (spirit yield) before distillation. Whisky malt, therefore, needs to contain high levels of saccharifying (sugar-producing) enzymes to convert the starch of malt itself as well as that from whichever adjunct materials are employed.

Grists for scotch malt whisky are 100% malt. Traditionally such malts were kilned over peat to impart the typical smoky and phenolic flavor characteristics of certain brands. This is still the practice for some pot-distilled brands.

Scotch grain whisky is most commonly produced from a grist of maize or wheat (as high as 90%) with the balance being "green" or, more frequently, lightly dried malts as rich sources of enzymes. As green malt is unstable, this generally demands that there be little distance between maltings and distillery. Of course, there are huge savings in kilning costs if green malt is used. In view of the high gelatinization temperature of maize starch, the maize must be cooked before addition of milled malt mixed in cold water to the cooled maize slurry. Exogenous enzymes and treatments to the malt, such as addition of gibberellic acid, are outlawed for Scotch whiskies.

Depending on economic factors, such as import levies, it may be cheaper in Scotch production to employ cereals other than maize, such as barley or, especially, wheat. These do not require precooking. However they may present other processing difficulties, such as the introduction of highly viscous polymers such as β-glucans (barley) and pentosans (wheat) into mashes.

Such adjuncts (and possibly oats or rye) may form part of the grist for Irish whisky, whereas in the United States the principal raw material for bourbon is maize (minimum 51%). Rye whisky is produced from a grist including some rye but largely maize. Malted wheat or malted rye may replace malted barley as the enzyme source.

For most beers, it is generally considered desirable that a residual level of nonfermentable dextrins survive fermentation; such dextrins supposedly provide body to the product. They are irrelevant to the flavor of whisky and, thus, total conversion of carbohydrate into alcohol is the rule. This is achieved through the use of high-enzyme malts (e.g., unkilned or lightly kilned ones) and mashing conditions that particularly facilitate enzyme action. Indeed, such mashes are not boiled, so that enzymes can survive into fermentation.

Far less emphasis is placed on the quality of yeast employed for whisky manufacture than for beer brewing. Indeed, the yeast may be largely surplus yeast derived from a brewing operation. The character of a beer is largely a function of a specific yeast strain(s). By contrast, the role of yeast in the production of whisky is essentially as a biocatalyst in the conversion of carbohydrate into alcohol, before concentration of the latter in a distillation phase.

Proteolysis is relevant only in terms of ensuring the availability of sufficient FAN for yeast metabolism. Optimizing proteolysis in search of a compromise between haze and foam stability is irrelevant for the distiller.

For the production of malt whisky, milled malt is customarily "mashed in" with the final "spray" from the previous mashing (Fig. 10). Mashing is typically at about 64.5° C for 1 hr, before the first worts are "run off." Mashes follow at 70, 80, and 90° C, with the first two worts going forward via coolers as washes for fermentation and the latter two used to mash-in fresh malt.

Yeast is pitched into the wash and allowed to ferment at 20–21° C for two or more days, until the alcohol content has attained a maximum. The contents are then transferred to the stills. The function, design, and operation of stills is amply described elsewhere (Whitby, 1992).

For grain whiskies, the malt component is milled and mixed with cold water before addition of the heated (for maize-cooked) cereal slurry, which raises the temperature to about 65° C. Once saccharification is complete, the mixture is cooled and pumped to fermentation. Yeast is added to the entire mash and, by diminishing sugar levels, alleviates any osmolar or feedback inhibitory interference of sugars with enzyme action. Fermentation may start at 20° C, and the temperature is allowed to rise to over 30° C. Once fully fermented, the wash is pumped intact to the still.

Many of the specifications placed on malt for distilling are comparable to those employed for brewing malt (Table 5). The major overlaps are moisture, HWE, modification, and fermentability. A high DP is needed for malts employed as enzyme sources for converting high levels of unmalted adjunct in grain distilling.

The principal measurement on distilling malt is spirit yield per tonne of malt. This is derived by application of a standard fermentation test to the Institute of Brewing coarse-grind HWE measure (Dolan, 1983).

Moisture in malt for distilling is a compromise between too low (<4%), which may indicate excessive kilning and loss of amylolytic activity, and too high (>6%), when milling is impaired.

Some distillers demand measurement of FAN or SNR to confirm that sufficient proteolysis has occurred in malting to support yeast metabolism.

Finally, a specification for peat smokiness may be applied, based either on extraction of malt with an organic solvent or by steam-distillation before extraction. The phenolic substances extracted are then quantified either by gas chromatography or colorimetry (Thomson, 1982).

Food safety issues concern the distiller as much as the brewer. Thus maximum nitrosamine figures are specified. Much recent research has been devoted to

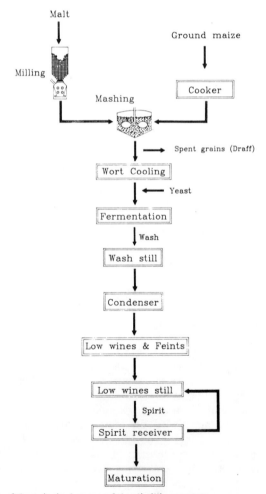

Fig. 10. Scheme of the principal stages of the distilling process.

the origin of ethyl carbamate in whisky (see above). The level of the precursor, cyanogenic glycoside, seems to be variety-dependent, and certain varieties have been highlighted as preferred because of being "nonproducers" of ethyl carbamate (Cook and Oliver, 1991).

Vinegar

Vinegars are produced by the bacterial oxidation of alcohol (e.g., wine, cider, or beer) to acetic acid.

Malt vinegars are produced from either all-malt grists or grists incorporating a proportion of raw cereal. As in the case of distilling, the requirement is for high fermentability of the grist so as to maximize ethanol production, as a forerunner to high yields of acetic acid. Accordingly, a high diastatic malt may be employed, which will be capable of converting starch in the adjunct.

Mashes are not boiled but, as for beer and malt whisky, worts are separated from spent grains before pitching with *Saccharomyces cerevisiae* and a highly attenuating yeast such as *S. diastaticus*. Amyloglucosidase (EC 3.2.1.3) may be added as an alternative means for maximizing the production of fermentable sugars.

Acetic acid bacteria (such as *Acetobacter aceti*) are employed to oxidize ethanol, before maturation of the vinegar in vessels containing beechwood chips. The acidic conditions ensure efficient protein precipitation and separation.

The specifications of malt for vinegar manufacture relate to yield of soluble material (HWE and modification) and yield of fermentable material (fermentability and DP). Moisture is routinely specified for similar reasons as for beer and whisky.

Other Food Uses

Malt enters into the formulation of many foodstuffs (Table 4; Baker-Munton, 1977). It may serve as a source of enzymes or sweetness or may afford nutritional benefits (provision of vitamins, amino acids, etc.). Malt is, however, more specifically employed to enhance color or flavor (principally through the roasted characters developed in relatively intense kilning regimes).

A list of colored malt types is given in Table 4.

Principal among the malt products are soluble extracts of colored malts, which present alternatives to caramels, about which there are increasing health concerns. Methods by which the color and flavor contributions from such malts can be separated have recently been described (Walker and Westwood, 1991). Essentially, the flavorsome materials are of low molecular weight and the colorful substances of high molecular weight. They can thus be split by size-exclusion fractionation.

The colored malts may be used without prior extraction as coffee extenders and in brown breads.

Clearly, the color developed during kilning (see above) is a function of the precise kilning regime balanced against the moisture content of the malt and the degree of modification of the green malt before kilning. High modifications (i.e., high FAN and sugar contents) facilitate a greater degree of melanoidin (color) formation.

Similarly, the flavor development in such malt products is due to a myriad of chemical reactions, which in turn are a function of variables such as degree of modification or of kilning strategy (temperature regime versus moisture content).

Certainly, it is at present impractical to specify flavor attributes for colored malt products in anything other than a relatively crude manner. Individual chemical constituents are not specified.

Color is easier to define, with increasing appreciation of the fact that measurement at a single wavelength is an insufficient index, leading to development of chromaticity and tristimulus quantification (Hunt, 1987).

Regarding enzymatic activity, appropriate malt extracts are frequently viewed as a preferable alternative to microbial sources of enzymes. Certainly, with regard to α-amylase, malt provides a rich supply of a heat-resistant activity, although for other enzymes (for example, β-glucanase), microbial sources tend to be more thermally robust. High-enzyme extracts (or malts) are prepared from higher nitrogen batches of barley, germinated over prolonged periods at relatively cooler temperatures before the malt is dried in mild kilning regimes.

The production of malt extracts has been reviewed by Burbridge and Hough (1970). For extracts used in baking, essentially a brewing-style mashing, wort separation, and boiling process is followed by cooling, filtration of settled precipitated protein, and concentration of the filtrate to about 80% solids in a multiple-effect evaporator. If required in a solid form, these syrups are spray-dried.

ACKNOWLEDGMENTS

The Director of BRF International and the Directors of Bass PLC are thanked for permission to publish this chapter. The numerous helpful comments by John MacDonald, Roger Hammond, and Mike Proudlove are greatly valued, as is the perseverance, skill, and patience of Sue Tomlinson. Gary Freeman is acknowledged for his drawings.

LITERATURE CITED

AASTRUP, S. and ERDAL, K. 1987. A mass balance study of β-glucan in malt, spent grains and wort using the Calcofluor method. Pages 353-360 in: Proc. Congr. Eur. Brew. Conv. 21st, Madrid.

AASTRUP, S., RIJS, P., and HANSEN, J. R. 1989. High vigor—The basis for high malting barley quality. Pages 171-178 in: Proc. Congr. Eur. Brew. Conv. 22nd, Zurich.

AASTRUP, S., BRANDT, J., and RIJS, P. 1991. Malt specifications and analyses (sense and nonsense). Louvain Brew. Lett. 4:16-20.

AHLUWALIA, B., and ELLIS, E. E. 1984. A rapid and simple method for the determination of starch and β-glucan in barley and malt. J. Inst. Brew. 90:254-259.

AMERICAN SOCIETY OF BREWING CHEMISTS. 1976. Methods of Analysis, 7th ed. The Society, St. Paul, MN.

ANDERSON, I. W., DICKENSON, C. J., and ANDERSON, R. G. 1989. β-Glucan in production malting. Pages 213-220 in: Proc. Congr. Eur. Brew. Conv. 22nd, Zurich.

ANNESS, B. J., and BAMFORTH, C. W. 1982. Dimethyl sulphide—A review. J. Inst. Brew. 88:244-252.

ANNESS, B. J., and REED, R. J. R. 1985. Lipids in wort. J. Inst. Brew. 91:313-317.

AXCELL, B., JANKOVCHY, D., and MORRELL, P. 1983. Steeping—The crucial factor in determining malt quality. Brew. Dig. 58:20-23.

BAKER-MUNTON, M. H. 1977. Recent developments—Malt extracts, cereal syrups. Chem. Ind. 446-448.

BALLANCE, G. M., and SVENDSEN, I. 1988.

Purification and amino acid sequence determination of an endo-1,3-β-glucanase from barley. Carlsberg Res. Commun. 53:411-419.

BAMFORTH, C. W. 1981. Enzymolysis of β-glucan. Pages 335-346 in: Proc. Congr. Eur. Brew. Conv. 18th, Copenhagen.

BAMFORTH, C. W. 1982. Barley β-glucans. Their role in malting and brewing. Brew. Dig. 57:22-27, 35.

BAMFORTH, C. W. 1983. Superoxide dismutase in barley. J. Inst. Brew. 89:420-423.

BAMFORTH, C. W. 1985. Cambridge prize lecture: Biochemical approaches to beer quality. J. Inst. Brew. 91:154-160.

BAMFORTH, C. W. 1986. Enzymes from the grist. Brewer 72:427-434.

BAMFORTH, C. W. 1989. β-Glucan solubilase. J. Inst. Brew. 95:314-315.

BAMFORTH, C. W., and MARTIN, H. L. 1981. The development of β-glucan solubilase during barley germination. J. Inst. Brew. 87:81-84.

BAMFORTH, C. W., and MARTIN, H. L. 1983. The degradation of β-glucan during malting and mashing: The role of β-glucanases. J. Inst. Brew. 89:303-305.

BAMFORTH, C. W., and PARSONS, R. 1985. New procedures to improve the flavor stability of beer. J. Am. Soc. Brew. Chem. 43:197-202.

BAMFORTH, C. W., and PROUDLOVE, M. O. 1992. The evaluation of barley for malting. Pages 90-106 in: Proc. Cereals R and D Conf. Home-Grown Cereals Authority, Cambridge, U.K.

BAMFORTH, C. W., and QUAIN, D. E. 1989. Enzymes in brewing and distilling. Pages 326-366 in: Cereal Science and Technology. G. H. Palmer, ed. Aberdeen University Press, Aberdeen.

BAMFORTH, C. W., CLARKSON, S. P., and LARGE, P. J. 1991. The relative importance of polyphenol oxidase, lipoxygenase and peroxidases during wort oxidation. Pages 617-624 in: Proc. Congr. Eur. Brew. Conv. 23rd, Lisbon.

BARRETT, J., and KIRSOP, B. H. 1971. The relative contributions to wort nitrogen of nitrogenous substances solubilized during malting and mashing. J. Inst. Brew. 77:39-42.

BARRETT, J., CLAPPERTON, J. F., DIVERS, D. M., and RENNIE, H. 1973. Factors affecting wort separation. J. Inst. Brew. 79:407-413.

BATHGATE, G. N. 1979. The determination of endo-β-glucanase activity in malt. J. Inst. Brew. 85:92-94.

BATHGATE, G. N. 1989. Cereals in Scotch whisky production. Pages 243-278 in: Cereal Science and Technology. G. H. Palmer, ed. Aberdeen University Press, Aberdeen.

BATHGATE, G. N., and PALMER, G. H. 1973. The in vivo and in vitro degradation of barley and malt starch granules. J. Inst. Brew. 79:402-406.

BATHGATE, G. N., PALMER, G. H., and WILSON, G. 1974. The action of endo-β-glucanases on barley and malt β-glucans. J. Inst. Brew. 80:278-285.

BATHGATE, G. N., MARTINEZ-FRIAS, J., and STARK, J. R. 1978. Factors controlling the fermentable extract in distillers malt. J. Inst. Brew. 84:22-29.

BAXTER, E. D. 1976. The use of hordein fractions to estimate proteolytic activity in barley and malt. J. Inst. Brew. 82:203-208.

BAXTER, E. D. 1982. Lipoxidases in malting and mashing. J. Inst. Brew. 88:390-396.

BAXTER, E. D. 1984. Recognition of two lipases from barley and green malt. J. Inst. Brew. 90:277-281.

BAXTER, E. D., and DAWE, C. J. 1990. Storage of malting barley. Ferment 3:159-162.

BAXTER, E. D., and O'FARRELL, D. D. 1983. Use of the friabilimeter to assess homogeneity of malt. J. Inst. Brew. 89:210-214.

BAXTER, E. D., and WAINWRIGHT, T. 1979. Hordein and malting quality. J. Am. Soc. Brew. Chem. 37:8-12.

BEST, S., and MULLER, R. E. 1991. Use of the Hagberg falling number apparatus to determine malt and barley quality. J. Inst. Brew. 97:273-278.

BOURNE, D. T., and WHEELER, R. E. 1982. Laboratory prediction of brewhouse extract and performance. J. Inst. Brew. 88:324-328.

BOURNE, D. T., and WHEELER, T. 1984. Environmental and varietal differences in total β-glucan content of barley and the effectiveness of its breakdown under different malting conditions. J. Inst. Brew. 90:306-310.

BOURNE, D. T., and WHEELER, R. E. 1985. Physiological and biochemical indications of vigor in barley and their relationship to malt modification. Pages 627-634 in: Proc. Congr. Eur. Brew. Conv. 20th, Helsinki.

BOURNE, D. T., JONES, M., and PIERCE, J. S. 1976. Beta glucan and beta glucanases in malting and brewing. Tech. Q. Master Brew. Assoc. Am. 13:3-7.

BOURNE, D. T., POWLESLAND, T., and WHEELER, R. E. 1982. The relationship between total β-glucan of malt and malt quality. J. Inst. Brew. 88:371-375.

BREDDAM, K. 1985. Enzymatic properties of malt carboxypeptidase II in hydrolysis and aminolysis reactions. Carlsberg Res.

Commun. 50:309-323.

BREDDAM, K., and SORENSEN, S. B. 1987. Isolation of carboxypeptidase III from malted barley by affinity chromatography. Carlsberg. Res. Commun. 52:275-283.

BREDDAM, K., SORENSEN, S. B., and OTTESEN, M. 1983. Isolation of a carboxypeptidase from malted barley by affinity chromatography. Carlsberg. Res. Commun. 48:217-230.

BRIGGS, D. E. 1978. Barley. Chapman and Hall, London.

BRIGGS, D. E. 1987. Endosperm breakdown and its regulation in germinating barley. Pages 441-532 in: Brewing Science, Vol. 3. J. R. A. Pollock, ed. Academic Press, London.

BRIGGS, D. E. 1990. Overcoming dormancy in malting barley. Ferment 3:156-158.

BROOKES, P. A. 1992. Dormancy in malting barley: A review. Pages 107-133 in: Proc. Cereals R and D Conf. Home-Grown Cereals Authority, Cambridge, U.K.

BROWN, P. H., and HO, T.-H. D. 1986. Barley aleurone layers secrete a nuclease in response to gibberellic acid. Plant Physiol. 82:801-806.

BRUNSWICK, P., MANNERS, D. J., and STARK, J. R. 1988. Degradation of isolated barley endosperm cell walls by purified endo (1-3)(1-4)-β-D-glucanases and malt extracts. J. Cereal. Sci. 7:153-168.

BURBRIDGE, E., and HOUGH, J. S. 1970. Malt extracts. Process Biochem. 5(4):19-22.

BUSH, D. S., STICKER, L., VAN HUYSTEE, R., WAYNE, D., and JONES, R. L. 1989. The calcium requirement for stability and enzymatic activity of two isoforms of barley aleurone α-amylase. J. Biol. Chem. 264:19392-19398.

CARBONELL, J., and JONES, R. L. 1984. A comparison of the effects of Ca^{++} and gibberellic acid on enzyme synthesis and secretion in barley aleurone. Physiol. Plant. 63:345-350.

CANADA GRAINS COUNCIL. 1991. Page 48 in: Canadian Grains Industry Statistical Handbook. The Council, Winnipeg, Manitoba, Canada.

CANAS, B. J., HAVERY, D. C., ROBINSON, L. R., SULLIVAN, M. P., JOE, F. R., and DIACHENKO, G. W. 1989. Ethyl carbamate levels in selected fermented foods and beverages. J. Assoc. Off. Anal. Chem. 72:873-876.

CANTRELL, I. C., ANDERSON, R. G., and MARTIN, P. A. 1981. Grain-environment interaction in production steeping. Pages 39-46 in: Proc. Congr. Eur. Brew. Conv. 18th, Copenhagen.

CHAPON, L., GROMUS, J., ERBER, H. L., and KRETSCHMER, H. 1980. Physical methods of the determination of malt modification and their relationship to wort properties. Pages 45-70 in: Eur. Brew. Conv. Symp. on The Relationship Between Malt and Beer, Helsinki.

CLARKSON, S. P., LARGE, P. J., and BAMFORTH, C. W. 1992. Oxygen-scavenging enzymes in barley and malt and their effects during mashing. J. Inst. Brew. 98:111-115.

CLUTTERBUCK, V. J., and BRIGGS, D. E. 1973. Enzyme formation and release by isolated barley aleurone layers. Phytochemistry 12:537-546.

COHEN, D., and PALEG, L. G. 1967. Physiological effects of gibberellins. X. The release of gibberellin-like substances by germinating barley embryos. Plant Physiol. 42:1288-1296.

COOK, R., and OLIVER, W. B. 1991. Rapid detection of cyanogenic glycoside in malted barley. Pages 513-519 in: Proc. Congr. Eur. Brew. Conv. 23rd, Lisbon.

COOK, R., McCAIG, N., McMILLAN, J. M. B., and LUMSDEN, W. B. 1990. Ethyl carbamate formation in grain-based spirits, Part III. The primary source. J. Inst. Brew. 96:233-244.

CRABB, D. 1971. Changes in the response to gibberellic acid of barley endosperm slices during storage. J. Inst. Brew. 77:522-528.

CRABB, D., and KIRSOP, B. H. 1970. Water sensitivity in barley: Inhibitors from barley embryos. J. Inst. Brew. 76:158-162.

CRAIG, S. A. S., and STARK, J. R. 1985. Chromatofocussing as a method for comparing β-D-glucan hydrolases from germinating cereals. Carbohydr. Res. 138:344-350.

DAUSSANT, K., MAYER, C., and MacGREGOR, A. W. 1987. Immunochemical characterisation of the debranching enzyme of barley and malt. Pages 305-312 in: Proc. Congr. Eur. Brew. Conv. 21st, Madrid.

DAVIES, N. L. 1989. Patterns of hydration in barley endosperm during steeping and their relation to malting performance. Pages 221-228 in: Proc. Congr. Eur. Brew. Conv. 22nd, Zurich.

DAVIES, N. L. 1991. Use of X-ray microanalysis to study hydration patterns in barley. J. Cereal Sci. 14:85-94.

DAVIES, N. L. 1992. A new malting index: Prediction of malting quality by endosperm hydration. J. Inst. Brew. 98:43-46.

DEIKMAN, J., and JONES, R. L. 1986. Regulation of barley α-amylase isoenzyme in RNA. Plant Physiol. 80:672-675.

DOLAN, T. C. S. 1983. Determination of fermentability of unboiled malt worts—A method for use in the distilling industry. J. Inst. Brew. 89:84-86.

DONHAUSER, S., EGER, C., and WINNEWISSER, W. 1990. Immunochemical detection of gibberellic acid in malt. Monatsschr. Brauwiss. 43:264-268.

EASTMOND, R., and GARDNER, R. J. 1974. Effect of various polyphenols on the rate of haze formation in beer. J. Inst. Brew. 80:192-200.

ELLIS, R. P. 1976. The use of high amylose barley for the production of whisky malt. J. Inst. Brew. 82:280-281.

ENARI, T.-M., and MIKOLA, J. 1967. Characterisation of the soluble proteolytic enzymes of green malt. Pages 9-16 in: Proc. Congr. Eur. Brew. Conv. 11th, Madrid.

ENARI, T.-M., and SOPANEN, T. 1986. Centenary review. Mobilisation of endosperm reserves during the germination of barley. J. Inst. Brew. 92:25-31.

ESSERY, R. E., KIRSOP, B. H., and POLLOCK, J. R. A. 1956. Studies in barley and malt. V. Determination of husk content and mealiness of barley. J. Inst. Brew. 62:150-152.

EUROPEAN BREWERY CONVENTION. 1987. Analytica, 4th ed. Brauerei und Getränke Rundschau, Zurich.

FINCHER, G. B. 1975. Morphology and chemical composition of barley endosperm cell walls. J. Inst. Brew. 81:116-122.

FINCHER, G. B. 1989. Molecular and cellular biology associated with endosperm mobilisation in germinating cereal grains. Annu. Rev. Plant Physiol. Plant Mol. Biol. 40:305-346.

FINCHER, G. B., and STONE, B. A. 1986. Cell walls and their components in cereal grain technology. Pages 207-295 in: Advances in Cereal Science and Technology, Vol. 8. Y. Pomeranz, ed. Am. Assoc. Cereal Chem., St. Paul, MN.

FORREST, I. S., and WAINWRIGHT, T. 1977. The mode of binding of β-glucans and pentosans in barley endosperm cell walls. J. Inst. Brew. 83:279-286.

FRENCH, B. J., and McRUER, G. R. 1990. Malt quality as affected by various steep aeration regimes. Tech. Q. Master Brew. Assoc. Am. 27:10-14.

FULCHER, R. G., SETTERFIELD, G., McCULLY, M. E., and WOOD, P. J. 1977. Observations on the aleurone layer. II. Fluorescence microscopy of the aleurone-subaleurone junction with emphasis on possible β-(1→3)-glucan deposits in barley. Aust. J. Plant. Physiol. 4:917-928.

GIANNAKOUROS, T., KARAGIORGOS, A., and SIMOS, G. 1991. Expression of β-galactosidase multiple forms during barley (*Hordeum vulgare*) seed germination. Separation and characterization of enzyme isoforms. Physiol. Plant 82:413-418.

GOLDBACH, H., and MICHAEL, G. 1975. Abscisic acid content of barley grains during ripening as affected by temperature and variety. Crop. Sci. 16:797-799.

GOTHARD, P. G., JENKINS, G., and MORGAN, A. G. 1978. Comparative malting performance of old and new barley varieties. J. Inst. Brew. 84:332-336.

GUERIN, J. R., LANCE, R. C. M., and WALLACE, W. 1992. Release and activation of barley beta-amylase by malt endopeptidases. J. Cereal. Sci. 15:5-14.

HAMMERTON, R. W., and HO, T.-H. D. 1986. Hormonal regulation of the development of protease and carboxypeptidase activities in barley. Plant Physiol. 80:692-697.

HARDIE, D. G. 1975. Control of carbohydrase formation by gibberellic acid in barley endosperm. Phytochemistry 14:1719-1722.

HARDWICK, W. A., LADISH, W. J., MEILGAARD, M. C., and JANGAARD, N. O. 1981. Technical report of the USBA on nitrosamines. Tech. Q. Master Brew. Assoc. Am. 18:92-108.

HARRIS, G., MacWILLIAM, I. C., and PHILLIPS, A. W. 1957. Studies on enzymes affecting the fermentability of wort carbohydrates. Pages 173-181 in: Proc. Congr. Eur. Brew. Conv 6th, Copenhagen.

HEJGAARD, J. 1978. "Free" and "bound" β-amylases during malting of barley. Characterisation by two-dimensional immunoelectrophoresis. J. Inst. Brew. 84:43-46.

HEJGAARD, J., and CARLSEN, C. 1977. Immunoelectrophoretic identification of a heteroisomer β-amylase in extracts of barley grain. J. Sci. Food Agric. 28:900-924.

HEJGAARD, J., JACOBSEN, S., and SVENDSEN, I. 1991. Two anti-fungal thaumatin-like proteins from barley grain. FEBS Lett. 291:127-131.

HENRY, R. J. 1989. Factors influencing the rate of modification of barleys during malting. J. Cereal. Sci. 10:51-59.

HERRERA, V. E., and AXCELL, B. C. 1991. Induction of premature yeast flocculation by a polysaccharide fraction isolated from malt husk. J. Inst. Brew. 97:359-366.

HICKMAN, E., and BUCKEE, G. K. 1982. Separation of nitrogenous constituents of malt, wort and beer using high performance liquid chromatography. J. Inst. Brew. 88:382-384.

HILL, R. D., and MacGREGOR, A. W. 1988.

Cereal α-amylases in grain research and technology. Pages 217-261 in: Advances in Cereal Science and Technology, Vol. 9. Y. Pomeranz, ed. Am. Assoc. Cereal Chem., St. Paul, MN.

HODGE, J. E. 1953. Dehydrated food, chemistry of browning reactions in model systems. J. Agric. Food. Chem. 1:928-943.

HØJ, P. B., HARTMAN, D. J., MORRICE, N. A., DOAN, D. N. P., HOY, J. L., MACAULEY, B. J., and FINCHER, G. B. 1981. Cellulases of plant and microbial origin in germinating barley. J. Inst. Brew. 87:77-80.

HØJ, P. B., HOGENRAAD, N. J., HARTMAN, D. J., YANNAKENA, H., and FINCHER, G. B. 1989. Purification of (1→3)-β-glucan endohydrolase isoenzyme II from germinated barley and determination of its primary structure from a cDNA clone. Plant Mol. Biol. 13:31-42.

HUNT, R. W. G. 1987. Measuring Color. Ellis Horwood, Chichester, England.

INSTITUTE OF BREWING. 1991. Recommended Method of Analysis. The Institute, London.

JACOBSEN, J. V. 1973. Interaction between gibberellic acid, ethylene and abscisic acid in control of amylase synthesis in barley aleurone layers. Plant Physiol. 51:198-202.

JACOBSEN, J. V., and CHANDLER, P. M. 1987. Gibberellin and abscisic acid in germinating cereals. Pages 164-193 in: Plant Hormones and Their Role in Plant Growth and Development. P. J. Davies, ed. Martinus Nijhoff, Netherlands.

JACOBSEN, J. V., and HIGGINS, T. J. V. 1982. Characterisation of the α-amylases synthesised by aleurone layers of Himalaya barley in response to gibberellic acid. Plant Physiol. 70:1647-1653.

JACOBSEN, S., MIKKELSEN, J. D., and HEJGAARD, J. 1990. Characterisation of two antifungal endochitinases from barley grain. Physiol. Plant. 79:554-562.

JONES, R. L., and CARBONELL, J. 1984. Regulation of the synthesis of barley aleurone α-amylase by gibberellic acid and calcium ions. Plant Physiol. 76:213-218.

JONES, R. L., and JACOBSEN, J. V. 1983. Calcium regulation of the secretion of α-amylase isoenzymes and other proteins from barley aleurone layers. Planta 158:1-9.

JØRGENSEN, O. B. 1965. Barley malt α-glucosidase. VI. Localization and development during barley germination. Acta Chem. Scand. 19:1014-1015.

KELLY, L., and BRIGGS, D. E. 1992. The influence of the grain microflora on the germination physiology of barley. J. Inst. Brew. 98:395-400.

KITAMURA, Y., NOSHIRO. A., and YAMADA, K. 1990. Activities of dehydrogenases in barley during steeping and germination. Monatsschr. Brauwiss. 43:151-154.

KRINGSTAD, H. 1969. Use of color indicators as tests for the modification of malt. Pages 131-138 in: Proc. Congr. Eur. Brew. Conv. 12th, Interlaken.

KRINGSTAD, H., and KILHOVD, J. 1957. Weitere studien uber die proteolytischen enzyme von gerste und malz. Pages 16-71 in: Proc. Congr. Eur. Brew. Conv. 6th, Copenhagen.

KUSABA, M., KOBAYASHI, O., YAMAGUCHI, I., TAKAHASHI, N., and TAKEDA, C. 1991. Effects of gibberellin on genetic variations in α-amylase production in germinating barley seeds. J. Cereal. Sci. 14:151-160.

LAWRENCE, M. 1988. World barley production and end-uses. Pages 3-9 in: Alternative End Uses of Barley. D. H. B. Sparrow, R. C. M. Lance, and R. J. Henry, eds. Cereal Chemistry Division, Royal Australian Chemical Institute, Parkville, Victoria, Australia.

LEAH, R., MIKKELSEN, J. K., MURPHY, J., and SVENDSEN, I. 1987. Identification of a 28000 dalton endochitinase in barley endosperm. Carlsberg Res. Commun. 52:31-37.

LEE, W. J. 1990. Phytic acid content and phytase activity of barley malt. J. Am. Soc. Brew. Chem. 48:62-65.

LEE, W. J., and PYLER, R. E. 1984. Barley limit dextrinase: Varietal, environmental and malting effects. J. Am. Soc. Brew. Chem. 42:11-17.

LEE, W. J., and PYLER, R. E. 1985. Nucleic acid degrading enzymes of barley malt. I. Nucleases and phosphatases. J. Am. Soc. Brew. Chem. 43:1-6.

LEE, W. J., and PYLER, R. E. 1986. Nucleic aid degrading enzymes in barley malt. III. Adenosine nucleosidase from malted barley. J. Am. Soc. Brew. Chem. 44:86-90.

LI, Y., REHMANJI, M., ABRAMS, S. R., and GUSTA, L. V. 1991. Effect of abscisic acid analogs on extract yield, alpha-amylase and diastatic power during malting of barley. J. Am. Soc. Brew. Chem. 49:135-139.

LITTS, J. E., SIMMONS, C. R., KARRER, E. E., HUANG, N., and RODRIGUEZ, R. L. 1990. The isolation and characterisation of a barley (1→3)-(1→4)-β-glucanase gene. Eur. J. Biochem. 194:831-838.

LONGSTAFF, M. A., and BRYCE, J. H. 1991. Levels of limit dextrinase activity in malting barley. Pages 593-600 in: Proc. Congr. Eur. Brew. Conv. 23rd, Lisbon.

LUNDGARD, R., and SVENSSEN, B. 1987. The four major forms of barley β-amylase. Purification, characterisation and structural relationship. Carlsberg Res. Commun. 52:313-326.

MacDONALD, J., REEVE, P. T. V., RUDDLESDEN, J. D., and WHITE, F. H. 1984. Current approaches to brewery fermentations. Pages 47-198 in: Progress in Industrial Microbiology, Vol. 19. M. E. Bushell, ed. Elsevier, Amsterdam.

McFADDEN, G. I., AHLUWALIA, B., CLARKE, A. E., and FINCHER, G. B. 1988. Expressive sites and developmental regulation of genes encoding (1→3,1→4) β-glucanases in germinated barley. Planta (London) 173:500-508.

MACEY, A. 1977. Malting in the seventies. Brew. Guardian 106(9):81-85.

MacGREGOR, A. W. 1978. α-Amylase I from malted barley—Physical properties and action pattern on amylose. Cereal Chem. 55:754-765.

MacGREGOR, A. W. 1987. α-Amylase, limit dextrinase and α-glucosidase enzymes in barley and malt. CRC Crit. Rev. Biotechnol. 5:117-128.

MacGREGOR, A. W., and LENOIR, C. 1987. Studies on α-glucosidase in barley and malt. J. Inst. Brew. 93:334-337.

MacGREGOR, A. W., and MORGAN, J. E. 1986. Hydrolysis of barley starch granules by alpha-amylases from barley malt. Cereal Foods World 31:688-693.

MacGREGOR, A. W., and YIN, X. S. 1990. β-Glucan solubilase from barley—Further observations. J. Am. Soc. Brew. Chem. 48:82-84.

MacGREGOR, A. W., MARCHYLO, B. A., and KRUGER, J. E. 1988. Multiple α-amylase components in germinated cereal grains determined by isoelectric focusing and chromatofocusing. Cereal Chem. 65:326-333.

MacGREGOR, A. W., BALLANCE, G. M., and DUSHNICKY, L. 1989. Fluorescence microscopy studies on (1→3)-beta-D-glucan in barley endosperm. Food Microstruct. 8:235-244.

MACKAY, D. B. 1972. The measurement of viability. Pages 172-208 in: Viability of Seeds. E. H. Roberts, ed. Chapman and Hall, London.

MacLEOD, A. M., and McCORQUODALE, H. 1958. Comparative studies of embryo and endosperm. J. Inst. Brew. 64:162-170.

MacLEOD, A. M., and PALMER, G. H. 1966. The embryo of barley in relation to modification of the endosperm. J. Inst. Brew. 72:580-589.

MacLEOD, A. M., and PALMER, G. H. 1967. Gibberellin from barley embryos. Nature (London) 216:1342-1343.

MacLEOD, A. M., and PALMER, G. H. 1969. The interaction of indoleacetic acid and gibberellic acid in the synthesis of α-amylase by barley aleurone. New Phytol. 68:295-304.

MacLEOD, A. M., DUFFUS, J. H., and JOHNSTON, C. S. 1964. Development of hydrolytic enzymes in germinating grain. J. Inst. Brew. 70:521-528.

MAJOR, W., and ROBERTS, E. H. 1968. Dormancy in cereal seeds. I. Effects of enzyme and respiratory inhibitors. J. Exp. Bot. 19:90-101.

MARTIN, H. L., and BAMFORTH, C. W. 1980. The relationship between β-glucan solubilase, barley autolysis and malting potential. J. Inst. Brew. 86:216-221.

MARTIN, H. L., and BAMFORTH, C. W. 1981. An enzymic method for the measurement of total and water-soluble β-glucan in barley. J. Inst. Brew. 87:88-91.

MARTIN, H. L., and BAMFORTH, C. W. 1983. Application of a radial diffusion assay for the measurement of β-glucanase in malt. J. Inst. Brew. 89:34-37.

MASAK, J., and BASAROVA, G. 1991. Endosperm cell wall degradation during the malting and brewing of feed barleys. Monatsschr. Brauwiss. 44:262-267.

McCLEARY, B. V. 1988. Solubility properties of barley β-glucan. Pages 117-120 in: Alternative End Uses of Barley. D. H. B. Sparrow, R. C. M. Lance and R. J. Henry, eds. Cereal Chemistry Division, Royal Australian Chemical Institute, Parkville, Victoria, Australia.

McCLEARY, B. V., and CODD, R. 1989. Measurement of β-amylase in cereal flours and commercial enzyme preparations. J. Cereal. Sci. 9:17-33.

McCLEARY, B. V., and GLENNIE-HOLMES, M. 1985. Enzymic quantification of (1→3)(1→4)-β-D-glucan in barley and malt. J. Inst. Brew. 91:285-295.

McCLEARY, B. V., and SHAMEER, I. 1987. Assay of malt β-glucanase using azo-barley glucan: An improved precipitant. J. Inst. Brew. 93:87-90.

McCLEARY, B. V., and SHEEHAN, H. 1987. Measurement of cereal α-amylase: A new assay procedure. J. Cereal Sci. 6:237-251.

MELCHER, U., and VARNER, J. E. 1971. Protein release by barley aleurone layers. J. Inst. Brew. 77:456-461.

MOIR, M. 1989. Effects of raw materials on flavor and aroma. Brew. Guardian 18(Sept.):64-71.

MOLL, B. A., and JONES, R. L. 1982. α-Amylase secretion of barley aleurone. Plant

Physiol. 70:1149-1155.

MOONEN, J. H. E., GRAVELAND, A., and MUTS, G. C. J. 1987. The molecular structure of gel protein from barley, its behaviour in wort-filtration and analysis. J. Inst. Brew. 93:125-130.

MUNCK, L., GIBBONS, G., and AASTRUP, S. 1981. Chemical and structural changes during malting. Pages 11-30 in: Proc. Congr. Eur. Brew. Conv. 18th, Copenhagen.

MUNCK, L., MUNDY, J., and VAAG, P. 1985. Characterization of enzyme inhibitors in barley and their tentative role in malting and brewing. J. Am. Soc. Brew. Chem. 43:35-38.

MUNDY, J. 1984. Hormonal regulation of α-amylase inhibitor synthesis in germinating barley. Carlsberg Res. Commun. 49:439-444.

MUNDY, J., and FINCHER, G. B. 1986. Effects of gibberellic acid and abscisic acid on levels of translatable mRNA for (1→3,1→4)-β-D-glucanase in barley aleurone. FEBS Lett. 198:349-352.

MUNDY, J., and MUNCK, L. 1985. Synthesis and regulation of hydrololytic enzymes in germinating barley. Pages 139-148 in: New Approaches to Research in Cereal Carbohydrates. R. D. Hill and L. Munck, eds. Elsevier, Amsterdam.

MUNDY, J., SVENDSEN, I. B., and HEJGAARD, J. 1983. Barley α-amylase/subtilisin inhibitor. I. Isolation and characterisation. Carlsberg Res. Commun. 48:81-90.

NARZISS, L., and LINTZ, D. 1975. Uber enzymverlauf und eiweissabbau beim maischen. Brauwissenschaft 28:305-315.

NARZISS, L., and SEKIN, Y. 1974. Uber das verhatten der katalase wahrend des malzungs und maisch processes. Brauwissenschaft 27:121-129.

NOLAN, R. C., LIN, L.-S., and HO, T.-H. D. 1987. The effect of abscisic acid on differential expression of α-amylase iso-enzymes in barley aleurone layers. Plant Mol. Biol. 8:13-22.

ORIVE, M., BATALLA, G., CERVERO, J. A., and TORRENT, J. 1991. Non-conventional methods for rapid production and malting/brewing quality evaluation of new barley varieties. Pages 153-160 in: Proc. Congr. Eur. Brew. Conv. 23rd, Lisbon.

PALMER, G. H. 1971. Mode of action of gibberellins during malting. Pages 59-71 in: Proc. Congr. Eur. Brew. Conv. 13th, Estoril.

PALMER, G. H. 1972. Transport of ¹⁴C-gibberellic acid in the barley embryo. J. Inst. Brew. 78:470-471.

PALMER, G. H. 1975. Influence of endosperm structure on extract development. Proc. Am.

Soc. Brew. Chem. 33:174-180.

PALMER, G. H. 1987. Influence of cell wall structure on enzyme breakdown of the endosperm of germinated barley. J. Inst. Brew. 93:105-107.

PALMER, G. H. 1988. Enzyme development in the embryos and aleurone of Galant and Triumph barleys. J. Inst. Brew. 94:61-63.

PALMER, G. H. 1989. Cereals in malting and brewing. Pages 61-242 in: Cereal Science and Technology. G. H. Palmer, ed. Aberdeen University Press, Aberdeen.

PALMER, G. H., and HARVEY, A. E. 1977. The influence of endosperm structure on the behaviour of barleys in the sedimentation test. J. Inst. Brew. 83:295-299.

PALMER, G. H., and TAYLOR, J. A. 1980. Dormancy, drying and pre-germination of malting barley. Brewer 66:105-110.

PALMER, G. H., GERNAH, D. I., McKERNAN, G., NIMMO, D. H., and LAYCOCK, G. 1985. Influence of enzyme distribution on endosperm breakdown (modification) during malting. J. Am. Soc. Brew. Chem. 43:17-28.

PETTERS, H. I., FLANNIGAN, B., and AUSTIN, B. 1988. Quantitative and qualitative studies of the microflora of barley malt production. J. Appl. Bacteriol. 65:279-297.

PHILLIPS, H. A., and WALLACE, W. 1989. A cysteine endopeptidase from barley malt which degrades hordein. Phytochemistry 28:3285-3290.

PIENDL, A. 1973. Malt modification and mashing conditions as influencing factors on the carbohydrates of wort. Brew. Dig. 48:58-72, 84.

PITZ, W. J. 1991. Rapid and objective methods for the estimation of pregermination and viability in barley. J. Am. Soc. Brew. Chem. 49:119-127.

POULLE, M., and JONES, B. L. 1988. A proteinase from germinating barley. I. Purification and some physical properties of a 30kD cysteine endoproteinase from green malt. Plant Physiol. 88:1454-1460.

PREECE, I. A., and MacDOUGALL, M. 1958. Enzymic degradation of cereal hemicelluloses. II. Pattern of pentosan degradation. J. Inst. Brew. 58:353-362.

PROUDLOVE, M. O., and MULLER, R. E. 1989. Immunological detection of gibberellin in barley during malting. Pages 243-250 in: Proc. Congr. Eur. Brew. Conv. 22nd, Zurich.

PROUDLOVE, M. O., DAVIES, N. L., and McGILL, W. 1990. Quality requirements for malting barley and their measurement. Ferment 3:173-176.

PYLER, R. E., and THOMAS, D. A. 1991. Malted cereals: Production and use. Pages

815-832 in: Handbook of Cereal Science and Technology. K. J. Lorenz and K. Kulp, eds. Marcel Dekker Inc., New York.

RADLEY, M. 1967. Site of production of gibberellin-like substances in germinating barley embryos. Planta (Berlin) 75:164-171.

RADLEY, M. 1969. Effect of the endosperm on the formation of gibberellin by barley embryos. Planta (Berlin) 86:218-223.

RANKI, H. 1990. Secretion of α-amylase by the epithelium of barley scutellum. J. Inst. Brew. 96:307-309.

RANKI, H., SOPANEN, T., and VOUTILAINEN, R. 1990. Localisation of carboxypeptidase I in germinating barley grain. Plant Physiol. 93:1449-1452.

RIJS, P., and BANG-OLSEN, K. 1991. Germination profile—A new term in barley analysis. Pages 101-108 in: Proc. Congr. Eur. Brew. Conv. 23rd, Lisbon.

RIJS, P., AASTRUP, S., and HANSEN, J. R. 1989. Controlled rapid and safe removal of dormancy in malting barley. Pages 195-202 in: Proc. Congr. Eur. Brew. Conv. 22nd, Zurich.

ROBERTS, E. H., and SMITH, R. D. 1977. Dormancy and the pentose phosphate pathway. Pages 385-411 in: The Physiology and Biochemistry of Seed Dormancy and Germination. A. A. Khan, ed. Elsevier, Amsterdam.

SAGE, G. C. M. 1992. Current and future breeding of barley for malting and brewing. Brew. Guardian 121(2):24-29.

SCOTT, R. W. 1972. Solubilisation of β-glucans during mashing. J. Inst. Brew. 78:411-412.

SEATON, J. C. 1987. Malt types and beer. Pages 177-188 in: Proc. Congr. Eur. Brew. Conv. 21st, Madrid.

SERRE, L., and LAURIERE, C. 1989. Limit dextrinase in cereal seeds (a review). Sci. Aliments 9:645-663.

SHINKE, R., and MUGIBAYASHI, N. 1971. Studies on barley and malt amylases. XVIII. Determination of total α-amylase activity and gibberellin acid-enhanced activation of zymogen α-amylase during germination of barley. Agric. Biol. Chem. 35:1391-1397.

SKRIVER, K., OLSEN, F. L., LEAH, R., and MUNDY, J. 1991. Gene promoter analysis of malting enzymes. Pages 117-124 in: Proc. Congr. Eur. Brew. Conv. 23rd, Lisbon.

SLACK, P. T., and BAMFORTH, C. W. 1983. The fractionation of polypeptides from barley and beer by hydrophobic interaction chromatography: The influence of their hydrophobicity on foam stability. J. Inst. Brew. 89:397-401.

SLACK, P. T., BAXTER, E. D., and

WAINWRIGHT, T. 1979. Inhibition by hordein of starch degradation. J. Inst. Brew. 85:112-114.

SLADE, A. M., HØJ, P. B., MORRICE, N. A., and FINCHER, G. B. 1989. Purification and characterisation of three (1→4)-β-D-xylan endohydrolases from germinated barley. Eur. J. Biochem. 185:533-539.

SLAKESKI, N., and FINCHER, G. B. 1992. Barley (1→3, 1→4)-β-glucanase isoenzyme EI gene expression is mediated by auxin and gibberellic acid. FEBS Lett. 306:98-102.

SLAKESKI, N., BAULCOMBE, D. C., DEVOS, K. M., AHLUWALIA, B., DOAN, D. N. P., and FINCHER, G. B. 1990. Structure and tissue-specific regulation of genes encoding barley (1→3, 1→4)-β-glucan endohydrolases. Mol. Gen. Genet. 224:437-449.

SMITH, D. B., MORGAN, A. G., and AASTRUP, S. 1980. Variation in the biochemical composition of acid extracts from barleys of contrasting malting quality. J. Inst. Brew. 86:277-283.

SOLE, S. M., STUART, D. T., and SCOTT, J. C. R. 1987. Viability of the aleurone in (proanthocyanadin-free) barley. Pages 243-250 in: Proc. Congr. Eur. Brew. Conv. 21st, Madrid.

SOPANEN, T., and LAURIERE, C. 1989. Release and activity of bound β-amylase in a germinating barley grain. Plant Physiol. 89:244-249.

STICKER, L., and JONES, R. L. 1991. Isolation and partial characterization of a factor from barley aleurone that modifies α-amylase in vitro. Plant Physiol. 97:936-942.

STUART, I. M., LOI, L., and FINCHER, G. B. 1986. Development of (1→3)(1→4)-β-D-glucan endohydrolase isoenzymes in isolated scutella and aleurone layers of barley (*Hordeum vulgare*). Plant Physiol. 80:310-314.

SUN, Z., and HENSON, C. A. 1990. Degradation of native starch granules by barley α-glucosidases. Plant Physiol. 94:320-327.

TAIZ, L., and HONIGMAN, W. A. 1976. Production of cell wall hydrolysing enzymes by barley aleurone layers in response to gibberellic acid. Plant Physiol. 58:380-386.

TAIZ, L., and JONES, R. L. 1970. Gibberellic acid, β-(1→3)-glucanase and the cell walls of barley aleurone layers. Planta (London) 92:73-84.

THOMSON, F. J. 1982. The estimation of total phenols on malt as a guide to the degree of peating of peated distilling malts. Pages 273-278 in: Current Developments in Malting, Brewing and Distilling. F. G. Priest and I. Campbell, eds. Institute of Brewing, London.

TURNER, B. K. 1986. Malty colored. Food (Sept.):63-65.

ULLRICH, S. E., CLANCY, J. A., CUTI, J. G., and TOMPKINS, C. M. 1991. Analysis of β-glucans in barley and malt: A comparison of four methods. J. Am. Soc. Brew. Chem. 49:110-115.

VAN AARLE, P. G. M, De BARSE, M. M. J., VELDINK, G. A, and VLIEGENTHART, J. F. G. 1991. Purification of a lipoxygenase from ungerminated barley. Characterization and product formation. FEBS Lett. 280:159-162.

VAN EERDE, P. 1983. Are you familiar with your malt? A modernised malt quality control method. J. Inst. Brew. 89:195-199.

VAN WAESBERGHE, J. W. M. 1991. Microflora management in industrial malting plants. Outlook and opportunities. Ferment 4:302-308.

VASCONCELOS, L., JESUS, A. C., ANDRADE, A., and MELLO-SAMPAIO, T. 1991. Rapid method of identification and analysis of barley varieties in a malting plant. Pages 161-167 in: Proc. Cong. Eur. Brew. Conv. 23rd, Lisbon.

VIETOR, R. J., ANGELINO, S. A. G. F., and VORAGEN, A. G. J. 1991. Arabinoxylans in barley, malt and wort. Pages 139-146 in: Proc. Cong. Eur. Brew. Conv. 23rd, Lisbon.

WAINWRIGHT, T. 1986. Nitrosamines in malt and beer. J. Inst. Brew. 92:73-80.

WAINWRIGHT, T., O'FARRELL, D. D., HORGAN, R., and TEMPORE, M. 1986. Ammonium persulphate in malting: Control of NDMA and increased yield of malt extract. J. Inst. Brew. 92:232-238.

WALKER, M. D., and WESTWOOD, K. T. 1991. Postfermentation adjustment of beer quality using extracts from speciality malts. J. Am. Soc. Brew. Chem. 50:4-8.

WEBSTER, R. D. J., and PORTNO, A. D. 1981. Analytical prediction of lautering performance. Pages 153-160 in: Proc. Congr. Eur. Brew. Conv. 18th, Copenhagen.

WESELAKE, R. J., MacGREGOR, A. W., and HILL, R. D. 1983. An endogenous α-amylase inhibitor in barley kernels. Plant Physiol. 72:809-812.

WHITBY, B. R. 1992. Traditional distillation in the whisky industry. Ferment 5:261-267.

WOOD, P. J., FULCHER, R. G., and STONE, B. A. 1983. Studies on the specificity of interaction of cereal cell wall components with Congo red and Calcofluor. Specific detection and histochemistry of (1→3)(1→4)-β-D-glucan. J. Cereal Sci. 1:95-110.

WOODWARD, J. R., and FINCHER, G. B. 1982a. Purification and chemical properties of two (1→3)(1→4)-β-glucan endohydrolases from germinating barley. Eur. J. Biochem. 121:663-669.

WOODWARD, J. R., and FINCHER, G. B. 1982b. Substrate specificities and kinetic properties of two (1→3)(1→4)-β-D-glucan hydrolases from germinating barley (Hordeum vulgare). Carbohydr. Res. 106:111-122.

WOODWARD, J. R., MORGAN, F. J., and FINCHER, G. B. 1982. Amino acid sequence homology in two (1→3)(1→4)-β-glucan endohydrolases from germinating barley (Hordeum vulgare). FEBS Lett. 138:198-200.

WOODWARD, J. R., FINCHER, G. B., and STONE, B. A. 1983. Water soluble (1→3),(1→4)-β-D-glucan from barley (Hordeum vulgare) endosperm. II. Fine structure. Carbohydr. Polym. 3:207-225.

WROBEL, R., and JONES, B. L. 1992. Electrophoretic study of substrate and pH dependence of endoproteolytic enzymes in green malt. J. Inst. Brew. 98:471-478.

YAMASHITA, H., VEHARA, H., TSUMURA, Y., HAYAYSE, F., and KATO, H. 1987. Precipitate-forming reactions of β-(1→4)-D-glucanase (I) in malt. Agric. Biol. Chem. 51:655-664.

YIN, X. S., and MacGREGOR, A. W. 1988. An approach to the identification of a β-glucan solubilase from barley. J. Inst. Brew. 94:327-330.

YIN, X. S., and MacGREGOR, A. W. 1989. Substrate specificity and nature of action of barley β-glucan solubilase. J. Inst. Brew. 95:105-109.

YIN, X. S., MacGREGOR, A. W., and CLEAR, R. M. 1989. Field fungi and β-glucan solubilase. J. Inst. Brew. 95:195-198.

YOSHIDA, T., YAMADA, K., FUJINO, S., and KOUMEGAWA, J. 1979. Effect of pressure on physiological aspects of germinating barleys and quality of malts. J. Am. Soc. Brew. Chem. 37:77-84.

CHAPTER 8

NONMALTING USES OF BARLEY

R. S. BHATTY
Crop Development Centre
Department of Crop Science and Plant Ecology
University of Saskatchewan
Saskatoon, Saskatchewan
Canada

INTRODUCTION

Nonmalting uses of barley include its utilization in feed, food, and industrial applications other than malting. This terminology is relatively new and reflects a rapidly developing interest in improvements of barley for feed and food utilization. Barley contains as much as, if not more, total dietary fiber (TDF) and soluble dietary fiber (SF) as oats, due to its higher β-glucan content (Ranhotra et al, 1991). The hypocholesterolemic effect of oat SF, although recently challenged (Swain et al, 1990), has been generally accepted (Hurt et al, 1988; Anderson et al, 1990b; Kestin et al, 1990; Bridges et al, 1992). Barley SF has been reported to exhibit similar properties in animal and human studies (Fadel et al, 1987; Klopfenstein and Hoseney, 1987; Newman et al, 1989; McIntosh et al, 1991; Ranhotra et al, 1991). In addition, barley, like oats, contains inhibitors of cholesterol biosynthesis (Qureshi et al, 1985, 1991). The potential utilization of barley in foods will undoubtedly be influenced by these findings.

At present, very little barley is used in human foods in the developed countries (Table 1); the high users are Korea and the West Asia-North Africa region, particularly Morocco, where per capita consumption of barley is 68 kg per year. The demand for barley for use in food in the West Asia-North Africa region has been projected to increase from 3 to 5 million tonnes by the year 2000 (Somel, 1988). However, per capita consumption of barley in Korea has decreased from 29 kg per year in 1977 to about 8 kg per year in 1987 and was expected to drop further to about 2 kg per year in 1991 (Tremere and Bhatty, 1989). In view of these statistics, barley remains predominantly a feed grain.

Barley used for feed is not necessarily unfit for human consumption or for industrial utilization. Physical features of the grain (such as bright and white kernel, higher bushel weight, uniform and plump kernel) required in select grades of malting barleys are equally preferred in food and feed barleys, albeit for appearance and marketability. Hull-less barley, which has been eaten for centuries by many Eastern cultures, is an excellent feed for swine and some classes of poultry. Therefore it is not always possible to distinguish feed, food, or malting barleys; the only such distinction is ipso facto, i.e., after the grain has been consumed.

FOOD USES OF BARLEY

Historical

Several recent studies (Newman and McGuire, 1985; Foster and Prentice, 1987; Newman et al, 1988; Oakenfull and Hood, 1988; Bhatty, 1992a) have referred to the use of barley as a staple food in the Near East several thousand years ago. Much of this information was taken from historical and archaeological evidence presented by Harlan (1979), Wendorf et al (1979), and Wiebe (1979). The latter traced the introduction of barley into the New World by European settlers from the time of Columbus. Clark (1967) reported that a two-rowed barley, derived from the wild form, was cultivated 9000 years ago in Northern Mesopotamia. About 2500 B.C., six-rowed barley was introduced from this region to the Indus Valley Civilization, and from there it spread to different parts of the Indian Subcontinent (Kajale, 1974). Ancient

TABLE 1
Utilization of Barley in Animal Feeds and Human Foods in Various Countries

Country	Feed[a] (% of total utilization)	Country	Food[b] (kg/person/year, 1986–1988)
Canada	89	Morocco	68.3
Turkey	88	Ethiopia	19.0
Denmark	87	Algeria	18.1
Spain	87	Afghanistan	15.4
Finland	86	Iraq	11.5
Italy	86	Tunisia	10.6
France	85	Libya	8.9
Sweden	85	Korea Republic	7.5
Norway	81	Iran	7.1
Austria	79	Poland	6.1
Switzerland	79	Peru	4.8
Ireland	78	Japan	1.1
United States	72	Netherlands	0.9
Germany, FDR	71	New Zealand	0.9
United Kingdom	70	Germany, FDR	0.7
Yugoslavia	67	United States	0.7
Netherlands	64	Canada	0.5
Belgium-Luxembourg	62	France	0.4
Australia	60	Australia	0.3
Japan	59	Denmark	0.3
New Zealand	47	Italy	0.3
Portugal	47	United Kingdom	0.3

[a] Organization for Economic Cooperation and Development (1988).
[b] Food and Agriculture Organization of the United Nations (1990), *personal communication.*

Indian literature, published about 1500 B.C., described the organoleptic properties of barley as astringent, cold, rough, light, and sweet; its physiological
functions included increasing fecal bulk, regulation of body heat, and the
production of body fluids (Grivetti, 1991). In *Food: The Gift of Osiris*, Darby
et al (1977) reported that barley preceded wheat as a food grain in ancient
Egypt and Nubia; other evidence presented included the use of barley brewing
as a medium of exchange, in therapeutics, and for feeds to animals; barley
was assigned a value three-fifths that of wheat. Barley was the chief form
of nourishment of Greeks in Homeric times (800 B.C.), when it was eaten
as *alphita*. This was roasted, ground barley mixed with water and eaten with
the addition of oil and other condiments (Beaven, 1947). Later, barley became
the general food of the Roman gladiators, who were known as *hordearii* (Kent,
1983). *Rieska*, an unleavened barley bread, was the earliest of all breads in
Finland. In medieval England, bread made from barley formed the staple
diet of the peasant and poor people, whereas the nobles ate wheaten bread
(Kent, 1983). As late as the beginning of the 20th century, barley was the
main food in rural Denmark (Munck, 1981). Only since the beginning of
this century has barley been systematically replaced by wheat and rice in
human foods, in the former case because of the superior quality of its gluten
for making baked products and in the latter because of its organoleptic
properties.

Barley is still used in many countries in traditional dishes such as *kasha*
in Russia and Poland, *tsampa* and others in Tibet, *miso* in Japan, and *sattu*
or popped barley (Chatterjee and Abrol, 1977) in India. In Korea, barley
is the second most important food crop (after rice) and is used (Ryu, 1979)
in several ways: 1) pearled barley as a rice extender, 2) pearled barley inoculated
with *Aspergillus* sp. for the production of soy paste and soy sauce, 3) roasted
barley used as tea or coffee substitute, and 4) barley-wheat composite flour
used for making cookies, cakes, and noodles. In the West Asia-North Africa
region, much of the barley is consumed as pearled grain in soups, flour in
flat bread, and ground grain in cooked porridge. In the Western countries,
small quantities of barley (pot or pearled) are used in breakfast cereals, soups,
stews, porridge, bakery blends, and for baby foods. Barley products such
as pot and pearled barley, grits, flakes, and barley and malt flours are
commercially available. Many national and international recipes based on
barley products, particularly flour, have been developed.

BARLEY FOOD PRODUCTS

Pearled Barley

Pearling is part of the milling process that produces blocked (dehulled)
barley, pot and pearled barley, barley flakes, and finally barley flour by roller-
milling of blocked or pearled barley. Pot and pearled barley are prepared
by gradual removal of hull, bran, and germ by abrasive action in a stone
mill. Production of pot barley is the first stage of pearling, which may remove
7–14% of the weight of the grain. Further abrasion results in the removal
of seed coat (testa and pericarp), aleurone, subaleurone layers, and the germ,
leaving behind a central endosperm rich in carbohydrates (largely starch and

β-glucans) and proteins (hordeins and glutelins). The final product of fine pearl may not constitute more than 60–70% of the grain, the average being 67% (Kent, 1983). Han (1979) reported pearling yields of 59–63% for hulled barley and 67–71% for hull-less barley in Korea. During the pearling process, the hull and seed coat largely appeared in the 0–11% fraction and the germ and aleurone in the 11–25% fraction; the endosperm formed the majority of the greater than 25% fraction (Pedersen et al, 1989a). Pearling rates of 30–40% were most desirable, as at these levels insoluble dietary fiber and acid detergent fiber were minimal, whereas SF and β-glucans were maximum (Fig. 1).

Barley preferred for pearling should be uniform, free from discolored grain, plump (kernel weight about 45 mg), white, medium hard, and thin-hulled (Pomeranz, 1974; Kent, 1983; Foster and Prentice, 1987). Two-rowed barleys are more likely to meet these requirements. In Germany, pearled barley may be made from imported blue aleurone barley, in which case bleaching of the grain with 0.04% sulfur dioxide is required (Kent, 1983). Koreans prefer a shallow crease and a clear white color for pearled barley. As barley is boiled with rice, its gelatinization temperature should be similar; the barley should preferably be waxy to give a sticky pap (Bae, 1979).

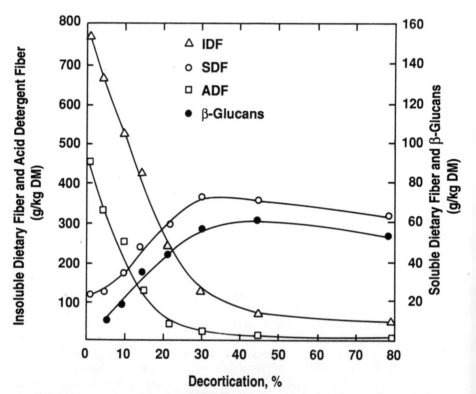

Fig. 1. Relationships between milling rate (decortication) and insoluble dietary fiber (IDF), soluble dietary fiber (SDF), acid detergent fiber (ADF), and β-glucan fractions of barley. (Reprinted from Pedersen et al, 1989a, with permission of S. Karger, AG, Basel)

The sequence of the pearling process (Kent, 1983) may be as follows: 1) preliminary cleaning, 2) conditioning or tempering to about 15% moisture, 3) bleaching (blue aleurone barley), 4) blocking or shelling, 5) aspiration, 6) size grading by sifting, 7) groat cutting, 8) pearling of blocked barley or large barley groats, 9) grading and sifting, and 10) polishing. Barley flakes are made by: 1) predamping of the barley groat, 2) steam cooking of groats or pearled barley, 3) flaking, and 4) drying of flakes in hot air. Barley flour is made by roller-milling of pearled or blocked barley. There may be many variations to the above sequence. Figure 2 shows a flow sheet for processing of barley into various foods, as used by one manufacturer in the United States. Another process used by a different company has been described by Weaver et al (1981).

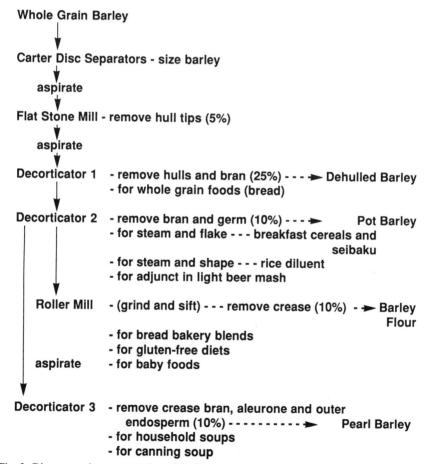

Fig. 2. Diagrammatic representation of barley processing into various food products. Courtesy of F. W. Sosulski, University of Saskatchewan, Saskatoon, SK, Canada.

Barley Milling

Traditionally, unpearled barley has not been roller-milled, as have wheat and oats, to produce flour and bran. Most barley flour has been obtained by milling pot or pearled barley, and, in some cases, brewers' spent grain (BSG) has been milled to produce barley bran. In the pearling process, bran is lost as part of the outer coverings, which are mixed with hull (dust or polishings) and used as animal feed (Weaver et al, 1981). Rarely have true barley bran and flour been produced and investigated. Barley reacts differently than wheat to conventional roller-milling. The bran is brittle and shatters regardless of tempering conditions, unlike wheat bran, which separates as large, stable flakes. Furthermore, barley flour may flow less easily. Nevertheless, barley can be milled, dry or tempered, with the equipment routinely used in wheat milling, as has been reported in a number of studies from different countries (Pomeranz et al, 1971; Cheigh et al, 1975; McGuire, 1979; Bhatty, 1986b, 1987b, 1992b, 1993b). Korean workers (Cheigh et al, 1975) milled hulled and hull-less barley tempered to 14 and 15% moisture, respectively, in a Buhler mill. The flour yields varied from 61.2 to 74.3% and were 10% greater for hull-less barley. McGuire (1979) reported milling yields of 16 diverse genotypes of barley, tempered to 13% moisture, in a similar mill. The average flour yield was 68% (range 51–72%). A range in flour yield for the same samples was also obtained on milling in an Allis-Chalmers mill. One sample of barley milled in a Miag-Multomat mill yielded 63% flour, 23% shorts, and 13% bran. Pomeranz et al (1971) milled five malting cultivars of barley in a similar mill, after tempering for 30 min with 0.5% water, and reported an average extraction of 65%.

In two separate studies, Bhatty (1986b, 1987b) reported milling of hulled and hull-less barley under different tempering conditions in an Allis-Chalmers experimental mill using a modified short-flow procedure. The flour yield was, on the average, 72%; the bran plus shorts, which were not separated, yielded 28% (Bhatty, 1986b). Neither tempering time (8–22 hr), tempering stage, nor growth location (four sites) had a major influence on flour yield (Bhatty, 1987b). Subsequently, 15 diverse genotypes and cultivars of hulled and hull-less barley were dry-milled (grain moisture 9–10%) using a similar procedure (Bhatty, 1992b). The average flour and bran yields were 69.7 and 30.3%, respectively, of the recovered product. The coefficient of variation for flour yield was 1.4% and for bran 3.3%, indicating that barley can be dry-milled to consistent flour and bran yields. In the Allis-Chalmers experimental mill, the bran and shorts do not separate. However, barley bran and shorts may be separated in other mills. Scout hull-less barley dry-milled on a larger scale in a Buhler mill gave the following yields, expressed as percent of the total recovered product: flour, 74%; shorts, 15%; bran, 11% (Bhatty, 1993). The potential use of barley as a source of SF may encourage direct roller-milling of barley under optimized conditions. The flour may be incorporated directly into various food products, processed into starch, or converted to sweeteners. Technology for such processing and conversion has been described (Bos, 1980; Linko, 1988). Hull-less, waxy barley is more suitable for such processing.

Pedersen and Eggum (1983) and Hegedus et al (1985) reported the composition and quality of barley extracted at different rates. At extraction rates of 69–75%, there were major losses of B vitamins, trace elements, phytate phosphorus, and tannins. However, energy and protein digestibilities of the fractions improved (Table 2). Weaver et al (1981) reported losses, on milling of barley, of 8% in protein, 14% in copper, and 30–36% in manganese, zinc, iron, and nickel. Vose and Youngs (1978) pin-milled and air-classified dehulled barley and malted barley to obtain barley or malt starch flour fractions in about 65% yield; the starch flour fraction contained 9–10% protein, 64–72% starch, and 1–3% fiber. Danish workers at the Carlsberg Research Centre have developed a disc mill (UMS MHA-600) for dry-milling of barley. The milling process may also be used for manufacture of barley starch (Munck et al, 1988).

Barley Flour

Table 3 shows physicochemical properties of barley flour and, for comparison, hard red spring wheat flour milled in an Allis-Chalmers experimental mill under identical conditions. Barley flour was as white as wheat flour, and it had generally similar protein but higher ash contents,

TABLE 2
Composition and Nutritive Quality of Barley Milled at Different Extraction Rates[a]

Component, dry basis	Extraction Rate, %	
	100	69–75
Ash, %	2.0	0.8–1.0
Protein (N × 6.25), %	10.8	8.9–9.3
Ether extract, %	3.3	1.7–1.9
Starch + sugar, %	67.2	81.9–84.0
Crude fiber, %	5.0	0.9–0.9
Tannin, %	0.7	0.4–0.4
Calcium + phosphorus, mg/g	4.1	1.8–2.2
Phytate-phosphorus, mg/g	2.3	<0.1–0.1
Zinc + copper + iron, ppm	90.8	23.4–29.4
True protein digestibility, %	87.4	93.0–94.1
Energy digestibility, %	80.5	94.2–94.5
B-vitamins, μg/g	57.5[b]	16.7–24.3[b]

[a] Source: Pedersen and Eggum (1983); used by permission.
[b] Data from Hegedüs et al (1985).

TABLE 3
Physiochemical Properties of Wheat and Tupper Hull-less (Six-Rowed) Barley Flour Dry Milled in an Allis-Chalmers Experimental Mill[a]

Property	Barley Flour	Wheat Flour[b]
Moisture, %	9.9	12.9
Ash, %	1.1	0.6
Protein, % (N × 5.75)	14.9	14.8
Oil absorption, %	128.3	134.2
Water absorption, mg/g	1.7	0.8
Whiteness (L)	+90.3	+88.4

[a] Source: Bhatty (1987b); used by permission.
[b] Hard red spring wheat tempered to 14% moisture and milled under conditions identical to those used for barley flour.

lower oil absorption, and twice the water absorption of wheat flour. Although water absorption is influenced by protein content and damaged starch, in the case of barley flour it was largely due to β-glucan. The high water absorption of barley flour reflected its higher viscoamylogram viscosity (swelling power), as well as higher set-back viscosity after cooling to $50°C$, due to formation of a viscous gel (Fig. 3). Comparative physicochemical properties of barley and wheat flours are described in greater detail elsewhere (Bhatty, 1993b).

Barley flour may be used as a food thickener or wheat flour additive, for making flat or dense breads, and in many other nonbread bakery products, but it is less suited for making yeast-leavened bread due to its weak and nonelastic gluten, readily observed from its mixogram behavior (Fig. 4). However, 5–10% barley flour may be added to wheat flour without affecting loaf volume and bread appearance (Bhatty, 1986b). Further additions depress loaf volume, essentially by diluting wheat gluten; the functionality of barley starch is similar to that of wheat starch (Hoseney et al, 1978). Addition of salt at a level of 2% to a dough made from a 60:40 blend of wheat and barley flours improved loaf volume by 20%; salt decreased farinograph water absorption of the dough mixture (Linko et al, 1984). Swanson and Penfield (1988) reported the use of 20% laboratory-milled, whole-grain hull-less barley flour in wheat flour, with the addition of 2% salt to the baking formula. A similar level of barley flour of 60% extraction was added to wheat flour or whole wheat meal to make satisfactory Norwegian wheat bread (Magnus et al, 1987). Longer prefermentation and addition of shortening proved beneficial for the use of barley flour.

Newman et al (1990a) reported the suitability of barley flour of 51–66% extraction for making muffins. Barley flour muffins had only slightly lower volume, density, and moisture but similar height and tenderness as wheat flour muffins and were preferred by a taste panel. Berglund et al (1992) substituted waxy hull-less barley for wheat flour in many food products in amounts

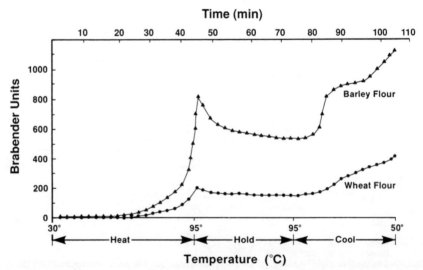

Fig. 3. Viscoamylogram of wheat flour and dry-milled barley flour. (Data from Bhatty, 1987b)

ranging from 25 to 100%. Barley substitutions increase TDF and SF and produce high-fiber food products.

Barley Bran

Barley bran (excluding the hull) consists of testa and pericarp, germ, the tricellular aleurone, and the subaleurone layers. Pedersen and Eggum (1983) reported that barley grain contains 8% testa and pericarp, 3% germ, and 8% aleurone. The levels of these fractions may vary considerably, however, depending on method of preparation and degree of purity. Simmonds (1978) reported 3% embryo + scutellum and 18% pericarp in barley; the aleurone was included with the endosperm. Although barley bran needs to be defined, 25–30% of the outer grain coverings may approximate bran and allow flour yields of 70–75%. The composition and functional properties of unpearled, roller-milled barley bran have been described in detail for the first time (Bhatty, 1993b). Use of roller-milled barley bran in various food products needs development research. The composition of BSG used in many baked products has been extensively reported (Prentice and D'Appolonia, 1977; Tsen et al, 1983; Weber and Chaudhary, 1987).

Several studies have reported use of BSG bran or flour in various bakery products. Chaudhary and Weber (1990) compared barley bran flour with other brans as dietary ingredients in white bread. Barley bran flour added at a level of 15% caused the smallest decrease in loaf volume, produced a loaf with substantially increased dietary fiber and reduced calories, and gave the highest score of the different fiber-enriched breads. Prentice and D'Appolonia (1977) found 5–10% inclusion of malt-corn grits BSG satisfactory for making

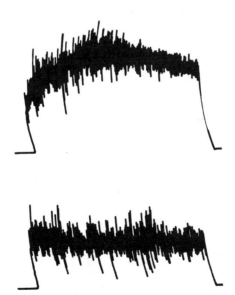

Fig. 4. Mixograms of wheat flour and dry-milled barley flour. Upper, wheat flour; lower, barley flour. (Adapted from Bhatty, 1986b)

high-fiber bread. High-fiber sugar cookies containing as much as 15% BSG were reported by Prentice et al (1978). Dreese and Hoseney (1982) reported decreased loaf volume and deleterious effect on crumb grain on addition of 15% BSG bread to wheat flour. These conditions were improved by adding shortening or dough improvers. In another study, Tsen et al (1983) reported that BSG flour, added at 10%, improved loaf volume, crumb grain, and color of bread. The inconsistency of these results is due to the heterogenous nature of the BSG. Several BSG products containing high TDF and low SF are commercially available. The barley bran flour used as a source of dietary fiber by Chaudhary and Weber (1990) contained 67% TDF and 3% SF. Nyman et al (1985) investigated the fermentation of dietary fiber extracted from different cereals at two different rates (65 and 100%). Barley fiber, like rice and sorghum fibers, consisting mainly of nonlignified glucans, was fermented more extensively when the proportion of SF was high. Thus BSG bran or bran flour would probably act as a fecal bulking agent.

Hull-less barley bran in about 30% yield has been obtained from several cultivars of barley milled in an Allis-Chalmers experimental mill. The composition of hull-less barley bran and, for comparison, commercial oat bran is given in Table 4. Barley bran had lower protein and ether extract but generally similar total carbohydrates and β-glucan as commercial oat bran. Barley bran had higher TDF and SF, although the ratio of SF to TDF was similar in both the brans. The sum of essential amino acids of barley bran or oat flour (Table 5) was not significantly different from that of oat bran or flour. There were small differences in individual essential amino acids of barley and oat bran and flour. As expected, the major differences in amino acid composition of barley and oat bran and flour were in glutamic acid and proline.

MALTED AND GERMINATED BARLEY FOOD PRODUCTS

Small quantities of (hulled) barley malt, malt extract, and malt syrups are routinely added to many foods, the largest use being in fermented bakery

TABLE 4
Comparative Composition (%) of Barley (Scout, Two-Rowed)
and Oat Bran Fractions[a]

Component	Barley Bran[b]	Oat Bran[c]
Moisture	8.5	10.3
Protein (N × 5.7)	16.5	17.6
Ether extract	4.1	8.4
Ash	2.6	2.5
Carbohydrates	49.9	48.7
β-Glucan	6.5	6.9
Total dietary fiber (TDF)	18.4	12.5
Soluble fiber (SF)	6.4	4.2
SF/TDF × 100	35	34

[a] Source: Ranhotra et al (1991); used by permission.
[b] Milled in an Allis-Chalmers experimental mill to yield 70% flour and 30% bran.
[c] Commercial sample obtained locally from Robin Hood Multifoods, Inc.

products. Malt extracts enhance soluble sugars, protein, and α-amylase in the dough; promote yeast activity, bread texture, and loaf volume; and impart flavor, color, and aroma to the finished product. Nonfermented applications include use in soda crackers, cookies, rolls, muffins, and dark variety breads.

Malt extracts are prepared by vacuum concentration of the wort to obtain extracts and syrups of different colors, solids content, and enzyme activity. The process of water extraction promotes the final conversion of starch to maltose and dextrins and of protein to low-molecular-weight peptides and amino acids. Depending on the drying temperature, malt extracts or syrups with diastatic activities varying from 0 to 200 L may be produced (Hickenbottom, 1983).

The hull content of barley is a limiting factor for use of barley malt in food applications. For this reason, hull-less barley is ideally suited for making specialized food-grade malt. Such a malt would be easily distinguished from brewers' malt, which must be made from select grades of hulled barley. Although the quality and desirable properties of food-grade malt are not known, such a malt may be free of hulls and have white color, enhanced protein (unlike brewers' malt), and improved functional properties. Conditions for malting hull-less barley and their effects on the quality of such a malt need to be established.

Germinated barley has been added to some food preparations. Alexander et al (1984) reported the nutritional value of barley germinated in light and dark. Protein quality evaluation showed improvements in protein efficiency ratio, net protein ratio, and net protein utilization. Germination of barley

TABLE 5
Amino Acid Composition (g/16 g of N) of Barley and Oat Bran and Flour Fractions

Amino Acid	Barley[a]		Oat[b]	
	Bran	Flour	Bran	Flour
Alanine	4.1	3.9	4.7	5.0
Arginine	5.7	4.6	7.2	7.3
Aspartic acid	6.4	5.7	9.7	10.7
Cystine	2.3	2.1	2.9	3.1
Glutamic acid	26.6	28.5	22.5	23.2
Glycine	3.9	3.4	4.9	5.0
Histidine	2.2	2.2	2.4	2.7
Isoleucine[c]	3.4	3.5	3.6	3.7
Leucine[c]	6.6	6.6	7.7	7.8
Lysine[c]	3.3	3.4	3.9	4.4
Methionine[c]	1.7	1.6	1.5	1.6
Phenylalanine[c]	5.4	5.5	5.2	5.6
Proline	11.9	12.8	5.3	5.4
Serine	4.4	4.4	5.0	5.2
Threonine[c]	3.2	3.0	2.4	2.1
Tryptophan[c]	1.3	1.4	1.9	1.8
Tyrosine	3.3	2.9	3.4	3.6
Valine[c]	4.7	5.4	5.6	5.9
Sum of EAA[c]	29.6	30.4	31.8	32.9

[a] Tupper (six-rowed) hull-less barley grown locally and milled in an Allis-Chalmers experimental mill to yield 70% flour and 30% bran.
[b] Oat bran and flour obtained locally from Robin Hood Multifoods, Inc.
[c] Essential amino acid (EAA).

in the dark was preferable; incorporation of meal from such barley into muffins produced an attractive and palatable product. A novel use of barley in weanling foods for the developing countries was proposed by Hansen et al (1989) and Pedersen et al (1989b). High-lysine barley (Ca 700202) was milled into whole meal and semirefined and refined fractions, decorticated, and ground into flour with a hammer mill. Gruels were prepared from germinated and nongerminated grain. Germination improved energy density of the gruels by two to three times, bringing it to the desired level of about 1.0 kcal/kg. Protein utilization and energy digestibility data obtained by rat feeding suggested that the high-lysine barley provided a safe level of protein intake for infants and small children.

INDUSTRIAL (NONMALTING) UTILIZATION OF BARLEY

Barley starch and, to a lesser extent, $(1\rightarrow3),(1\rightarrow4)$-$\beta$-D-glucan ($\beta$-glucan) have commercial potential. Barley cultivars containing waxy or glutenous ($<1\%$ amylose) and high-amylose starches are available (see below). Native starch and starch derivatives are extensively used in the food industry; waxy starches have specialized uses due to their high swelling power and colloidal stability (Greenwood, 1988). On the other hand, high-amylose starches have unique gelling and film-forming properties. Munck et al (1988) have listed many nonfood applications of cereal starches, particularly in the paper industry. Use of barley starch in food and nonfood applications needs to be evaluated in light of the abundant availability of low and normal waxy corn starches and normal wheat starch as by-products of the gluten industry.

Barley has been used in some countries for the production of ethanol, glucose, maltose syrups, and β-amylase. The syrup production process involves starch extraction from the grain, usually by wet-milling, followed by its conversion to sugars in a batch or continuous process. High-maltose syrup has special properties for use in food and pharmaceutical industries. It is prepared from enzyme- or acid-liquefied starch by saccharification with β-amylase; in the case of very high maltose content, pullulanase is added to avoid excessive production of maltotriose (Linko et al, 1983b). Goering et al (1980) developed a process for the production of high-maltose syrup from roller-milled waxy barley (Washonupana) flour. Barley starch readily converted to simple sugars. The syrup contained 3–7% glucose, 58–66% maltose, 16–20% maltotriose, and 10–18% higher oligosaccharides.

The most integrated process for industrial utilization of barley has been developed in Finland by Linko and co-workers (Linko et al, 1983a,b; Linko, 1988). Commercial barley starch, liquefied in a twin-screw high-temperature, short-time extrusion cooker employing thermostable α-amylase, compared favorably with that prepared using the conventional batch liquefaction process (Linko et al, 1983a). Linko et al (1983b) described a novel process for the production of high-maltose syrup from barley starch without the use of α-amylase. Another process described in Fig. 5 (Linko, 1988) uses wet-milling technology for the production of β-amylase and barley starch, which is subsequently processed to various sweeteners and maltodextrins.

β-Glucans may be extracted and purified from barley or its β-glucan-enriched (1.4-fold) bran fraction (Bhatty, 1993a). Isolated β-glucan has potential as a thickening agent in foods, as an industrial hydrocolloid, and in pharmaceuticals. Such applications need investigations of the rheological and functional properties of the isolated β-glucan. Hydrolyzed β-glucan has been suggested as a bulking agent for replacement of sucrose (Cowan and Mollgaard, 1988).

Many solvents have been used to extract β-glucan from barley for its subsequent quantitative determination, but none has been used in commercial production. McCleary (1988) has discussed the solubility properties of barley β-glucans, which may be extracted almost entirely with water at 40, 65, and 95° C. The major proportion (40–60%) of β-glucan was soluble in water at 65° C in a number of barleys; this fraction was of greater molecular size than that extracted at 40° C, based on extract viscosity values. Carr et al (1990) found $1N$ NaOH the best solvent for β-glucan from different cereal-based foods. Other solvents such as urea, perchloric acid, and water were less satisfactory.

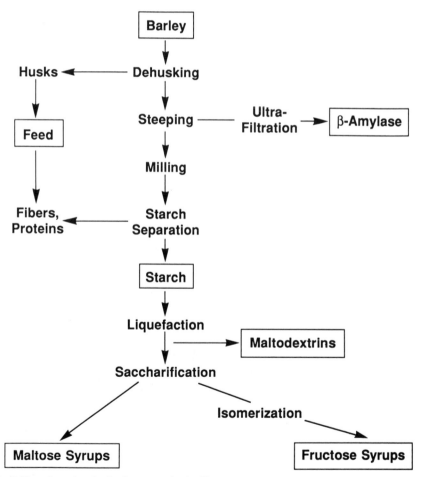

Fig. 5. Flow sheet showing barley processing by Finnsugar in Finland. (Reprinted, with permission, from Linko, 1988)

β-Glucan has been commercially extracted from oat fractions using 20% Na_2CO_3 (Wood et al, 1989). The same procedure used for β-glucan extraction from barley and barley bran gave a lower enrichment index, which took into account the yield and purity of the β-glucan preparations, than was obtained with $1N$ NaOH (Bhatty, 1993a). Furthermore, sodium hydroxide extracts more pentosans than other solvents. These nonstarch polysaccharides (NSP) enhance the viscometric properties of β-glucan, a desirable feature in food applications. Freeze-dried barley β-glucan was a light, white, fluffy material. Its chemical composition and, for comparison, that of β-glucan extracted with 20% Na_2CO_3 from commercial oat bran under identical conditions are given in Table 6. Barley β-glucan was less pure, largely because of its higher arabinoxylan and ash contents, as both the fractions contained low levels of nitrogen and starch. Lipids were not detected in the preparations. The purity of β-glucan could be improved further by removing ash, either by washing with water or by dialysis. However, sodium hydroxide is the preferable solvent for enrichment of β-glucan from barley or oat bran.

Cowan and Mollgaard (1988) reported a pilot-plant-scale procedure for the preparation of hydrolyzed β-glucan from barley. In this procedure, starch was first removed from wet- or dry-milled barley by treatment with Termamyl α-amylase and amyloglucosidase. Hydrolysis of β-glucan was achieved by Finizyme β-glucanase; it yielded, on concentration and spray-drying, a white, free-flowing powder that compared favorably with sucrose in its properties when added to various food products.

HYPOCHOLESTEROLEMIC EFFECTS

Soluble Fiber

The hypocholesterolemic effects of barley are partly due to its SF fraction. The SF may be chemically defined as NSP and lignin. The NSP include cell wall components such as β-glucan, arabinoxylans or pentosans, cellulose, fructans, and glucomannans. Physiologically, SF may be defined as NSP and lignin resistant to digestion by mammalian enzymes in the digestive tract. Gordon (1989) included in TDF ingested polymers in foods not broken down by digestive enzymes in the small intestine. The significance of a small amount

TABLE 6
Composition (%) of β-Glucan Isolated from Tupper Hull-less Barley Bran
(Six-Rowed) and Commercial Oat Bran[a]

Component	Barley Bran[b]	Oat Bran[c]
β-Glucan	57.9	79.7
Nitrogen	0.5	0.5
Starch	1.1	1.2
Ether extract	0.0	0.0
Pentosans[d]	7.8	1.1
Ash	9.5	3.7
Total monosaccharides	59.3	63.9

[a] Source: Bhatty (1993a); used by permission.
[b] Bran obtained in 30% yield on dry milling of barley in an Allis-Chalmers experimental mill.
[c] Oat bran obtained locally from Robin Hood Multifoods, Inc.
[d] Sum of xylose plus arabinose $\times$ 0.88.

of resistant starch in the NSP is not clear and has been the subject of controversy (Englyst and Cummings, 1987). The SF tends to increase intestinal transit time, particularly in the small intestine, delays gastric emptying, and slows glucose absorption. These actions lower postprandial blood glucose concentrations and decrease serum cholesterol (Anderson et al, 1990a). Procedures for the measurement of SF, insoluble fiber, and TDF have been described (Englyst et al, 1982; Cummings and Englyst, 1987; Prosky et al, 1988; Schweizer, 1989; Mongeau and Brassard, 1990).

Several studies have described the TDF and SF fractions of barley and barley products (Newman et al, 1989; Bengtsson et al, 1990; Ranhotra et al, 1991). Figure 6 shows the proportions of various components in the TDF (about 21%) of Azhul hull-less barley, of which about one-third was SF (Ranhotra et al, 1991). TDF and SF isolated from Scout hull-less barley bran and flour according to the procedure of Prosky et al (1988) contained β-glucan, resistant starch, Klason lignin (except SF), arabinoxylans, and uronic acid (Bhatty, 1993b). In the case of bran TDF, β-glucan formed 39%, arabinoxylans 34%, and uronic acid 6% of the components measured.

Animal and Human Feeding Experiments

De Groot et al (1963) have been credited with being the first to show the hypocholesterolemic effects of rolled oats in rats and humans. Oat lipids and nonlipid materials contributed almost equally to this effect. The same study included barley as well, although its hypocholesterolemic effects in rats were not as dramatic as those of rolled oats. Nevertheless, rats fed barley or barley plus whole milk powder showed cholesterol levels that were about 50% that of the control group fed the basal diet. More definitive studies were reported later by Qureshi and co-workers. In an initial study, Qureshi et al (1980) reported that barley-based diets reduced plasma and liver cholesterol in

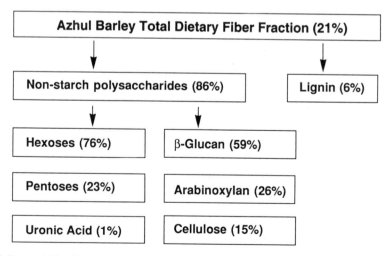

Fig. 6. Composition of Azhul hull-less barley total dietary fiber fraction recalculated from Bengtsson et al (1990). Figures in brackets indicate percent of the preceding fraction.

chickens by 45 and 35%, respectively. The lower cholesterol levels were accompanied by a 79% reduction in activity of hydroxy-β-methylglutaryl coenzyme A (HMG-CoA) reductase, a rate-limiting enzyme in the biosynthesis of cholesterol. The barley-based diet exerted a second effect on lipid metabolism. Fatty acid synthetase activity in livers of birds fed the barley-based diet increased fivefold compared to levels in those fed the corn-based diet. In another study conducted with pigs as experimental animals (Qureshi et al, 1982), the barley-based diet lowered cholesterol by 18% in comparison with the corn-based diet. HMG-CoA reductase activities were lower, while those of fatty acid synthetase were higher in the liver, adipose tissue, intestine, lung, and muscle of pigs that had received the barley-based diet. These findings suggested that the hypocholesterolemic effect of barley was not solely the result of fiber-enhanced excretion of cholesterol metabolites such as bile acids (Qureshi et al, 1985). They may indicate a number of effects on lipid metabolism in the liver. Subsequently, high-protein barley flour (the commercial pearling fraction consisting of aleurone, subaleurone, and germ sequentially extracted with solvents of increasing polarity such as petroleum ether, ethyl acetate, methanol, and water) was devoid of cholesterol-suppressive activity; each of the solvent fractions contained material suppressive to HMG-CoA reductase (Burger et al, 1984). Purification by chromatography of the fraction of high-protein barley flour soluble in nonpolar petroleum ether yielded two inhibitors of cholesterogenesis (inhibitors I and II) in vivo and in vitro. Inhibitor I was identified as d-α-tocotrienol (Qureshi et al, 1986), an isomer of vitamin E (α-tocopherol) that acts as a natural antioxidant in foods. Figure 7 shows the structures of α-tocotrienol and α-tocopherol, which differ only in double bonds in the isoprene chain. Of the four tocotrienols, α, β, γ, and δ, α-

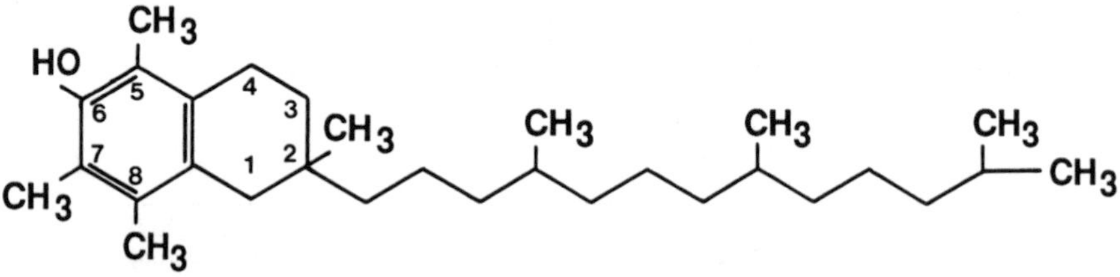

α-TOCOPHEROL (5, 7, 8-trimethyltocol)

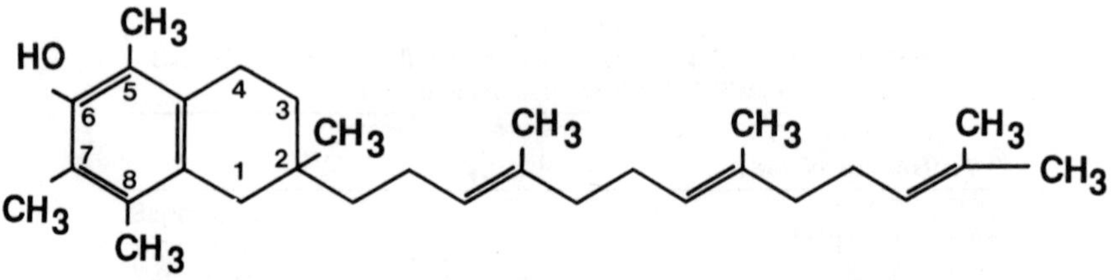

α-TOCOTRIENOL (5, 7, 8-trimethyltocotrienol)

Fig. 7. Chemical structures of α-tocotrienol and α-tocopherol.

tocotrienol has the highest biological activity (Andrikopoulos, 1989). Barley is rich in α-tocotrienol, which forms 81% of the total tocols compared with 15% in corn, 61% in wheat, 62% in rye, and 71% in oats (Qureshi et al, 1986).

Other studies have claimed that barley SF, particularly β-glucan, is directly responsible for serum cholesterol reduction. This view is in agreement with the results of Chen et al (1981), obtained on feeding a variety of oat products to rats, and of Anderson et al (1990a), who fed oat bran to healthy and hyperlipidemic subjects. Oat bran selectively lowered plasma cholesterol and increased high-density-lipoprotein cholesterol; these effects appeared to be related to oat water-soluble gum (Chen et al, 1981). In another human feeding study, the oat bran-cereal diet lowered serum total cholesterol and serum low-density-lipoprotein (LDL) cholesterol concentrations significantly, by 5.4 and 8.5%, respectively, compared with a corn flakes diet (Anderson et al, 1990b). Klopfenstein and Hoseney (1987) reported that rats fed glucan-rich bread had lower serum and liver cholesterol levels than those fed the control bread; the physiological function of β-glucan survived the baking process. Fadel et al (1987) reported the hypocholesterolemic properties of two cultivars of barley having similar β-glucan content. Only waxy barley, which had higher SF content, caused a significant reduction in both total (16%) and LDL- (30%) cholesterol. These effects were reversed by supplementing the diet with β-glucanase, thus clearly establishing the hypocholesterolemic effect of β-glucan. In another study, Azhul hull-less barley containing 10–11% β-glucan, when fed to chicks, reduced total serum cholesterol and LDL-cholesterol by 26 and 52%, respectively (Newman et al, 1987b). The chick-feeding studies were followed by clinical studies with human subjects, who gave a definite indication of hypocholesterolemia in those subjects with high initial cholesterol levels (Newman et al, 1989). Table 7 summarizes the hypocholesterolemic effects of barley and its products reported by different researchers. The data need to be interpreted cautiously, as not all differences may be statistically significant.

TABLE 7
Serum Cholesterol and High Density Lipoprotein (HDL)-Cholesterol (mg/100 ml)
of Subjects Fed Control and Barley or Barley-Product Diets
Reported by Various Researchers[a]

Reference	Subject	Serum Cholesterol		HDL-Cholesterol	
		Control	Barley	Control	Barley
de Groot et al (1963)	Rat	100[b]	50[b]	...	...
Qureshi et al (1980)	Chicken	139	76	...	...
Klopfenstein and Hoseney (1987)	Rat	104	85	64	75
Fadel et al (1987)	Chicken	158	137[c]	65	82[c]
Newman et al (1989)	Human	198	173	43	34
Ranhotra et al (1991)	Rat	373[d]	166[e]	22[d]	38[e]

[a] Data comparable only within each experiment.
[b] Serum cholesterol percent of group fed basal diet.
[c] Washonupana barley.
[d] Commercial oat bran.
[e] Azhul hull-less barley bran of 30% extraction.

Mechanisms

Two different factors, SF and α-tocotrienol, have been implicated in the cholesterol metabolism of different animals and humans fed barley-based diets. In barley, inhibition of cholesterogenesis by α-tocotrienol has been proposed (Qureshi et al, 1985, 1991); in the case of SF, the evidence has been largely obtained from oat products and other commercial gums (Anderson et al, 1990a,b).

Figure 8 gives an overview of cholesterol synthesis from acetyl-CoA through the formation of mevalonate. The rate-limiting step in this sequence is the conversion of HMG-CoA to mevalonate by HMG-CoA reductase. This enzyme is inhibited by mevalonate as well as by cholesterol, the end-product of the pathway (Lehninger, 1982). Qureshi et al (1985), based on their earlier studies, reported highly significant correlations between HMG-CoA reductase activity and total serum cholesterol ($r = 0.88$) and serum LDL-cholesterol ($r = 0.87$) but no correlation ($r = 0.02$) between HMG-CoA reductase activity and high-density-lipoprotein cholesterol. These relationships indicated the impact of HMG-CoA reductase activity on the LDL-cholesterol level of poultry fed barley diets essentially free of cholesterol. Their conclusion (Qureshi et al, 1986) was that the suppression of mevalonate biosynthesis by dietary d-α-tocotrienol through the inhibition of HMG-CoA reductase results in the lowering of serum LDL-cholesterol in poultry. Their most recent evidence was obtained with BSG and its high-protein flour, which were devoid of all starch, β-glucan, or pentosans but were rich sources of tocopherols and tocotrienols. The reduction in HMG-CoA reductase activity by two fractions of brewers'

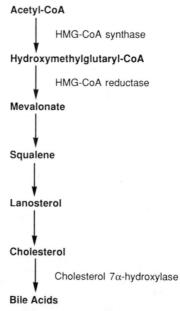

Fig. 8. Overview of the synthesis of cholesterol and bile acids from acetyl-coenzyme A (CoA), showing the rate-limiting enzyme hydroxymethylglutaryl (HMG)-CoA reductase.

grain, added to the corn-soybean meal control, was about 50% (Qureshi et al, 1991).

A number of mechanisms largely based on oat bran have been proposed to account for the hypocholesterolemic effects of SF. Because of the similarity in composition and structure of oat and barley β-glucans, barley SF is thought to have a physiological function similar to that of oat bran. These mechanisms originate in the large intestine, particularly the ascending colon, where large numbers of bacteria ferment SF, resistant starch, and some of the insoluble fiber, resulting in the production of carbon dioxide, hydrogen, methane, and short-chain fatty acids—acetic, butyric, and propionic. This results, in the case of SF, in a large bacterial mass and small fiber residue in the colon, and a reverse situation in the case of insoluble dietary fiber, as illustrated in Fig. 9.

Figure 10 shows the fate of short-chain fatty acids produced from dietary fiber and starch in the colon. Apparently, butyric acid does not enter the liver and is used, perhaps entirely, as a energy source in the regulation and proliferation of colon cells (Roediger, 1982). Both acetic and propionic acids enter the liver; propionic acid has been implicated in suppressing cholesterol

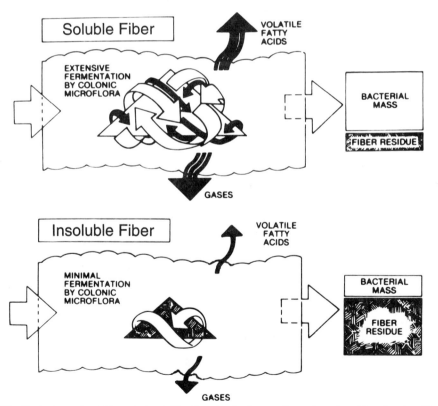

Fig. 9. Action of soluble and insoluble fiber in the human large intestine. (Reprinted, with permission, from Phillips and Stephen, 1981; ©Williams and Wilkins)

synthesis. Supporting data for this hypothesis have been obtained from rat studies in which propionic acid significantly reduced serum cholesterol (Anderson et al, 1990a). The actual mechanism is not completely understood but may involve inhibition of HMG-CoA synthase, an enzyme that converts acetyl-CoA to HMG-CoA, as well as of HMG-CoA reductase (Fig. 8), which is involved in cholesterol synthesis (Chen et al, 1984).

Illman and Topping (1985) concluded that increased concentrations of volatile fatty acids in the blood of rats fed oat bran were too low to influence cholesterol synthesis. In their opinion, fecal excretion of bile acids and neutral sterol were the most likely cause of the cholesterol-lowering effect of oat bran. Vast literature has been reported on changes in bile acid absorption and reabsorption; the reader is referred to reviews on the subject (Anderson and Gustafson, 1988; Gordon, 1989; Anderson et al, 1990a). A simplistic hypothesis

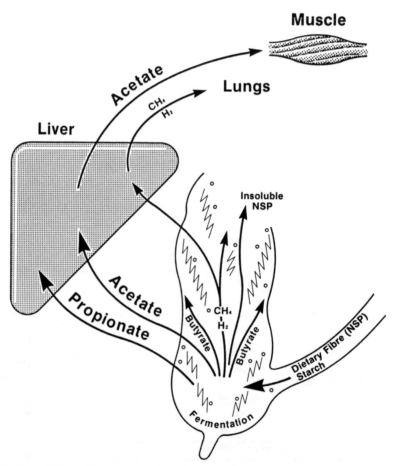

Fig. 10. Fate of dietary fiber and starch in the human large intestine. (Courtesy of A. M. Stephen, University of Saskatchewan, Saskatoon, SK, Canada)

may be that bile acids synthesized in the liver from serum cholesterol are bound by SF, thereby decreasing their absorption. Alternatively, SF may not bind bile acids but, because of its viscosity, may physically prevent their reabsorption. This results in less bile acid return to the liver, which then synthesizes more, decreasing the amount of cholesterol available for lipoprotein synthesis. However, not all SF increases fecal bile acid excretion; beans, which also lower cholesterol, do not increase fecal bile acid excretion (Anderson et al, 1984b). The relative contributions of effects of SF on bile acid absorption and on cholesterol metabolism in the liver are yet to be determined.

FEED USES OF BARLEY

Barley, one of the four major feed grains of the world (corn, barley, oats, and wheat), is widely used as a livestock feed. The grain may be used as a major source of energy, protein and, in addition, fiber as a source of roughage for ruminants; a major source of energy and protein for swine (Munck, 1981; Newman et al, 1981; NAS-NRC, 1988); and to support egg production in laying hens (Table 14 and references therein). Only broiler chicks require treatment of barley, for elimination of β-glucans. Digestible energy (DE) or metabolizable energy (ME) remains the single most important quality criterion in feed barley, particularly for monogastric animals. Use of barley in livestock feeds in different countries varies from a low of 47% to a high of about 90% (Table 1).

This section deals with the use of barley grain in livestock feeds. Barley by-products such as silage and distillers' and brewers' dried grains, which are used only marginally in livestock feeds, have been excluded. These products were covered in an earlier review (Newman and McGuire, 1985), and not much new information has since been added. Mineral and vitamin compositions of barley have been excluded as well, since minerals and vitamins are routinely supplemented in barley diets. The literature review has been largely restricted to the last 30 years.

The feed quality of barley is influenced by many factors, some of which are difficult, if not impossible, to account for when comparing barley cultivars or barley with other cereals. Such variability has contributed to much inconsistent and sometimes contradictory data on the feed quality of barley for various classes of livestock. Factors that affect feed quality of barley may be physical and/or chemical.

Physical Factors

Physical characteristics of barley grain may include color, plumpness (kernel size), 1,000-kernel weight (KW), test or bushel weight (BW), barley type (two- or six-rowed), and hull (hulled or hull-less). Most of the physical grain characteristics such as plumpness, large KW, high BW, or high bulk density are interrelated. They improve grain appearance and marketability, but, except for hull, their influence on feed quality of barley is not clear. Furthermore, barley is rarely fed to livestock as whole grain; the importance of certain physical factors may be lost on processing of barley.

SIZE OF GRAIN

Table 8 shows ranges in BW, KW, and plumpness in a number of barley cultivars and their effects on energy digestibility (D, expressed as %) and DE measured with mice as experimental animals (Bhatty et al, 1974). Their effects on ME were also studied (Table 9), using adult roosters (Sibbald and Price, 1976a). In the mouse-feeding study (Table 8), in spite of 18, 65, and 482% ranges in BW, KW, and plumpness, respectively, no positive correlations were obtained with DE. However, both BW and plumpness were positively related with D. In the poultry-feeding experiment, the ranges in BW and KW were 56 and 182%, respectively (Table 9). Only weak positive correlations were obtained between KW and ME and between BW and ME. Fewer barley samples have been used to determine such relationships in large animal-feeding experiments. Hinman (1978) and Middaugh et al (1989) reported positive influences of higher BW in cattle and swine, respectively. A higher BW thus

TABLE 8
Simple Correlations Between Physical or Chemical Characters
and Digestion Coefficient (D) or Digestible Energy (DE) in Barleys ($n = 29$),
Determined by Mouse-Feeding[a]

Component	Range	Mean	Correlation (r) with D	Correlation (r) with DE
Bulk weight, kg/hl	62.3–73.6	68.5	0.55[b]	0.19
1,000-Kernel weight, g	34.5–57.0	42.9	0.35	0.28
Plumpness, %	17.0–99.0	69.9	0.45[c]	0.28
Protein, %	12.7–17.2	14.3	0.29	0.41[c]
Ether extract, %	1.4–2.7	2.1	0.50[c]	0.28
Starch, %	43.7–56.2	49.8	0.10	−0.02
Amylose, %	23.5–33.0	28.7	0.26	0.16
Fiber, %	2.3–6.2	4.9	−0.52[b]	−0.29
β-Glucan, %	1.3–3.3	1.9	−0.16	−0.10
Gross energy, kcal/kg	4,032–4,415	4,274	0.19	0.82[b]
DE, kcal/kg	3,184–3,558	3,390	0.72[b]	1.00

[a] Source: Bhatty et al (1974); used by permission.
[b] $P < 0.01$.
[c] $P < 0.05$.

TABLE 9
Simple Correlations Between Physical or Chemical Characters and Metabolizable Energy (ME)
in Barleys ($n = 40$), Determined by Rooster-Feeding[a]

Component	Range	Mean	Correlation (r) with ME
Bulk weight, kg/hl	45.7–71.4	60.3	0.58[b]
1,000-Kernel weight, g	17.1–48.3	32.8	0.53[b]
Protein, %	10.8–16.8	14.0	−0.06
Ether extract, %	1.0–2.6	1.6	0.49[b]
Starch, %	53.8–70.0	61.9	0.21
Fiber, %	4.2–9.6	6.4	−0.59[b]
Gross energy, kcal/kg	4,210–4,590	4,440	0.05
ME, kcal/kg	2,360–3,470	3,060	1.00

[a] Source: Sibbald and Price (1976a); used by permission.
[b] $P < 0.01$.

seems desirable, as it increases the proportion of grain and hence the readily digestible nutrients and correspondingly reduces the fibrous hull.

In other studies, two- and six-rowed barleys have been compared in animal-feeding experiments. The results have been inconsistent. Taverner (1988) reported identical DE values (3,488 kcal/kg) for five six-rowed and 66 two-rowed barleys for pigs; these data were in agreement with those reported earlier by Bhatty et al (1975, 1979), using rats and pigs as experimental animals. Hinman (1979) was not able to distinguish two- and six-rowed barleys grown on irrigated and dryland fields in a cattle-feeding experiment. There were no significant differences in average daily gain and carcass characteristics of steers fed the four barley samples. On the other hand, Honeyfield et al (1989) concluded from many years of feeding data that two-rowed barley was better than six-rowed for feeding to pigs. The apparent superiority of two-rowed as compared to six-rowed barley may partly be caused by a lower degree of variability in its physical characteristics and chemical composition.

HULL

Hull constitutes 10–13% of the dry weight of barley grain (Bhatty et al, 1975) and may be easily determined either mechanically by dehulling or chemically by boiling barley in 50% sulfuric acid (Essery et al, 1956) or alkaline sodium hypochlorite (Whitmore, 1960). Barley hull consists mainly of cellulose, hemicellulose, lignin, pectins, and a small quantity of protein. It is the major contributor to crude fiber in barley. Removal of hull reduces the crude fiber content of barley (hull-less) to that of corn and wheat (Bhatty, 1986a).

Hull has a major detrimental effect on DE of barley, particularly for swine. This influence is brought about either by dilution of available nutrients or by physical or chemical inhibition of nutrient digestion and utilization (Larsen and Oldfield, 1961). In France, Perez et al (1980) reported a significant negative correlation (0.96) between DE and crude cellulose content in seven cultivars of barley; 93% of the variation in DE was attributable to crude cellulose. Simulated barley containing 0–30% hull gave highly significant negative correlations (0.90) between percent hull, percent crude fiber, and D (Bell et al, 1983). Studies conducted with 30 cultivars of barley have provided further evidence of the negative effect of acid-detergent fiber (ADF) on DE for swine (Froseth et al, 1989). These workers found that as the ADF content increased, D of barley for pigs decreased (−0.98). Just (1982) reported that an increase in dietary fiber by 1% depressed D by approximately 3.5%.

Utilization of crude fiber by pigs varies considerably, depending on fiber source, degree of lignification, level of inclusion, extent of processing, and type of analysis. Fiber utilization may also be influenced by the physical and chemical composition of the total diet, level of feeding, age and weight of the animal, and individual differences among pigs. When these factors are taken into account, it is not surprising that digestibility of crude fiber has been shown to vary widely and that the literature contains conflicting reports about the effects of crude fiber on digestibility of nutrients (NAS-NRC, 1988).

Crude fiber content may range from 3 to 6% in hulled barley and from 1.5 to 3% in hull-less barley (Bhatty et al, 1974). Ullrich et al (1984a) reported a range of 2.5–4.8% in crude fiber (mean 3.5%), 10.2–19.6% in neutral detergent fiber (NDF; mean 15.2%), and 4.7–8% in ADF (mean 6.1%) for 20 cultivars of hulled barley grown over different locations. Generally similar ranges in ADF (4.0–6.8%) and NDF (10.4–19.9%) for nine cultivars of barley of variable backgrounds were reported by Oram (1988). Measuring ADF is now the accepted method for crude fiber determination, whereas a modified NDF method is an assay for dietary fiber in cereal grains. ADF estimates the content of cellulose and lignin, while NDF estimates cellulose, hemicellulose, and lignin; the difference between the two methods estimates hemicellulose (Wisker et al, 1985).

CHEMICAL FACTORS

Protein

In contrast to the extensive studies performed to improve the quality of protein in barley (see section on lysine), few attempts have been made to improve the quantity of its protein. Progress in this direction has been limited due to a combination of factors: generally negative relationships between protein and starch (Fig. 11), protein and lysine (Kirkman et al, 1982 and

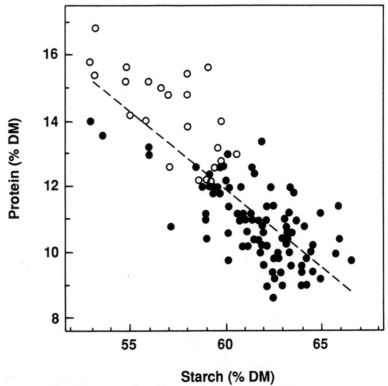

Starch (% DM)

Fig. 11. Relationship between grain protein and starch for two- and six-rowed barleys grown in Sweden (dark circles) and Montana, U.S.A. (white circles). $y = 40.4 - 0.47x$; $r^2 = 0.65$. (Reprinted, with permission, from Åman and Newman, 1986)

references therein), and protein and grain yield (Scholz, 1976; Persson, 1984); the lower protein requirement in malting barley, most of which ends up as feed barley; and a strong environmental influence on the protein content of grain. The difficulties in breeding for high protein yields in barley were discussed by Scholz (1976), who concluded that the potential to increase the protein yield per unit area by breeding appears to be limited. Even less optimistic conclusions were drawn by Persson (1984) from barley research at Svalöf, Sweden.

Torp et al (1981) found that protein content of barley could vary between 8.1 and 14.7% in the same genotype grown at different locations, even at similar nitrogen fertilization levels. Fourteen hundred lines of barley analyzed for protein gave a range of 8.5–21.2% with a mean of 13.1% (Miller, 1958). The mean protein content of Western Canadian samples of malting barley (*n*, 3,817) was 12.2% on a dry basis (LaBerge and Tipples, 1989). Friedman and Atsmon (1988) suggested that an increased protein content and nutritional quality of cultivated barley could be obtained by crossing it with *Hordeum spontaneum*, which contains 65% more protein. However, the wild barley contained 9% less total carbohydrate, 38% less starch, 65% more total fiber, and 14% more fat.

In spite of a large range and variability, most barley can meet the protein requirements of animals at a level of about 12% or less (Fig. 12). A feed barley containing about 15% protein and other attributes of normal barley such as low fiber and high lysine, starch, and DE or ME may be the most desirable. Such a protein concentration would greatly reduce or even eliminate the need to provide external protein supplements, which are required in many barley-based diets. Whether such a protein concentration is feasible in view of the many constraints mentioned above remains to be established.

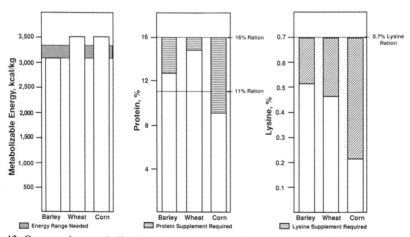

Fig. 12. Comparative metabolizable energy, protein, and lysine contents of hulled barley, wheat, and corn and corresponding concentrations required by swine. Shaded areas indicate requirements. (Adapted from Canada Grains Council, 1970)

Lysine

The low contents of lysine and threonine (first and second limiting amino acids for swine, respectively) in regular barley are essentially due to its major protein fraction, hordein, which contains only 0.6 and 2.4 mol% of these amino acids, respectively. In contrast, the albumin and globulin fractions contain 5.0 and 6.0 mol% and the glutelin fraction 4.6 and 5.7 mol% (Bhatty and Whitaker, 1987). Lysine and threonine values reported for the same three protein fractions of barley by Shewry et al (1984) were: albumins plus globulins, 4 and 5 mol%, respectively; hordein, <1 and 3 mol%; and glutelins, 4 and 7 mol%. Small differences in lysine and threonine values in these two studies were the result of method of protein fractionation and amino acid recoveries. Of the two major hordeins, hordein-1 (C or sulfur-poor hordein) contained only traces of lysine and sulfur amino acids, whereas hordein-2 (B or sulfur-rich hordein) contained about 0.5 mol% each of lysine and methionine and 2.5 mol% cysteine (Shewry and Miflin, 1985).

Animal nutritionists usually express lysine concentration as percent of the meal or diet. Using this expression, Pomeranz et al (1976) reported a mean lysine value of 0.45% for 113 genotypes of barley obtained from the USDA World Barley Collection. Barley is thus deficient in lysine by one-third in a diet requiring 0.75% lysine and one-half in a diet requiring 1% lysine (Fig. 12). Nitrogen fertilization decreases the lysine content of barley because of increased relative synthesis of the lysine-poor hordein fraction (Kirkman et al, 1982). This was reported in many earlier studies as well. Munck et al (1969) reported a correlation of −0.89 between the concentrations of protein and lysine in 16 commercial cultivars of barley. Viuf (1969) tested 650 barley lines and reported 4.2% lysine as a percent of total protein in barley lines containing 9.5–10.9% protein and 2.7–3.1% lysine in lines containing 17.8–18.1% protein.

The discovery of high-lysine mutants (opaque-2 and floury-2) in maize, first reported by Mertz et al (1964) and Nelson et al (1965) and later in sorghum by Singh and Axtell (1973), prompted a search for high-lysine barley. In 1970, Munck et al reported discovery of the first naturally occurring high-lysine mutant of barley, Hiproly (CI 3947) from the USDA World Barley Collection. Hiproly contained 19.6% protein and 4.1% lysine compared with 18.7 and 3.2% protein and lysine, respectively, in a sister line (CI 4362) isolated from the same collection. In the same year, Bansal (1970) isolated two mutants from an ethylmethanesulfonate-treated population of NP-113 barley. The kernels of these mutants carried a dorsal depression and hence the mutants were called notch-1 and notch-2. They contained 20 and 40% more protein and lysine, respectively, than NP-113. Later, Ingversen et al (1973) discovered Risø 1508, a mutant from a Danish two-rowed spring barley cultivar Bomi treated with ethyleneimine. It had increases in lysine and threonine contents of 42 and 36%, respectively. This mutant, among all barley mutants discovered, had an amino acid composition that was most similar to the requirements of growing pigs (Bang-Olsen et al, 1987). Doll et al (1974) and Doll (1976) described a number of additional chemically induced mutants of barley.

Hiproly is not considered a hordein mutant. The hordein content is nearly normal (Table 10); the increase in lysine is due to the salt-soluble protein fraction (Tallberg, 1982). "Free" β-amylase, protein Z, and two different chymotrypsin inhibitors CI-1 and CI-2, with lysine contents of 5.0, 7.1, 9.5, and 11.5 g/100 g of protein, respectively, were identified in Hiproly by immunoelectrophoresis (Hejgaard and Boisen, 1980). Jonassen (1980) reported two albumin proteins, SP IIA and SP IIB, which accounted for 37% of the increase in the lysine content of Hiproly compared to that in barley having a normal lysine content. The SP proteins were identified as chymotrypsin inhibitors CI-2b and CI-2c (Svendsen et al, 1980).

Unlike Hiproly, Risφ 1508 has a greatly reduced concentration of lysine-poor hordein-1 and hordein-2 proteins, increased lysine-rich albumins and globulins, as well as free lysine (Ingversen et al, 1973; Brandt, 1976). The embryo (and scutellum) is enlarged, forming 6.9% of the seed compared to 3.6% in Bomi. However, differences in lysine and other amino acids between the two are entirely due to endosperm proteins despite the altered embryo-endosperm ratio (Tallberg, 1977).

The *lys3a* gene in Risφ 1508 impairs starch synthesis and affects endosperm morphology due to pleiotropic effects (Kreft, 1987). The endosperm is shrunken, causing a decrease in small starch granules (Burgess et al, 1982). The poorly filled cells collapse upon grain dessication. Poor starch filling of the cells is either due to a block in the conversion of sucrose to starch as the former accumulates in the mutant or to faster degradation of the starch responsible for the low grain yield and shrunken endosperm of the mutant (Doll and Koie, 1978; Kreis, 1978; Koie and Doll, 1979). The relationship between concomitant impairment of hordein and starch synthesis in Risφ 1508 has not been established and may involve an enzyme deficiency in the sucrose-starch pathway (Kreis and Doll, 1980).

The availability of high-lysine genes from Hiproly and Risφ 1508 led to lysine improvement programs in barley in many countries, particularly in those where barley was a major livestock feed (Berdahl and Bhatty, 1979; Seko and Kato, 1981; Ullrich et al, 1984b; Tallberg and Eggum, 1986; Oram, 1988). Munck (1992) has written an excellent historical review on high-lysine barley breeding in different countries. No high-lysine cultivar of barley has yet been licensed, because of the low grain yield and problems in breaking the linkage between high lysine and shrunken endosperm. Nevertheless, progress has been made in developing better-yielding, high-lysine lines of barley (Persson and Karlsson, 1977; Seko and Kato, 1981, Ullrich et al, 1984b; Newman et al, 1990b). Bang-Olsen et al (1987) described a Risφ 1508-derived line of barley

TABLE 10
Protein Fractions (% of meal protein) of Regular Barley (Bomi) and of High-Lysine Mutants

Protein Fraction	Bomi[a]	Risφ 1508[a]	Hiproly[b]	Notch-1[b]
Albumins and globulins	27	46	25	28
Hordeins	29	9	22	25
Glutelins	39	39	45	41
Residue	5	6	8	6
Total	100	100	100	100

[a] Data from Ingversen et al (1973).
[b] Data from Balaravi et al (1976).

(Ca 700202) that, in spite of a lower KW, had a DE value similar to that of Triumph, a normal-lysine cultivar of barley. A comparison of the composition and nutritional qualities of Triumph and Ca 700202 barleys is given in Table 11. The improved DE of line Ca 700202 was the result of an increase in both starch and fat contents over those of Risφ 1508. Recently, Newman et al (1990b) confirmed the improved nutritional quality of Ca 700202 by chemical analysis, rat growth studies, and nitrogen-balance trials and described this line as a major advance in the development of high-lysine feed barley. Although mutant barley protein has higher biological value because of its higher lysine content, it has lower digestibility than protein of regular barley (Munck et al, 1970; Bansal et al, 1977; Bhatty and Whitaker, 1987). The reasons for the lower digestibility of mutant protein are not completely understood, although they may be partly caused by alterations in the proportions of endosperm proteins. Silano (1977) has written an excellent review on factors affecting digestibility and availability of cereal proteins.

Carbohydrates

In normal barley, total carbohydrates (starch, free sugars, oligosaccharides, and NSP) vary from 78 to 84% of the grain dry weight (Henry, 1988). The free sugars (glucose, fructose, and sucrose) vary from 0.7 to 5.8%, sucrose being the major sugar. The oligosaccharides (fructans) vary from trace to 1.0%, the NSP (arabinoxylans, β-glucans, and cellulose) from 9.5 to 19.0%, and starch from 50 to 65% (Åman and Hesselman, 1984; Åman et al, 1985; Åman and Newman, 1986; Bach Knudsen et al, 1987a; Henry, 1987a).

STARCH

Starch averaged about 57% in U.S. barleys (Åman and Newman, 1986), 61% in Swedish two- and six-rowed barleys (Åman et al, 1985), and 58% in Australian barleys (Henry, 1987a). It is thus the single major source of DE in barley for livestock. Starch undergoes hydrolysis in the small intestine by a combination of pancreatic and mucosal enzymes. The products of hydrolysis, mainly glucose, galactose, and fructose are rapidly absorbed. Digestibility of barley starch in poultry, swine, and cattle has been reported to vary from 95 to 100% (Hayer et al, 1961; Taylor et al, 1985; Graham

TABLE 11
Comparative Composition, Protein Quality, and Available Energy
of Triumph (Normal-Lysine) and Ca700202 (High-Lysine) Barleys[a]

	Triumph	Ca700202
Fat, %	3.5	4.8
Lysine, g/kg	3.8	6.8
Lysine, g/16 g of N	3.8	5.5
Protein, %	9.2	11.7
True protein digestibility, %	87.4	83.4
Biological value, %	75.6	87.4
Net protein utilization, %	66.1	72.9
Energy digestibility, %	83.5	81.9
Digestible energy, kJ/g	14.9	14.9

[a] Source: Bang-Olsen et al (1987); used by permission.

et al, 1986; Edney et al, 1989). Thus less than 5% of barley starch may escape digestion in the small intestine; this may be termed "resistant starch." Bach Knudsen et al (1987b) reported a highly significant correlation (0.77) between DE and starch in a rat-feeding experiment.

Although large populations of barley have not been analyzed for starch because of its difficult, rapid quantitative determination, normal barleys contain only a limited range (12–20%) in starch content (Åman et al, 1985; Åman and Newman, 1986; Henry, 1987a). Furthermore, the range may largely be environmentally induced due to variations in protein content of barley, which is negatively correlated with starch content (Fig. 11). Hull-less barley contained about 9% more starch than normal hulled barley grown under identical conditions; their protein content was generally similar (Åman and Newman, 1986), but this comparison may be partially confounded by barley hull. The same study reported that chemically induced barley mutants contain 21.2–45.9% starch and a greatly increased sucrose content due to impaired starch synthesis. Among the cereals, only rice contains substantially more starch than barley (Henry, 1988). Because barley starch is almost completely digestibile, animal nutritionists have, not surprisingly, investigated other components of barley carbohydrates in greater detail.

LOW- AND HIGH-AMYLOSE BARLEY STARCHES

Normal barley starch contains 20–30% amylose (70–75% amylopectin), which may vary from less than 1 to 45% in waxy and high-amylose starches, respectively (Merritt, 1967; Goering et al, 1973; Morrison et al, 1986; Henry, 1988). The source of the waxy gene in barley was waxy Oderbrücker, introduced into U.S. Compana barley by Goering et al (1973). High-amylose barley Glacier (Pentland), a Scottish mutant of the Canadian six-rowed Glacier barley, was identified by Merritt (1967).

Wilson and McNab (1975) reported significant increases in feed intake and body weight of broiler chicks fed the high-amylose Glacier barley compared to conventional barley. In a series of studies, Newman and co-workers (Calvert et al, 1976, 1977, 1981; Newman et al, 1978; Moss et al, 1983) compared waxy and normal high-amylose barleys in rat-, pig-, and chicken-feeding experiments. They were unable to detect any effect of starch composition on barley digestibility. Calvert et al (1977) and Newman et al (1978) concluded that the major nutritional differences in feed value of waxy and high-amylose Glacier barleys compared to those of the normal isotypes were due to protein and amino acid differences rather than to starch. In feeding trials with purified diets, waxy starch was digested equally as well as starch from normal barley and maize starches (Calvert et al, 1976). The high-amylose starch was less efficiently used by rats and pigs than starch from normal Glacier barley and maize. The differences between the two barleys were confounded by the higher lysine levels in the protein of high-amylose Glacier barley (Newman et al, 1978; Calvert et al, 1981).

NONSTARCH POLYSACCHARIDES

Of the three NSP of barley, cellulose and hemicellulose are present largely in the hull, with β-glucans and arabinoxylans (pentosans) in the endosperm. Barley is unique among cereals in that almost all of the β-glucan is present in the endosperm, compared to 47–48% in wheat and oats and 70% in rye. The pentosans are the predominant fraction of wheat and rye endosperms, whereas only 12–22% of the pentosans of barley and oats are found in this fraction (Henry, 1987b). Barley containing low and high levels of β-glucans may be identified by the thickness of the endosperm cell walls following staining with Calcofluor and observation under a fluorescence microscope (Aastrup, 1983; Aastrup and Munck, 1985; Bhatty et al, 1991). Fluorometric flow injection analysis is the most rapid quantitative method for β-glucan determination in barley and its products (Aastrup and Jørgensen, 1988; Sendra and Carbonell, 1989).

The level of β-glucan in barley may vary considerably, depending on cultivar, method of determination, and growing conditions (Anderson et al, 1978; Henry, 1986; Åman and Graham, 1987; Lehtonen and Aikasalo, 1987b). A range of 2–11% has been published in the literature (Table 12). Two-rowed barley contained, on the average, somewhat more β-glucans than six-rowed barley (Lehtonen and Aikasalo, 1987b). It may be desirable to reduce the content of β-glucan in feed barley, particularly for broiler chicks.

Barleys containing highly variable acid-extract viscosity (AEV) are available (Aastrup, 1979a; Bhatty, 1987a; Campbell et al, 1989; Bhatty et al, 1991). AEV of low- and high-β-glucan barleys was completely abolished on the addition of β-glucanase, suggesting that the viscosities were largely due to soluble β-glucan (Bhatty et al, 1991). Low-viscosity barley required less addition of enzymes and may allow the use of unsupplemented barley diets for poultry under some conditions (Campbell et al, 1989).

Barley has been reported to contain 4–11% pentosans, depending on the method of analysis and environmental influences (Henry, 1986; Lehtonen and Aikasalo, 1987a). They formed 20–25% of the endosperm matrix poly-saccharides (Fincher, 1975). Their effect on the nutritional quality of barley is not known, but they may contribute to AEV and should be taken into consideration (Bhatty et al, 1991).

TABLE 12
β-Glucan Content of Barley Reported by Different Researchers[a]

β-Glucan (%)	References
2.7–5.2	Jorgensen and Aastrup (1988b)[b]
3.6–6.4	Anderson et al (1978)[c]
1.9–6.8	Aastrup (1979b)[c]
3.2–5.8	Smith et al (1980)[c]
3.8–4.8	McCleary and Glennie-Holmes (1985)[c]
6.1–10.7	Bamforth and Martin (1981)[d]
4.3–6.0	Ahluwalia and Ellis (1984)[e]
3.5–4.0	Åman and Hesselman (1985)[f]

[a] Data and references from Jorgensen and Aastrup (1988a).
[b] Calcofluor fluorescence and flow injection analysis.
[c] Enzymatic method, *Bacillus subtilis* β-glucanase.
[d] Enzymatic method, *Trichoderma reesei* cellulase system.
[e] Enzymatic method, *Penicillium funiculosum* cellulase system.
[f] Enzymatic method, *Rhizomucor pusillus* β-glucanase.

Lipids

Another reason (after hull) for the lower DE or ME of barley, particularly compared to corn, is its lower lipid content. Based on many genotypes and cultivars grown in different countries, barley was found to contain 2.1–2.8% lipids (Bhatty et al, 1974; Fedak and De la Roche, 1977; Welch, 1978). On the basis of several studies, Morrison (1978) suggested that the lipid concentration in barley ranged from 0.9 to 3.3%. These ranges are narrow and of little practical importance for improving the lipid content of barley. There is thus a need to identify barley lines that contain a lipid content more similar to that present in corn. This should increase the intrinsic energy of barley, as lipids contain 2.25 times more gross energy (GE) than carbohydrates. Yet little, if any, effort has been expended in this direction. Barley mutant Risϕ 1508 contained 3.4–3.8% lipid, which was stable under different environments (Bhatty and Rossnagel, 1979), and a line derived from it (Ca 700202) contained 4.8% lipid (Bang-Olsen et al, 1987). However, the high lipid content of these lines was incidental to their high lysine content. Parsons and Price (1974) visually screened the USDA Barley Collection for embryo size and isolated 60 entries. Line CI 12116 contained 4.6% lipid, which was 35% higher than the lipid content of Prilar (hull-less) barley. This line, grown at two locations across Canada (Ottawa and Saskatoon), gave the same lipid content as the local check cultivars (Fedak and De la Roche, 1977; Bhatty and Rossnagel, 1979), suggesting a strong environmental influence on lipid content in barley. The genetics and control mechanism of lipids in barley have not been investigated.

In regular barleys, the embryo, including the scutellum, contains about 3.0–3.6% of the seed weight, and in mutant barley (Risϕ 1508) it contains 5.7% (Bhatty and Rossnagel, 1980; Bhatty, 1982). However, the lipid distribution in embryo fractions of regular and mutant barleys was generally similar (22.3–23.8% of total lipid). Thus, in barley, unlike in corn, about three-quarters of the lipids are distributed in the endosperm. This distribution is similar to that found in oats (Morrison, 1978). Genetic improvement in barley lipid will thus require an increase in endosperm lipid rather than in embryo lipid. Neutral or nonpolar lipids were the major component (about 65%) of the endosperm lipids (Price and Parsons, 1979; Bhatty, 1982); the major fatty acids were palmitic (16.4–20.5%), oleic (16.6–22.5%), and linoleic (51.9–56.8%).

Polyphenols

Polyphenols of barley, the proanthocyanidins and catechins, are distributed in the hull, seed coat (testa-pericarp), and aleurone layer (Jende-Strid, 1981; Foster and Prentice, 1987). Foster and Prentice (1987) listed a number of phenolic compounds present in barley. Polyphenols impart various colors to barley. Total polyphenols in barley, expressed as gallic acid, were 0.2–0.4% of grain (Bendelow and LaBerge, 1979), or about 0.2% as measured by the vanillin reaction with catechin as a standard (Bhatty and Whitaker, 1987).

The effect of polyphenols on the feed quality of barley has been investigated by comparing regular barleys with proanthocyanidin-free mutants, particularly *ANT* 13-13 (Newman et al, 1984, 1987a). Chicks fed the *ANT* 13-13 mutant grew more efficiently than those fed Nordal barley. Nitrogen balance data obtained with rats showed improved protein digestibility and confirmed the chick growth data (Newman et al, 1984). In a later study (Newman et al, 1987a), six normal barleys and their proanthocyanidin-free mutants were compared in rat and chick trials. Chick body weight gain, feed consumption, or feed-gain ratio did not vary with barley type. The authors concluded that available energy (starch content) and β-glucan levels possibly cancelled out any beneficial effects of the *ANT* gene. In the rat-feeding experiment, the overall mean true digestible protein value for normal barley (83.3%) was lower than that obtained with the proanthocyanidin-free barley (85.7%). Eggum and Christensen (1975) reported a negative correlation between true protein digestibility and tannin content in 29 cultivars of barleys. Similarly, Ekman (1981) reported a highly significant negative correlation (-0.74) between polyvinylpyrrolidine-extracted tannins and protein digestibility of barley.

The development of proanthocyanidin-free barley mutants has major implications in malting barleys. The significance of polyphenols in feed barleys, however, remains questionable in view of their low concentration and the lack of consistent data on deleterious effects in animals.

Inhibitors

Barley contains inhibitors of mammalian trypsin, chymotrypsin, and serine proteases (Mikola and Suolinna, 1969; Mikola and Kirsi, 1972; Kirsi, 1973; Warchalewski and Skupin, 1973; Boisen, 1976; Boisen et al, 1981). These inhibitors have different molecular weights and amino acid compositions than trypsin inhibitors of legume seeds (Mikola and Suolinna, 1969). Boisen (1983) reviewed protease inhibitors of cereals. Barley contains inhibitors in the endosperm as well as in the germ. In a more recent study, Friedman and Atsmon (1988) compared trypsin inhibitory activity, chymotrypsin inhibitory activity (CIA) and hemagglutinating activity of wild and cultivated barleys. The cultivated barley contained about one-sixth the trypsin inhibitory activity and CIA and about half the hemagglutinating activity of raw soya flour. The wild barley (*H. spontaneum*) contained twice the CIA of cultivated barley.

Neither the deleterious effect of barley inhibitors in livestock feeding nor their stability under various processing conditions has been established. Ironically, two inhibitors of chymotrypsin isolated from barley were rich in lysine (9.5–11.5 g/g of protein); Risø 1508 contained fivefold and Hiproly 24-fold more inhibitors than normal cultivars of barley (Boisen et al, 1981).

BARLEY FOR POULTRY FEEDING

Barley is less suited for feeding to poultry, particularly broiler chicks, than to swine. It has low ME or true ME (TME) compared to wheat and corn; in addition, β-glucans present in both hulled and hull-less barley increase gastric viscosity, interfere with nutrient availability, and cause sticky droppings, leading to litter management problems. Traditionally, therefore, barley has not been a preferred grain for poultry. In Sweden, where barley is the main grain used in poultry diets, its use is limited to 20–25% in broiler diets and 25–35% in layers diets (Gohl et al, 1978). In Canada, barley has not been used in starter rations for chicks, and its use has generally been limited to 10–15% in broiler-finisher diets, 20% in growing bird diets, and 40% in laying hen feed formulations. However, improvements have been made in the use of barley in poultry feeds in the last 30 years. The availability of hull-less barley, which has a crude fiber content similar to that of wheat and corn (Bhatty, 1986a), combined with the use of commercial enzyme preparations has largely eliminated the deleterious effects of barley β-glucans in poultry feeds (Campbell and Bedford, 1992).

Processing of Barley for Poultry Feed

Barley is rarely fed to poultry as whole grain. The grain may be broken down to a form that can be fed on its own or blended with other ingredients for formulation of balanced poultry feeds. It may be cracked, crushed, crimped, flaked, or pelleted in various mills. The effects of milling may be augmented by steaming or pressure cooking. The objective of reducing grain size and disrupting its structure is to facilitate nutrient digestibility and improve availability. Hamm et al (1960) and McIntosh et al (1962) reviewed earlier studies on the influence of feeding pelleted cereal diets to poultry. In the study of Hamm et al (1960), conducted with a large number of broiler chicks and turkey poults, pelleting improved the feeding value of barley diets essentially by decreasing deleterious effects of fiber and increasing the density of the feed. Hussar and Robblee (1962) reported that chicks fed pelleted diets consumed 15% more feed, gained 25% more weight, and had an efficiency of feed utilization that was 10% higher than the values for those fed the same diet in mash form. Pelleting had no effect on apparent ME (AME), nor did it influence grain lysine content due to heating. However, not all studies agree on the usefulness of pelleting barley for poultry. McIntosh et al (1962) studied effects of grinding, pelleting, and grit feeding on availability of energy to six-week old chicks. The overall conclusion was that grinding or pelleting had little effect on ME, although grit feeding was, in general, beneficial, probably due to its grinding action in the gizzard. Generally, similar results were obtained in a later study (Sibbald, 1976), in which cold pelleting increased TME of barley by only 0.9%. Pelleting of barley offered no advantage in energy availability over nonfibrous grains like wheat or corn, nor did the degree of fineness to which cultivars of hull-less barley were ground have any effect on TME (Sibbald, 1982). If anything, fine grinding decreased energy availability, possibly due to heat damage of protein. Al-Bustany and Elwinger (1988) reported better performance by laying hens fed mash diets than by those given whole-grain diets. Hens consumed less feed and had lower mortality, better eggshells, and better interior egg quality.

Another common processing factor of poultry feeds is heat treatment. Distinction needs to be made between barley meal heated directly and that heated after other treatments. Petersen (1969) reported a slight decrease in nutritive value of barley that had been dried at 90–110°C. Herstad and McNab (1975) heated barley meal to 100–120°C for 1 hr or autoclaved it at 120°C for 0.5 hr. Heat treatment increased weight gain significantly in only one experiment. Autoclaving resulted in a significant decrease in dry matter digestibility. Autoclaved barley became slightly darker in color, an indication of browning (Maillard) reaction and possibly deterioration of protein quality. Willingham et al (1960) reported lowering the nutritional quality of Eastern (U.S.) barley by enzyme inactivation. Using heat treatment after soaking barley for 18 hr gave lower weight gains and feed efficiency ratios in broiler chicks (Thomke and Hellberg, 1976). Amino acid composition (lysine, histidine, and glutamic acid) and protein quality, determined by mouse and rat feeding experiments, were not affected by the heat treatment. These effects were attributed to changes in the viscosity of the treated, as compared to the untreated, barley.

Metabolizable Energy Content of Barley for Poultry

Wide variations have been reported in ME content of barley for poultry. This variability partly reflects the physical condition of grain (maturity and BW), its chemical composition, and the experimental procedures used to determine ME. In many cases, ME has been predicted from chemical analysis of barley (Coates et al, 1977; Sibbald et al, 1980; Campbell et al, 1986). However, few of the published equations can explain more than 80% of the variability in ME, as analytical techniques are not absolute and do not measure grain constituents that may be digested and absorbed by the bird; nor do such analyses take into account inter- and intranutrient interactions (Sibbald, 1979). ME is a generic rather than a specific term, and descriptions reported in the literature include AME, TME, and AME_n (AME corrected to nitrogen equilibrium). AME_n is most commonly used to express the DE content of the diet or a component within the diets (Sibbald, 1979, 1982).

Variability in ME due to barley composition relates to its GE, which is determined by relative proportions of carbohydrates, protein, and lipids; their energy contents are 4.0, 5.7, and 9.0 cal/g, respectively (Bhatia and Rabson, 1987). Furthermore, TME of barley varies inversely with its crude fiber content (Sibbald and Price, 1976b). Thus, barley varying appreciably in any of these constituents is likely to have a different ME. Nevertheless, the NAS-NRC (1984) recommends that poultry feeds contain ME of 2,900–3,300 kcal/kg; however, the ME of untreated (with enzyme) barley does not exceed 2,750 kcal/kg compared with 3,320 kcal/kg for corn and 3,250 kcal/kg for wheat (Bhatty, 1986a). Thus, compared with wheat and corn, barley fed to poultry may be deficient in ME content by 5–20%. Table 13 summarizes the ME values of barley, wheat, and corn reported in a number of poultry-feeding

TABLE 13
Metabolizable Energy Content of Wheat, Corn, and Barley Reported by Different Researchers

Reference	Adult Bird	Actual, kcal/kg			Relative, %		
		Corn	Wheat	Barley	Corn	Wheat	Barley
McNab and Shannon (1974)	Hens	3,160	2,910	2,660	100	92	84
Sibbald and Price (1976a)	Roosters	...	3,520[a]	3,060[a]	...	...	...
NAS-NRC (1984)	Birds	3,350	2,800	2,640	100	84	79
Smith et al (1988)	Cockerels	3,712	3,822	3,438	100	103	93
Mean		3,407	3,263	2,950	100	93	85

[a] Means of 35 samples of Canadian wheat and 40 samples of Canadian barley.

studies. Taking corn as 100%, the relative ME values, on the average, were 93% for wheat and 85% for barley. In determining the adequacy of barley for poultry feeding, distinction needs to be made between broiler chicks (less than a week old) and adult birds. Roosters and laying hens are less sensitive to the β-glucan content of barley (Bhatty, 1986a). In their cases, the hull content of barley may be the only major limiting factor, whereas in broiler chicks both hull and β-glucan tend to reduce ME values.

Barley for Laying Hens

A number of studies have been conducted using barley as the sole ingredient in feeds for laying hens. Arscott and Rose (1960) observed no differences in egg production in New Hampshire or White Leghorn layers fed barley and corn diets. Body weight appeared depressed in hens fed the barley diet. Barley fed at a level of 78–80% gave egg production comparable to that obtained with corn, milo, and wheat. Slightly more feed was required to produce a dozen eggs with barley. Later studies reported by Brown and Hale (1965) in Ireland and Dunstan (1973) in Australia came to similar conclusions; in the latter study, feed consumption and feed required per dozen eggs were greater with diets based on barley than with those based on wheat. Lillie and Denton (1968) fed barley, wheat, and corn as sole grains at three protein levels to caged layers. Overall average egg production (hen-day) was 55.1, 59.0, and 62.7% for hens fed diets containing barley, wheat, and corn, respectively. In another study (Lockhart and Bryant, 1965), corn and barley fed at 16% protein gave 75.3 and 78.0% egg production, respectively; at 14% protein, the values were similar (78.0%). Feed efficiencies (feed per dozen eggs) were 8.6 and 9.3 kg for corn and barley, respectively. Al-Bustany and Elwinger (1988) also reported a similar overall performance when hens were fed diets containing barley and wheat.

Hull-less barley has also been evaluated as a feed grain for laying hens. Anderson et al (1960) fed hull-less barley at a level of 78–80% and compared it with hulled barley, wheat, corn, and milo in laying hens. Egg production was comparable to that obtained with the other cereals. Slightly more feed was required to produce a dozen eggs with barley. In a more recent study, Classen et al (1988b) reported that hull-less barley fed at levels of 71–80% to laying hens proved equal to wheat and superior to conventional (hulled) barley. Campbell (1984) has summarized the results of many studies conducted on the relative performance, over a complete laying cycle, of laying hens fed barley, wheat, and corn as the sole source of energy (Table 14). Clearly, barley supported egg production equal to that obtained with wheat and even corn in some experiments. Relative feed efficiency values calculated from these studies showed that corn-based diets were superior to wheat-based diets which, in turn, were superior to barley-based diets in terms of amount of feed required to produce a given weight of egg. Certain considerations need to be taken into account for a comparison of barley with wheat and corn. First, because of its low energy density, barley has lower ME than wheat and corn (Table 13). Laying hens adjust feed intake to compensate for this difference. As a result, most data reported in literature showed that when barley was used as sole source of grain, there was greater feed intake and consequently more feed required per dozen eggs. This may be remedied by making diets isocaloric by addition of fat or other supplements. An advantage of barley is that it contains more protein and a better amino acid balance than corn, and consequently barley-based diets require lower protein supplementation. Many studies have attempted to improve the feed quality of barley for laying hens by treatment with water or various enzyme preparations. Berg (1959, 1961) reported that barley treated with water, with fungal and bacterial enzyme preparations, or with addition of barley malt did not affect rate of lay, feed per dozen eggs, body weight gain, hatch of fertile eggs, nor egg quality characters such as weight, shell quality, albumin quality, yolk color, or the age at which enzyme preparations were added to barley. Similar results showing lack of response to enzyme treatment of barley in egg production were reported by Arscott and Rose (1960) and Al-Bustany and Elwinger (1988).

Broiler Chicks

Broiler chicks are traditionally fed higher-energy corn- or wheat-based diets to promote rapid growth and development. The high fiber content of hulled barley and the sensitivity of young chicks to β-glucan have made it less attractive, compared with wheat and corn, for this class of poultry. Earlier studies conducted on feeding barley to broiler chicks have been reviewed (Mannion, 1981; Hesselman et al, 1982; Newman and McGuire, 1985). All reported barley to be an inferior feed grain compared to wheat and corn. Classen et al (1985) reported a linear decrease in three-week body weight of chicks fed hull-less barley at 0–60%. Hulled barley fed at the highest level was only a little better than hull-less barley fed at the same level (Fig. 13). However, utilization of barley by chicks may be greatly improved by aqueous or enzyme treatment of grain, by γ-irradiation, or by lincomycin (antibiotic) addition, as shown in Fig. 13. A simple treatment was reported more than 30 years ago by Fry et al (1957). Ground barley soaked in an equal weight of water at 40°C, followed by drying in a forced draft oven at 70°C, gave performance equal or even superior to that of corn in supporting growth and feed efficiency. More recent studies on barley treatment have concentrated

TABLE 14
Percent Hen-Day Egg Production of Single-Comb White Leghorn Hens
Fed Various Cereal-Based Diets[a]

Source of Data	Number of Hens per Treatment Group	Hen-Day Production, %		
		Wheat	Barley	Corn
Sell (1971)	72	82.8	82.4	82.4
Campbell (1974)	96	78.8	77.7	...
Campbell (1974)	112	79.7	81.6	...
Dunstan (1973)	240	63.2	63.6	...
Sell and Johnson (1974)	192	80.9	...	81.2
Sell (1971)	96	...	75.3	74.4
Brown and Hale (1965)	204	...	68.8	70.0
Han and Kim (1973)	80	...	83.5	85.3
Campbell (1984)	1,152	81.2	81.6	...
Mean		77.8	76.8	78.7

[a] Data and references from Campbell (1984).

on the use of various preparations of β-glucanase (Hesselman et al, 1982; Classen et al, 1985; Broz and Frigg, 1986; Elwinger and Saterby, 1987; Newman and Newman, 1987; Classen et al, 1988a; Edney et al, 1989; Rotter et al, 1989b,c; 1990b; Campbell and Bedford, 1992). Table 15 shows data selected from literature in which Swedish, Canadian, and United States-grown hulled, hull-less, waxy, and nonwaxy barleys were enzyme-treated and used in chick performance experiments. The results can be compared only within each experiment due to different methods used for data expression. Most experiments reported improvement in weight gain of chicks fed enzyme-treated barley, although in some experiments differences between treated and untreated samples were probably not statistically significant. The differences reported in chick weight gain in different experiments are not surprising, as barley cultivars having different starch and β-glucan composition and, most importantly, different sources and levels of β-glucanase preparations were used. The differences in feed conversion ratios between untreated and treated barley were, in general, small, although feed intake was improved with enzyme treatment.

Addition of enzyme improves the ME value of barley (Potter et al, 1965; Herstad and McNab, 1975; Mannion, 1981; Rotter et al, 1990a). In the latter study, enzyme treatment significantly increased AME_n of barley for young chicks only and not for adult roosters fed the same diet. Furthermore, there was differential response with barley cultivars; the greatest increase in energy availability (25%) was obtained with Scout (hull-less) and the least (none)

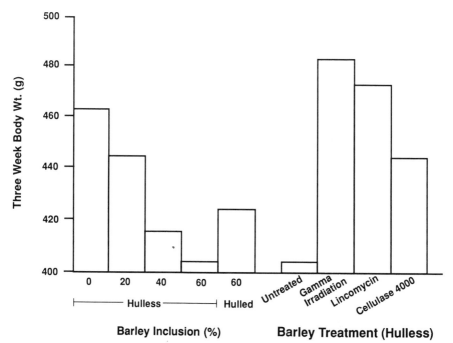

Fig. 13. Influence of level of hull-less barley in the diet and treatment of barley on body weight gains of broiler chicks. (Reprinted, with permission, from Classen et al, 1985)

with Bedford (hulled) barley. Enzyme treatment of barley for broiler diets is now well accepted in many countries (Campbell and Bedford, 1992). Commercial crude enzyme preparations of fungal (*Trichoderma reesei, Aspergillus niger*, etc.) or bacterial (*Bacillus subtilis*) origin are available. The degree of response to enzyme treatment varies considerably, depending on the barley cultivar used for treatment, its β-glucan content, and the activity of β-glucanase in the preparation (Rotter et al, 1989a,c).

Enzymatic treatment of barley was also beneficial in a six-week commercial broiler feeding experiment using 8,700 chicks (Univ. Manitoba, 1990). Chicks fed the barley plus enzyme diet were heavier, had reduced mortality, and gave better feed conversion than chicks fed a wheat-corn diet (Table 16). The decision to use commercial enzyme preparations for treatment of barley is largely determined by economic considerations. This is all the more reason to develop feed barley for poultry having a low content of β-glucan or at least a low content of acid-soluble β-glucan.

Mechanism of Action of β-Glucan

The deleterious action of barley β-glucan is generally associated with its partial solubilization in the gastrointestinal tract, which induces a viscous condition that interferes with nutrient absorption. White et al (1981) reported that β-glucan added to a corn-based diet increased the viscosity of chick intestinal content by threefold and that viscosity was reduced to that of the control diet on addition of a culture filtrate from *Trichoderma viride*. Campbell

TABLE 15
Performance of Chicks Fed Nonenzyme-Treated (−) and Enzyme-Treated (+) Barleys[a,b]

References	Barley Type	Feed Consumption, g −	Feed Consumption, g +	Weight Gain, g −	Weight Gain, g +	Feed Conversion Ratio −	Feed Conversion Ratio +
White et al (1981)	Hulled	560	611	267	317	0.48	0.52
Hesselman et al (1982)	Hulled	734	835	391	483	1.88	1.73
Campbell (1984)	Hulled (?)	3,520	3,738	1,781	1,891	2.05	1.99
Elwinger and Saterby (1987)	Hulled	2,569	2,551	1,470	1,485	1.80	1.77
Newman and Newman (1987)	Hulled	...	...	571	604	1.63	1.52
	Hull-less	...	...	558	605	1.68	1.51
Rossnagel et al (1988)	Hull-less	...	...	263	289	1.69	1.57
Froseth et al (1988)	Hulled	26	32	215	311	1.60	1.37
	Hull-less	27	30	229	310	1.58	1.29
Newman and Newman (1988)	Hulled	...	...	657	688	1.61	1.57
	Hull-less	...	...	670	709	1.61	1.51
Rotter et al (1989a)	Hulled[c]	235	248	102	120	2.36	2.07
	Hull-less[d]	233	246	111	126	2.10	1.95

[a] Results may be compared only within each experiment due to different methods used for expression of data and level and different sources of enzyme.
[b] − = Control without enzyme; + = enzyme added.
[c] Means of two cultivars.
[d] Means of five samples of Scout and Tupper barleys.

et al (1989) reported that chicks fed low-viscosity barleys gained faster and converted feed more efficiently than those given high-viscosity barleys. Enzyme supplementation improved chicks' performance with both barley types. However, the response was greater for high-viscosity barleys. Earlier studies (Gohl et al, 1978; Hesselman et al, 1981, 1982; Broz and Frigg, 1986; Hesselman and Åman, 1986) had reported that enzyme supplementation significantly increased the dry matter content of chick excreta, suggesting a reduced water-holding capacity of hydrolyzed β-glucan. Crude β-glucanase preparations may hydrolyze both β-glucans and pentosans of barley, decreasing their molecular weight and, as a consequence, their viscosity (de Silva et al, 1983). Low gastric viscosity therefore seems largely responsible for improved utilization of enzyme-treated barley. This improvement was not likely to have been caused by glucose availability from β-glucan hydrolysis (White et al, 1983), as the starch and protein contents of low- and high-viscosity barleys are generally the same (Hesselman and Åman, 1986).

Several studies reported improved fat, starch, nitrogen, and amino acid absorption by chicks fed enzyme-treated barleys (Classen et al, 1985; Hesselman and Åman, 1986; Edney et al, 1989). How increased viscosity interferes with nutrient absorption is not understood. White et al (1983) suggested that higher viscosity of intestinal contents may slow the rate of mixing of digestive enzymes and also may change transport properties of nutrients at the mucosal surface. The reduced nutrient absorption encourages growth of gut microflora. Another plausible explanation has been simply the physical hindrance offered by unhydrolyzed β-glucan present in cell walls to intracellular starch and protein, thus necessitating hydrolysis of cell walls for improved utilization of barley (Hesselman and Åman, 1986).

BARLEY FOR SWINE-FEEDING

Barley is a traditional feed for swine in many countries, particularly in northern countries where corn cannot be grown successfully. It may supply 80–90% of the animal's energy and 50–80% of its protein requirements (Munck, 1981; Newman et al, 1981). In western Canada and the Pacific region of the United States, barley is the preferred feed for swine (Castell and Bowren, 1980; Honeyfield et al, 1986; Weltzien and Aherne, 1987). The feeding value of barley for swine is highly variable, as it is influenced by type of barley (two- or six-rowed), cultivar, physical characteristics of the grain, and chemical

TABLE 16
Performance of Broiler Chicks Fed Wheat-Corn and Enzyme-Supplemented Barley Diets in a Six-Week Commercial-Scale Experiment[a]

Parameter	Wheat-Corn	Barley[b] + Enzyme
Age (days)	42	42
Number of chicks	8,700	8,700
Mortality, %	5.9	4.8
Average weight, kg	1.93	1.99
Feed-grain ratio	2.08	1.98

[a] Source: Univ. Manitoba (1990); used by permission.
[b] Bedford (hulled) barley treated with crude β-glucanase preparation used at 1 kg/t.

composition (Castell and Bowren, 1980; Honeyfield and Froseth, 1983; Anderson et al, 1984a; Taylor et al, 1985; Honeyfield et al, 1986).

Morgan and Whittemore (1982) reported that DE is preferable in describing the energy requirements of swine and the energy content of swine feeds. It is more easily and precisely measured than ME, and it overestimates ME by only 3–6%. Small losses of energy in urinary and gaseous nitrogen account for the differences between DE and ME (Farrell, 1979). Honeyfield et al (1989) used a mobile nylon bag technique to measure the DE content of barley for swine. This technique involved duodenal insertion, was faster, required only 30–50 g of barley, and was highly correlated (+0.90) with the conventional method of measuring DE.

Several studies have reported that barley is deficient in available energy, compared with wheat and corn, for growing-finishing pigs (Gill et al, 1966; Hollis and Palmer, 1971; Kromann et al, 1976; Wu and Ewan, 1979; Borg et al, 1988; Taverner, 1988). It has been assigned a value of about 90% that of wheat or corn (Taylor et al, 1985; Honeyfield et al, 1986). However, in growing pigs (under 40 kg), there appears to be little difference in performance associated with dietary grain source (Bowland, 1974; Mitchall et al, 1976). The data in Table 17, taken from many studies, show that the DE of barley for pigs may vary from about 2,900 to 3,700 (mean, 3,300) kcal/kg and may be 6–7% lower than that of wheat or corn, taking a DE value of 3,530 kcal/kg for the latter (NAS-NRC, 1988). Taverner (1988) reported a mean DE of 3,512 kcal/kg (range 3,106–3,918) for 76 samples of barley. Because of the lower DE, feed intake of barley-based diets by swine is generally greater and weight gain and feed-to-gain ratio poorer than for wheat- or corn-based diets (Greer et al, 1965; Wu and Ewan, 1979).

Processing Barley for Swine Feeds

A variety of processes such as grinding, pelleting, steaming, rolling, cubing, heating, and cooking have been used to prepare barley for swine feed. The

TABLE 17
Digestible Energy Values of Wheat and Barley for Swine
Reported by Different Researchers

Reference	Swine Weight (kg)	Digestible Energy (kcal/kg)	
		Wheat	Barley
Lawrence (1970)	27–57	3,261	2,888
Bowland (1974)[a]	5.6–7.5	3,561	3,489
Kromann et al (1976)		3,510	3,120
Wu and Ewan (1979)[b]	5.1	3,820	3,760
Wu and Ewan (1979)[c]		3,680	3,390
Castell and Bowren (1980)	52	...	3,236
Taylor et al (1985)	21	...	3,536
NAS-NRC (1988)		3,402	3,120
Mean		3,539	3,317

[a] Mean of five cultivars of wheat and one of barley.
[b] Author's own data.
[c] Based on several studies reviewed by the authors.

purpose is to improve feed intake and to increase bulk density and nutrient availability and digestibility. Processing of barley may rupture and gelatinize starch granules and facilitate digestion (Burnett and Neil, 1964). Furthermore, the processed grain is easier to mix with other nutrients for the preparation of a balanced diet. Haugse et al (1966) reported that weight gain and feed efficiency ratio were greater for fattening swine fed a pelleted diet compared to values for those fed a meal diet. Pelleted barley improved rate of gain and feed intake and apparently improved feed conversion, unlike steamed barley (Hintz and Garrett, 1967). Larsen and Oldfield (1960) reported that pigs fed pelleted barley gained weight more rapidly and had significantly improved efficiency of feed conversion.

The influence of grist (particle size) was investigated by Simonsson (1978a,b). Daily weight gain and feed efficiency did not relate significantly to grist size, nor did particle size of barley milled in four different types of mills have any influence on daily weight gain, feed conversion efficiency, or carcass quality in growing pigs. The fineness of grind determines surface area exposed to digestive enzymes. However, a particle size that is too fine has been reported to cause esophagogastric lesions in swine (Lawrence et al, 1980).

Micronization of barley followed by flaking had no effect on growth rate, feed conversion, deposition of back fat, etc., in pigs (Fernandes et al, 1975), although the process markedly improved starch availability in vitro. Beames and Ngwira (1978) reported growth and digestibility data for growing-finishing pigs fed a diet containing whole or ground barley. Feed efficiency of whole barley was inferior to that obtained with ground barley. Fadel et al (1988, 1989) investigated extrusion cooking and baking of hull-less barley at different moisture and temperature levels using cannulated pigs. Extrusion cooking caused a shift of insoluble NSP to soluble NSP and altered ileal but not fecal digestibilities of dietary components. Increased energy utilization of extruded diet in the upper tract occurred, primarily due to increased digestion of starch (Fadel et al, 1988). Digestibility of NSP measured at the ileum and in feces of pigs fed the baked, hull-less barley diets was about 10% higher than in pigs fed the uncooked diet (Fadel et al, 1989). Borg et al (1988) reported superior performance of pigs fed pelleted barley diets compared to those fed ground or dry rolled barley. Thus pelleting of barley-based diets seems to be the method of choice. Barley is usually ground to a medium or fine particle size before pelleting. The benefit of pelleting barley may be due largely to increased bulk density as well as to increased starch availability, as Graham et al (1989) reported that pelleting increased β-glucan solubility from 45 to 62% and preileal apparent starch digestibility from 91.5 to 95.3%. They concluded that treatments that disrupted endosperm cell walls improved utilization of nutrients.

β-Glucanase Treatment of Barley for Swine Feeds

A few studies have been conducted on the effect of β-glucanase supplementation of barley-based diets for swine. The results obtained so far have been contradictory. Markstrom et al (1985) reported small increases in apparent D, crude protein, and urinary nitrogen in weanling pigs fed fine- and coarse-ground barley diets supplemented with β-glucanase. Taylor et al

(1985) concluded that the β-glucan content of barley was a major factor in determining its feed value for growing swine. This conclusion was based on the high β-glucan and viscosity of Steptoe barley harvested in 1984, which gave the lowest percentage of dry matter and energy digestibilities, although the starch and protein digestibilities of this barley sample were higher than those of barley harvested in 1983. Enzyme treatment to verify the effect of β-glucan on pig performance was not included in this study. In contrast, Graham et al (1986) reported that control and enzyme-supplemented barley fed to pigs produced similar fecal digestibilities of starch (99.2–99.3%), dry matter (76.2–77.1%), protein (75.9–79.3%), and β-glucan (100%). In their opinion, the poor response to β-glucanase supplementation was due to the substantial degradation of β-glucan by endogenous feed enzymes and microbial activity in the pig stomach and small intestine. A similar conclusion was reached by Graham et al (1989). In one of the earlier studies, Newman et al (1980) reported no effect of enzyme supplementation (bacterial diastase) in growing pigs fed Washonupana, a waxy hull-less barley. However, a small improvement in growth and feed conversion due to enzyme supplementation was observed in Unitan, a covered barley. In a latter study, Newman et al (1983) reported that bacterial diastase supplementation improved DE and protein digestibility in pigs fed Washonupana barley. This contradiction was apparently due to adverse environmental effects on the barley used in the earlier study (Newman et al, 1980). Cromwell et al (1988) reported a complete lack of response to β-glucanase supplementation of barley diets by growing-finishing pigs. Age of pigs may influence response to enzyme supplementation; growing pigs may respond better than finishing pigs. According to Graham et al (1989), dietary fiber degradation before the ileum may increase with pig age; such degradation inevitably reduces the benefit of β-glucanase supplementation. Weltzien and Aherne (1987) reported ileal digestibility of barley β-glucan to be 79.6% with a range of 76.0–82.2%. Graham et al (1986) also reported high ileal digestibility of barley β-glucan in pigs and attributed this to endogenous feed enzymes and the presence of a large population of lactobacilli in the small intestine of pigs. In two Canadian studies (Thacker et al, 1988b, 1989), β-glucanase supplementation of hull-less barley significantly improved dry matter, protein, and energy digestibilities. However, these improvements were not reflected in significant differences in average daily gain, feed intake, and feed efficiency. Supplementation of the diet with sodium bentonite, an inert colloidal clay used as a binding agent during pelleting of barley, did little to enhance the effect of β-glucanase supplementation (Thacker et al, 1989). Newman and Newman (1990) recently compared Minerva and Minerva-737 (high and low β-glucan) barleys in weanling pig performance. Although the low-β-glucan barley seemed desirable, β-glucanase supplementation was of questionable value. Thus, there seems to be little justification for β-glucanase supplementation of barley for swine feeds.

Lysine Supplementation of Barley for Swine

Figure 12 and Table 18 show that barley is deficient in lysine for swine diets. Although lysine requirements may vary, NAS-NRC (1988) recommendations are 6.2–7.0 g/kg for 20–50 kg liveweight pigs and 5.7–6.2 g/kg for 50–90 kg liveweight pigs. An average barley sample may supply about two-thirds of the lysine requirement of a growing pig (Table 18). Barley may supply about one-half of the threonine, methionine, cystine, isoleucine, and tryptophan requirements of a growing (20–50 kg) pig (Taverner, 1988). As lysine, and to a lesser extent threonine, is the most limiting amino acid in barley, the response to its supplementation has been investigated in a number of pig-feeding studies. In one of the earlier studies, Soldevila and Meade (1964) reported that supplementation of a barley-urea diet with 0.15 and 0.30% L-lysine or 0.1 and 0.2% DL-methionine alone or in combination significantly improved weight and efficiency of gain in weanling Yorkshire pigs. In another study (Reimer et al, 1964), a basal barley diet supplemented with 0.06 or 0.12% L-lysine or 0.05 and 0.10% DL-methionine alone or in combination did not improve rate and efficiency of gain or have an effect on the carcass characteristics. In later studies, Chung and Beames (1974) reported a growth response in growing pigs by the addition of 0.05% threonine to a barley-lysine diet containing 0.75% lysine and 0.24% threonine. Aw-Yong and Beames (1975) also reported that threonine (0.37%) added to a similar barley-lysine diet improved growth response, whereas the addition of 0.1% methionine to the diet gave no additional response. Other researchers have shown that lysine supplementation also improved weight gain in growing and finishing pigs (Alaviuhkola and Partanen, 1975; Nasi, 1985; Giles et al, 1986, 1987; Bell et al, 1988).

A number of studies (Newman et al, 1977, 1990b; Thomke et al, 1978; Misir and Sauer, 1980) used Hiproly-type barleys (with high protein and lysine) as a source of protein and amino acids in diets of growing-finishing pigs and reported superior performance relative to those obtained with a regular type of barley. Use of such barleys greatly reduced the need for protein and amino acid supplementation.

Lysine and threonine are poorly absorbed by the pig; the availability of lysine may vary from 65 to 77%, depending on the age of pig (Sauer et al, 1974). Lysine availability may be determined either by fecal or ileal analysis. Fecal analysis may confound true lysine availability due to its interconversion

TABLE 18
Essential Amino Acid Composition of Barley and Corn
Compared with Requirements of Pig

Amino Acid	Barley[a] (%)	Corn[b] (%)	Requirement[c] (25-kg pig)
Arginine	0.59	0.43	0.25
Histidine	0.28	0.27	0.22
Isoleucine	0.49	0.35	0.46
Leucine	0.89	1.19	0.60
Lysine	0.45	0.25	0.75
Methionine and cystine	0.51	0.40	0.41
Phenylalanine and tyrosine	1.06	0.84	0.66
Threonine	0.42	0.36	0.48
Tryptophan	0.09[c]	0.09	0.12
Valine	0.67	0.48	0.48

[a] Means of 113 samples from the USDA World Collection (Pomeranz et al, 1976).
[b] Taverner (1988).
[c] NAS-NRC (1988).

by microflora in the lower intestine of the pig. Sauer et al (1981) reported that barley cultivars varied in apparent lysine availability (64.9–72.5%) when determined by ileal analysis but were the same when measured by fecal analysis. Ileal analysis thus seemed to be more sensitive in measuring amino acid availability, although the differences between the two methods were influenced by the type of cereal grain used and its processing condition (Sauer et al, 1977). However, in both methods of analysis, apparent availability values were influenced by protein levels in the diet (Taverner et al, 1981). Therefore, true rather than apparent amino acid concentrations are likely to provide a more accurate value of availability. Although lysine remains the first limiting amino acid in barley for pigs, the response to its supplementation has generally been small and inconsistent.

Hull-less Barley for Swine Feeds

The superiority of hull-less barley over hulled barley, wheat, and corn in supporting swine growth was reported 69 years ago (Joseph, 1924). When fed without supplement, hull-less barley promoted weight gain 8–15% greater than that of hulled barley. Bhatty et al (1979) reported a difference of 14.7% in DE (2,962 vs. 3,398 kcal/kg) and 11% in D (73.2% vs. 77.3%) between hulled and hull-less isogenic lines of barley grown under identical conditions. In another study, with rats as experimental animals, differences in DE and D between 10 hulled and six hull-less genotypes of barley, varying widely in physical and chemical composition, were, on the average, 7.9 and 8.2%, respectively (Bhatty et al, 1975). Several other workers reported use of hull-less barley in swine feeds. Larsen and Oldfield (1961) reported that pearled barley yielded superior average daily gain and feed-gain ratio in swine compared to that obtained with hulled barley. Barley hull (40%) added to a diet containing pearled barley depressed dry matter digestibility more than cellulose (6%) added to a corn-based swine diet, even though the crude fiber contents of the two diets were generally similar (8.4 vs. 9.2%). Gill et al (1966) reported that Utah hull-less barley yielded performance values in growing-finishing swine that were equal to those of wheat and significantly better than that obtained with Hannchen (hulled) barley. Different results were obtained in two studies reported by Newman and co-workers. Newman et al (1968) reported superior rate and efficiency of gain in pigs fed hull-less Compana compared to those fed normal Compana, but no difference was obtained between Glacier hulled and hull-less barleys when fed to young pigs. Similarly, no differences were observed in pig performance during starter and growing periods with Compana (hulled) and Nupana (hull-less) barleys. However, rate and efficiency of gain were significantly greater for the finisher diets prepared with Nupana barley compared with those prepared from Compana barley (Newman and Eslick, 1970). Truscott et al (1988) reported similar rates of gain, feed consumption, and feed-gain ratios in pigs fed Betzes hulled and hull-less barleys, although the hull-less isotype had 2.9% more DE than the covered type. Taverner (1988) reported DE values, compiled from the literature, for hulled and hull-less barleys. The means for five hull-less and 70 hulled barleys were 3,846 kcal/kg and 3,488 kcal/kg, respectively. This evidence supported that reported in France by Perez et al (1980).

A number of Canadian studies have reported comparisons of hulled and hull-less barleys in swine diets (Mitchall et al, 1976; Bell et al, 1983; Bell and Keith, 1988; Spicer and Aherne, 1988, 1990; Thacker et al, 1988b). The protein and energy digestibility data from some of these studies are included in Table 19. Energy digestibility value gives a better comparison between hulled and hull-less barleys than DE, as the latter is influenced, to a small extent, by differences in GE, which is used in calculation of DE (DE = D × GE). The average D of hull-less barleys was about 7% greater, whereas protein digestibility was only 2.5% greater than those of hulled barleys. However, individual studies (Table 19) have reported differences in D of hulled and hull-less barleys, ranging from 3 to 11% (Mitchall et al, 1976, Bhatty et al, 1979; Thacker et al, 1988a). Part of the reason for the inconsistencies in D may be due to the barleys used for comparison. These data would suggest that insufficient attention has been paid to the physical characteristics and chemical composition of barleys used for comparison. For example, Thacker et al (1988a) compared Scout hull-less barley with Harrington, a thin-hulled malting barley with a high BW. Such a comparison is likely to minimize differences in D of hulled and hull-less barleys.

The reasons for the lower protein digestibilities of hull-less barleys, 2.6% (Newman et al, 1968) and 4–6% (Mitchall et al, 1976), are not clear. On the other hand, Thacker et al (1988a) and others (Table 19) reported higher protein digestibilities of hull-less barley. There is some disagreement concerning the influence of crude fiber on protein digestibility (NAS-NRC, 1988).

Unlike the differences in D between hulled and hull-less barley reported by various workers (Table 19), swine performance data have not clearly established the advantage of hull-less barleys over hulled barleys. Mitchall et al (1976) reported no significant differences between hulled and hull-less barley (and wheat) in growth and feed utilization by 22- to 50-kg pigs. Similar results were reported by Thacker et al (1988a), except for feed efficiency. There were also no differences in carcass traits such as carcass weight, dressing percentage, back fat, or carcass value index in pigs fed hulled and hull-less barleys. Bell and Keith (1988) compared wheat (HY 320), Tupper hull-less barley, and yellow corn in growing-finishing (23–100 kg) swine. There was little difference in rate of gain, efficiency of feed utilization, or carcass quality among pigs fed wheat, hull-less barley, or corn. However, pigs that were fed

TABLE 19
Protein and Energy Digestibilities of Hulled and Hull-less Barley
Determined by Swine Feeding by Different Researchers[a]

Reference	Swine Weight (kg)	Protein Digestibility, %		Energy Digestibility, %	
		Hulled	Hull-less	Hulled	Hull-less
Newman et al (1968)	9	78.1	76.1	87.5	92.7
Mitchall et al (1976)	34	73.2	69.7	73.2	77.3
Bhatty et al (1979)	17	61.5	66.0	73.6	81.8
Thacker et al (1988a)	20	71.7	74.9	77.2	79.3
Truscott et al (1988)		74.0	74.6	81.8	84.2
Bell and Keith (1988)	21–100	68.6	76.5	71.5	81.2
Mean		71.2	73.0	77.5	82.7

[a] Data may be compared only across the rows.

wheat, hull-less barley, or corn grew 8–20% faster and 10–30% more efficiently and had a higher dressing percentage, more back fat, and lower lean yield than pigs fed hulled (Johnson) barley.

Despite lack of consistent data for hulled and hull-less barleys, hull-less barley seems potentially superior to hulled barley as a feed grain for swine. The DE of hull-less barley may approach that of wheat and corn in many cases. In spite of early evidence of its superiority in swine feeds (Joseph, 1924), hull-less barley has not, as yet, become popular with swine nutritionists. Probable reasons are lack of consistent supplies of hull-less barley in sufficient quantities, poor incentives for farmers to grow hull-less barley to compensate for its lower yield compared with that of hulled barley, and lack of attention by plant breeders to the development of high-yielding, stable cultivars of hull-less barley. This situation is likely to change, due to renewed interest in development of superior cultivars of hull-less barley (Bhatty, 1986a; Edney et al, 1992).

BARLEY FOR RUMINANTS

Barley is an excellent source of energy and protein for cattle and sheep and may be fed whole, ground, pelleted, or steam- or dry-rolled. Processing affects availability of starch for fermentation in the rumen. Whole barley is resistant to digestion in the rumen, and the starch is not readily available for microbial fermentation. In contrast, physically processed barley is rapidly fermented in the rumen. Barnes and Orskov (1982) have reviewed the literature on processing of grain for ruminants. Their conclusion was that no processing of barley was necessary for small ruminants such as sheep and goats. In their case, processing was detrimental due to excessive production of propionic acid (low pH) and depressed liveweight gain, resulting in poor feed conversion. In contrast, some processing of barley was necessary for large ruminants, which do not produce soft fat despite an increase in the proportion of propionic acid in the rumen. However, excessive feeding of barley followed by rapid fermentation of the starch in the rumen causes digestive disturbances such as acidosis, rumenitis, and liver abscess (Orskov, 1986). Starch digestion in ruminants has been slowed down by treatment of barley with formaldehyde (Van Ramshorst and Thomas, 1988; McAllister et al, 1990), which increases the passage of starch and protein into the small intestine. Starch digested in the small intestine provides 30–50% more energy for the ruminant than that digested in the rumen. In addition, reduction in ruminal starch digestion results in pH that is more favorable for fiber digestion in cattle fed a mixed diet of grain and forage (McAllister et al, 1990). Production of volatile fatty acids (VFA), such as acetic, propionic, and butyric, from glucose obtained from starch and cellulose hydrolysis by rumen fermentation is a major criterion of energy availability in ruminants. Longer-chain VFA such as propionic and butyric acids are better utilized than acetic acid. Net energy content of barley was similar to that of milo in fattening cattle (Garrett et al, 1964), and there were no differences in net energy content values of the two grains due to method of processing (Garrett, 1965). Similarly, no differences in digestibilities of GE, crude protein, and starch were found in steam- or dry-rolled barley fed to beef cattle; their digestion coefficients were 79.7, 74.6, and 95.2%, respectively (Hayer et al, 1961).

Molar concentrations of VFA in rumen fluid of cattle were 23.9, 59.5, and 8.7 for acetic, propionic, and butyric acids, respectively, for dry-rolled barley and 32.6, 49.1, and 10.1, respectively, for steam-rolled barley. The high production of propionic acid suggested, in part, the efficient feed-gain conversion of the all-barley fattening ration (Hayer et al, 1961). However, excess production of propionic acid from an all-barley diet fed to early-weaned lambs produced soft, fat carcass containing an increased proportion of *n*-fatty acids, possessing an odd number of carbon atoms, and monomethyl branched-chain fatty acids and a decreased proportion of stearic acid (Orskov et al, 1975). Lambs fed whole maize or whole wheat also produced an unusual proportion of these fatty acids, whereas those fed whole oats produced only a small proportion of such acids (Duncan et al, 1974). However, Clark et al (1977) did not find appreciable differences in branched-chain or odd-numbered fatty acids in lambs fed barley- or lucern-based diets supplemented with corn oil. The oil-supplemented barley diet increased linolenic acid (18:2) content in the fat. In their opinion, this was probably due to selection and development of different rumen populations of bacteria and protozoa, as feeding of barley apparently results in decreased ability of rumen microbiota to hydrogenate fatty acids of dietary origin.

Leat (1977) reported that barley-fed cattle gained weight, fattened, and accumulated 16:1 and 18:1 fatty acids in subcutaneous fat more rapidly than hay-fed cattle. Hinman (1978) investigated the influence of BW on beef cattle performance. Average daily gain decreased as barley (Steptoe) weight decreased from 650 to 542 g/L. Feed required per kilogram of gain increased from 7.3 to 7.8 kg for the heavy and light barleys, respectively. Differences in barley BW, however, did not influence carcass characteristics. In another study, barley cultivars could not be distinguished, as determined by the performance of cattle (Hinman, 1979). Comparison of Steptoe (six-rowed feed) and Klages (two-rowed malt) barleys, grown on irrigated and dryland fields, showed no significant difference in average daily gain, feed consumption, feed-gain ratio, or carcass characteristics. Differences in β-glucan (3.5–4.8%), starch (56.5–65.6%), and ADF (5.7–9.7%) contents of six lots of barley had no detectable effects on daily gains, dry matter intake, or the ratio of dry matter to gain in feed lot cattle. Apparent digestibilities of β-glucan and starch were 98.6 and 98.1%, respectively (Engstrom et al, 1992).

In lactating cows, the response to barley may depend on the physical form of the grain, the proportion in the diet, and the basal diet. With a high level of barley feeding, dietary fiber may limit rumen fermentation and milk fat production. Tommervik and Waldern (1969) reported similar yields of milk, solids-not-fat, fat-corrected milk, and milk protein in cows fed pelleted grain rations containing 95.7% of either wheat, barley, oat, sorghum, or maize. Barley, when fed at levels of 98% as meal or pellets to lactating dairy cows, was superior to wheat-mixed feed in dry matter and energy digestibilities and in total digestible nutrients (Waldern and Cedeno, 1970). In a trial with lactating cows, conducted with the same grains, differences in production of fat-corrected milk, percentage of solids-not-fat, and percentage protein of milk among meal and pelleted rations were small. In young calves fed starter concentrate rations containing either 100% barley or oats, dry matter digestibilities were 83.2% for barley and 80.7% for oats and protein digestibilities were 78.2 and 82.3%, respectively (Moss and Prier, 1981). Moran (1986) reported similar voluntary dry matter intake of wheat, barley, and oats by lactating cows; the organic matter digestibilities were greatest for wheat, less for barley, and least for oats. Moss et al (1980) compared the nutritional quality of waxy and normal barley for beef steers, whether-lambs, and lactating dairy cows. In each case, no differences were detected for the two barleys, suggesting that both types of barley starch are highly digestibile in the rumen.

CONCLUSIONS AND FUTURE DIRECTIONS

Barley is identified in many countries with malting and brewing for the production of alcoholic beverages and as a feed grain. A feed barley is often an unsold or "failed" malting barley, although in many countries 80–90% of it may be used as feed (Table I). Only recently, some attention is beginning to be paid to the development of a feed barley, which needs to have high DE or ME, protein, and lysine and low β-glucan for use in poultry (broiler chicks) diets. Although development of low-β-glucan barley may be achievable by plant breeding, its implications in affecting endosperm structure are not clear, in spite of the fact that other cereals (except oats) have little or none of these nonstarch polysaccharides. The development of plump, high-lysine barley has so far been elusive due to the pleotropic effect of the high-lysine gene (*lys3a* in Risø 1508) on kernel shriveling in induced mutants, although progress has been made by the development of a Risø 1508-derived line of barley (Bang-Olsen et al, 1987). In the natural high-lysine mutant Hiproly, in which the high lysine is due to the lysine-rich trypsin inhibitor proteins (SP II), kernel shriveling is even more severe. Enhancement of barley lipids to levels present in corn may enhance the intrinsic energy of barley, yet little attention has been expended in this direction. This task may prove daunting because of the lack of availability of a stable, high-lipid line of barley and also because the lipids are largely in the endosperm rather than in the embryo, unlike in corn. Hull-less barley has the potential to meet some of the above requirements and also to be used in food and industrial applications other than the production of brewers' or distillers' malt. To promote its production, price incentives will be needed to compensate for its lower grain yield.

Barley has been largely forgotten as a food grain, particularly in the Western countries. In the last 100 years or more, its decline has paralleled the increase in consumption of wheat and rice, with the result that barley has now been relegated to a coarse grain largely fit for livestock feed. However, barley may yet be "rediscovered" as a food grain. One of its redeeming features may be the level and range (2–11%) of β-glucan, a major component of the SF implicated in hypocholesterolemia and postprandial hypoglycemia, as reported in many human and animal studies conducted with oats and to a lesser extent with barley. The promotion of barley and barley products in human foods has started in the light of this evidence, although far more medically creditable research using controlled human experiments is needed. For use in human foods, roller-milled barley products such as flour and bran are more suited for incorporation into bread, cookies, noodles, muffins, and other baked products as a source of SF than are pot or pearled barley, which have hitherto been used in human foods. However, much applied and basic research needs to be done on the milling quality of barley and the use, functionality, and behavior of barley bran and flour under different conditions of processing, product development, food preparation, and food preservation. Secondly, industrial exploitation of barley (preferably hull-less) for the production of glucose syrups, β-amylase, and β-glucan for use in food and the pharmaceutical industries promises new uses of an old grain. Technology for some of these processes has already been developed and used in northern countries, particularly Finland. The availability of barley cultivars having thin or no hull, normal or waxy starch, low or high lysine, high or low β-glucan, and no known antinutritive factors makes barley uniquely suitable for use in many feed and food products.

ACKNOWLEDGMENTS

The author appreciates the assistance of Lori Jackson in collecting literature and Bonita Wong in typing the manuscript. Partial financial assistance from the University of Saskatchewan Publication Fund is gratefully acknowledged.

LITERATURE CITED

AASTRUP, S. 1979a. The relationship between the viscosity of an acid flour extract of barley and its β-glucan content. Carlsberg Res. Commun. 44:289-304.

AASTRUP, S. 1979b. The effect of rain on β-glucan content in barley grains. Carlsberg Res. Commun. 44:381-393.

AASTRUP, S. 1983. Selection and characterization of low β-glucan mutants from barley. Carlsberg Res. Comm. 48:307-316.

AASTRUP, S., and JØRGENSEN, K. S. 1988. Application of the Calcofluor flow injection analysis method for determination of β-glucan in barley, malt, wort, and beer. J. Am. Soc. Brew. Chem. 46:76-81.

AASTRUP, S., and MUNCK, L. 1985. A β-glucan mutant in barley with thin cell walls. Pages 291-296 in: New Approaches to Research on Cereal Carbohydrates. R. D. Hill and L. Munck, eds. Elsevier, Amsterdam.

AHLUWALIA, B., and ELLIS, E. E. 1984. A rapid and simple method for the determination of starch and β-glucan in barley and malt. J. Inst. Brew. 90:254-259.

AL-BUSTANY, Z., and ELWINGER, K. 1988. Whole grains, unprocessed rapeseed and β-glucanase in diets for laying hens. Swed. J. Agr. Res. 18:31-40.

ALAVIUHKOLA, T., and PARTANEN, J. 1975. Protein supplement in the utilization of high protein barley in the diets of growing-finishing pigs. Ann. Agric. Fenn. 14:277-285.

ALEXANDER, J. C., GABRIEL, H. G., and

REICHERTZ, J. L. 1984. Nutritional value of germinated barley. Can. Inst. Food Sci. Technol. J. 17:224-228.

ÅMAN, P., and GRAHAM, H. 1987. Analysis of total and insoluble mixed-linked $(1\rightarrow3),(1\rightarrow4)$-$\beta$-D-glucans in barley and oats. J. Agric. Food Chem. 35:704-709.

ÅMAN, P., and HESSELMAN, K. 1984. Analysis of starch and other main constituents of cereal grains. Swed. J. Agric. Res. 14:135-139.

ÅMAN, P., and HESSELMAN, K. 1985. An enzymatic method for total mixed-linkage β-glucan in cereal grains. J. Cereal Sci. 3:231-237.

ÅMAN, P., and NEWMAN, C. W. 1986. Chemical composition of some different types of barley grown in Montana, U.S.A. J. Cereal Sci. 4:133-141.

ÅMAN, P., HESSELMAN, K., and TILLY, A. 1985. The variation in chemical composition of Swedish barleys. J. Cereal Sci. 3:73-77.

ANDERSON, D. M., SAUER, W. C., JORGENSEN, H., and THACKER, P. A. 1984a. The total and digestible yield of nutrients in barley cultivars grown in the Peace River area of Alberta fed to growing swine. Can. J. Anim. Sci. 64:479-485.

ANDERSON, J. O., WAGSTAFF, R. K., and DOBSON, O. C. 1960. Value of barley and hulless barley in rations for laying hens. Poult. Sci. 39:1230.

ANDERSON, J. W., and GUSTAFSON, N. J.

1988. Hypocholesterolemic effects of oat and bean products. Am. J. Clin. Nutr. 48:749-753.

ANDERSON, J. W., STORY, L., SIELING, B., CHEN, W.-J. L., PETRO, M. S., and STORY, J. 1984b. Hypocholesterolemic effects of oat-bran or bean intake for hypercholesterolemic men. Am. J. Clin. Nutr. 40:1146-1155.

ANDERSON, J. W., DEAKINS, D. A., FLOORE, T. L., SMITH, B. M., and WHITIS, S. E. 1990a. Dietary fiber and coronary heart disease. Crit. Rev. Food Sci. Nutr. 29:95-147.

ANDERSON, J. W., SPENCER, D. B., HAMILTON, C. C., SMITH, S. F., TIETYEN, J., BRYANT, C. A., and DELTGEN, P. 1990b. Oat-bran cereal lowers serum total and LDL cholesterol in hypercholesterolemic men. Am. J. Clin. Nutr. 52:495-499.

ANDERSON, M. A., COOK, J. A., and STONE, B. A. 1978. Enzymatic determination of 1,3:1,4-β-glucans in barley grain and other cereals. J. Inst. Brew. 84:233-239.

ANDRIKOPOULOS, N. K. 1989. The tocopherol content of Greek olive oils. J. Sci. Food Agric. 46:503-509.

ARSCOTT, G. H., and ROSE, R. J. 1960. Studies on the use of enzymes and pelleting barley for layers. Abstr. Poult. Sci. 39:1231-1231.

AW-YONG, L. M., and BEAMES, R. M. 1975. Threonine as the second limiting amino acid in Peace River barley for growing-finishing pigs and growing rats. Can. J. Anim. Sci. 55:765-783.

BACH KNUDSEN, K. E., ÅMAN, P., and EGGUM, B. O. 1987a. Nutritive value of Danish-grown barley varieties. I. Carbohydrates and other major constituents. J. Cereal Sci. 6:173-186.

BACH KNUDSEN, K. E., EGGUM, B. O., and JACOBSEN, I. 1987b. Nutritive value of Danish-grown barley varieties. II. Effect of carbohydrate composition on digestibility of energy and protein. J. Cereal Sci. 6:187-195.

BAE, S. H. 1979. Barley breeding in Korea. Pages 26-43 in: Proc. Joint Barley Utilization Seminar. Korean Sci. Eng. Foundation, Suweon, Korea.

BALARAVI, S. P., BANSAL, H. C., EGGUM, B. O., and BHASKARAN, S. 1976. Characterisation of induced high protein and high lysine mutants in barley. J. Sci. Food Agric. 27:545-552.

BAMFORTH, C. W., and MARTIN, H. L. 1981. β-Glucan and β-glucan solubilase in malting and mashing. J. Inst. Brew. 87:365-371.

BANG-OLSEN, B., STILLING, B., and MUNCK, L. 1987. Breeding for yield in high-lysine barley. Pages 865-870 in: Barley Genetics V. Proc. 5th Int. Barley Genet. Symp. S. Yasuda and T. Konishi, eds. Maruzen Co., Okayama, Japan.

BANSAL, H. C. 1970. A new mutant induced in barley. Curr. Sci. 39:494.

BANSAL, H. C., SRIVASTAVA, K. N., EGGUM, B. O., and MEHTA, S. L. 1977. Nutritional evaluation of high protein genotypes of barley. J. Sci. Food Agric. 28:157-160.

BARNES, B. J., and ORSKOV, E. R. 1982. Grain for ruminants—Simple processing and preserving techniques. World Anim. Rev. 42:38-44.

BEAMES, R. M., and NGWIRA, T. N. 1978. Growth and digestibility studies with growing-finishing pigs receiving whole barley or ground barley by various feeding methods. Can. J. Anim. Sci. 58:319-328.

BEAVEN, E. S. 1947. Barley. Fifty Years of Observation and Experiment. Duckworth, London.

BELL, J. M., and KEITH, M. O. 1988. Comparisons of HY-320 wheat, Tupper hulless barley and yellow corn in feeding grower-finisher pigs. Annu. Rep. Prairie Swine Centre, University of Saskatchewan, Saskatoon, Canada.

BELL, J. M., SHIRES, A., and KEITH, M. O. 1983. Effect of hull and protein contents of barley on protein and energy digestibility and feeding value for pigs. Can. J. Anim. Sci. 63:201-211.

BELL, J. M., KEITH, M. O., and DARROCH, C. S. 1988. Lysine supplementation of grower and finisher pig diets based on high protein barley, wheat, and soybean meal or canola meal, with observations on thyroid and zinc status. Can. J. Anim. Sci. 68:931-940.

BENDELOW, V. M., and LaBERGE, D. E. 1979. Relationships among barley, malt, and beer phenolics. J. Am. Soc. Brew. Chem. 37:89-90.

BENGTSSON, S., ÅMAN, P., and GRAHAM, H. 1990. Chemical studies on mixed-linked β-glucans in hull-less barley cultivars giving different hypocholesterolaemic responses in chickens. J. Sci. Food Agric. 52:435-445.

BERDAHL, J. D., and BHATTY, R. S. 1979. Protein fractions and lysine distribution in barley lines derived from Hiproly. Can. J. Plant Sci. 57:1135-1139.

BERG, L. R. 1959. Enzyme supplementation of barley diets for laying hens. Poult. Sci. 38:1132-1139.

BERG, L. R. 1961. Effect of adding enzymes to barley diets at different ages of pullets on laying house performance. Poult. Sci. 40:34-39.

BERGLUND, P. T., FASTNAUGHT, C. E., and HOLM, E. T. 1992. Food uses of waxy hull-less barley. Cereal Foods World 37:707-714.

BHATIA, C. R., and RABSON, R. 1987. Relationship of grain yield and nutritional quality. Pages 11-43 in: Nutritional Quality of Cereal Grains: Genetic and Agronomic Improvement. R. A. Olson and K. J. Frey, eds. Am. Soc. Agron., Madison, WI.

BHATTY, R. S. 1982. Distribution of lipids in embryo and bran-endosperm fractions of Riso 1508 and Hiproly barley grains. Cereal Chem. 59:154-155.

BHATTY, R. S. 1986a. The potential of hull-less barley. A review. Cereal Chem. 63:97-103.

BHATTY, R. S. 1986b. Physicochemical and functional (breadmaking) properties of hull-less barley fractions. Cereal Chem. 63:31-35.

BHATTY, R. S. 1987a. Relationship between acid extract viscosity and total soluble and insoluble β-glucan contents of hulled and hulless barley. Can. J. Plant Sci. 67:997-1008.

BHATTY, R. S. 1987b. Milling yield and flour quality of hulless barley. Cereal Foods World 32:268, 270, 272.

BHATTY, R. S. 1992a. Dietary and nutritional aspects of barley in human foods. Pages 913-923 in: Barley Genetics VI. Vol. 2. Proc. 6th Int. Barley Genet. Symp. L. Munck, ed. Munksgaard Int. Publ., Copenhagen.

BHATTY, R. S. 1992b. β-Glucan content and viscosities of barleys and their roller-milled flour and bran products. Cereal Chem. 69:469-471.

BHATTY, R. S. 1993a. Extraction and enrichment of $(1\rightarrow3),(1\rightarrow4)$-$\beta$-D-glucan from barley and oat brans. Cereal Chem. 70:73-77.

BHATTY, R. S. 1993b. Physicochemical properties of roller-milled barley bran and flour. Cereal Chem. 70:397-402.

BHATTY, R. S., and ROSSNAGEL, B. G. 1979. Oil content of Riso 1508 barley. Cereal Chem. 56:586.

BHATTY, R. S., and ROSSNAGEL, B. G. 1980. Lipids and fatty acid composition of Riso 1508 and normal barley. Cereal Chem. 57:382-386.

BHATTY, R. S., and WHITAKER, J. R. 1987. In vivo and in vitro protein digestibilities of regular and mutant barleys and their isolated protein fractions. Cereal Chem. 64:144-149.

BHATTY, R. S., CHRISTISON, G. I., SOSULSKI, F. W., HARVEY, B. L., HUGHES, G. R., and BERDAHL, J. D. 1974. Relationship of various physical and chemical characters to digestible energy in wheat and barley. Can. J. Anim. Sci. 54:419-427.

BHATTY, R. S., BERDAHL, J. D., and CHRISTISON, G. I. 1975. Chemical composition and digestible energy of barley. Can. J. Anim. Sci. 55:759-764.

BHATTY, R. S., CHRISTISON, G. I., and ROSSNAGEL, B. G. 1979. Energy and protein digestibilities of hulled and hulless barley determined by swine-feeding. Can. J. Anim. Sci. 59:585.

BHATTY, R. S., MacGREGOR, A. W., and ROSSNAGEL, B. G. 1991. Total and soluble β-glucan contents of hulless barley and their relationship to acid extract viscosity. Cereal Chem. 68:221-227.

BOISEN, S. 1976. Characterisation of the endospermal trypsin inhibitor of barley. Phytochemistry 15:641.

BOISEN, S. 1983. Protease inhibitors in cereals. Occurrence, properties, physiological role, and nutritional influence. Acta Agric. Scand. 33:369-381.

BOISEN, S., ANDERSEN, C. Y., and HEJGAARD, J. 1981. Inhibitors of chymotrypsin and microbial serine proteases in barley grains. Physiol. Plant. 52:167-176.

BORG, B. S., HAMILTON, C. R., LIBAL, G. W., and WAHLSTROM, R. C. 1988. The effect of processing method and lysine and energy concentration on performance of pigs fed barley based diets. Abstr. J. Anim. Sci. (Suppl. 1) 66:129.

BOS, C. 1980. Engineering technology for the manufacture of sugars from cereals. Pages 75-96 in: Cereals for Food and Beverages. G. E. Inglett and L. Munck, eds. Academic Press, New York.

BOWLAND, J. P. 1974. Comparison of several wheat cultivars and a barley cultivar in diets for young pigs. Can. J. Anim. Sci. 54:629-638.

BRANDT, A. 1976. Endosperm protein formation during kernel development of wild type and a high-lysine barley mutant. Cereal Chem. 53:890-901.

BRIDGES, S. R., ANDERSON, J. W., DEAKINS, D. A., DILLON, D. W., and WOOD, C. L. 1992. Oat bran increases serum acetate of hypercholesterolemic men. Am. J. Clin. Nutr. 56:455-459.

BROWN, W. O., and HALE, R. W. 1965. Efficiency of egg production of three types of caged layers fed diets containing maize, oats or barley as the main cereal ingredient. Br. Poult. Sci. 6:119-124.

BROZ, J., and FRIGG, M. 1986. Effects of β-glucanase on the feeding value of broiler diets based on barley or oats. Arch. Gefluegelk. 50:41-47.

BURGER, W. C., QURESHI, A. A., DIN, Z. Z., ABUIRMEILEH, N., and ELSON, C. E. 1984. Suppression of cholesterol biosynthesis by constituents of barley kernel. Atherosclerosis 51:75-87.

BURGESS, S. R., TURNER, R. H., SHEWRY, P. R., and MIFLIN, B. J. 1982. The structure of normal and high-lysine barley grains. J. Exp. Bot. 33:1-11.

CALVERT, C. C., NEWMAN, C. W., ESLICK, R. F., and GOERING, K. G. 1976. Comparison of waxy, high-amylose and normal barley starches in purified rat diets. Nutr. Rep. Int. 14:55-61.

CALVERT, C. C., NEWMAN, C. W., ESLICK, R., GOERING, K. G., MOSS, B. R., and EL-NEGOUMY, A. M. 1977. Waxy vs normal barley in rat and pig diets. Nutr. Rep. Int. 15:157-164.

CALVERT, C. C., NEWMAN, C. W., EL-NEGOUMY, A. M., and ESLICK, R. F. 1981. High amylose Glacier barley in swine diets. Nutr. Rep. Int. 23:29-36.

CAMPBELL, G. L. and BEDFORD, M. R. 1992. Enzyme applications for monogastric feeds: A review. Can. J. Anim. Sci. 72:449-466.

CAMPBELL, G. L., SALMON, R. E., and CLASSEN, H. L. 1986. Prediction of metabolizable energy of broiler diets from chemical analysis. Poult. Sci. 65:2126-2134.

CAMPBELL, G. L., ROSSNAGEL, B. G., CLASSEN, H. L., and THACKER, P. A. 1989. Genotypic and environmental differences in extract viscosity of barley and their relationship to its nutritive value for broiler chickens. Anim. Feed Sci. Technol. 26:221-230.

CAMPBELL, L. D. 1984. Low energy barley-based diets for laying hens. Pages 102-121 in: Proc. 5th Western Nutrition Conference, Calgary. University of Alberta, Edmonton, AB, Canada.

CANADA GRAINS COUNCIL. 1970. Feed Grains of Canada. The Council, Winnipeg, Manitoba.

CARR, J. M., GLATTER, S., JERACI, J. L., and LEWIS, B. A. 1990. Enzymic determination of β-glucan in cereal-based food products. Cereal Chem. 67:226-229.

CASTELL, A. G., and BOWREN, K. E. 1980. Comparison of barley cultivars in diets for growing-finishing pigs. Can. J. Anim. Sci. 60:159-167.

CHATTERJEE, S. R., and ABROL, Y. P. 1977. Protein quality evaluation of popped barley grains (*Sattu*). J. Food Sci. Technol. 14:247-250.

CHAUDHARY, V. K., and WEBER, F. E. 1990. Barley bran flour evaluated as dietary fiber ingredient in wheat bread. Cereal Foods World 35:560-562.

CHEIGH, H.-S., SNYDER, H. E., and KWON, T.-W. 1975. Rheological and milling characteristics of naked and covered barley varieties. Korean J. Food Sci. Technol. 7:85-90.

CHEN, W.-J. L., ANDERSON, J. W., and GOULD, M. R. 1981. Effects of oat bran, oat gum and pectin on lipid metabolism of cholesterol-fed rats. Nutr. Rep. Int. 24:1093-1098.

CHEN, W.-J. L., ANDERSON, J. W., and JENNINGS, D. 1984. Propionate may mediate the hypocholesterolemic effects of certain soluble plant fibers in cholesterol-fed rats (41791). Proc. Soc. Exp. Biol. Med. 175:215-218.

CHUNG, A. S., and BEAMES, R. M. 1974. Lysine, threonine, methionine and isoleucine supplementation of Peace River barley for grower pigs. Can. J. Anim. Sci. 54:429-436.

CLARK, H. H. 1967. The origin and early history of the cultivated barleys. A botanical and archaeological synthesis. Agric. Hist. Rev. 15:1-18.

CLARK, R. T. J., BAUCHOP, T., and BODY, D. R. 1977. Effect of dietary corn oil on the linolenic acid content of adipose tissue lipids in barley-fed lambs. J. Agric. Sci. 89:507-510.

CLASSEN, H. L., CAMPBELL, G. L., ROSSNAGEL, B. G., BHATTY, R. S., and REICHERT, R. D. 1985. Studies on the use of hulless barley in chick diets: Deleterious effects and methods of alleviation. Can. J. Anim. Sci. 65:725-733.

CLASSEN, H. L., CAMPBELL, G. L., and GROOTWASSINK, J. W. D. 1988a. Improved feeding value of Saskatchewan-grown barley for broiler chickens with dietary enzyme supplementation. Can. J. Anim. Sci. 68:1253-1259.

CLASSEN, H. L., CAMPBELL, G. L., ROSSNAGEL, B. G., and BHATTY, R. S. 1988b. Evaluation of hulless barley as replacement for wheat or conventional barley in laying hen diets. Can. J. Anim. Sci. 68:1261-1266.

COATES, B. J., SLINGER, S. J., ASHTON, G. C., and BAYLEY, H. S. 1977. The relation of metabolizable energy values to chemical composition of wheat and barley for chicks, turkeys and roosters. Can. J. Anim. Sci. 57:209-219.

COWAN, W. D., and MOLLGAARD, A. 1988. Alternative uses of barley components in the food and feed industries. Pages 35-41 in: Alternative End Uses of Barley.

D. H. B. Sparrow, R. C. M. Lance, and R. J. Henry, eds. Waite Agricultural Research Institute, Glen Osmond, Australia.

CROMWELL, G. L., CANTOR, A. H., STAHLY, T. S., and RANDOLPH, J. H. 1988. Efficacy of beta-glucanase addition to barley-based diets on performance of weanling and growing-finishing pigs and broiler chicks. Abstr. J. Anim. Sci. (Suppl. 1) 66:46.

CUMMINGS, J. H., and ENGLYST, H. N. 1987. The development of methods for the measurement of 'dietary fiber' in food. Pages 188-220 in: Cereals in a European Context. I. D. Morton, ed. Ellis Horwood publishers, Chichester, England.

DARBY, W. J., GHALIOUNGUI, P., and GRIVETTI, L. 1977. Food: The gift of Osiris, Vol. 2. Academic Press, London.

de GROOT, A. P., LUYKEN, R., and PIKAAR, N. A. 1963. Cholesterol-lowering effect of rolled oats. Lancet 2:303-304.

de SILVA, S., HESSELMAN, K., and ÅMAN, P. 1983. Effects of water and β-glucanase treatment on non-starch polysaccharides in endosperm of low and high viscous barley. Swed. J. Agric. Res. 13:211-219.

DOLL, H. 1976. Genetic studies of high lysine barley mutants. Pages 542-546 in: Barley Genetics III. Proc. 3rd Int. Barley Genet. Symp. H. Gaul, ed. Verlag Karl Theimig, Munich.

DOLL, H., and KOIE, B. 1978. Influence of the high-lysine gene from barley mutant 1508 on grain, carbohydrate and protein yield. Pages 107-114 in: Seed Protein Improvement by Nuclear Techniques. Int. Atomic Energy Agency, Vienna.

DOLL, H., KOIE, B., and EGGUM, B. O. 1974. Induced high lysine mutants in barley. Radiat. Bot. 14:73-80.

DREESE, P. C., and HOSENEY, R. C. 1982. Baking properties of the bran fraction from brewer's spent grains. Cereal Chem. 59:89-91.

DUNCAN, W. R. H., ORSKOV, E. R., and GARTON, G. A. 1974. Effect of different dietary cereals on the occurrence of branched-chain fatty acids in lamb fats. Abstr. Nutr. Soc. Proc. 33:81A.

DUNSTAN, E. A. 1973. The performance of laying hens on diets using barley as the main energy source. Aust. J. Exp. Agric. Anim. Husb. 13:251-256.

EDNEY, M. J., CAMPBELL, G. L., and CLASSEN, H. L. 1989. The effect of β-glucanase supplementation on nutrient digestibility and growth in broilers given diets containing barley, oat groats, or wheat. Anim. Feed Sci. Technol. 25:193-200.

EDNEY, M. J., TKACHUK, R., and

MacGREGOR, A. W. 1992. Nutrient composition of the hulless barley cultivar, Condor. J. Sci. Food Agric. 60:451-456.

EGGUM, B. O., and CHRISTENSEN, K. D. 1975. Influence of tannin on protein utilization in feedstuffs with special reference to barley. Pages 135-143 in: Breeding for Seed Protein Improvement Using Nuclear Techniques. Int. Atomic Energy Agency, Vienna.

EKMAN, R. 1981. Determination of protein digestibility in barley and evaluation of the breedability for the character. Pages 263-270 in: Barley Genetics IV. Proc. 4th Int. Barley Genet. Symp. R. N. H. Whitehouse, ed. Edinburgh University Press, Edinburgh.

ELWINGER, K., and SATERBY, B. 1987. The use of β-glucanase in practical broiler diets containing barley or oats. Effect of enzyme level, type and quality of grain. Swed. J. Agric. Res. 17:133-140.

ENGLYST, H. N., and CUMMINGS, J. H. 1987. Resistant starch, a 'new' food component: A classification of starch for nutritional purposes. Pages 221-233 in: Cereals in a European Context. I. D. Morton, ed. Ellis Horwood, Chichester, England.

ENGLYST, H., WIGGINS, H. S., and CUMMINGS, J. H. 1982. Determination of the non-starch polysaccharides in plant foods by gas-liquid chromatography of constituent sugars as alditol acetates. Analyst 107:307-318.

ENGSTROM, D. F., MATHISON, G. W., and GOONEWARDENE, L. A. 1992. Effect of β-glucan, starch, and fiber content and steam vs dry rolling of barley grain on its degradability and utilization by steers. Anim. Feed Sci. Technol. 37:33-46.

ESSERY, R. E., KIRSOP, B. H., and POLLOCK, J. R. A. 1956. Studies in barley and malt. V. Determination of husk content and mealiness of barley. J. Inst. Brew. 62:150-152.

FADEL, J. G., NEWMAN, R. K., NEWMAN, C. W., and BARNES, A. E. 1987. Hypocholesterolemic effects of beta-glucans in different barley diets fed to broiler chicks. Nutr. Rep. Int. 35:1049-1058.

FADEL, J. G., NEWMAN, C. W., NEWMAN, R. K., and GRAHAM, H. 1988. Effects of extrusion cooking of barley on digestibility of dietary components in pigs. Can. J. Anim. Sci. 68:891-897.

FADEL, J. G., NEWMAN, R. K., NEWMAN, C. W., and GRAHAM, H. 1989. Effects of baking hulless barley on the digestibility of dietary components as measured at the ileum and in the feces of pigs. J. Nutr. 119:722-726.

FARRELL, D. J. 1979. Energy systems for pigs

and poultry: A review. J. Aust. Inst. Agric. Sci. 45:21-34.

FEDAK, G., and De la ROCHE, I. 1977. Lipid and fatty acid composition of barley kernels. Can. J. Plant Sci. 57:257-260.

FERNANDES, T. H., HUTTON, K., and SMITH, W. C. 1975. A note on the use of micronized barley for growing pigs. Anim. Prod. 20:307-310.

FINCHER, G. B. 1975. Morphology and chemical composition of barley endosperm cell walls. J. Inst. Brew. 81:116-122.

FOSTER, E., and PRENTICE, N. 1987. Barley. Pages 337-396 in: Nutritional Quality of Cereal Grains: Genetic and Agronomic Improvement. R. A. Olson and K. J. Frey, eds. Am. Soc. Agron., Madison, WI.

FRIEDMAN, M., and ATSMON, D. 1988. Comparison of grain composition and nutritional quality in wild barley (Hordeum spontaneum) and in a standard cultivar. J. Agric. Food Chem. 36:1167-1172.

FROSETH, J. A., GARBER, M. J., and PUBOLS, M. H. 1988. Effects of the addition of a mixed enzyme including β-glucanase activity to chick diets containing barleys with varying levels of β-glucans. Proc. West. Sect. Am. Soc. Anim. Sci. 39:170-172.

FROSETH, J. A., HONEYFIELD, D. C., PETERS, D. N., and ULLRICH, S. E. 1989. Nutrient composition and feeding value for various barley cultivars for swine. Barley Newsl. 33:145.

FRY, R. E., ALLRED, J. B., JENSEN, L. S., and McGINNIS, J. 1957. Influence of water-treatment on nutritional value of barley. Proc. Soc. Exp. Biol. Med. 95:249-251.

GARRETT, W. N. 1965. Comparative feeding value of steam-rolled or ground barley and milo for feedlot cattle. J. Anim. Sci. 24:726-729.

GARRETT, W. N., LOFGREEN, G. P., and MEYER, J. H. 1964. A net energy comparison of barley and milo for fattening cattle. J. Anim. Sci. 23:470-476.

GILES, L. R., BATTERHAM, E. S., and DETTMANN, E. B. 1986. Amino acid and energy interactions in growing pigs. II. Effects of food intake, sex and live weight on responses to lysine concentration in barley-based diets. Anim. Prod. 42:133-144.

GILES, L. R., BATTERHAM, E. S., DETTMANN, E. B., and LOWE, R. F. 1987. Amino acid and energy interactions in growing pigs. III. Effects of sex and live weight and cereal on the responses to dietary lysine concentration when fed ad libitum or to a restricted food scale on diets based on wheat or barley. Anim. Prod. 45:493-502.

GILL, D. R., OLDFIELD, J. E., and

ENGLAND, D. C. 1966. Comparative values of hulless barley, regular barley, corn and wheat for growing pigs. J. Anim. Sci. 25:34-36.

GOERING, K. J., ESLICK, R., and DeHAAS, B. W. 1973. Barley starch. V. A comparison of the properties of waxy Compana barley starch with the starches of its parents. Cereal Chem. 50:322-328.

GOERING, K. J., DeHAAS, B. W., CHAPMAN, D. W., and ESLICK, R. F. 1980. New process for production of ultra high maltose syrup from special genetically derived barley. Starch/Staerke 32:349-352.

GOHL, B., ALDEN, S., ELWINGER, K., and THOMKE, S. 1978. Influence of β-glucanase on feeding value of barley for poultry and moisture content of excreta. Br. Poult. Sci. 19:41-47.

GORDON, D. T. 1989. Functional properties vs. physiological action of total dietary fiber. Cereal Foods World 34:517-518, 520-525.

GRAHAM, H., HESSELMAN, K., JONSSON, E., and ÅMAN, P. 1986. Influence of β-glucanase supplementation on digestion of a barley-based diet in the pig gastrointestinal tract. Nutr. Rep. Int. 34:1089-1096.

GRAHAM, H., FADEL, J. G., NEWMAN, R. K., and NEWMAN, C. W. 1989. Effect of pelleting and β-glucanase supplementation on the digestibility of a barley-based diet in the pig gastrointestinal tract. J. Anim. Sci. 67:1293-1298.

GREENWOOD, C. T. 1988. Barley starches—Basic concepts. Pages 67-72 in: Alternative End Uses of Barley. D. H. B. Sparrow, R. C. M. Lance, and R. J. Henry, eds. Waite Agricultural Research Institute, Glen Osmond, Australia.

GREER, S. A. N., HAYS, V. W., SPEER, V. C., McCALL, J. T., and HAMMOND, E. G. 1965. Effects of level of corn and barley base diets on performance and body composition of swine. J. Anim. Sci. 24:1008-1013.

GRIVETTI, L. E. 1991. Nutrition past—Nutrition today: Prescientific origins of nutrition and dietetics. Nutrition Today 26:13-24.

HAMM, D., JAEN, J., TOLLETT, J., and STEPHENSON, E. L. 1960. Broiler and poult rations. Effects of pelleting, water soaking the grain, enzyme additions and limited feedings. Agric. Exp. Stn. Bull. 631. University of Arkansas, Fayetteville.

HAN, P. J. 1979. A seminar on the barley pearling and its utilization in food and feed. Pages 72-88 in: Proc. Joint Barley Utilization Seminar. Korean Sci. Eng. Foundation, Suweon, Korea.

HANSEN, M., PEDERSEN, B., MUNCK, L.,

and EGGUM, B. O. 1989. Weaning foods with improved energy and nutrient density prepared from germinated cereals. 1. Preparation and dietary bulk of gruels based on barley. Food Nutr. Bull. 11:40-45.

HARLAN, J. R. 1979. On the origin of barley. Pages 9-31 in: Barley: Origin, Botany, Culture, Winter Hardiness, Genetics, Utilization, Pests. Agricultural Handbook 338. U.S. Dept. Agric., Sci. and Educ. Admin., Washington, DC.

HAUGSE, C. N., DINUSSON, W. E., ERICKSON, D. O., and BOLIN, D. W. 1966. Effect of physical form of barley in rations for fattening pigs. Res. Rep. 17. N.D. State Univ. Agric. Exp. Stn., Fargo.

HAYER, W. T., TAYLOR, R. E., and HUBBERT, F. 1961. Apparent digestibility and volatile fatty acid studies with all barley fattening rations for beef cattle. J. Anim. Sci. 20:666.

HEGEDÜS, M., PEDERSEN, B., and EGGUM, B. O. 1985. The influence of milling on the nutritive value of flour from cereal grains. 7. Vitamins and tryptophan. Qual. Plant. Plant Foods Hum. Nutr. 35:175-180.

HEJGAARD, J., and BOISEN, S. 1980. High-lysine proteins in Hiproly barley breeding: Identification, nutritional significance and new screening methods. Hereditas 93:311-320.

HENRY, R. J. 1986. Genetic and environmental variation in the pentosan and β-glucan contents of barley, and their relation to malting quality. J. Cereal Sci. 4:269-277.

HENRY, R. J. 1987a. Variation in the carbohydrate composition of barley. Pages 763-766 in: Barley Genetics V. Proc. 5th Int. Barley Genet. Symp. S. Yasuda and T. Konishi, eds. Sanyo Press, Okayama, Japan.

HENRY, R. J. 1987b. Pentosan and $(1\rightarrow3),(1\rightarrow4)$-β-glucan concentrations in endosperm and wholegrain of wheat, barley, oats and rye. J. Cereal Sci. 6:253-258.

HENRY, R. J. 1988. The carbohydrates of barley grains—A review. J. Inst. Brew. 94:71-78.

HERSTAD, O., and McNAB, J. M. 1975. The effect of heat treatment and enzyme supplementation on the nutritive value of barley for broiler chicks. Br. Poult. Sci. 16:1-8.

HESSELMAN, K., and ÅMAN, P. 1986. The effect of β-glucanase on the utilization of starch and nitrogen by broiler chickens fed on barley of low- or high-viscosity. Anim. Feed Sci. Technol. 15:83-93.

HESSELMAN, K., ELWINGER, R. K., NILSSON, M., and THOMKE, S. 1981. The effect of β-glucanase supplementation, stage of ripeness, and storage treatment of barley in diets fed to broiler chickens. Poult. Sci. 60:2664-2671.

HESSELMAN, K., ELWINGER, R. K., and THOMKE, S. 1982. Influence of increasing levels of β-glucanase on the productive value of barley diets for broiler chickens. Anim. Feed Sci. Technol. 7:351-358.

HICKENBOTTOM, J. W. 1983. Malts in bakery foods. Am. Inst. Baking Technol. Bull. 5:1-5.

HINMAN, D. D. 1978. Influence of barley bushel weight on beef cattle performance. Proc. West. Sect. Am. Soc. Anim. Sci. 29:390-391.

HINMAN, D. D. 1979. A comparison of malting vs. feed barley varieties on beef cattle performance. Proc. West. Sect. Am. Soc. Anim. Sci. 30:49-50.

HINTZ, H. F., and GARRETT, W. N. 1967. Steam pressure processing and pelleting of barley for growing-finishing swine. J. Anim. Sci. 26:746-748.

HOLLIS, G. R., and PALMER, A. Z. 1971. Wheat and barley vs. corn for growing-finishing pigs. (Abstr.) J. Anim. Sci. 32:381.

HONEYFIELD, D. C., and FROSETH, J. A. 1983. Components of barley that predict its feeding value for finishing pigs. Swine Information Days Proc. Washington State Univ., Pullman, WA.

HONEYFIELD, D. C., TAYLOR P. F., and FROSETH, J. A. 1986. Barley cultivars for swine diets: Effect of year, cultivar and barley type on performance. Swine Information Days Proc. Washington State Univ., Pullman, WA.

HONEYFIELD, D. C., FROSETH, J. A., and ULLRICH, S. E. 1989. Use of the mobile nylon bag technique to determine digestible energy of new barley breeding lines early in the WSU cultivar development program. Barley Newsl. 33:201-206.

HOSENEY, R. C., LINEBACK, D. R., and SEIB, P. A. 1978. Role of starch in baked foods. Baker's Dig. 52:11-14, 16, 18, 40.

HURT, H. D., MATHEWS, R., and INK, S. L. 1988. Biomedical considerations of oat dietary fiber and beta-glucans. Pages 206-222 in: Proc. 3rd Int. Oat Conf. Lund. B. Mattsson and R. Lyhagen, eds. Svalöf, Sweden.

HUSSAR, N., and ROBBLEE, A. R. 1962. Effects of pelleting on the utilization of feed by the growing chicken. Poult. Sci. 41:1489-1493.

ILLMAN, R. J., and TOPPING, D. L. 1985. Effects of dietary oat bran on faecal steroid excretion, plasma volatile fatty acids and lipid synthesis in rats. Nutr. Res. 5:839-846.

INGVERSEN, J., KOIE, B., and DOLL, H.

1973. Induced seed protein mutant of barley. Experientia 29:1151-1152.

JENDE-STRID, B. 1981. Characterization of mutants in barley affecting flavonoid synthesis. Pages 631-634 in: Barley Genetics IV. Proc. 4th Int. Barley Genet. Symp. R. N. H. Whitehouse, ed. Edinburgh University Press, Edinburgh.

JONASSEN, I. 1980. Characteristics of Hiproly barley. II. Quantification of two proteins contributing to its high lysine content. Carlsberg Res. Comm. 45:59-68.

JORGENSEN, K. G., and AASTRUP, S. 1988a. Determination of β-glucan in barley, malt, wort and beer. Pages 88-108 in: Modern Methods of Plant Analysis. Vol.7, Beer Analysis. H. F. Linskens and J. F. Jackson, eds. Springer-Verlag, New York.

JORGENSEN, K. G., and AASTRUP, S. 1988b. Quantification of $(1\rightarrow3)$ $(1\rightarrow4)$-β-D-glucan using Calcofluor complex formation and flow injection analysis. II. Determination of total β-glucan content of barley and malt. Carlsberg Res. Commun. 53:287-296.

JOSEPH, W. E. 1924. Feeding pigs in drylot. Mont. Agric. Exp. Stn. Bull., Bozeman, MT.

JUST, A. 1982. The influence of crude fiber from cereals on the net energy value of diets for growth in pigs. Livest. Prod. Sci. 9:569-580.

KAJALE, M. D. 1974. Ancient grains from India. Bull. Deccan College Postgrad. Res. Inst. 34:55-74.

KENT, N. L. 1983. Technology of Cereals, 3rd ed. Pergamon Press, Oxford, U.K.

KESTIN, M., MOSS, R., CLIFTON, P. M., and NESTEL, P. J. 1990. Comparative effects of three cereals brans on plasma lipids, blood pressure and glucose metabolism in mildly hypercholesterolemic men. Am. J. Clin. Nutr. 52:661-666.

KIRKMAN, M. A., SHEWRY, P. R., and MIFLIN, B. J. 1982. The effect of nitrogen nutrition on the lysine content and protein composition of barley seeds. J. Sci. Food Agric. 33:115-127.

KIRSI, M. 1973. Formation of proteinase inhibitors in developing barley grain. Physiol. Plant. 29:141-144.

KLOPFENSTEIN, C. F., and HOSENEY, R. C. 1987. Cholesterol-lowering effect of beta-glucan-enriched bread. Nutr. Rep. Int. 36:1091-1098.

KOIE, B., and DOLL, H. 1979. Protein and carbohydrate components in the Risø high-lysine barley mutants. Pages 205-215 in: Seed Protein Improvement in Cereals and Grain Legumes, I. Int. Atomic Energy Agency, Vienna.

KREFT, I. 1987. Pleiotropic effects of high-lysine genes and possibilities for breeding high yielding barley with improved nutritional quality. Pages 861-863 in: Barley Genetics V. Proc. 5th Int. Barley Genet. Symp. S. Yasuda and T. Konishi, eds. Sanyo Press Co. Ltd., Okayama, Japan.

KREIS, M. 1978. Starch and free sugars during kernel development of Bomi barley and its high-lysine mutant 1508. Pages 115-120 in: Seed Protein Improvement by Nuclear Techniques. Int. Atomic Energy Agency, Vienna, Austria.

KREIS, M., and DOLL, H. 1980. Starch and prolamin level in single and double high-lysine barley mutants. Physiol. Plant. 48:139-143.

KROMANN, R. P., FROSETH, J. A., and MEISER, W. E. 1976. Interactional digestible, metabolizable and net energy values of wheat and barley in swine. J. Anim. Sci. 42:1451-1459.

LaBERGE, D. E., and TIPPLES, K. H. 1989. Quality of Western Canadian malting barley. Crop Bull. 180. Canadian Grain Commission, Winnipeg.

LARSEN, L. M., and OLDFIELD, J. E. 1960. Improvement of barley rations for swine. II. Effects of pelleting and supplementation with barley malt. J. Anim. Sci. 19:601-606.

LARSEN, L. M., and OLDFIELD, J. E. 1961. Improvement of barley rations for swine. III. Effect of fibre from barley hulls and purified cellulose in barley and corn rations. J. Anim. Sci. 20:440-444.

LAWRENCE, T. L. J. 1970. High level cereal diets for the growing/finishing pig. J. Agric. Sci. 74:539-548.

LAWRENCE, T. L. J., THOMLINSON, J. R., and WHITNEY, J. C. 1980. Growth and gastric abnormalities in the growing pig, resulting from diets based on barley in different physical forms. Anim. Prod. 31:93-99.

LEAT, W. M. F. 1977. Depot fatty acids of Aberdeen Angus and Friesian cattle reared on hay and barley diets. J. Agric. Sci. 89:575-582.

LEHNINGER, A. L. 1982. Principles of Biochemistry. Worth Publishers, Inc., New York.

LEHTONEN, M., and AIKASALO, R. 1987a. Pentosans in barley varieties. Cereal Chem. 64:133-134.

LEHTONEN, M., and AIKASALO, R. 1987b. β-Glucan in two- and six-rowed barley. Cereal Chem. 64:191-193.

LILLIE, R. J., and DENTON, C. A. 1968. Evaluation of four cereal grains and three protein level combinations for layer performance. Poult. Sci. 47:1000-1004.

LINKO, P., HAKULIN, S., and LINKO, Y.-Y. 1983a. Extrusion cooking of barley starch for the production of glucose syrup and ethanol. J. Cereal Sci. 1:275-284.

LINKO, P., HÄRKÖNEN, H., and LINKO, Y.-Y. 1984. Effects of sodium chloride in the processing of bread baked from wheat, rye and barley flours. J. Cereal Sci. 2:53-62.

LINKO, Y.-Y. 1988. Novel approaches for biotechnical utilization of barley. Pages 87-92 in: Alternative End Uses of Barley. D. H. B. Sparrow, R. C. M. Lance, and R. J. Henry, eds. Waite Agricultural Research Institute, Glen Osmond, Australia.

LINKO, Y.-Y., MÄKELÄ, H., and LINKO, P. 1983b. A novel process for high-maltose syrup production from barley starch. Ann. N.Y. Acad. Sci. 413:352-354.

LOCKHART, W. C., and BRYANT, R. L. 1965. Barley for chickens? N.D. Farm Res. 32:17-21.

MAGNUS, E. M., FJELL, K. M., and STEINSHOLT, K. 1987. Barley flour in Norwegian wheat bread. Pages 377-384 in: Cereals in a European Context. I. D. Morton, ed. Ellis Horwood publishers, Chichester, England.

MANNION, P. F. 1981. Enzyme supplementation of barley based diets for broiler chickens. Aust. J. Exp. Agric. Anim. Husb. 21:296-302.

MARKSTROM, B., PETTERSSON, D., and HESSELMAN, K. 1985. Supplementation of β-glucanase to finely and coarsely ground barley—A feeding trial with weanling pigs. Rep. 149. Dept. of Animal Nutrition and Management, Swedish University of Agricultural Sciences, Uppsala, Sweden.

McALLISTER, T. A., CHENG, K.-J., RODE, L. M., and BUCHANAN-SMITH, J. G. 1990. Use of formaldehyde to regulate digestion of barley starch. Can. J. Anim. Sci. 70:581-589.

McCLEARY, B. V. 1988. Solubililty properties of barley beta-glucan. Pages 117-120 in: Alternative End Uses of Barley. D. H. B. Sparrow, R. C. M. Lance, and R. J. Henry, eds. Waite Agricultural Research Institute, Glen Osmond, Australia.

McCLEARY, B. V., and GLENNIE-HOLMES, M. 1985. Enzymatic quantification of (1→3) (1→4)-β-D-glucan in barley and malt. J. Inst. Brew. 91:285-295.

McGUIRE, C. F. 1979. Roller milling and quality evaluation of barley flour. Pages 89-93 in: Proc. Joint Barley Utilization Seminar. Korean Sci. Eng. Foundation, Suweon, Korea.

McINTOSH, G. H., WHYTE, J., McARTHUR, R., and NESTEL, P. L. 1991. Barley and wheat foods: Influence on plasma cholesterol concentrations in hypercholesterolemic men. Am. J. Clin. Nutr. 53:1205-1209.

McINTOSH, J. I., SLINGER, S. J. SIBBALD, I. R., and ASHTON, G. C. 1962. Factors affecting the metabolizable energy content of poultry feeds. 7. The effects of grinding, pelleting and grit feeding on the availability of the energy of wheat, corn, oats and barley. 8. A study on the effects of dietary balance. Poult. Sci. 41:445-456.

MERRITT, N. R. 1967. A new strain of barley with starch of high amylose content. J. Inst. Brew. 73:583-585.

MERTZ, E. T., BATES, L. S., and NELSON, O. E. 1964. Mutant gene that changes protein composition and increases lysine content in maize endosperm. Science 45:279-280.

MIDDAUGH, K. F., FROSETH, J. A., ULLRICH, S. E., and MALES, J. R. 1989. The relationship among chemical composition, digestibility and feeding value of dryland and irrigated barleys for young pigs. Proc. Wash. State Univ. 4:17-24.

MIKOLA, J., and KIRSI, M. 1972. Differences between endospermal and embryonal trypsin inhibitors in barley, wheat, and rye. Acta Chem. Scand. 26:787-795.

MIKOLA, J., and SUOLINNA, E.-M. 1969. Purification and properties of a trypsin inhibitor from barley. Eur. J. Biochem. 9:555-560.

MILLER, D. F. 1958. Composition of cereal grains and forages. Publ. 585. National Academy of Sciences, National Research Council, Washington, DC.

MISIR, R., and SAUER, W. C. 1980. Nutritional evaluation of high lysine barley for growing pigs. Abstr. Can. J. Anim. Sci. 60:1052.

MITCHALL, K. G., BELL, J. M., and SOSULSKI, F. W. 1976. Digestibility and feeding value of hulless barley for pigs. Can. J. Anim. Sci. 56:505-511.

MONGEAU, R., and BRASSARD, R. 1990. Determination of insoluble, soluble, and total dietary fiber: Collaborative study of a rapid gravimetric method. Cereal Foods World 35:319-323, 325.

MORAN, J. B. 1986. Cereal grains in complete diets for dairy cows: A comparison of rolled barley, wheat and oats and of three methods of processing oats. Anim. Prod. 43:27-36.

MORGAN, C. A., and WHITTEMORE, C. T. 1982. Energy evaluation of feeds and compounded diets for pigs. A review. Anim. Feed Sci. Technol. 7:387-400.

MORRISON, W. R. 1978. Cereal lipids. Pages 221-348 in: Advances in Cereal Science and Technology, Vol. 2. Y. Pomeranz, ed. Am.

Assoc. Cereal Chem., St. Paul, MN.
MORRISON, W. R., SCOTT, D. C., and KARKALAS, J. 1986. Variation in the composition and physical properties of barley starches. Starch/Staerke 38:374-379.
MOSS, B. R., and PRIER, S. G. 1981. High levels of barley in rations for calves and lactating cows. J. Dairy Sci. (Suppl. 1) 64:128.
MOSS, B. R., LAUDERT, S. B., STOCKTON, G., MILLER, C., and BALDRIDGE, D. 1980. Nutritional value of waxy versus normal barley for ruminants. Nutr. Rep. Int. 21:487-495.
MOSS, B. R., EL-NEGOUMY, A. M., and NEWMAN, C. W. 1983. Nutritional value of waxy barleys for broiler chickens. Anim. Feed Sci. Technol. 8:25-34.
MUNCK, L. 1981. Barley for food, feed and industry. Pages 427-460 in: Cereals, A Renewable Resource. Y. Pomeranz and L. Munck, eds. Am. Assoc. Cereal Chem., St. Paul, MN.
MUNCK, L. 1992. The case of high-lysine barley breeding. Pages 573-601 in: Barley: Genetics, Biochemistry, Molecular Biology and Biotechnology. P. R. Shewry, ed. CAB International, Wallingford, U.K.
MUNCK, L., KARLSSON, K. E., and HAGBERG, A. 1969. Selection and characterization of a high-protein, high-lysine variety from the World Barley Collection. Pages 544-558 in: Barley Genetics II. Proc. 2nd Int. Barley Genet. Symp. R. A. Nilan, ed. Washington State University Press, Pullman, WA.
MUNCK, L., KARLSSON, K. E., HAGBERG, A., and EGGUM, B. O. 1970. Gene for improved nutritional value in barley seed protein. Science 168:985-987.
MUNCK, L., REXEN, F., and HAASTRUP, L. 1988. Cereal starches within the European Community—Agricultural production, dry and wet milling and potential use in industry. Starch/Staerke 40:81-87.
NASI, M. 1985. Replacing protein supplements in barley-based diets for growing pigs with free lysine and methionine. J. Agric. Sci. (Helsinki) 57:245-253.
NAS-NRC. 1984. Nutrient Requirements of Poultry. 8th rev. ed. National Academy of Sciences, National Research Council, Washington, DC.
NAS-NRC. 1988. Nutrient Requirements of Swine. 9th rev. ed. National Academy of Sciences, National Research Council, Washington, DC.
NELSON, O. E., MERTZ, E. T., and BATES, L. S. 1965. Second mutant gene affecting the amino acid pattern of maize endosperm proteins. Science 150:1469-1470.

NEWMAN, C. W., and ESLICK, R. F. 1970. Barley varieties for swine diets. Proc. West. Sect. Am. Soc. Anim. Sci. 21:111-116.
NEWMAN, C. W., and McGUIRE, C. F. 1985. Nutritional quality of barley. Pages 403-456 in: Barley Agronomy Monogr. 26. D. C. Rasmusson, ed. American Society of Agronomy, Madison, WI.
NEWMAN, C. W., and NEWMAN, R. K. 1990. Improved performance of weanling pigs fed a low β-glucan barley. Proc. West. Sect. Am. Soc. Anim. Sci. 41:223-226.
NEWMAN, C. W., THOMAS, O. O., and ESLICK, R. F. 1968. Hulless barley in diets for weanling pigs. J. Anim. Sci. 27:981-984.
NEWMAN, C. W., ESLICK, R. F., MOSS, B.R., and EL-NEGOUMY, A. M. 1977. Hiproly barley as a source of protein and amino acids for growing-finishing pigs. Nutr. Rep. Int. 15:383-390.
NEWMAN, C. W., ESLICK, R. F., CALVERT, C. C., and EL-NEGOUMY, A. M. 1978. Comparative nutritive value of Glacier and high amylose Glacier barleys. J. Anim. Sci. 47:448-455.
NEWMAN, C. W., ESLICK, R. F., PEPPER, J. W., and EL-NEGOUMY, A. M. 1980. Performance of pigs fed hulless and covered barleys supplemented with or without a bacterial diastase. Nutr. Rep. Int. 22:833-837.
NEWMAN, C. W., EL-NEGOUMY, A. M., and ESLICK, R. F. 1981. Genetic factors affecting the feed quality of barley. Pages 299-304 in: Barley Genetics IV. Proc. 4th Int. Barley Genet. Symp. R. N. H. Whitehouse, ed. Edinburgh University Press, Edinburgh.
NEWMAN, C. W., ESLICK, R. F., and EL-NEGOUMY, A. M. 1983. Bacterial diastase effect on the feed value of two hulless barleys for pigs. Nutr. Rep. Int. 28:139-146.
NEWMAN, C. W., NEWMAN, R. K., BOLIN-HEINTZMAN, K., ROTH, N. J., and HOCKETT, E. A. 1987a. Factors affecting protein utilization in proanthocyanidin-free barley. Pages 833-840 in: Barley Genetics V. Proc. 5th Int. Barley Genet. Symp. S. Yasuda and T. Konishi, eds. Sanyo Press Co. Ltd., Okayama, Japan.
NEWMAN, C. W., OVERLAND, M., NEWMAN, R. K., BANG-OLSEN, K., and PEDERSEN, B. 1990b. Protein quality of a new high-lysine barley derived from Riso 1508. Can. J. Anim. Sci. 70:279-285.
NEWMAN, R. K., and NEWMAN, C. W. 1987. β-Glucanase effect on the performance of broiler chicks fed covered and hulless barley isotypes having normal and waxy starch. Nutr. Rep. Int. 36:693-699.
NEWMAN, R. K., and NEWMAN, C. W. 1988. Nutritive value of a new hull-less barley

cultivar in broiler chick diets. Poult. Sci. 67:1573-1579.

NEWMAN, R. K., NEWMAN, C. W., EL-NEGOUMY, A. M., and AASTRUP, S. 1984. Nutritional quality of proantho-cyanidin-free barley. Nutr. Rep. Int. 30:809-816.

NEWMAN, R. K., NEWMAN, C. W., FADEL, J., and GRAHAM, H. 1987b. Nutritional implications of β-glucans in barley. Pages 773-780 in: Barley Genetics V. Proc. 5th Int. Barley Genet. Symp. S. Yasuda and T. Konishi, eds. Sanyo Press Co. Ltd., Okayama, Japan.

NEWMAN, R. K., NEWMAN, C. W., and McGUIRE, C. F. 1988. Barley for food products: Functionality and health implications. Pages 55-59 in: Alternative End Uses of Barley. D. H. B. Sparrow, R. C. M. Lance, and R. J. Henry, eds. Waite Agricultural Research Institute, Glen Osmond, Australia.

NEWMAN, R. K., LEWIS, S. E., NEWMAN, C. W., BOIK, R. J., and RAMAGE, R. T. 1989. Hypocholesterolemic effect of barley foods on healthy men. Nutr. Rep. Int. 39:749-760.

NEWMAN, R. K., McGUIRE, C. F., and NEWMAN, C. W. 1990a. Composition and muffin-baking characteristics of flours from four barley cultivars. Cereal Foods World 35:563-566.

NYMAN, M., ASP, N.-G., PEDERSEN, B., and EGGUM, B. O. 1985. Fermentation of dietary fibre in the intestinal tract of rats— A comparison of flours with different extraction rates from six cereals. J. Cereal Sci. 3:207-219.

OAKENFULL, D. G., and HOOD, R. 1988. Do barley beta-glucans lower plasma cholesterol? The evidence from studies with oat bran. Pages 43-47 in: Alternative End Uses of Barley. D. H. B. Sparrow, R. C. M. Lance, and R. J. Henry, eds. Waite Agricultural Research Institute, Glen Osmond, Australia.

ORAM, R. N. 1988. High lysine mutants in barley. Pages 83-86 in: Alternative End Uses of Barley. D. H. B. Sparrow, R. C. M. Lance, and R. J. Henry, eds. Waite Agricultural Research Institute, Glen Osmond, Australia.

ORGANIZATION FOR ECONOMIC COOPERATION AND DEVELOPMENT. 1988. Food Consumption Statistics. 1976-1985. The Organization, Paris, France.

ORSKOV, E. R. 1986. Starch digestion and utilization in ruminants. J. Anim. Sci. 63:1624-1633.

ORSKOV, E. R., DUNCAN, W. R. H., and CARNIE, C. A. 1975. Cereal processing and

food utilization by sheep. 3. The effect of replacing whole barley by whole oats on food utilization and firmness and composition of subcutaneous fat. Anim. Prod. 21:51-58.

PARSONS, J. G., and PRICE, P. B. 1974. Search for barley (*Hordeum vulgare* L.) with higher lipid content. Lipids 9:804-808.

PEDERSEN, B., and EGGUM, B. O. 1983. The influence of milling on the nutritive value of flour from cereal grains. 3. Barley. Qual. Plant. Plant Foods Hum. Nutr. 33:99-112.

PEDERSEN, B., BACH KNUDSEN, K. E., and EGGUM, B. O. 1989a. Nutritive value of cereal products with emphasis on the effect of milling. World Rev. Nutr. Diet. 60:1-91.

PEDERSEN, B., HANSEN, M., MUNCK, L., and EGGUM, B. O. 1989b. Weaning foods with improved energy and nutrient density prepared from germinated cereals. 2. Nutritional evaluation of gruels based on barley. Food Nutr. Bull. 11:46-52.

PEREZ, J. M., RAMOELINTSALAMA, B., and BOURDON, D. 1980. Energy evaluation of barley for pigs. Prediction from analyses of fibre content. J. Rech. Porc. Fr. 12:273-284.

PERSSON, G. 1984. Methods for the genetic improvement of quality and quantity in barley. Pages 105-110 in: Cereal Grain Protein Improvement. Int. Atomic Energy Agency, Vienna.

PERSSON, G., and KARLSSON, K.-E. 1977. Progress in breeding for improved nutritive value in barley. Cereal Res. Comm. 5:53-58.

PETERSEN, V. E. 1969. A comparison of the feeding value for broilers of corn, grain sorghum, wheat and oats and the influence of various grains on the composition and taste of broiler meat. Poult. Sci. 48:2006-2013.

PHILLIPS, S. F., and STEPHEN, A. M. 1981. The structure and function of the large intestine. Nutr. Today 16:4-12.

POMERANZ, Y. 1974. Food uses of barley. Crit. Rev. Food Technol. 4:377-394.

POMERANZ, Y., KE, H., and WARD, A. B. 1971. Composition and utilization of milled barley products. I. Gross composition of roller-milled and air-separated fractions. Cereal Chem. 48:47-58.

POMERANZ, Y., ROBBINS, G. S., SMITH, R. T., CRADDOCK, J. C., GILBERTSON, J. T., and MOSEMAN, J. G. 1976. Protein content and amino acid composition of barleys from the world collection. Cereal Chem. 53:497-504.

POTTER, L. M., STUTZ, M. W., and MATTERSON, L. D. 1965. Metabolizable energy and digestibility coefficients of barley for chicks as influenced by water treatment or by presence of fungal enzyme. Poult. Sci.

44:565-573.

PRENTICE, N., and D'APPOLONIA, B. L. 1977. High-fiber bread containing brewer's spent grain. Cereal Chem. 54:1084-1095.

PRENTICE, N., KISSELL, L. T., LINDSAY, R. C., and YAMAZAKI, W. T. 1978. High-fiber cookies containing brewers' spent grain. Cereal Chem. 55:712-721.

PRICE, P. B., and PARSONS, J. 1979. Distribution of lipids in embryonic axis, bran-endosperm, and hull fractions of hulless barley and hulless oat grain. Agric. Food Chem. 27:813-815.

PROSKY, L., ASP, N.-G., SCHWEIZER, T. F., DeVRIES, J. W., and FURDA, I. 1988. Determination of insoluble, soluble and total dietary fiber in foods and food products: Interlaboratory study. J. Assoc. Off. Anal. Chem. 71:1017-1023.

QURESHI, A. A., BURGER, W. C., PRENTICE, N., BIRD, H. R., and SUNDE, M. L. 1980. Regulation of lipid metabolism in chicken liver by dietary cereals. J. Nutr. 110:388-393.

QURESHI, A. A., BURGER, W. C., ELSON, C. E., and BENEVENGA, N. J. 1982. Effects of cereals and culture filtrate of *Trichoderma viride* on lipid metabolism of swine. Lipids 17:924-934.

QURESHI, A. A., BURGER, W. C., PETERSON, D. M., and ELSON, C. 1985. Suppression of cholesterogenesis by plant constituents: Review of Wisconsin contributions to NC-167. Lipids 20:817-824.

QURESHI, A. A., BURGER, W. C., PETERSON, D. M., and ELSON, C. E. 1986. The structure of an inhibitor of cholesterol biosynthesis isolated from barley. J. Biol. Chem. 261:10544-10550.

QURESHI, A. A., CHAUDHARY, V., WEBER, F. E., CHICOYE, E., and QURESHI, N. 1991. Effects of brewer's grain and other cereals on lipid metabolism in chicken. Nutr. Res. 11:159-168.

RANHOTRA, G. S., GELROTH, J. A., ASTROTH, K., and BHATTY, R. S. 1991. Relative lipidemic responses in rats fed barley and oat meals and their fractions. Cereal Chem. 68:548-551.

REIMER, D., MEADE, R. J., and GRANT, R. S. 1964. Barley rations for swine. III. Lysine and methionine supplementation: Effects on rate and efficiency of gain and on carcass characteristics. J. Anim. Sci. 23:404-408.

ROEDIGER, W. E. W. 1982. Utilization of nutrients by isolated epithelial cells of the rat colon. Gastroenterology 83:424-429.

ROSSNAGEL, B. G., CAMPBELL, G. L., CLASSEN, H. L., and BHATTY, R. S. 1988.

Barley for poultry feeding. Pages 111-114 in: Alternative End Uses of Barley. D. H. B. Sparrow, R. C. M. Lance, and R. J. Henry, eds. Waite Agricultural Research Institute, Glen Osmond, Australia.

ROTTER, B. A., MARQUARDT, R. R., GUENTER, W., BILIADERIS, C., and NEWMAN, C. W. 1989a. In vitro viscosity measurements of barley extracts as predictors of growth responses in chicks fed barley-based diets supplemented with a fungal enzyme preparation. Can. J. Anim. Sci. 69:431-439.

ROTTER, B. A., NESKAR, M. GUENTER, W., and MARQUARDT, R. R. 1989b. Effect of enzyme supplementation on the nutritive value of hulless barley in chicken diets. Anim. Feed Sci. Technol. 24:233-245.

ROTTER, B. A., NESKAR, M., MARQUARDT, R. R., and GUENTER, W. 1989c. Effects of different enzyme preparations on the nutritional value of barley in chicken diets. Nutr. Rep. Int. 39:107-120.

ROTTER, B. A., FRIESEN, O. D., GUENTER, W., and MARQUARDT, R. R. 1990a. Influence of enzyme supplementation on the bioavailable energy of barley. Poult. Sci. 69:1174-1181.

ROTTER, B. A., MARQUARDT, R. R., GUENTER, W., and CROW, G. H. 1990b. Evaluation of 3 enzymatic methods as predictors of in vivo response to enzyme supplementation of barley based diets when fed to young chicks. J. Sci. Food Agric. 50:19-27.

RYU, S. 1979. Grain quality of barley for human diet. Pages 94-108 in: Proc. Joint Barley Utilization Seminar. Korean Sci. Eng. Foundation. Suweon, Korea.

SAUER, W. C., GIOVANNETTI, P. M., and STOTHERS, S. C. 1974. Availability of amino acids from barley, wheat and triticale and soybean meal for growing pigs. Can. J. Anim. Sci. 54:97-105.

SAUER, W. C., STOTHERS, S. C., and PHILLIPS, G. D. 1977. Apparent availabilities of amino acids in corn, wheat and barley for growing pigs. Can. J. Anim. Sci. 57:585-597.

SAUER, W. C., KENNELLY, J. J., AHERNE, F. X., and CICHON, R. M. 1981. Availabilities of amino acids in barley and wheat for growing pigs. Can. J. Anim. Sci. 61:793-802.

SCHOLZ, F. 1976. Problems of breeding for high protein yield in barley. Pages 548-556 in: Barley Genetics III. Proc. 3rd Int. Barley Genet. Symp. H. Gaul, ed. Verlag Karl Theimig, Munich.

SCHWEIZER, T. F. 1989. Dietary fibre

analysis. Lebensm. Wiss. Technol. 22:54-59.

SEKO, H., and KATO, I. 1981. Breeding for high-lysine hull-less barley. Pages 336-340 in: Barley Genetics IV. Proc. 4th Int. Barley Genet. Symp. R. N. H. Whitehouse, ed. Edinburgh University Press, Edinburgh.

SENDRA, J. M., and CARBONELL, J. V. 1989. Determination of β-glucan in wort and beer by its binding with Calcofluor, using a fluorometric flow-injection-analysis (FIA) method. J. Inst. Brew. 95:327-332.

SHEWRY, P. R., and MIFLIN, B. J. 1985. Seed storage proteins of economically important cereals. Pages 1-83 in: Advances in Cereal Science and Technology 7. Y. Pomeranz, ed. Am. Assoc. Cereal Chem., St. Paul, MN.

SHEWRY, P. R., BRIGHT, S. W. J., BURGESS, S. R., MIFLIN, B. J. 1984. Approaches to improving the nutritional quality of barley seed proteins. Pages 227-239 in: Cereal Grain Protein Improvement. Int. Atomic Energy Agency, Vienna, Austria.

SIBBALD, I. R. 1976. The effect of cold pelleting on the true metabolizable energy values of cereal grains fed to adult roosters and a comparison of observed with predicted metabolizable energy values. Poult. Sci. 55:970-974.

SIBBALD, I. R. 1979. A new technique for estimating the ME content of feeds for poultry. Pages 38-43 in: Standardization of Analytical Methodology for Feeds, IDRC-134e. W. J. Pigden, C. C. Balch, and M. Graham, eds. International Development Research Centre, Ottawa, Canada.

SIBBALD, I. R. 1982. The effect of grinding on the true metabolizable energy value of hull-less barley. Poult. Sci. 61:2509-2511.

SIBBALD, I. R., and PRICE, K. 1976a. Relationships between metabolizable energy values for poultry and some physical and chemical data describing Canadian wheat, oats and barleys. Can. J. Anim. Sci. 56:255-268.

SIBBALD, I. R., and PRICE, K. 1976b. True metabolizable energy values for poultry of Canadian barleys measured by bioassay and predicted from physical and chemical data. Can. J. Anim. Sci. 56:775-782.

SIBBALD, I. R., PRICE, K., and BARRETTE, J. P. 1980. The metabolizable energy values for poultry of commercial diets measured by bioassay and predicted from chemical data. Poult. Sci. 59:808-811.

SILANO, V. 1977. Factors affecting digestibility and availability of proteins in cereals. Pages 13-46 in: Nutritional Evaluation of Cereal Mutants. Int. Atomic Energy Agency, Vienna, Austria.

SIMMONDS, D. H. 1978. Structure, composition and biochemistry of cereal grains. Pages 105-138 in: Cereals '78: Better Nutrition for the World's Millions. Y. Pomeranz, ed. Am. Assoc. Cereal Chem., St. Paul, MN.

SIMONSSON, A. 1978a. Some effects of the fineness of ground barley on the performance of growing pigs: Growth rate, feed conversion efficiency, digestibility and carcass quality. Swed. J. Agric. Res. 8:75-84.

SIMONSSON, A. 1978b. Some effects of including barley processed by different mill types in the diet of growing pigs: Growth rate, feed conversion efficiency, digestibility and carcass quality. Swed. J. Agric. Res. 8:85-96.

SINGH, R., and AXTELL, J. D. 1973. High lysine mutant gene (hl) that improves protein quality and biological value of grain sorghum. Crop Sci. 13:535-539.

SMITH, D. B., MORGAN, A. G., and AASTRUP, S. 1980. Variation in the biochemical composition of acid extracts from barley of contrasting malting quality. J. Inst. Brew. 86:277-283.

SOLDEVILA, M., and MEADE, R. J. 1964. Barley rations for swine. II. The influence of L-lysine and DL-methionine supplementation of barley-soybean meal diets upon the rate and efficiency of gain and upon nitrogen retention of growing swine. J. Anim. Sci. 23:397-403.

SOMEL, K. 1988. The importance of barley in food production and demand in West Asia and North Africa. Curr. Top. Vet. Med. Anim. Sci. 47:27-35.

SPICER, H., and AHERNE, F. X. 1988. An evaluation of a new variety of hulless barley (TR607) for young pigs. 66th Annual Feeders' Day Rep. University of Alberta, Edmonton, Canada.

SPICER, H., and AHERNE, F. X. 1990. Nutritional evaluation of hulless barley (Condor) for starter and growing pigs. 69th Annual Feeders' Day Rep. University of Alberta, Edmonton, Canada.

SVENDSEN, I., MARTIN, B., and JONASSEN, I. 1980. Characteristics of Hiproly barley. III. Amino acid sequences of two lysine-rich proteins. Carlsberg Res. Comm. 45:79-85.

SWAIN, J. F., ROUSE, I. L., CURLEY, C. B., and SACKS, F. M. 1990. Comparison of the effects of oat bran and low-fiber wheat on serum lipoprotein levels and blood pressure. New Engl. J. Med. 322:147-152.

SWANSON, R. B., and PENFIELD, M. P. 1988. Barley flour level and salt level selection for a whole-grain bread formula. J. Food Sci. 53:896-901.

TALLBERG, A. 1977. The amino-acid composition in endosperm and embryo of a barley variety and its high lysine mutant. Hereditas 87:43-46.

TALLBERG, A. 1982. Characterization of high-lysine barley genotypes. Hereditas 96:229-245.

TALLBERG, A., and EGGUM, B. O. 1986. Grain yields and nutritional qualities of some high-lysine barley hybrids. J. Cereal Sci. 4:345-352.

TAVERNER, M. R. 1988. Nutritional constraints to the feeding value of barley for pigs and poultry. Pages 29-34 in: Alternative End Uses of Barley. D. H. B. Sparrow, R. C. M. Lance, and R. J. Henry, eds. Waite Agricultural Research Institute, Glen Osmond, Australia.

TAVERNER, M. R., HUME, I. D., and FARRELL, D. J. 1981. Availability to pigs of amino acids in cereal grains. II. Apparent and true ileal availability. Br. J. Nutr. 46:159-171.

TAYLOR, P. F., FROSETH, J. A., ULLRICH, S. E., and MALES, J. R. 1985. The effect of cultivar and growing season on the feeding value of barley for growing swine. Proc. West. Sec. Am. Soc. Anim. Sci. 36:260-264.

THACKER, P. A., BELL, J. M., CLASSEN, H. L., CAMPBELL, G. L., and ROSSNAGEL, B. G. 1988a. The nutritive value of hulless barley for swine. Anim. Feed Sci. Technol. 19:191-196.

THACKER, P. A., CAMPBELL, G. L., and GROOTWASSINK, J. W. D. 1988b. The effect of β-glucanase supplementation on the performance of pigs fed hulless barley. Nutr. Rep. Int. 38:91-99.

THACKER, P. A., CAMPBELL, G. L., and GROOTWASSINK, J. W. D. 1989. The effect of sodium bentonite on the performance of pigs fed barley-based diets supplemented with beta-glucanase. Nutr. Rep. Int. 40:613-620.

THOMKE, S. O., and HELLBERG, A. 1976. Effect of different treatments on the feeding value of barley harvested at two stages of ripeness. Acta Agric. Scand. 26:25-32.

THOMKE, S. O., RUNDGREN, M., and ELWINGER, K. 1978. Evaluation of Hiproly-type barleys fed to rats, pigs, broilers and laying hens. Swed. J. Agric. Res. 8:39-53.

TOMMERVIK, R. S., and WALDERN, D. E. 1969. Comparative feeding value of wheat, corn, barley, milo, oats, and a mixed concentrate ration for lactating cows. J. Dairy Sci. 52:68-73.

TORP, J., DOLL, H., and HAAHR, V. 1981. Genotypic and environmental influence upon the nutritional composition of barley grain. Euphytica 30:719-728.

TREMERE, A. W., and BHATTY, R. S. 1989. Food uses of barley. Pages 123-128 in: Proc. Prairie Barley Symp. University of Saskatchewan, Saskatoon, Canada.

TRUSCOTT, D. R., NEWMAN, C. W., and ROTH, N. J. 1988. Effect of hull and awn type on the feeding value of Betzes barley. III. Growth performance, carcass characteristics and nitrogen and energy digestibilities by pigs. Nutr. Rep. Int. 38:221-230.

TSEN, C. C., WEBER, J. L., and EYESTONE, W. 1983. Evaluation of distillers' dried grain flour as a bread ingredient. Cereal Chem. 60:295-297.

ULLRICH, S. E., HONEYFIELD, D. E., and FROSETH, J. A. 1984a. Variation in the composition of Western grown barley. Proc. West. Sec. Am. Soc. Anim. Sci. 35:163-166.

ULLRICH, S. E., KLEINHOFS, A., COON, C. N., and NILAN, R. A. 1984b. Breeding for improved protein in barley. Pages 93-103 in: Cereal Grain Protein Improvement. Int. Atomic Energy Agency, Vienna, Austria.

UNIV. MANITOBA. 1990. 36th annual progress review. University of Manitoba, Faculty of Agriculture, Winnipeg.

VAN RAMSHORST, H., and THOMAS, P. C. 1988. Digestion in sheep of diets containing barley chemically treated to reduce its ruminal degradability. J. Sci. Food Agric. 42:1-7.

VIUF, B. T. 1969. Breeding of barley varieties with high-protein content with respect to quality. Pages 23-28 in: New Approaches to Breeding for Improved Plant Protein. Int. Atomic Energy Agency, Vienna, Austria.

VOSE, J. R., and YOUNGS, C. G. 1978. Fractionation of barley and malted barley flours by air classification. Cereal Chem. 55:280-286.

WALDERN, D. E., and CEDENO, G. 1970. Comparative acceptability and nutritive value of barley, wheat mixed feed and a concentrate ration in meal and pelleted form for feeding cows. J. Dairy Sci. 53:317-324.

WARCHALEWSKI, J. R., and SKUPIN, J. 1973. Isolation and properties of trypsin and chymotrypsin inhibitors from barley grits after storage. J. Sci. Food Agric. 24:995-1009.

WEAVER, C. M., CHEN, P. H., and RYNEARSON, S. L. 1981. Effect of milling on trace element and protein content of oats and barley. Cereal Chem. 58:120-124.

WEBER, F. E., and CHAUDHARY, V. K. 1987. Recovery and nutritional evaluation of dietary fiber ingredients from a barley by-product. Cereal Foods World 32:548-550.

WELCH, R. W. 1978. Genotypic variation in oil and protein in barley grain. J. Sci. Food Agric. 29:953-958.

WELTZIEN, E. M., and AHERNE, F. X. 1987. The effects of anaerobic storage and processing of high moisture barley and its ileal digestibility by, and performance of growing pigs. Can. J. Anim. Sci. 67:829-840.

WENDORF, F., SCHILD, R., EL HADIDI, N., CLOSE, A. E., KOBUSIEWICZ, M., WIECKOWSKA, H., ISSAWI, B., and HAAS, H. 1979. Use of barley in the Egyptian Late Paleolithic. Science 205:1341-1347.

WHITE, W. B., BIRD, H. R., SUNDE, M. L., PRENTICE, N., BURGER, W. C., and MARLETT, J. A. 1981. The viscosity interaction of barley beta-glucan with *Trichoderma viride* cellulase in the chick intestine. Poult. Sci. 60:1043-1048.

WHITE, W. B., BIRD, H. R., SUNDE, M. L., and MARLETT, J. A. 1983. Viscosity of β-D-glucan as a factor in the enzymatic improvement of barley for chicks. Poult. Sci. 62:853-862.

WHITMORE, E. T. 1960. Rapid method for determination of the husk content of barley and oats. J. Inst. Brew. 66:407-408.

WIEBE, G. A. 1979. Introduction of barley into the new world. Pages 2-8 in: Barley: Origin, Botany, Culture, Winter Hardiness, Genetics, Utilization, Pests. Agricultural Handbook 338. U.S. Dept. Agric., Sci. and Educ. Admin., Washington, DC.

WILLINGHAM, H. E., LEONG, K. D., JENSEN, L. I., and McGINNIS, J. 1960. Influence of geographical area of production on response of different barley samples to enzyme supplements or water treatment. Poult. Sci. 39:103-108.

WILSON, B. J., and McNAB, J. M. 1975. Diets containing conventional, naked and high-amylose barleys for broilers. Br. Poult. Sci. 16:497-504.

WISKER, E., FELDHEIM, W., POMERANZ, Y., and MEUSER, F. 1985. Dietary fiber in cereals. Pages 169-238 in: Advances in Cereal Science and Technology, Vol 7. Y. Pomeranz, ed. Am. Assoc. Cereal Chem., St. Paul, MN.

WOOD, P. J., WEISZ, J., FEDEC, P., and BURROWS, V. D. 1989. Large-scale preparation and properties of oat fractions enriched in $(1{\rightarrow}3)(1{\rightarrow}4)$-β-D-glucan. Cereal Chem. 66:97-103.

WU, J. F., and EWAN, R. C. 1979. Utilization of energy of wheat and barley by young swine. J. Anim. Sci. 49:1470-1477.

CHAPTER 9

POTENTIAL IMPROVEMENT OF BARLEY QUALITY THROUGH GENETIC ENGINEERING

K. J. KASHA
D. E. FALK
A. ZIAUDDIN
Crop Science Department
University of Guelph
Guelph, Ontario
Canada N1G 2W1

INTRODUCTION

The parallel evolution of improvements in plant cell culture systems and molecular technology has created new opportunities for the genetic engineering of plants. Thus, we can look forward to improvements in malting or feed quality through 1) altering the barley grain composition by DNA manipulation or the stabilization of gene expression and 2) developing methods for identification of important genes or their expression products and of cultivars. A great deal of industry time and money can be wasted by being unable to identify the cultivars or the level of purity in seed lots. Molecular tools and genetic engineering may be able to overcome such obstacles. The potential impact of these tools is limited by our knowledge of the important processes (biochemical pathways and their control) and DNA organization within the cells and plants. Although progress is amazingly rapid, many applications may be years away.

The popular view of genetic engineering equates it with transformation, i.e., the stable integration of DNA or genes into a new genome. Although this sounds simple enough, there are a multitude of prerequisites to that final phase. First, an understanding is needed of how a trait is inherited, how many genes are involved, their location on chromosomes, and the stability of gene expression. These can be examined through molecular mapping and tagging tools such as restriction fragment length polymorphism (RFLP) or random amplified polymorphic DNAs (RAPDs). In barley, a number of such efforts are in progress (Graner et al, 1990; Blake et al, 1991; Heun et al, 1991). Ideally, the next major step would be to isolate and characterize the important genes in a malting process such as α-amylase or β-glucanase genes.

419

Subsequently, the genes would need to be cloned and linked with effective promoters and selection markers to ensure that the genes would be expressed and identified in transformation experiments. Finally, a cell culture system is desired where, ideally, single cells can be transformed and regenerated into plants. In cereals, the development of an effective single-cell culture system has been lagging behind work in other species, but it is feasible in barley at this time (Kasha et al, 1992; Lörz and Lazzeri, 1992). However, the need to isolate important genes to manipulate in barley is a major limitation for transformation at present.

Transformation is not the only aspect of genetic engineering that could be utilized for crop improvement. Understanding the inheritance of traits and tagging desired alleles with DNA markers is equally important to breeding and transformation. The major challenge in breeding is to identify desirable genetic variability and then to select for it genotypically rather than phenotypically (Cubitt, 1991). Molecular tags will allow breeders to follow specific alleles through the breeding generations and, by increasing selection efficiency, decrease population sizes. Most molecular approaches are too costly at present, and their widespread use in breeding will depend upon the evolution of improved and simplified procedures. However, Cubitt (1991) indicates that nearly all the major plant breeding companies in the world have programs on RFLP mapping.

Traditionally, genetic modification of crops has been achieved by plant breeding, which will continue to be the major approach for improvement. Plant breeding requires a source of genetic variation (germ plasm collections, mutation, or related species), followed by hybridization and selection of recombinants to produce adapted cultivars. The techniques of molecular biology offer a whole new focus on more specific and precise changes to desired traits that may be incorporated into new cultivars.

In this chapter we examine areas that might be improved relative to malting, brewing, feed, and food uses of barley. While recognizing that vast amounts of work are still needed, we then discuss possible approaches to achieve genetic modifications through genetic engineering.

POTENTIAL AREAS OF IMPROVEMENT
FOR MALTING, BREWING, FEED, AND FOOD USES

Barley is an ancient crop with a long history of association with civilized peoples. Originally domesticated as a major staple food crop (Harlan, 1968), barley was put to use in various ways by an evolving society as the special properties of barley were recognized. In most cultures, barley has largely been replaced as a food crop by wheat because of the leavening ability of the gluten proteins that wheat contains. Barley has been relegated to the category of "coarse grains" because of its use primarily as a feed grain. The use of barley in producing malt and brewing beer is quite old, dating from Egyptian times (Hardwick, 1977). The ability of barley to develop high levels of amylolytic enzymes and then convert large amounts of carbohydrates to highly fermentable sugars has earned it a unique place among domesticated plant species.

Although the end-uses of barley are somewhat diverse, the quality criteria often overlap and in many cases are not greatly different (Table 1). These are discussed briefly.

Comparison of Traits

STARCH

The primary function of barley for all end-uses is to provide a source of energy in the form of carbohydrate (starch). This energy is used for growth or maintenance in humans and animals or for conversion to fermentable sugars for yeast fermentation such as in the brewing and distilling industries. The starch content can vary greatly, depending on environmental and genetic factors. The starch in barley generally contains about 75% amylopectin and 25% amylose (Foster and Prentice, 1987). Genetic factors can alter this ratio to produce nearly 100% amylopectin (waxy barley) (Goering and Eslick, 1976) or elevated levels of amylose (Merritt, 1967). The ratio of amylose to amylopectin is under genetic control and could be altered across a wide range to provide various types of starches for specific industrial processes. The gene structure and the control of expression of the enzymes responsible for the conversion of sucrose are currently under intensive investigation by a collaborative group of Nordic scientists (Shulman et al, 1991).

PROTEINS

After energy or starch, protein is probably next in importance in barley. Levels of 14–15% protein are desirable for human consumption or animal feeding (Price, 1980), whereas in brewing, high levels of protein are undesirable because protein forms a matrix in the endosperm that reduces access of the amylolytic enzymes to the starch granules during mashing. The soluble protein in malted barley needs to be balanced with the carbohydrate content for optimum brewing performance. Use of high-protein malt in brewing leads to excessive head retention in the final product. Genetic factors control protein quantity in barley cultivars, although the environment also has a major influence on protein content.

Protein quality is nearly as important a consideration in nonruminant nutrition as quantity. For monogastric animals, barley is deficient in lysine

TABLE 1
Ideal Quality Parameters in Food, Feed, and Malting Barleys

Parameter	End-Use		
	Food	Feed	Malting
Starch content	High	High	High
Proteins			
Total	High	High	Low
Lysine	High	High	NA[a]
Lipids	NA	High	NA
β-Glucan	High	Low	Low
Enzymes (malt)	NA	NA	High
Phenolics	NA	NA	Low
Husk	Absent	Absent	Present, thin

[a] Not applicable.

and, to a lesser extent, threonine and must be supplemented to obtain optimum growth. Genetic factors have been identified that control the proportion of some amino acids in the protein. High-lysine genotypes have been developed, but they have not been commercially successful because of a close association between shrunken seed and high lysine (Persson, 1984). When the incoming photosynthate is redirected to develop an altered protein profile, the amount of carbohydrate (starch) produced in the seed is greatly reduced, and grain yield is significantly lower. Although it would be highly desirable to increase total protein and alter the protein balance, conventional and mutation breeding have not been successful because of the associated reduced energy per unit area. The associated effects (pleiotropy) cannot be predicted when such major biochemical changes are produced, and pleiotropy may occur with genetic engineering changes as well. When enzymes are altered to give a modified product in one specific part of the plant, the effect of that modification on other products may be quite dramatic. Thus, a positive increase in protein may result in a significant decrease in starch (Køie and Doll, 1979).

LIPIDS

Lipids are present in barley but at levels generally below 4% (Skarsaune and Banasik, 1972) and mainly in the embryo, scutellum, and aleurone tissues. They vary somewhat among genotypes, but no major genes have been identified that affect lipid content per se. In some oilseeds, lipid composition has been altered considerably by genetic means to make it more suitable for human consumption or for industrial uses (Röbbelen and Nitsch, 1975; Kondra and Wilson, 1976; Miller et al, 1987). In barley, there is an apparent pleiotropic effect of the lysine (*lys*) gene from Risø 1508 that gives increased lipid levels primarily in the bran-endosperm fraction (Bhatty and Rossnagel, 1979). Lipids can provide significant amounts of energy but would require major increases in quantity to have an impact on barley metabolizable energy. Higher lipid content would be undesirable in brewing.

β-GLUCAN

The viscosity of barley extract as it moves through the digestive tract of animals or of the wort as it is filtered through the lauter tun is a major concern for animal feeders and brewers alike (Newman et al, 1981; Ullrich et al, 1981; Morgan et al, 1983a). High viscosity, primarily associated with $(1\rightarrow3),(1\rightarrow4)$-β-D-glucans, reduces digestibility of the feed in the animal and reduces flow rates in the brewery. In animals, high levels of endogenous soluble β-glucans have been associated with reduced feed efficiency compared to other feed grains such as wheat or maize. β-Glucanase, which is synthesized during malting, is active in breaking down the β-glucan in the grain during malting and mashing. If sufficiently high levels of β-glucanase are present, most of the β-glucan may be broken down and will not create a problem during wort filtration.

The amount of β-glucan is influenced by both environment and genotype, whereas genotype alone has the major influence on the level of β-glucanase (Morgan et al, 1983b).

ENZYMES

The level of amylolytic and proteolytic enzymes produced during germination (malting) has little or no effect on digestibility and so is not a factor in food or feed uses of barley. The brewing industry, however, is greatly concerned with these enzymes. The amount of enzymatic activity determines the length of time needed to convert a specific quantity of starch to sugar. Higher levels of enzymes mean shorter mashing periods and allow for the addition of other sources of starch (adjunct) to the mashing process. The ability of the barley to develop a high level of enzymatic activity in a short germination time is under genetic control (Hockett and Nilan, 1985). There are wide differences among genotypes, and this property is relatively stable across environments.

PHENOLICS

Phenolic substances are undesirable in malting barley because they conjugate with proteins in beer to give a precipitate upon cooling (chill haze). Their role in the digestibility of barley is largely unknown. If the anthocyanogens in barley were reduced, the cost of stabilizing beer would be reduced, with a substantial saving to the breweries. Attempts to genetically alter the anthocyanogen content of barley have been successful, although most genotypes with lowered levels have not performed as well as their normal counterparts (Larsen et al, 1987). The majority of mutants to date have an altered pathway at a relatively early stage (Erdal, 1986), thus causing the plants to be anthocyanin-free, proanthocyanidin-free, and catechin-free. However, the lack of catechins appears to reduce the background resistance of the plants to numerous pathogens and results in yield reductions. Attempts are currently being made to develop proanthocyanidin-free barley with normal levels of anthocyanin and catechin (Jende-Strid, 1991).

HUSK

The husk (lemma and palea) of most barley cultivars adheres tightly to the pericarp of the seed. This is a decided advantage in malting, as the husk protects the growing acrospire from damage while the barley is germinating. This allows for a thorough mixing and turning of the grain during malting to maintain uniform temperature and humidity. Acrospire damage at this time adversely affects the quality of the resulting malt by lowering the enzyme level and reducing the degree of modification. The husks also form an efficient filter bed for the lautering process after mashing is complete. The quantity of husk in a normal barley is also influenced by genetic factors. Malting barley should have a tightly adhering husk, but it should be as thin as possible.

From a food or feed point of view, the husk is highly undesirable, as it is composed primarily of cellulose and hemicellulose, both of which are highly indigestible (Pond and Maner, 1974). Passing this excess of indigestible bulk through the digestive tract of an animal reduces feed efficiency considerably. A recessive gene (*n*) results in the hull not adhering tightly to the grain. The hull then threshes free of the grain to leave a naked grain much like wheat in appearance. This gene is present in many food barleys and in some feed types.

Genetic Control of Quality Factors

The potential for changing various quality factors by genetic engineering will depend upon the identification of major genes and the control of their expression. Examples of some of these are provided in the next section. In this section, we provide brief summary comments about the inheritance of quality traits and their relative potential for manipulation by genetic engineering.

The carbohydrate content of barley is largely under environmental control, but the type of starch can be altered genetically and is a logical target for genetic engineering manipulation (Schulman et al, 1991). Visser and Jacobsen (1993) have reviewed the goals and biotechnology strategies for the genetic alteration of starch content and composition.

Relative protein content and quality are both highly influenced by genes in barley and so should be fairly easy to alter through genetic engineering. The negative association between protein content and total yield was virtually impossible to overcome using traditional and mutation methods (Scholz, 1976).

Lipid content is closely associated with embryo size and oil content in normal barleys and, as such, could not be altered dramatically without influencing the relative size and/or function of the embryo. Special genotypes such as Risø 1508 appear to have an increased lipid content in the bran-endosperm, but a lower starch content (Bhatty, 1982). Although it may be feasible to alter lipid content by genetic engineering, it would not likely be a priority.

The level of enzyme activity in malted barley is often under the control of many genes (quantitative genetic control), and it may be possible to alter levels by manipulation of regulatory genes that turn on a number of such genes (Olsen et al, 1991). It may also be possible to change the nature of some of the enzymes in such a way as to alter the substrate specificity.

Numerous lines have been developed that are anthocyanogen-free, but none has proven to be of commercial value (Larsen et al, 1987). Even though conventional mutation breeding has shown that anthocyanogen-free lines are possible, it has not been successful in producing high-yielding genotypes. Improvement of this factor could also be attempted with genetic engineering.

The presence or absence of the husk is under simple genetic control and so does not need to be addressed via genetic engineering. The thinness of the husk is a minor factor in malting quality, and so it would not be worth applying genetic engineering technology for improvement.

BIOTECHNOLOGICAL APPROACHES TO GENETIC MODIFICATION OF BARLEY

Molecular Technology

Relative to the malting, brewing, and food quality of barley, some major genes have been identified, isolated, and cloned, e.g., those for α-amylase and β-glucanase. However, most kernel traits described in the preceding section, such as kernel size and oil or protein content, are controlled by a few or many genes with small effects. Attempts to recognize and select such traits have led to the development of highly refined statistical procedures that attempt to distinguish genetic variation from environmental effects. Thus, methods of identifying and tagging genes to simplify their selection have been a top priority for many years.

The markers most often available for use as tags have been morphological traits that could have undesirable pleiotropic effects on yield or quality. Such markers include chlorophyll, floral, or seed mutants and those altering the plant architecture. Isozymes also have been investigated as markers that would not have pleiotropic effects on agronomic traits. Marchylo (1987) used 65 combinations of patterns for B, C, and D hordein proteins on a survey of 100 Canadian barley cultivars, but many biotypes shared the same combinations and were indistinguishable. Furthermore, these types of electrophoretic variants have not proven to be plentiful enough to cover the plant genome as markers. Thus, development of DNA markers for tagging genes in plant breeding (e.g., Helentjaris et al, 1985) has rapidly evolved.

The use of molecular technology for crop improvement requires more information on a number of topics including: 1) understanding the inheritance of traits, 2) development of molecular probes and linkage maps, 3) tagging the genes with molecular markers, 4) studying the expression of genes, 5) developing procedures to identify, isolate, and transform genes. These topics can be consolidated into two sections for further discussion, namely, molecular marker techniques and identification and isolation of genes.

MOLECULAR MARKER TECHNIQUES

Molecular marker techniques are evolving rapidly. In 1980, Botstein et al reported on the use of RFLP for mapping of eukaryotes. Speed and safety considerations have led to the development of polymerase chain reaction (PCR) sequence amplification procedures for mapping. One such modification currently in use in mapping is the RAPDs (Williams et al, 1990). Another alternative is to develop primers for known DNA sequences such as RFLPs or genes so that PCR may be used and hazardous radioactive labeling avoided. Waugh and Powell (1992) have compared the advantages and efficiencies of RFLPs and RAPDs.

Fragment length polymorphism of DNA occurs when the DNA base pair sequences of a region are different between genotypes. Restriction enzymes recognize specific short segments of base pairs and can cut the DNA into fragments by attacking those sequences. When the DNA of one cultivar is isolated and digested by a specific restriction enzyme, the DNA is cut into a large number of fragments. These fragments can be isolated by electrophoresis, cloned in plasmids, and used as labeled probes to detect differences in base pair sequences in other genotypes. This is checked by digesting the DNA of other genotypes with the same enzyme; if a restriction site is different, the fragment hybridized by the labeled probe may be different in length and migrate a different distance in southern blot electrophoresis analysis. This RFLP serves as a molecular marker or probe for that region of the barley genome. Since there are almost infinite numbers of such RFLP probes, they can be used to generate a high-density linkage map of the barley genome. For most crop species, it is easy to obtain large numbers of these single-copy DNA probes to produce a linkage map. The advantages of RFLP markers are that 1) they behave in a codominant manner so that both polymorphic sizes are identifiable within one plant; 2) they are phenotypically neutral so that they will not alter quality or agronomic traits of importance during selection in breeding programs; 3) they are free from epistatic interactions, i.e., their presence should not alter the expression of other traits or RFLPs; and 4) allelic variation is quite high so that the number of RFLPs available is not limiting.

With a dense barley RFLP linkage map (one marker for every five to 10 cross-over units [in centiMorgans]), it should be feasible to identify and map genes for traits controlled by many loci, i.e., quantitative trait loci (Lander and Botstein, 1989; Knapp and Bridges, 1990). If a gene is found to be closely linked to an RFLP probe, the probe can then be used as a tag to follow and select a desirable allele in segregating populations of breeding programs.

To date, there have been a number of reports on RFLP mapping in barley (Graner et al, 1990; Shin et al, 1990; Blake et al, 1991; Cannell et al, 1991; Heun et al, 1991). We are aware of at least five groups working on the development of molecular marker maps in barley. The largest group, the North American Barley Genome Mapping Project, has developed populations to specifically study malting quality as well as agronomic traits. The objective is to construct a linkage map for each of the seven barley chromosomes, which will include RFLPs, RAPDs, isozymes, and isolated genes. The ability to produce doubled haploids in barley from the F_1 of selected crosses provides a rapid method for producing a population of recombinant pure lines for both mapping and studying the inheritance of quantitative traits in field trials. These molecular probes from the North American project and most other groups are intended to be publicly available. In addition, there are a number of private efforts on RFLP mapping (Cubitt, 1991).

Another important application of RFLP or PCR technology is the fingerprint identification of cultivars. Since each cultivar has its own unique DNA, it also has a unique pattern of electrophoretic bands when molecular techniques are used. Thus, the development of RAPDs can be valuable for varietal identification. Although this work is feasible, only preliminary studies with RFLPs have been reported in barley (Molnar and McKay, 1991).

IDENTIFICATION AND ISOLATION OF GENES

Although a gene may be closely linked to a molecular marker on a linkage map, the gene and marker are most likely many thousands of DNA base pairs apart, so DNA sequencing of RFLPs is not feasible for the isolation of individual genes at the molecular level. Since gene isolation is the first essential step for transformation research, approaches other than mapping are required.

To be able to identify genes, one must find the gene product, either as the mRNA transcribed from DNA or as the translated protein product mRNA. From the product (a protein), one can work back toward the DNA structure and try to synthesize oligonucleotides (copy or cDNA) that could hybridize with a segment of the gene. Through hybridization of the nucleotides to restriction-enzyme-digested denatured genomic DNA, one might isolate small fragments of DNA that contain coding regions for the gene. This is tedious and laborious work for a specific gene. However, once a gene is isolated from one species, it can serve as the hybridization probe to isolate the gene from other species, as there is often much DNA homology among such genes (Moore et al, 1993). A partial list of genes that have been isolated and sequenced in barley using cDNAs is shown in Table 2. This list includes only those of possible interest to malting or feed uses.

Originally it was hoped that storage proteins (hordeins) could be isolated and characterized so that they could be modified to contain additional DNA codons for the amino acid lysine at a site in the gene that did not alter the synthesis, deposition, and utilization of proteins. The problem encountered was that hordeins are a series of polymorphic proteins specified by a family of genes (Miflin et al, 1981). Thus, several modified genes would have to be inserted to significantly affect the amino acid content of a protein.

With the use of cDNA techniques, many sequences of the seed proteins have been determined. Leah and Mundy (1989) have cloned and sequenced a full-length cDNA from barley for a member of the trypsin inhibitor family. This barley protein is a specific inhibitor for endogenous α-amylase 2 of germinating barley (the major α-amylase component of barley malt) and of the bacterial serine protease subtilisin. It is interesting to note that the high-lysine barleys showed two- to fourfold higher levels of barley α-amylase/ subtilisin inhibitor mRNA compared to the controls. Information from such studies could be useful in elucidating steps in processing and deposition of barley endosperm proteins.

Kreis et al (1986) have isolated, characterized, and cloned cDNAs for chymotrypsin inhibitors 1 and 2. They are encoded by small multigene families (a group of related function genes) that specify several subfamilies of mRNA. Six DNA-binding proteins have been identified that might recognize and interact with the putative regulatory sequences in the B_1 hordein gene.

Plant breeders use genetic recombination to exchange large chromosome segments, whereas transformation concentrates on one or very few genes. These genes may need large control regions or a series of genes in order to function properly in a "new home." Thus, there is also interest in transferring larger segments of DNA. Newer techniques that allow for the separation of larger (many kilobase) segments of DNA are field inversion gel electrophoresis (van Daelen et al, 1989), pulse field gel electrophoresis (PFGE), and yeast artificial

TABLE 2
Some Barley Genes That Have Been Isolated and Cloned and That Control End-Use Quality Components

Gene Symbol	Function	Reference[a]
Adh 1	Alcohol dehydrogenase	Good et al (1988)
Amy 1, Amy 2	α-Amylase	Khursheed and Rogers (1989)
Bmy 1, Bmy 2	β-Amylase	Kreis et al (1986)
BASI[b]	α-Amylase/subtilisin inhibitor	Leah and Mundy (1989)
...	β-Glucanase	Loi et al (1988)
Cl-1, Cl-2	Chymotrypsin inhibitors 1 and 2	Kreis et al (1986)
Glb 1, Glb 2	Glucohydrolases	Fincher et al (1986)
Hor 2, Hor 3	Storage protein, hordeins	Sorenson (1989)
Nar 1	Nitrate reductase	Melzer and Kleinhofs (1987)
Wx, Glx	Waxy locus, starch synthase	Rohde et al (1988)

[a] Only one recent reference is given for each clone.
[b] Barley α-amylase/subtilisin inhibitor.

chromosomes (Ganal et al, 1990). Adapting PFGE, Sorenson (1989) studied the *Hor* 2 locus in barley to investigate the organization of multiple genes within a single genetic locus. A detailed analysis of the arrangement of genes within the complex hordein loci will provide the basis for more information on the regulatory aspects of the hordein gene.

Malting and brewing contain many steps to keep in balance, and it may be simpler to put some key genes into yeast rather than barley. A large portion of the malt β-glucanase is irreversibly heat-inactivated during kilning, and the remaining activity is rapidly destroyed during mashing (Loi et al, 1987). Therefore, thermostable $(1\rightarrow3),(1\rightarrow4)$-$\beta$-glucanases of fungal or bacterial origin are often added during mashing. The best-characterized bacterial $(1\rightarrow2),(1\rightarrow4)$-$\beta$-glucanases are those from *Bacillus subtilis* and *B. amyloliquefaciens*, and the genes encoding these enzymes have been cloned and sequenced (Hofemeister et al, 1986). It has been shown that the β-glucanase gene from *B. macerans* is more thermostable than the *B. subtilis* and *B. amyloliquefaciens* enzymes (Borris et al, 1988). According to D. von Wettstein (*unpublished data*), efforts to do molecular breeding of microbial $(1\rightarrow3),(1\rightarrow4)$-$\beta$-glucanases are in progress. Hybrid genes have been constructed with the aid of the DNA PCR technology, expressed in *Escherichia coli*, and the enzymes produced have been tested with regard to heat stability. In these studies, a first case of hybrid vigor for heat stability was obtained by intragenic recombination. The best result was achieved with hybrid 3[H3] containing the 16 NH_2 terminal amino acids from the *B. amyloliquefaciens* β-glucanase and the 198 amino acids of the *B. macerans* enzyme. Whether these more heat-stable β-glucanase genes can be placed and expressed in barley awaits further development of barley transformation procedures. Genetic engineering of yeast for other enzymes might be achieved. The advantages of yeast are the smaller genome size, availability of transformation procedures, and much more rapid life cycle, compared to those of barley.

Plant Cell Cultures

Cell culture techniques have been used routinely for a number of years for doubled haploid production in barley. However, with more recent advances in techniques, cell cultures are also being used for genetic manipulation and selection. A good regenerable single-cell culture system to serve as the targets for transformation research in barley is needed, although larger tissues are suitable for testing vector constructs. Some of the different areas in which cell cultures are currently in use for genetic advancement of barley are haploid production, somaclonal variation, in vitro selection, exotic gene introgression, and production of targets for genetic transformation.

HAPLOID PRODUCTION

Haploid production is important for barley breeding and research, as it provides a means of producing pure lines (doubled haploids). This pure line occurs in one step when the single set of chromosomes in the haploid gamete is returned to the normal two sets by chromosome doubling. Although a number of procedures have led to the production of haploids in barley (Kasha and Seguin-Swartz, 1983), the limitation for use is the production of large numbers of haploids from any genotype. The system that has led to the production of many new barley cultivars is the bulbosum method (Kasha and Kao, 1970), in which *Hordeum bulbosum* is used to pollinate barley and subsequently *H. bulbosum* chromosomes are eliminated during embryo development (Subrahmanyam and Kasha, 1973). More recently, Hayes and Chen (1989) have improved the Bulbosum method by culturing the pollinated florets. As evidence of efficiency, from three F_1 plants they have been able to produce about 700 haploids for the North American Barley Genome Mapping Project (P. M. Hayes, *personal communication*). The production of a population of pure lines (recombinant inbreds) for molecular mapping permits their maintenance and continued use by other researchers, as well as field evaluation of malting, feed, and agronomic traits.

However, dramatic improvements of haploid production in barley have also been obtained with the anther-microspore culture procedures (Hunter, 1988; Kasha et al, 1990, 1992). With improvements in donor plant growth, culture media, and pretreatments of anthers or microspores, 10–20 green plants can be produced from a single anther of some genotypes. In addition, many of these plants are spontaneously doubled haploids, eliminating the necessity for extra treatments and time in order to double the chromosome number and obtain pure lines.

The production of doubled haploids in barley via embryo culture from F_1 hybrids or via anther culture not only speeds up the breeding program but produces completely homozygous lines for evaluation of quantitative traits. Detection of mutations is also facilitated with the use of haploids. Since most of the mutations are usually recessive, haploidy allows expression of both recessive and dominant mutations. Selection in breeding requires techniques that can produce large numbers of haploid plants. Alternatively, selection could be made for traits at the cellular level during the culturing of microspores, if selective agents can be applied in cultures. Examples are herbicide resistance or pathogen resistance where toxins are available. Selection for enzymes involved in quality might be investigated at advanced culture stages.

SOMACLONAL VARIATION

Somatic cells or tissue, when introduced into culture media, are induced to grow rapidly with the aid of hormones in the media. As such, variations, termed "somaclonal variation," may be induced during such cell culture growth (Larkin and Scowcroft, 1981). Chromosomal structural rearrangements have been observed in a number of *Hordeum* cell cultures and subsequently regenerated plants (Mix et al, 1978; Orton, 1980; Ziauddin and Kasha, 1990). Therefore, for creating novel variation, one can utilize some of the variation that occurs during the callus phase of tissue culture. However, only part of this variation may be stable and useful in breeding.

IN VITRO SELECTION

In vitro selection is a process of screening cell cultures for desired mutations by applying a selective agent in the culture media. This is most often done with resistance to herbicides or antibiotics linked to a gene during transformation studies (described below). Selection at the cellular level has many advantages over the traditional whole-plant selection, if the trait selected at the cellular level is also expressed in the whole plant. Advantages include working with large numbers (millions of cells), small space (flasks), rapid screening, economics, and ease of handling. The difficulty often encountered is to obtain efficient plant regeneration from the cell cultures.

One means of overcoming the problem of regeneration has been the use of embryos as a selection unit on media. Seeds can be used intact where there is no effect of the breakdown of seed reserves on the process being studied. Quality traits such as threonine accumulation (Bright et al, 1982a; Kuruvinashetti, 1985) and stress tolerance via proline production (Bright et al, 1982b) have been successfully selected in barley at the petri plate level. Where a trait cannot be directly selected, it is necessary to cotransform with specifically selectable markers that are either dominant or that repair a deficiency in the recipient (Miflin et al, 1981). An example of selectable markers would be chlorophyll-deficient mutations that would not survive to the reproductive stage without being transformed.

EXOTIC GENE INTROGRESSION

A number of significant advances in cereal improvement have been obtained by the introgression of alien genes. An example of this is the transfer of stem rust resistance from *Agropyron* to common wheat (Knott, 1961). Orton (1980) cultured *H. vulgare* × *H. jubatum* immature ovary tissue and regenerated plants. Even though the haploid plants were morphologically similar to *H. vulgare*, some of them exhibited *H. jubatum* gene expression (esterase isozymes and perenniality), suggesting gene introgression. Crosses with alien species and rescue of the developing embryonic tissue provide access to increased genetic variation. Crosses between barley and *H. bulbosum* can also produce interspecific hybrids as well as barley haploids. Introgression of *H. bulbosum* DNA into barley has occurred when such hybrids are backcrossed to barley (Xu and Kasha, 1992) or undergo anther culture (Pickering and Fautrier, 1993) and could be a source of useful genes.

TARGETS FOR TRANSFORMATION

Foreign vectors are most often used to transfer DNA into higher plant cells. In this way, desired traits or enhanced expression of traits due to increased copies of genes may be effected. The most widely used vector has been the tumor-inducing (Ti) plasmid carried by *Agrobacterium tumefaciens*. While very effective in dicots, this system has shown little promise in monocots such as barley. Thus, a number of other techniques by which DNA may be delivered into plant cells have been examined. These include direct DNA uptake by protoplasts (Potrykus et al, 1985) or dried embryos (Senaratna et al, 1991), microinjection (Neuhaus et al, 1987), or the Biolistic particle gun (Sanford, 1990). The lack of plant regeneration from barley protoplasts to date has limited the potential for direct DNA uptake accompanied by chemicals or electroporation. Thus, microinjection and Biolistic particle gun approaches have received the most interest in barley. Recently, two groups of researchers have reported successful stable maize transformations with genes conferring herbicide tolerance (Fromm et al, 1990; Gordon-Kamm et al, 1990). Stable particle bombardment transformation in maize indicates that it is likely that other cereals can also be stably transformed. Transient gene expression has been observed in several cereal species. Barley suspension cultures have transiently expressed β-glucuronidase (GUS), neomycin phosphotransferase II (NPT II), and chloramphenicol acetyltransferase reporter genes (Kartha et al, 1989; Mendel et al, 1989; Creissen et al, 1990). Integration of the new DNA into the germ cell line and plant regeneration from these cells remain as main obstacles. To avoid the problem of chimeras arising from multicellular targets, the single cell is the target of choice for genetic transformation procedures, and therefore extensive research on regeneration of plants from single-cell cultures or microspores is being conducted. Work on the transformation of barley protoplasts (Lörz and Lazzeri, 1992) and of microspores in our own laboratory is most encouraging.

Plant cell cultures can also serve as a vehicle for testing the value of specific gene changes on transcription and translation. For example, Lee et al (1989) studied transient gene expression in aleurone protoplasts isolated from immature seeds of barley and wheat. They demonstrated the control of gene expression from gene constructs introduced into the protoplasts using polyethylene glycol treatment of the protoplasts. While plants could not be regenerated, the system could be useful in studying developmental gene control of cereal seed proteins or starch. Olsen et al (1991) have been searching for gene promoters that will direct transcription in different tissues of developing barley grains. In maize, Klein et al (1989) have studied gene expression in intact aleurone and embryo cells using microprojectiles to deliver genes. This system offers a method to study genetic and tissue-specific regulation of gene expressions and a means of evaluating promoter constructs. Such procedures have led to the identification of the active region in front of the initiation codon of the α-amylase gene (Huttly and Baulcombe, 1989), which responds to gibberellins.

FUTURE CONSIDERATIONS

In the near future, one can visualize rapid improvement of new improved cultivars by tagging genes with RFLPs and RAPDs. These techniques will also allow for automated cultivar identification for grain purchasers so that quality traits for specific purposes can be identified. Such systems will eliminate the difficulties of breeders having to use morphological traits for specific uses, i.e., the blue aleurone color for six-rowed malting barleys in Canada.

The markers in high-density RFLP maps can be used to break down complex genetic traits into their single-gene components (Tanksley et al, 1989). Once tightly linked markers have been found associated with a gene of interest, and a physical map has been constructed using PFGE, the entire region between these markers must be cloned to identify and isolate the gene. A very recent cloning system based on a eukaryotic host, yeast, appears promising (Ganal et al, 1990). Yeast artificial chromosomes have large insert capacities and can clone large segments of DNA for further analysis.

Even though many recent advances have been made in molecular techniques, there are still many specific areas that need to be resolved. These include isolation of genes, directing foreign genes to specific sites in the genome, and regulating the expression of inserted genes in specific tissues. However, the prospect of transferring desired genes to barley from other plant species or even other organisms makes the entire process of genetic engineering attractive. As seen in Table 2 and the list of Cannell et al (1991), a number of genes that might influence the composition of the barley kernel have been cloned. These are related mainly to enzymes, carbohydrates, and proteins of the barley kernel, but no doubt genes for other components can also be isolated. Comparative genome mapping from other species, cereals in particular, should greatly facilitate the isolation of more genes in barley (Moore et al, 1993). As we learn more about the genetics of barley, we will have greater opportunity to modify the barley kernel for specialized uses in industry or food and beverages.

LITERATURE CITED

BHATTY, R. S., and ROSSNAGEL, B. G. 1979. Oil content of Risø barley. Cereal Chem. 56:586.

BHATTY, R. S. 1982. Distribution of lipids in embryo and bran/endosperm fractions of Risø 1508 and Hiproly barley grains. Cereal Chem. 59:154-155.

BLAKE, T., et al 1991. An RFLP map of barley, North American Barley Genome Mapping Project. Pages 245-248 in: Barley Genetics VI, Vol. 1. Proc. 6th Int. Barley Genet. Symp. L. Munck, ed. Munksgaard Int. Publ., Copenhagen.

BORRIS, R., MANTEUFFEL, R., and HOFEMEISTER, J. 1988. Molecular cloning of a gene coding for thermostable beta-glucanase from *Bacillus macerans*. J. Basic Microbiol. 28:3-10.

BOTSTEIN, D., WHITE, R. L., SKOLNICK, M., and DAVIS, R. W. 1980. Construction of a genetic linkage map in man using restriction fragment length polymorphisms. Am. J. Hum. Genet. 32:314-331.

BRIGHT, S. W. J., MIFLIN, B. J., and ROGNES, S. E. 1982a. Threonine accumulation in the seeds of a barley mutant with an altered aspartate kinase. Biochem. Genet. 20:229-243.

BRIGHT, S. W. J., KEUH, J. S. H., FRANKLIN, J., and MIFLIN, B. J. 1982b. Proline accumulating mutants. Pages 858-863 in: Barley Genetics IV. Proc. 4th Int. Barley Genet. Symp. R. N. H. Whitehouse, ed. Edinburgh University Press, Edinburgh.

CANNELL, M., KARP, A., SHEWRY, P., and ISAACS, P. 1991. Restriction fragment length polymorphism analysis in barley and assignment of characterized probes to chromosome arms. Pages 249-253 in: Barley Genetics VI, Vol. 1. Proc. 6th Int. Barley Genet. Symp. L. Munck, ed. Munksgaard Int. Publ., Copenhagen.

CREISSEN, G., SMITH, C., FRANCIS, R., REYNOLDS, H., and MULLINEAUX, P.

1990. Agrobacterium- and microprojectile-mediated viral DNA delivery into barley microspore-derived cultures. Plant Cell Rep. 8:680-683.

CUBITT, I. R. 1991. The commercial application of biotechnology to plant breeding. Plant Breed. Abstr. 61(2):151-158.

ERDAL, K. 1986. Proanthocyanidin-free barley malting and brewing. J. Inst. Brew. 92:220-224.

FINCHER, G. B., LOCK, P. A., MORGAN, M. M., LINGELBACH, K., WETTENHALL, R. E. H., MERCER, J. F. B., BRANDT, A., and THOMSEN, K. K. 1986. Primary structure of the $(1{\to}3,1{\to}4)$ β-D-glucan 4-glucanohydrolase from barley aleurone. Proc. Natl. Acad. Sci. USA 83:2081-2085.

FOSTER, E., and PRENTICE, N. 1987. Barley. Pages 337-396 in: Nutritional Quality of Cereal Grains. R. A. Olson and K. J. Frey, eds. American Society of Agronomy, Madison, WI.

FROMM, M. E., MORRISH, F., ARMSTRONG, C., WILLIAMS, R., THOMAS, J., and KLEIN, T. M. 1990. Inheritance and expression of chimeric genes in the progeny of transgenic maize plants. Bio/Technology 8:833-839.

GANAL, M. W., MARTIN, G. B., MESSEGUER, R., and TANKSLEY, S. D. 1990. Application of RFLPs, physical mapping and large DNA technologies to the cloning of important genes from crop plants. AgBiotechnol. News Inform. 2:835-840.

GOERING, K. J., and ESLICK, R. F. 1976. Barley starch. VI. A self-liquefying waxy barley starch. Cereal Chem. 53:174-180.

GOOD, A. G., PELCHER, L. E., and CROSBY, W. L. 1988. Nucleotide sequence of a complete barley Adh 1 cDNA. Nucleic Acids Res. 16:7182.

GORDON-KAMM, W. J., SPENCER, T. M., MANGANO, M. L., ADAMS. T. R., DAINES, R. J., START, W. G., O'BRIEN,

J. V., CHAMBERS, S. A., ADAMS, W. R., Jr., WILLETS, N. G., RICE, T. B., MACKEY, C. J., KREUGER, R. W., KAUSCH, A. P., and LEMAUX, P. G. 1990. Transformation of maize cells and regeneration of fertile transgenic plants. Plant Cell 2:603-618.

GRANER, A., SIEDLER, H., JAHOOR, A., HERRMANN, R. G., and WENZEL, G. 1990. Assessment of the degree and the type of restriction fragment length polymorphism in barley (*Hordeum vulgare*). Theor. Appl. Genet. 80:826-832.

HARDWICK, W. A. 1977. History of brewing in the Americas. Pages 1-12 in: The Practical Brewer. H. M. Broderick, ed. Master Brewers Assoc. of the Americas, Madison, WI.

HARLAN, J. R. 1968. On the origin of barley. Pages 9-31 in: Barley Origin, Botany, Culture, Winterhardiness, Genetics, Utilization, Pests. Agric. Handbook 338. U.S. Dep. Agric., Washington, DC.

HAYES, P. M., and CHEN, F. Q. 1989. Genotypic variation for *Hordeum bulbosum* L. mediated haploid production in winter and facultative barley. Crop Sci. 29:1184-1188.

HELENTJARIS, T., KING, G., SLOCUM, M., SIEDENSTANG, C., and WEGMAN, S. 1985. Restriction fragment polymorphisms as probes for plant diversity and their development as tools for applied plant breeding. Plant Mol. Biol. 5:109-118.

HEUN, M., KENNEDY, A. E., ANDERSON, J. A., LAPITAN, N. L. V., SORRELLS, M. E., and TANKSLEY, S. D. 1991. Construction of a restriction fragment length polymorphism map for barley (*Hordeum vulgare*). Genome 34:437-447.

HOCKETT, E. A., and NILAN, R. A. 1985. Genetics. Pages 187-230 in: Barley. D. C. Rasmusson, ed. American Society of Agronomy, Madison, WI.

HOFEMEISTER, J., KURTZ, A., BORRIS, R., and KNOWLES, J. 1986. The β-glucanase gene from *Bacillus amyloliquefaciens* shows extensive homology with that of *Bacillus subtilis*. Gene 49:177-187.

HUNTER, C. P. 1988. Plant regeneration from microspores of barley, *Hordeum vulgare*. Ph.D. thesis, Wye College, University of London.

HUTTLY, A. K., and BAULCOMBE, D. C. 1989. A wheat α-Amy 2 promoter is regulated by gibberellin in transformed oat aleurone protoplasts. EMBO J. 8:1907-1913.

JENDE-STRID, B. 1991. A new type of proanthocyanidin-free barley. Pages 504-506 in: Barley Genetics VI, Vol. 1. Proc. 6th Int. Barley Genet. Symp. L. Munck, ed. Munksgaard Int. Publ., Copenhagen.

KARTHA, K. K., CHIBBAR, R. N., GEORGES, F., LEUNG, N., CASWELL, K., KENDALL, E., and QURESHI, J. 1989. Transient expression of chloramphenicol acetyltransferase (CAT) gene in barley cell cultures and immature embryos through microprojectile bombardment. Plant Cell Rep. 8:429-432.

KASHA, K. J., and KAO, K. N. 1970. High frequency of haploid production in barley (*Hordeum vulgare* L.). Nature 225:874-876.

KASHA, K. J., and SEGUIN-SWARTZ, G. 1983. Haploidy in crop improvement. Pages 19-68 in: Cytogenetics of Crop Plants. M. S. Swaminathan, P. K. Gupta, and U. Sinha, eds. MacMillan Press, New Delhi, India.

KASHA, K. J., ZIAUDDIN, A., and CHO, U.-H. 1990. Haploids in cereal improvement: Anther and microspore culture. Pages 213-235 in: Gene Manipulation in Plant Improvement II. J. P. Gustafson, ed. Plenum Press, New York.

KASHA, K. J., CHO, U.-H., and ZIAUDDIN, A. 1992. Application of microspore cultures. Pages 793-806 in: Barley Genetics VI, Vol. 2. Proc. 6th Int. Barley Genet. Symp. L. Munck, ed. Munksgaard Int. Publ., Copenhagen.

KHURSHEED, B., and ROGERS, J. C. 1989. Barley α-amylase genes and thiol protease gene aleurain: Use of a single poly (A) addition signal association with a conserved pentanucleotide at cleavage site. Proc. Natl. Acad. Sci. USA 86:3987-3991.

KLEIN, T. M., KORNSTEIN, L., SANFORD, J. C., and FROMM, M. E. 1989. Genetic transformation of maize cells by particle bombardment. Plant Physiol. 91:440-444.

KNAPP, S. J., and BRIDGES, W. C. 1990. Using molecular markers to estimate quantitative trait locus parameters: Power and genetic variances for unreplicated and replicated progeny. Genetics 126:769-777.

KNOTT, D. R. 1961. The inheritance of rust resistance. VI. The transfer of stem rust resistance from *Agropyron elongatum* to common wheat. Can. J. Plant Sci. 41:109-123.

KØIE, B., and DOLL, H. 1979. Protein and carbohydrate components in the Risφ high-lysine barley mutants. Pages 205-215 in: Seed Protein Improvement in Cereals and Grain Legumes, Vol. 1. International Agency for Atomic Energy (Food and Agriculture Organization), Vienna.

KONDRA, Z. P., and WILSON, T. W. 1976. Selection for oleic, linoleic and linolenic acid content in F_2 populations of rape. Can. J. Plant. Sci. 56:961-966.

KREIS, M., WILLIAMSON, M. S., FORDE, J., SCHMUTZ, D., CLARK, J., BUXTON,

B., PYWELL, J., MARRIS, C., HENDERSON, J., HARRISON, N., SHEWRY, P. R., FORDE, B. G., and MIFLIN, B. J. 1986. Differential gene expression in the developing barley endosperm. Philos. Trans. R. Soc. London B 314:355-365.

KURUVINASHETTI, M. S. 1985. In vitro selection for lysine and threonine mutants in barley (*Hordeum vulgare* L.). Ph.D. thesis, Univ. of Guelph, Guelph, Canada.

LANDER, E. S., and BOTSTEIN, D. 1989. Mapping Mendelian factors underlying quantitative traits using RFLP linkage maps. Genetics 121:185-199.

LARKIN, P. J., and SCOWCROFT, W. R. 1981. Somaclonal variation—A novel source of variability from cell cultures for plant improvement. Theor. Appl. Genet. 60:197-214.

LARSEN, J., ULLRICH, S., INGUERSEN, J., NIELSEN, A. E., COCHRAN, J. S., and CLANCY, J. 1987. Breeding and malting behaviour of two different proanthocyanidin-free barley gene sources. Pages 767-772 in: Barley Genetics V. Proc. 5th Int. Barley Genet. Symp. S. Yasuda and T. Konishi, eds. Sanyo Press, Okayama, Japan.

LEAH, R., and MUNDY, J. 1989. The bifunctional α-amylase/subtilisin inhibitor of barley: Nucleotide sequence and pattern of seed specific expression. Plant Mol. Biol. 12:673-682.

LEE, B., MURDOCK, K., TOPPING, J., KREIS, M., and JONES, M. G. K. 1989. Transient gene expression in aleurone protoplasts isolated from developing caryopses of barley and wheat. Plant Mol. Biol. 13:21-29.

LOI, L., BARTON, P. A., and FINCHER, G. B. 1987. Survival of barley (1→3, 1→4) β-glucanase isoenzymes during kilning and mashing. J. Cereal Sci. 5:45-50.

LOI, L., AHLUWALIA, B., and FINCHER, G. B. 1988. Chromosomal location of genes encoding barley (1→3, 1→4)-β-glucanohydrolases. Plant Physiol. 87:300-302.

LÖRZ, H., and LAZZERI, P. A. 1992. In vitro regeneration and genetic transformation of barley. Pages 807-815 in: Barley Genetics VI, Vol. 2. Proc. 6th Int. Barley Genet. Symp. L. Munck, ed. Munksgaard Int. Publ., Copenhagen.

MARCHYLO, B. A. 1987. Barley cultivar identification by SDS gradient page analysis of hordein. Can. J. Plant Sci. 67:927-944.

MELZER, J. M., and KLEINHOFS, A. 1987. Molecular genetics of barley. Pages 481-491 in: Barley Genetics V. Proc. 5th Int. Barley Genet. Symp. S. Yasuda and T. Konishi, eds. Sanyo Press, Okayama, Japan.

MENDEL, R. R., MULLER, B., SCHULZE, J., KOLESNIKOV, V., and ZELENIN, A. 1989. Delivery of foreign genes into intact barley cells by high-velocity microprojectiles. Theor. Appl. Genet. 78:31-34.

MERRITT, N. R. 1967. A new strain of barley with starch of high amylose content. J. Inst. Brew. 73:583-585.

MIFLIN, B. J., BRIGHT, S. W. J., and THOMAS, E. 1981. Towards the genetic manipulation of barley. Pages 858-863 in: Barley Genetics IV. Proc. 4th Int. Barley Genet. Symp. R. N. H. Whitehouse, ed. Edinburgh University Press, Edinburgh.

MILLER, J. F., ZIMMERMAN, D. C., and VICK, B. A. 1987. Genetic control of high oleic acid content in sunflower oil. Crop Sci. 27:923-926.

MIX, G., WILSON, H. M., and FOROUGHI-WEHR, B. 1978. The cytological status of plants of *Hordeum vulgare* L. regenerated from microspore callus. Z. Pflanzenzuecht. 80:89-99.

MOLNAR, S. J., and McKAY, A. 1991. Restriction fragment analysis of ribosomal and hordein genes in eastern Canadian two-rowed barleys. Genome 34:298-302.

MOORE, G., GALE, M. D., KURATA, N., and FLAVELL, R. B. 1993. Molecular analysis of small grain cereal genomes: Current status and prospects. Bio/Technology 11:584-589.

MORGAN, A. G., GILL, A. A., and SMITH, D. B. 1983a. Some barley grain and green malt properties and their influence on malt hot water extract. I. β-Glucan, β-glucan solubilase and endo-β-glucanase. J. Inst. Brew. 89:283-291.

MORGAN, A. G., GILL, A. A., and SMITH, D. B. 1983b. Some barley grain and green malt properties and their influence on malt hot water extract. II. Protein, proteinase and moisture. J. Inst. Brew. 89:292-298.

NEUHAUS, G., SOPANGENBERG, G., MITTELSTEN-SHERD, O., and SCHWEIGER, H. G. 1987. Transgenic rapeseed plants obtained by microinjection of DNA into microspore-derived proembryoids. Theor. Appl. Genet. 75:30-36.

NEWMAN, C. W., EL-NEGOUMY, A. M., and ESLICK, R. F. 1981. Genetic factors affecting the feed quality of barley. Pages 299-304 in: Barley Genetics IV. Proc. 4th Int. Barley Genet. Symp. R. N. H. Whitehouse, ed. Edinburgh University Press, Edinburgh.

OLSEN, O.-A., KLEMSDAL, S. S., KALLA, R., LØNNEBERG, A., AALEN, R. B., FERSTAD, H.-G. O., and LINNESTAD, G. 1991. Barley grain tissue- and stage-specific gene promoters. Isolation and use in strategies to improve sprouting resistance.

Pages 148-150 in: Barley Genetics VI, Vol. 1. Proc. 6th Int. Barley Genet. Symp. L. Munck, ed. Munksgaard Int. Publ., Copenhagen.

ORTON, T. J. 1980. Haploid barley regenerated from callus cultures of *Hordeum vulgare* × *H. jubatum.* J. Hered. 71:780-782.

PERSSON, G. 1984. Ideas and methods for genetic improvement of quality and quantity of barley. Pages 105-109 in: The Use of Nuclear Techniques for Cereal Grain Protein Improvement. STI/PUB/664. International Agency for Atomic Energy (Food and Agriculture Organization), Vienna.

PICKERING, R. A., and FAUTRIER, A. G. 1993. Anther culture-derived regenerants from *Hordeum vulgare* × *H. bulbosum* crosses. Plant Breed. 110:41-47.

POND, W. G., and MANER, J. H. 1974. Swine Production in Temperate and Tropical Environments. W. H. Freeman and Co., San Francisco.

POTRYKUS, I., SHILLITO, R. D., SAUL, M. W., and PASZKOWSKI, J. 1985. Direct gene transfer. State of the art and future potential. Plant Mol. Biol. Rep. 3:117-128.

PRICE, P. B. 1980. Barley proteins. S.D. State Univ. Ext. Circ. FS759.

RÖBBELEN, G., and NITSCH, A. 1975. Genetical and physiological investigation on mutants for polyenoic fatty acids in rapeseed. I. Selection and description of new mutants. Z. Pflanzenzuecht. 75:93-105.

ROHDE, W., BECKER, D., and SALAMIN, F. 1988. Structural analysis of the waxy locus from *Hordeum vulgare.* Nucleic Acids Res. 16:7185-7186.

SANFORD, J. C. 1990. Biolistic plant transformation. Physiol. Plant. 79:206-209.

SCHOLZ, F. 1976. Problems of breeding for high protein yield in barley. Pages 548-556 in: Barley Genetics III. Proc. 3rd Int. Barley Genet. Symp. H. Gaul, ed. Verlag Karl Theimig, Munich.

SENARATNA, T., MCKERSIE, B. D., KASHA, K. J., and PROCUNIER, J. D. 1991. Direct DNA uptake during the imbibition of dry cells. Plant Sci. 79:223-228.

SHIN, J. S., CHAO, S., CORPUZ, T., and BLAKE, T. 1990. A partial map of the barley genome incorporating restriction fragment length polymorphism, polymerase chain reaction, isozyme and morphological marker loci. Genome 33:803-810.

SHULMAN, A. H., BOJKO, M., DEIBER-HOAG, A., JANSSON, C., KLECZKOWSKI, L. A., MARCUSSEN, J., MOTAWIA, M. S., MØLLER, B. L., OLESEN, P., OLSEN, C. E., OLSEN, O.-A., PESSA, E., POUTANEN,

K., SUN, C., SUORTII, T., TOUMI, T., TYYNELÄ, J., and VILLAND, P. 1991. The molecular genetic, biochemical, and physical analysis of starch synthesis in barley: A Nordic collaboration. Pages 125-129 in: Barley Genetics VI, Vol. 1. Proc. 6th Int. Barley Genet. Symp. L. Munck, ed. Munksgaard Int. Publ., Copenhagen.

SKARSAUNE, S. K., and BANASIK, O. J. 1972. Lipids of postharvest barley. Am. Soc. Brew. Chem. Proc. pp. 94-97.

SORENSON, M. B. 1989. Mapping of the *Hor 2* locus in barley by pulsed field gel electrophoresis. Carlsberg Res. Comm. 54:109-120.

SUBRAHMANYAM, N. C., and KASHA, K. J. 1973. Selective chromosomal elimination during haploid formation in barley following interspecific hybridization. Chromosoma 42:111-125.

TANKSLEY, S. D., YOUNG, N. D., PATERSON, A. H., and BONIERBALE, M. W. 1989. RFLP mapping in plant breeding: New tools for an old science. Bio/Technology 7:257-173.

ULLRICH, S. E., COON, C. N., and SEVER, J. M. 1981. Relationships of nutritional and malting quality traits of barley. Pages 225-233 in: Barley Genetics IV. Proc. 4th Int. Barley Genet. Symp. R. N. H. Whitehouse, ed. Edinburgh University Press, Edinburgh.

VAN DAELEN, R. A. J., JONKERS, J. J., and ZABEL, P. 1989. Preparation of megabase-sized tomato DNA and separation of large restriction fragments by inversion gel electrophoresis (FIGE). Plant Mol. Biol. 12:341-352.

VISSER, R. G. F., and JACOBSEN, E. 1993. Towards modifying plants for altered starch content and composition. TIBTECH 11:63-68.

WAUGH, R., and POWELL, W. 1992. Using RAPD markers for crop improvement. TIBTECH 10:186-191.

WILLIAMS, J. G. K., KUBELIK, A. R., LIVIK, K. J., RAFALSKI, J. A., and TINGEY, S. V. 1990. DNA polymorphisms amplified by arbitrary primers are useful as genetic markers. Nucleic Acids Res. 18:6531-6535.

XU, J., and KASHA, K. J. 1992. Transfer of a dominant gene for powdery mildew resistance and DNA from *Hordeum bulbosum* into cultivated barley (*H. vulgare*). Theor. Appl. Genet. 84:771-777.

ZIAUDDIN, A., and KASHA, K. J. 1990. Long-term callus cultures of diploid barley (*Hordeum vulgare*). II. Effect of auxins on chromosomal status of cultures and regeneration of plants. Euphytica 48:279-286.

CHAPTER 10

WHOLE-CROP UTILIZATION OF BARLEY, INCLUDING POTENTIAL NEW USES

P. BJØRN PETERSEN
L. MUNCK[1]
Carlsberg Research Laboratory
DK-2500 Valby Copenhagen, Denmark

INTRODUCTION

The exponential growth of the world population has been dependent on increased production of cereals, including barley, which is today mainly used for feed and to some extent food. The recent rapid development in the industrialized world has been driven not only by the defense industries but also and most importantly by the industrialization of agriculture at all levels in the production chain from farm to consumer. This development has taken place in an economic environment where input of human labor has been minimized and inputs from machinery, chemicals, and energy have been maximized, strongly stimulating industrialization and creating affluence in Western society. The success of industry in exploiting the agroindustrial option is exemplified by the fact that in 1988 the Danish farmer earned an average of only about 2% of the retail price of food for his private consumption. Increasing prices of fossil resources and increasing awareness of the limits of our biosphere as a receptor of pollution are now slowly bringing us to contemplate another strategy for using and maintaining our renewable resources, one that, instead of maximizing production, aims at maximizing the efficiency of conversion in the production chain (Munck, 1993).

A hundred years ago, the manufacturing industry used relatively more cereal raw material than it does today. Starch, for example, was used extensively in the textile industry, and straw was utilized as a source for paper pulp. Since then, other raw materials from mineral oil, wood, etc., have reduced the use of cereal raw materials for nonfood purposes.

In the last two decades, oil prices have fluctuated enormously, displaying a significant upward trend (Fig. 1), whereas prices on the international market for maize, for example, have been more stable. The energy crises in 1973,

---

[1]Present address: Department of Dairy and Food Science, Royal Veterinary and Agricultural University, Frederiksberg C, Denmark.

1979, and 1990 were crises in confidence of delivery rather than a lack of underground resources. The ratio between the price of one tonne of maize and the price of one barrel of crude oil is thus greatly diminished compared to the ratio when oil was really cheap (Fig. 2). This is today reflected in the fact that, for example, palm oil fractions and maize can compete with crude oil on the world market as a fuel. This is, however, a marginal exercise. With our present way of life, in which we annually consume about 39 × 10^6 gigawatt hours (GWh) of crude oil, and with a global production of starch in all grains of 6 × 10^6 GWh, it is not at all realistic to replace the crude oil used today with biomass for fuel and industry. Fossil fuels will be available for many years if we learn more about how to utilize them efficiently and avoid pollution constraints. Thus, the Ten Commandments should be expanded with an Eleventh Commandment: "Thou shalt not burn fuel (of any kind) rather than utilizing mechanical energy." With investments in heat pumps and electric generators, energy consumption for heating and cooling energy could be diminished to one-third of today's use in the industrialized societies, which are the great wasters of energy. With such changes and with the use of modern insulation technology and solar panels, we could further decrease our demand for energy. Thus the presently produced nonfood biomass could make a significant local contribution, e.g., as pyrolysis and biogas for driving

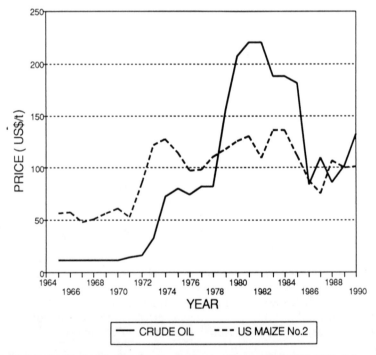

Fig. 1. Maize price (dashed line) vs. crude oil price (continuous line) 1965–1990. Prices of maize (U.S. No. 2 yellow, FOB Gulf, Chicago) from FAO (1968–1990). Prices of crude oil: for 1965–1986 (Arabian light) from Myklebust et al (1986); for 1986–1990 (Dubai light) from the Shell Oil Company, Amsterdam.

engines for heat pumps and electric generators. Because of transportation problems, this option is feasible only in a decentralized society. Large processing industries and central electric generators still will have to use fossil fuels in the foreseeable future.

Even if energy prices occasionally could go down further between now and the year 2000, we must recognize the long-term need to save and steadily decrease the amount of energy and other raw materials used per unit of agricultural product. By doing so, we simultaneously reduce pollution, which is merely a sign of inadequate management of resources. In most cases, biomass, including its components such as starch, cellulose, and fat, is too valuable as a food, feed, or industrial raw material to be burned on a large scale or to be used to produce ethanol, which also is a wasteful process. Hence there is no alternative but to improve the overall efficiency of agriculture, including increasing its structural flexibility. Such a policy will not be at all inconsistent with our present apparent surpluses in the Western industrialized world. These surpluses are only some evident signs of an obsolete agroindustrial structure and a policy incapable of handling problems.

In the following discussion, the potential use of the whole barley plant (seed and straw) for industry is evaluated, mainly concentrating on the

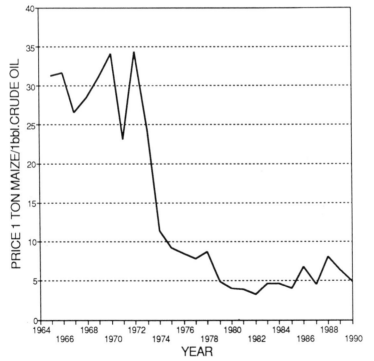

Fig. 2. Ratio of prices of maize to prices of crude oil, showing commodity price trends for 1965-1990. Prices of maize (U.S. No. 2 yellow, FOB Gulf, Chicago) from FAO (1968-1990). Prices of crude oil: for 1965-1986 (Arabian light) from Myklebust et al (1986); for 1986-1990 (Dubai light) from the Shell Oil Company, Amsterdam.

fascinating natural polymers, starch and cellulose. In Fig. 3, the potential options for utilizing the whole barley plant are described. Our experience in this area is built on research projects developed during 1983–1988 mainly for the Commission of the European Communities (Rexen and Munck, 1984; Munck, 1986a; F. Rexen and L. Munck, *unpublished report to the EC, 1986*; Munck 1987a; Petersen, 1988; Munck and Rexen, 1990), including the total spectrum of agricultural resources in an area (north/western Europe) where spring and winter barleys are as important in agricultural production as is maize in the Midwest of the United States. In this chapter, production figures and relationships from the countries of the European Community (EC) of 12, which has an economy comparable in size to that of North America, are cited as examples. At the end of the chapter, we further discuss how agriculture and industry could cooperate to realize the potential nonfood options of the barley raw material as an important part of the whole agro-industrial panorama and visualize under which circumstances such cooperation would be profitable.

BARLEY AS AN INDUSTRIAL RAW MATERIAL

Barley is used worldwide for malting, which is its only large-scale industrial utilization so far outside of its use for the feed industry. The marketing of brewing enzymes produced industrially from microorganisms has not been able to replace malt from the brewing market, in spite of the fact that a reasonable beer can be brewed from cereal adjuncts and nonmalt enzymes.

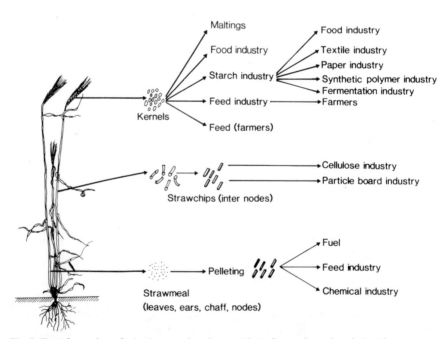

Fig. 3. Transformation of a barley crop into intermediates for use in various industries.

In the present "green movement" of consumers, this is not likely to happen. The barley aleurone, just one to three cells thick, is one of the most effective tissues for enzyme secretion among all living organisms. Through the gibberellic acid control mechanism, the embryo/scutellum (Mundy et al, 1989) is able to direct protein synthesis of the aleurone layer to just a few proteins such as α-amylase, which is the main protein produced by this tissue. In the near future, when gene transfer can be made regularly with barley, nonbarley genes, e.g., those coding for peptides of pharmaceutical importance, may be transferred and inserted into the aleurone layer to produce specific nonbarley proteins instead of barley α-amylase by induction through gibberellic acid (Rogers, 1985,[2] *personal communication*). If this could be accomplished, and if methods for wet peeling of the aleurone layer and for concentrating and purifing the protein products designed by genetic engineering could be made competitive with the microbiological production alternative, a malt house could be turned into a pharmaceutical industry.

From a genetic point of view, barley is diploid and is genetically simpler than the polyploid wheat, which displays many more copies of each gene. Thus, in maize (Nelson, 1985) and barley there are simple Mendelian genes that control the branching of starch and the ratio between the linear amylose and the branched amylopectin molecules, which is of paramount importance for the swelling and gelling properties of starch (Munck, 1985, and Chapter 5). Similarly in maize and barley, there exist regulatory genes that radically change the endosperm protein pattern of those cereals (called high-lysine genes); this is of importance for the nutritional quality of the protein (Munck, 1992). Similar genes with such drastic effects have not been identified in wheat. It is conceivable that the diploid barley would be easier to manipulate with the new techniques of molecular genetics than the polyploid wheat.

At present, maize is superior to both wheat and barley for starch production because it has a narrow size range of starch granules giving almost 100% A-starch. In wheat and barley, small starch granules (B-starch) that adhere to protein are produced in starch processing as an unwanted product; they are of inferior quality compared to A-starch, which constitutes the major product. Thus, it would be of interest in wheat and barley to engineer a plant that produced only large starch granules in the seed to make these cereals competitive with maize in starch production. Such an endeavor would have a greater expectation of success in barley than in wheat, as discussed previously.

In industrial processes, the whole process scheme from the agricultural raw material to the final product must be evaluated; not only the major products but also the by-products are of paramount importance for the economy of the process. In starch manufacturing, maize has a considerable advantage, first because it has a high yield potential, second because it produces almost exclusively A-starch, third because it gives a high-priced edible oil as a by-product, and fourth because the concentrated steeping liquor is an ideal fermentable product for the microbiological industry, e.g., for penicillin production.

The major advantage of wheat for starch production is the by-product vital

[2]J. C. Rogers, Washington University, School of Medicine, Div. of Hematology-Oncology, St. Louis, MO.

gluten, which has a unique quality in baking and in textured products and which can be sold at quite a high price in the market, provided it is not overproduced. Wheat has no other advantages in starch manufacturing compared to maize, and barley has none whatever. It is not surprising, therefore, that we know of only one starch/syrup factory based on (spring) barley. This is situated in Finland, where maize cannot be imported without heavy levies, maize for seeds cannot be grown, and wheat production for starch is rather insecure due to severe winters and troublesome conditions during harvesting, including a relatively short growing season.

Cereal straw is a downgraded material for industrial use, in spite of the fact that as much or more straw (in tonnes) than grain is produced in the world from cereals. Thus, straw is usually either burned, ploughed under, used for bedding, or fed to ruminants. A hundred years ago, most paper was produced from annual plants. There still exist a few straw-based cellulose factories, most in the developing countries and a few in the EC, including one in Denmark. Also the scientific and technological knowledge of cereal straws is very limited; this encouraged us to produce a preliminary inventory of cereal plants valid for northern European conditions. Tables 1 and 2 display our results from a preliminary investigation, studying the botanical and chemical composition of various cereals harvested as whole plants. The yield and crude composition of barley seed and straw are compared to those of other cereals, giving a rough overview of barley as a starch and cellulose producer. Assuming a grain-to-starch ratio of 1:1, 1 ha of barley crop producing 5 t of seeds and 5 t of straw would potentially yield 3.1 t of starch and 1.6 t of cellulose. The yield of paper pulp would be about 2.4 t, considering that the hemicellulose in this product is partly included with the α-cellulose. Cellulose pulp has for long periods had a world market price more than

TABLE 1
Yield and Composition (dry matter) of Cereals Grown in Denmark in 1985—Grain and Straw

Species	Straw, t/ha			Grain, t/ha			Straw-Grain Ratio			Starch, % dry matter		
	n	Mean	Max and Min	n	Mean	Max and Min	n	Mean	Max and Min	n	Mean	Max and Min
Spring barley	18	3.92	5.54 2.76	18	5.12	6.33 3.56	20	0.78	1.01 0.52	69	62.5	69.3 55.5
Winter barley	4	2.83	3.66 2.00	4	4.21	4.52 3.85	4	0.67	0.81 0.52	16	60.0	60.2 54.1
Spring wheat	5	5.80	7.34 3.93	5	4.09	5.70 2.59	5	1.51	2.22 1.04	12	65.1	68.0 62.2
Winter wheat	14	6.10	8.46 3.66	14	6.91	9.10 3.83	14	0.92	1.63 0.68	53	67.1	70.2 61.6
Winter rye	6	6.42	7.53 5.29	6	4.89	5.40 4.60	6	1.31	1.58 1.10	16	62.8	68.7 58.2
Oats	2	5.66	7.13 4.20	2	4.25	5.40 3.09	2	1.34	1.36 1.32	2	41.9	43.2 40.6
Maize	5	6.64	10.57 0.25	5	6.24	6.86 5.73	5	1.06	1.74 0.72	23	71.8	75.4 68.5

TABLE 2
Composition (% of dry matter) of Hand-Dissected Leaves, Nodes, and Internodes from Straw of Cereals Grown in Denmark in 1985[a]

Species	Botanical Components	Weight Distribution			α-Cellulose		Lignin			Protein			Ash			Silicon		
		n	Mean	Max/Min	n	Mean	n	Mean	Max/Min	n	Mean	Max/Min	n	Mean	Max/Min	n	Mean	Max/Min
Spring barley	Internode	21	50.4	55.1/44.7	2	38.3	14	18.3	22.1/14.0	21	2.0	3.4/1.1	21	4.52	7.08/1.54	21	0.5	1.2/0.0
	Leaf	21	41.6	48.4/33.9	2	28.2	15	13.0	14.8/11.7	21	3.9	5.6/3.2	21	6.25	9.68/3.41	21	1.4	2.8/0.4
	Node	21	5.4	4.0/1.0														
Winter barley	Internode	4	53.0	56.2/50.2		n.d.	2	20.0	21.7/18.2	4	2.8	3.1/2.4	4	3.72	4.93/2.24	4	0.1	0.1/0.0
	Leaf	4	40.0	44.4/35.6			2	15.0	15.6/14.3	4	6.2	9.1/4.6	4	4.52	5.90/3.36	4	0.5	1.0/0.1
	Node	4	4.2	4.8/3.7														
Spring wheat	Internode	5	58.8	61.4/52.5		n.d.	3	17.6	18.2/16.5	5	2.7	3.5/1.8	5	4.05	6.32/1.95	5	0.9	1.6/0.2
	Leaf	5	32.4	35.1/30.3			4	16.3	17.6/15.6	5	4.0	6.6/3.2	5	6.94	11.4/3.38	5	1.7	3.7/0.8
	Node	5	4.2	5.2/2.6														
Winter wheat	Internode	16	55.0	63.0/49.8	2	42.2	7	18.0	20.9/15.6	16	3.0	6.3/1.6	16	4.59	9.25/2.18	16	1.0	2.1/0.0
	Leaf	16	38.7	44.2/31.6	2	29.3	8	15.4	18.9/13.6	16	5.2	9.2/2.9	16	8.38	13.8/9.20	16	2.3	5.4/0.5
	Node	16	4.8	7.0/3.4														
Winter rye	Internode	6	67.7	68.7/66.7	1	41.3	4	17.9	19.2/16.5	6	3.0	6.8/2.5	6	3.68	5.73/2.37	6	0.5	1.1/0.0
	Leaf	6	23.9	25.4/20.7	1	29.8	3	16.1	16.7/15.4	6	5.9	7.7/4.8	6	5.71	7.38/3.81	6	1.2	2.1/0.2
	Node	6	5.2	6.5/2.8														
Oats	Internode	2	50.4	53.4/47.3	2	39.2	2	17.3	17.6/17.0	2	2.3	2.6/1.9	2	4.57	5.16/3.97	2	0.2	0.3/0.0
	Leaf	2	42.1	45.5/38.7	2	30.3	2	13.2	13.3/13.1	2	3.2	3.5/2.9	2	7.38	9.94/4.82	2	1.9	3.2/0.6
	Node	2	4.4	5.1/3.7														
Maize	Internode	9	46.6	52.0/40.4	1	39.5	1	17.0		9	3.7	4.9/2.4	9	6.29	8.92/2.54	9	0.2	0.4/0.0
	Leaf	9	42.1	46.4/34.3			1	13.7		9	8.3	11.3/5.2	9	7.86	10.3/3.83	9	1.4	2.0/0.6
	Node	9	11.9	16.6/8.7														

[a] Material same as in Table 1.

twice that of starch. Cellulose production based on straw is likely to be more costly than starch manufacturing, including higher costs for transportation and storage. This, on the other hand, is partly counterbalanced by the fact that straw is a cheaper raw material than seeds; it also helps to compensate for the lower yield of cellulose pulp than of starch. Thus, the cellulose component should be considered seriously for the future. This requires integration of raw material production, handling, transportation, processing, and marketing, as has been done by the wood-based cellulose industry. Such logistics are largely unheard of in the agricultural sector, with the exception of the sugarbeet-based industry. There is no reason why the straw-handling problem could not be solved so that straw could compete with wood.

The use of barley should be considered in conjunction with all the other potential crops at each site of production. Spring barley, with a very short season from sowing to harvest, is one of the most flexible crops in the world, being able to survive and yield near the polar circle as well as in dry, hot, and salty deserts near the Equator. However, it cannot stand a humid and hot tropical climate, where maize yields exceptionally well but demands much more input of resources than barley. Winter barley produces high yields in Europe, on the level of winter wheat, but is less reliable in northern Europe (Denmark) than winter wheat due to inferior frost resistance. In conclusion, barley, being the number four cereal in the world, defends its role in agriculture well. Thus, we should exploit the broadest possible range of plant species with different agricultural and industrial qualities to buffer our ecosystem, which has been so heavily influenced by humans.

Another aspect of the total utilization of agriculturally produced resources such as barley seeds and straw is that these commodities are rather nonhomogeneous and consist of different botanically defined tissues with quite different compositions and the potential to be used for various purposes, which are exemplified in the following discussion. A deeper understanding of the nature of these intrinsic inhomogeneities is the key to efficient agroindustrial utilization of agricultural plants.

INVENTORIES TO ASCERTAIN THE POTENTIAL USE OF BARLEY AND OTHER CEREALS

In spite of an impressive amount of work published about plants, we have very little interrelated, systematic information on how modern varieties yield or on their composition in relation to their botanical and chemical components. The whole plant material collection, analyzed and shown in Tables 1 and 2, is small and fragmentary but is still unique and absolutely necessary to elucidate the subject of this chapter.

A well-cultivated field of a cereal crop is an incredibly efficient factory during seed filling for converting CO_2 and light into starch. Maize, being a C_4-pathway plant in photosynthesis, is rated here as more efficient than barley, which follows the C_3 scheme (Mac Key, 1981). Theoretically, it takes the energy of 1.2 glucose units to produce 1 g of starch or cellulose, which is much less than in the production of protein and oil, for which 2.5 and 3.1 glucose units, respectively, are needed (Mac Key, 1981). It is thus obvious that starch and cellulose production give more tonnage per hectare than protein and oil production according to the internal "economy" of the plant. Starch and cellulose are thus the agricultural chemical commodities that can be produced at the lowest energy price per unit of dry matter.

As seen in Tables 1 and 2 and in Fig. 4, there is, as expected, a high correlation between starch yield and grain yield, irrespective of plant species. A poorer but significant positive correlation was found within barley between yield of straw and yield of grain.

DRY AND WET MILLING OF BARLEY FOR STARCH

In our EC investigation, quite a large variation in the starch content of different cereal species was found (Table 1). Maize and winter wheat have the highest starch content, but, surprisingly, spring barley (variety Triumph) can reach almost 70% starch in spite of the fact that the kernels contain hulls.

Industrial barley milling is a minute branch of the present milling industry. The dry-milling process aims at separating the husk (palea and lemma), pericarp, testa, aleurone, and germ from the endosperm, which can be used further for food and as brewers' grits (Munck and Lorenzen, 1977) or for

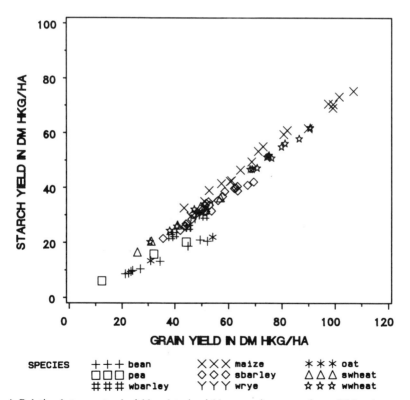

Fig. 4. Relation between starch yield and grain yield; s = spring, w = winter, DM = dry matter. (From F. Rexen and L. Munck, *unpublished report to the EC, 1986*)

manufacturing starch and sugars through a wet-milling process (Rexen and Munck, 1984). Compared to wheat, the barley seed has a shallower crease and is thus suitable for decortication in a carborundum dehuller (pearling). On the other hand, barley, in contrast to wheat, has a multicellular aleurone layer with thick cell walls. The endosperm cell walls are also thick and consist mainly of β-glucan. The texture (elasticity) of the barley endosperm is also different from that of wheat. This implies difficulties in milling a barley flour with a low ash and fiber content compared to milling wheat; the resulting flour is much more fluffy and less dense than wheat flour.

As in wheat, seed texture and density play a great role in barley dry milling for wet starch processing. Hard, dense feed barley tends to contain less starch and more β-glucan than malting varieties. In Fig. 5, a flotation experiment in sodium nitrate solution is shown. The three barley varieties, the mealy malting barley Triumph (β-glucan, 4.2% dry matter [DM]), the steely feed barley Minerva (β-glucan, 5.9% DM), and the mealy, low-β-glucan mutant of Minerva, M 737 (β-glucan, 2.7% DM) (Aastrup and Munck, 1985; Munck, 1987b), display differences in density. Minerva sinks because it is most dense, followed by Triumph and M 737, which show an increased number of floaters. Table 3 shows that when a sample of Triumph is separated by flotation, the mealy, light fraction is richer in starch and lower in protein than the more dense fractions. There is slightly less β-glucan in the mealy seed fraction but considerably less soluble β-glucan than in the other fractions. This is advantageous because soluble β-glucan is a major problem in the wet starch

Fig. 5. Flotation experiments on three barley varieties in NaNO$_3$ solution, showing 68% (Triumph), 39% (Minerva), and 97% (M 737) floating grains.

separation of the dry-milled barley flour because it impairs separation of starch by centrifugation. The same β-glucan quality criterion is also operative in the malting and brewing industry. Thus, the optimal barley raw material for both malt and dry-milling for starch manufacture is a large-seeded, soft (mealy) kernel with a high level of starch and a low level of (soluble) β-glucan. This implies that the kernel has more slender endosperm cell walls and larger cells.

During disc milling of barley, there is a direct relationship between β-glucan content and milling capacity at a given work load (Munck, 1981) (Table 4).

Normally in barley dry-milling for starch, the barley is decorticated in a carborundum dehuller and thereafter milled with rollers or a hammer mill.

The Carlsberg Research Laboratory has developed a dry-milling technology involving a newly designed disc mill, UMS MHA-600, for barley and wheat processing (Andersen, 1987; Gram et al, 1989). It is a dry-milling step producing flour for further wet-milling for extraction of starch and gluten. The machine has a first-break capacity of 800–1,100 kg/hr. As in the old stone mills, the disc mill consists of a stationary and a rotary disc (Fig. 6). Unlike the stone mills, these discs are made of steel and mounted vertically. The rotary disc has a velocity of 3,600 rpm, which means that the speed is 350 km/hr on the periphery in the first break of the 50-cm discs. The grinding surface consists of 24 specially corrugated hard metal segments (Fig. 6B) mounted on the periphery of each disc so that each segment covers an angle of 15°. The elements can be easily changed when needed without elaborate tools. The capacity of the mill is about 1 t of grain per hour. The grain is fed to the mill through the center of the stationary disc, and by centrifugal force and the crossing angle between the grinding elements it is thrown toward the periphery of the discs, where the grain is ground.

TABLE 3
Analyses of Three Fractions of Triumph Barley Seeds Obtained by Flotation
in Sodium Nitrate Solution[a]

	Barley Fraction		
	"Mealy"	Intermediate	"Steely"
Hectoliter weight, kg	64.85	69.41	70.66
Thousand-kernel weight, g	40.13	41.85	43.08
Protein, % DM[b]	9.45	10.45	11.70
Starch, % DM	65.70	61.90	60.10
Total β-glucan, % DM	4.04	4.34	4.36
Soluble β-glucan, % DM	0.43	0.63	0.74

[a] Source: Munck (1987b).
[b] DM = dry matter.

TABLE 4
Milling of Barley Grits with a United Milling Systems MHA Disc Mill, Type 400[a]

	Capacity (kg/hr)	Electricity Load A	β-Glucan (% dry matter)
Triumph	400	9.5	4.44
Lami	300	10.5	5.22
Minerva	225	10.5	6.36

[a] Source: Munck (1981).

In Table 5, data from raw material and products from a typical barley trial in the dry-milling process (Fig. 7), preceding wet barley starch manufacture, are outlined. After one passage through the UMS MHA-600 disc mill, 51.1% flour and 7.3% coarse bran could be sifted off. Middlings 1 (41.6%) were further processed in the disc mill, and middlings 2 are recycled twice. If a very high flour yield is wanted, as in barley milling for starch, the remaining fractions after the four disc mill passages are mixed and milled in a corrugated roller mill, giving a total yield of 88% with an ash content of around 2%.

The new dry-milling techniques could be combined advantageously for barley with the new efficient wet-milling high-pressure-steeping techniques developed by Meuser et al (1985). In Table 6, a typical experiment of such an extraction of barley starch is demonstrated. The high-pressure disintegration technique

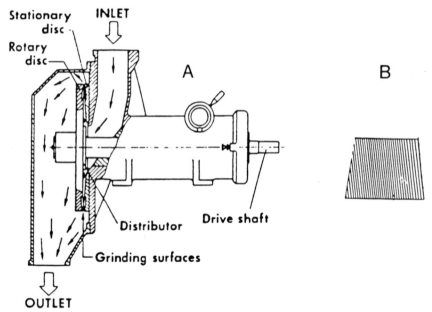

Fig. 6. Cross section of the United Milling Systems disc mill MHA 600 (A) with a disc section (B). (Reprinted, by permission, from Gram, 1989)

TABLE 5
Composition (% dry matter) of Whole Barley
Dry-Milled with the United Milling Systems MHA-600 Disc Mill Process
Optimized for Subsequent Wet-Milling of Flour[a,b]

	Ash	Protein	Starch	Fat	Fiber	Milling Yield (%)
Raw material	2.61	11.7	59.3	2.1	5.1	...
Flour	2.09	11.7	65.2	3.8	2.4*	88.0**
Coarse bran	5.58	3.3	3.8	0.7	35.4	7.3
Fine bran	5.26	13.0	24.5	0.7	35.4	4.7
Bran (fine + coarse combined)	...	...	11.9***	...	...	...

[a]Source: Munck et al (1988); used by permission.
[b]Industrial specifications: * = < 3.0, ** = > 86.0, *** = < 14.0.

when applied during steeping gives higher yields of starch (especially B starch) and less solubles, making steeping with SO_2 unnecessary. The separation and yield of starch with this method would be improved if barley flour from disc-milled barley were included instead of flour from conventionally dehusked barley.

Further research should be conducted if cereals ever can be specially bred to suit dry and wet processes, simplifying starch production and improving

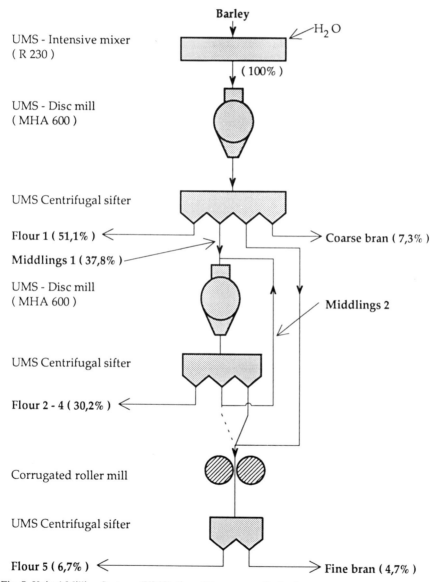

Fig. 7. United Milling Systems (UMS) disc milling process for barley.

economy. Such procedures could also include use of specific enzymes to loosen the starch granules (Olsen and Christensen, 1984).

UTILIZATION OF STARCH

Barley starch, even after purification, has a grayish look compared to wheat and maize starch and contains larger amounts of protein and minerals (e.g., 0.2% DM of protein in wheat starch compared to 1.0–1.5% in barley starch; see Table 6). Barley starch has a viscosity profile similar to that of potato starch and has a similar range of applications. For most applications that are mentioned in the following discussion, barley starch can be used but will meet strong price competition from other starches.

Today, the utilization of cereals in the nonfood sector is very limited. The main component in cereal seeds is starch, and one year's production of cereals in the EC contains as much as 100 million tonnes of starch (Munck et al, 1988). Most of the starch is used for food or feed; only a minor part is processed by industry. The total production of native starch in the EC is only about 4 million tonnes, of which 1.3 million tonnes is used in nonfood industries. Of the 4 million tonnes, approximately 800,000 t are derived from potatoes. In the EC in 1983, 51% of the manufactured starch was used in the food industry, 4.8% for animal feed, 20% for paper and board, 1.7% for textiles, 2.4% for adhesives, and 9.5% for chemical and pharmaceutical purposes. The starch is used either as such, as a derivative, or after hydrolysis. Figure 8 reviews the potential uses of starch (Rexen and Munck, 1984; Munck, 1993).

Starch consumption in the paper and board industry has increased considerably during recent years, mainly due to the favorable development of the price relationship between starch and cellulose. As a matter of fact, native starch is today cheaper than cellulose. In addition, the starch manufacturing industry has succeeded in developing new and improved derivatives for the cellulose industry. For example, the introduction of cationic starches in the paper industry has substantially increased the market for starch to 1) improve the strength of paper, 2) increase filler, pigment, or dye retention without losing sheet strength, 3) increase size retention, and 4) increase the rate of paper production. With the cationic starches, the paper industry for the first

TABLE 6
Wet Separation of Starch from Dehusked Barley
Obtained from Two Different Wet-Milling Procedures[a]

Product	Distribution, %	
	Steeping with SO_2	High-Pressure Disintegration
Barley	100	100
Fiber	10.5	5.0
Solubles	6.8	5.3
B-starch	25.0	31.5
A-starch	57.7	58.2
Recovery	99.7	98.6
Protein content of the A-starch, dry basis	1.5	1.2

[a] Adapted from Meuser et al (1986).

time obtained a starch with an affinity for negatively charged surfaces like cellulose. The retaining capability of cationic starches makes them excellent flocculants, for example, for finely dispersed anionic particles in sewage treatment.

Starch consumption in the textile industry has decreased during recent years and is destined to be reduced further because the textile industry in the EC is declining and starch products are exposed to tough competition from petrochemically based products. Also the adhesive market is rather small for starch production.

The chemical and pharmaceutical industries consume approximately 10% of the total starch production, mainly in the form of starch hydrolysates. Hydrolysates are used in fermentation processes to produce commodity chemicals such as alcohols and organic acids and also fine chemicals and pharmaceuticals.

Other fields of industrial applications of starch are in the mining industry and in oil exploration (flocculating agent, increasing the viscosity of drilling muds). Also the synthetic polymer industry uses starch products, although in very limited amounts. They are mostly used as fillers in biodegradable plastics or as chemical intermediates, e.g., sorbitol.

The outlet for starch in the synthetic polymer industry can be increased considerably. Starch may be used directly as a filler, e.g., in polyvinylchloride (Griffin, 1985), to reduce the cost and make the product more or less biodegradable. Such starch polymer films may be used for carrier bags and

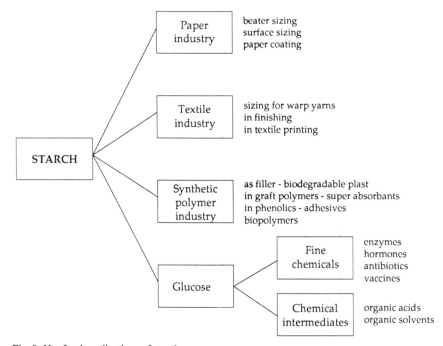

Fig. 8. Nonfood applications of starch.

as an agricultural mulch for plants to diminish evaporation under dry growing conditions.

Starch may also act as an active component in a graft copolymer with a synthetic polymer (Otey, 1985). The synthetic polymer may be a polyester, polyamide, polyacrylonitrile, etc. A wide variety of monomers have been graft polymerized into granular and gelatinized starch, and several of the polymers show promise as thickeners, flocculants, clarification aids, retention aids, and for many other uses. Such products may also be used in controlled-release fertilizers, coating of seeds, agricultural sprays, etc.

Starch has been used successfully in the production of phenol resin, partly substituting for formaldehyde, e.g., for making a glue for straw and wood fiber boards (Woelk, 1981), and it can be used to produce polyols, e.g., glucosides, which may find large-scale application in the production of urethane foams, alkyds, surfactants, etc.

Finally, microbial polymers produced from starch and starch hydrolysates have been proposed for a wide variety of industrial applications, for example, pullulans, xanthan, and polyhydroxybutyrate.

The market potential for starch in the polymer industry is thus substantial—up to 800,000 t for the EC has been mentioned (Rexen and Munck, 1984).

There are thus reasonably large potential new outlets for starch in the cellulose, chemical and pharmaceutical, and synthetic polymer industries.

The European fiber industry is only about 40% self-sufficient and cannot meet the demand for cellulose fibers; the EC has to import still larger quantities of wood, cellulose pulp, and paper. Therefore, there is growing interest within the EC in using alternative sources of fibers such as recycled fibers and fibers from annual plants (straw). The quality of pulp for paper manufacturing depends on both chemical and structural characteristics. The occurrence of parenchyma cells, for example, is unique to straw raw material. The addition of starch derivatives could improve the paper strength of straw cellulose so that a paper of a reasonable quality could be produced entirely from agricultural resources. Native starch is cheaper than cellulose, and so it would be worthwhile to extend the upper limits for starch additions. Too much starch makes the paper brittle and transparent. However, up to 30% starch has been added in laboratory-scale studies with satisfactory results, and new starch derivatives might increase further the use of starch in paper-making.

The chemical industry is dominated by the capital-intensive petrochemical complexes, which naturally are interested in conserving the present industrial structure. In theory, however, no technical obstacles prevent starch from being used as raw material even for the production of basic chemicals. On economic grounds, this is not very likely to happen. Biomass, such as starch and cellulose-rich raw materials, will remain more expensive to produce and process for basic chemicals than oil and natural gas, as long as we have free access to the fossil raw materials. The use of 10% ethanol for automobile fuel would consume about 35 million tonnes of cereals in the EC, which would be infeasible from an economic point of view. It is mainly in their nonhydrolyzed state that the natural polymers, starch and cellulose, and their derivatives will be able to compete with petrochemicals in the future (Rexen et al, 1988).

A few commodity chemicals are produced today by fermentation of starch products. These chemicals are, e.g., ethanol, glycerol, acetone, butanol, acetic acid, propionic acid, citric acid, and lactic acid. A much larger outlet could be found in the production of commodity chemicals if the competitive strength of starch over fossil raw materials were increased. The total potential in this field in the EC corresponds to approximately 5 million tonnes of starch.

Presumably, the pharmaceutical and fine chemical sectors will be the first to expand consumption. However, in the EC, even a doubling of the consumption in these sectors, for example, will lead only to a comparatively moderate increase (500,000 t) in the demand for raw materials (sugar or starch).

It will take a long time to reach the above-mentioned total potentials unless a lasting change in price in favor of biomass over fossil carbon sources is maintained. Then it is reasonable to believe that starch will become a more attractive raw material for the future chemical industry, stimulating improvement in raw materials, starch processing, and fermentation technology.

UTILIZATION OF CEREAL STRAW

The potential industrial applications of cellulose from straw are outlined in Fig. 9 (Rexen and Munck, 1984; Munck, 1993). This section concentrates on the use of straw fractions for paper, particle boards, feed, and fuel, which seem most feasible. Because of the difficulty in hydrolyzing cellulose to glucose, starch is often preferred for the preparation of hydrolysates and chemicals, and because cellulose in the foreseeable future will be more expensive than starch, we think that intact cellulose components will be more economical to market than cellulose hydrolysate (Rexen et al, 1988). Further references may be found in Rexen and Munck (1984), Petersen (1988, 1989), and F. Rexen and L. Munck, *unpublished report to the EC, 1986.*

To obtain maximum utilization of cereal straw, it is important to have knowledge of its chemical and botanical composition.

Chemical Composition

The chemical constituents of straw from annual plants can be classified into three groups: the polysaccharides (70%), lignin (20%), and other constituents (10%) such as minerals, protein, free phenolic acids. and waxes (Theander and Åman, 1984).

POLYSACCHARIDES

These are mainly the high-molecular-weight carbohydrates cellulose and hemicellulose.

Cellulose is composed of $(1{\rightarrow}4)$-β-D-anhydroglucopyranosyl units with every second unit turned $180°$; because of this type of bond, cellulose is a linear molecule (Fig. 10a). The glucan chains in cellulose are bound together in parallel by hydrogen bonds to form microfibrils that again aggregate into larger fibrils. A large part of cellulose occurs in crystal form, which accounts for its mechanical strength and its resistance to enzymatic and chemical hydrolysis (Krässig, 1984; Haigler, 1985).

Hemicellulose is, in contrast, a heteroglycan (Fig. 10b). The backbone of hemicellulose in straw is a chain of β-D-$(1{\rightarrow}4)$-linked D-xylopyranose residues with a few attached groups of L-arabinofuranosyl units, D-glucopyranosyl-uronic acids, and/or its 4-methyl ether. Small amounts of mannose and galactose are also found in the hemicellulose of cereal straw (Wilkie, 1979). The degree of polymerization in hemicellulose is lower than that in cellulose (Theander and Åman, 1984). This and the fact that the xylan chains cannot associate easily because of the side chains make hemicellulose less resistant to enzymatic or chemical attack. The chemical structure of straw hemicellulose resembles that of hardwood (deciduous trees), whereas softwood (conifers) hemicellulose is rich in mannan polymers (Fan et al, 1982). In cell-wall preparations from cereals, *O*-acetyl groups have been detected in amounts of 1–2% (Bacon et al, 1975).

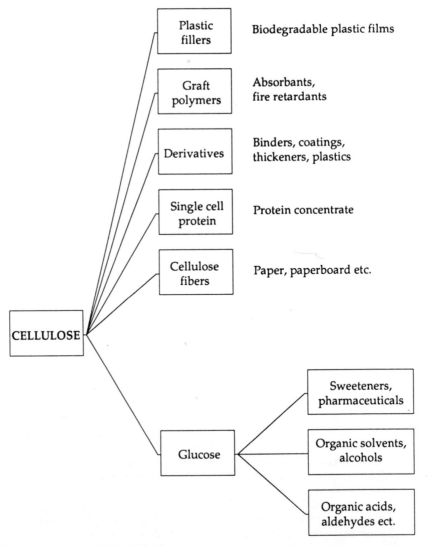

Fig. 9. Industrial applications of cellulose.

LIGNIN

Lignin, a complex polymer built of phenylpropane units, has various functions in the plant; it gives structural rigidity, acts as a bonding agent between cells, reduces the permeation of water across the cell walls of the xylem, and effectively resists microbiological attack (Sarkanen and Hergert, 1971).

The three main precursors for lignin are: *p*-coumaryl alcohol (Fig. 10c,

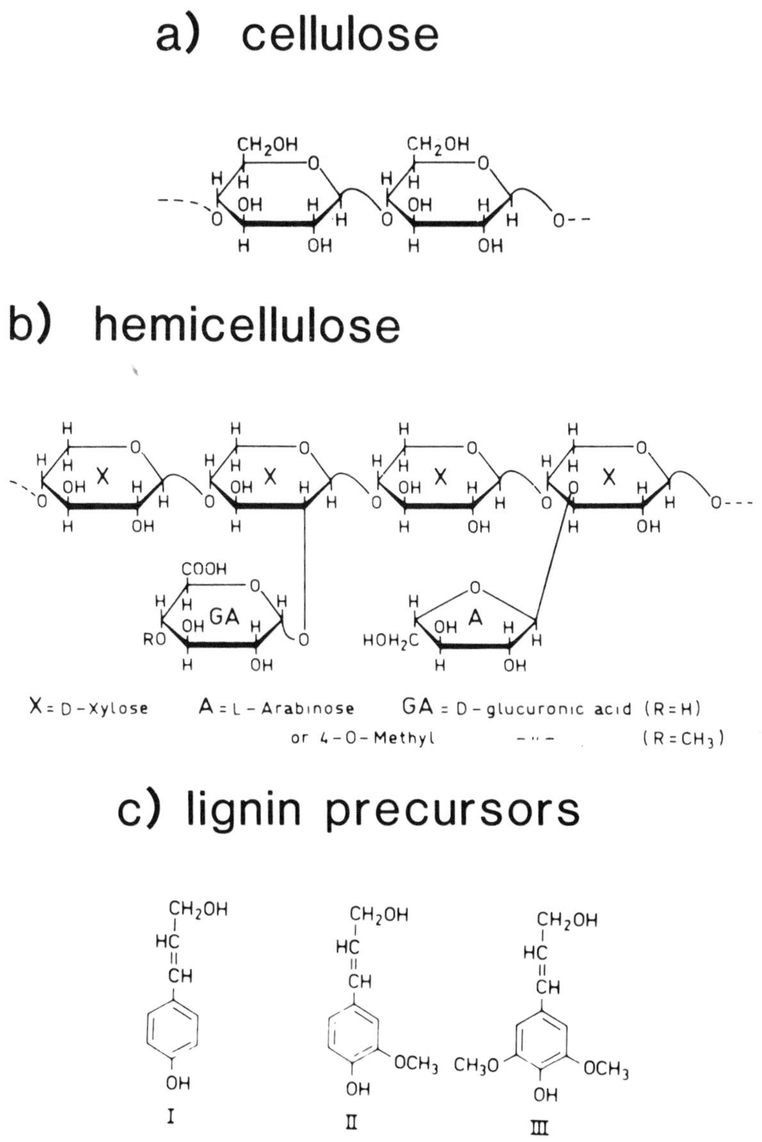

a) cellulose

b) hemicellulose

X = D-Xylose   A = L-Arabinose   GA = D-glucuronic acid (R=H)
                 or 4-O-Methyl   - " -   (R=CH₃)

c) lignin precursors

Fig. 10. Chemical composition of straw constituents: a) cellulose, b) hemicellulose, c) lignin.

I), coniferyl alcohol (Fig. 10c, II) and sinapyl alcohol (Fig. 10c, III). Softwood lignin is mainly a condensation product of coniferyl alcohol, whereas hardwood lignin comes from coniferyl and sinapyl alcohols. All three classes are represented in lignin of cereals (Sarkanen and Hergert, 1971; Theander and Åman, 1984). The respective structural elements in the lignin polymer are called *p*-hydroxyphenyl, guaiacyl, and siringyl, and they are held together by carbon-carbon, aryl ether, and alkyl ether bonds.

RESIDUAL CONSTITUENTS

This group represents constituents such as protein, waxes, free phenolic acids, low-molecular weight carbohydrates, and minerals.

The protein content of cereal straw (2–10%) is dependent upon time of harvest but is low in mature straw and is known to have low digestibility.

The dominating components of the minerals are potassium and silicon (Theander and Åman, 1984). The insoluble ash content is much greater in straw than in wood; silicon is especially abundant in straw (Fan et al, 1982).

Although the residual constituents form only a small quantity of the straw, their presence is significant not just because of their biological and physiological functions but also for their mainly negative influence on, for example, pulping and bleaching of cellulose fibers (Fan et al, 1982). Silicon can cause serious scaling on boiler surfaces during evaporation of the process fluid in the straw cellulose industry, making recycling difficult and impairing energy conservation and antipollution measures.

Botanical Components

Cereal straw is composed of three major botanical parts: leaves, internodes, and nodes (Fig. 11). The internodes are separated by the nodes, from which the leaves emerge. The leaf organ includes both the leaf blade and the leaf

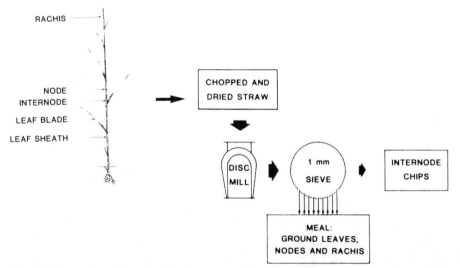

Fig. 11. Botanical constituents of barley straw and their mechanical separation in disc milling.

sheath. The leaf sheath envelopes the lower part of the internodes. At the top part of the straw is the rachis, which carries the seeds and is composed of nodes and very short internodes (Müller, 1960; Theander and Åman, 1984).

The weight distribution of the straw components is shown in Table 2 and differs among the species of cereals. In rye, the internodes may constitute up to 70% of the straw, whereas barley and oats have a higher proportion of leaves. The nodes component is a minor constituent of the straw, with a weight of 4–6% of the whole straw.

The variation in botanical composition depends on species, variety, climatic factors, and growth conditions. Botanical components of straw have different physical strength properties; the leaves are very fragile, but the internodes are tough and strong as they are built to carry the weight of both the grain and the leaves.

Chemical Composition of Leaves and Internodes

The botanical components of straw differ in their chemical composition (Müller, 1960; Theander and Åman, 1984).

Taking the spring barley variety Triumph grown in Denmark as an example (Fig. 12), it was found that the content of cellulose was higher in the internodes than in the leaves; the leaves contained higher levels of protein and minerals, especially silica, and the internodes were more lignified than the leaves. Also the composition of the hemicellulose in the leaves and internodes varied (Fig. 12). The leaves had a higher proportion of both arabinose and galactose in their hemicellulose than did the internodes, which had a higher content of xylose.

For industrial utilization of straw, the protein content of the leaves and the yield of internodes, as well as the ash, silicon, and lignin contents of the internodes, are all important factors. The influence of barley variety and growing location on these factors have been evaluated (Table 7).

The coefficients of variation show that the protein in leaves and the ash and especially silicon content in internodes varied with the place of growth. It was found earlier that cereals grown on loamy soils accumulate more minerals than those grown on sandy soils (Petersen, 1988). The variation in leaf protein among different growing locations may have been influenced by different fertilization procedures.

Variation among different cultivars of spring barley was less pronounced, but the ash and lignin contents seemed to vary most.

The varieties and place of growth showed only a small influence on the weight distribution of internodes in these trials, although a lower yield of internodes was obtained in 1986 than in 1985.

The composition of carbohydrates was found to vary between the botanical fractions in both spring and winter barley (Table 8). Higher contents of glucose and xylose were found in the internodes in accordance with earlier observations (Åman and Nordquist, 1983; Theander and Åman, 1984). The higher glucose content corresponded to a higher α-cellulose content in the internodes in accordance with Fig. 12, whereas the leaves had a larger proportion of arabinose and galactose, indicating that the hemicellulose of internodes is more homogeneous in its composition of carbohydrates. A difference in physical behavior of the hemicellulose during, for example, cellulose pulping could be expected between the internodes and leaves because of the difference in carbohydrate composition.

The hemicellulose composition seemed to vary with place of growth, showing the influence of both climatic and agronomic factors.

Straw Milling and Fractionation

Cereal straw in general is considered to be a uniform biomass but is in fact much more complex and interesting in terms of its botanical constituents

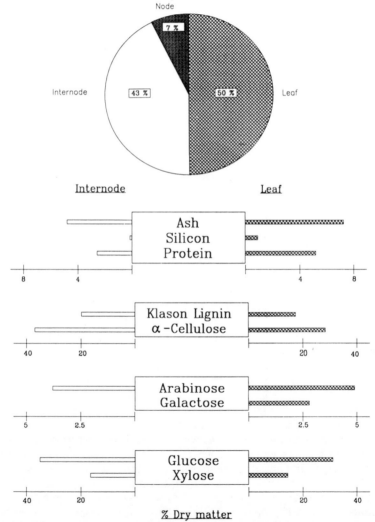

Fig. 12. Botanical composition of hand-dissected spring barley, variety Triumph (top) and chemical composition (% dry matter) of the internodes and leaves (bottom).

and their chemical composition. Today, straw is used as a bulk material, but it is definitely advantageous to separate straw into its botanical components before utilization.

The botanical components of straw can be separated mechanically (Fig. 11). This is done by milling the straw dry and screening it into different fractions. Before processing, the straw must be chopped into 3- to 5-cm pieces, and the moisture content should be less than 15%. The principle in the milling system depends on a difference in physical behavior between leaves and internodes when milled in a disc mill. Thus, when milling the straw, two fractions are obtained: a fraction of internode chips and a meal consisting of ground leaves, nodes, and rachis. The leaf meal is separated from the internode chips by sieving on a 1-mm screen.

The internodes are strong and result in flaked, flat particles (1–3 cm long), whereas the leaves and nodes are fragile, so they are easily pulverized between the discs and are hence ground into a fine powder.

Fractions of milled barley straw are shown in Fig. 13.

The milling equipment was developed by the Carlsberg Research Laboratory in cooperation with United Milling System A/S, Copenhagen, Denmark. The disc mill (see Fig. 6) has a stationary and a rotary disc, both equipped with hard metal grinding segments made especially for straw grinding. Different rotation speeds can be used, and the distance between the discs and the rotation direction can be changed. Specific process conditions can be chosen depending on the straw type to be milled.

The yield of internode chips varies with species milled, depending on the difference in botanical composition. In the case of barley, the yield ranges from 40 to 55% DM. The mechanical separation was defined as optimal if the same weight proportion of internode chips could be obtained as when the straw was manually separated into its botanical components. All straw

TABLE 7
Variation in Content of Protein, Ash, Silicon, and Lignin
in Hand-Dissected Leaves and Internodes, as well as Weight Distribution
of Internodes Depending on Variety and Place of Growth

| | | Leaf | Internode | | | |
		Protein (%)	Percent of Straw	Ash (%)	Silicon (%)	Lignin (%)
Spring barley	Mean	3.6	53	5.81	0.9	18.1
(Varieties: 6,[a]	CV[b]	8	4	15	10	17
Locations: 1,	Max	3.9	55	7.08	1.0	19.4
Year: 1985)	Min	3.2	50	4.65	0.8	14.0
Spring barley	Mean	6.3	41	6.40	0.6	21.3
(Variety: Triumph,	CV	39	12	26	116	9
Locations: 5,	Max	9.8	46	8.99	1.5	23.9
Year: 1986)	Min	3.6	33	4.80	0	19.7
Winter barley	Mean	6.3	52	5.35	0.9	24.2
(Variety: Igri,	CV	30	8	44	109	6
Locations: 6,	Max	9.0	56	9.90	2.6	25.6
Year: 1986)	Min	4.0	46	3.60	0	21.6

[a] Varieties: Ca 700202, Galant, Lami, R-1508, Sewa, and Triumph.
[b] CV = coefficient of variation.

separations were run at a fixed set of processing conditions, but since the species of cereals have different straw strength properties, individual process conditions should be used for each of the cereals (Petersen, 1988). Chemical analyses were made on both the manually and the mechanically separated fractions to test the efficiency of the milling process.

In the case of two winter barley varieties, Igri and Gerbel, different behavior during milling was found. When Igri was milled, the optimal yield of internode chips could be obtained, but when Gerbel was milled under the same conditions,

TABLE 8
Carbohydrates[a] (given as % w/w of straw dry matter) in Hand-Dissected Internodes
and Leaves of Spring and Winter Barley

		Spring Barley Triumph, Locations: 3		Winter Barley Igri, Locations: 6	
		Mean	Range	Mean	Range
Glucose	Internode	35.2	36.4–34.1	33.5	36.9–31.3
	Leaf	28.6	31.1–24.9	29.5	31.3–27.5
Xylose	Internode	15.7	16.7–14.1	15.0	16.8–13.2
	Leaf	12.7	14.4–10.6	11.5	15.3–12.8
Arabinose	Internode	2.8	4.9–1.4	1.9	4.0–1.1
	Leaf	3.8	3.8–2.0	3.4	5.5–2.2
Galactose	Internode				(0.4)
	Leaf	3.2	6.1–0.8	3.4	6.1–1.0

[a] Mannose was detected only in very low quantities (<0.2%).

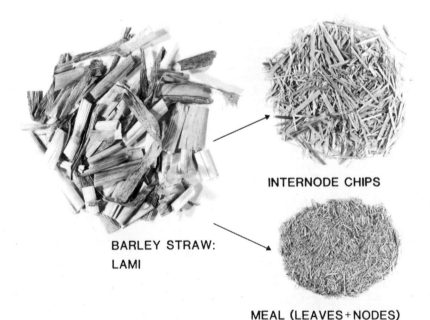

INTERNODE CHIPS

BARLEY STRAW:
LAMI

MEAL (LEAVES+NODES)

Fig. 13. Raw material and fractions from disc-milled straw after sieving.

only 75% of the optimal yield could be reached (Petersen, 1988). This meant that part of the internode was ground into the meal with the leaves. Igri, a two-rowed barley, is known to have a stiffer straw than Gerbel, which is six-rowed.

Uses of Mechanically Processed Fractions from Straw

Since the leaves and internodes of straw have individual physical and chemical characteristics, they have different industrial application areas. The internode chips, having a high cellulose content approaching that of wood and a low content of minerals, are well suited as raw material for the cellulose industry. They are ideal for the production of particle boards because of their high physical strength properties.

The leaf-node meal, on the other hand, is excellent as fodder or can be used as energy sources for local processing, e.g., drying of biomass.

CELLULOSE FROM INTERNODE CHIPS

Straw of annual plants is generally characterized as a short-fiber cellulose material. The average fiber length of whole, unprocessed straw ranges from 1.1 to 1.5 mm, whereas that of hardwood ranges from 0.6 to 1.0 mm and that of softwood from 2.0 to 5.7 mm (Rexen and Munck, 1984). There is, however, a difference in fiber length distribution between the leaves and internodes of straw (Fig. 14), which is of great practical interest.

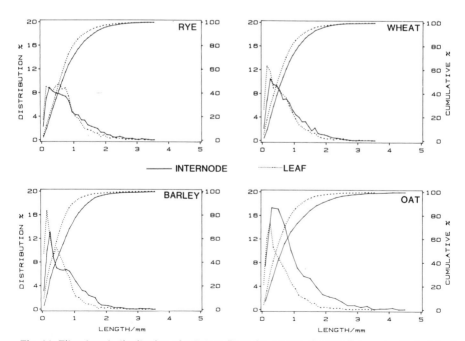

Fig. 14. Fiber length distribution of cellulose fibers from hand-dissected internodes (dotted line) and leaves (continuous line) from rye, wheat, barley, and oats.

The fiber length was measured on 20,000–25,000 fibers using a Kajaani fiber size analyzer FS-200 (Bichard and Scudamore, 1988).

This preliminary study (see Fig. 14 and Table 9, analyzing one variety each of rye, wheat, barley and oats), clearly indicated a distinction in quality of cellulose fibers between the internodes and leaves, the internodes having a higher average fiber length. Whole straw from wheat and rye is generally known to have longer fibers, so these cereals are normally preferred as whole-straw raw material in the cellulose industry. Surprisingly, the oats variety collected in this material had a high average fiber distribution.

A large difference in average fiber length was found between the leaves and internodes of barley. The barley leaves had much shorter fibers than did the internodes; the fibers of barley internodes were comparable in fiber length to fibers from wheat internodes. Whole-barley straw normally gives shorter-fiber cellulose compared to the cellulose of wheat and rye. This may be explained by the large weight percentage of leaves (see Table 2), which have low average fiber length. Thus, paper quality should improve considerably using barley internodes compared to whole barley (and should make it a competitive raw material).

The coarseness of the fibers (Table 9) is also an important quality parameter; fine fibers result in a different quality of paper, with different application possibilities than those for coarse fibers (Britt, 1965). The coarseness of internodes and leaves of barley, oats, rye, and wheat was found to vary with the botanical components of the straw. The leaf fibers seemed coarser than the fibers of the internodes.

To study varietal differences, four barley varieties were selected; the internodes were pulped, and the average fiber length distribution and coarseness were determined (Table 10).

The internodes of Golden Promise gave a high yield of α-cellulose and a high average fiber length with relatively low coarseness compared to the other varieties. The internode fibers of Golf were much coarser than the fibers of the other varieties. When producing cellulose from straw, the most suitable varieties giving optimal quality for specific applications should be chosen as raw material. Golden Promise was shown to be superior in the properties tested and so should be the best raw material for paper pulp manufacturing.

The ratio of arabinose to xylose is thought to influence the water-holding capacity of dietary fibers (Southgate and Englyst, 1985; Cummings, 1986). In a study on brewers' spent grain, a positive correlation between water-holding

TABLE 9
Length-Weighted Distribution and Coarseness of Chemical, Bleached Pulp from Rye, Wheat, Barley, and Oats, Made from Hand-Dissected Botanical Components

Cereal Variety		Rye (Petcus)	Wheat (Kraka)	Barley (Triumph)	Oats (Risø)
Average fiber length,[a] mm	Internode	0.83	0.77	0.74	0.91
	Leaf	0.74	0.63	0.53	0.63
Coarseness, mg/m	Internode	0.081	0.082	0.091	0.103
	Leaf	0.085	0.112	0.114	0.118

[a] Length-weighted fiber length average $= \Sigma(n_i \times \text{length}^2_i)/\Sigma(n_i \times \text{length})$, where $n_i =$ number of fibers in each length class (Bichard and Scudamore, 1988).

capacity and the arabinose-xylose ratio was found (Grøndal, 1990). Highly branched arabinoxylans favor the intramolecular binding of water, whereas cellulose and xylan are less hydrophilic. The ratio of arabinose to xylose was found to vary between the botanical components of straw (see Table 8). Thus, because of a lower arabinose-xylose ratio, cellulose pulp from internodes could possibly obtain better drainage time than pulp made from whole straw.

Summing up, because of the higher cellulose content, the lower ash (silicon) content, and the better fiber length distribution, the internodes are the most suitable part of straw for making cellulose pulp and are considerably better than the unseparated straw.

Whole barley straw today is not considered to be a good raw material for production of cellulose. Experience with whole barley straw in the cellulose industry has shown a lower yield of cellulose and difficulties during production and that the cellulose is not easily bleached (Fredericia Cellulose A/S,[3] 1990, *personal communication*). The use of barley internodes instead of the whole barley straw will certainly improve the fiber length distribution and the yield of cellulose and thereby the quality of the resulting paper. Thus, the use of barley straw for production of cellulose must be reviewed.

PARTICLE BOARDS FROM INTERNODES

Particle boards of internode chips have been produced industrially at Baltic Board, Bornholm, Denmark (Andreasen et al, 1988; Munck and Rexen, 1990). The factory normally produces thin wood particle boards for the furniture industry. The plant is a "Mende"-plant using a continuous-calender press, which operates at a lower pressing temperature ($160°C$) and reduces the pressing time in comparison with the conventional multiple-calender press. The wood boards normally produced have a thickness of 2–8 mm and a density of 600–700 kg/m^3. Particle boards of barley, wheat, and rape mixed with wood have been produced (Fig. 15).

Internode chips of the different cereals, dried to a moisture content of 1–3%, were intermixed with wood in weight ratios of 0–50%. Ordinary 10% urea formaldehyde was used, and the manufactured boards had a thickness of 2.5–3.0 mm. The density and the bending strength of the boards were tested (Table 11).

[3]Fredericia Cellulose Fabrik A/S, 7000 Fredericia, Denmark.

TABLE 10
Yield of α-Cellulose, Average Fiber Length, and Coarseness of Chemical, Bleached Pulp from Hand-Dissected Internodes of Different Barley Varieties

Variety	α-Cellulose (%)	Average Fiber Length[a] (mm)	Coarseness (mg/m)
Golf	40.1	0.83	0.160
Triumph	40.1	0.86	0.086
Corgi	39.5	0.85	0.086
Golden Promise	42.7	1.02	0.092

[a]Average length-weighted fiber length. See Table 9 for definition.

The DIN standard value for the bending strength of boards with a thickness of up to 13 mm is 18 MPa (Deutsche Industry Norm standard 68761). Particle boards from rape partly complied with the standard norms, but the boards made of wheat and barley internode chips had lower bending strength. These results are still encouraging because the same process conditions (temperature, pressing time, etc.) had been used as for wood, and these might not be optimal for straw.

The surfaces of barley and wheat internodes, as compared with those of rape, are covered with a waxy layer that makes the binding of glue and hardener difficult. Enlarging the binding area on the straw internode chips would make it possible to increase the intermixing and binding of straw and still obtain

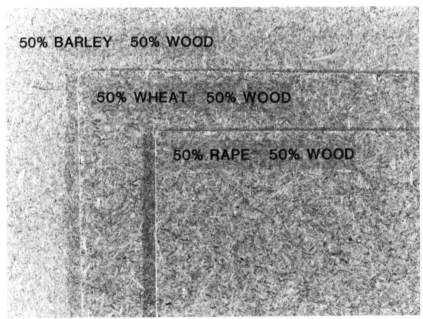

Fig. 15. Texture of particle boards, tested in Table 10, made from wood chips and machine-separated chips (internodes) from barley straw.

TABLE 11
Density and Bending Strength of Particle Boards Produced from Barley, Wheat, Rape, and Wood Chips Made at Bornholm in Full-Scale Production

	n^a	Density (kg/m³)	Bending (MPa)	Strength[b] (MPa)[c]
25% barley + 75% wood	10	597	12.3	15.2
50% barley + 50% wood	10	587	11.2	13.3
50% wheat + 50% wood	10	632	13.7	14.7
50% rape + 50% wood	10	625	16.2	17.2
100% wood	10	605	16.3	19.1

[a] Number of boards tested.
[b] Bending strength is given as an average of all boards tested with a 5% quantile of outcome.
[c] Bending strength extrapolated to a board density of 650 kg/m³.

reasonable strength properties. It is possible to etch the surface by mechanical treatment and thereby increase the number of binding sites to improve the strength of the straw board. Another glue, polymeric diphenyl-methan-4,4-diisocyanat, with other physical properties, may be used with success (von Sachs, 1977; Tröger and Pinke, 1988).

Use of Straw Meal (Leaves) as Fodder

Cereal straw, especially from barley and oats, is used as ruminant feed. Straw can be chemically treated to improve the feeding value; treatments with ammonia or sodium hydroxide are commonly employed. The treatment with ammonia increases the content of crude protein in addition to the digestibility.

The botanical components of straw have had different rates of rumen degradation in in vitro experiments (Åman and Nordquist, 1983; Caper, 1986; Ramanzin et al, 1986), with the leaves being more degradable than the nodes, which in turn were more degradable than the internodes.

The leaf meal and internode chips from mechanically separated straw were tested for in vitro digestibility of dry matter. The experiments were performed at the Rowett Institute in Scotland (Chesson and Ørskov, 1984), using the nylon bag technique (Fig. 16).

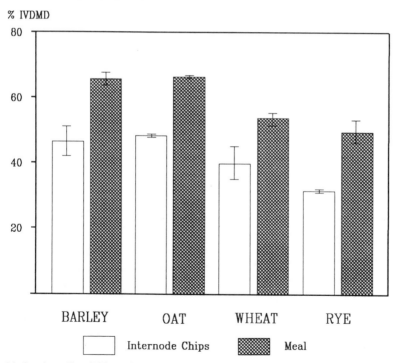

Fig. 16. In vitro digestibility (48 hr) of internode chips and leaf meal dry matter (IVDMD) for mechanically separated barley (Sewa, Ca 700202, from two locations), oats (Risø, from two locations), wheat (Rektor, Walter, Bert, and Kraka), and rye (Danko, from two locations). Maximum and minimum values are given.

For the species and varieties tested, it was found that the leaf meal had the higher digestibility, with leaf meal of barley and oats reaching the highest levels. These results show that a straw fraction with increased digestibility for ruminants can be obtained by mechanically separating the leaf fraction from the internodes. The feeding value can then be increased to the level of that of hay or chemically pretreated straw.

Oats and barley display a large proportion of leaves (see Table 2), the most degradable part of straw, and thus oat and barley straw have a higher feeding value than straw from other species. A positive difference in degradability between the leaves of the cereal species in favor of oats and barley contributes further to the increased feeding value.

In vivo digestibility experiments have been performed on barley leaf meal and internode chips. Like the in vitro experiments, they showed that the leaf meal had significantly higher digestibility than internodes (Table 12).

The use of leaf meal in ruminant feeding is restricted because this product lacks the physical structure typical of intact straw, which to some extent is essential for the microbiological functions of the rumen. The possibility of including leaf meals from straw in ruminant diets is, therefore, somewhat limited.

Use of Straw Meal for Energy

Straw meal could be used as fodder or as an energy source (Table 13).

Rape leaf meal was found to have the highest calorific value, reaching the level of wood. The leaf meals of barley and wheat had acceptable calorific values and so could be used as energy sources. The use of barley leaf meal for energy consumption would, however, compete with its use as a feed.

TABLE 12
Apparent in vivo Organic Matter Digestibility
of Mechanically Separated Barley Fractions[a]

	Apparent in vivo Organic Matter Digestibility (%)
Barley leaf meal	51.3 ± 2.3
Barley internode chips	41.0 ± 1.1

[a] Digestibility is given as a mean with standard deviation. Five sheep were used for the feeding trials during a period of seven days.

TABLE 13
Calorific Value of Different Straw Meals from the Bornholm Factory
and Commercially Available Pellets

	Calorific Value (MJ/kg dry matter)
Barley meal	16.8
Wheat meal	17.8
Rape meal	18.2
Wood pellets[a]	18.4
Straw pellets[a]	17.0

[a] Commercially available products.

REALIZING THE INDUSTRIAL POTENTIAL OF STARCH AND CELLULOSE FROM CEREAL PLANTS

If cereal starch and cellulose are to be utilized as bulk industrial commodities, agricultural production must be made more efficient, both in absolute terms and on a cost-benefit basis. In 1982 and again in 1990 when the energy crisis was again at its height, the price of starch on the world market on a weight basis was not far from that of crude oil—not bad for a highly purified and well-defined product such as starch (Fig. 17). Cellulose, on the other hand, compared to both crude oil and starch (Fig. 17), is a highly priced commodity that should benefit the cereal farmer if an efficient pulp production system, including collection, based on straw could be organized. Between 1980 and 1990, oil prices declined but cereal prices were also reduced, resulting in only small changes in the relationship between the prices of cereal commodities and crude oil (see Fig. 2).

The present agriculture in industrialized countries is in a deep crisis due to overproduction, but this also means new opportunities (Rexen and Munck, 1984; Munck, 1985, 1986b, 1987a; Munck and Rexen, 1990).

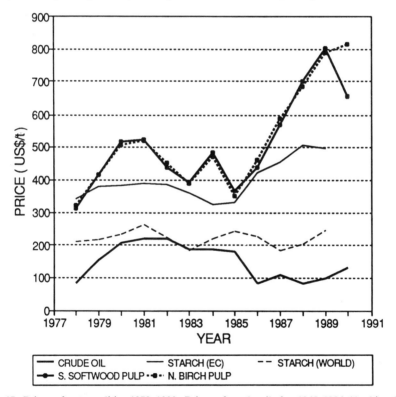

Fig. 17. Prices of commodities 1978-1990. Prices of crude oil: for 1965-1986 (Arabian light) from Myklebust et al (1986); for 1986-1990 (Dubai light) from the Shell Oil Company, Amsterdam. Starch (maize) prices from Eurostat, Import and Export. Cellulose pulp prices, CIF North Europe, include northern birch pulp (short-fiber pulp) and southern softwood pulp (long-fiber [conifer] pulp).

Agriculture has been used by industry as an outlet for huge amounts of machinery, fertilizers, pesticides, etc. This is in fact one of the main reasons for the success of our industry in the Western world. This overconsumption in agriculture, however, implies that there is really much to be done to improve the cost-benefit ratio of inputs in agriculture. The main point in this connection is to gain better control of the cereal plant. Plant parasites such as mildew decrease starch production and, remarkably, spray irrigation seems to lower starch yield compared with irrigation to the roots from below. With the help of modern biotechnology (Munck, 1985, 1986b, 1987c), it will be possible to temper the plant and adapt it to the steadily changing seasonal demands that will indeed further increase the reliability of production and yield. It will thus be possible to grow crops with high yield of seeds and straw with a minimum of pollution problems compared to the way crops are grown now.

To increase the efficiency of individual farms or the local farming community, there is a need for local collaboration with industry, which we have expressed with the concept of agricultural refineries (Fig. 18). The agricultural refinery takes care of the whole crop produced from 2,000–10,000 ha, including harvesting and drying, and utilizes local energy sources such as straw leaf meal for self-sufficiency. The crop is mechanically separated into different

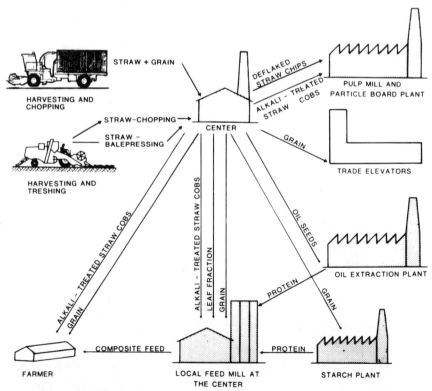

Fig. 18. The biorefinery concept. (Reprinted, by permission, from Rexen and Munck, 1984)

homogeneous fractions for use in, e.g., starch and cellulose industries. In this way, products with improved value can be obtained for use as fodder (a leaf fraction with a high level of digestible energy and protein) and in the cellulose and board industry (an internode fraction with a high content of cellulose).

Using the preliminary analysis presented here, the approximate total production of the different botanical fractions of cereals has been calculated (Table 14 with the EC as an example). In 1985, the EC produced approximately 98 million tonnes of starch and 28.5 million tonnes of cellulose from internodes. Only about 4 million tonnes of starch are purified out of the above-mentioned potential. Out of 73 million tonnes of internodes, about 36 million tonnes of paper pulp theoretically may be produced. In the EC today, only about 0.2 million tonnes (chemical and semichemical) is produced from straw.

ECONOMIC CONSIDERATIONS OF THE USE OF STARCH AND CELLULOSE

The theoretical possibilities for utilization of starch in the synthetic polymer industry are numerous. Until now, however, only a few have been explored in practice.

Most research on starch utilization has been limited to the food industry and to some extent the textile and paper industries. Comparatively little has been done in other industrial areas such as the synthetic polymer industry. For quite a number of years, however, a few private and government research centers have done research on the application of starch and starch-derived products to the synthetic polymer industry. Promising results from some of this work have been published (Griffin, 1985; Otey, 1985), and starch has begun to receive more serious attention for use in the polymer industry, especially in the United States. A contributory cause is the changing price relationship between starch and petroleum-derived raw materials. This change began with the oil crisis in the early 1970s. Starch, especially if its world market price is used for comparison, is a cheaper raw material than synthetic polymers, polyethylene (Fig. 19), and polypropylene (Rexen and Munck, 1984). The trends indicate that this price relationship might be even more favorable for starch in the years to come.

For both technical and economic reasons, however, it is of course unrealistic

TABLE 14
Harvest 1985 (EUROSTAT) EC Total Yield and Yield of Botanical Components, Cellulose, and Starch from Cereal Crops (million tonnes)[a]

Crop	Grain	Starch	Straw	Internodes	Cellulose from Internodes	Leaves
Barley	51.3	30.0	37.4	19.0	7.6	15.7
Wheat	71.5	46.0	64.9	37.0	14.1	22.7
Maize	24.4	17.0	18.8	9.0	3.6	7.7
Oats	7.8	3.0	10.5	5.0	2.0	4.4
Rye	3.2	2.0	4.2	3.0	1.2	1.0
Total	157.2	98.0	135.8	73.0	28.5	51.5

[a]From F. Rexen and L. Munck, *unpublished report to the EC on Projects 8610 and 8611,* 1986.

to expect starch to totally replace petroleum-derived raw materials in the synthetic polymer industry. On the other hand, it seems realistic that some polymers derived from starch, cellulose, and petroleum will complement one another in a wide range of combinations, together creating new opportunities both technological and economic. Today, the incorporation of native starch in synthetic polymers is limited to a narrow range of applications, which, however, could be considerably expanded through new developments. As an example of this complementation, the utilization of starch in the preparation of phenol resins can be mentioned (Woelk, 1981).

According to starch, paper, and board manufacturers, consumption of starch is likely to increase considerably in the future because native starch is cheaper than cellulosic fibers, especially at the world market level.

It has been calculated (Rexen and Munck, 1984) that the total potential demand for internodes for pulp production in the EC would be 10–17 million tonnes if all printing and writing paper, corrugated board, and solid board produced in the EC by the year 2000 contained 30–50% straw pulp and 10% solid board (as in Denmark in 1984). The short-fiber cellulose from cereal internodes combined with a suitable starch derivative could thus alleviate the deficit in the EC of raw materials for paper and board products.

It is obvious that both the starch and the cellulose industries would benefit from the improved economy of integrated, agricultural production that is cost-benefit efficient, which would ensure that starch and agricultural cellulose

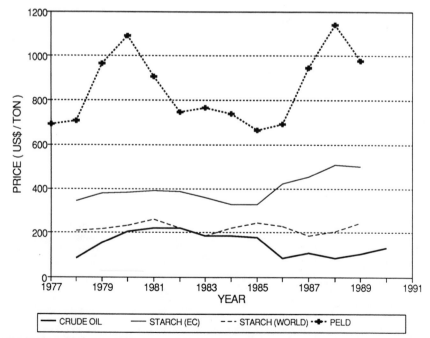

Fig. 19. Comparison between prices of crude oil, starch, and a synthetic polymer (low-density polyethylene [PELD]).

would be still more competitive in relation to their substitutes than is the case today.

CONCLUSION

The utilization of the whole barley crop is an important part of the utilization of renewable agricultural resources, but it can be evaluated fully only when compared with competing plants and alternative raw materials in a wide range of widely different environmental and economic conditions.

There are a great number of potential uses for cereal starch and cellulose in industry. In the industrialized countries, most of these will not be utilized until the price of the current raw materials has increased and made them competitive.

We can in the short run see a conflict between industries and organizations favoring fossil fuels versus renewable resources, but in the long run sound cooperation should be possible. For instance, why shouldn't oil companies stimulate the use of agricultural products for industry as a supplement to oil if they could participate in this development themselves? First, it is in their own interest to stimulate the agricultural sector, which is one of their basic markets for delivery of chemicals. Second, there will always be a need for fossil fuels, and it might be economical to leave more of them in the ground to obtain a better price. The present trend of plant breeding companies being sold to chemical and oil industries is a sign that the large industrial sector is interested in this problem, but restructuring from fossil fuels to renewable resources will not be allowed to go too far by these multinational companies because of their present huge investments.

It is obvious that it will take time to realize these perspectives in industrialized countries because their realization is to a very high degree dependent on the production costs of biomass versus energy.

In most developing countries that lack raw materials such as mineral oil, gas, and coal, and where hard currency for imports is not available, the options of utilizing cereal starch and cellulose locally and even for export are economical now if the structural and cultural problems could be overcome. Instead of exporting cereals from the EC and other industrialized countries to developing countries, which destroys the incentives of the local farmers, we should export a "package of technology" for the self-sufficiency of the developing countries based on their own agricultural produce (Munck and Rexen, 1985).

Western starch, cellulose, and chemical industries knowledgeable in the manufacture and industrial utilization of starch and cellulose should, together with machine manufacturers, convince the aid organizations and FAO of the need for setting up such a program for self-sufficiency of foods and agriculturally derived industrial products in developing countries, utilizing local starch and cellulose sources for industry. Also, politicians and other industrialists in the industrialized world should listen because, under present conditions, the developing countries will never become a profitable market for imported products. This will be a reality only when they are self-sufficient in their basic needs and have obtained an industrial infrastructure. We can thus envisage quite another type of agricultural refinery in these countries (Munck and Rexen, 1985), which could create local jobs.

Modified starch and cellulose products that could be introduced economically into developing countries could certainly be introduced later into the industrial countries themselves when suitable structural and economical conditions are available. The amount of cereals used as raw materials in industry would constitute only a part of the total production with the greatest expansion possibilities for straw uses, and barley could here have a minor but locally important role. It is probable that paper pulp from barley straw internodes would have a better chance of being developed by industry than would barley starch. The former is less different in quality from competing cereal raw materials than is starch. Thus, utilization of the whole plant crop would be of great value for employment and environment, being economic first in the developing countries. This would slowly introduce the necessary concept of an ecologically balanced system into a world where barley has an important role as the fourth largest cereal crop.

ACKNOWLEDGMENTS

We are indebted to the financial and laboratory support from the EC Commissions in Bruxelles, DG VI and DG XII (projects 8610/8611), and from the Carlsberg Research Laboratory in Copenhagen. We are grateful for having been able to draw on the experience of Finn Rexen, formerly at the Carlsberg Research Laboratory, now with the EC ECLAIR Programme in Bruxelles. Kirsten Kirkegaard is acknowledged for her active assistance in the preparation of this manuscript.

LITERATURE CITED

AASTRUP, S., and MUNCK, L. 1985. A β-glucan mutant in barley with thin cell walls. Pages 291-296 in: New Approaches to Research on Cereal Carbohydrates. R. D. Hill and L. Munck, eds. Elsevier Science Publishers, Amsterdam, The Netherlands.

ÅMAN, P., and NORDQUIST, E. 1983. Chemical composition and in vitro degradability of botanical fractions of cereal straw. Swed. J. Agric. Res. 13:61-67.

ANDERSEN, M. 1987. Method of milling and apparatus for carrying out the method. U.S. patent 4,667,888.

ANDREASEN, L., MUNCK, L., PETERSEN, B., and REXEN, F. 1988. Projekt Biomasseraffinaderi Bornholm. Rapport fra forsøgsarbejdet 1986/87. Carlsberg Research Laboratory, Copenhagen.

BACON, J. S. D., GORDON, A. H., and MORRIS, E. J. 1975. Acetyl groups in cell wall preparations from higher plants. Biochem. J. 149:485-487.

BICHARD, W., and SCUDAMORE, P. 1988. An evaluation of the comparative performance of the Kajaani FS-100 and FS-200 fiber length analyzers. Tappi 71(12):149-155.

BRITT, K. W. 1965. Determination of fiber coarseness in wood samples. Tappi 48(1): 7-11.

CAPER, B. S. 1986. The feeding value of straw from different genotypes of barley when given to Awassi sheep. Anim. Prod. 42:337-342.

CHESSON, A., and ØRSKOV, E. R. 1984. Microbial degradation in the digestive tract. Pages 305-339 in: Straw and Other Fibrous By-Products as Feed. F. Sundstøl and E. Owen, eds. Elsevier Science Publishers, Amsterdam, The Netherlands.

CUMMINGS, J. H. 1986. The effect of dietary fiber on fecal weight and composition. Pages 212-213 in: Handbook of Dietary Fiber in Human Nutrition. G. Spiller, ed. CRC Press, Inc., Boca Raton, FL.

FAN, L. T., YOUNG-HYUN, L., and GHARPURAY, M. M. 1982. The nature of lignocellulosics and their pretreatments for enzymatic hydrolysis. Adv. Biochem. Eng. 23:158-187.

FAO. 1965-1986. Production yearbooks. Food and Agriculture Organization of the United Nations, Rome, Italy.

GRAM, L. E., ANDERSEN, M., and MUNCK, L. 1989. A short milling process for wheat. Pages 445-455 in: Wheat Is Unique. Y. Pomeranz, ed. Am. Assoc. Cereal Chem., St. Paul, MN.

GRIFFIN, G. J. L. 1985. Starch granules, their properties and industrial applications. Pages 201-210 in: New Approaches to Research on Cereal Carbohydrates. R. D. Hill and L.

Munck, eds. Elsevier Science Publishers, Amsterdam, The Netherlands.

GRØNDAL, J. 1990. Utilization of brewers spent grains fractions as ingredients in the food and feed industry. Project No. 244. Danish Academy of Technical Sciences, Copenhagen, Denmark.

HAIGLER, C. H. 1985. The functions and biogenesis of native cellulose. Chapter 2 in: Cellulose Chemistry and Its Applications. T. P. Nevell and S. H. Zeronian, eds. Ellis Horwood Ltd., W. Sussex, England.

JACOBSON, A. 1990. Har priserna nått botten? Allt pekare på ett stabilt 1990. (In Swedish.) Plast Nordica 1/2:30-32.

KRÄSSIG, H. A. 1984. Cellulose: Structur und Eigenschaften. In: Cellulose, Schriftenreihe des Fonds der Chemischen Industrie. Heft 24, VCI-Symposium "Cellulose and Stärke."

MAC KEY, J. 1981. Cereal production. Pages 5-23 in: Cereals—A Renewable Resource; Theory and Practice. Y. Pomeranz and L. Munck, eds. Am. Assoc. Cereal Chem., St. Paul, MN.

MEUSER, F., GERMAN, H., and HUSTER, H. 1985. The use of high-pressure disintegration technique for the extraction of starch from corn. Pages 161-180 in: New Approaches to Research on Cereal Carbohydrates. R. D. Hill and L. Munck, eds. Elsevier Science Publishers, Amsterdam, The Netherlands.

MEUSER, F., WITTIG, J., HUSTER, H., and HOLLEY, W. 1986. Recent developments in the extraction of starch from various raw materials. Pages 97-111 in: Proc. EC—EFB DECHEMA 2nd Workshop "Agricultural Surpluses." DECHEMA, Frankfort, Germany.

MÜLLER, F. M. 1960. On the relationship between properties of straw pulp and properties of straw. Tappi 43:209A-218A.

MUNCK, L. 1981. Barley for food, feed and industry. Pages 427-460 in: Cereals—A Renewable Resource; Theory and Practice. Y. Pomeranz and L. Munck, eds. Am. Assoc. Cereal Chem., St. Paul, MN.

MUNCK, L. 1985. The impact on industry of development of cereals through genetic biotechnology. Pages 287-301 in: Proc. Biotech'85 Asia Conference, Singapore.

MUNCK, L. 1986a. Stimulation of the agro-industrial interface—Future perspectives in structure improvements as reflected in a programme suggested for research and development. Pages 223-253 in: Proc. EC—EFB DECHEMA 2nd Workshop "Agricultural Surpluses." DECHEMA, Frankfort, Germany.

MUNCK, L. 1986b. The use of surplus "grain" in the production of fuel and chemical

commodities. Pages 163-176 in: Proc. International Grain Forum, Amsterdam.

MUNCK, L. 1987a. A new agricultural system for Europe? TIBTECH 5(1):1-4.

MUNCK, L. 1987b. Quality of barley. Pages 61-78 in: Cereal Science and Technology. Proc. 23rd Nordic Cereal Congress. The Danish Cereal Society. (c/o Carlsberg Research Laboratory, Copenhagen)

MUNCK, L. 1987c. Utilization of modern biotechnology in the production chain of cereal varieties. Pages 319-328 in: Proc. International Symposium on "Rice Farming Systems: New Directions." International Rice Research Institute, Manila, The Philippines.

MUNCK, L. 1992. The case of high-lysine barley breeding. Pages 573-601 in: Barley: Genetics, Biochemistry, Molecular Biology and Biotechnology. P. R. Shewry, ed. C.A.B. International, Wallingford, England.

MUNCK, L. 1993. On the utilization of the renewable resources. Pages 500-522 in: Plant Breeding: Principles and Prospects. M. D. Hayward, N. O. Bosemark, and I. Romagosa, eds. Chapman and Hall, London.

MUNCK, L., and LORENZEN, K. 1977. New possibilities in the production of brewers grits from grain through abrasive milling. Pages 369-376 in: Proc. Congr. Eur. Brew. Conf., 16th, Amsterdam.

MUNCK, L., and REXEN, F. 1985. Increasing income and employment in rice farming areas—Role of whole plant utilization and mini rice refineries. Pages 271-280 in: Impact of Science on Rice. International Rice Research Institute, Manila, The Philippines.

MUNCK, L., and REXEN, F. 1990. Agriculture: Agricultural Refineries—A Bridge from Farm to Industry. EUR 11583 EN. Proc. EC Workshop "Agricultural Refineries—A Bridge From Farm to Industry." Commission of the European Communities, Brussels, Belgium.

MUNCK, L., REXEN, F., and HAASTRUP PEDERSEN, L. 1988. Cereal starches within the European Community—Agricultural production, dry and wet milling and potential use in industry. Starch/Staerke 40(3):81-87.

MUNDY, J., LEAH, R., OLSEN, F. L., STILLING, B., SKRIVER, K., and MUNCK, L. 1989. Gene regulation by gibberellic and abscisic acids. Pages 36-47 in: Proc. European Brewery Convention Symp. "Plant Biotechnology." E.B.C., Amsterdam.

MYKLEBUST, S., STENSETH, B., and SØBYE, P. E. 1986. North Sea Oil and Gas Yearbook. Norwegian University Press, Oslo, Norway.

NELSON, O. E. 1985. Genetic control of starch synthesis in maize endosperms—A review.

Pages 19-28 in: New Approaches to Research on Cereal Carbohydrates. R. D. Hill and L. Munck, eds. Elsevier Science Publishers, Amsterdam, The Netherlands.

OLSEN, H. S., and CHRISTENSEN, F. M. 1984. Modern enzymatic processing of basic foodstuffs. Pages 335-356 in: Proc. International Symposium "Industrial Basic Foodstuffs for the Food Industry." APRIA.

OTEY, F. H. 1985. New starch-based polymer technologies. Pages 191-200 in: New Approaches to Research on Cereal Carbohydrates. R. D. Hill and L. Munck, eds. Elsevier Science Publishers, Amsterdam, The Netherlands.

PETERSEN, P. B. 1988. Separation and characterization of botanical components in straw. Agric. Progress 63:8-23.

PETERSEN, P. B. 1989. Industrial application of straw. Pages 179-183 in: Proc. 5th International Meeting on Wood and Pulping Chemistry. Technical Association of the Pulp and Paper Industry, Raleigh, NC.

RAMANZIN, M., ØRSKOV, E. R., and TUAH, A. K. 1986. Rumen degradation of straw. Anim. Prod. 43:271-278.

REXEN, F., and MUNCK, L. 1984. Cereal Crops for Industrial Use in Europe. EUR 9617 EN. Rep. for the Commission of the European Communities. E.C., Brussels, Belgium.

REXEN, F., PEDERSEN, P. B., and MUNCK, L. 1988. Exploitation of cellulose and starch polymers from annual crops. Trends Biotechnol. 6:204-205.

SARKANEN, K. V., and HERGERT, H. L. 1971. Classification and distribution. Pages 43-94 in: Lignins—Occurrence, Formation, Structure and Reactions. K. V. Sarkanen and C. H. Ludwig, eds. Wiley-Interscience, New York.

SOUTHGATE, D. A. T., and ENGLYST, M. 1985. Dietary fibre: Chemistry, physical properties and analysis. Pages 31-56 in: Dietary Fibre, Fibre Depleted Foods and Disease. M. Trowell, D. Burkitt, and K. Heaton, eds. Academic Press, London.

THEANDER, O., and ÅMAN, P. 1984. Anatomical and chemical characteristics. Pages 45-78 in: Straw and Other Fibrous Byproducts as Feed. F. Sundstøl and E. Owen, eds. Elsevier Science Publisher, Amsterdam, The Netherlands.

TRÖGER, F., and PINKE, G. 1988. Beitrag zur Herstellung PMDI-verleimter Spanplatten mit verschiedenen Strohanteilen. Holz Roh- Werkst. 46:389-395.

VON SACHS, H. I. 1977. Isocyanate als Bindemittel für Spanplatten. Holz-Zentralbl. 20:295-296.

WILKIE, K. O. B. 1979. The hemicelluloses of grasses and cereals. Adv. Carbohydr. Chem. Biochem. 36:215-264.

WOELK, H. U. 1981. Stärke als Chemierohstoff. Möglichkeiten und Grenzen. Starch/Staerke 33(12):397-408.

INDEX

Abscisic acid, 248, 251, 255, 279, 301
Acetobacter aceti, 345
Acid phosphatases, 253, 255, 269
Acid-extract viscosity, 384
Acrospire, 225, 226, 323, 324, 325, 423
Acrotrisomics, 17
Adaptation, of plant to environment, 4
Additives, in malting, 322–324
Adenosine nucleosidase, 270
Adenosine triphosphatases, 250, 251
Adjuncts, to malt, 333, 343
Agricultural refineries, 468–469
Agrobacterium tumefaciens, 180, 430
Agropyron, 12, 430
Air rests, in steeping, 301, 314, 315, 320
Airflow, for drying and kilning, 316, 318, 329
Albumins
  amino acid composition, 133, 135, 380
  content, 64, 65, 132
  and defense of grain, 272–273
  in developing grain, 50–51, 52
  in Hiproly barley, 381
Aleurain, 269
Aleurone
  Ca²⁺ in, 255
  description, 251
  development, 54–56
  enzymes, 253–255
  function, 251, 302
  during germination, 248, 251–255
  lipase in, 221
Aleurone-specific proteins, 156–157
Alkalis, additives, 323
Alternaria spp., 316
Amino acids
  amounts in seed, 133, 135,

160, 168
  in developing grain, 58, 62
  in flour and bran, 364
  free, 134
  during germination, 257, 267
  in processed feed, 388
  sequences, 139, 141, 142, 144, 162
  of hordeins, 169, 170, 172, 173, 175, 176, 180
  of hydrolases, 260, 263, 264–265, 266, 268–269
  of inhibitor proteins, 146, 148, 152, 153
Aminopeptidases, 267
Ammonium persulfate, 323, 339
α-Amylase
  and abscisic acid, 251
  in developing grain, 60
  during germination, 258, 264–265, 267, 271
  and gibberellic acid, 249, 250
  isoforms, 265, 307
  during malting, 307
  inhibitor, 60, 151, 153, 154–155, 280
  pI groups
    high, 264, 279, 282, 307
    low, 264, 271, 307
  polymorphism, 181
  secretion, 156, 249, 250, 255
  and starch hydrolysis, 90, 91
α-Amylase/subtilisin
  inhibitor, 155–156, 280, 307, 427
β-Amylase
  amino acid sequence, 140
  content, 137
  in developing grain, 60, 138–139
  genes for, 140, 271
  during germination, 265–266, 267
  inhibitor, 155–156
  during malting, 308
  polymorphism, 137, 181

and starch hydrolysis, 90
  synthesis, 139
Amylopectin
  branching, 77–78
  chains, 77, 78, 79
  in developing grain, 47, 48, 94
  in mature grain, 77–80
  in starch granule, 81, 82, 95, 264
  and swelling factor of starch, 232
Amyloplasts, 256
Amylose
  branching, 75–76
  complexes with lipids, 223
  in developing grain, 47, 52, 53, 94
  gel formation, 76
  and lipid content, 209–212, 228
  in mature grain, 75–76
  in starch granule, 81, 82, 87–89, 95, 264
  structure, 76
Amylose-amylopectin ratio, 421
Amylose-lipid complexes, 82, 92, 223, 232, 234
Aneuploids, 17–18
Animal nutrition
  effects of β-glucans on, 103
  energy requirements, 388, 394
  lysine requirements, 380, 396–397
  protein requirements, 379
Anther culture, 21
Anthocyanin, 423
Anthocyanogens, 423, 424
α-Arabinofuranosidase, 263
Arabinose, 98, 457
Arabinose-xylose ratio, 462–463
Arabinosyl residues, 306
Arabinoxylans
  and brewing, 53
  in cell walls
    content, 97, 258, 303, 306

475

organization, 112
physical properties, 111
structure, 108–111
content in grain, 53, 64,
112–113
in developing grain, 53
during germination, 255,
262–264
in mature grain, 65
quality, effects on, 112–114
solution, behavior in, 111
Aspartic proteases, 157–158
Aspergillus spp., 229, 318,
357, 392
Autotetraploids, 17
Autoxidation, 224, 226, 232
Auxins, 301
Axial ratios, of
polysaccharides, 101
Azide, 11
Azidoalanine, 11

Bacillus spp., 392, 428
Baker's asthma, 152, 153, 280
Bakery products, from barley
flour and bran, 362,
363–364, 365
Barley α-amylase/subtilisin
inhibitor (BASI), 155–156,
279
Barley-producing countries,
5–7
Barley-producing states and
provinces, 6–7
Bean, endochitinase, 143
Beer
ale-type, 310
foam stability, 104, 140,
235
frozen, 305
hazes, 104, 114, 140, 234,
259
head retention, 235
high-lipid, 234, 235
lager-type, 234, 310
lipids in, 234
low-calorie, 283
off-flavor, 227, 234, 235
storage, effect of
β-glucans, 104
value of barley in, 8
Bile acids, 370, 374–375
Bins, storage, 319–320, 332
Biolistic particle gun, 430
Biomass, 438, 452, 453
Blue value, of starch, 86
Bound lipids, 200, 201, 202,
208, 214, 229
Bran, 214, 221, 363–364
Breeding, 18–24, 420

for β-glucan levels, 108
for hull-less barley, 400
for malting quality, 314
methods, 19–24
Brewers' spent grains, 360,
363, 364
Brewing
chill haze, 104, 423
lipids in, 233–236
problems, 53, 104, 259, 308
process, 332–334
rate of filtration, 104
soluble nitrogen ratio,
338–339, 344
yeast growth, 104, 235

Calcium (Ca^{2+}) ion, 250, 251,
255, 271, 301
Calcofluor, 106, 337
Callose, 115, 116
Canada
production of barley, 5, 6,
7
use of barley for feed, 386,
393
Carbohydrate. *See also*
individual carbohydrates
content, 64, 73, 382, 424
in grain
cell wall poly-
saccharides,
96–116
other, 116–118
starch, 74–96
metabolism, in developing
embryo, 34
Carbon transport in
endosperm, 48
Carboxypeptidases, 258, 265,
267–268, 307
and cell wall
solubilization, 303–305
Catabolic processes in developing grain, 59–61
Catechin, 423
Cell culture techniques,
428–431
Cell division, 44
Cell walls, 96–98
breakdown, 231, 259
theories concerning,
303–306
germination, changes
during, 258–264
modification, 254–255, 257
polysaccharides in, 96–116
Cellulase, 262
Cellulose
in barley straw, 442–443,
457

in cell walls, 53, 96, 114,
262
in cereal straws, 453
fiber length, 462
in husk, 64, 97
production, 469
strength, 462–463
Chiasmata, 15
Chitin, 144
Chloramphenicol
acetyltransferase, 431
Cholesterol
high-density-lipoprotein,
371
low-density-lipoprotein,
371, 372
metabolism, 372
serum, 371, 372
synthesis, 216, 372
inhibitors, 370
Chlorophyll-deficient
mutations, 10, 11
Chloroplast genome, 14
Choline, 222, 223
Chromosomes
homology, 12
number, 8, 16–18
satellite, 9
structure, 18
Chymotrypsin inhibitors,
279, 381, 427
CM proteins, 150–154, 181,
279–280
Coarse-fine difference, 336
Coldhardiness, 98
Convicilin, 160
Corn, 390, 394. *See also*
Maize
p-Coumaric acid, 109
Cross cells, 41
Crystalline microfibrils, 114
Crystallinity, of starch, 81–82
Crystalloids, 55, 252
Culms, 330, 332
Cultures, single cell, 431
Cuticular layers, in testa, 39
Cytogenetics, and study of
barley, 16–18
Cytokinins, 301
Cytology, of barley, 8–9

Debranching enzyme, 60
Defense, against pests and
pathogens. *See also*
Protection, of grain
by inhibitor proteins, 160,
154, 156
by mechanical barriers,
273
by other proteins, 157

by proteins C and T, 144, 145
by thionins, 143
Density, of seed, 446
Dextrins, in beer, 343
Diacylglycerol, 204, 230, 234
Diastase activity, 282–283
Diastatic power, 281, 340–341
Dietary fiber, 104, 113
  soluble, 355, 364, 369
  hypocholesterolemic effects, 355, 368–375
  total, 355, 364, 368, 369
Digalactosyldiglyceride, 205, 207, 209
Digestible energy, 375, 376, 377, 394, 396, 399
Digestibility
  of extracted barley, 361
  of feed, 387, 388, 395, 396, 400, 401, 402
  of hull, 377, 398
  of internode chips, 466
  of leaf meal, 466
Dimethyl sulfide, 311, 323, 341
Diol lipids, 209
Distilling, 342–345
DNA
  direct uptake, 430
  markers, 420, 425
  sequencing, 11, 426
cDNA
  for hydrolases, 270–272
  probes, use of, 271, 273, 277
Dormancy
  break in, 229
  and lipids, 229
  and maltability, 313–314
Doubled-haploids
  analysis of, 16
  in breeding, 20–21
  use in molecular technology, 426, 427, 428
Drum kilns, 330
Drum plants, for malting, 328
Dryers, types, 316
Drying, of barley for malting, 316–319
Durum wheat, 4

Elymus, 12
Embryo, development, 33
  carbohydrate metabolism in, 34
  enzymes in, 226
  lipids in, 230

Endochitinases, 145, 147, 309
  defense of plant, role in, 278–279
  protein C, 143–144
  protein T, 144–145
Endopeptidases, 251, 255, 268–269, 271, 306–307
Endoplasmic reticulum, 52, 141, 177, 178, 231
  during germination, 251, 252, 253, 254, 256
Endosperm
  development, 43–56
  aleurone, 54–56
  starchy, 45–53
  during germination, 257–270
  cell walls, 258–264
  nucleic acids, 269–270
  reserve proteins, 267–269
  starch, 264–267
Endoxylanases, 255
Energy
  digestible, 375, 376, 377, 393, 396, 399
  metabolizable, 375, 376, 389, 391, 388–389
  requirements, for kilns, 330
Environmental effects
  on β-glucan level in grain, 107
  on developing grain, 65–67
  on lipids, 214
  stress, and abscisic acid, 251, 279
  on straw components, 457, 458
Enzymatic tests of malt modification, 337
Enzymes. *See also individual enzymes*
  during germination, secretion of, 253–255
  hydrolytic
    genes for, 270–273
    germination, role in, 303
    for lipids, 220–227
    pH optima, 258
    for polysaccharides, 254, 255
    production of, 248, 249, 250, 301, 302
    for starch, 90
  inhibitors of fungal growth, 274–279
  level of activity, genetic influence, 423, 424
  transfer within grain,

mechanism, 253–255
  treatment of animal diets with, 392, 393, 395–396
Ergosterol, 235
Erisiphe sp., 278
Escherichia coli, 428
Esterase, 231, 255
Ethanol, 301, 320
Ethanolamine, 223
Ethyl carbamate, 323–324, 345
Ethylene, 301
Euploids, 16
Evolution, 3–4
Exotic gene introgression, 430
Exporters of barley, 6

Fatty acid methyl esters, 199–200, 209
Fatty acids
  in beer, 234, 235, 236
  in the colon, 373
  free, 204, 205, 207, 209, 214, 228
  in germinating barley, 229, 230, 253
  in nonstarch lipids, 214–216
  oxidation of, 308–309
  in starch lipids, 80, 219–220
  in stored barley, 228, 229
  in whole grain, 201
Feed, barley as, 355–356
  leaf meal, 465–466
  from pearling, 360
  pellets, 322, 332, 387
  processing of, 387–388, 394–395, 400
  quality factors
    carbohydrates, 382–384
    hull, 377–378
    inhibitors, 386
    lipids, 385
    lysine, 380–382
    polyphenols, 385–386
    protein, 378–379
    size of grain, 376–377
Feed efficiency, 389, 395
Feed-grade barley
  export of, 6
  β-glucan levels in, 106
  value of, 8
Feeding studies
  chicks, 103, 384, 390–392
  hens, 389–390
  pigs (swine), 103, 393–400
  poultry, 103, 113, 387–393

ruminants, 400–402, 465, 466
Fermentation, of malt, 334
Fertilization, nitrogen, 214, 380
Ferulic acid, 109, 263, 303
Fiber. *See also* Dietary fiber
acid-detergent, 377, 378
crude, 377, 378, 387
neutral detergent, 377, 378
Fingerprinting, of cultivars, 426
Flavonoids, 11
Flavors, of malt, 310, 333, 334, 339
Floor malting, 324, 325
Flour
malted, supplement for wheat flour, 156
properties, 233, 361–362, 446
uses, 362
yields, 360, 363, 448
Fluorescein, 231
Food, barley as
consumption, by area, 355
hypocholesterolemic effects, 369–375
products, 357–364
malted and germinated, 364–366
uses, historical, 356–357
Formaldehyde, 323
Formazin, 313
Free lipids, 200, 202, 204, 205, 208, 214, 229, 233
Friabilimeter, 337
Fructans, 52, 64, 117–118
Fructosan, 61
Fructose, 116
Fructosyl residues, 61, 117
Fusarium spp.
and grain heating, 316
inhibition of, 144, 145, 147

Galactose, 116, 457
β-Galactosidase, 263
Gelatinization, of starch, 92–96
effect of lipids, 232
Gene pools, 12
Gene promoters, 281, 282, 431
Genes
activation, 279
from alien species, 430
ant or *ANT*, 11, 386
cer, 11
for economic traits, 16
expression, regulation of,

271–273, 281
hap, 21
for high lysine, 178, 422
lys1, 147, 156
lys3a, 154, 156, 381
for hordein, 168–169, 173–174, 178–181
for hydrolytic enzymes, 270–273, 283
regulation, 271–273
structure, 270–271
identification and isolation, 426–428
for inhibitor proteins, 149, 152, 154, 155, 156, 279
multigene family, 282
multiple, 13
regulatory, 424
structure, 270–271
subfamilies, in hordein, 166, 167, 180
"supergene" family, 277
waxy, 383
Genetic analysis
of barley grain, 9–16
of barley proteins, 140, 141
of β-glucan, 106–107
Genetic engineering
genetic modification, techniques, 424–431
cloning, 14
identification and isolation of genes, 426–428
molecular markers, 425–426
plant cell cultures, 428–431
potential use, 280–283, 420–424, 441
process, 281, 419
transformation, 419–420, 427, 430–431
Genetic recombination, 427
Genetic studies, barley in, 8, 10, 147
aleurone layer as model, 248
hordein polypeptides as markers, 182–183
Genome, of barley, 14, 15
Germ plasm sources, 10, 12, 19
Germinated barley, in foods, 366
Germination
aleurone, function, 251–255, 302, 303
biochemistry of, 301–303
cell walls, changes,

258–264
embryo, function, 301
hormones, action, 248–251, 301
initiation, 247–248
lipids, changes, 229, 230–231
and lipoxygenase activity, 225, 226
nucleic acids, 269–270
reserve proteins, 267–269
scutellum, function, 256–257, 302
starch, 264–267
starchy endosperm, function, 257–270
Germination capacity, 313, 315
Germination index, 313
Germinative energy, 313, 314, 315
Gibberella fujikuroi, 323
Gibberellic acid, 221, 225, 226, 230, 342
as additive, in malting, 323, 325
gene transcription, effect on, 271, 273
germination, action during, 248, 249–251, 255, 265, 269, 301
Gibberellins, 301
Globoids, 55
Globulins
7S, 156, 157, 158–160
12S, 160–163
amino acids in, 133, 135
content, 64, 65, 132
and defense of grain, 272–273
in developing grain, 50
lysine in, 380
threonine in, 380
(1→4)-α-Glucan, 48, 265, 266
(1→3)-β-Glucan, 115–116, 304
(1→4)-β-Glucan, 114, 234
(1→3),(1→4)-β-glucan 4-glucanohydrolases, 259
(1→3)-β-Glucanase, 274–278, 305
and cell wall solubilization, 303–304
isoforms, 274
(1→4)-β-Glucanase, 305
(1→3),(1→4)-β-Glucanase. *See also* β-Glucanase
content, 278
developmental patterns, 55, 255, 258, 261

evolution, 277, 305
during germination, 114,
251, 255, 259-262, 263
heat-stable genes, 428
hormones, affected by, 301
isoenzymes
EI, 260, 261, 262, 273,
282, 305
EII, 260, 261, 262, 273,
305
and malt extract values,
259
and rainfall, 108
stability, 310. *See also*
Thermostability, of
β-Glucans
(1→3),(1→4)-β-D-Glucans.
See also β-Glucans
and breeding, 108
in cell wall, 97, 98-103,
258, 303
organization, 102-103
structure, 98-100
and cell wall thickness, 106
commercial uses, 366-367
content in grain, 53, 64,
105-108, 384
genotype, influence, 422
measurement of,
105-106
depolymerization of,
259-262
in developing grain, 48, 53
extraction procedures,
367-368
in feed, 53, 103, 390,
392-392
genes for, 271
in human nutrition, 104
in malting and brewing,
53, 104-105, 259
molecular weight of,
100-101
shape of, 101
solubility, 367, 392, 395
solutions, behavior in,
100-102
β-Glucan solubilase, 262,
304, 305, 306
β-Glucanase. *See also*
(1→3),(1→4)-β-
Glucanase
content, genetic influence,
422
and gibberellic acid, 306
measurement in malt, 341
and pathogen inhibition,
145, 147
solubilization of cell wall,
304

treatment for animal feeds,
391, 395-396
β-Glucans. *See also*
(1→3),(1→4)-β-D-
Glucans
content, 22, 300
measurement of, in malt,
337
solubilization, initial,
303-306
Glucoamylase, and starch
hydrolysis, 90
Glucodifructose, 61
Glucomannans, 53, 115
Glucose, 116
α-Glucosidase, 60, 266-267,
308
β-Glucosyl residues, 98, 100,
101, 102, 114, 259, 262
β-Glucuronidase, 431
Glutelins
amino acid composition,
135
content, 64, 65
in developing grain, 50, 51
lysine in, 380
threonine in, 380
Glycolipids, 201, 202, 203,
206-207, 208, 230, 234
Glycoside, 324
Glyoxylate pathway, 253
Golgi apparatus, 252, 254
Golgi complex, 254, 256, 257
Grain
composition, 64-65
development
amino acids, changes in,
62
catabolic processes,
59-61
chemical changes dur-
ing, 61-65
early stages, 31-33
embryo, 33-34
endosperm, 43-56
environmental effects
on, 65-67
hordeins, 178
husk, 43
lipids, 210, 220, 227-228
minerals, changes in, 64
nucellar tissue, role of,
34-37
nutrient supply, 56-59
pericarp, 39-42
photosynthesis in
pericarp, 43-43
protease inhibitors in,
155, 156
protection, from attack,

see Protection, of
grain
sugars, changes in, 61
testa, 37-39
heating, effects, 204
in storage, 228-229
yield, 442, 443, 445
Granule annealing, 94
Gushing, 235

Haploids, 16-17
production of, 428-429
Haze, in beer, 234
and β-glucan, 104, 114,
259
and proteins, 140, 338, 339
Heating
and enzyme activity, 225,
226, 308
of feed, effects, 387
lipid losses, 218
of respiration, in malting,
325
in storage, 316
Hemicellulose
in barley straw, 457
in cereal straws, 453-454
Hens, on barley diets,
389-390
Herbicide resistance, selection for, 429
Hexokinase, 59
High-amylose barley
cv. Glacier, 383
starch, 84, 91, 94
High-lysine lines, 137, 140,
179, 422
Ca 700202, 382, 385
inhibitor proteins in, 147,
149
use in foods, 366
High-maltose syrup, 366
Hiproly, 380, 381, 386
History, of barley growth
and use, 3, 356-357, 420
Hops, 333, 334
Hordeins
amino acid composition,
167-168
amino acid sequences,
168-174
and brewing, 51
conformations, 175-177
content, 64, 65
in developing grain, 51, 52
disulfide structure,
177-178
evolutionary relationships,
174
gene structure and expres-

sion, 178–181, 427, 428
genetics, 167
γ-hordein, 167, 170, 171,
174
B hordein, 52, 67, 164–166,
178, 183
amino acids in, 380, 381
genetic structure,
170–171, 175
C hordein, 52, 67,
164–166, 177, 183
amino acids in, 380, 381
genetic structure,
171–174, 175, 176, 177
D hordein, 167, 174, 178
polymorphism, 166–167
polypeptides as genetic
markers, 182–183
protein in, 380
and sulfur content, 164,
174–175
synthesis and deposition,
178
Hordeum
bulbosum, 12, 16, 20, 21,
429, 430
jubatum, 430
spontaneum, 108, 113, 379,
386
taxonomy, 2–3
vulgare agriocrithon, 3
vulgare spontaneum, 3, 4,
9, 12, 17
vulgare vulgare, 3, 12
Hordothionins, 141–143
Hormones, during germina-
tion, 248–251
Hull. *See also* Husk
in animal feed, 377
components, 377, 384
Hull-less barley, 208
bran, 364
in feeds, 389, 390
in foods, 365
production of, 7
starch in, 383
for swine feed, 398–400
use, 346, 358
Husk, 214. *See also* Hull
development, 43
as a filter in malting, 333,
423
genetic influences, 423, 424
Hybrids, 12, 23
Hydrocarbons, 207
Hydrogen peroxide, 323, 309
Hydroperoxide, 226
Hydroxy-β-methylglutaryl
coenzyme A reductase,
370, 372, 374

Hypochlorite, 323

Importers of barley, 6
Induced mutants
in breeding, 21, 22
sources of variation, 10–12
Industrial uses of barley,
366–368
Insects, 332
International Triticeae Mapping Initiatives, 16
Internode chips, 459, 460
cellulose from, 461–463
for paper, 463, 470, 472
for particle boards,
463–465
Internodes, in cereal straw,
456, 457
composition, 457–458
milling, 458–461
surface, 464
Inulins, 117
Invertase, 34, 59
In vitro selection, 429–430
Iodine-amylose complex, 76,
86
Iodine-binding capacity, of
starch, 86, 88
Isovaleraldehyde, 311

Junction zones, 102, 103, 112

Ketols, 227
Kilning, 298–299
airflow, 329
changes during, 309–311
energy requirements, 330
and enzyme activity, 225,
226
heat recovery systems, 330
kilns, 329–330
relative humidity, 329
and resistant starch, 92
screening, 330
temperature, 329
traditional, 329, 330
Kolbach index, 338

Laminarin, 274
Lausmann malting system,
328
Lautering, 333–334, 423
Leaf meal, 459, 461, 465–466
Leaves, 143, 274,
280
chemical composition,
457–458
in cereal straw, 456–457
fiber length, 462
milling, 459

Lectins, 157
Lemma, 43
Levans, 117
Lignin
in cell wall, 97
in cereal straws, 455–456
in dietary fiber, 368, 369
in husk, 97
in straw, 457
Limit dextrinase
brewing, importance in,
283
during germination, 266
during malting, 308
and starch hydrolysis, 90
Linkage maps, 8, 9, 15–16,
17, 425, 426
Linoleate, 224, 228, 229
Linoleate hydroperoxide, 225
Linoleate hydroperoxide
isomerase, 224, 225–226,
227
Linoleic acid, 214, 225, 226
Linolenate, 224, 228, 229
Linolenic acid, 214, 225
Lipase, 220–221, 231, 253,
308
Lipid-starch complex, 88
Lipids
and amylose content,
209–212
bound, 200, 201, 202, 208,
214, 229
in brewing, 233–236
in the caryopsis, 204–212
classes, 200
complexes
with amylose, 82, 92,
223, 232, 234
with starch, 88, 234
content
in caryopsis, 209, 210,
212
in developing grain, 228
genetic control of, 424
in germinating grain,
230
in mutants, 384, 385,
422, 424
in stored grain, 229
and swelling factor, 233
in whole grain, 64, 65,
201, 385
in developing grain, 52–53,
227–228
enzymes acting on,
220–227
fatty acids, 52, 214–216,
219–220
free, 202, 204, 205, 208,

214, 229, 233
genetic engineering,
considerations, 422, 424
in germinating barley, 229,
230–231
glycoplipids, 201, 202, 203
and lysine, 422
during malting, 308–309
methods of analysis,
199–201
nonpolar, 201, 202, 203,
204, 208, 219, 230, 234
nonstarch, 201, 204–209,
214–216
phospholipids, 201, 202,
204, 205, 206, 216
polar, 52, 204, 235
and protein, 230
in starch granules, 80,
209–212, 219–220
on starch surface, 201,
214, 229
in stored grain, 202,
228–229
tocopherols in, 216–219
in whole grain, 201–204
Lipoperoxidase, 224
Lipoxygenase, 157, 218,
224–227, 230, 234, 235, 308
Lysine. *See also* Mutants,
high-lysine
and β-amylase, 137
animal requirements for,
380, 396–397
breeding programs for, 381
content, 12, 22, 380,
421–422
in high-amylose barley,
383
in hordeins, 51, 380
in processed feed, 387
and protein Z, 140, 381
and shrunken endosperm,
381, 422
supplements in swine diets,
396–398
Lysophospholipase, 223, 231
Lysophospholipids, 52, 209,
210, 212, 220, 223, 228,
231
lysophosphatidylcholine,
205, 209, 220, 222, 228
lysophosphatidylethanolamine,
205, 209, 222
lysophosphatidylglycerol,
205, 209
lysophosphatidylinositol,
205, 209

Maillard reaction, 310, 388

Maize, 333, 342, 343
genetic transformation in,
430, 431
high-lysine mutants, 380
starch, 441, 442
Male sterility, 11, 23
Male-sterile-facilitated recurrent selection, 19–20, 21,
22
Malic acid, 258
Malt
color, 310, 330, 333, 340
colored malt, 310, 330,
345–346
flavor, 310, 333, 334, 339,
341–342
green, 231, 259, 325, 328,
342
high-enzyme, 343
lipase activity in, 221, 231
lipids in, 230, 233, 234
nitrosamines in, 310, 342,
344
quality indices
barley variety, 341
color, 340
enzyme measurement,
340–341
fermentability, 339, 343,
345
filtration rate, 340
flavor, 341–342
free amino nitrogen,
339, 343, 344, 346
hot water extract,
334, 336, 343. 345
modification level,
336–337, 343, 345
moisture content, 340
nitrosamine content, 342
soluble nitrogen ratio,
338–339, 344
roasted, 340
specifications for quality,
334, 335
starch in, 308
uses for, 332–346
water content, 340
for whiskey, 342
whole, 231
Malt dressing, 330
Malt extract
genetic engineering,
possibilities for, 280, 181
production, 346, 365
values, 104, 114, 259
Malt vinegar, 345
Maltability, of barley,
311–314
Malted barley, 252

Malting
biochemistry, 299–311
drying, 316–319
germination, *see*
Germination
β-glucan level, effect on,
107–108, 259
kilning, *see* Kilning
lipids, changes during, 230
modification
biochemistry, 303–309
indices of, 336–338
moisture level, 324
monitoring, 325
process, 297–299
quality, 183
purchase requirements,
315
selection for, 314
reason for, 334
respiration of grain,
324, 325
steeping, 299–301, 320–324
storage, 319–320
technology, 315–332
temperature control, 324
transfer of grain from
steep to, 325
turning of grain, 325
types, 324
vessels, 325, 328
Malting loss, 315
Malting-grade barley, 6, 301
Maltose
content, 61, 116
release of, 265
Mannose, 116
Mapping of genes, *see* Linkage maps
Markov chain, 99
Mashing, 332
Metabolizable energy, 375,
376, 389, 391
animal requirements,
388–389
Methyl linoleate, 225
S-Methyl methionine, 323,
332, 341–342
2-Methylfurfural, 235
Microorganisms. *See also*
Protection, of grain
enzymes from 305, 309
factors promoting growth,
273
on surface of grain, 262,
305, 309, 314
Milling, 360–361
disc mill, 447, 448, 449
dry, 445, 446, 447, 448
fractions, lipids in,

207-208
and β-glucan, 446-447
losses, 361
of straw, 458-461
wet, 446, 448
Minerals, 64
Mitochondrial genome, 14
Mitosis, 43
Modification, 298
biochemistry of, 303-309
indices of, 336-338
Moisture. See also Water
content in mature grain,
64, 67
for kilning, 329
for malting, 315, 324
for steeping, 299, 301, 320,
321
during storage, 316, 318
stress, and (1→3)-β-
glucans, 116
Molecular genetics
analysis of barley by,
13-15
isolation of barley genes,
270
Molecular tags, 420, 425-426
Molecular technology,
424-426
Monoacylglycerol, 204, 230,
234
Monoclonal antibodies, 14
Monogalactosyldiglyceride,
205, 207, 209
Monogalactosylmonoglyceride,
209
Mutants. See also Hiproly;
Risø 1508
high-lysine, 137
induced, 10-12, 21, 22
proanthocyanidin-free,
385-386
seg1, 41
spontaneous , 9-10
starch in, 383
Mutation breeding, 21-23

Naked barley, see Hull-less
barley
Near-infrared reflectance
spectroscopy, 106
Neomycin
phosphotransferase II, 431
Neurospora spp., 145
Nitrate content, 12
Nitrogen
effect on grain develop-
ment, 65-66
uptake in developing
grain, 58

Nitrosamines, 311, 323, 330,
342, 344
Nodes, in cereal straw, 456.
457
trans-2-Nonenal, 227, 235,
308
Nonpolar lipids, 201, 202,
203, 204, 216, 230, 234
in caryopsis, 204, 208, 209
Nonstarch lipids, 204-209,
214-216
Nonstarch polysaccharides,
53, 368-369, 384
Nordic Gene Bank, 10, 12, 19
North American Barley
Genome Mapping Project,
15, 23, 426, 429
Nucellar projection, 35, 36,
37
Nucellar tissue, in grain
development, 34-37
Nuclear genome, 14
Nucleases, 255
Nucleic acids, during germi-
nation, 269-270
Nucleosidases, 269
Nucleotidases, 269
Nucleotides G+C, 271

Oats
flour, 231
globulins, 161, 162
soluble fiber, 355
straw, 457
Osborne solubility groups, 50
Ostertag Wanderhaufen
malting system, 328
Oxygen
during steeping, 301
storage at low levels, 319
uptake in developing
grain, 42, 43, 59

Palea, 43
Palmitate, 229
Parboiling, 221
Particle boards, from
internode chips, 463-465
Pearled barley, 208, 216,
357-359
process, 359, 446
Pelleting
benefits of, 395
of by-products, 322, 332
nutrients, effect on, 387
and resistant starch, 92
Penicillium spp., 318
Pentosans, 384
Pentose phosphate pathway,
313

Peptidases, 253, 267
Peptides, 134, 257
Pericarp
development, 39-42
photosynthesis in, 42-43
Peroxidase, 157, 255
Phenolic acids, 109, 423
Phosphatidic acid, 222, 223
Phosphatidyl methanol, 223
Phosphatidylcholine, 204,
205, 209, 222, 223, 228
and gibberellic acid, 250
Phosphatidylethanolamine,
204, 205, 209, 223
Phosphatidylglycerol, 204,
205
Phosphatidylinositol, 204,
205, 209
Phosphatidylserine, 205
Phosphodiesterases, 269
Phosphoglucomutase, 59
Phospholipases, 222-224,
228, 305
Phospholipid transfer pro-
tein, 155
Phospholipids, 201, 202, 204,
205, 208, 216, 222, 223,
230
N-acyl, 206
in beer, 234
diacyl, 205, 206, 223
in germination, 253
synthesis, 231
Phosphomonoesterases, 269
Phosphorus, 209
Photosynthesis
by barley ear, 56-57
in developing pericarp,
42-43
Phycomyces spp., 145
Phytase, 253, 309
Phytin, 55, 252, 253
Pigs (swine)
amino acid requirements,
380
feeding of, 393-400
and storage-deteriorated
barley, 229
Plant Gene Resources, 19
Plasma membrane, 253, 254,
257
Pleotropy, 381, 402, 422
Ploidy, 2, 16
Polar lipid acyl hydrolase,
221-222, 223
Polymerase chain reaction
technique, 425, 428
Polymorphism, of proteins,
133, 137, 181-183
Polyphenols, 309, 333-334,

340, 341, 385–386
Polysaccharides
in cell walls, 96–98
nonstarch, *see* Nonstarch
polysaccharides
Pot barley, 357
Potassium, in cereal straws,
456
Potassium bromate, 323
Potato starch, 79, 80, 82, 450
Poultry, feeding of, 103, 113,
387–393
Preharvest sprouting, 116
Proanthocyanidin, 22
-free barley, 385–386, 423
Probable amylase/protease
inhibitor (PAPI), 154–155,
157, 158, 279
Production, of barley plant,
5–8
Prolamins. *See also*
Hordeins
in developing grain, 50, 51
low-molecular-weight, 181
Propionic acid, 373, 400, 401
Protease inhibitors, 147–156
α-amylase/subtilisin
inhibitor, 155–156
chymotryptic inhibitors
CI-1 and CI-2, 147–150
probable amylase/protease
inhibitor, 154–155
trypsin/α-amylase
inhibitor family,
150–154
Proteases, 157–158
Protection, of grain,
273–280, 304, 309. *See also*
Defense, against pests and
pathogens
Proteinase K, 304
Protein C, 143–144
Protein disulfide isomerase,
177
Protein K, 145–147
Protein N, 158
Protein Q, 158
Protein T, 144–145
Proteins. *See also* Seed
proteins
and animal requirements,
379
in cell wall, 96–97, 98, 303,
304
content, 64, 315, 379, 421,
424
degradation, during
malting, 306–307
digestibility, 382, 386, 399
genetic engineering, poten-

tial for, 421–422
quality, 67, 421–422, 424
quantity, need to increase,
379
reserve, during germina-
tion, 267–269
salt-soluble fraction,
133–134, 157, 380
in starch, 80–81
study of genes for, 14
in straw, 456, 457
supplementation in animal
feeds, 379, 390
synthesis and deposition,
48–52, 55, 145
toxicity, to microbes or
insects, 273, 280
trans-acting, 178, 181
Protein Z, 140–141, 308
Proteins S1–S4, 158
Protoplast fusion, 14

Quality
for feed, 421
chemical factors,
378–386
physical factors,
375–378
for food, 421
for malting and brewing,
421
diastatic power, 281
and (1→3),(1→4)-β-
glucanase levels, 281,
422
malt extract, 280
procedures for
determining, 334–342
purchase requirements
for malting, 315
selection for, in breed-
ing, 314

Radiation, in genetic studies,
10
Raffinose, 61, 64, 117, 118
Random amplified
polymorphic DNAs
(RAPDs), 419, 425, 426,
431
Recombination, of genes,
study of, 15
Recurrent selection, 19
male-sterile-facilitated,
19–20
Regeneration, of barley
plant, 281, 282
Resistance
to disease, 12, 15, 22, 183
to insects, 12

Restriction fragment length
polymorphism (RFLP)
in barley analysis, 15, 16,
23, 425–426, 431
in breeding, 420
usefulness, 183
Rhizoctonia sp., resistance
to, 145
Ribonucleases, 269
Rice, 212, 333, 383
Ricin, 145, 146
Risø 1508
amino acids in, 380, 386
and hordeins, 179
and inhibitors, 147, 149
lipids in, 201, 385, 422
sequencing, 170
and starch, 381, 382
RNA, in germination, 253,
269
mRNA
of α-amylase, 265
of carboxypeptidase, 268
of endopeptidases, 269
of β-glucanase, 261
of hordein, 52
levels, in germinating
grain, 271
stability of, 271
synthesis, effect of
gibberellic acid, 271, 273
Roasting, 214
Rootlets, 214, 225, 226, 301,
324, 329, 330
Roots, 277
Ruminants, and barley feed,
400–402
Rye
crosses with wheat, 12
β-glucans in, 384
lipase activity in, 231
starch granules in, 84
straw, 447, 462
in whiskey, 343

*Saccharomyces
cerevisiae*, 334, 345
diastaticus, 345
Scutellum
description, 256
function, 256, 302
during germination, 251,
256–257, 302
Secale, see Rye
Seed coat, 214. *See also*
Testa
Seed proteins. *See also* indi-
vidual proteins
aleurone-specific, 156–157
classification, 131–132

fingerprinting, 183
nonstorage, 132–158
albumins and globulins,
132–133
β-amylase, 137–140
aspartic proteases,
157–158
endochitinases, 143–145
globulins, 134–136,
158–163
hordein, see *Hordein*
hordothionins, 140–143
lectin, 157
lipoxygenase, 157
low-molecular-weight
prolamins, 181
peroxidase, 157
protein C, 143–144
protein K, 145–147
protein N, 158
protein Q, 158
protein T, 144–145
protein Z, 140–141
proteins S1–S4, 158
residual, 136
storage, 158–181
synthesis inhibitors,
145–147
varietal identification,
181–183
Selenium, 216
Semidwarfism, 22
Serum cholesterol, 371
Silica, 97, 457
Silicon, 456, 457
Silos, 320, 332
Sitosterol, 231, 235
Six-rowed barley
for animal feeding, 377
β-glucan levels in, 106, 384
lipids, in, 201
protein, 315
spikelets, fertility, 31
Slack malt, 332, 340
Sodium azide, use for mutation induction, 10
Somaclonal variation, 22, 23,
429
Soya, 224
Soybean trypsin inhibitor,
279
Spent grains, 332
Spikelet, 31, 42
Spring barley, 444
Staining test of malt modifi-
cation, 337
Starch
A-type granules, 47, 52,
53, 82, 84, 210, 212, 441
amylolysis, 235

amylopectin, *see*
Amylopectin
amylose, *see* Amylose
blue value, 86
B-type granules, 47, 82, 84,
210, 212, 441
cationic, 450
commercial uses, 366
compared to wheat and
maize starches, 441–442
content, 64, 75, 382, 383,
421
crystallinity, 81–82
degradation, 59–60, 264
in developing grain, 33,
46–48
digestibility, 382, 383, 395
gelatinization and pasting,
92–96
genetic engineering, potential for, 421, 424
germination, changes dur-
ing, 264–267
granules, 80–82
crystallites, 94
enzymatic hydrolysis of,
90–92
growth rings, 82
hydrolysis of, 90, 264
size distribution, 82–85
structure, 81
high-amylose, 89, 95, 96,
210, 212, 366, 383. *See
also* High-amylose
barley
hydrolysis, 90–91, 156
iodine, interactions with,
76, 85–87, 88
lipids in, 80, 209–212,
219–220, 228
low-amylose, 383
during malting, 307–308
milling yield, 442, 445
production, 74–75, 469
resistant, 92, 369, 383
swelling factor, 232–233
synthesis, 47–48, 381
utilization, of all cereal
starches
in chemical and pharma-
ceutical industries,
451
as commodity
chemicals, 452–453
as graft copolymer, 452
for microbial polymers,
452
in mining and oil
industries, 451
in paper industry, 442,

450, 452, 470, 471
for phenol resin, 452,
470
for polyols, 452
for synthetic polymers,
469–470
in textile industry, 451
waxy, 81, 86, 96, 209, 210,
212, 220. *See also* Waxy
barley, hydrolysis of
Starch synthase, 48
Starchy endosperm
development, 45–53
function, 251
during germination,
257–270
mealiness, and malting,
299, 301
Steeping
additives, 322–324
aeration, 320
air rests during, 301, 314,
315, 320
chemistry of, 299–301
flush steeping, 321
hot water steeping, 321
and lipoxygenase activity,
225
moisture content in,
320, 321
resteeping, 321
spray steeping, 321
traditional method,
320–321
vessels, 321–322
Sterols, 231, 234
Steryl ester hydrolase, 231
Steryl esters, 204, 209, 234
Storage
of grain
conditions, optimum,
316, 318
lipid changes in, 202,
218, 221, 228–229
systems, types, 319–320
of malt, 330, 332
Straw
composition, 443
in cereals, 453–458
milling, 458–461
paper pulp from, 442, 443
utilization, of cereal
straws, 461–466
yield, 442, 445
Subtilisin, 279
Sucrose
content, 61, 117, 118
in germination, 231
metabolism, in developing
grain, 34, 58–59

Sucrose synthase, 65
Sugars
  changes during grain development, 61
  sucrose metabolism, in developing grain, 58–59
Sulfur, effect on grain development, 67
Sweet wort, 333
Swelling, of starches, 95, 212, 232–233
Swine, *see* Pigs
Syrups, from barley, 366

Tanning reaction, 309
Tannins, 341
Taxonomy, 2–3
Telotrisomics, 17
Temperature
  and dormancy, 313, 318
  of drying of grain, 316
  and enzymes, 231
  of gelatinization, 92, 95, 212, 232, 308
  measurement, 92–94
  during grain filling, effects, 94, 95, 214
  of growth, effects, 212
  of kilning, 233, 259, 329
  during malting, 324
  of mashing, 233, 332
  for optimum growth, 33
  and starch granule development, 47, 65
  of starch swelling, 232
  of storage, 316
Tenebrio molitor, inhibition of, 151, 153
Testa, development, 37–39
Tetrazolium test, 313
Thermostability, of β-glucanases, 259–260, 261, 282
Thiols, 314
Thionins
  defense mechanism, 280
  and lipids, 208–209
Tocopherols, 201, 216–219, 228
  α-tocopherol, 370
α-Tocotrienol, 370
Tower malting, 328
Transformation, genetic, 419–420, 427, 430–431
Translation inhibitor, 145, 146
Translocations, of genes, 18
Triacylglycerol
  in germinating grain, 230, 231

  in lipids, 204, 206, 207, 214
  in pericarp, 221
  in ripening grain, 228
Trichoderma spp., 143, 144, 145, 147, 392, 393
Trilinolein, 225
Triploids, 17
Trisomics, 17
Triticale, 12
Triticin, 162–163
Triticum, see Wheat
Trub, 234, 235, 334
Trypsin inhibitor, 152, 279
Tube cells, development, 41
Turbidity, in beer, 234
Two-rowed barleys
  for animal feeding, 377
  β-glucan levels in, 106, 384
  kernel size, optimum, 315
  lipids in, 201
  for pearling, 358
  production of, 7
  protein, 315
  spikelets, fertility, 31

United States, types of barley grown, 6–7
Uridine diphosphate-dependent sucrose synthase, 59
USDA Seed Storage Laboratory, 10, 12
USDA Small Grains Collection, 19
USDA World Barley Collection, 380, 385
Use of barley. *See also* Starch; Straw
  feed, 375–378
  food, 356–359, 361–366
  industrial, 366–368, 440–444, 463
  by United States and Canada, 7
USSR (former), and barley production, 5, 6

Variants, *see* Mutants
Variation, genetic, 9–13
Variety, 312, 315
Viability, 313
Vicilins, 159, 160
Vinegar, malt, 345
Viscosity
  acid-extract, 384
  of arabinoxylans, 113–14
  of C hordein, 177
  of β-glucan, problems from, 100–101, 103, 392–393, 422

lipids, effect on, 233, 235
peak, 96
of starch during gelatinization, 95
test of malt modification, 338
Vitamin B, 361
Vitamin E, 216, 370

Water
  absorption, by barley flour, 362
  binding, by wall polysaccharides, 98
  control of, 207
  in developing grain, 37, 41, 42, 46
  during germination, 247–248
  for steeping, 321, 322
  uptake during steeping, 299–301
Water sensitivity, 314, 320
Waxy barley
  development, 7, 383
  genetic expression, 13
  starch, 84, 89, 91, 383
  gelatinization of, 94, 95, 233
Weight of grain, quality factor, 376
Wheat
  as adjunct, 333, 343
  amino acids in, 62
  for animal diets, 390, 394
  crosses with barley, 12
  ear photosynthesis, 57
  flour, with barley flour added, 156, 362
  germ, agglutinin, 143
  β-glucans, 384
  glutenin, 177
  legumins, 161, 162
  lipase, 221, 231
  lipids, 201, 202, 206, 228
  prolamin genes, 179
  starch, 441–442, 445
  starch granules in, 84, 94, 95
  straw, 462, 463, 464
  thioredoxin, 143
Wheat-barley addition lines, 12–13
Whiskey, 342
Wild species, 8, 9, 12, 108, 379, 386
Winter barleys
  production of, 7, 21
  milling of, 460–461
  yields from, 444

Winterhardiness, 4, 12, 20
Wort, 235, 333
  attenuation, 235
  lipids in, 233–234, 235
  run-off, 235
Wounding, and $(1 \rightarrow 3)$-β-
  glucans, 116

Xenia, 13
Xylanases, 255, 263, 306
Xylobiose, 306
Xylopyranosidase, 263
Xylose, 98, 263
Xylose-arabinose ratio, 109,
  100, 113

Yeast
  in distilling, 343
  genetic engineering of, 428
  growth, 104, 235
  in wort, 334
Yield, 5, 13

/